D1563769

THE CREDIT RISK OF COMPLEX DERIVATIVES

The Credit Risk
of Complex
Derivatives

Third Edition

ERIK BANKS

First published 2004 by
PALGRAVE MACMILLAN
Houndmills, Basingstoke, Hampshire RG21 6XS and
175 Fifth Avenue, New York, N.Y. 10010
Companies and representatives throughout the world

PALGRAVE MACMILLAN is the global academic imprint of the Palgrave Macmillan division of St. Martin's Press, LLC and of Palgrave Macmillan Ltd. Macmillan® is a registered trademark in the United States, United Kingdom and other countries. Palgrave is a registered trademark in the European Union and other countries.

ISBN 1–4039–1669–1

MIL

This book is printed on paper suitable for recycling and made from fully managed and sustained forest sources.

A catalogue record for this book is available from the British Library.

A catalog record for this book is available from the Library of Congress.

Editing and origination by
Curran Publishing Services, Norwich

10   9   8   7   6   5   4   3   2   1
13   12   11   10   09   08   07   06   05   04

Printed and bound in Great Britain by
Antony Rowe Ltd, Chippenham and Eastbourne

To my wife, Milena

Contents

List of Figures

List of Tables

Preface

Since the publication of the second edition of *The Credit Risk of Complex Derivatives* in 1997 the world of derivatives has again gone through a period of very dramatic change – in the external operating environment, underlying products and markets, and risk management techniques.

Changes in the external operating environment have been dramatic.

■ The global corporate credit environment has deteriorated; after a decade of de-leveraging and re-equitization, a new cycle of leverage (some fuelled by the technology, media, and telecom boom), coupled with an economic slowdown, has brought corporate defaults back to levels not seen since 1991–2.

■ Global stock markets have experienced tremendous bouts of volatility from the late 1990s into the new millennium.

■ Financial and accounting scandals, some ending in bankruptcy, have shaken the corporate world and investor confidence (including Enron, Tyco, Global Crossing, Daewoo, Vivendi, Swissair, and Ahold, among others).

■ The Japanese economy, the second largest in the world, has been crippled by asset deflation and a bad loan crisis for the past decade; Japanese banks and corporations, historically active participants in the derivatives market, have been forced to renegotiate their credit dealing terms to take account of their weakened financial condition.

■ Monetary union has arrived in Europe, causing consolidation of the currency and interest rate markets and growth in pan-European equity and credit investment.

■ Emerging market crises have appeared with frequency, impacting local and offshore credit and derivative counterparties (such as those in Mexico in 1994, Korea, Indonesia, Thailand, and Malaysia in 1997, Russia in 1998, Brazil in 1999 and 2002, Argentina in 2000, Venezuela in 2002 and 2003). Systemic credit problems, which spread and deepened throughout the 1990s, continue to plague the banking systems of some Asian countries (Indonesia and Thailand for instance).

■ Hedge funds, always significant derivative players, have been through a boom and bust cycle of their own, culminating in the spectacular bailout of the Long Term Capital Management (LTCM) behemoth by a consortium of international banks in 1998.

The underlying derivative products and markets have changed in tandem, sometimes in response to macro events:

■ Derivative product availability has increased steadily; new structures (such as volatility swaps, first-to-default swaps, and others) and new asset classes (such as non-catastrophic weather, bankruptcy, and inflation) are now part of the financial marketplace.

■ Once-exotic and unique instruments, such as barrier options and credit default swaps, have become part of the mainstream of financial activity.

■ Some of the "pioneering" derivative instruments of the early 1980s, such as vanilla interest rate swaps, have become so common and liquid that they are now traded on leading exchanges as listed futures contracts.

■ Overall trading volumes and liquidity have expanded, bid-offer spreads have tightened, and transaction maturities have lengthened.

■ New players have entered different segments of the market (insurance and reinsurance companies, for example, are increasingly active in credit and catastrophe derivatives, and electronic trading networks are delivering vanilla products) while established players are consolidating (for example, mergers of intermediaries, including some long-standing derivative pioneers, have commenced).

■ Derivative-related losses, from market, credit, operational, and legal risks, have continued to mount, but have not yet created broad systemic problems. Special purpose vehicles, including those with embedded derivatives, have come under accounting and regulatory scrutiny.

To cope with these macro and industry changes, risk management techniques and rules are being redesigned:

- Credit and market risk exposures are drawing closer together and are increasingly being managed on an enterprise-wide basis.

- New credit analysis tools and portfolio credit risk models have been developed by industry leaders. Computing power and analytical sophistication have increased, allowing for more timely and accurate quantification and management of exposures.

- Portfolio management of credit exposures has taken greater hold; sensitivity to credit stress scenarios and correlated counterparty credit exposures is becoming standard operating procedure.

- Use of collateral, third-party clearing services, and other risk mitigation tools and vehicles has expanded.

- Derivative documentation standards have been strengthened and clarified, sometimes as a result of disputes and lawsuits; netting of derivatives has gained wider support around the world.

- New regulatory capital requirements for the credit risks of derivatives have been created, new disclosure rules have been enacted, and accounting treatments have been refined – all in hopes of creating more meaningful and equitable consideration of risk and capital.

- Sensitivity to risk issues – including disclosure and governance – is on the rise.

Clients, intermediaries, and regulators continue to focus on risk education, risk management, and risk disclosure in order to make participation in derivatives more secure, transparent, efficient, and beneficial. Given these changes, and a desire to continue conveying valuable information on the state of the derivative credit risk sector, the second edition of *The Credit Risk of Complex Derivatives* has been fully revised. The new edition has been substantially reorganized, updated, and expanded.

- Several new chapters have been added, including:
  - Chapter 2: Derivative Losses. This chapter provides an updated view on market, operational, legal, and credit-related derivative losses.
  - Chapter 3: Risk Governance and Risk Management. This chapter

discusses important board-level and executive management governance requirements related to risk, credit risk, and derivatives.

- Chapter 4: Regulatory and Industry Initiatives. This chapter outlines unfolding regulatory and industry efforts centered on credit risk, derivatives, capital, and "best practice" risk management.

- Chapter 12: Credit Risk Portfolio Models. This chapter reviews advances in "next stage" portfolio credit risk management tools that have appeared in recent years – those applicable to credit sensitive instruments generally (for example, loans and bonds) and derivatives specifically.

■ In addition, the new edition has been updated throughout to convey the latest product and control information. The book includes:

- Definitions, explanations, and examples of new derivative structures that have appeared in the marketplace in recent years.

- Discussion of documentation issues, including those that have arisen through formal legal proceedings; this has particular relevance for the credit derivative market, which has been at the center of a host of documentary and definitional issues.

- Review of alternate transaction and portfolio quantification techniques. As in the second edition, the new edition continues to focus on a volatility-based risk equivalency process as the primary quantification framework for discrete derivative transactions. However, alternative credit quantification techniques based on simulation and option statics, are discussed.

- Analysis of portfolio risk management models and techniques and capital allocation processes.

- An expanded and updated glossary.

I would like to express my sincere gratitude to Andrea Hartill at Palgrave Macmillan for her support and guidance on this project (as well as many others) over the past decade. Thanks are also due to the production and marketing teams at Palgrave Macmillan.

E.B.
Redding, Connecticut
July 2003
ebbrisk@netscape.net

PART I

Derivatives, Credit, and Risk Management

CHAPTER 1

An Overview
of the
Derivatives Marketplace

We've spoken with the client and we're ready to sell him a two-year, 10 percent out-of-the-money Asian/average price two-power put on the Hang Seng Index with a quanto into yen; the client will pay us 12 month yen Libor plus 50 as premium.

> (Derivatives salesman in conversation with his sales manager)

I do not for one moment wish to suggest that you have got it all wrong. What I do ask is, are you quite sure you have got it all right?

> (R. Farrant, Deputy Head of Banking Supervision, Bank
> of England, March 1992, in an address to participants at
> International Swaps and Derivatives Association (ISDA)
> conference)

These increasingly complex financial instruments have especially contributed, particularly over the past couple of stressful years, to development of a far more flexible, efficient, and resilient financial system than existed just a quarter century ago.

> (A. Greenspan, Chairman, Federal Reserve Board,
> November 2002 speech)

[D]erivatives are financial weapons of mass destruction, carrying dangers that, while now latent, are potentially lethal.

> (W. Buffett, Chairman and CEO, Berkshire Hathaway, March
> 2003, in the Berkshire Hathaway annual report)

DERIVATIVES MARKET SCOPE

Financial derivatives – or contracts that derive their value from financial market references – were created by global intermediaries and exchanges starting in the 1970s as a mechanism for capitalizing on, or protecting against, movements in increasingly volatile markets. Although basic derivatives on commodities had already existed for many decades, the market volatility present from the early 1970s onward led to increased innovation and participation in the financial segment of the marketplace.[1] After several decades as part of the "mainstream," financial derivatives have proven they can be useful in helping institutions achieve certain goals; at the same time, losses and other problems reflect the fact that they can also be quite destructive. The debate on whether derivatives are useful or dangerous will obviously carry on for some time; strong views exist on both sides of the issue. However, the question of whether derivatives are "good" or "bad" may actually be moot, as activity and volumes are so significant, and reliance on such contracts so widespread, that they are now a permanent element of the global marketplace. There is, however, a point that still deserves attention in the marketplace of the millennium: making sure that intermediaries, end users, regulators, and others understand how derivatives work so they can be used to obtain the benefits expected in a properly controlled manner. If appropriate knowledge exists there is a greater likelihood that derivative activity will remain useful and not pose a threat either to individual companies or the global financial system at large.

The earliest derivatives of the modern financial era were based on standardized *exchange-traded derivatives*, which gained widespread acceptance during the 1970s, and simple, customized *over-the-counter (OTC) derivatives* (forwards, swaps, and options), which gained popularity during the 1980s; these were supplemented by basic *structured products* (convertible bonds, hybrid – putable and callable – bonds) which became more widely used during the same period. Most of these instruments are extremely common in the marketplace of the twenty-first century, and are actively used by both end users (investors and issuers that utilize the products for specific asset, liability, or risk management purposes) and intermediaries (investment and commercial banks that create, package, and trade the products). This group of instruments includes:

- *Futures*: standard exchange contracts that enable participants to buy or sell an underlying asset at a predetermined forward price.

- *Forwards*: customized off-exchange contracts that permit participants to buy or sell an underlying asset at a predetermined forward price.

- *Swaps*: customized off-exchange contracts that enable participants to exchange periodic flows based on an underlying reference.

- *Options*: standard exchange or customized off-exchange contracts that grant the buyer the right, but not the obligation, to buy or sell an underlying asset at a predetermined strike price.

- *Structured products*: financing/capital market instruments that contain embedded derivatives that alter risk and return characteristics.

As a result of widespread acceptance and active use, aspects of the OTC segment have become "commoditized." Many products can be created quickly in standard form by bank trading and origination desks for clients without the need for extensive negotiation or complex documentation, and can often be repurchased or resold in a liquid, and tightly priced, secondary market. Many financial institutions still rely on such "commoditized" products for a stream of regular (albeit declining) profits; not surprisingly, extreme competition on standard structures has driven spreads and fees down dramatically over the past few years.

Being sensitive to customer requirements and the need for new revenue sources, financial institutions with strong capabilities in product origination began creating new derivative instruments and strategies in the 1990s to provide more customized types of risk protection and investment opportunity. The innovation process continues into the twenty-first century. Although these "second generation" derivative products are based on fundamental instruments such as forwards, swaps, and options (and, indeed, share similarities with such contracts), most are enhanced to provide participants with even more unique payoff/protection profiles.[2] Examples of OTC products and strategies that have appeared over the past decade (many of which we consider later in the text) include:

- *Complex options*: options that are modified with respect to time, price, and/or payoff to produce unique and specific results.

- *Complex swaps*: swaps that are modified with respect to time, price, notional size, and/or payoff to produce unique and specific results.

- *Compound option strategies*: multiple packages of options that provide unique and specific results.

- *Complex structured notes*: financing/capital market instruments that contain embedded complex derivatives that alter risk and return characteristics in unique ways.

Although the variety of derivative products currently available in the financial marketplace is substantial we summarize, for purposes of this discussion, the major categories of first and second-generation derivatives in Figure 1.1.

While all the derivatives illustrated in the figure form an integral part of the global financial market, our focus in this text is on the OTC derivative sector, not only because it has experienced the most dramatic growth and innovation in recent years, but also because it is the segment where derivative credit risks, which we define as "the risk of loss arising from a counterparty's failure to perform on its contractual obligations," are at the forefront. Since this text is devoted to an understanding of the credit risks of complex derivatives, the emphasis on OTC instruments is appropriate. When dealing with exchange-traded futures and options, participants regularly post initial and variation margins with centralized clearing houses in

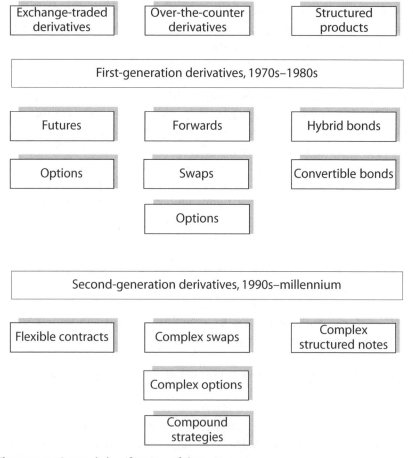

Figure 1.1 General classification of derivatives

order to mitigate the effects of credit risk. This does not mean exchange-traded products are risk-free; improper use, particularly in terms of broad risk management and control, can lead to considerable losses (this point has been highlighted very dramatically in the past, with futures-related losses at merchant bank Barings (where unauthorized trading by its Singapore office in index/bond futures and options over a period of several years resulted in losses of approximately US$1.4 billion) and Japanese trading company Sumitomo Corporation (where unauthorized trading in copper futures over 11 years resulted in losses of US$2.5 billion); we shall discuss these, and other, cases in further detail in the next chapter). Despite the fact that market-related losses can occur in this sector of the market, credit risk is not a central concern.

When dealing with structured products (for example, hybrid bonds, convertible and exchangeable bonds, bonds with warrants, structured notes with embedded derivatives, and collateralized debt obligations), credit risk is centered on the issuer of the bonds or notes, rather than on the derivatives embedded in the securities.[3] This risk, which we term "credit inventory risk," exposes investors to *credit spread risk* losses as the issuer of the structured note deteriorates in credit quality, and *credit default risk* losses in the event the issuer is unable to pay principal and/or interest on the notes. Credit risks related to the embedded derivatives, however, are of no particular consequence as they are contained within the securities, not transacted directly with counterparties. Though we shall consider credit inventory risks in the context of credit portfolio management in Part III, detailed discussion is beyond the scope of this text.[4]

Although we again simplify and summarize the large number of OTC derivatives available in the twenty-first century marketplace, Figures 1.2 and 1.3 illustrate major categories of OTC swaps and options.[5] These illustrations are by no means all-inclusive, simply designed to provide the reader with an indication of the myriad financial instruments available to those actively seeking risk protection, yield enhancement, or outright market exposure. Financial engineering is fast-paced and creative, so new structures are constantly being developed and marketed (though many are variations of products we consider in this book). Note that we have attempted to keep the classifications as general as possible, indicating that many of the instruments can be applied equally to the fixed income, equity, currency, credit, and commodity markets; a select few, however, are more readily applicable to specific markets (as we shall discuss in Chapter 10).

In addition to pioneering new derivative structures on well-established asset classes (for example, fixed income, currencies, equities), some intermediaries have expanded their offerings into new asset classes in recent years, introducing vanilla or complex derivatives on "other" references,

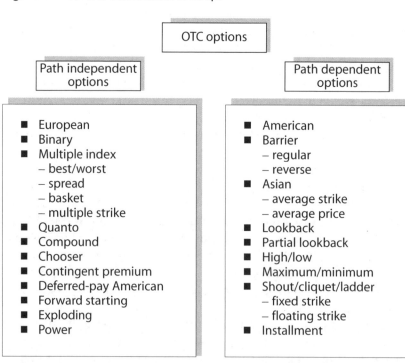

OTC swaps

- Vanilla
- Basis
- Discount/premium
- Zero coupon
- Puttable/callable
- Accreting
- Amortizing
- Arrears
- Forward starting
- Index principal/reverse index principal
- Mortgage
- Differential
- Inverse floater
- Leveraged
- Total return
- Hybrid/embedded
- Volatility

Figure 1.2 General classification of swaps

OTC options

Path independent options

- European
- Binary
- Multiple index
  - best/worst
  - spread
  - basket
  - multiple strike
- Quanto
- Compound
- Chooser
- Contingent premium
- Deferred-pay American
- Forward starting
- Exploding
- Power

Path dependent options

- American
- Barrier
  - regular
  - reverse
- Asian
  - average strike
  - average price
- Lookback
- Partial lookback
- High/low
- Maximum/minimum
- Shout/cliquet/ladder
  - fixed strike
  - floating strike
- Installment

Figure 1.3 General classification of options

including property, taxes, macroeconomic indicators,[6] bankruptcy, inflation, electricity, catastrophic events (hurricane, windstorm, earthquake)
and non-catastrophic weather (temperature, precipitation). In addition to
derivatives on the direction of conventional or new market references,
transactions can also be arranged on relationships involving those references, including volatilities, correlations, basis movements, curve movements, and spread movements. Although many of these are in their infancy
and still quite illiquid (for example, "by appointment only") it is possible
some will become as common as directional interest rate, currency, equity,
commodity, and credit derivatives are in the market of the twenty-first
century. Figure 1.4 provides a summary view of asset classes on which
OTC derivatives can be bought or sold.

As we shall discover during the course of this book, many derivative
instruments are complex from a pricing, hedging, or credit risk quantification standpoint; it is our objective to discuss the descriptive and credit
risk aspects of such instruments in order to clarify some of these complex-
ities. Understanding the function and risk of these instruments is an integral component of an effective risk management framework as it permits
the appropriate identification, measurement and management of risks; this
is a topic we will take up in greater detail in Chapter 3.

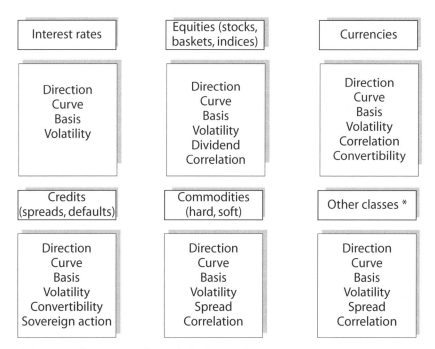

* Including catastrophe, non-catastrophic weather, bankruptcy, inflation, macroeconomics, and so on.

Figure 1.4 Derivative asset classes

Before embarking on a discussion of risk process and a detailed analysis of complex derivative products, it is useful to first consider market volatility and its impact on the growth of derivatives activity, and general risk/return and risk management considerations. This helps explain why derivatives have continued to be expand in size, scope, and liquidity in recent years, and why they continue to represent an important source of trading, marketing, and origination revenues for financial institutions.

MARKET VOLATILITY AND THE GROWTH OF DERIVATIVES

Volatility in the world's financial markets has been present for decades and has been a prime factor in the development and growth of derivatives. Fundamentally, institutions enter into derivative transactions to protect against, or take advantage of, market volatility; this can be accomplished by establishing simple or compound derivative hedge or speculative positions in particular markets. If successful, the derivative position provides the necessary protection or payoff; if unsuccessful, it can result in a loss.

Financial institutions have developed derivative transactions because the volatile market environment creates demand for such products. Banks are by now skilled in risk management techniques and are generally adept at managing the risks inherent in their own businesses (though major market dislocations and spectacular bankruptcies, such as those discussed in Chapter 2, can lead to temporary setbacks). They are willing, therefore, to transfer knowledge of risk and investment management to institutional clients so that they can protect against, or capitalize on, movement created by market volatility. Transferring this knowledge, of course, is not free. By creating derivative structures financial intermediaries earn substantial fee income; they supplement this by earning money on their own derivative trading positions. Although much of the now standard business of interest rate and currency swaps is only modestly profitable – with earnings per discrete transaction down to just a few basis points (given both widespread participation by a large number of institutions and the relative ease with which transactions can be assembled and executed) – the complex/structured business is profitable as it involves a certain amount of creativity, financial engineering expertise, and risk management capability. Single complex transactions can earn for an institution what dozens, or even hundreds, of "plain vanilla" transactions can earn. As long as banks are able to earn sufficient profits by providing expertise, it is likely they will continue to be active participants in the derivatives market.

From the perspective of the end user (for example, an investor, borrower/issuer or corporate hedger), the presence of market volatility means properly structured derivative instruments can be employed to: lower funding costs, enhance investment returns, gain upside (or downside) participation in a given market, or obtain price-rate protection for a liability, asset, input, or output. End users might also utilize derivatives to overcome specific accounting or regulatory barriers (though this activity has come under scrutiny in the aftermath of the various corporate scandals appearing since the late 1990s and may ultimately fade).

We highlighted in Figures 1.2 to 1.4 derivatives that intermediaries and end users might employ to solve a specific problem or address a given requirement. Major financial institutions develop these structures to respond to the needs of end users. Though many of these products are, indeed, profitable for bank originators, they exist primarily because of client demand. If issuers or investors are not interested in utilizing particular derivatives, they will soon disappear from the market place. Thus, popular derivative structures prosper because supply and demand (that is, intermediary and end user) forces are at work. Fabozzi and Modigliani (1992) have summarized it succinctly:

> New financial instruments are not created simply because someone on Wall Street believes that it would be fun to introduce an instrument with more bells and whistles than existing instruments. . . . The demand for new instruments is driven by the needs of borrowers and investors based on their asset/liability management situation, regulatory constraints (if any), financial accounting considerations, and tax considerations.[7]

An examination of volatility data from a number of the world's main financial markets/indexes helps indicate why so many institutions attempt to protect or profit by entering into derivative trades. Figures 1.5 to 1.11 illustrate the historical price volatility of various key market references over the past 15 years.

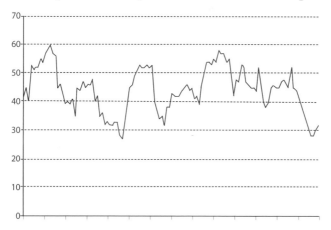

Figure 1.5 Eurodollars (US$ Libor), 15-year average volatility (%), 1988–2002

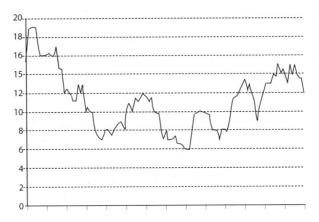

Figure 1.6 30-Year US Treasury bond, 15-year average volatility, 1988–2002

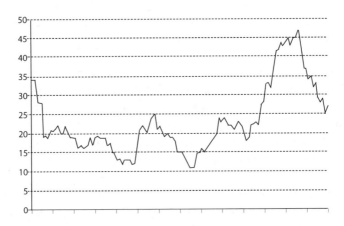

Figure 1.7 S&P500 Index, 15-year average volatility, 1988–2002

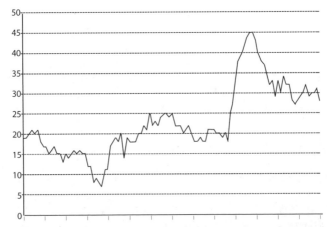

Figure 1.8 Crude oil (light sweet crude), 15-year average volatility, 1988–2002

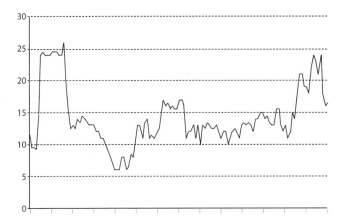

Figure 1.9 Gold, 15-year average volatility, 1988–2002

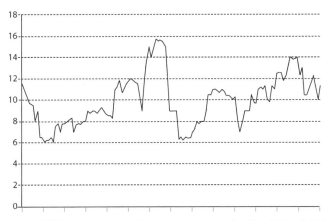

Figure 1.10 US$/Japanese yen, 15-year average volatility, 1988–2002

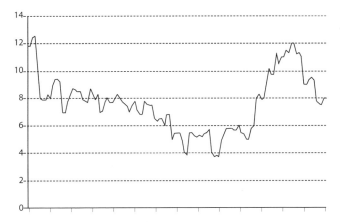

Figure 1.11 US$/Pound Sterling, 15-year average volatility, 1988–2002

Volatility has clearly been a driving force in the development and use of derivatives and it seems logical to presume that while it exists, originators and end users will continue to develop and demand new derivative products; this will invariably expand overall volumes and credit exposures. Indeed, there is little to suggest market volatility will decline or disappear, particularly in a marketplace characterized by global capital movements, deregulation, rapid information dissemination and increased profit pressures.

To place the growth of the derivatives market in context, we cite the findings of the annual International Swap and Derivatives Association (ISDA, the industry trade group) derivatives survey, which shows notional derivative outstandings increasing from US$865 billion in 1987 to more than US$87 trillion in 2002; interest rate and currency derivatives accounted for US$82 trillion of the outstandings in 2002 (credit derivatives accounted for a further US$1.6 trillion and equity derivatives for US$2.3 trillion). While notional amounts are not an accurate representation of risk (as we shall discuss in Part II) they provide a general benchmark regarding the size and growth of the market. Figure 1.12 summarizes the ISDA survey data. A more accurate representation of true risk, gross replacement value (for example, the cost of replacing derivative contracts, without granting the beneficial effects of netting) reflects dramatic growth. According to surveys by the Bank for International Settlements (BIS), gross replacement cost has risen from US$3.2 trillion at the end of 1998 to US$6.4 trillion at the end of 2002. Figure 1.13 reflects the BIS results.

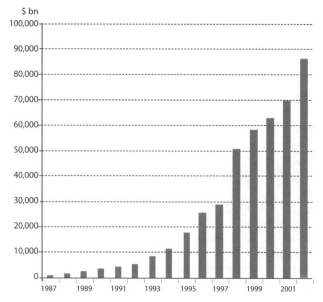

Figure 1.12 Notional outstandings, OTC derivative contracts, 1987–2002

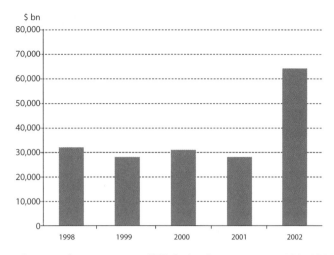

Figure 1.13 Gross replacement cost, OTC derivative contracts, 1998–2002

GENERAL DERIVATIVE RISK AND RETURN CONSIDERATIONS

Market volatility is obviously an important driver of derivatives growth, but it is not the sole driver; an appropriate economic framework must reinforce the market if activity is to occur. Institutions are unlikely to engage in derivatives if they are not receiving some economic benefit; this is particularly true for the intermediaries that are responsible for creating, and risk-managing, individual derivative transactions. Accordingly, it is essential for participants to focus on the risks and returns characterizing specific products and markets. The structure and function of all products (including risk, return, flows, obligations, and termination) must be thoroughly understood by end users and intermediaries. Sometimes it is just necessary to review key aspects of a transaction as reflected in a term sheet or flowchart. Other times more rigorous analysis is required; this may include a detailed review of structural aspects of a particular transaction as well as basic or sophisticated scenario-simulation analysis (we have included, as Appendix 2, a list of "20 Questions" a risk officer dealing with derivatives may wish to pose to a specialist when attempting to capture the unique details of a given product or structure). In trying to understand a given derivative product it is useful to focus on the basic elements and trade-offs common to all financial transactions: return and risk.

The gross return of a given instrument is generally the concern of bank trading/sales desks or origination units. These groups design the function and parameters of derivative instruments and ensure that the products meet customer requirements; if customers are not interested in products being developed, there will be little demand for them and they will ultimately cease to exist. When creating derivative instruments, the trader or originator knows generally what type of gross return is possible or necessary, depending on the originality/complexity of the product, competitive pressures, liquidity conditions, customer demand, hedging requirements and challenges, and so on. Profit may be derived from an upfront fee, a bid-offer spread, or an above market rate, and may be guaranteed or contingent. Such profit parameters must naturally be well understood by the product professional and agreed by senior bank management. Note that gross return is only one aspect of profitability; net return, which factors in items such as funding charges, overhead costs, taxes, and specific risk reserves (discussed below), is an increasingly important measure of a product's true profitability.

The second component of the risk-return equation focuses on the specific risk characteristics of an instrument. Risk, as we shall discuss in the next chapters, comes in many different forms, including credit, market, liquidity, settlement, operational, legal, and sovereign. Not all risks are present in every transaction, but an appropriate risk-return mechanism should account for any elements that do exist. A basic tenet of finance demands that greater risk carry greater return. Accordingly, a derivative with large or complex hedging, liquidity, and market or operational risks should feature a larger gross spread: one that accounts for the added challenges and uncertainties. By extension, a prudent pricing mechanism should reflect the credit quality of the counterparty: transactions executed with weaker (higher risk) credits should carry higher spreads and vice versa. This is a fundamental concept of credit pricing.

The theory of risk-adjusting returns to account for dimensions of credit risk has become more widely accepted with growth and liquidity in the credit derivative market. Though pricing credit risk has been the subject of widespread discussion among banks and dealers for many years, there is greater willingness to specifically weigh risk against return. Although some commercial banks have been successful in pricing traditional loan products according to credit quality for many years, extending the credit pricing framework to derivatives, in particular customized packages of derivatives, has taken much longer to achieve. However, the availability of an increasingly liquid, transparent, and reliable credit derivative market has made the exercise more feasible and reference prices on a broader range of credits are available.

While more work remains to be done in this area, the increasing focus on risk-adjusted profitability has moved the issue to the forefront. One critical aspect of the risk-adjustment process is the allocation of specific risk reserves for derivative products; as indicated above, net return, a more accurate measure of profitability, reflects gross profitability less the costs and reserves allocated to cover actual or perceived risks (including credit risks). It is increasingly apparent that firms that measure profitability on a risk-adjusted basis are actually evaluating their performance more accurately. Balancing risk and reward properly (that is, in a risk-adjusted framework) is an essential element of prudent risk management. Figure 1.14 summarizes aspects of the risk-adjusted return process; we shall discuss the process at greater length in Chapter 11.

As indicated above, in determining how a new product functions it is vital to focus closely on the risk parameters of the instrument. This enables a finance or corporate professional to decipher the logic in executing a transaction and permits specific quantification of potential losses (and gains). Although there is often pressure to react quickly to a given structure, deal, or opportunity, patience and diligence are necessary when evaluating complex structures. Misunderstanding aspects of risk can be damaging to the bank originating a product, the issuer or investor active as an end user, and the regulator charged with specific oversight of markets, institutions, and products; we consider each in turn.

The financial intermediary, as the originator, structurer, and/or trader of derivative products, has at least two interests in ensuring a thorough understanding of derivative risks at all levels within the institution; preventing losses in its own operations and ensuring that it retains an active and interested client base. If an intermediary is unable to understand and control the risk emanating from its own derivatives book it will eventually realize losses; though this may seem obvious, it is often a problem, as we shall note in Chapter 2. The responsible banking institution must therefore ensure that all levels of management are educated about derivatives and their associated

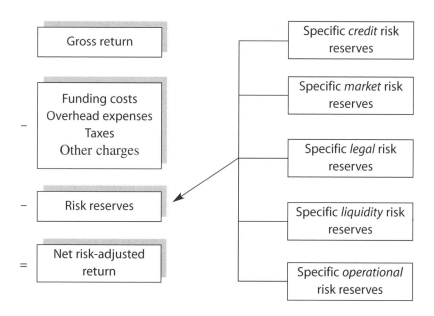

Figure 1.14 Risk-adjusted returns

risks: senior bank managers, law and compliance professionals, credit officers, risk managers, operations managers, financial controllers, and so on. In short, any group that has responsibility for aspects of derivatives must understand how they function and what risks they generate and those responsible for establishing a firm's risk tolerance must have a particularly good understanding. In addition to protecting its own business, the intermediary has a strong interest (some might argue responsibility) in ensuring its client base is fully aware of profit, loss, and risk profiles of derivatives. If an intermediary adopts a "short-term" view with a client and simply attempts to structure and sell a given instrument without taking time to explain benefits, risks, and costs, it will only be a matter of time before a client is harmed financially. When this occurs, it is likely that an intermediary's franchise and reputation will sustain some level of damage; there have certainly been many examples of this, as we shall discuss in Chapter 2.

Derivative clients may be active as issuers, investors, or corporate hedgers, and they must always ensure a thorough analysis and understanding of any structure. A client that can undertake a complete analysis of a transaction gains comfort that it is receiving the economic gain it is expecting; either a lower funding cost or an enhanced yield, or perhaps exposure to, or protection against, the upside/downside of a given market. The client also gains a more thorough understanding of the credit, liquidity, and market risks that exist or might arise (it is important to remember that the client often faces many of the same risks as the financial intermediary). And, as with the intermediary, it is vital that all relevant parties at the client institution, including senior managers and treasury/financial officers, be aware of the transactions and associated risks. Although many end users are quite sophisticated regarding financial engineering (for instance, pension fund managers, treasury units of large multinational corporations), not all client institutions have the same level of knowledge and expertise. It is in their own interests to exercise care, reviewing all structures with an objective and analytical eye. The client cannot, and should not, rely on the intermediary for a detailed understanding of deals and risks; it must assume that task itself. This point bears emphasizing as a result of the large derivative losses sustained by numerous end users during the 1990s and into the millennium.

The regulator is charged with ensuring safety, stability, and control in the financial market place; regulations are applied to financial businesses, including derivatives, to ensure participants are adequately protected. There has been a great deal of press in recent years regarding regulatory concerns about the pace of growth in derivatives and the increased level of sophistication and complexity involved in the business. Certain regulators have expressed fears that they are being "left behind," that senior bank managers are unaware of the structures the "high-powered" trading desks are creating and that clients are being sold instruments they may not completely understand. Regulators must be aware of these transactions so that they may impose, on a reasonable and fair basis, regulation that fosters orderly and secure markets and appropriate use of derivative products. Failure by regulatory authorities to understand all aspects of these transactions may result in disparate views and ineffective, or unfair, regulation. (Note that formal regulation is supplemented by self-regulation by market participants and institutions, who must remain diligent and vigilant as well. In fact, this "self-policing," which we consider in our regulatory discussion in Chapter 4, is a vital element of the regulatory structure).

ADDRESSING DERIVATIVE RISK MANAGEMENT ISSUES

The growing complexity of the derivatives business, coupled with greater market volatility, weak economic and credit cycles, and a higher incidence of derivative-related losses, has led financial and corporate institutions and regulators to adopt a stricter posture regarding derivative risk management controls. This focus has been constructive. It should provide a more secure operating environment, and help the derivatives business expand prudently over the coming years. Specific enhancements that financial and regulatory professionals have emphasized over the past few years include:

- implementing independent internal risk management controls

- enhancing client sales disclosures

- employing comprehensive risk-mitigation techniques

- managing exposures accurately and actively.

We consider each of these points in summary form below and discuss them at greater length in Chapters 3 and 4.

Implementing internal risk management controls

As a result of losses sustained by intermediaries and end users, financial institutions, regulators, and industry groups have recommended implementation of internal risk management controls at various points over the past decade. Such controls are suggested as a means of ensuring an institution's risks are appropriately and continuously identified, measured, managed, and controlled; they are now standard operating procedure at many firms, though quality and efficacy still varies widely. For instance, the Group of 30 (an industry group comprised of intermediaries, end users and academics) released *Derivatives: Practices and Principles* in 1993. The document contained a series of recommendations regarding the implementation of robust, independent credit and market risk management policies and controls. The Derivatives Policy Group (DPG, comprised of officers from the six largest US investment banks) published *A Framework for Voluntary Oversight* in early 1995, echoing many of the sentiments outlined in the work of the Group of 30. In addition, the Counterparty Risk Management Group (comprised of 12 leading financial institutions) released *Improving Counterparty Risk Management Practices* in 1999 to focus attention on strengthening credit and risk management controls, information sharing and disclosure, market practices/conventions, and regulatory reporting. These efforts have been reinforced by formal recommendations from supranational and national regulators (for instance, the Bank for International Settlements, Securities and Exchange Commission, and the Financial Services Authority).

Enhancing client sales disclosure

A key issue arising from derivative losses relates to appropriate client disclosure. Many end users (some suffering significant losses) have claimed lack of accurate disclosure –that is, clear explanations, term sheets, scenario analyses – has led to ill-advised or imprudent dealing in derivatives; some have also indicated that lack of ongoing, independent valuation has compounded the problem. Various financial intermediaries have disputed this argument, claiming end users are sophisticated institutions responsible for their actions.

There is, at present, no industry consensus on what proper client disclosure should encompass, though most players seem to agree that it should be sufficiently detailed and transparent. Certain institutions voluntarily provide clients with a great deal of upfront and ongoing information, while others are less forthcoming. Intermediaries on the leading edge of client disclosure often provide detailed term sheets with scenario analyses reflecting the potential upside and downside of derivative transactions under various market scenarios, the effect of transactions when considered as part of a hedge (for example, the effect of movements on both the derivative and the underlying exposure being hedged), and ongoing valuation and reporting of existing derivative transactions (perhaps weekly or monthly). At the opposite end of the spectrum are intermediaries following a *caveat emptor* approach; this suggests client institutions must rely on their own skills and resources in initially understanding, and subsequently valuing, derivative transactions. Various technology and risk consulting companies provide standard software packages that can be used to value positions on a market value basis. However, "unbundling" or "decomposing" exotic derivatives can be a difficult exercise and obtaining a truly "independent" price on a complicated structure a challenge.

While the industry has not achieved consensus regarding client disclosure guidelines, and though certain institutions actively warn clients they are "on their own" when it comes to understanding, managing, and valuing derivatives, the industry has generally moved in the direction of providing clients with more, rather than less, upfront and ongoing information. The DPG, for instance, put forward minimum *voluntary* standards regarding client disclosure in its 1995 document: advocating development and use of generic risk disclosure (designed to provide end users with information on the risks of any derivative transaction under consideration), fair and accurate marketing materials, detailed transaction proposals, and comprehensive scenario analyses (particularly for complex transactions); recommending the use of well-documented agreements, confirmations, and term sheets to avoid confusion or dispute; and, urging care and good faith on the part of intermediaries in determining ongoing transaction valuations for end users who are unable to perform their own valuations. Other groups have put forth similar efforts, but more work remains to be done in this area.

Employing comprehensive risk mitigation techniques

As we have noted above, the expansion of the derivatives market has been dramatic, in terms of both products and volume. The increase in activity has had at least two direct effects on the credit dimension of the business: derivative dealers have large exposures to other dealers, and they have opportunities to deal with a larger number of lower-rated clients (for example, lower-rated counterparties in industrialized nations and local counterparties in lower-rated emerging nations). Both of these have been drivers in the development of risk mitigation techniques. Though we describe risk mitigation in greater detail in Chapter 13, we briefly summarize the most common techniques as a means of highlighting their importance in the overall derivative risk management control framework:

- *Diversification*: using portfolio techniques (for example, correlations and optimization) to minimize concentrations of credit exposure and create a balanced set of risks.

- *Netting*: documenting portfolios of derivatives so payments can be made on a net, rather than gross, basis.

- *Collateralization/credit enhancement*: taking assets as security against a derivative exposure or requiring a counterparty to contract with a third-party of higher credit quality to support a derivative exposure.[8]

- *Recouponing*: reviewing the value of a derivative portfolio and arranging a net settlement in order to eliminate the actual, or mark-to-market, exposure of the portfolio.

- *Assignment*: transferring a derivative exposure from the original counterparty to a third party.

- *Intermediation*: executing a derivative through a second intermediary rather than the end user (included in this category are credit clearing houses that stand between the intermediary and end user).[9]

- *Downgrade/termination options*: employing options to terminate a derivative transaction at pre-specified points in time or in the event of credit deterioration.

- *Credit derivative hedging*: using credit options, forwards or swaps, structured products (for example, basket notes, collateralized debt obligations) to shift the derivative credit exposure from the original counterparty to a third party.

Netting, in particular, has emerged as perhaps the most popular credit exposure management tool. Bilateral netting is the process by which multiple derivative credit exposures with a given counterparty are condensed into a single payment made by one of the two parties (depending on the level and movement of the market). Though we shall discuss different aspects of netting in greater detail throughout the text, we introduce the topic here to stress the importance of accurate measurement and management of net exposures in the overall risk management process. Netting can take the form of:

- *Payment netting*: an institution and its non-defaulting counterparty agree to net payments in the normal course of business.

- *Closeout netting*: an institution and the defaulting counterparty agree to terminate the transactions and net payments.

- *Set-off*: an institution and the defaulting counterparty agree to terminate the derivative transactions and apply any net payments against amounts due, or owed, under other financial transactions.

In order for netting to be effective it must be governed by a master agreement (which we consider in Chapter 4) and have legal basis in the appropriate jurisdiction. ISDA (in its role as the industry's representative), working in concert with regulators, legislators, and law firms worldwide, has spent the past decade clarifying the status of netting in different countries throughout the world. Though netting is not legally enforceable everywhere, various countries have changed their insolvency laws to permit netting (see Table 1.1).[10] In addition, ISDA has gathered positive opinions regarding the acceptability of netting in a number of other countries and formal changes to national bankruptcy codes in many may appear in the future. While financial intermediaries have long favored netting, the BIS provided regulatory support in 1994 when it announced that it would accept capital allocations against derivative transactions on a net, rather than gross, exposure basis (as long as the operating jurisdictions provide appropriate legal comfort that netting is permissible). As the acceptability of netting increases, many institutions have turned toward the use of net potential exposure measures to manage their derivative businesses; this ultimately results in a more accurate and efficient use of corporate resources and a more accurate representation of risk.

Again, by utilizing risk mitigation techniques more actively the industry makes dealing more secure and reduces the chance of systemic problems, particularly among dealers.[11] In addition, it also creates greater credit capacity by reconstituting credit portfolios and releasing credit limits. Figure 1.15 summarizes common risk mitigation techniques.

Table 1.1 Countries amending legislation to accept netting

Australia	Austria	Belgium
Canada	Denmark	England*
Finland	France	Germany
Hungary	Ireland	Italy
Japan	Luxembourg	Mexico
New Zealand	Norway	Portugal
South Africa	Spain	Sweden
Switzerland	United States	

* Accepted without specific statutory recognition.

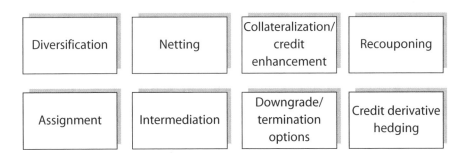

Figure 1.15 Common credit risk mitigation techniques

Managing exposures more accurately and actively

Credit risk management of derivatives (and other credit-risky instruments, such as loans or bonds) is no longer based on a "binary" decision-making framework calling for credit professionals to either approve or reject incremental transactions, or for credit risk transactions to be originated and held until maturity.

Through improvements in transaction risk quantification, portfolio risk aggregation, risk mitigation, and credit technologies, the financial industry is gradually improving its ability to manage derivative credit exposures in a more accurate and dynamic fashion. This means the binary "yes" or "no" decisions that have historically characterized the credit function are giving way to a continuum of decisions; in many instances credit professionals are active participants in the management of exposures, proposing alternate structures, managing risks on a portfolio, rather than individual transaction, basis, and enforcing credit pricing to ensure an institution is being appropriately compensated for assuming particular risks. It also means that institutions actively shed or assume different credit risks on an ongoing basis; directly or synthetically. According to a 2002 survey sponsored by ISDA and the Risk Management Association (conducted by Rutter Associates), 80 percent of major financial institutions surveyed have a credit portfolio management function; 75 percent of those use portfolio management as a "defensive" mechanism (for example, to protect credit exposures), while 25 percent use it as a proactive, or revenue-generating, mechanism.

As this process takes greater hold, financial institutions (and, indeed, sophisticated end users) can manage their businesses more efficiently and accurately; this means a greater focus on return, instead of pure volume. This also suggests excessive credit exposures are not applied against credit limits, capital allocations are more accurate, and pricing more equitable. It also means credit exposures are not understated; this is obviously critical in ensuring an institution maintains a prudent risk profile. Dynamic management of credit exposures necessarily means management information must be more accurate and comprehensive than ever before. In addition, the information must be readily available upon request. In many instances financial institutions are investing significant financial and human resources in the expansion and enhancement of credit technology and systems. Third party vendors have also developed analytic, data, portfolio, and aggregation tools over the past few years.

Though active management of credit exposures is occurring, it has more ground to cover before it is fully implemented, even in the most sophisticated and forward-looking firms. Active credit risk management requires financial intermediaries with a credit culture (for instance, loan origination capabilities) to assume a market risk/trading mindset. This means a willingness to constantly manage, monitor, and readjust portfolios, and to ensure infrastructure is available to price and compute risks in a more dynamic manner. It also demands cross-business unit cooperation and a willingness to sacrifice the "territoriality" that sometimes characterizes credit-related business. Though certain institutions have adopted a more active stance towards management of portfolios of risks, it is still unclear which model is best: a dedicated, independent credit risk management function which absorbs all of a firm's credit risks; a team within a central credit division charged with central management of risks; individual business units working in cooperation with one another; or, some other model. Capital allocated to credit risks must, of course, be a prominent feature in any dynamic risk allocation and management process, as we shall discuss at length throughout the book.

OVERVIEW OF THE TEXT

As indicated above, one of the keys to addressing derivative risk management issues is understanding, identifying, measuring, and managing risks, including credit risks. The focus of this text is thus on gaining an understanding of the credit risk aspects of "next generation" derivatives. In the remainder of Part I we focus on risk process.

■ Chapter 2 provides an overview of derivative risk losses that have plagued the market over the past 20 years; this helps set the stage for our discussion on risk management and controls.

■ Chapter 3 focuses on risk governance/risk management in the context of credit risks generally, and derivative risks specifically. We explore some of the issues that center on creating a proper governance framework that simultaneously constrains risks and maximizes shareholder value.

■ Chapter 4 turns attention to regulatory and self-regulatory initiatives and advances related to the general field of credit risk. Global regulators and industry organizations/conduits have spent a great deal of time and effort trying to create a more secure and equitable playing field and we consider their progress.

In Part II we shift our focus from risk process and control to the actual description and quantification of credit risks which characterize compound option strategies, complex options, and complex swaps.

■ Chapter 5 provides initial background on the classification of risk, risk equivalency and general methods of quantifying credit risk. Although we introduce a variety of risk quantification techniques, our focus is on the development of a volatility-based risk equivalency process.

- Chapter 6 reviews the quantification methodology for conventional put and call options (including a review of alternate techniques).

- Chapter 7 presents product description and credit risk quantification of compound option strategies.

- Chapter 8, in turn, focuses on the product description and credit risk quantification of complex options, including path dependent and path independent structures.

- Chapter 9 provides a review of swap risk quantification techniques (including review of a detailed model).

- Chapter 10 presents product description and credit risk quantification for a series of complex swap products.

Following a review of transaction-specific credit risk, we turn our attention to portfolio and credit risk management issues in Part III.

- Chapter 11 provides a detailed discussion on the quantitative aspects of derivative credit risk management, including aggregating individual transactions into portfolios and developing and implementing the expected/unexpected credit loss framework for determining portfolio credit reserves and capital allocations.

- Chapter 12 then considers credit risk portfolio models that have been created over the past few years, analyzing the essential qualities of a credit portfolio model and examining the capabilities of various "first" and "second" generation credit risk portfolio tools.

- Chapter 13 focuses on qualitative portfolio risk management issues, including managing credit exposures on a dynamic basis (through risk mitigation, simulations/stress tests, and active limit management) and addressing ancillary risk issues that are at the forefront of the derivative industry (that is, transaction motivation/suitability, lengthening transaction maturities, and ability versus willingness to pay).

CHAPTER 2

Derivative Losses

Derivatives have become a central element of the world's financial system. The size of the market, the speed at which it has grown, and the range of participants it has attracted indicate that it is part of the mainstream of global financial and capital flows. Though the marketplace has become well established and proven itself to be extremely useful in shifting risks and providing investment and funding opportunities, it has also suffered from a series of setbacks and problems, including client and dealer losses. As we expand our discussion on derivative risk management, it is helpful to consider how and why derivative losses occur. This gives us a sense of the pitfalls that exist and provides insight into the need for institutional and regulatory control efforts, some of which we discuss in Chapters 3 and 4.

SOURCES OF DERIVATIVE LOSSES

Dealing in derivatives, whether as intermediary or end user, means an institution is exposed to a range of risks that can lead to losses; this is true even when a firm is using derivatives to hedge rather than speculate. Though some risks are mitigated or eliminated when hedging, others can arise including:

- *market risk*, or risk of loss due to adverse market movements (including liquidity risk as a special subset)

- *credit risk*, or risk of loss due to counterparty non-performance (our main focus in this book)

- *model risk*, or risk of loss due to errors in mathematical models

- *operational risk*, or risk of loss due to operational errors or control failures

■ *legal risk*, or risk of loss due to suitability issues, documentation problems, or legal difficulties.

Over the past few years intermediaries and end users have lost money in derivatives as a result of mispricing or mishedging complex structures, misunderstanding risk payoff profiles of transactions (particularly those with excessive leverage), circumventing internal controls, dealing outside legal authorities, and so on. Interestingly, losses attributable to counterparty credit losses have been relatively modest in relation to the size of the market. Although counterparties with large derivative portfolios have defaulted (for example, Drexel Burnham Lambert, Enron, hedge funds), portfolios have either resulted in "manageable losses" for counterparties or been unwound or transferred with little or no loss to the non-defaulting parties.

Derivative instruments at the center of losses have ranged from the relatively straightforward (for instance, foreign exchange forwards) to the very esoteric (for instance, leveraged, or "ratio," swaps based on complex payoff formulae). This helps reinforce the point that *all derivatives* can present intermediaries and end users with potential risk; participants must therefore strive to understand the upside and downside of all transactions, whether straightforward or exotic. A vanilla derivative transaction that is misused or mismanaged can be more damaging than an exotic transaction that is properly used and controlled, and vice versa.

In some cases derivative losses have been, and can be, especially large and cause considerable financial problems. In the most extreme situations financial collapse can follow (for example, the failure of merchant bank Barings and the forced bailout and subsequent wind-down of hedge fund Long Term Capital Management (LTCM)). However, it is important to remember that even in such extreme cases it is not the derivative contracts themselves, but the way in which they are used, that creates losses and problems – reinforcing the need for strong risk management awareness within every organization.

Given the size of the market, overall derivative losses (which began appearing in the late 1980s with the collapse of the US savings and loan sector and continue to the present time) have remained relatively modest – certainly in comparison with other credit-sensitive instruments, including bonds and loans. Despite a relatively strong track record over the past two decades, the financial press has reported, quite appropriately, on the negative side of the business: losses sustained by intermediaries and end users on large or highly complex positions in derivatives; lack of appropriate risk controls at both intermediaries and end users; insufficient disclosure on key issues such as derivative transaction risk and ongoing valuation; "inappropriate transactions" executed with relatively unsophisticated players, and so on. Most of these losses have been well contained, however, impacting only a limited number of parties at any one time.

Indeed, only on two occasions have broader systemic concerns arisen. The first occurred during the LTCM crisis of late 1998. LTCM, as noted below, was a highly leveraged hedge fund with very large positions in derivatives that encountered difficulties during the market turmoil of June to October 1998 (triggered initially by Russia's domestic debt default). The fund's large losses in a range of derivative (and cash) markets raised serious fears that other funds and dealers would collapse as well. Panic set in among the financial markets at large, and a wide range of assets were negatively impacted, including global equity volatilities, high grade corporate credit spreads, and off-the-run US Treasury bonds. This led to broader concerns about liquidity, pricing, hedging, and collateral management for a period of several weeks in September and October. In the event, a multi-bank bailout group prevented a systemic collapse, but the "negative aspects" of derivatives were widely publicized. The second major event occurred in 2001 when Enron, the largest player in the energy derivatives market (holding up to a 25 percent share in some segments), admitted to accounting problems, restated its earnings, and went through a period of rapid financial deterioration. Once again, there was concern that the collapse of the firm would lead to the failure of other dealers and energy companies (as many had dealt with the company on an unsecured basis since it maintained an investment grade rating until two months before its collapse). The bankruptcy and subsequent unwinding of positions was organized; although some firms sustained losses, the process was orderly and no systemic damage occurred. Despite the specter of deeper problems in both cases it became clear that the reasons for the dislocations related primarily to weak corporate governance and risk management, not the functioning of derivatives themselves.[1]

Highlighted below is a summary of significant OTC and exchange-traded derivative losses of the past 20 years. This list is not all-inclusive, merely a sampling of the most interesting and dramatic losses that have occurred since the mid-1980s. Again, the nature and source of the losses is quite varied, and includes market, model, operational/control, legal, and credit risks. Although our particular focus is on counterparty credit risks that arise from dealing in derivatives, it should be clear that they cannot be analyzed or managed in isolation. As we shall note in Chapter 3, the strong corporate governance function ensures proper coordination and communication on key issues – such as derivative risk and management – across all business units and control functions.

A SAMPLING OF DERIVATIVE LOSSES

As noted above, derivative losses can arise from a number of different sources, including market risk, model risk, operational/control risk, legal risk, and credit risk. While exchange-traded derivative losses are typically confined to market risks and operational/control risks, OTC derivatives are subject to those risk sources and also to model, legal, and credit risks. We consider each of these in turn by highlighting representative examples.

Market risk losses

Market risk losses from derivative contracts can come from a variety of sources, including market movements (for example, the derivative reference moves in a manner opposite to the one expected), *mishedging* (for example, a poorly constructed hedge, or one that changes over time, fails to provide the protection required), or a breakdown in financial relationships/assumptions that govern the price and hedge parameters of a transaction (for example, historical volatility, correlations, dividend payments, or basis/spreads used to trade or hedge become irrelevant in the face of some dislocation). A firm active in derivatives might sustain market-related losses from a number of sources:

- *Delta*: losses from small, adverse moves in the direction of a market reference (for instance, interest rate, bond price, equity price, and credit spread).

- *Gamma*: losses from large, adverse moves in the direction of a market reference; this is particularly true in the instance of options that have been sold (as we shall discuss in Part II).

- *Vega*: losses from adverse movement in the level of implied market volatility.

- *Theta*: losses from time decay, or the passage of time.

- *Correlation*: losses from adverse movement in correlations (price relationships) underpinning a derivative contract or derivative trading/hedging strategy.

- *Skew*: losses from adverse movement in the volatility relationship between out-of-the-money put and call options.

- *Smile*: losses from adverse movement in the volatility relationship between in-, out-, and at-the-money options.

- *Curve*: losses from adverse movement in the shape of the reference curve (price/maturity relationship).

- *Spread*: losses from adverse movement in the differential between two reference assets that may not have a common link.

- *Basis*: losses from adverse movement in the differential between two reference assets that are related but not perfectly fungible.

Mishedging is a frequent source of losses in the derivatives market, particularly among active derivative intermediaries that deal in complex products. The collapse of historical or implied price, rate, or volatility relationships can also create market-related losses. This often manifests itself during periods of extreme market stress, when investors, end users, and intermediaries abandon certain assets and risks in favor of others, causing supply and demand imbalances and price distortions. Market losses can be compounded by the presence of *illiquidity*, which is the inability to realize value on a derivative position when needed. For instance, if a dealer cannot liquidate a bad position or establish a protective hedge as a result of general illiquidity, it might sustain additional losses.

Noted below are several examples of publicly reported market-based derivative losses. Where available, we have cited specific derivative instruments that have caused the market-related losses. (Some of the market risk-related losses sustained by corporate end users have led to legal actions against the derivative providers/intermediaries; we consider those losses in the legal risk section below.)

- First Boston lost US$50m in 1987 from dealing in OTC bond options (primarily due to risk management difficulties).

- JP Morgan lost an estimated US$50m in 1991 from dealing in mortgage derivatives.

- Allied Lyons lost approximately US$220m in 1991 from dealing in foreign exchange derivatives.

- Nippon Steel Chemical lost US$154m in 1993 from dealing in foreign exchange derivatives.

- Tokai Corporation lost US$43m in 1993 from Australian dollar and US dollar currency options and forwards.

- Metallgesellschaft lost US$1.3b in 1993 from mishedging long-term oil exposures with short-term futures contracts.

- Air Products and Chemicals lost US$107m in 1994 from a series of leveraged US dollar swaps.

- Berjaya Industrial lost US$14m in 1994 from Australian dollar and Deutschemark leveraged interest rate swaps.

- China International Petroleum and Chemical Company lost US$44m in 1994 from dealing in foreign exchange derivatives.

- China National Metals and Mineral Import and Export Company lost US$52.5m in 1994 from dealing in foreign exchange derivatives.

- Dharmala Sakti Sejahtara lost US$64m in 1994 from leveraged swaps and Libor barrier swaps.

- Chemical Bank lost US$70m in 1994 from currency derivatives.

- Federated Paper Board lost approximately US$47m in 1994 from interest rate derivatives.

- Gibson Greetings lost US$23m in 1994 from Libor-linked ratio swaps, leveraged Treasury swaps and spread locks, leveraged inverse knock-out calls, and periodic floors.

- Kashima Oil lost US$1.77b in 1994 from dealing in forward foreign exchange contracts/historical rate rollovers.

- Procter and Gamble lost US$195m in 1994 from US and German leveraged yield curve swaps and ratio swaps.

- Glaxo lost US$190m in 1994 from asset backed securities and derivatives.

- TPI Polene lost US$31m in 1994 from mishedging an underlying Deutschemark exposure with a currency swap.

- Tokyo Securities lost US$325m in 1994 from dealing in currency options.

- Orange County lost US$1.7b in 1994 from leveraged interest rate products and derivatives.

- Postipannki lost US$110m in 1995 from mortgage derivatives.

- Mattel lost US$20m in 1995, primarily from Mexican peso derivatives.

- Capital Corporate Federal Credit Union lost US$126m in 1995 from mortgage derivatives.

- Wisconsin Investment Board lost US$95m in 1995 from interest rate and currency derivatives.

- Kanematsu Corporation lost US$83m in 1995 from dealing in crude oil futures.

- Nippon Sanso lost US$132m in 1995 from yen yield curve swaps.

- Overseas Chinese Bank lost up to US$60m in 1995 from a series of quanto swaps.

- Commonfund lost US$138m in 1995 from stock index futures and options.

- Sinar Mas Group companies (Indah Kiat Pulp and Paper, Pabrik Kertas Tjiwi Kimia, and Sinar Mas Agro Resources) lost US$69m in 1995 from interest rate and currency derivatives.

- Various international banks lost heavily from the market risk positions on their derivative books as a result of disruptions from August to October 1998, caused by Russia's domestic debt default and hedge fund LTCM's growing financial stress (which culminated in a US$3.6b bank bailout of the fund in late September 1998). Specific details on actual losses were not widely published. When information was disclosed it was typically done as an overall loss figure, combining cash trading and derivative trading losses: for instance, CSFB and Goldman Sachs reported that they lost over US$1b each in market risk positions, ING Barings just under US$1b, and so on.

- Goldman Sachs, CSFB, and other dealers suffered "large losses" in 1999 in sterling swaptions when covering short positions in long-dated swaption volatility.

- French insurer Scor lost approximately US$40m on credit derivatives in late 2002.

Model risk losses

Model risk losses can arise from analytics errors (for instance, errors
with the underlying mathematical analytics used to value derivative
transactions) and technological implementation flaws (for example,
errors in software coding). As we shall note at length in this text, market
and credit risk quantification (for pricing, risk exposure, and hedging
purposes) is heavily dependent on the use of models. Any errors
centered in quantitative methods can lead to potentially significant
losses. This is especially true in derivative markets that do not feature
much two-way flow or price transparency. While it is simple to get
accurate quotes for vanilla interest rate or currency swaps, equity index
options, and so forth, the same is not true for esoteric, longer-dated, or
less active market references such as complex, multi-option packages,
20 or 30 year transactions, and structures referencing illiquid indexes.
In such instances an intermediary or end user is forced to rely on a
mark-to-model rather than mark-to-market valuation, meaning that the
underlying parameters and assumptions that are used to construct that
model are of paramount importance and, if not handed correctly, can
generate losses. Examples of derivative-based model risk losses
include:

- Chemical Bank lost US$33m in 1989 from dealing in interest rate
  options, primarily as a result of mispricing in its commercial
  paper/Libor options book.

- National Westminster Bank (now part of Royal Bank of Scotland
  Group) lost US$139m in 1997 from modeling errors and mispricings
  in sterling interest rate derivatives.

- Bank of Tokyo Mitsubishi lost US$83m in 1997 from modeling errors
  in its swap and option books.

- UBS lost US$420m in 1997 from mispriced transactions in its global
  equity derivatives unit (including model errors that affected its positions in Japanese convertible bonds, UK equity index derivatives, and
  long-dated European options).[2]

- Natexis Banques Populaires lost a "significant" amount (for example,
  reported estimates of €30m) in the second half of 2002 from model
  valuation errors in its structured equity product and exotic option
  book.

Operational/control risk losses

Operational/control risk losses can come from a variety of sources and in some cases can be particularly devastating. Although there are many ways of categorizing operational/control risk losses, for our purposes we define them to include:

- Operational errors (for example, errors in trade tickets or reconciliations).

- Control failures (for example, problems with proper segregation of duties, inadequate policies and procedures, and ineffective audits/financial controls).

- Collateral management failures (problem tracking, valuing, and monitoring collateral taken as security against derivative transactions).

- Business interruption (for example, inability to access systems, data, technology, telecommunications, or physical infrastructure in order to engage in business).

Within the derivatives sector, some of the most significant losses have come from control failures, where inadequate controls/checks and balances (technological, operational, financial, and audit) and/or lack of segregation between front and back-office activities has led to instances of unauthorized trading in a variety of derivative instruments. Failure to monitor and manage collateral processes properly can also be a significant source of losses. This is because elements of the derivatives market rely on collateral to secure exposures properly, and an inability to track, value, liquidate, return, or request additional security can result in problems. Examples of operational/control risk losses from the derivatives market follow:[3]

- Merrill Lynch lost approximately US$377m in 1987 from dealing in mortgage derivatives (partly due to unauthorized trading).

- Salomon Brothers (now part of Citibank) reported US$281m in operational risk losses in 1994 from unreconciled balances in its New York and London derivative operations from 1988–93.

- Codelco lost US$174m in 1994 from dealing in copper futures (due to unauthorized trading).

- CITIC Shanghai lost US$42m in 1994 from dealing in copper futures (much apparently due to unauthorized trading).

- Showa Shell lost nearly US$1.4b in 1994 from dealing in forward foreign exchange contracts/historical rate rollovers (much reportedly due to unauthorized trading).

- Barings lost US$1.4b in 1995 from dealing in futures and options on Japanese Government Bonds, Euroyen, and Nikkei 225 (due to unauthorized trading and manipulation of controls/systems).

- Tokyo Securities lost US$355m in 1995 from dealing in over-the-counter options on US Treasuries and UK gilts (primarily due to unauthorized trading).

- Daiwa Bank lost US$1.1b in 1995 from dealing in US Treasury bonds and Treasury bond derivatives (due to unauthorized trading and manipulation of controls/systems).

- Sumitomo Corporation lost US$2.6b in 1996 from dealing in copper futures (due to unauthorized trading and manipulation of controls/systems).

- Griffin, a Chicago-based commodity futures firm, collapsed in late 1998 after an independent London trader clearing through the firm lost US$10m in Eurex bund futures trading (well in excess of authorized clearing limits).

- Allfirst/AIB lost US$691m in 2002 from dealings in ¥/$ forwards and options (due to unauthorized trading and manipulation of controls/systems).

Legal risk losses

Legal risk losses can occur as a result of:

- Lack of proper documentation (or documentation that fails to adequately protect against potential losses, for example, poorly or vaguely defined terms).

- Lack of legal basis in the national system where a particular dispute is being adjudicated (for example, netting is not enforceable).

- Dealing outside of legal scope (for example, *ultra vires*, meaning a counterparty has no legal authorization to conduct certain types of commercial or financial activities).

■ Unsuitable transactions (for example, derivative dealing that is found to have an excess of risk, poor disclosure of potential losses, bad or irregular communication of periodic valuations).

It is worth noting that in some cases legal risk losses on derivative contracts occur directly, rather than indirectly. For instance, rather than face the public spectacle and press coverage related to a court case, an intermediary may decide to settle the case out of court by paying a "damaged party" some recompense – whether or not there would have been a legal case against the intermediary. Some firms believe that it is far more important to protect reputation and goodwill (since these are the essence of any financial business) and will thus go to great lengths to keep the matter relatively quiet (it should be noted that many such settlements often occur on a "no contest" basis so that the intermediary neither admits nor denies guilt).

■ Several international banks lost varying amounts in the UK local authorities swap cases in 1991 (including the key Hammersmith and Fulham case), following a House of Lords determination that local authorities executed swaps outside their empowered authorities. The final losses ultimately amounted to US$178m, though a potential US$900m was originally at stake.[4]

■ Bankers Trust (BT) lost hundreds of millions of dollars through out of court settlements paid to corporate customers that felt they had been misled by the bank into executing a series of complex leveraged swaps; they included Procter and Gamble, Gibson Greetings, Federal Paper Board, Air Products, and Sandoz. While the financial losses were large, damage to reputation was even more severe and was a catalyst in the eventual sale of the BT to Deutsche Bank.[5]

■ Merrill Lynch agreed to pay Orange County US$437m to settle potential claims related to the financing and derivative transactions it had provided the county (which created the US$1.7b loss cited above); Merrill Lynch pleaded "no contest" in settling the lawsuits. Nomura Securities settled separately on similar transactions.

■ Merrill Lynch and JP Morgan Chase paid US$275m and US$125m, respectively, to Sumitomo Corporation after being sued by the company for their role in providing its trader with excessive financing for the illegal copper futures trade that produced the US$2.6b loss. UBS and Credit Lyonnais ultimately settled with the firm as well.

- Merrill Lynch paid the Kingdom of Belgium US$100m in 2000 in an out-of-court settlement related to exotic currency options. During the early 1990s Belgium purchased a variety of leveraged barrier options on CHF/$ from Merrill Lynch. After the Kingdom sustained market losses on the positions (which reached US$1.4b on an unrealized basis at their peak) it closed down the positions and sued the bank.

- Citibank (via the Yosemite special purpose entity among others) and JP Morgan Chase (via Mahonia) settled regulatory charges related to "prepaid swaps" executed with Enron.[6] The banks were accused of arranging "derivative transactions" that actually functioned as loans and allowed the company to understate its leverage position. Merrill Lynch paid US$80m to regulatory authorities for its part in arranging transactions that ultimately helped Enron hide losses and understate debt levels: one of the Merrill Lynch strategies involved a series of round-trip energy swaps. In all three cases the banks pleased "no contest."

- Allied Irish Bank (AIB) sued Bank of America and Citibank in mid-2003 for their role in helping rogue trader Rusnak conceal US$691m in currency option losses. AIB claimed the two firms, acting as prime brokers, failed to request collateral on exposures with Allfirst (standard industry practice), which would have revealed the fraud at a much earlier stage.

Credit risk losses

Credit risk losses can arise from failure by a counterparty to perform on its contractual derivative obligations, as a result of unwillingness or inability to pay what is due under a specific contract. This can occur with individual companies as well as government-supported organizations and sovereigns.

If a defaulting counterparty is particularly active in derivatives, it might have an entire portfolio of transactions with a number of dealers/counterparties, all of which will become due and payable under standard cross-default clauses. Alternatively, if a counterparty defaults on bond or loan obligations, it will cross-default its derivative transactions – again, making them due and payable.

When a counterparty becomes insolvent, a bankruptcy receiver or administrator will often seek to transfer a derivatives portfolio in its entirety to a third-party in order to preserve value. When this can be done successfully, counterparties to the now-insolvent company might not sustain any credit losses. For instance:

- In late 1989 Development Finance Corporation of New Zealand (DFC) defaulted on its debt obligations, leaving a derivative portfolio of NZ$3b notional (covering 100 transactions with 70 counterparties). The portfolio was transferred in its entirety to Barclays Bank, which assumed DFC's role in the transactions.

- In 1990 Drexel Burnham Lambert (DBL) defaulted on its debt obligations, leaving a derivative portfolio of US$25b notional (covering 250 counterparties). The entire portfolio was unwound during bankruptcy proceedings with a net gain of US$10m to DBL and no losses to counterparties.

- In early 1990 British and Commonwealth Merchant Bankers (BCMB) defaulted on its debt obligations, leaving a derivative portfolio of £1.5b notional (covering 130 transactions with 40 counterparties). The portfolio was transferred in its entirety to Barclays Bank, which assumed BCMB's role in the transactions.

- In 1992 Olympia and York (O & Y) defaulted on its debt obligations. Following an out of court agreement, parties to O & Y derivatives were able to preserve the value inherent in their transactions.

At other times, however, real losses ensue; this is especially true when a large market player is involved, or broader systemic forces damage an entire sector or industry group.

- The 1998 Russia/hedge fund crisis, where many international banks and fund managers engaged in a variety of OTC derivative transactions tied to credit baskets, emerging market bonds and currencies, global equity volatility, and so forth, led to a broad range of credit losses. Although specific losses generally were not detailed, they are known to have been quite substantial. Though many of the derivatives were structured with collateral, the very significant market dislocations that occurred ultimately left some firms unsecured (for example, lags in obtaining additional collateral, inability to liquidate collateral near carrying values) and thus exposed to loss. Some of the transactions were highly correlated (for instance, a total return swap with a Russian bank using a Russian bond as reference) meaning the probability of a credit loss was much greater, as the creditworthiness of the bank would decline at the same time the value of the reference bond was deteriorating and the exposure of the offshore counterparty increasing. International banks and funds that did such transactions using Russian, Korean, Argentine, Indonesian, and similar emerging market assets/counterparties sustained a variety of credit losses.

- Various financial institutions suffered credit losses on their dealings with hedge fund LTCM (which was bailed out by a group of international banks in September 1998 – though not before significant value had eroded). UBS, for instance, wrote off US$693m on its LTCM exposure.

- US energy company Enron defaulted on its debt obligations – including loans, bonds, and derivatives – in December 2001. Many counterparties had dealt with Enron either directly or indirectly (through the Enron Online platform, a conduit that permitted electronic trading of "standardized" derivative contracts on energy, weather, and commodity references). Those that did not take collateral from the company suffered loses on contracts with positive value whereas those that were secured emerged relatively, or completely, unharmed.

It is worth noting that in many of the other rather spectacular bankruptcies occurring at the turn of the millennium, including WorldCom, Global Crossing, Swissair, Adelphia Communications, Kmart, Daewoo Corporation, Qwest, Lernout and Hauspie, and Railtrack, the discipline characteristic of the derivatives marketplace meant that no meaningful credit-related derivative losses occurred.[7] Most of the companies cited above were sub-investment grade and, to the extent they engaged in derivatives, were required to post collateral as standard operating procedure. This "self regulatory" characteristic of the OTC derivatives market, which we discuss in Chapter 4, has served participants well over the years. While many bond and loan holders lost billions of dollars as direct, unsecured lenders (or secured lenders unable to realize expected value from their security holdings) the same was not necessarily true of derivatives parties. This does not suggest that large, credit-related derivative losses cannot or will not happen, simply that they have been avoided in the past as a result of important market discipline.

It should be relatively clear from the examples and discussion above that derivatives can cause losses when they are not properly considered and managed. Though the contracts themselves can be relatively benign, they should only be used in a properly controlled environment that incorporates key aspects of an integrated risk management process. An institution seeking to be an active derivatives participant – whether as end user or intermediary – must ensure an adequate level of understanding and protection before commencing any activities. This means considering very closely the types of losses that might arise in the normal course of derivatives dealing. Though our focus in this book is limited to the credit risk dimension of derivative activities we stress the point that risk management in the "enlightened" organization is holistic and thoroughly considers all elements and sources of risk, including market, model, operational, legal, and credit aspects. In the next chapter we consider risk governance and risk management structures that are designed to help an institution avoid some of the derivative-based losses we have cited above.

CHAPTER 3

Risk Governance and Risk Management

CORPORATE AND RISK GOVERNANCE

Corporate governance, which we define as the responsibility a corporation has to its stakeholders generally and its shareholders specifically, focuses on many different theories, concepts, and practices, most of them well outside the scope of this book.[1] However, governance can be narrowed considerably for our purposes, so that we can investigate its use in the context of credit risk management. Under such a focused view, credit risks must be properly considered, managed, and controlled so that stakeholder expectations and requirements are met.

Financial risks are diverse and pervasive. As we have already noted, financial and corporate institutions with any degree of operating scope are required to deal with credit, market, liquidity, legal, and operational risks on an ongoing basis (as well as pure operating risks, which are beyond our scope). To do so properly demands a process that:

- defines an appropriate risk appetite and capital framework

- assigns accountabilities and responsibilities throughout the organization

- establishes proper controls, including policies, control units, reporting, and infrastructure and audit verification.

The process created by a company's directors – as agents of shareholders – to manage risks must be reviewed and approved by regulators and supervisors. Although these authorities vary by industry (for example, bank, insurance company, investment management firm, and so on) they must ensure that institutions are operating according to prudent guidelines. Where relevant, they must make certain that every institution is adhering to overarching policies, procedures, and financial standards so that the possibility of stakeholder mistreatment and systemic disruption are reduced.

Failure to create a proper risk governance framework can ultimately lead to unexpected losses and financial distress. Such losses might come from taking too much risk or being unaware of risks taken; they can harm enterprise value and, thus, shareholder interests. A firm must therefore seek to avoid "surprise" losses and ensure efficient and profitable use of capital. A robust credit risk management process, operating in concert with other risk and control functions, can help achieve this goal.

CREDIT RISK MANAGEMENT PROCESSES

The credit governance process is created by the board of directors and managed on a daily basis by executive management and the independent control functions. In practical terms risk management is a combination of awareness, culture, controls, clarity, and disclosure, and operates through a multi-stage process centered on identification, measurement, management, and reporting. An effective credit risk process, acting as part of a broader suite of governance measures, can combat common problems that might otherwise appear, including poor credit standards, inadequate transaction-level or portfolio-based risk measures, inattention to counterparty financial deterioration, and/or insufficient transparency regarding true risks (for example, concentrations, correlations, non-nettable exposures, "missing" information, and other problems that might skew the true counterparty risk profile).

Board level risk duties

The board of directors in any public company has certain responsibilities it must pursue in the prudent discharge of its fiduciary duties. While directors obviously have many responsibilities, some relate specifically to the treatment of financial risks including credit risks.[2] In particular, directors, in representing shareholders and providing ultimate oversight over executive management, must approve and review a firm's credit risks. This involves, initially and/or continuously:

■ Defining an appropriate level of credit risk exposure; this should ideally be related to the firm's:

   – business lines, strategies, and client/market focus

   – financial resources and ability to withstand losses

   – profit hurdles and risk/return considerations

- shareholder expectations

- technical expertise.

■ Creating an independent control function (for example, corporate risk management division) to monitor and manage the risk process.

■ Delegating certain management, authority, and monitoring duties to executive management and independent control functions.

■ Reviewing and communicating, internally and externally, the firm's risk exposures and risk tolerance levels.

These high level duties are summarized in Figure 3.1.

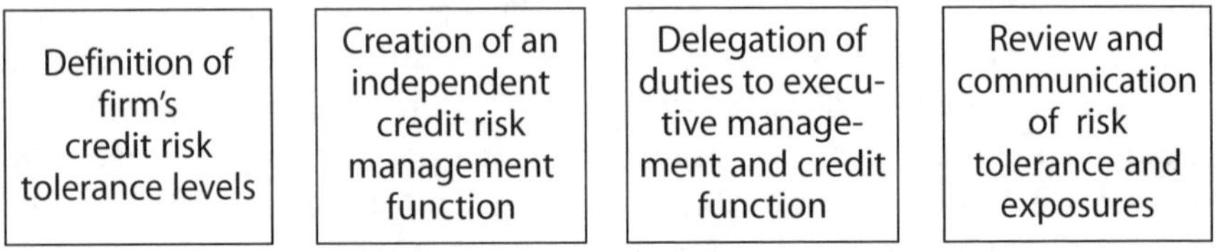

Definition of firm's credit risk tolerance levels	Creation of an independent credit risk management function	Delegation of duties to execu- tive manage- ment and credit function	Review and communication of risk tolerance and exposures

Figure 3.1 Board level credit risk management duties

Once a board has defined overall tolerance levels (related, in some meaningful way, to the financial resources, goals, and expectations of the firm), it must discharge the daily operation of risk management to those most qualified to oversee matters. It must ensure the independent control functions create policies and procedures that properly constrain exposures and foster a safe operating environment. It should also require regular reporting on the status of exposures and significant control issues. Indeed, directors must be kept informed of all significant risk issues/profile/trend, top exposures, exceptions, and violations.

Corporate risk management duties

The corporate risk management function – the independent body charged by the board with overseeing the daily risk process – has grown in many institutions to include specialists focused on credit risk, market risk, and operational (or process) risk. This unit is typically responsible for:

■ Creation and enforcement of all relevant risk policies.

■ Establishment of appropriate risk limits (related specifically to the firm's tolerance).

■ Allocation of risk limits to individual business units and ongoing decisions/monitoring.

■ Continuous identification, quantification, management, and reporting of risks to all relevant parties.

These duties are summarized in Figure 3.2.

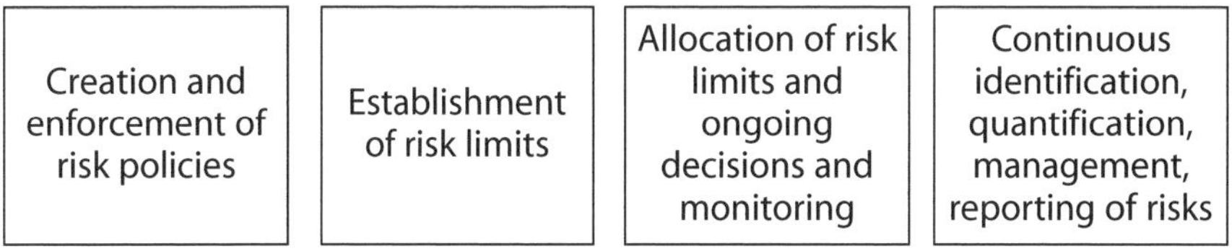

Creation and enforcement of risk policies	Establishment of risk limits	Allocation of risk limits and ongoing decisions and monitoring	Continuous identification, quantification, management, reporting of risks

Figure 3.2 Corporate risk management duties

The board should make certain that adequate resources exist to attract the correct level of skills and experience into the function. Risk managers must have the stature and experience necessary to properly manage the firm's risks. Sufficient resources must also exist for other essential risk management requirements, including technology (in any complex organization systems must be used to keep track of exposures; indeed, many of the algorithms and analytics we consider in this text demand considerable computing power, particularly at the portfolio level). Naturally, the risk function must be independent of business units that actually take risks. Accordingly, it must report up through the office of the CFO or directly into executive management. The head of the function should also have direct access to the board of directors in order to communicate sensitive issues. Under no circumstances must the risk group have any compensation, reporting, or management ties with risk-taking business units. The corporate risk function must focus on risk identification, measurement, management, and reporting on a daily basis and the entire process must be supported by the appropriate infrastructure. We consider each point in brief.

Identification

The risk management process begins with identification of risks – if a firm does not know what risks it has, it cannot then quantify and manage them. Credit risks in modern corporate institutions – non-financial, but especially financial – are diverse. In a large firm they may be particularly diffuse, appearing in a variety of instruments and products across multiple business units. Credit spread (or migration) risks and credit default risks can exist through a firm's balance sheet and off-balance sheet activities; delivery/ settlement risks (which are sometimes classified as credit risks and other times as operational risks) might exist in some business lines as well. Though our primary interest in this text is on credit default risks that arise from derivatives activity, we would be remiss in excluding from our discussion other credit risks that can impact a firm. This is particularly true when we start considering portfolio risk management issues that are influenced by all credit-sensitive instruments and transactions; an holistic, or enterprise-wide, view demands that all credit risks be considered in unison. Thus, where appropriate, we shall broaden our focus and discussion.

Figure 3.3 illustrates sources of credit risk that might be found in a typical financial institution.

Credit risk activity has been expanded (and some might say complicated) by the growing liquidity of credit derivatives – instruments that can hedge, transfer, or synthetically reproduce a credit spread or credit default position. Though this provides new risk management opportunities (as we shall discuss in Chapters 8 and 10), it also makes the identification of credit risks

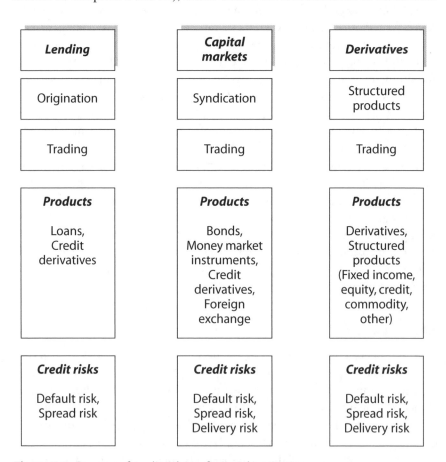

Figure 3.3 Sources of credit risk in a financial institution

more challenging on both a micro and macro basis. Indeed, it can be very hard to determine where in an institution and the financial system credit risks actually reside, since they can be shifted among business units, institutions, and markets with relative ease (and at reasonable cost).

Risk identification functions best when the corporate risk function works cooperatively with business units and other control functions. In addition to standard credit committees to review particular credit proposals, the process can be strengthened by the addition of new product, capital commitment, and suitability functions. For instance, a new product committee can evaluate the risks inherent in any new marketplace, product or client relationship, a capital commitment committee might review the credit risk implications of new lending or financing transactions, and a suitability committee can determine whether the nature of proposed client transactions is appropriate from both a firm and client perspective (this is particularly true in the case of complex derivative transactions, which are not always simple to understand). By adding such mechanisms in the identification process a firm can help define the precise nature and scope of credit risks and help minimize the chance of problems and losses, including those we have mentioned in Chapter 2.

Measurement

Once specific sources of credit risk have been identified (for example, default risk from derivative transactions or loans, settlement risk from foreign exchange transactions, and convertibility risk from placement of local assets in a country that might impose capital controls) they must be measured. The credit risk function, often in conjunction with a quantitative research or market risk function, should be able to quantify three different elements: transactions, portfolios, and counterparties. This, as we shall note in subsequent chapters, is an essential, and sometimes non-trivial, task.

Measuring the magnitude of the firm's risk exposure on transactions and portfolios is critical for initial decision-making and ongoing credit portfolio management. As part of any quantification process, good governance demands that models and analytics used to mathematically measure risks be independently reviewed and stress tested (in order to capture the "unthinkable"). These steps can help provide comfort regarding the intellectual integrity and rigor of an approach and possible "worst-case" scenarios that might actually impact a firm's portfolio (and capital levels). Quantification techniques should also focus on correlated exposures that might appear in the portfolio during changing market conditions (for instance, times of market stress) to determine whether unwanted risk concentrations might appear. We shall consider each one of these issues in greater detail in Part III of the book.

The quantification process must also focus on counterparty credit ratings – the process of financially analyzing and rating each of the firm's counterparties in order to estimate the likelihood of default. The ratings process must be based on thorough, fundamental credit analysis and include current and prospective analysis of all relevant financial statements and associated information (for example, income statement, balance sheet, cash flows, corporate hierarchies, related-party transactions, legal status/ability to engage in business, and off-balance sheet activities). Prudent credit analysis stresses the performance of the counterparty in a "down cycle" (for example, a weak credit environment brought on by industrial slowdown or global recession). The ideal counterparty rating system is driven by a firm's independent rating analysis, which should be monitored continuously. To be useful the process should reflect internal and external consistencies so that similar companies are analyzed and rated in a similar fashion. Thus, a German steel manufacturer with particular leverage and liquidity characteristics, and a Japanese steel company with a similar financial profile, should carry the same performance risk. Consistency across counterparties helps ensure that an AA or BBB rated credit means the same thing to every credit risk officer or business manager. Third party benchmarking (for example, via consultants, supervisors, markets) can create a useful link to the external environment and help reinforce a particular view. When an internal ratings approach cannot be accommodated for resource reasons, there must be some minimum reference to work supplied by external agencies (for example, Moody's, Standard and Poor's, Fitch, and so on). Of course, relying solely on external ratings must be considered carefully as it effectively puts a portion of the credit management process in the hands of a third party. Rigor in the ratings process is especially critical when ratings are linked explicitly to a firm's risk tolerance and allocation process. For instance, if a firm is only comfortable taking a certain amount of credit risk with a borderline investment grade counterparty (for example, BBB-/Baa3 in terms of external ratings) then it must be certain that the counterparties that it rates in that category are actually in that category –and not really in a sub-investment grade category.

Since the quantification effort related to credit risks is driven heavily by models and analytic processes, it is very important to stress that models are simply an approximation of financial reality – they cannot always accurately convey the reality of the marketplace or human nature, and can only be one dimension of a risk management framework. The governance process must always emphasize the importance of using models in a proper context – conservatively and realistically rather than "blindly," with due consideration of shortcomings and potential flaws. Human judgment should always override model-driven results when it seems prudent to do so.

Management

Ongoing management of risks centers on balancing the firm's credit exposures in light of its authorized risk appetite. Counterparties must be reviewed and rated as part of the quantification process. Credit transactions or facilities must then be considered by gaining a thorough understanding of the specifics of a structure: the nature of the facility, the rationale for the transaction, sources of repayment,[3] the nature of potential risk mitigants (for example, collateral, netting), credit seniority, suitability, authority to deal, and so on. Active management of collateral securing credit exposures is vital. Though collateral should never be the sole (or even primary) source of repayment, it can facilitate the execution of business. This means that processes and technologies must be able to cope with collateral valuations and calls, as well as possible liquidation. Any collateral process must also have a link back to exposure computations, to reflect possible lags in receiving requested security. Ongoing management of risks covers many disciplines and all relevant control groups must work in a coordinated manner if risk governance is to function effectively.

As the portfolio of counterparty exposures builds, and the sum total of portfolios across industries, countries, and ratings classes grows in tandem, the overall business must be managed in light of the firm's risk appetite. Where exceptions are needed, a procedure for obtaining proper executive management (or even board level) sanction must be put in place and followed. Exceptions should be just that – exceptions – and strictly limited in size and maturity. Proper management also demands a focus on the returns that can be obtained from credit-related businesses. As we shall note later in the book, it is vital that the extension of risk capital command a fair price. If one of the key goals of good governance is to provide shareholders with a fair return on capital invested, then that philosophy and metric must exist throughout the firm. If resources are not priced to maximize returns, then shareholders will not earn what they deserve. As already indicated, the increasing growth of the credit derivatives market and liquidity of underlying classes of credit risks mean that pricing is more transparent than ever before; every firm should have in place a framework for the evaluation of risk-adjusted returns on credit capital.

Most firms discharge the management of risk appetite through a risk limit structure, with an explicit tie back to the firm's stated risk tolerance. Risk limits, which must be properly documented in order to establish an appropriate audit trail, are intended to constrain the maximum amount of business that can be done in different risk classes, including credit risks. Effective management means diligent monitoring and management of such limits. Those who violate limits must be penalized through a properly designed, and diligently enforced, process. Failure to do so renders the independent risk management function ineffective and weakens the entire governance process. Credit approval authorities should be explicitly granted and risk managers should follow the proper chain of command when exceptions are sought; decisions should be taken on the basis of established procedures rather than subjective actions.

Daily management also requires a focus on portfolio management. Because credit risks exist in so many different parts of a firm, and because they are becoming increasingly liquid (for example, even once-illiquid par loans have developed a secondary market of their own) the migration towards true credit portfolio management is finally a reality – rather than an academic or theoretical exercise. Active management requires appropriate infrastructure. While it is simple to talk about enterprise-wide credit management from both a control and return-maximization standpoint, it is quite another to actual implement it. To be effective, credit risk portfolio management requires data, analytics, technology, and, most importantly, the proper mindset.

Naturally, effective management requires that those responsible for credit risks work in close cooperation with their colleagues in Finance (on reserve issues), Treasury (liquidity management), Legal (suitability and credit workout issues), Audit (business and risk controls), and Operations (settlement risks). The legal dimensions of credit relationships serve as a good example of cross-unit cooperation. Credit officers monitoring distressed credit exposure must work with lawyers to determine appropriate legal protections and actions in the event of insolvency and the two groups should regularly discuss the common "credit events" that can impact a counterparty – such as failure to meet obligations, bankruptcy/moratorium, repudiation, debt restructuring, or acceleration. Collateral management serves as another good example. As events of the past few years have shown, an effective collateral process is central to good governance. A robust technical environment must surround any collateral that is securing credit exposures (particularly those which are sub-investment grade). The process requires perfecting a security interest upfront, creating proper "haircuts" (discounts) in initial security taken, recognizing potential lags that might exist in receiving additional collateral, remaining aware of contingent market risk that might arise through correlation between collateral and credit risks, attending to valuation of positions and calling for additional security when needed, and so forth. These are important issues that cross functional boundaries: credit, technology, operations, finance, and legal. Credit risks cannot be managed in a vacuum – many intersections and dependencies exist, and the closer the inter-departmental links, the lower the likelihood of surprise losses. Internal and external auditors must regularly review the risk function to ensure adherence to corporate policies (including those sanctioned by the board) and regulatory requirements. This is an important tie back to board-driven directives.

Reporting

Without proper reporting mechanisms and infrastructure, the credit risk management exercise, and the overall risk governance effort, becomes ineffective. Relevant parties must have access to meaningful, accurate, and reasonably timely information on credit risk exposures – including counterparty exposures versus limits, concentrations, top risks, actual and future exposures, credit reserves, netting agreements, and collateral.

Reporting exposures in a large firm is not an easy task; it demands an investment in technology, creation of data templates with minimum counterparty and transaction parameters, and controls around the entire process. The inputs must be sufficiently flexible to accommodate new business products, clients, and markets, while the outputs must be sufficiently meaningful and transparent that a broad range of users can interpret and use the information. Reporting must also be timely. This does not mean real-time reporting of exposures – that, in most cases, is both technically impossible (absent great expense) and unnecessary. It is much more important for the reporting mechanism to supply complete and accurate credit risk exposure information after the close of business or the start of the next business day. Unlike market risk exposures, which have to be managed dynamically during the course of the day (reinforcing the need for real-time exposure reporting), the same urgency does not really exist with credit risk exposures. A standard suite of close-of-business reports should be circulated to appropriate parties. In a typical organization these might include such things as top exposures by counterparty, largest movement in exposures, sub-investment grade credit exposures, high-risk exposures, concentrations, long-maturity and aged exposures, and credit reserve estimates and movements.

Executive managers and board directors should receive summarized reports on a regular, but somewhat less frequent, cycle. These reports should contain enough information to put them in command of the important credit risks of the firm and how they relate to stated tolerance levels. In order to complete the governance cycle board directors must be aware at all times of the firm's top risks, including its top credit risks, and the state of the firm's risk profile in the context of approved appetite. It should also be advised of any potential credit problems, movement in credit reserves, documentary backlogs, exceptions, legal or client suitability issues, and so forth. In short, any event that could materially impact the firm's reputation or financial position, and in some way jeopardize shareholders capital.

Infrastructure

As noted, an appropriate level of infrastructure, including technology, data and analytics must support the entire credit risk governance process. Many of the identification, management, and reporting tasks that form the core of the process can only be performed with appropriate computing platforms – this is true in any large firm with various sources of credit risk coming from multiple geographic and product areas. Accurate aggregation of risk is critical, particularly when trying to manage concentrations. Data flowing into analytic process must be "clean" and surrounded by controls that ensure integrity. In addition, analytic models used to compute credit risk information must be intellectually robust and computationally sound. Though we shall discuss in Part III different analytic models that firms may use to compute, manage, and report credit exposures, we introduce the concept in brief here. Firms most often select between one of two approaches:

- Counterparty exposure models, which measure and aggregate the exposure of all transactions with a given counterparty. For derivative transactions in particular, this may occur via a regulatory "add-on" method or, in a more accurate and sophisticated light, through a simulation process. Leading-edge counterparty exposure simulations can easily handle netting, collateral, and correlated portfolio effects. Counterparty exposure models are most often used for limit management and reporting purposes.

- Portfolio credit risk models, which measure and compute possible credit losses and the capital needed to support business. Again, leading-edge portfolio credit risk simulations can handle portfolio correlations and dynamically changing credit exposures (in a consistent framework). Portfolio credit risk models are typically used for capital allocation and portfolio optimization purposes.

With these basic governance mechanisms in place, a firm is prepared to cope with the challenges of dealing in a risky environment. Figure 3.4 summarizes our discussion of the credit risk governance process. Again, it is important to stress that the risk governance function must never operate in isolation from other business and controls units. The interdependencies, particularly with other control functions, are very significant, so a constructive relationship and open lines of communication are vital. It is also worth emphasizing that a risk culture must be driven from the top of the organization down: board directors and executive managers must believe in the risk process, use it and reinforce it. If they do not, others in the firm will not either.

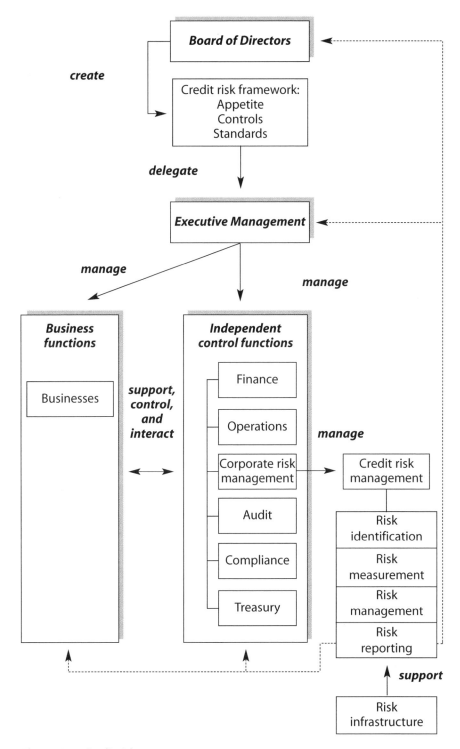

Figure 3.4 Credit risk governance process

CHAPTER 4

Regulatory and Industry Initiatives

Regulation in the derivatives market has evolved steadily over the past three decades through the efforts of national/supranational supervisors, self-regulatory organizations, and financial intermediaries. The process has developed gradually, in response to the natural evolution of the market and the problems that periodically appear. Regulation of derivatives takes two forms: formal regulation through supervisory agencies and self-regulation through market and industry discipline. Both are ultimately necessary to ensure a safe and controlled operating environment and reinforce the governance efforts we have outlined in Chapter 3. When appropriate regulatory processes (and associated legal protections) exist, governance can be truly effective. In this chapter we consider important initiatives and advances that have taken place in both sectors in recent years.

REGULATORY EFFORTS

Regulators – central banks, securities/banking commissions, and monetary authorities – are interested in the risks carried by financial institutions and other counterparties operating in their jurisdictions, and go to considerable lengths to develop broad-based frameworks that help reinforce sound risk management. The underlying premise is good: to ensure that institutions with financial risk exposures (and credit risk exposures specifically, in the context of our discussion) understand the nature of those risks so that they can manage them and have sufficient financial resources to protect against any potential problems. The first issue – understanding the nature of the risks – is central to the governance issues we highlighted in Chapter 3 and shall discuss at length in Part II. The second issue – ensuring the availability of enough financial resources to protect against potential losses – is the focus of our discussion on credit portfolio management in Part III. Though regulations are generally well intended and effective, efforts sometimes fall "short of the mark" and lend themselves to a certain amount of dispute, criticism, and "arbitrage." This happens when efforts are inefficient in protecting participants – what we might term "form over substance" – and can lead to broader problems.

Though many formal regulatory and supervisory regimes exist at a local, regional, or national level, and across specific industries (for example, insurance companies, investment managers, banks, broker-dealers), we focus our attention on the overarching regulations and advances that affect the largest number of players in the financial markets generally, and the derivative markets specifically. In particular, we consider the regulatory framework put forth by the Bank for International Settlements (BIS), since BIS regulations serve as minimum standards for large international banking institutions, most of which are very active in the derivative market.[1] The same applies to the self-regulatory framework. Though many industries and companies have put forth different control frameworks over the years, we are mainly interested in those "best practice" initiatives developed and implemented by market leaders, such as consortia of global financial institutions and industry representatives.

The BIS, credit risk, and capital

The BIS, in its role as the central banker to the world's central banks, has been at the forefront of regulatory initiatives for several decades. Though the mandate of the BIS is broad, we consider in this section its initiatives related to credit risk and capital – both of considerable interest to any institution active in derivatives (and other credit-risky instruments).

Capital is needed to protect an institution against unexpected losses; it provides a financial cushion, or buffer, that permits a firm to continue operating safely. From a credit perspective, capital is allocated to protect against risk of loss arising from an excess of counterparty defaults. By establishing minimum capital requirements the BIS (through national regulatory enforcement) attempts to ensure that an institution has sufficient financial resources to avoid a situation that might lead to financial distress, including potential insolvency. The definition of capital is a central area of focus and debate, and we can consider at least two different forms:

- *Regulatory capital*: capital that institutions must keep on hand in order to satisfy regulatory requirements.

- *Economic capital*: capital that institutions keep on hand to internally manage the risks of their businesses (also known as "management capital").

These two figures are generally not equivalent, primarily because regulators and financial institutions have different ways of defining capital and use different methods to compute how much capital is required to manage a financially risky business. Regulatory capital is most often defined to include Tier 1 and Tier 2 capital:

- Tier 1 (core) capital includes common stock, retained earnings, and disclosed reserves (including loan loss reserves).

- Tier 2 (supplemental) capital includes hybrid securities (for example, mandatory convertibles), long-term subordinated debt with maturities greater than five years, perpetual securities, unrealized gains on investment assets, and hidden reserves.

(Tier 3 capital, used only to cover certain market risks, includes short-term, unsecured subordinated debt.)

It should be noted that Tier 2 capital is limited to a maximum of Tier 1 capital; this helps preserve a higher quality of capital resources (that is, equity-driven rather than debt-driven).

Economic capital, as measured by a financial institution, relates almost exclusively to common stock and retained earnings: the true buffers that management relies on in the event of losses (some institutions also include perpetual preferreds in their definition). These forms of capital are summarized in the balance sheet depicted in Figure 4.1.

The amount of regulatory and economic capital held against risks can vary as a result of computation differences. Individual institutions often employ specific internal models to compute what they view as an appropriate level of capitalization given risk and potential for loss; more often than not, results diverge from those suggested by regulatory models. In an ideal world regulatory and economic capital would be computed in the same way: that is, institutions and regulators would agree on how much capital is needed to protect a business, set relevant hurdles, and calculate according to agreed formulas. With cohesive views, all parties would follow the capital allocation and monitoring process very diligently. However, since there has historically been a considerable difference in views and methodologies, discrepancies exist and arbitrages can occur (for example, if an institution feels that regulatory capital charges are too high compared with what it believes real risks to be, it might move to an alternate, unregulated regime where such high charges are not imposed). As we shall note below, modeling initiatives introduced at the turn of the millennium are leading in the direction of greater unity, which ultimately stands to benefit all parties.

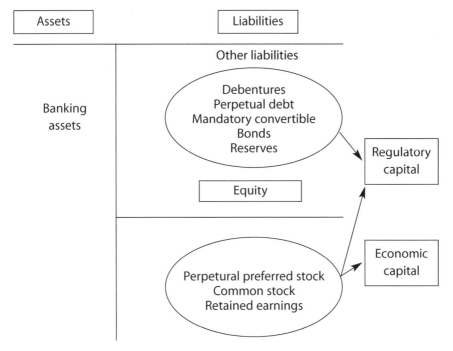

| Assets | Liabilities |

Figure 4.1 Forms of regulatory and economic capital

The 1988 Accord, 1994–5 enhancements, and the 1996 Amendment

In 1988 the BIS promulgated new capital requirements for banking institutions in member countries.[2] The effort was driven largely by the need to ensure global financial institutions had sufficient capital to cover credit risks in their loan portfolios. Many banks had suffered considerable losses during the Latin American debt crisis of the mid-1980s, and the BIS was eager to ensure that institutions would not again be caught short of capital (and possibly create systemic problems). The original BIS requirement called for an institution to maintain a total of 8 percent capital against risk-weighted capital (including a minimum of 4 percent in the form of Tier 1 and 4 percent in Tier 2 – again, with Tier 2 not counting for more than 100 percent of Tier 1). The generic form of the credit capital assignment took the following form:

$$k = RW * Exp * 0.08 \qquad\qquad (4.1)$$

where k is capital; RW is a risk weighting, and Exp is the credit exposure.

The RW risk-weighting factor was based on the characteristics rather than the credit quality of the obligor. Thus, the Organization for Economic Cooperation and Development (OECD) government obligations had a

0 percent weighting, non-OECD banks 100 percent, derivative counter-parties 50 percent, and so forth. The *Exp* exposure component, in turn, was broadly dependent on the nature of the credit obligation. Thus, exposures on loans and guarantees were counted as 100 percent of notional (under the assumption that default on a loan would equal a 100 percent loss – a very conservative stance which ignores possible recoveries), while exposures on derivatives were related to their current and/or potential future value. More specifically, swap exposure was computed through the current exposure method (CEM) and the original exposure method (OEM). The development of CEM and OEM was seen as an appropriate, if embryonic, step toward the uniform allocation of capital in support of swap credit risk. Though many of the elements of the original swap framework were criticized, they provided an early focus on the topic. To understand how the framework has subsequently evolved (and to appreciate the concepts that remain valid to the present time), we review some of the main points of the original process.

Under the CEM approach swap credit risk is the sum of *replacement cost* (or mark-to-market (MTM) value) and future credit exposure, where the future credit exposure is estimated by a CEM factor (not unlike the risk factor we discuss at greater length in the next chapter). The OEM approach ignores replacement cost and focuses strictly on future credit exposure through an OEM factor. These equations are given as:

$$CEM = MTM + (CEM_{factor} * N) \tag{4.2}$$

and

$$OEM = (OEM_{factor} * N) \tag{4.3}$$

where *MTM* is the mark-to-market value of the swap; CEM_{factor} is a predefined *CEM* risk factor supplied by the BIS; OEM_{factor} is a pre-defined *OEM* risk factor supplied by the BIS; and *N* is the notional of the swap.

The formulae by which to allocate capital to swaps via CEM and OEM are given by:

$$CR = \frac{k}{CEM * RW} \tag{4.4}$$

and

$$CR = \frac{k}{OEM * RW} \tag{4.5}$$

where *CR* is an institution's target BIS ratio; *k* is the capital required to support a transaction (and represents an unknwn to be solved); and other terms are as defined above.

Knowing that the standard Tier 1 and Tier 2 capital ratio for member institutions must be a minimum of 8 percent allows a bank to determine the relevant amount of capital, k, needed for a single swap transaction (or a portfolio of swap transactions). We can thus restate the equations above as:

$$k = CEM * CR * RW \tag{4.6}$$

and

$$k = OEM * CR * RW \tag{4.7}$$

Using the CEM approach, assume a bank has a US\$100m swap with a current MTM value of US\$10m; the associated CEM_{factor} is 5 percent and the swap has been executed with a second OECD bank with a risk weighting of 20 percent. In order to generate a capital ratio of 8 percent the required capital is:

$$
\begin{aligned}
k &= ((US\$10m + (US\$100m * 0.05)) * 0.08 * 0.2) \\
&= US\$240,000
\end{aligned}
$$

Note that as the mark-to-market fluctuates and the maturity of the swap declines, the capital associated with the position changes. We shall explore this concept later in the book.

The BIS's original 1988 exposure factors for the CEM and OEM are contained in Tables 4.1 and 4.2. An examination of the tables reveals that 1988 OEM factors are significantly higher than CEM factors, particularly for long-term transactions. This occurs because the OEM does not value the ongoing replacement cost inherent in a swap once it is under way.

Several years after the introduction of the CEM and OEM framework, shortcomings became increasingly apparent. For instance, the Accord treated risks, obligors, and instruments inconsistently and did not allow for portfolio and netting effects or improvements based on internal models.[3] Dealers active in the market wanted to ensure more realistic and equitable

Table 4.1 BIS CEM factors, 1988 (percentages)

Swap maturity	Interest rates	Currency rates
< 1 year	0.0	1.0
> 1 year	0.5	5.0

Table 4.2 BIS OEM factors, 1988 (percentages)

Swap maturity	Interest rates	Currency rates
< 1 year	0.5	2.0
1–2 years	1.0	5.0
> 2 years	additional 1.0 p.a.	additional 3.0 p.a.

treatment of derivative credit risks and the capital allocated against such exposures so as not to stifle market growth and competition, and lobbied for changes. Accordingly, between mid-1994 and mid-1995 the BIS announced several significant alterations to the original CEM methodology – although it did not address all of the shortcomings noted above. As an interim step, it:

■ created risk factors for several new underlying references

■ increased the risk factors for long-term interest rate and currency swaps

■ developed a new formula for determining the risk factor "add-on" amount for swaps based on net, rather than gross, credit exposures.

The first and second changes in the BIS methodology, the creation of CEM factors for new references and longer maturities, occurred as a result of structural developments in the market that gathered momentum during the early 1990s. While the swap market of the 1980s was based primarily on standard short to intermediate maturity interest rate and currency swaps, the market of the 1990s featured strong growth in equity, precious metal and commodity swaps, and long-term interest rate and currency swaps. The new CEM factors arising from the structural market changes are given in Table 4.3.

The third change in the methodology, the introduction of an add-on

Table 4.3 BIS CEM factors, 1994–5 (percentages)

Swap maturity	Interest rates	Currency rates/gold	Equities	Precious metals	Other commodities
< 1 year	0.0	1.0	6.0	7.0	10.0
1–5 years	0.5	5.0	8.0	7.0	12.0
> 5 years	1.5	7.5	10.0	8.0	15.0

computation based on net, rather than gross, credit exposure, came as a result of legal developments that started in the early 1990s. As more institutions active in derivatives began utilizing master agreements and dealing in jurisdictions that recognized and accepted netting of credit exposures, the move to a net exposure valuation for regulatory capital purposes was seen as a justifiable refinement. Through the bilateral netting process, as we mentioned in Chapter 1 (and which we discuss at greater length in Part III), an institution active on both sides of a market with a given counterparty (for example, paying and receiving fixed rates on a portfolio of transactions) can use netting to reduce its credit exposures. When netting is accepted in a given jurisdiction, the true amount of exposure at risk is the difference between the exposure of the fixed payer and receiver swaps; this figure may, at any time, be positive or negative.[4] If counterparties are legally able to net exposures across a portfolio of swap trades they eliminate the risk of a bankruptcy receiver "cherry picking" only those contracts favorable to the defaulting counterparty.

Consider the following example. A credit officer at Bank X establishes a swap limit of US$100m for business with Bank Y in a jurisdiction that accepts netting. If Bank X has a series of swap trades with Bank Y on both sides of the market (and all trades are governed by a master agreement) the portfolio can be condensed into a single net exposure figure. If X's gross potential exposure to Y is US$100m but its net potential exposure is only US$50m (that is, the net figure due X, including future market movements, nets to a value of US$50m) a further US$50m of swaps can be accommodated under the credit line. More importantly, in the event of a default by Y the loss to X is based on net, not gross, mark-to-market exposure. If, in the example above, Bank X's actual mark-to-market exposure on the fixed payer swaps is US$20m (that is, Y owes X a total of US$20m), but the mark-to-market on the fixed receiver swaps is –US$30m (that is, X owes Y a total of $30m), the net payment in bankruptcy, assuming close-out, is US$10m from X to Y. While a bankruptcy receiver would seek to dismiss the US$20m fixed payer swaps and enforce only the US$30m fixed receiver swaps, it will not be able to do so if an enforceable netting agreement exists and the jurisdiction accepts netting. If close-out netting is not allowed (or no master agreement exists), gross credit exposures cannot be reduced to a net balance. Indeed, it is possible that upon default a bankruptcy receiver will honor only those contracts with value to the defaulting counterparty, and dismiss those with a detrimental effect (which are of value to the non-defaulting counterparty). For instance, in the example above a bankruptcy receiver might seek to dismiss the US$20m fixed payer swaps and enforce the US$30m fixed receiver swaps; under a favorable judgment for Y, X would be forced to pay a full U$30m to Y, instead of the U$10m it was expecting to pay.

Given the legal acceptability of netting in the jurisdictions noted in Chapter 1 the BIS agreed in its 1994–5 revisions to permit offsetting of claims on a net, rather than gross, replacement cost basis and altered its original CEM formula. In proposing its new formula, however, it included a scaling factor to ensure a sufficient "prudency" cushion.

The new CEM formula, which replaced the one cited in Equation 4.2, is given as:

$$CEM = (MTM + (0.4 * N * CEM_{factor}) + (0.6 * N * CEM_{factor} * NGR)) \quad (4.8)$$

where NGR is current netted market value/current gross market value (a figure between 0 and 1) and other terms are as defined above.

Further indirect benefits accrued from the 1996 Amendment to the 1988 Accord. The 1996 Amendment related primarily to market risks (rather than credit risks), with a specific focus on activity in the trading, rather than banking or lending, book. To compute market risk capital, the Amendment allowed institutions to use regulatory models or internal models (for example, internal Value-at-Risk (VAR) models, which we shall consider in greater detail in Chapter 11) if they proved sufficiently robust and could withstand regulatory scrutiny. Indeed, those capable of providing specific risk treatment (for example, security-specific exposure) receive more favorable treatment under the assumption that they can more readily monitor and manage concentrated market risks. The willingness to approve internal market risk models created important parallels and precedents for credit quantification and modeling techniques to come. In fact, the 1996 Amendment was a catalyst in moving credit risks to the "market oriented" regime/mindset that appeared with the new Accord. Many institutions opted to use their own internal models, believing them to be more realistic and consistent with proprietary views of risk.

The new Basel Capital Accord and the internal ratings-based approach

As the derivative markets developed further, new crises unfolded, modeling techniques improved, and credit resources became scarcer, the industry once again began pressuring the BIS to consider enhancements and refinements to the regulatory credit capital framework. As noted, experience gained through market-based VAR models helped fuel the process; success in managing market risk capital through internally developed models led banks to seek similar treatment for their credit risks.

The BIS recognized that it needed to enhance its 1988 Accord in order to make it more useful. From a credit risk perspective, this centered on several different areas:

■ Consistency: credit risks must be treated uniformly. "Like" products (for example, loans, bonds, and derivatives) that have the same economic characteristics should be treated the same – or else opportunities for "internal arbitrage" will appear. For instance, pricing, capital, and accounting policies for the credit risk embedded in the loan book, credit derivatives desk, or bond trading desk should be treated consistently.

■ Credit quality: capital allocation must be linked to credit quality (that is, probability of default), rather than credit type (that is, the arbitrary categorization/bucketing approach). The original 1988 Accord obligor "bucket approach" failed to properly link into actual credit risks (for example, OECD credits, regardless of creditworthiness, receive certain weightings, non-OECD credits less favorable weightings). An appropriate framework must take account of the credit rating process and the value that it adds.

■ Transaction dynamics: dynamic credit risk exposures and maturities must be incorporated. The derivative market, in particular, is based on constantly changing variables and parameters that should be reflected in the analytic framework.

■ Risk mitigation: a broad array of risk mitigating devices must be considered. Even after the 1994–5 enhancements only basic close-out netting was accepted, while other strategies, such as termination options and recouponing, were ignored. Since that time even more instruments, such as credit derivatives, collateralized debt obligations (CDOs), and other securitization vehicles have been employed to manage credit risk exposures.[5]

Ultimately, these forces led to collaboration between the industry and regulators in creating new approaches to the capital treatment of credit risks. In June 1999 the BIS circulated a consultative paper to solicit feedback from industry practitioners and academics on a new Basel Capital Accord (the so-called "three pillars"), designed to improve, and expand, on the original 1988 Accord. The three pillars center on:

■ Minimum recommended capital requirements (including modification of 1988 risk weightings to correspond to external or internal ratings methods, elimination of the OECD/non-OECD distinction, application of 100 percent risk weights for low quality credits, elimination of maximum 50 percent weightings for derivative counterparties, and the creation of new operational risk charges).[6]

■ Supervisory review of capital adequacy by individual national regulators.

■ Proper risk discipline and disclosure.

Additional drafts were circulated in 2001 and 2002, with a goal of implementing the new agreement in the second half of the decade.

As the BIS embarked on its consultative process discussion quickly turned to the use of internal credit risk models for capital allocations. Rather than requiring use of prescribed methodologies, the BIS expressed willingness to consider the adoption of internal models when computing credit risk capital. (This, as we shall note, is dependent on regulatory satisfaction that a bank can accurately assess counterparties and exposures). To be truly useful, regulators and practitioners agreed that the framework needed a stronger link between real credit risk and capital allocation: the stronger the linkage, the closer the definition and concepts of regulatory and economic capital, the more useful and effective the risk management process. In absence of such regulatory/economic capital convergence, disparities necessarily persist.[7]

From a credit perspective the BIS's new *Internal Ratings Based (IRB) Approach* to credit risk capital allocation represents a significant change to the original 1988 framework. The IRB approach has been welcomed by many academics, practitioners, and supervisors because it adds greater realism to the process and helps bring the regulatory and economic capital frameworks closer together (it also allows institutions to participate more proactively).[8]

In developing the IRB framework, the BIS has allowed for two distinct, but evolutionary, phases: the *foundation methodology* and the *advanced methodology*. The framework centers on two components: counterparty ratings/risk of default and credit exposures/credit losses. Under the foundation approach, banks provide input on counterparty risk of default but use BIS-supplied risk factors to compute credit risk exposures. This is deemed an appropriate starting point for banks that are able to demonstrate a robust internal ratings framework and an independent credit risk management process, but lack the capability of evaluating stochastic credit exposures and generating complete credit loss distributions. Under the advanced approach, banks not only use internal models to compute counterparty default risk (as in the foundation approach) but also exposure estimates, loss given default, the impact of a range of risk mitigants, and the relationship of counterparty exposures to other exposures in the portfolio. This obviously requires an increased level of sophistication and more rigorous control framework. Once regulators permit use of the advanced methodology, there is no need to rely on BIS-supplied risk factors to compute exposures. When this occurs, we might argue that economic and regulatory capital are virtually the same. Figure 4.2 summarizes the two approaches.

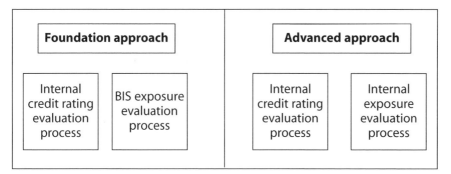

Figure 4.2 BIS IRB approaches

The essential *inputs* under the full IRB (which we shall review in our own form throughout the text) include:

- probability of counterparty default

- exposure at default

- loss given default (as a percentage of exposure)

- maturity

- granularity (for example, level of counterparty-specific measurement, including correlations between counterparty exposures).

Since credit risk mitigation measures can have a significant impact on probability of default, exposure at default, and loss given default, it features prominently in the IRB framework; this is in contrast, of course, to the original 1988 framework.

Broadly speaking, the capital allocation under the IRB approach follows a multi-step process:

- Classification of exposures into one of six broad classes, including corporates, sovereigns, banks, retail, project finance, and equity.

- For each type of exposure, computation of risk inputs using the standard parameters mentioned immediately above. These inputs can be obtained through supervisory rules (under the foundation approach) or internal assessment (under the advanced approach).

  - When determining the probability of counterparty default, the BIS recommends that firms take a conservative, long-run view (either point in time (for example, based on the rating of a counterparty at any specific moment) or through-the-cycle (for example, based on the rating of a counterparty as it passes through the worst part of its economic cycle)). The ratings assignment process, as discussed in the last chapter, typically focuses on thorough financial/credit analysis and industry group/peer comparisons. Some firms might also choose to consider ratings on specific credit facilities (for example, "one notch" below the counterparty rating for each level of subordination) and adjust ratings to reflect the presence of a support provider (such as a guarantor) or a credit derivative hedge provider.

– *Loss given default* (LGD, which we define as 1 less recoveries in subsequent chapters, or the actual loss sustained after default and bankruptcy proceedings) is most likely to be facility-specific (taking account of collateral benefits), and related to the structural and seniority characteristics of a given transaction. Under the foundation approach the BIS has put forth a 45 percent LGD for senior, unsecured facilities (which would include most OTC derivatives) and 70 percent for subordinated facilities (transactions that are backed by real estate receive special treatment that takes particular account of real estate collateral). Again, under the advanced methodology an institution makes its own assessment; however, the BIS recommend a focus on long-term, average views.

– *Exposure at default* (which we define as risk equivalent exposure in the next chapter) is also facility-specific. For balance sheet items this is generally the full notional value (for example, a funded loan), while for off-balance sheet transactions it varies. For instance, unfunded loan commitments are assigned a 75 percent drawdown value, performance bonds 50 percent of notional, forwards 100 percent, note issuance facilities 50 percent, and so on. Under the foundation approach OTC derivatives follow the same CEM method outlined above (hence its continued relevance for some firms), while under the advanced approach internal models that can provide a robust estimate of future exposures may be used (we shall defer discussion of this until Chapters 11 and 12). In all cases, the effects of credit risk mitigants, such as netting, are taken into account.

– The maturity dimension is specific to each transaction or an entire portfolio of transactions, though the BIS allows use of a 2.5-year average maturity. When the 2.5-year constant maturity is used, risk weightings are determined solely by probability of counterparty default and loss given default.

■ Determination of risk weights. Under the foundation approach, institutions select from between five weights ranging from 0 to 150 percent.

These are based on probability of default, LGD, and maturity estimates. The generic form of the equation (for the foundation approach with a maturity constant of 2.5 years) produces a risk weight that is the lesser of:

$$RW = LGD/50 * BRW(Pdef), \text{ or } (12.50 * LGD) \qquad (4.9)$$

Under the advanced approach, or the foundation approach that does not use the maturity constant, the risk weight is:

$$RW = LGD/50 * BRW(Pdef) * [1 + b(Pdef) * (M - 2.5)]$$
$$\text{or } (12.50 * LGD) \qquad (4.10)$$

where *LGD* is the loss given default; *BRW(Pdef)* is the corporate benchmark risk weight associated with a given probability of default; *b* is the maturity factor (slope); and $[1+b(Pdef)*(M - 2.5)]$ is a multiplicative maturity-scaling factor.

■ Determination of risk weighted assets. This is accomplished by multiplying risk weights by exposure at default and then adding the resulting amounts across the portfolio. An adjustment factor (standard supervisory index) is applied to total risk-weighted assets to reflect the granularity of the portfolio – the greater the granularity, the lower the adjustment factor, under the assumption that a more granular portfolio results in greater ability to identify idiosyncratic risks and diversify them away (for example, through use of uncorrelated positions; this is similar to the specific risk treatment of market VAR). Inability to track credit risks at a granular level results in a "penalty" in the form of a more conservative capital allocation, on the basis that a firm might find itself with excess concentration risk generated by highly correlated credit exposures.

The complete IRB formula takes the following form:

$$K = [RW * (Exp + G)] * 0.08 \qquad (4.11)$$

where *G* is a granularity adjustment; *Exp* is exposure at default; and *RW* is as defined above.

■ Minimum requirements of process compliance reinforce the quantitative elements defined above. The IRB framework is not simply about creating robust internal models, but surrounding the entire process with checks and balances, including integrity, audits, daily review, active usage, management attention, and so on. Under the foundation approach this focuses on:

- differentiation of credit risk categories

- completeness and integrity in credit rating processes

- oversight and review of credit ratings

- robust estimates of probability of default

- solid data collection and technology infrastructure

- active monitoring and usage

- internal and external validation.

■ Under the advanced method, an institution demonstrates the same minimum ratings-based criteria, and supplements this by demonstrating efficacy and strength in its advanced models (for example, loss given default and exposure at default analytics). Through this phase of the process the BIS wants national regulators to be certain a firm has a proper credit environment, sound credit processes/standards and administration, appropriate controls promulgated by the board, and executive management and relevant supervisory oversight – many of the governance items we noted in Chapter 3.

The dimensions of the IRB approach we have summarized (and which we expand on in Part III) represent the desire of the BIS to move to a more accurate capital allocation regime. Given intensive input from practitioners and academics, this framework should prove more efficient than the original framework in providing a fair, but still prudent, treatment of credit risk capital allocation. Though full implementation of the IRB approach is not expected until the latter part of the decade (giving national regulators and participating institutions several years during which to create the necessary processes), various interim phases will appear before then.

INDUSTRY EFFORTS

The derivative market relies heavily on self-regulation and market discipline to help ensure appropriate control and safety. Such self-regulation has developed gradually, over a period of years, and now forms a central part of marketplace control. Indeed, some might argue that self-regulation is even more valuable than formal regulation because it is exercised on a daily basis and grounded in useful practice; it also contains enough flexibility to adapt to changing markets, products, conditions, and national systems with relative ease. Like formal regulation, industry-based self-regulation represents an important element of the governance process.

When a market is mature enough to accept self-regulation, it operates through a disciplined process that centers on expectations and conventions. When excesses occur and the conventions start to change, the market can be brought back in line by eliminating abusive practices and squeezing out unworthy participants or creating a new series of best practice recommendations. In fact, the industry has evolved in this fashion since the 1980s, developing important governance and control measures, including standardized documentation, netting, risk modeling, reporting, and client disclosure and suitability standards.

Risk process advances

New financial crises tend to bring out new control reviews and initiatives; this is true for financial markets at large (for example, the emerging market debt crisis, the S&L crisis) and for derivative markets as a particular subset. Self-regulation in the derivatives market has appeared following specific dislocations, including those in 1993, 1996, and 1998–9 (other measures have, of course, been put forward; these, however, represent the most significant).

We briefly expand on some of the key efforts referred to in Chapter 1 to demonstrate the nature of derivative market self-regulation:

- The Group of 30 (G30) released its *Derivatives Principles and Practices* guidelines in 1993, following a number of counterparty credit defaults and credit losses brought on by global economic recession and excess corporate leverage.[9] Some of the guidelines relate very closely to aspects of general risk governance. In particular, G30 urged institutions to center their efforts on:
    - developing derivative mark-to-market policies and valuation methods
    - promoting greater use of master swap agreements and furthering efforts on the acceptability of netting
    - implementing robust systems capable of tracking and controlling all front/back office aspects of derivatives businesses
    - ensuring accounting, disclosure, and tax policies are consistent with industry norms
    - delineating appropriate authority levels for derivative professionals within intermediary and end user institutions, and ensuring senior management is aware of their activities
    - developing an independent market risk management function with specific responsibility for setting market risk limits and monitoring

exposures against such limits, verifying the accuracy of derivative pricing models, identifying sources of profit and loss, and performing stress tests/simulations on portfolios of market risks (including those generated by derivatives); and, most important for purposes of our discussion in this text:

- developing an independent credit risk management group with specific responsibility for analyzing counterparty creditworthiness, establishing counterparty credit risk limits and monitoring usage against limits, aggregating exposures by counterparty and across counterparties, managing concentrations of exposures, quantifying the risk of credit-sensitive derivative transactions on a mark-to-market/potential exposure basis, promoting use of risk reduction techniques, and determining appropriate credit reserves/capital based on expected default ratios or probabilities of counterparty default.

■ The Derivatives Policy Group (DPG) released the *Framework for Voluntary Oversight* "best practices" guidelines in 1995, following the derivatives marketing failures we summarized in Chapter 2.[10] DPG, consisting of six of the largest derivative dealers, focused its efforts on:

- ensuring effective, independent credit and market risk functions (for example, those responsible for measuring/monitoring risks, establishing appropriate risk limits, gathering and analyzing risk-related data, implementing valuation methodologies, and establishing mechanisms for managing risks that deviate from guidelines)

- creating and implementing specific, uniform methodologies for treating credit and market risks

- developing and using proper client risk disclosures that include fair and accurate marketing materials, downside scenarios, and proper legal documentation (including netting and/or collateral documents, authorizations).

■ The Counterparty Risk Management Group (CRMG) released *Improving Counterparty Risk Management Practices* following the LTCM/Russian crisis of late 1998.[11] CRMG, a consortium of leading financial institutions, centered its efforts on implementation of stronger credit and market risk practices, including:[12]

- transparency and counterparty assessment, based on: performing comprehensive and detailed credit analyses on counterparties prior to dealing (and monitoring their performance on a continuous basis thereafter); creating confidentiality standards to protect proprietary information; utilizing a credit risk management framework that takes due account of leverage, market risk, funding risk, and liquidity risk; and, ensuring a proper level of skills in dealing with risk management issues

– internal risk measurement, management, and reporting, based on: utilizing robust credit exposure tools that take account of adverse market movements and illiquidity; employing credit risk limits and monitoring tools based on replacement costs (gross and net of collateral), liquidation exposure, and potential exposure; performing market and credit risk stress tests to determine hidden correlations and concentrations; establishing credit practices for management of collateral; creating incentives for ongoing valuation and dynamic management of exposures; developing a suite of relevant credit reports including those related to large and concentrated risks

– market practices and conventions, based on: developing written policies governing documentation risks (for example, unsigned master agreements, netting agreements, confirmations) and modifying standard ISDA documents to take account of quotation and valuation practices

– regulatory reporting, based on: communicating with regulators formally and informally on the nature of quantitative and qualitative risks; providing additional informative detail as, and when, requested.

Table 4.4 summarizes these three major self-regulatory efforts.

Interestingly, no enhancements appeared in the aftermath of the Enron collapse, despite the fact that the company's downfall was tied, in some of the popular press, to derivatives (especially through special purpose entities (SPEs)).[13] In fact, the Enron case strengthens the case for derivatives' self-regulation. Had Enron been truthful about its financial position (for example, not used derivatives/SPEs either to lower its leverage, improve its earnings, or reduce its earnings volatility), its borderline investment grade credit rating would have been squarely sub-investment grade – meaning less credit losses would have occurred as market discipline would have kept counterparties from extending unsecured credit to such a company.[14]

It is difficult for the credit officer, no matter how astute, experienced, and insightful, to compete against financial fictions perpetrated by insiders who fully intend to deceive; this is particularly true when it includes senior executives. Regulators seeking to strengthen controls based on the lessons of Enron must necessarily focus on accounting controls, board oversight, internal and external audit efficacy, and conflicts of interest rather than derivatives. In fact, the US Sarbanes–Oxley Act of 2002 (passed in

Table 4.4 Best practice self-regulation

Year	Best practice study/sponsor	Focus
1993	Derivatives Principles and Practices Group of 30	Implementation of independent credit and market risk management functions, creation of robust valuation policies, encouraging use of netting, client risk disclosures
1995	Framework for Voluntary Oversight Derivatives Policy Group	Implementation of specific market and credit risk duties, creation and use of client risk disclosures
1999	Improving Counterparty Risk Management Practices Counterparty Risk Management Group	Implementation of robust credit analysis, management, and reporting processes, with a focus on liquidity, correlation and concentrations and market stress scenarios

response to the problems of Enron and other companies) deals explicitly with regulations related to corporate controls and behavior, and not at all with derivatives. The most relevant portion of the legislation from the perspective of derivative counterparties relates to increased transparency of financial statements and dealings – a move which all market participants are likely to welcome.

All of these "crisis-induced" self-regulatory initiatives arise because the industry attempts to learn from very expensive lessons related to controls, client suitability, risk concentrations, liquidity, correlated exposures, and so on. Industry leaders generally follow these "guidelines" as a matter of good practice. When such leaders participate, others are usually quick to join. Once best practices have been adopted, they often become second nature – and thus a central part of the operating culture and organization. This helps strengthen the governance process we discussed in Chapter 3.

Derivative documentation advances

ISDA (the industry trade group) has been at the forefront of creating, promoting, and administering a variety of critical issues related to derivatives, including those focused on netting, collateral management, valuation procedures/standards, and so forth. Perhaps its most valuable contribution has been in the creation and dissemination of standardized legal documentation templates that can be used for documenting trading and netting relationships between counterparties (this has also been supplemented by arranging for legal opinions related to netting under ISDA documents, as noted in Chapter 1). The centerpiece is the ISDA Master Agreement, which was formalized in 1992 and has been enhanced at various intervals over the past decade. As market circumstances change – that is, new products develop, definitions are revised, market-dealing conventions change, and dislocations arise – ISDA has refocused industry efforts on enhancing documentation standards. Over the past few years the group has added particular amendments in response to new features and conventions in the marketplace at large. In 2002 it introduced a new consolidated version of the Master Agreement, a document that will ultimately replace previous versions of the Agreement. The process is, of course, continuous. Although the 2002 version amends, consolidates, and updates much of what has been used over the past years, it will be subject to further revision as the underlying markets continue to evolve. (It is important to note that, although ISDA's Master Agreement is a central document in the derivatives marketplace, and certainly reflects the continued evolution of self-regulation, it is not the only legal framework that can be (or is) used by derivatives participants; other regimes exist, such as the German Rahmenverstrag Agreement and the French Association Francaise de Banque (AFB) Agreement.)

In this section we briefly review some of the key changes contained in the 2002 ISDA Master Agreement (the full agreement is reproduced in Appendix 3). In a general sense the Master Agreement can be considered one over-arching document comprised of various "components," including the printed form of the Master Agreement, the Schedule, the ISDA dictionary, the Credit Support Annex (detailing credit terms and provisions, including collateral, as we discuss at greater length in Chapter 13), and individual confirmations. With a Master Agreement in place, parties to the agreement can use "short-form" confirmations for each trade (rather than more extensive "long-form" versions), which reduces operational risks and costs. The Agreement, created by the ISDA Documentation Committee with input from 100-plus members, replaces the 1992 version. Though the basic architecture of the 1992 agreement remains intact, many of the subsequent changes, additions, and enhancements that have occurred are embedded in the new version (which is now 50 percent longer than the previous one). Although we shall not review all the changes in detail (but urge interested readers to do so), we highlight several of the key advances that are continued in the new Agreement:

- Early termination payments: the section on calculating early termination payments (damages) has been completely revised. The former method-ologies (first and second method, and market quotation and loss) have been replaced by the "close out amount."[15] The intent behind the revision is to make the close out process related to early termination more transparent and efficient (and, hopefully, objective). The new close out amount calculates a payment that provides the non-defaulter (or non-affected party in the event of early termination) the economic equivalent of the terminated transaction. The intent is to make sure the non-defaulter is in "the same economic position" as if the deals had not been terminated (the non-defaulter must still make a payment if so required under the terms of the transaction). Under the new agreement the non-defaulter is entitled to calculate value as the determining party (for example, it must act in good faith, use commercially reasonable procedures to produce results, use a market quotation approach or "relevant market data" provided by third parties, or rely on quotes from its own models/data if it uses such in the normal course of business – but only if it believes in good faith that the alternates would not satisfy business standards).

- Cure periods: the period within which to rectify a problem or clarify a situation is much shorter under the new version. For instance, the cure period for payment default has been reduced from three to one local business days and the period to obtain dismissal of involuntary bankruptcy/insolvency proceedings has been shortened from 30 to 15 days.

- Default under specified transactions: the definition of a specified transaction (which can trigger default) has been broadened considerably. Whereas the 1992 version was confined strictly to common OTC derivatives, the 2002 version references credit derivatives, repurchase/reverse repurchase agreements, buy/sell backs, securities lending, securities and commodity forwards, capital markets/trading transactions, and so forth.[16]

- Credit event upon merger: the credit event upon merger termination event is expanded and the affected party must now be "materially weaker" after one of three events (note that the term "materially weaker" is not explicitly defined): (1) reorganization, reincorporation, or reconstitution, (2) direct/indirect change in beneficial ownership of equity securities having the power to elect a majority of the board of directors or exercise of control, or (3) a substantial change in the capital structure (via debt, convertible bonds, or preferred securities).

- Force majeure termination event: a new clause has been added (deemed necessary and prudent in the aftermath of the 1998 Russia crisis and the 2001 terrorist acts) that reflects the impossibility for a party to perform (for example, make/receive a payment) as a result of physical disruption. If an event occurs, affected parties can defer the obligation for up to eight local business days, after which either party can terminate based on mid-market values.

The 2002 version includes various other clarifications and changes related to cross-default thresholds, interest accruals, tax representations, and so forth. As in the 1992 version, elections and amendments to the standard form are made through a separate schedule. In 2002 new definitions and clarifications were also issued for equity derivatives and credit derivatives; these, again, were intended to solidify market practice or provide relevant explanations. Like the Master Agreement, these definitional amendments must be viewed as a part of a continuous process; since the market is so dynamic, the underlying documentation and "rules" governing dealing must be equally dynamic, enhanced, and refined as needed. For instance, within the equity derivatives sector the 2002 definitions provide clarification and enhancements to guidelines established in 1996; many of the changes are expected to be included in confirmations:

- Product coverage: while the 1996 definitions centered on a rather narrow scope of American and European options and swaps, the 2002 version handles products such as Bermudan options, barriers, and forward contracts with prepayments with greater precision. Settlement mechanisms no longer depend on product type – physical or financial settlement can be applied to any instrument.

- Potential adjustment events: adjustments can be made based on a more clearly defined set of events, including "poison pills" (a broad range of anti-takeover defenses) and reverse mergers. The calculation agent can also take account of changes in volume, liquidity, stock lending rules, and so forth when determining valuation. Cancellation and payment amounts are synchronized to the new close out amount referenced above. When financial consideration of a merger event is combined (for example, new shares and "other" value), then the "partial cancellation and payment" approach results in cancellation of a portion of the transaction represented by "other value" and continuation of the balance represented by the new shares.

- Market disruption: the market disruption language is expanded to include not only disruption in trading, but also events that cause disruption in trading (for example, exchange closure). Thus, if closure continues for eight local business days, the calculation agent will terminate the transaction based on good faith estimates of value.

Similar clarifications and refinements have been put forth by ISDA for the rapidly growing credit derivatives market. Although the group released credit derivative definitions in 1999 that were intended to address legal, operational, and basis risk issues, aspects of the process were still not precise enough for many market participants. Accordingly, several supplements were issued relating to areas such as identification of successors to reference credit entities, the scope of insolvency, treatment of exchangeable and convertible debt, and restructurings. We summarize a few key points:

- Restructurings: it has been difficult to gain agreement on the treatment of credit derivatives in the event of restructuring, so the 2002 framework permits some flexibility. Participants can choose from among:
  - Restructuring maturity limitation and fully transferable obligation: this limits the range of obligations deliverable under a physically settled credit derivative to those that are "fully transferable" (for example, transferable without consent), maturing no later than 30 months following the scheduled termination date of the relevant transaction.
  - Modified restructuring maturity limitation and conditionally transferable obligation: this approach, reflecting a European standard, allows delivery of loan obligations where consent to transfer is required but is not expected to be unreasonably withheld/delayed. The maturity is limited to scheduled termination of the transaction or 60 months following restructuring, whichever is later.

    Non-inclusion of restructuring as a credit event: this approach specifies whether multiple holder obligation treatment is applicable; if it is, it will exclude restructuring of bilateral loans from constituting a credit event. Note that redenomination of an obligation into an OECD currency is no longer considered a restructuring event.

- Repudiation: repudiation or moratorium is now taken to be a two stage event that includes (a) declaration of repudiation of obligations by an authorized officer and (b) failure to pay within a given period (for example, 60 days).

- *Notice of physical settlement*: the seller of a credit derivative has the right to close out all or a portion of a transaction by buying in assets when the buyer fails to comply with delivery obligations.

The 2002 credit derivative framework deals with other provisions related to consistent use of guarantees – for example, classic downstream guarantees (qualifying affiliate), upstream or sidestream guarantees (qualifying) – operational standards for notices, more precise definitions of subordination, and so on.

Ultimately, regulation must achieve some specific benefit. In a world that is characterized by lower barriers to entry and competitive pressures, participants must evaluate the nature and extent of proper regulation. If regulation can produce better results than deregulation (or lack of regulation) or if it can enhance or strengthen self-oversight, then the process is likely to be beneficial. If some market failure has occurred and requires regulatory repairs that, too, can be beneficial. If, however, regulation is simply imposed to create another layer of rules, then inefficiencies are likely to arise (for example, cost of compliance) and the supposed benefits of the market will start to contract – perhaps even disappear. Regulation and self-regulation must be handled carefully and aim towards the same final goals.

PART II

The Credit Risk
of Complex
Derivatives

CHAPTER 5

Classification and Quantification of Credit Risk

BACKGROUND

As noted in Chapter 3, proper governance and control require a firm to identify, measure, manage, and monitor variables that represent uncertainty or risk to the normal functioning of operations. This is especially true in the financial industry, where the essence of the business is to reward an institution for risks it assumes. The effective management of risks is typically accomplished through a framework that lets an institution control the different risks inherent in its line of businesses; this allows potential losses to be managed to firmwide tolerance levels and profits to be maximized.

As we have already indicated, any global financial institution involved in a variety of traditional banking services and products is subject to a broad range of financial risks. To review, these can include credit risk, market risk, liquidity risk, model risk, legal risk, and operational risk. In order for a bank to manage its affairs properly, it must consider all dimensions of risk. Through a governance structure, management and control units can be established to assume responsibility for each element. We know, for instance, that the corporate risk management department might be responsible for overseeing market risk, model risk, liquidity risk, and, through dedicated credit specialists, credit risk; the legal/regulatory department may be responsible for aspects of legal risk (including client suitability); the operations and systems departments might be responsible for operational and settlement risks. Although this type of departmental control framework is by now well established in many financial institutions, it may be less formalized or structured in others (particularly in corporate end users, despite the fact that they often face similar risks). With current industry and regulatory efforts pointed towards stronger governance and internal controls, however, it is likely that even more institutions will come to feature similar control functions in coming years.

While addressing all aspects of risk is vital to the continuing success of an institution, discussion of each is well beyond the purview of this book. In fact, our sole focus is on the credit risk discipline. Implementation of a credit risk framework, part of a corporate governance process that involves counterparty management and product risk management, allows an institution to evaluate individual counterparties and manage its credit exposure, and potential credit losses, to such counterparties. While a credit officer must be able to accurately assess counterparty risk – which we again define as the risk that a counterparty to a transaction will fail to perform as expected, for reasons of financial deterioration or collapse – and must incorporate specific details on credit quality in the decision-making process and the expected credit loss framework, the purpose of this book is not to review what makes a counterparty a good or bad credit.[1] Instead, we focus our attention on the product risk evaluation segment of the credit framework and, more specifically, of complex derivatives. This part of the process centers on valuing the credit risk an institution assumes when it enters into a derivative transaction with a counterparty. In a worst-case scenario, failure by the counterparty to perform on a contracted obligation will lead to a credit loss in an amount that can be estimated by determining the risk in existence at the time of default (less any special considerations, such as collateral or other forms of risk mitigation we have discussed). The loss estimate is typically determined by examining market risk, for reasons we consider at greater length below. We shall also provide a general commentary on the appropriateness and suitability of derivative transactions for counterparties of varying degrees of creditworthiness.

Since the book is limited to derivative transactions we will not concern ourselves with other forms of product risk that affect credit limits (that is, settlement risk, credit inventory risk, or contingent risk) until Part III, when we introduce a few additional concepts to aid in our consideration of credit portfolio risks.[2] Our focus for now is on market risk, why derivative products carry market risk, and methods of estimating market risk for purposes of credit quantification. In this chapter we begin with a basic definition of market risk and then discuss risk equivalency: the banker's means of placing market risk-based derivative products on a "loan equivalent" basis. We then discuss the development of risk factors, a key method by which to measure risk equivalency, and conclude by reviewing alternate risk quantification methodologies.

MARKET RISK

Market risk can be defined as the risk of loss due to an adverse movement in market prices or rates (note that when we discuss market risk and market loss we confine ourselves to the topic as related to counterparty default, not to periodic profit and loss adjustments to a bank's income statement, as might occur through credit spread movements, for instance). Market risk exists because interest rates, currency rates, stock prices, index levels, credit spreads, commodity prices, or other references governing a given derivative transaction fluctuate. As noted in Chapter 1, without movement in any of these indicators there would be no concern over market risk (and little need for derivative products, since these instruments seek to take advantage of, or protect against, market movements). When a bank or company enters into a derivative, it expects the market variable(s) under-lying the transaction to change during the life of the trade; this derivative transaction is said to be market risk-based and must be quantified through a process known as risk equivalency or risk adjustment.

As indicated, during the life of a derivative trade, prices/rates will fluc-tuate. If, for example, a bank buys a call option on a stock giving it the right, but not the obligation, to purchase a share of stock for US$100, the option will increase or decrease in value as the current price of the equity moves above or below the strike price (the value will also change due to certain other factors, such as the passage of time, or changes in the risk-free rate, but we set these aside for the moment). As the price of the stock changes, the level of risk exposure – the amount a bank stands to lose if a counterparty defaults – changes as well. If the current price of the stock moves above the strike price so that the call has value, and the counterparty fails, the bank will not receive the money it is owed. (In reality it is expect-ing shares from the counterparty in exchange for cash at a below-market price; it may then sell the shares in the market at the higher current price or retain them in its portfolio. The economic effect is the same.) Once this occurs, the bank becomes an unsecured creditor of the bankrupt company and may receive a certain residual value following bankruptcy proceed-ings. Such value, if any, will generally be considerably less than originally anticipated. When the current market price is above the strike price in the case of calls (vice versa in the case of puts), market risk exposure is said to be positive and implies the bank has exposure to its counterparty. When the current market price is below the strike price in the case of calls (again, vice versa in the case of puts), market risk exposure is negative and indi-cates that the bank has no exposure to its counterparty (this assumption ignores any upfront premium payment, which generally accompanies the transaction; we shall explore this in greater detail in later chapters). Note that the same general concept applies to other derivatives, such as forwards and swaps. Market risk may therefore be positive or negative during the life of a given derivative transaction; when positive, the bank must take account of its credit exposure, but when negative, it need not be concerned. The central point is that market movements influence market risk, which influences credit risk exposure. In a standard unsecured transaction, counterparty default when market risk exposure is positive results in a loss to the bank in an amount equal to the existing risk exposure. A counterparty default when market risk is negative generates no loss.

Under a medium to long-term transaction (that is, a transaction with a final maturity of more than one or two years), market risk becomes especially critical. As we might expect, the longer the time to final maturity, the greater the opportunity for market movements. Since a long time horizon allows a market to move by a greater amount (which implies a transaction can acquire further value), risk exposure to the counterparty can grow. In addition, transactions that are based on volatile rates or prices can lead to an increase in market risk exposure. Many of the derivative trades common in the markets of the twenty-first century have multi-year maturities and are written on volatile indexes, stock prices, currency rates, commodity prices, and other measures. Therefore, credit professionals must be very sensitive to transactions with long maturities and volatile references; these two elements, not coincidentally, play a leading role in defining the risk factor, a key risk equivalency measure for derivative instruments. We shall discuss the development and implementation of risk factors in greater detail below.

In order for credit officers to assess market risk so that correct credit decisions can be made, it is helpful to segregate market risk into two separate components: potential market risk and actual market risk. Potential market risk is often referred to as deemed risk, time-to-decay risk, pre-settlement risk, expected exposure, or fractional exposure, while actual market risk is often known as mark-to-market risk, replacement cost, or actual exposure (we shall use these terms interchangeably throughout the text). We consider basic definitions of potential and actual market risk in order to highlight the importance of each in the decision-making and exposure management processes.

■ *Potential market risk (PMR)* is the risk exposure a bank (or any corporate institution) allocates against a counterparty's credit limit at the inception of a transaction; it provides a credit officer with the *ex ante* exposure information needed to make a reasoned credit decision. We know that market risk exists and affects the value of derivative instruments. Potential market risk attempts to quantify future market movements that can affect a bank's exposure to a counterparty over the life of a transaction. It can be viewed as a component that reflects the most likely "worst-case" risk exposure a bank might encounter. The actual calculation of PMR is determined through the risk equivalency process discussed below. It should be noted that PMR declines as the maturity of a transaction draws nearer since the opportunity for market movement falls. At maturity PMR is equal to zero as no more market movement, which might affect the value of the transaction, can occur.

■ *Actual market risk (AMR)* measures the true value of risk exposure once a derivative trade is underway. Since it is understood that rates or prices governing an underlying transaction will move between trade date and maturity date (in a magnitude that, in most instances, should be less than PMR estimates through the risk equivalency process), AMR represents the quantification of actual market movements and is the amount a bank loses if default occurs at a specific point in time. This can be interpreted as the cost a bank must bear in replacing the transaction in the market. As indicated above, in certain instances AMR is actually negative, implying no risk of loss if default occurs (that is, there is no cost in replacing a trade – indeed, a profit is earned). Note that for standard, on-market trades AMR is always equal to zero at inception, since market movements will not yet have commenced.

Both PMR and AMR are essential for initial credit decisions and ongoing exposure management. Total credit risk exposure is generally reflected as a sum of the PMR and AMR components; this approach is widely accepted in the industry and by regulators.[3] The discussion above is summarized in Table 5.1.

The discussion above indicates that market risk exists in some form during the life of a trade. Market risk can either be "theoretical," as measured by PMR, or "real," as measured by AMR. A bank sustains a credit loss only if AMR is positive at the time of default. The value of PMR is not relevant at the time of default, even though it will certainly be positive (because PMR will only be zero when market rates/prices can no longer impact the value of the transaction; this occurs at maturity, when no more market movement can take place). PMR is only utilized to estimate how much a bank might lose if a bank defaults at some future point. This, as we shall note throughout the text, is vitally important for credit decision, credit reserve, and capital allocation purposes. Without PMR a credit officer

Table 5.1 PMR and AMR over trade life

	Potential market risk	Actual market risk
At the inception of a trade	+	0
During the life of a trade	↓	0, ↓ , ↑
At the maturity of a trade	0	+, –, 0

Note: For on-market trades only.

would find it difficult to make a credit decision; likewise, allocation of reserves and capital would be inaccurate. Table 5.2 summarizes the interaction between counterparty risk, market risk, and resulting losses, where maximum counterparty risk is counterparty default, and maximum market risk includes both AMR and PMR.

Our focus in dealing with derivative products is therefore on market risk, since it is market movement that adds or reduces credit exposure in a transaction. In the next section we consider risk equivalency, a mechanism for estimating the credit risk exposure generated by a derivative transaction.

RISK EQUIVALENCY

Risk equivalency is the process by which the notional amount of a transaction is evaluated in light of its characteristics (for example, payoff profile, maturity, initial rate, and frequency of payments) in order to arrive at a figure that most accurately reflects potential risk. *Risk equivalent exposure* (REE), also known as "risk-adjusted exposure," "credit equivalent risk," or "loan equivalent risk," is the end-result of the risk equivalency process. In standard form REE is precisely equal to the sum of potential and actual market risk. Since AMR is zero at the inception of an on-market trade, it follows that REE is simply equal to PMR. Over time, however, it becomes a blend of PMR and AMR.

Unlike drawn loans or advances, most derivative instruments are not funded transactions.[4] In virtually all derivative trades, notional amounts are used only as a reference point to calculate interest, currency, commodity, or index amounts payable and/or receivable. Since the notional is not granted or exchanged in a unilateral manner, as in a traditional bank loan, it is not at risk; therefore, credit risk is usually smaller than the notional (with the exceptions noted below). In addition, market movements continuously affect the value of the derivative transaction, so the ongoing amount of risk exposure is dynamic (while in a fully drawn bullet loan it is completely static); this presents significant challenges in quantification, as discussed below.

Table 5.2 Counterparty risk, market risk, and losses

Counterparty risk	Market risk	Resulting loss
Minimum	Minimum	0
Minimum	Maximum	0
Maximum	Minimum	0 or minimum
Maximum	Maximum	Maximum

Risk equivalency is the process of adjusting the notional of a derivative so that the exposure is accurately reflected in terms that are logical to the banker or credit officer. For instance, a US$100m five-year unsecured loan extended by a bank represents US$100m of risk to the counterparty. A US$100m five-year interest rate swap may only represent US$2m of risk, since the risk is bilateral and only the net interest flows, rather than the notional, are exchanged. The US$2m represents the REE of the transaction and may be quantified in different forms. Note that derivative instruments do not always carry less risk than unsecured loans; most do, but some do not. Cross currency swaps, zero coupon swaps, leveraged or "power" derivatives, or those which contain "all-or-nothing" payouts are examples of derivatives where the REE may be very large indeed. The main point to stress at this stage is that derivatives must be risk-adjusted so that the correct credit and business decisions can be made.

Developing a risk equivalency framework can be accomplished through one of several methods, including the volatility method and the simulation method. This chapter (and, indeed, this text) focuses on the volatility-based framework, though we shall also consider alternate approaches such as the simulation process. Each technique has its own benefits and drawbacks and there is no "perfect" solution to the development of a risk equivalency framework. Indeed, the estimation of credit risk exposure of derivative transactions is a difficult challenge – and most assuredly not an exact science. A volatility framework, however, provides an institution with a straightforward and workable process that generates quality estimates of maximum credit risk exposure.

The process of quantifying volatility-based REE in a derivative transaction is twofold: first, a risk factor, which reflects the underlying movement in rates or prices governing the derivative, must be calculated and, second, the risk factor must be applied to a broader equation which is specific to the derivative under consideration. The REE that results from combining these two elements is the figure ultimately used by the credit analyst in arriving at a credit decision. Knowing the REE, a credit officer can determine whether the relative risk under consideration is appropriate for the counterparty. REE is also used as an ongoing measurement tool to permit management and monitoring of exposures once they are booked (for example, the AMR component of the framework).

The next section of this chapter is devoted to understanding the development of the volatility-based risk factor; we then discuss the use of the risk factor in a simple risk equivalency equation. At the end of this chapter we provide a brief description of the simulation risk methodology (which we shall revisit again in later chapters). Part III of this book employs risk factors in specific risk equations introduced for individual products and strategies.

RISK FACTORS

The risk factor (RF) is the central tool for converting the notional value of a derivative transaction into REE. To examine the potential loss that might arise from a market risk-based product, it is helpful to understand qualitatively what is being measured. When a bank enters into a derivative transaction, it assumes an obligation that will increase and/or decrease in value during its life. A rise or fall in value is traced primarily to the rise or fall in rates/prices governing the transaction. If the underlying index moves in a certain direction, the transaction becomes more valuable to the bank and, therefore, reflects increased credit risk exposure; there is therefore a positive correlation between the value of the transaction and the credit risk exposure it generates. As value increases, risk increases, and as value decreases (or becomes negative), risk decreases (though rarely will a bank apply a negative risk figure against credit limits). In order to determine risk, the value of underlying rates/prices must be estimated. Transaction maturity must also be considered. As we have mentioned, the longer the maturity of a transaction, the greater the opportunity for a given price or rate to move. Rates or prices can only move so far in one week, but they have the potential of moving much farther in a month or a year. Consequently, an effective measure of risk must also include a time dimension. These two parameters, market movement and maturity, are the foundation of the RF. In order to develop RF we turn our attention to the lognormal distribution, square root of time, and historical volatility: several key assumptions underpinning financial option pricing models.

The lognormal distribution

Many option-pricing models attempt to estimate future prices through a *stochastic process*, a mathematical framework that generates the path of a stochastic variable (one that changes in an uncertain manner continuously or at certain points in time). A stochastic process may involve *continuous time* (the variable can change at any moment) or *discrete time* (the variable can only change at certain intervals) and it may involve a *continuous variable* (which can take on any value) or a *discrete variable* (which can only assume one of a set of values). A *Markov process* is a stochastic process that indicates that only the current price of a variable is relevant in determining what may happen in the future. That is, previous prices and the number of periods preceding the current observation are irrelevant.

One of the defining assumptions of the Markov process *Black–Scholes model* (a key analytic, price-based option model of the financial industry) is that the return of the market variable follows a lognormal continuous time stochastic process (sometimes also known as a *"geometric Brownian motion"* (GBM)).[5] Under this assumption the movement of the variable is random in continuous time; the instantaneous return (defined as the change in the price of the variable divided by the price of the variable) has a constant mean and a constant variance (which we define below). The resulting distribution of the variable is lognormal, which is equivalent to saying that the natural logarithm of the variable is normally distributed. A lognormal distribution is skewed slightly to the right; its upper bound is infinite and its lower bound is zero. This is distinguished from the normal distribution, with the familiar "bell shaped" curve; Figures 5.1 and 5.2 illustrate these two distributions. Use of a lognormal distribution is generally thought to be reasonable for many financial

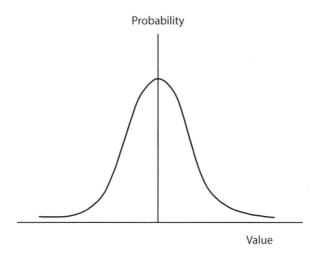

Figure 5.1 Normal distribution

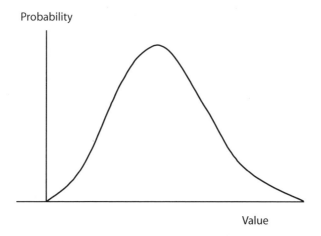

Figure 5.2 Lognormal distribution

prices as rates, as the lognormal does not permit negative prices/rates but allows very high prices/rates; a normal distribution allows for negative rates or prices.[6]

A continuous time stochastic process is often referred to as a *diffusion process*, meaning that the market variable exists in continuous time and its probability density function is continuous. The variable changes on a random and continuous basis and, as the time interval becomes larger, uncertainty in the returns increases in a predictable fashion (because the probability function is known). Returns over long time periods are lognormally distributed while returns on an instantaneous (or continuously compounded) basis are normally distributed. Note that the diffusion process does not account for sudden "jumps" in variables, it simply assumes they move smoothly and continuously in small increments. Critics argue that continuous price behavior is not always realistic and point to instances where prices surge up or down dramatically (for instance, stock prices during the October 1987 stock market crash, currency rates during the 1997 Asian currency crises, credit and swap spreads, during the 1998 Russian/hedge fund crisis). To overcome this limitation certain pricing models (for example, Cox and Ross, Merton) explicitly incorporate "jump processes."[7]

For the purposes of this discussion, however, we follow the diffusion approach. A diffusion process, together with the lognormal distribution, means that the market variable can take any value from zero to infinity at any point in time, T. Let us consider the movement of stock price S (though we might just as easily consider the movement of an equity index, a currency rate, a commodity price, and so on). The diffusion process can be defined as:

$$\frac{\Delta S}{S} = \mu \Delta t + \sigma \varepsilon \sqrt{\Delta t} \qquad (5.1)$$

where ΔS is the change in the stock price; S is the stock price; $\Delta S/S$ is the return of the stock price; μ is the expected return; Δt is a small time interval; σ is the volatility; and ε is a random sample from a normal distribution with mean 0 and standard deviation 1.

Since $\Delta S/S$ is equal to the return of the stock price, it can be written as:

$$\frac{\Delta S}{S} = \frac{(S_T + \Delta t - S_T)}{S_T} \qquad (5.2)$$

with time equal to T. In qualitative terms this means that the return of the stock price is equal to the expected return μ plus the standard deviation σ, adjusted for an error term ε (which is included as a normally distributed random sample that can impact the total return at any point in time).

We may convert the equation above into the following form:

$$\frac{dS}{S} = \mu dt + \sigma dz \tag{5.3}$$

or

$$dS = \mu S dt + \sigma S dz \tag{5.4}$$

where dz is a Weiner process and both the expected return and the variance of returns are functions of the stock price S and time t. A Weiner process is a stochastic process that is normally distributed with expected value of 0 and variance of 1 at each time interval t. Under a Weiner process, values at time t and $t+1$ have a correlation of 0 (that is, they are independent of one another, as indicated above; thus, a Weiner process is also a Markov process). After a certain amount of calculus, we can determine that:[8]

$$\ln\left[\frac{S_T}{S}\right] = \mu - \frac{\sigma}{2}\tau + \sigma\sqrt{\tau} \tag{5.5}$$

and, through algebra,

$$S_T = Se^{\mu - \frac{\sigma^2}{2}\tau + \sigma\sqrt{t}} \tag{5.6}$$

That is, the stock price at time T is equal to the continuously compounded stock price at $(T - t)$, normally distributed with mean $\mu - (\sigma^2/2)\tau$ and variance $\sigma\sqrt{\tau}$. Based on this summary discussion we can say that the stock price $S(T)$ is lognormally distributed with a standard deviation proportional to the square root of time. The variance about the mean is said to increase as time increases. In fact, if the variable in question follows the diffusion process, then the variance of the changes is proportional to time; thus, the standard deviation (which is the square root of the variance) of the changes is proportional to the square root of time. (Knowing that the standard deviation is the square root of the variance leads us to conclude, for instance, that σ p.a. $= \sqrt{\sigma^2_\tau \tau}$ for a given time interval τ. This becomes $\sqrt{\sigma^2_\tau} * \sqrt{\tau}$, or $\sigma_\tau\sqrt{\tau}$, assuming τ interval results are independent.) This is known as the "square root rule," a concept that we incorporate in the RF model. The concepts above demonstrate that asset price changes can be estimated by Equation 5.6, which indicates that the changes are (a) lognormally distributed and (b) vary in proportion to the square root of time; both of these facts have a bearing on the development of derivative risk factors used to estimate the potential market movements (and, therefore, potential credit exposure) inherent in derivative instruments.

Historical volatility

Historical volatility is a means of quantifying the historical movement of price changes; this, of course, is what is measured by standard deviation. When attempting to determine the volatility parameter for option pricing purposes, traders often utilize *implied volatility* (which is a forward-looking measure defined as the volatility "implied" by option prices quoted in the market).[9] When implied volatility is unavailable (or appears suspect), historical volatility, a backward-looking measure, is often used as a proxy. Historical volatility is also utilized in various risk measurement models (including the market VAR models we discuss in Chapter 11).

There are many ways of calculating historical volatility or standard deviation. One of the most common approaches is to determine the mean and standard deviation of the natural log of the price relatives, S(T)/S(T − 1). Using *s* as an estimate of the standard deviation parameter, we show this as:

$$s = \sqrt{\frac{1}{n-1} \sum_{T=1}^{n} (r_T - \bar{r})^2} \qquad (5.7)$$

where T is the time interval; n is the number of observations; $S(T)$ is the price at time T; $r(T)$ is $\ln(S(T)/S(T-1))$; and is the mean of the natural log of price relatives defined by r.

The value of s provides an estimate of the standard deviation of the price relatives, but only after the result has been adjusted for the time dimension denoted by T. If the price relatives are based on daily observations, the resulting s measures the standard deviation of the daily price changes. Since most volatility figures are quoted on a per annum basis, s must be multiplied by the square root of the number of days during which the index or market is active (generally considered to be 250 active business days). Likewise, if monthly observations are taken (measuring the monthly volatility of the price changes), s must be multiplied by the square root of the months during which activity takes place (again, an estimate calls for 8.3 months per year). Note that certain methodologies call for adjustment by 365 days or 12 months; it is left for the reader to employ whichever method appears most logical – though the latter is certainly more conservative. In order to obtain a per annum historical volatility estimate (HV p.a.) we simply need to calculate:

$$HVp.a. = s\sqrt{m} \qquad (5.8)$$

where m is equal to the size of the interval during which observations are taken (that is, 250 or 365 for days, 8.3 or 12 for months and so on). There are other ways of computing historical volatility but the method above provides a reasonable estimate and is computationally simple to implement.

The optimal number of observations that should be taken to develop a volatility measure is an important and complex topic in statistics. While there are many factors to consider, it is generally understood that more, rather than fewer, observations are better (with the caveat that too many historical data points may lead to the inclusion of irrelevant figures in the measure). When employing weekly or monthly data it is reasonable to utilize at least two to three years of observations points; when employing daily data, three to six months of rolling observations can be sufficient to provide a good estimate.[10] However, in all instances, due allowance must be made for the current state of the markets.

At this point we have a volatility figure that is adjusted to represent annual movement in the price, rate, or index governing a transaction. This is obviously a crucial parameter in the development of RF, as it provides a starting point in dictating how far, based on historical market movements (and the other assumptions covered above), a given variable is expected to move over a given period of time. This, in turn, allows us to estimate how future market movements will act to increase (or decrease) the credit risk exposure encountered in a transaction.

Confidence levels

Once historical data has been identified and gathered, and the standard deviation (or volatility) of the price movements calculated, we need to adjust the volatility to the appropriate statistical confidence level; this allows the historical volatility measure to assume a meaningful role in the decision-making process. Specifically, we want to ensure that the risk factor being utilized captures anticipated market movements 90, 95, or 99 percent of the time (that is, only in 10, 5, or 1 percent of cases will the movement be in excess of the volatility estimate). By doing so, we expect a future rate or price observation (underlying a given transaction) will be less than or equal to the calculated figure to a specified degree of confidence. We add a cautionary note: the actual shape of the distribution does not indicate how large the market movements might be the remaining 10, 5, or 1 percent of the time (that is, we do not know the potential magnitude of the observation in the extreme right-hand tail of the curve).

To determine the appropriate confidence level we use a standardized z factor to evaluate the confidence level $(1 - \alpha)$, where $z(\alpha)$ is the standardized normal value leaving α in one tail and $(1 - \alpha)$ under the remainder of the curve. Through standard statistical processes[11] we can determine the probability the unit normal variable Z will exceed $z(\alpha)$ with probability α via:

$$P\{Z > z\alpha\} = 1 - \Phi(Z\alpha) = \alpha \qquad (5.9)$$

An examination of standard statistical tables provides the information contained in Table 5.3.

We can therefore say that the confidence levels leaving α in one tail equate to the z factors ($\Phi(z(\alpha))$) highlighted in Table 5.4. A practical interpretation of these scores indicates that 1.28 standard deviations from the mean, on a one-tailed test, capture 90 percent of observations. Utilizing the information above, we can adjust the volatility measure to the relevant confidence level by multiplying the appropriate z factor against the calculated volatility. This process is summarized via:

$$HV = HVp.a * z \qquad (5.10)$$

(where we assume s, in HV(p.a.), has been adjusted to the appropriate time interval).

For example, if volatility is 10 percent, a 90 percent z factor of 1.28 yields a 90 percent confidence level volatility of 12.80 percent. To adjust a calculated volatility measure of 15 percent to a 95 percent confidence level, we multiply 15 percent by 1.64 to obtain 24.6 percent. This can be interpreted as saying we are confident that 95 percent of future price observations governing a transaction will be within 24.6 percent of the level on trade date. This implies the risk factor will capture the observations in at least 95 percent of all cases, which adds a degree of confidence to the credit decision-making process. Institutions opting for a more conservative standard can increase the confidence level to 99 percent or even 99.5 percent; the associated confidence level factors, as shown above, are 2.33 and 2.58, respectively. Once again, for those not wishing to delve into the statistics presented above, it is sufficient to note that a volatility measure can be adjusted to a confidence level by utilizing one of the z factors highlighted in Table 5.4.

Table 5.3 Probabilities and z factors

$\Phi(z(\alpha)) =$	$0.5 - prob = \alpha$	$(1 - \alpha)$
$\Phi(1.28) =$	$0.5 - 0.4000 = 0.10$	$1 - 0.10 = 0.90$
$\Phi(1.64) =$	$0.5 - 0.4495 = 0.05$	$1 - 0.05 = 0.95$
$\Phi(1.96) =$	$0.5 - 0.4750 = 0.025$	$1 - 0.025 = 0.975$
$\Phi(2.33) =$	$0.5 - 0.4900 = 0.01$	$1 - 0.01 = 0.99$
$\Phi(2.58) =$	$0.5 - 0.4950 = 0.005$	$1 - 0.005 = 0.995$

Table 5.4 Confidence levels and z factors

z(α)	F(z(α))	Confidence level
z(0.10)	1.28	90.0%
z(0.05)	1.64	95.0%
z(0.025)	1.96	97.5%
z(0.01)	2.33	99.0%
z(0.005)	2.58	99.5%

Note that we shall refer to $\Phi(z(\alpha))$ as z below and throughout the text.

Transaction maturity

We know from the discussion above that the standard deviation of the changes in the underlying variable is proportional to the square root of time; this is known as the *square root rule*. In order to take account of the maturity of a given transaction, we must incorporate this rule into our volatility estimate. That is, if we obtain an HV of 15 percent (recalling that HV has already been annualized by Equation 5.8 above and has been adjusted to the relevant confidence level), we know the expected movement of the index during the next 12 months will be within 15 percent of the starting point. If a particular transaction has a final maturity in six months, two years, or five years, we adjust the volatility measure to account for this change in time. The change is made by

$$HV_{adj} = HV * \sqrt{T} \tag{5.11}$$

where T is the maturity of the transaction, in fractions or multiples of one year (that is, T equals 2 for a two-year trade, 5 for a five-year trade, 0.5 for a six-month trade, and so forth (using 12, rather than 8.3, trading months)). Using HV of 15 percent, a two-year trade yields HV_{adj} of 21.2 percent while a six-month trade yields HV_{adj} of 10.6 percent.

The complete risk factor

The combination of:

- volatility (based on a lognormally distributed asset prices)

- confidence intervals (associated with bringing the volatility measure up to a specified confidence level)

- maturity (reflecting the time dimension of the transaction) leads to the development of the complete risk factor RF. We summarize these elements as:

$$RF = HV * \sqrt{T} * z \tag{5.12}$$

(Note that we shall continue to separate HV and $\sqrt{T}$, instead of combining as HV_{adj}, for purposes of clarity.)

With this information we are now able to estimate the potential future market movements for a given price, rate, or index, adjusted to a given confidence level and maturity.

To place this discussion in the context of an example, we can develop a series of risk factors that reflect the potential future market movements of the Nikkei 225 index. If the annualized volatility of the Nikkei 225 is 20 percent, we adjust HV to a 90 percent confidence level by multiplying by the 1.28 z factor, as outlined in Equation 5.10; this yields a 90 percent confidence level volatility measure of 25.6 percent. We are thus confident that in 90 percent of future cases, the one-year market movement will be within 25.6 percent of today's starting level (again, we are not certain how far it may travel in the remaining 10 percent of cases). We then take account of the time dimension by multiplying by the square root of trans-action maturity T, per Equation 5.11. To create a one-year risk factor there is no change to the confidence-level adjusted risk figure of 25.6 percent. A six-month risk factor, however, becomes:

25.6 percent * $\sqrt{0.5}$ = 18.1 percent (assuming 12 trading months)

and a two-year risk factor becomes:

25.6 percent * $\sqrt{2}$ = 36.2 percent (again, assuming 12 trading months)

We now have a series of risk factors for the Nikkei 225 index, which tell us that we expect, with 90 percent certainty, the six-month, one-year, and two-year movements of the Nikkei to be within 18.1, 25.6, and 36.2 percent of today's starting point, respectively. This is a measure of how estimated future index levels might impact the value of a market risk derivative transaction involving the Nikkei. We can easily create broader tables reflecting trans-action maturity and confidence level or volatility (depending on which variable we choose to hold constant). Tables 5.5 and 5.6 illustrate sample risk factors for a range of maturities, volatilities, and confidence levels.

The generalized RF process permits a bank to estimate the maximum expected market movement in the index and the maximum potential market risk exposure on the transaction. The same logic can be applied to any stochastic variable evaluated through the RF framework (for example, stock

Table 5.5 Sample table of Nikkei risk factors:
constant 10% volatility, varying confidence levels

10% HV	90.0%	95.0%	97.5%	99.0%	99.5%
1 yr	12.8%	16.4%	19.6%	23.3%	25.8%
2 yr	18.1%	23.2%	27.7%	33.0%	36.5%
3 yr	22.2%	28.4%	33.9%	40.4%	44.7%
4 yr	25.6%	32.8%	39.2%	46.6%	51.6%
5 yr	28.6%	36.7%	43.8%	52.1%	57.7%
6 yr	31.4%	40.2%	48.0%	57.1%	63.2%
7 yr	33.9%	43.4%	51.9%	61.6%	68.3%
8 yr	36.2%	46.4%	55.4%	65.9%	73.0%
9 yr	38.4%	49.2%	58.8%	69.9%	77.4%
10 yr	40.5%	51.9%	62.0%	73.7%	81.6%

Table 5.6 Sample table of Nikkei risk factors:
constant 97.5% confidence levels, varying volatilities

97.5% CL	10.0%	15.0%	20.0%	25.0%	30.0%
1 yr	19.6%	29.4%	39.2%	49.0%	58.8%
2 yr	27.7%	41.6%	55.4%	69.3%	83.2%
3 yr	33.9%	50.9%	67.9%	84.9%	101.8%
4 yr	39.2%	58.8%	78.4%	98.0%	117.6%
5 yr	43.8%	65.7%	87.7%	109.6%	131.5%
6 yr	48.0%	72.0%	96.0%	120.0%	144.0%
7 yr	51.9%	77.8%	103.7%	129.6%	155.6%
8 yr	55.4%	83.2%	110.9%	138.6%	166.3%
9 yr	58.8%	88.2%	117.6%	147.0%	176.4%
10 yr	62.0%	93.0%	124.0%	155.0%	185.9%

prices, currency rates and so on). Figure 5.3 illustrates the path of sample risk factors at 10 percent volatility and 97.5 percent confidence interval over varying maturities. Figure 5.4 illustrates the path of sample risk factors with

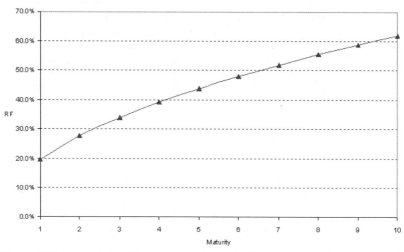

Figure 5.3 Path of the risk factor at 10% volatility, 97.5% confidence level

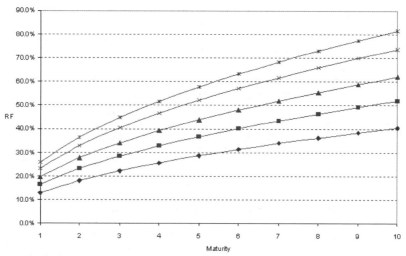

Figure 5.4 Path of the risk factor at 10% volatility, varying confidence levels (90–99%)

constant volatility and varying confidence levels. Figure 5.5 shows the same for constant confidence level and varying volatilities.

THE RISK EQUIVALENCY FRAMEWORK

The risk factor we have developed above can next be used in the appropriate risk equivalency calculation, which depends on the specific derivative product or strategy under consideration. The general form of the risk equivalency equation is:

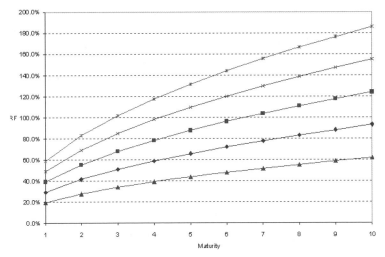

Figure 5.5 Path of the risk factor at 97.5% confidence level, varying volatilities (10–30%)

$$REE = RF * N \tag{5.13}$$

Where RF is the risk factor, and N is the notional amount of the transaction.

Thus, if a bank enters into a derivative transaction with a notional of US\$100m and an RF of 5 percent, the REE equals US\$5m. Based on the RF framework this is the maximum the bank expects to lose at any point during the life of the trade, to the confidence level specified. If the counterparty defaults during the life of the derivative, the bank expects the maximum credit loss to be less than, or equal to, US\$5m in x percent of cases, where x is the confidence interval selected. This figure is also equal to the potential market risk discussed earlier in the chapter. As we have noted, PMR, or REE at inception, is the *ex ante* figure required to make a credit decision.[12] Knowing the REE is US\$5m, for example, a risk officer considering a transaction (and bearing in mind other items such as transaction maturity, product suitability, and so forth) can make a rational credit decision. Without a measure such as REE, it is impossible for the analyst to know how to evaluate the risk on the US\$100m derivative. Actual market risk (AMR), though vital once a trade is under way, is equal to zero at inception and is therefore unsuitable for decision-making purposes. It should be noted that the standard REE equation given in Equation 5.13 is generally modified to take account of the characteristics of individual products, as we shall discuss in subsequent chapters; the form given above is generic. Figure 5.6 summarizes the steps involved in the risk equivalency process.

Obviously, the framework we have presented relies on a number of assumptions in order to be useful and can be altered to suit the individual

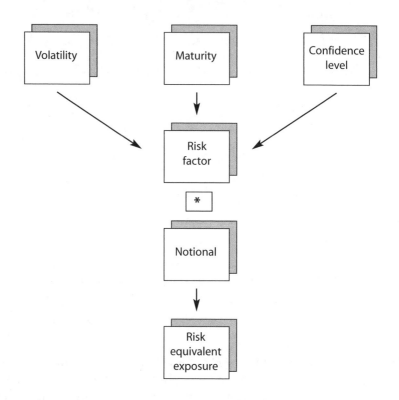

Figure 5.6 The risk equivalency process

requirements of a given institution. The process above is by no means the only effective representation of a risk equivalency framework; alternate methods exist and can be employed. That said, we have one straight-forward method by which to estimate potential market movements and, by extension, the potential credit risk exposure that might be encountered in a given derivative transaction under normal conditions.

It is important to stress that financial markets exhibit a fair degree of volatility, which sometimes exceeds the boundaries of what might be considered "normal." Instances of turmoil in certain markets lend weight to this: the global equity crashes in October 1987 and October 1989, the junk bond market crash in October 1989, the currency turmoil in Europe in September 1992, the Mexican peso crisis in late 1994, the Asian currency crisis of 1997, the Russian and hedge fund collapse of 1998, and so on. These market moves represent multiple standard deviation events (for example, 3, 5, 10+ standard deviations, most often depicted as a distribution with a "fat tail" (for example, leptokurtic statistical distribution)). No model is perfect, as derivative practitioners have found, particularly in times of extreme volatility. If decision making and transaction execution must occur during such periods, then the credit professional involved in a transaction must take account of this fact and modify the approach or decision accordingly by employing more relevant (that is, conservative) assumptions.

REFINING RISK EQUIVALENT EXPOSURE

The generic REE framework above is a mechanism for deriving what we refer to henceforth as terminal worst-case REE, or REE_{twc}. By its construction, REE_{twc} is a very conservative measure of credit risk exposure and it can most appropriately be thought of as credit exposure that is maximized at the conclusion of a transaction based on maximum market movement. Since it is an extreme measure we also want to introduce adjustments that provide a more "realistic" level of exposure; these center on the concepts of average and expected credit exposure.

In refining the REE framework we distinguish between four different versions:

■ *Terminal exposure*: credit exposure based on the final maturity of the transaction.

■ *Average exposure*: credit exposure based on the average maturity of the transaction.

■ *Worst-case exposure*: credit exposure based on an extreme market movement.

■ *Expected exposure*: credit exposure based on a mathematically expected market movement.

Using these definitions we can categorize credit exposure into four different classes:

■ *Terminal worst-case exposure*: calculation of credit exposure based on the final maturity of the transaction and an extreme market movement; this, as indicated above, is defined as REE_{twc}.

■ *Average worst-case exposure*: calculation of credit exposure based on the average maturity of the transaction and an extreme market movement; this is defined as REE_{awc}.

■ *Terminal expected exposure*: calculation of credit exposure based on the final maturity of the transaction and a mathematically expected market movement; this is defined as REE_{te}.

■ *Average expected exposure*: calculation of credit exposure based on the average maturity of the transaction and a mathematically expected market movement; this is defined as REE_{ae}.

These four classes of credit exposures reflect different levels of conservatism. When defining risk appetite through the governance process described in Chapter 3, an institution should decide which approach is most suitable given its own risk tolerance and philosophy: final versus average maturity and worst-case versus expected market moves, for example. As before, there is no single correct answer.

Let us consider a basic methodology for deriving each class of credit exposure. As indicated in equation 5.12, the derivation of the risk factor, RF, is based on the standard equation:

$$RF = HV * \sqrt{T} * z \tag{5.12}$$

Multiplying this basic equation by a notional amount N yields a standard *ex ante* REE figure. This figure represents the terminal worst-case REE, since no adjustments are made to account for either the average (rather than the final) maturity of the transaction or the expected (rather than worst-case) market movement of the stochastic variable underlying the derivative. In order to obtain average worst-case REE, we adjust RF so that it reflects the average, rather than final, maturity of the transaction. To begin, we convert the terminology of Equation 5.12 into the following notation

$$RF = \sigma * T^{1/2} * z \tag{5.14}$$

This permits us to manipulate the equation in a simpler fashion (for example, as illustrated in Note 12). Next, we assume that *s* is a daily, rather than annual, volatility measure. We also assume that the probability of counterparty default is uniformly distributed over the maturity of the transaction (T) and that default is independent of the size of the exposure (that is, a greater RF or REE will not increase the probability of default; we discuss this concept at greater length in Part III). In order to derive an average worst-case credit exposure we integrate, from 0 to T, the terminal worst-case exposure, and then divide by the maturity of the transaction.[13] The end result is an average worst-case risk factor RF_{awc} which, when applied to the notional N, yields an average worst-case REE, REE_{awc}:

$$REE_{awc} = REE_{twc} * (2/3) \tag{5.15}$$

In other words, the average worst-case credit exposure is estimated at two-thirds of terminal worst-case credit exposure. For institutions interested in utilizing this approach to measure and manage exposure, the two-thirds multiplier is a convenient "rule of thumb."

The next step in the refinement of REE converts worst-case exposure into expected exposure. Whereas the conversion of terminal into average exposure is related to the maturity of the transaction, the conversion of worst-case exposure into expected exposure is based on the movement of the underlying market variable governing the transaction. Expected exposure is defined as credit exposure that will be experienced during the transaction based on a mathematically expected, rather than worst-case, market movement. As before, several inputs are required, including maturity, volatility and confidence level. Given use of a two standard deviation (2σ) one-sided confidence interval (for example, 97.5 percent confidence level) to determine REE_{twc} we show that expected terminal REE (or REE_{te}) is equal to:[14]

$$REE_{te} = REE_{twc}/5 \tag{5.16}$$

This provides a terminal expected credit exposure based on a two standard deviation confidence level; different confidence levels will yield slightly different results.

We can generate REE_{ae} from REE_{te} through the same process we used for converting REE_{twc} into REE_{awc}. This, once again, is accomplished by integrating the expected terminal credit exposure from 0 to T and dividing by T. The end result is shown as:

$$REE_{ae} = REE_{te} * (2/3) \tag{5.17}$$

That is, average expected credit exposure is approximately equal to two-thirds of terminal expected credit exposure.

Let us consider the following example based on the discussion above: a bank enters into a 12-month derivative transaction which has US$10m of REE, based on REE_{twc} (adjusted to a 97.5 percent confidence level). If the bank feels use of terminal worst-case credit exposure is excessively conservative it might decide to use average worst-case exposure, REE_{awc}. Based on Equation 5.15, REE_{awc} amounts to US$6.66m. If it prefers to compute its REE based on expected, rather than worst-case, market movements, it can employ Equation 5.16 to calculate terminal expected exposure (again, to a 97.5 percent confidence level); this yields an REE of US$2m. As a final option, it can compute average expected exposure via Equation 5.17; this yields REE of US$1.33m. We can see the range of credit exposures that arises by applying different transaction maturity and market movement assumptions. While there is no single correct way of implementing the REE computation an institution should ensure that it is not excessively conservative or liberal; such can drive away business or encourage too much risk-taking. Table 5.7 and Figure 5.7 summarize the discussion above.

In this chapter we have focused on the REE quantification of single transactions through a volatility-based framework. While the REE quantification of single transactions is the critical starting point, the same framework can be extended to an entire portfolio of transactions. In order to incorporate REEs at the portfolio level, an institution must rely on correlations to take account of additive, or offsetting, effects generated through discrete derivative deals. For simplicity, in the remainder of Part II we continue to focus on the REE of individual transactions, with the understanding that the REE process can be extended to a full portfolio by utilizing a combination of REEs and correlations. A more detailed discussion of portfolio aggregation follows in Part III.

Table 5.7 Alternative REE computations*

Credit exposure	General computation
Terminal worst case credit exposure	REE_{twc}
Average worst case credit exposure	$REE_{awc} = REE_{twc} * 2/3$
Terminal expected credit exposure	$REE_{te} = REE_{twc} / 5$
Average expected credit exposure	$REE_{ae} = REE_{te} * 2/3$

* based on a 97.5 per cent, one-sided confidence level.

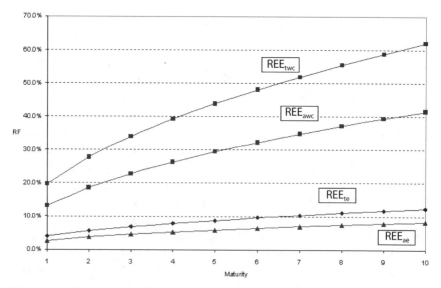

Figure 5.7 Alternative risk exposure paths

SIMULATION: AN ALTERNATIVE METHODOLOGY

We have presented above a common volatility approach for quantifying potential credit risk exposure of derivative transactions. It is certainly not the only means by which to quantify such risks; institutions use a variety of other proprietary or industry-accepted methods to generate risk equivalent exposures. Although it is not our intent to review in detail all alternate exposure evaluation methodologies, we present in summary form a discussion of the simulation approach, which is widely used by numerous financial institutions (particularly those with computing resources and analytics expertise). In fact, simulation processes drive many of the IRB and portfolio frameworks we mention in this book.

The simulation approach (often implemented via the Monte Carlo simulation process) is a computer-intensive statistical methodology that generates random paths of market variable(s) (for example, the underlying reference of a given derivative) based on select user inputs, valuing a derivative at select points during the life and/or at maturity of the transaction. This process is repeated tens of thousands of times in order to develop an average value of the derivative; comparing the starting value of the derivative with the average value at select points in time provides a profile of credit exposure over time.

The initial step in the simulation process involves the selection and definition of an equation that describes the path of asset prices. Earlier in the chapter we discussed use of the GBM as a means of describing the path of continuous, stochastic variables (which exhibit independence from one period to the next); equity and foreign exchange prices are often modeled in this fashion. Bond prices/interest rates generally follow a distinct process that takes account mean reversion and convergence to par at maturity (the "pull to par" effect).[15] For purposes of this example we shall illustrate the process via a GBM (knowing the same general steps apply to alternate models).

Restating the fundamental GBM equation given in Equation 5.4 to reflect time increments (t), we obtain:

$$dS_1 = \mu_1 S_1 dt + \sigma_1 S_1 dz \tag{5.18}$$

To convert continuous time to very small increments of time, the GBM equation becomes:

$$\Delta S_1 = \mu S \Delta t + \sigma S \Delta z \tag{5.19}$$

where Δt is a small time increment.

Integrating over a time interval yields:

$$S_T = S e^{\mu - \frac{\sigma^2}{2} \tau + \sigma \varepsilon \sqrt{\tau}} \tag{5.20}$$

where ε is a normal random variable with mean 0 and variance 1. (Note that this is effectively a restatement of Equation 5.6.) Expanding, we can generate the movement of the stock price from one time period to the next via:

$$S_{t+1} = S_t e^{\mu - \frac{\sigma^2}{2}\tau + \sigma\varepsilon\sqrt{\tau}} \tag{5.21}$$

To generate the price path of S we define the key parameters of Equation 5.21, including μ and σ, the starting level of $S(t)$, and the length of the time interval Δt. Once these variables are defined, it is necessary to generate a series of random numbers ε (at each time interval) that can be incorporated into the equation. Each random generation produces an incremental step in the price path until a complete path is created, from trade date until maturity date. At select time intervals along the path, and at maturity of the transaction, the derivative is valued and discounted back to the present. Completion of the periodic and terminal valuations along the simulated path comprises a single generation, or trial, of the process. Once tens of thousands of trials are run, the expected value of the derivative is computed as the average of all valuations. This expected value provides an indication of the economic worth of the derivative and can be used to determine expected credit exposure; such exposure can then be allocated against counterparty credit limits. If a counterparty defaults when the derivative has an expected value as determined through the simulation process, a bank suffers an economic loss of that amount. There is a trade-off between the number of price paths generated and the accuracy of the valuation; the more runs executed, the greater the accuracy, but the more time-consuming the process.

Figure 5.8 illustrates sample asset price paths bounded by confidence bands.[16]

The simulation approach allows for the development of an entire continuum of credit risk exposure over the life of the transaction. While it is often thought to provide the most accurate estimates of credit exposure, the approach has several drawbacks. Like the volatility technique, the simulation approach is very sensitive to the statistically defined "user inputs" and, as such, requires the use of certain underlying assumptions about distributions, movement of asset prices, and so on; any simulation model will reflect the nature of these inputs. In addition, the framework requires reasonably significant computing power and time to generate a simulation of the proposed transaction and not every institution has the resources needed to generate this type of analysis. From the perspective of the derivatives intermediary, credit analysts often do not have time to generate the required simulated credit exposure when dealing with "live" trades. The speed of market movements and the need to respond to client requests on a "real time" basis may render this an unworkable solution.

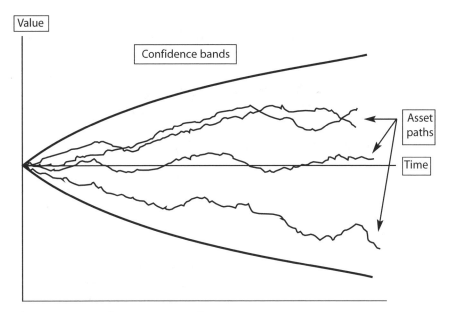

Figure 5.8 Sample asset price paths

Although the simulation approach is a valid method of computing REE, this book will continue to focus on the volatility-based RF framework (though we shall illustrate use of simulation at select points in the text). Having described approaches to estimating REE, we are prepared to implement RF in a broader product framework. Parts II and III of the book focus on use of RF and REE in the quantification of credit risk for a variety of complex derivatives.[17]

CHAPTER 6

Quantifying Option Credit Risk

OTC options can be bought and sold on any instrument and can be constructed to provide virtually any type of payoff or protection profile. Since options are so flexible it is not surprising that they are one of the fundamental building blocks of custom derivative packages. Given the importance of options in the financial markets we develop, in this chapter, an REE method for estimating credit risk in standard contracts, and apply these equations to option products and strategies analyzed in Chapters 7 and 8.

Put options (which, as noted earlier, give the buyer the right, but not the obligation, to sell an underlying instrument at a certain strike price) and call options (which give the buyer the right, but not the obligation, to buy an underlying instrument at a certain strike price) are available on virtually any market reference and may be settled in cash or physical form. The buyer can exercise options at any time until maturity (*American option*), at maturity (*European option*), or at specified periodic intervals (*Bermudan option*).

Since market movements impact options, they are defined as market risk-sensitive products and must be adjusted through the risk equivalency process in order to obtain an estimate of credit risk. This can be achieved through the REE process introduced in the previous chapter; it can also be accomplished through alternate methodologies, including the sensitivities approach and the simulation approach. In the section immediately following we discuss option credit risk exposure from a qualitative standpoint. We then develop various equations for estimating risk exposure that take account of the changing intrinsic and time value characteristics of the contracts. We conclude with an overview of alternate option credit risk quantification methodologies.

AN OVERVIEW OF OPTION CREDIT RISK

The credit risk exposure of OTC options is unilateral, with the buyer of the option bearing the credit risk of the seller.[1] The role of the option seller is to provide the buyer with an economic payoff should a certain strike level be reached; in exchange for this payoff the seller earns premium income. Once the seller receives its premium it is no longer dependent on the buyer for future performance and, as such, bears no credit exposure. When option contracts are independent (for example, not embedded in interest, currency, equity, or commodity swaps) premium is commonly paid upfront, within a five-business-day settlement period.[2] If the seller does not receive premium from the buyer within the cash-settlement time frame, it simply cancels the option contract.

The option buyer, in contrast, pays the seller for a potential financial gain (or receipt of an asset with implicit value) should a market move in a particular direction. If the option gains value during the life of the trans-action and the buyer exercises its right under the contract, it relies on performance by the seller in order to obtain its economic gain; it thus has economic exposure to the seller as its counterparty. If the seller defaults when the option is in-the-money, the buyer will not receive what it is owed and suffers an economic loss; this is the primary credit exposure of a long option position and relates strictly to the potential intrinsic value of the derivative. In addition, some element of premium, the payment the buyer made to secure the option, may be sacrificed. Option premium is comprised of intrinsic value and time value: *intrinsic value* measures the "moneyness" of the option. Options struck well out-of-the-money have no intrinsic value (for example, if exercised immediately no economic gain results), while those struck in-the-money have a great deal of intrinsic value (for example, if exercised immediately they generate an economic gain); options struck at-the-money have no intrinsic value but have the potential of gaining it very quickly. *Time value* measures the remaining time until maturity. Options with a long time to maturity have greater time value than those with only a short time.

Assuming an institution divides the value of the premium payment into time value and intrinsic value components, the credit risk of the initial premium payment can be treated with varying degrees of conservatism. Certain institutions ignore the time value component of the upfront premium payment as a credit risk exposure and simply count the intrinsic value of the option as true risk to the counterparty; others allocate the full amount of time value against credit limits and leave it unadjusted until expiry of the transaction; still other institutions count time value against credit limits and adjust it downward until it reaches zero at expiry (that is, reflecting the time decay concept). In this text we present a discussion based on the latter approach, where credit exposure of premium consists only of the time value element of the payment and, for simplicity, amortizes on a straight line basis; the intrinsic value component of option premium is estimated through a separate component of the overall credit risk equation.[3] The logic of this approach is as follows: if an institution buys a 12-month at-the-money option for US$100, and one month into the transaction the counterparty defaults while the option is still at-the-money, the institution loses the remaining time value of the option (for example, the chance that, over time, the market will move slightly and force the option in-the-money). This is a true economic loss for the institution because, though the underlying option still has no intrinsic value, it has the potential of gaining such during the remaining 11 months of the trade. Note that throughout this text when we refer to premium generically we refer to the time value component of premium.

To summarize, an option buyer has credit risk exposure on two fronts: exposure to loss of the economic gain resulting from the option moving in-the-money (that is, the intrinsic value component of the option's value) and exposure to loss of the time value component of premium. An option seller has no credit risk exposure as long as premium is received in a normal cash settlement time frame. For the purposes of this chapter we assume option purchases by an institution are made through an upfront payment of premium; likewise, option sales are only made when premium is received upfront. The reader should bear in mind that differences in exposure occur when premium payments are either deferred or amortized during the life of the transaction; we discuss such non-standard treatment of premium in subsequent chapters.

Quantifying option credit risk

With these comments as a general background we focus on the credit risk exposure generated by long option positions. We begin with the general risk equivalency equation introduced in Chapter 5, REE = RF * N, and make certain modifications so that it provides a more accurate reflection of the actual and potential economic value inherent in a long position.

The payoff of a long call, ignoring present value considerations, equals the difference between the current market price (which we term CMP) and the strike price (SP). The payoff of a long put is simply the difference between the strike price and current market price, or (SP − CMP). In attempting to estimate credit risk, it is appropriate to determine how far the underlying market price will move during the life of the transaction, since this ultimately determines the payoff of the option. The higher above, or below, the strike price the underlying reference moves (for calls and puts, respectively), the greater the payoff to the option purchaser,and the greater the payoff to the purchaser, the greater the purchaser's credit risk exposure to the seller. This movement can be crystallized by applying a risk factor, RF, against the CMP; subtracting the resulting value from SP (for a call) or subtracting SP from the resulting value (for a put) provides an estimate of the maximum expected payoff based on predicted market movements (which, as we know from the last chapter, can be estimated through historical volatility, adjusted by a confidence level and a time dimension). A variable reflecting the size of the transaction can then be applied to indicate the dollar value of the potential gain/exposure, which is ultimately what needs to be measured.

An option transaction can be denominated in either contract or notional terms. If denominated in contracts, any gain is reflected as the difference between the underlying price and strike price times the number of contracts. (There may be an additional step, where contracts are multiplied by a fixed "amount" to reflect a contract multiplier; for example, S&P 500 is multiplied by US$500, Osaka Nikkei 225 by ¥1000, and so on. We shall ignore this step for the sake of clarity and simply assume unit payoff against a contract.) If denominated in notional terms, any gain is reflected as the percentage difference between the underlying and strike; we discuss this refinement below. Based on these parameters, we define standard REE equations for contract-based options as:

$$REE = prem + (NC * (((1 + RFc) * CMP) - SP)) \qquad (6.1)$$

for calls, and

$$REE = prem + (NC * (SP - ((1 - RFc) * CMP))) \qquad (6.2)$$

for puts,

where *prem* is the time value component of option premium; *NC* is the number of option contracts; *RFc* is the risk factor, constantly adjusted for declining maturity; *SP* is the strike price; and *CMP* is the current market price.

Let us consider an example using Equation 6.1 for calls. Assume Bank CDE purchases a 12-month call on stock ABC from Dealer JKL. The call, which is based on 10,000 contracts (one contract/share) is struck at-the-money (US$50/share) and is worth US$10,000 in premium (which we know is strictly time value, since the option currently has no intrinsic value). Based on past historical volatilities and a 90 percent confidence level, CDE determines the initial RF on stock ABC is 35 percent. The REE, via Equation 6.1, is therefore:

$$\text{REE} = \text{US\$10,000} + (10,000 * (((1 + 0.35) * 50) - 50))$$

$$= \text{US\$10,000} + (10,000 * (67.5 - 50))$$

$$= \text{US\$10,000} + \text{US\$175,000}$$

$$= \text{US\$185,000}$$

This figure, representing time value of premium paid plus future credit exposure on the intrinsic value portion, is applied against the seller's credit limits. Based on a 90 percent confidence level RF, CDE estimates stock ABC will rise to a maximum of US$67.50/share in the next 12 months; if this occurs, the payoff on the long call is US$175,000. Thus, if JKL defaults when the underlying reaches its peak (as estimated by the 90 percent confidence level RF), CDE loses the full economic value of the call (plus any residual time value of premium, depending on whether exposure peaks before maturity). Using the equations above we can adjust the risk factors on an ongoing basis, via RFc, to reflect the declining potential market risk of the transaction; we can also substitute the latest CMP as the market changes.

A second adjustment can be made to reflect the intrinsic value of the option at inception and at subsequent points during the life of the trade; this may be thought of as measuring actual market risk (AMR), or current exposure, as outlined earlier. When an option is initially purchased, it may be out-of-the-money, at-the-money, or in-the-money. Options struck out-of-the-money (that is, those with no intrinsic value) have less economic value than those struck at-the-money or in-the-money. An option with less value carries less credit risk exposure than one with more value. Intuitively this seems sensible: if a bank purchases an option that is deeply out-of-the-money, it has less value and stands less chance of finishing in-the-money. If an option does not move in-the-money, the option buyer does not need to look to the option seller for performance, so its associated risk exposure is lower. For options which are deeply out-of-the-money, particularly with a short time to maturity (that is, little time value), it is reasonable to suppose market risk exposure will never be positive; that is, the option will not move in-the-money and the buyer will not look to the seller for the economic gain.[4] In such cases it seems appropriate only to count the risk of the time value component of premium as credit exposure. Conversely, options that are struck in-the-money have a greater chance of ending with value. Since it is highly probable the derivative will be exercised (prior to or at maturity, depending on exercise style), the buyer places increased reliance on the performance of the seller. Indeed, since the option is in-the-money at the inception of the trade, counterparty default immediately after commencement results in a certain loss of intrinsic value. The equations below take account of these facts by assigning credit risk exposure to the maximum of zero or the potential market risk movement (calculated by applying the risk factor to the current market price CMP, which is the relevant starting point), adjusted for the moneyness of the option (which is calculated by comparing CMP and SP). The new REE equations (which are similar to the equations above, though more transparent), are given as:

$$REE = prem + max(0, (NC*((RFc * CMP) + (CMP - SP)))) \qquad (6.3)$$

for calls, and

$$REE = prem + max(0, (NC*((RFc * CMP) + (SP - CMP)))) \qquad (6.4)$$

for puts,

where all terms are as defined above.

Note that we designate CMP as the starting point in tracking market movements and apply RF to that starting point. Intuitively this should make sense since RF, applied to the current market level, provides the maximum upward or downward movement expected during the life of the transaction. Use of (RF * CMP) provides a slight upward bias when CMP is higher than SP, a slight downward bias when it is lower than SP.[5] (Those preferring not to bias the risk factors may use (RFc * SP); there is no single correct answer.) Note that regardless of the method used, the intrinsic value component, (CMP – SP) or (SP – CMP), remains unchanged. Although it is left for the reader to decide which method is most appropriate, we shall continue to value options via the equations detailed above (and will use a similar approach in developing swap risk factors).

Consider the following example: Bank J buys 50,000 out-of-the-money put contracts (one contract/share) on stock DEF, struck at US$15 in a US$16.50 market (that is, 10 percent out-of-the-money). The maturity of the trade is 12 months and the premium paid to the seller, Bank Y, is US$50 000 (once again, the premium is comprised solely of time value since the option is struck out-of-the-money). Based on historical movements in the price of DEF the risk factor is determined to be 25 percent. The initial risk faced on this transaction, per equation 6.4, is:

REE = US$50,000 + max(0, (50,000 * ((0.25 * 16.50) +(15.00 - 16.50))))

= US$50,000 + max(0, (50,000 * ((4.125) + (21.50))))

= US$50,000 + US$131,250

= US$181,250

Although the option is struck 10 percent out-of-the-money (which subtracts from the total market risk exposure faced by Bank J), the long time to expiry translates into an initial 25 percent risk factor, which is applied to the starting price. This, in turn, more than offsets the out-of-the-money portion and adds potential risk exposure to the transaction. A short-term option, also struck 10 percent out-of-the-money, would have less time for market movement to force the contract in-the-money and would thus generate less credit risk exposure. If, in the example above, the maturity of the trade is lowered from 12 months to one month (with the associated risk factor falling from 25 to 7 percent), the second portion of the equation is negative; in such cases the only credit risk exposure is attributable to premium (time value).

Returning to the original example, we can track the credit risk exposure of the option trade every quarter, remembering at each evaluation point to substitute a new risk factor and lower the remaining time value of premium. The results, including hypothetical CMPs at each valuation point, are shown in Table 6.1.

Through this example we see how the option's risk changes over time. The premium (time value) declines throughout the life of the transaction as maturity draws nearer, reaching zero at the conclusion of the trade. (Once again, we assume straight line decay in the time value of the premium; this is an estimate for simplicity, as it is well known that time value decays at an increasing rate as maturity draws nearer.) The RFc declines each quarter (or each month, week, or day) in line with the declining maturity of the option. As the option moves in-the-money the second portion of the equation, (SP – CMP), becomes positive. Upon exercise of the option at maturity Bank J receives a payout of US$50,000, the difference between the strike (US$15.00) and the market price (US$14.00) times the number of contracts. If Bank Y, as seller of the put, defaults on day 180, Bank J sustains a certain loss of US$25,000 (that is, remaining time value of premium, but no intrinsic value, since the option is not yet in-the-money). If Y defaults just prior to maturity, J sustains a certain loss of US$50,000 (that is, intrinsic value, since the option is in-the-

Table 6.1 Ongoing credit risk of a put option

Day	REE	Premium(TV)	RFc	CMP	SP
t=0	$181,250	$50,000	0.25	$16.50	$15.00
90	$163,500	$37,500	0.22	$16.00	$15.00
180	$152,500	$25,000	0.17	$15.00	$15.00
270	$131,750	$12,500	0.13	$14.50	$15.00
360	$50,000	$0	0.00	$14.00	$15.00

money, but no time value as it is fully decayed). Not knowing when (or if) the option will move in-the-money or when (or if) the counterparty will default, means a credit officer assigns a potential worst-case risk exposure scenario to the transaction through the risk equivalency framework (though it is certainly possible to consider use of expected, rather than worst-case, credit exposure, as outlined in the last chapter).

As indicated earlier, there are instances when an option is expressed in notional, rather than contract, terms. When this occurs we adjust the equations illustrated above by substituting notional (N) for number of contracts (NC) and dividing terms of the equations by the strike price; Equations 6.3 and 6.4 become:

$$REE = prem + \max\left[0, \left[N * \left[\frac{(RFc * CMP)}{SP} + \frac{(CMP - SP)}{SP}\right]\right]\right] \qquad (6.5)$$

for calls

$$REE = prem + \max\left[0, \left[N * \left[\frac{(RFc * CMP)}{SP} + \frac{(SP - CMP)}{SP}\right]\right]\right] \qquad (6.6)$$

for puts,

where N is the notional of the option transaction and all other terms are as defined above.

Returning to the example above, where Bank J purchases a 12-month 10 percent out-of-the-money put option (SP of US$15.00 in a US$16.50 market) on US$750,000 notional (50,000 contracts * US$15.00) for US$50,000, the REE, per Equation 6.6, is:

REE = US$50,000 + max(0, (US$750,000 * ((0.25 * US$16.50)/US$15.00 + (US$15.00 − US$16.50)/US$15.00)))

= US$50,000 + max(0, (US$750,000 * ((0.275) + (20.10))))

= US$50,000 + US$131,250

= US$181,250

The result, not coincidentally, is identical to the result from the earlier contract-based example; the gains (and hence REE) are simply reflected as a percentage of the notional rather than an absolute value. Thus, Equations 6.3 and 6.4 are useful when dealing with numbers of contracts and Equations 6.5 and 6.6 are useful when dealing with notional amounts.

As a final note, it should be highlighted that the approach taken above is algebraically identical to the current market price approach assumed by certain other works, which value credit lines for options in terms of CMP rather than SP.[6] For instance, Arak, Goodman, and Rones (1986) define the adjustment to the out-of-the-money portion of a call option as (SP − CMP)/CMP (subtracted from the original risk factor value), while this author defines the adjustment as (CMP − SP)/CMP (added to the original risk factor value).[7] These are consistent with the discussion above when expressed as a percentage of the market value of the underlying. This may be accomplished, for example, by:

$$REE = prem + \max\left[0,\left[(RFc *NC * CMP) + \left[\frac{(CMP - SP)}{SP} * (NC *CMP)\right]\right]\right]$$

(6.7)

for calls, and

$$REE = prem + \max\left[0,\left[(RFc *NC * CMP) + \left[\frac{(SP - CMP)}{SP} * (NC *CMP)\right]\right]\right]$$

(6.8)

for puts.

Note that the notional amount N is the product of NC and CMP (rather than SP).

Returning to the example above we can show the results are identical:

REE = US$50,000 + max(0,(((0.25 * 50,000 * US$16.50) + ((US$15.00 − US$16.50)/US$16.50) * (50,000 * US$16.50)))

= US$50,000 + max(0, ((US$206,250) + (-US$75,000))))

= US$50,000 + US$131,250

= US$181,250

Although algebraically identical and consistent, it is intuitively simpler to discuss the above in terms of strike prices, rather than current market prices. As such, we focus on Equations 6.3 through 6.6 when valuing the credit risk of options.

At this point we have certain basic equations that can be used to estimate option credit risk. There are, of course, other ways to value such risks, but the equations above are intuitively easy to understand and mathematically simple to employ. We shall return to these standard equations at various points throughout the text as we explore the quantification of compound option strategies, complex options, and swaps with embedded options.

Alternate quantification methodologies

An institution can use other methods to estimate the REE of options. Although it is not our intent to provide detailed coverage of all available methods, we outline below certain interesting ones that are commonly used.

Simulation approach

The credit risk exposure of options is often determined using simulation analysis. As mentioned in the last chapter, simulations can be used to project the future path of key stochastic variables impacting the value of derivatives. Once an institution has a simulation procedure (for example, one which defines the stochastic process of the variable(s), the starting level of the variable, the confidence levels and time intervals, and so on), it can revalue the option at selected intervals. Tens of thousands of revaluations based on randomly generated market price paths permit the computation of an average value for the option (at selected intervals and maturity). The difference between the starting value of the option and the simulated average value provides a measure of future credit exposure at select points in time. Naturally, in simulating the value of the option one is jointly quantifying the time value and intrinsic value components of the option.

Sensitivities approach

The sensitivities approach to estimating option credit risk, presented in a number of studies, uses the comparative statics (or sensitivities) of options (for example, delta, gamma, vega, and theta) to estimate current and future credit exposure.[8] Traders generally measure and manage the market risk of option positions and trading strategies through statics (or "Greeks") and the quantification of credit risk makes use of the same information. By altering each of the model input parameters (for example, underlying price, volatility, time) through scenarios or RFs and recomputing the value of the option at selected time intervals, an increase or decrease in credit exposure can be determined. Before describing the framework we briefly review the major comparative statics: delta, gamma, theta, and vega (note that we shall not consider rho, sensitivity to changes in the risk-free rate, in this section).

Delta

Delta is the rate of change (or percentage change) in the price of the option for a unit change in the price of the underlying instrument; it thus measures the change in the value of an option for a small change in the price of the underlying. Options struck at-the-money typically have a delta near 0.5; that is, for a unit price change in the underlying instrument, the option price changes by 0.5. Options struck further in-the-money have deltas greater than 0.5 (which converge on 1.0 as they move deeper in-the-money), while options struck out-of-the-money have deltas of less than 0.5 (which converge on 0 as they move deeper out-of-the-money). Long calls and short puts have positive deltas, while long puts and short calls have negative deltas. Options with positive deltas gain in value when there is an increase in the value of the underlying, and options with negative deltas gain in value when there is a decrease in the value of the underlying. Delta is often employed in the calculation of appropriate hedge ratios; for instance, if a long call option has a delta of 0.5, 0.5 short units of the underlying are needed to hedge one long option. Establishing a delta-hedged position reduces, or neutralizes, exposure to local (small) moves in the underlying.

Gamma

Gamma is the rate of change (or percentage change) in the delta of the option for a unit change in the price of the underlying instrument. It effectively measures the risk of an option, while delta measures the risk of the underlying. Gamma is particularly useful when attempting to measure the risk of an option to non-local (large) moves in the underlying. Options struck at-the-money carry the highest gammas (which tend towards infinity as expiry draws near). High gamma options have deltas that are very sensitive to changes in the value of the underlying. Options struck either in- or out-of-the-money have lower gammas (which converge on 0 as time to expiry draws near). Low gamma options have deltas that are relatively insensitive to changes in the value of the underlying. Short options (whether puts or calls) have negative gammas and long options (puts or calls) have positive gammas. The seller of options therefore benefits when the movement of the underlying is stable, while the buyer benefits when the movement of the underlying is volatile.

Vega

Vega (sometimes called zeta, lambda, or kappa) is the rate of change in the value of the option for a percentage change in volatility. Options struck at-the-money have high vegas and display greater sensitivity to changes in volatility; options struck in or out-of-the-money have lower vegas and are relatively less sensitive to changes in volatility. As maturity draws nearer, vega begins to decline. Short option positions (whether puts or calls) have negative vegas, while long option positions (puts or calls) have positive vegas. A decrease in volatility is therefore beneficial to a seller of options while an increase is beneficial to a buyer.

Theta

Theta is the rate of change in the value of the option for a change in time; this is often known as time decay. Since an option's value is comprised of time value (and intrinsic value), and since time is a "wasting asset," the value of a long option decreases as time to maturity draws nearer, at a rate measured by theta. Options struck at-the-money have the highest thetas, indicating a greater sensitivity to the passage of time, while options struck in or out-of-the-money have lower thetas, meaning a lower sensitivity. The higher an option's theta, the greater the decay in the option's value; short-term options have the greatest rate of time decay. In general, long option positions (whether puts or calls) have negative thetas, suggesting premium time decay works against the buyer, while short option positions (puts or calls) have positive thetas, indicating premium time decay works in favor of the seller.

Returning to our discussion of the sensitivities approach, Ong's process focuses primarily on use of delta and gamma in deriving an REE for options. Under the methodology, a standard RF is multiplied by the port-folio delta (which consists of the delta of the option and the delta of the hedge) and the notional of the transaction; this yields an estimate of the total risk exposure of the option transaction. The magnitude of delta reflects the moneyness of the option and adjusts the RF (and hence the REE) accordingly (in a manner conceptually similar to the one we have discussed above). In a second step, the effects of gamma on an option's price (and hence its risk exposure) are considered; the gamma adjustment to the REE is generally small.[9]

The sensitivities approach proposed by Mark focuses on changes in the price and volatility of the underlying and changes in time in order to obtain possible changes in the price of an option. This approach incorporates a broader group of parameters (delta/gamma, vega, and theta), and makes use of scenario analysis to generate new values for the option. As the value of a long option position increases or decreases through changes in each of the statics, the credit exposure associated with the position increases or decreases. Note that under this approach the option can be valued as a simple position or as part of a delta-neutral (hedged) portfolio (which contains a long call or put, and a delta equivalent of short or long under-lying). The method is based on a simple price-based model (for example, Black futures model) and price and volatility scenarios covering multiple standard deviations. Scenarios are created by moving one parameter (for example, delta/gamma, or vega, or theta) while holding the others constant, and recomputing the value of the option; it can also be accomplished by moving all parameters in unison and determining a value for the option under each joint scenario. Under the first approach the changes in value from each scenario are not additive, since individual valuations are derived while holding two of three parameters constant. For a simple long option position, credit exposure increases as volatility rises (for example, the long position becomes more valuable as volatility rises); it also increases as the price of the underlying moves sharply upward (for a call) or downward (for a put). Analyzing a delta-hedged portfolio may yield slightly different results so the net value from the "up" and "down" scenarios must be considered. In all cases theta subtracts from the value of a long position (for example, the effects of time decay on option premium paid) and, hence, its credit exposure. This, again, is conceptually similar to the treatment of premium (time value) in Equations 6.3 to 6.6; we have shown that premium time value (and, hence, associated credit risk) declines on a continuous basis as time to maturity draws nearer.

Consider the following example: Bank A purchases a call from Bank C and wants to quantify its credit exposure based on the sensitivities approach. Given the position, Bank A knows its credit exposure increases as volatility rises (from vega) and as the price of the underlying rises (from delta/gamma); it also knows that one day's passage of time lowers the value and credit exposure of the option. Accordingly, Bank A runs a compound scenario where it increases the volatility and price of the underlying by two standard deviations; the combination of these scenarios, after accounting for the effects of theta, produces a value for the option which A then allocates against C's credit limits.

The sensitivities approach is best implemented by identifying multiple standard deviation moves in price or volatility (not unlike the REE process above); such moves may be associated with specific bank-determined confidence levels. The approach also requires use of the option pricing model most applicable to the derivative under consideration. Closed-form or analytic models are the simplest to implement, and appropriate for a range of vanilla price-based structures (for example, simple European exercise equity options, FX options, commodity options, short-term bond options on long-term bonds, and so on); these can also be used with compound positions such as straddles and strangles. Tree-based models (such as binomial and trinomial trees) are somewhat more complex to implement as they require greater computing power, while full simulation-based models are the most complex to implement (requiring even more time and computing power).

While the simulation and sensitivities methodologies are valid approaches for quantifying option credit risk exposure, we will continue to focus on the option REE process given in Equations 6.3 to 6.6 in subsequent chapters.

CHAPTER 7

The Credit Risk of Compound Option Strategies

An institution active in listed or OTC options for investment or risk management purposes often utilizes more than simple put or call positions to implement a strategy. Depending on desired results, a firm might use options in combinations that yield very particular payoff or protection profiles, including those that cannot be attained through simple positions. In the previous chapter we discussed the credit risk of standard put and call transactions. In this chapter we expand the discussion by exploring the credit risk of compound option strategies.

Our analysis of the credit risk aspects of compound option strategies begins with a descriptive overview of the most commonly used direction and volatility positions. We start with a review of simple directional strategies and then discuss compound directional and volatility positions, including vertical spreads, straddles, strangles, butterflies, condors, time spreads, ratio vertical spreads, and backspreads.

Following the product description, we analyze the credit risk aspects of compound strategies, building on the framework developed in the previous chapter. The reader should note that the strategies covered in this chapter are applicable to any underlying security or market, and relate equally to listed and OTC options (although OTC options clearly provide a great deal more flexibility and access); from a credit perspective our discussion obviously relates exclusively to OTC products.

PRODUCT DESCRIPTION

Directional strategies: simple positions

Establishing a simple naked position (short or long) in a put (the right to sell an underlying instrument at a certain strike price) or a call (the right to buy an underlying instrument at a certain strike price) implies taking a view on market direction. We briefly review these simple directional positions, for the time being ignoring the consequences of credit risk exposure. Note that when we indicate limited or unlimited risk, we refer to price risk that might cause an economic gain or loss for the investor, not credit risk. While price risk clearly has a bearing on credit risk, it is not the only determining factor in arriving at a credit exposure estimate. Full credit risk considerations are addressed later in the chapter.

- *Long call*: a bullish position taken when a market reference (for example, equity price, bond price, or currency rate) is expected to rise. Premium is paid in exchange for receipt of potential upside in the reference; returns are theoretically unlimited and economic downside is limited to loss of premium.

- *Short call*: a bearish position taken when a market reference is expected to fall. Premium is earned in exchange for payment of potential upside in the reference; returns are limited to the premium earned, while economic downside is theoretically unlimited.

- *Long put*: a bearish position taken when a market reference is expected to fall. Premium is paid in exchange for receipt of potential downside in the market reference; returns are limited only at the point where market prices reach zero, while economic downside is limited to loss of premium paid.

- *Short put*: a bullish position taken when a market reference is expected to rise. Premium is earned in exchange for payment of potential downside in the reference; returns are limited to premium earned, while economic downside is nearly unlimited (bounded only at the point where market prices reach zero).

These four positions are often categorized as *directional strategies* as they seek to take advantage primarily of the absolute direction of prices (though they also gain or lose from changes in volatility and time decay); the initial delta of these positions is always either positive or negative

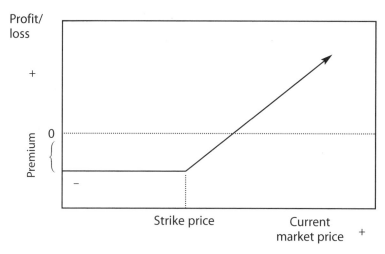

Figure 7.1 Long call payoff profile

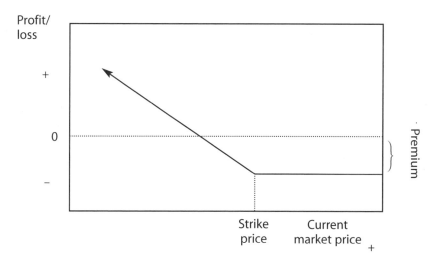

Figure 7.2 Long put payoff profile

(unlike compound volatility strategies, where the initial delta is often neutral). The payoff profiles of the basic positions described above are highlighted in Figures 7.1 to 7.4.

Table 7.1 summarizes the direction (positive, negative, or neutral) of key option risk parameters (for example, the comparative statics outlined in the last chapter), for each of the simple directional positions. The table also indicates whether the initial premium position results in a debit (payment) or a credit (receipt).

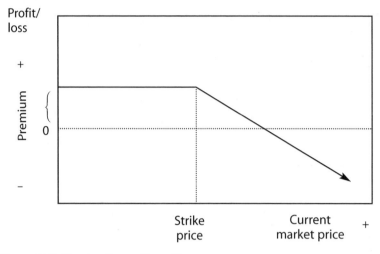

Figure 7.3 Short call payoff profile

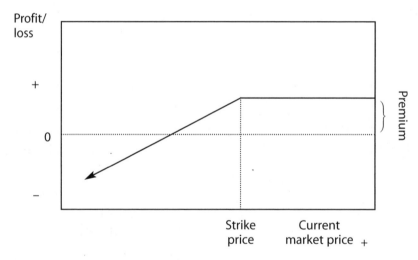

Figure 7.4 Short put payoff profile

Directional strategies: compound positions

Combining puts and/or calls into groups of two or more results in the creation of derivative packages with unique payoff profiles. Specific outcomes depend on the options used (for example, puts/calls), the positions taken (for example, long/short), the strike levels utilized (for example, identical/different), and the exercise dates employed (for example, identical/different). The most common compound directional positions include bullish vertical call spreads, bullish vertical put spreads, bearish vertical call spreads, and bearish vertical put spreads.

Table 7.1 Option risk sensitivities: simple position directional strategies

Position	Delta	Gamma	Vega	Theta	Premium
Long call	Positive	Positive	Positive	Negative	Debit
Short call	Negative	Negative	Negative	Positive	Credit
Long put	Negative	Positive	Positive	Negative	Debit
Short put	Positive	Negative	Negative	Positive	Credit

Vertical spreads

Vertical spreads (also known as price or money spreads) are the most common of the compound direction strategies. Vertical spreads consist of long and short positions in the same type of option (that is, calls or puts) with the same expiry date but different strike prices; spreads may be bullish or bearish to reflect a view on the market's direction.

Bullish vertical call spread

This spread is a combination of a long call with a low strike and a short call with a higher strike; the long position is struck closer to-the-money and is thus more expensive (resulting in a premium debit). For example, a bank might purchase a call struck at 101 and sell a call struck at 105 when the current market price (CMP) is 100. Once CMP exceeds 101, the bank has an in-the-money position that is only offset once CMP exceeds 105; the long position is always worth four points more than the short position once the short call strike is reached. This type of strategy is suitable when a bank is bullish and wants to generate market gains within a limited range. Note that the sale of the higher strike call reduces the overall premium paid.

Bullish vertical put spread

This spread is a combination of a long put with a low strike and a short put with a higher strike. Since the short position is struck closer to-the-money, the spread generates a premium credit, or inflow. As above, this strategy is taken when a bank expects the market to rise (or at least remain stable). For example, if the long put is struck at 95 and the short put is struck at 100 (in a market trading at 101) and the market subsequently rises to 105, both puts remain out-of-the-money but the bank retains its premium income.

Bearish vertical call spread

This is the reverse of the bullish vertical call spread and is created by combining a short call with a low strike and a long call with a higher strike; the sale of the more expensive call creates a premium credit. This spread is a bearish strategy taken when a bank expects the market to fall. For instance, if the short call is struck at 101 and the long call is struck at 105 and CMP falls to 99, both calls remain out-of-the-money but the bank retains its premium income.

Bearish vertical put spread

This spread is the reverse of the bullish vertical put spread and is established by combining a short put with a low strike and a long put with a higher strike; the purchase of the more expensive put results in a premium debit. This spread is a bearish position taken when a bank expects the market to fall. For example, if the short put is struck at 95, the long put is struck at 100 and CMP falls below the two strikes, a bank generates a gain of five points (the long spread in this example is always worth five points more than the short position once the short put strike has been reached).

Figures 7.5 and 7.6 illustrate the payoff profiles of a bullish vertical call spread and a bearish vertical put spread.

Table 7.2 highlights the option risk sensitivities and premium effect of compound directional positions. As with the simple directional strategies above, compound directional strategies typically begin with either positive or negative delta, reflecting a specific view of market direction.

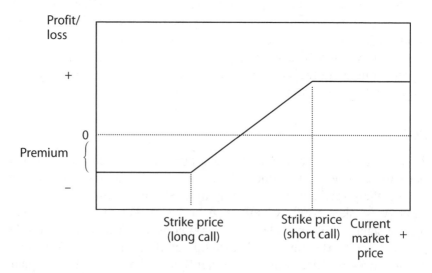

Figure 7.5 Bullish vertical call spread payoff profile

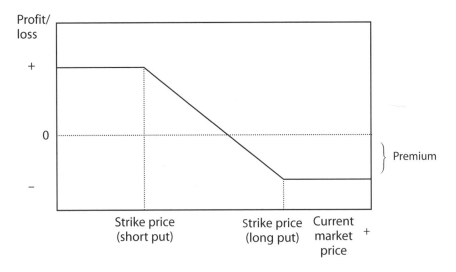

Figure 7.6 Bearish vertical put spread payoff profile

Table 7.2 Option risk sensitivities: compound position directional strategies

Position	Delta	Gamma	Vega	Theta	Premium
Bullish vertical call spread	Positive	Neutral*	Neutral*	Neutral*	Debit
Bullish vertical put spread	Positive	Neutral*	Neutral*	Neutral*	Credit
Bearish vertical call spread	Negative	Neutral*	Neutral*	Neutral*	Credit
Bearish vertical put spread	Negative	Neutral*	Neutral*	Neutral*	Debit

* Approximately neutral; depending on the specific strike levels, there may be a slight positive or negative bias but the overall magniture is generally negligible.

Volatility strategies: compound positions

Compound put/call positions can be created to take advantage of, or protect against, movements in volatility rather than market direction. Indeed, most volatility-based spreads are created with positive or negative vega but neutral delta. The most common compound volatility option strategies are straddles, strangles, butterflies, condor spreads, time spreads, backspreads, and ratio vertical spreads.

Straddles

Straddles are formed by combining puts and calls with equal strike prices and identical expiry dates. A long straddle is established by buying a put and a call with the same strike and maturity, and is taken in anticipation of a large upward or downward move in the market (that is, significant volatility) — when the anticipated direction of movement is uncertain. If the market moves by an amount greater than that dictated by the volatility reflected in the price of the options, the position results in a gain. For example, a bank might purchase a put at 100 and a call at 100, in a current market of 100. If the market remains relatively stagnant (that is, it displays little volatility), the position is not profitable and suffers time decay. If there is upward or downward price movement of significance, however, the position becomes profitable (that is, volatility rises and one of the two options moves in-the-money). From a payoff perspective, a long straddle is characterized by limited downside risk (premium paid) and unlimited profit potential.

A short straddle is the reverse of a long straddle, created through the sale of a put and a call with the same strike and maturity. A bank that believes the market will remain relatively stable for a period of time (that is, it will show little or no volatility) can sell a straddle; if there is little volatility, payoff to the buyer on the put or call position is minimal (and may, in fact, be zero). A short straddle is characterized by limited upside gain (premium income earned) and unlimited downside risk.

Figures 7.7 and 7.8 illustrate the payoff profiles of long and short straddles.

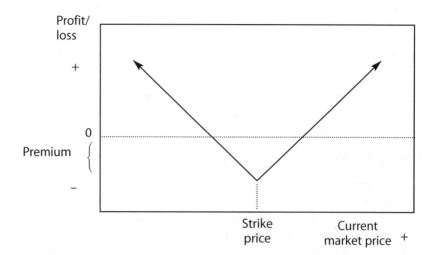

Figure 7.7 Long straddle payoff profile

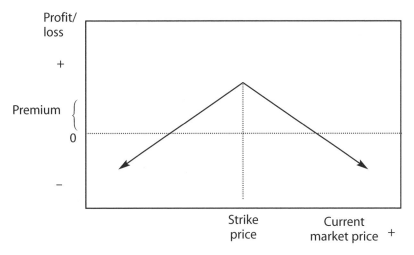

Figure 7.8 Short straddle payoff profile

Strangles

Strangles are formed by combining puts and calls with identical expiry dates but different strike prices; they are similar to straddles but require greater volatility before they move in-the-money (or deeper in-the-money). A long strangle is established by buying a put and a call with the same expiry but different strikes. For instance, a bank might purchase a put struck at 90 and a call struck at 110 in a current market of 100; it will not gain on either position when the underlying trades in a range of 90 to 110 and, as such, must wait until there is significant market movement (that is, a sharp increase in volatility) which pushes the underlying below 90 or above 110 (which is obviously in contrast to a straddle). A long strangle is characterized by limited downside risk (premium paid) and unlimited profit potential.

Short strangles are the reverse of long strangles and, like short straddles, are established when market volatility is expected to decline (or at least remain stable). A short strangle is established by selling a put and a call with the same expiry but different strikes; in exchange for upfront premium income, the seller faces theoretically unlimited downside. Unlike a straddle, the seller of a strangle typically has a greater margin of volatility before one side of the transaction moves in-the-money (assuming the original strangle is struck out-of-the-money; strangles which contain one in-the-money leg at the outset, sometimes referred to as "guts," generate both greater premium income and greater risk of payoff).

The payoff profiles of long and short strangles are shown in Figures 7.9 and 7.10.

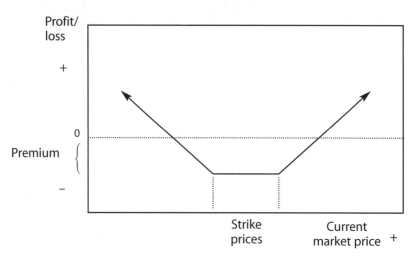

Figure 7.9 Long strangle payoff profile

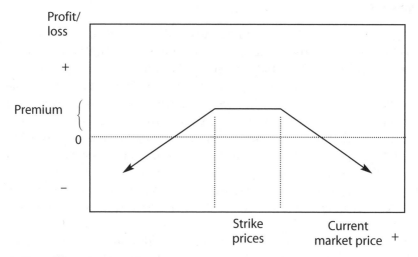

Figure 7.10 Short strangle payoff profile

Butterfly spreads

Butterfly spreads are combinations of four puts or calls with different strikes and identical expiries that provide payoff/protection similar to strad-dles. In fact, a long butterfly is similar to a short straddle with limited risk, while a short butterfly is similar to a long straddle with limited risk. A bank that believes market volatility will remain low can sell a straddle or purchase a butterfly – though the sale of the straddle exposes it to much greater downside risk if volatility trends up. Conversely, a bank believing volatility will rise can buy a straddle or sell a butterfly.

A long butterfly can be created by purchasing low and high strike options and selling middle strike options, all with the same expiry; the creation of a butterfly is typically done in the same ratio (that is, one low strike, two middle strikes, one high strike). For instance, a bank purchasing a call-based butterfly might establish a position by buying a call with a low strike (100), selling two calls with middle strikes (105) and buying a call with a high strike (110). This provides the bank with gains between 100 and 105. If the market price of the underlying falls below 100 the spread is worthless; if it rises above 110, the two long calls at 100 and 110 are offset by the two short calls at 105, for a net of zero. The only profit position in a butterfly is found in the range between the two long strikes, with the maximum profit coming at the middle strike of 105 (the long call with the 100 strike is worth five points, while the two short calls and long high strike call expire worthless); low volatility therefore benefits the long butterfly. The payoff profile of a long butterfly is highlighted in Figure 7.11 (readers should contrast this diagram with the short straddle highlighted in Figure 7.8).

A short butterfly is created by selling options with low and high strikes and purchasing options with middle strikes, all with the same expiry date. As indicated, this strategy is established when an institution believes volatility will increase; a sharp increase renders the package of options worthless but the institution retains premium income. The payoff profile of a short butterfly is shown in Figure 7.12 (once again, the reader may wish to compare the diagram with the long straddle depicted in Figure 7.7).

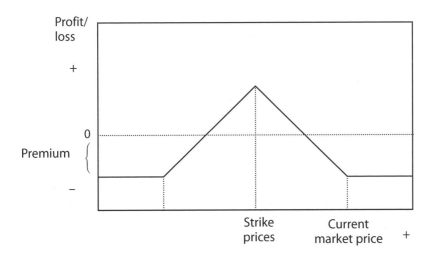

Figure 7.11 Long butterfly payoff profile

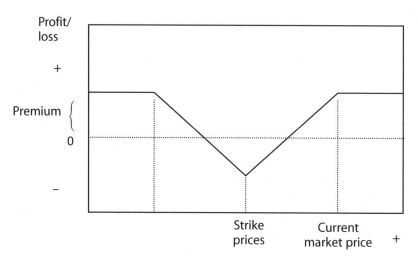

Figure 7.12 Short butterfly payoff profile

Condor spreads

Condor spreads are combinations of four puts or calls with different strikes and identical expiries, which provide payoff/protection similar to that of butterfly spreads. The primary difference between a condor and a butterfly is found in the spacing of the middle strikes: while a butterfly features two middle options with identical strikes, a condor has two middle options with different strikes. This difference results in a greater potential gain if the underlying moves in the proper direction; it also implies greater loss if the market moves in the opposite direction.

A long condor is established when volatility is expected to be low. For instance, an institution might purchase a call with a low strike (100), sell a call with a middle low strike (103), sell a second call with a middle high strike (107), and purchase a call with a high strike (110). If the market trades in a narrow range, say from 100 to 103, the long condor generates a gain of three points. If the market trades sharply higher, to 110, the condor expires worthless; for example, the long call generates a profit of 10 points (110 to 100), but the two short calls create a liability of 10 points ((110 to 107) and (110 to 103)). If the market trades sharply lower, say to 90, the entire package expires worthless; in either case, a sharp move in volatility proves detrimental. Note that the profile of a long condor is similar to a short strangle (just as a long butterfly is similar to a short straddle), except that downside risk is limited. Figure 7.13 illustrates the payoff profile of a long condor.

A short condor is created through the sale of high and low strike puts or calls and the purchase of middle strike low and high puts or calls. The payoff profile of a short condor is similar to a long strangle with limited risk, and requires an increase in volatility in order to generate profits. In the example above, high volatility pushes the market higher or lower and renders the package of options worthless, but premium income is retained; the position, therefore, favors an increase in volatility. Figure 7.14 highlights the payoff profile of a short condor.

Time spreads

A *time spread* is created when a bank buys (or sells) an option with a short time to expiry and simultaneously sells (or buys) one with a longer expiry

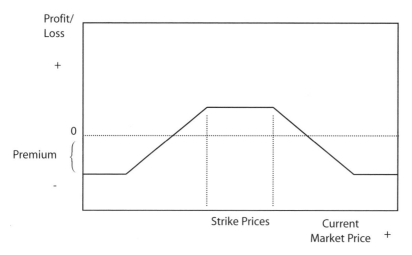

Figure 7.13 Long condor payoff profile

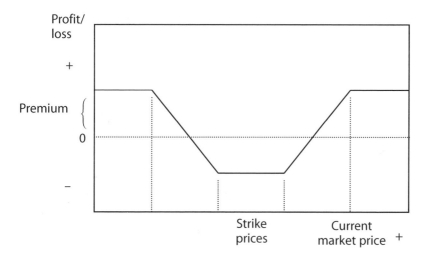

Figure 7.14 Short condor payoff profile

(this is also known as a ratio horizontal spread or calendar spread). This strategy seeks to capitalize on expected changes in volatility that might occur over time. The spreads are often established in multiples, rather than just one long option against one short option (the greater the multiple – for example one long option against two short options – the greater the potential risk and return). Spreads are established by utilizing the same type of option (that is, puts or calls, but not both) struck at the same level; a long time spread results in a net outflow of premium, while a short spread results in an inflow.

One of the key considerations in time spreads is theta, or time decay. Theta is central to time spreads as short-term options generally lose value more rapidly than longer-term ones (that is, short-term options have a higher theta). Time spreads thus attempt to take advantage of volatility as related to time. For instance, a bank expecting volatility to remain low can establish a long spread by purchasing the far call (for example, September 105s) and selling the near call (for example, March 105s). If volatility remains modest the short-term option with the higher theta (March 105s) loses more value, the spread widens, and the purchaser generates a gain. The opposite occurs with a short time spread, which requires greater volatility in order to generate a gain. If volatility is high, time value begins to decline as positions move sharply in or out-of-the-money. If an institution sells the time spread and the market moves down sharply the two options lose time value and the spread becomes worthless, but the institution retains its premium income.

Backspreads

A *backspread* is created when an institution buys more put or call contracts than it sells; all contracts have the same expiry date but, in order to remain delta-neutral, the spread requires the purchase of calls with higher strikes and the sale of calls with lower strikes (or the purchase of puts with lower strikes and the sale of puts with higher strikes). For instance, a bank might create a call backspread by buying ten March 100 calls and selling five March 95 calls. As the market moves upward (for instance, volatility increases), the value of the backspread rises; if it moves downward, the long and short calls expire worthless but the bank retains its premium income. An institution with a backspread gains as long as volatility increases; if volatility is low, the market remains stable, and the position expires with no gain. (The gains on a call backspread increase as the underlying price rises, and on a put backspread as the underlying price falls.) The opposite of a long backspread (a short backspread) is generally referred to as a ratio vertical spread (discussed immediately below). The payoff profile of a call backspread is illustrated in Figure 7.15.

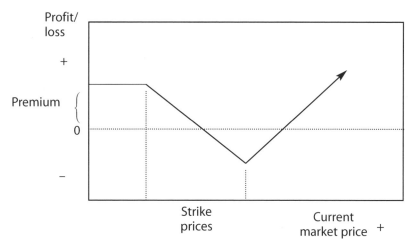

Figure 7.15 Call backspread payoff profile

Ratio vertical spreads

A *ratio vertical spread* is created when an institution sells more put or call contracts than it buys; all contracts have the same expiry date but, in order to remain delta-neutral, the spread requires the purchase of low strike calls and sale of high strike calls (or the purchase of high strike puts and sale of low strike puts). The ratio vertical strategy, which is the reverse of the backspread discussed above, attempts to capitalize on a market with low volatility. For example, a bank might buy ten March 100 calls and sell 20 March 105 calls; since it is buying closer-to-the-money options (albeit in smaller quantity), it is a net payer of premium. If there is little market volatility the bank is not forced to pay the upside on the short calls; it earns its maximum profit when the underlying price expires at the strike of the short calls. If, in contrast, there is a great deal of upside movement in the underlying price, the bank has unlimited risk. Note that the creation of a put-based ratio vertical spread exposes the bank to unlimited downside risk as the price of the underlying declines. The payoff profile of a call ratio vertical spread is illustrated in Figure 7.16.

Table 7.3 highlights the option risk sensitivities and premium effects of the compound volatility strategies described above. Note that most strategies are initially delta-neutral, reflecting the overall importance of volatility as a means of generating profits.

Other strategies

While the strategies described above are among the most common in the OTC and listed options markets, many others can be assembled to express a specific view of market direction or volatility, for example:

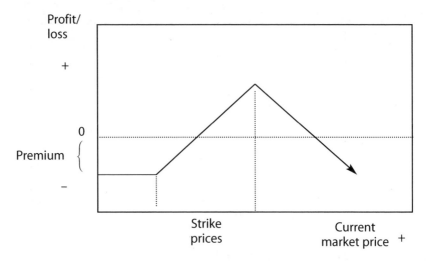

Figure 7.16 Call ratio vertical spread payoff profile

Table 7.3 Option risk sensitivities: compound position volatility strategies

Position	Delta	Gamma	Vega	Theta	Premium
Long straddle	Neutral	Positive	Positive	Negative	Debit
Short straddle	Neutral	Negative	Negative	Positive	Credit
Long strangle	Neutral	Positive	Positive	Negative	Debit
Short strangle	Neutral	Negative	Negative	Positive	Credit
Long butterfly	Neutral	Negative	Negative	Positive	Debit
Short butterfly	Neutral	Positive	Positive	Negative	Credit
Long condor	Neutral	Negative	Negative	Positive	Debit
Short condor	Neutral	Positive	Positive	Negative	Credit
Long time spread	Neutral	Negative	Positive	Positive	Debit
Short time spread	Neutral	Positive	Negative	Negative	Credit
Backspread	Neutral	Positive	Positive	Negative	Credit
Ratio vertical spread	Neutral	Negative	Negative	Positive	Debit

■ *Long strap*: long one put and long two calls with the same strike, characterized by unlimited profit potential and limited downside risk.

■ *Short strap*: short one put and short two calls with the same strike, characterized by unlimited downside risk and limited profit potential.

■ *Long strip*: long one call and long two puts with the same strike, characterized by unlimited profit potential and limited downside risk.

■ *Short strip*: short one call and short two puts with the same strike, characterized by unlimited downside risk and limited profit potential.

Synthetics

Combining long or short positions in underlying securities with long or short puts/calls on the same securities results in the creation of *synthetic options*. Consider the following:

■ If a bank is long a put and long the underlying, it is long a synthetic call. If the put strike and the underlying price are initially 100 and the price rises to 105, the put moves further out-of-the-money (and expires worthless), while the long underlying generates a gain. If the price falls to 95 the underlying generates a loss, but the loss is offset by gains on the long put as it moves in-the-money; hence the two scenarios result in a profit profile characteristic of a long call.

■ If a bank is long a call and short the underlying, it is long a synthetic put. If the call strike and the underlying price are initially 100 and the price falls to 95, the call moves out-of-the-money and expires worthless, but the short underlying generates a gain; if the price rises to 105 the short underlying generates a loss, but the loss is offset by gains on the long call.

■ If a bank is long the underlying and short a call, it is short a synthetic put. If the call strike and the underlying price are initially 100 and the price falls to 95, the underlying generates a loss while the call expires out-of-the-money; if the price rises to 105 the losses on the short call are offset by gains from the long underlying.

■ If a bank is short the underlying and short a put, it is short a synthetic call. Again, if the put strike and the underlying price are initially 100 and the price falls to 95, gains from the short underlying offset losses from the short put; if the price rises to 105, the short underlying generates a loss and the short put expires worthless.

These synthetic relationships, which are an important part of creating option strategies, are highlighted in Table 7.4.

Long or short put/call positions can also be used to create synthetic instruments. For instance, if a bank is long a call and short a put with the same strikes and expiries, it is synthetically long the underlying. If the options are struck at 100 and the underlying price increases to 105, the call gains in value, while the put expires worthless; if the price falls to 95 the call expires worthless and the put generates a loss. This is the same payoff profile as a long position in the underlying.

Conversely, if a bank is short a call and long a put with equal strikes and expiries, it is synthetically short the underlying. If the strikes are set at 100 and the underlying price falls to 95, the put gains in value and the call expires worthless; if the price rises to 105, the put expires worthless and the call generates a loss. This is the same payoff profile as a short position in the underlying. These synthetic relationships are summarized in Figures 7.17 and 7.18 and Table 7.5.

Table 7.4 Synthetic options

Synthetic =	Underlying	+	Option
Long call	Long underlying	+	Long put
Long put	Short underlying	+	Long call
Short put	Long underlying	+	Short call
Short call	Short underlying	+	Short put

Table 7.5 Synthetic underlyings

Synthetic =	Option	+	Option
Long underlying	Long call	+	Short put
Short underlying	Short call	+	Long put

CREDIT RISK QUANTIFICATION

Our discussion of the credit risk inherent in compound option strategies takes two forms: strategies which are created by an institution with a single counterparty and those that are created "synthetically," by splitting the

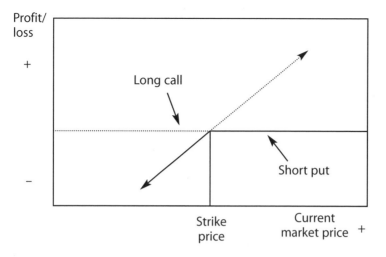

Figure 7.17 Synthetic long payoff profile

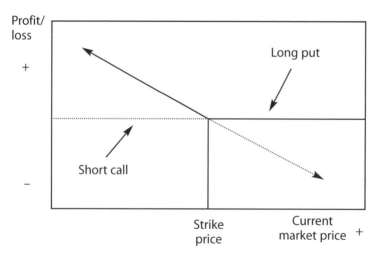

Figure 7.18 Synthetic short payoff profile

positions between two separate counterparties. Although it is far more common for specific strategies to be executed with a single counterparty, the same effects can be replicated synthetically using different counterparties; there are, in certain instances, different risk assessments for each scenario.

In many of the risk discussions below we refer to the original call/put risk equations developed in Chapter 6. As a reminder these equations, for contract-based calculations, are:

$$REE = prem + \max(0, (NC * ((RFc * CMP) + (CMP - SP)))) \qquad (6.3)$$

for calls, and

$$REE = prem + \max(0, (NC * ((RFc * CMP) + (SP - CMP)))) \qquad (6.4)$$

for puts,

where *prem* is the time value component of option premium; *RFc* is a constantly adjusted risk factor; *NC* is the number of option contracts; *CMP* is the current market price, and *SP* is the strike price.

Directional strategies: simple positions

Our discussion on the credit risk of simple directional strategies reverts to the analysis presented in Chapter 6; these are the very long/short put and call positions we have already covered.

Directional strategies: compound positions

Vertical spreads

A vertical spread is a combination of a long and short put (put spread) or a long and short call (call spread) with the same expiry dates. In a bullish call spread, the long position is struck closer to-the-money, indicating a net outflow of premium (debit); in a bullish put spread the short position is struck closer to-the-money, indicating a net inflow of premium (credit). Bearish spreads are constructed in the opposite manner.

Single counterparty transaction

If a bank executes a put or call spread with a single counterparty, and the spread is documented as a single transaction, the risk evaluation for each spread position is as shown below.

BULLISH VERTICAL CALL SPREAD
Under this strategy a bank faces credit risk on both net premium (time value; note that this is not a gross figure, since the deal is executed with one counterparty) and the potential intrinsic value of the long call position. We recall, however, that the bank's upside gain is limited once the short call position is in-the-money. The maximum market risk that can occur is simply the difference between the long call strike and the short call strike. We may show this as:

$$REE = net\ prem + (NC * (SP_{call2} - SP_{call1})) \qquad (7.1)$$

where *net prem* is the time value component of net option premium; *NC* is the number of option contracts; SP_{call1} is the strike price of the closer to-the-money long call; SP_{call2} is the strike price of the farther-from-the-money short call, and $SP_{call2} > SP_{call1}$.

Consider the following example: Bank EFG purchases a 12-month S&P call spread with the long call struck at 600 (in a 600 market) and the short call struck at 605. The notional is based on 100,000 contracts (which, for simplicity, pay off at US$1/contract), and net premium paid is US$100,000 (this consists entirely of time value as the spread is at-the-money, with no intrinsic value). The maximum REE EFG will encounter over the life of the transaction is limited to the differential between the two strikes:

REE = US$100,000 + (100,000 * (605 - 600))

    = US$100,000 + US$500,000

    = US$600,000

Since the maximum payoff of this spread is the differential between the strikes times the number of contracts (once both legs are in-the-money), Equation 6.3 is not applicable. Note that the formula above is generic, with no adjustments for moneyness. It is unlikely we would want to incorporate such adjustments (as we might with standard options) because maximum risk is bounded by the differential between the two options, not by market movements measured by RFc. The only exception to this treatment might occur when the spread between the long and short positions is excessively large (that is, the spread is wider than the amount dictated by RFc). In such cases, the risk valuation would follow the standard formula for calls indicated by Equation 6.3. If a particular spread is struck well out-of-the-money, it is conceivable that an institution might only count the time value of the premium as risk. We assume, however, that the spreads are struck at, in, or slightly out-of-the-money, so the focus is strictly on the differential.

BULLISH VERTICAL PUT SPREAD

Under this strategy the bank has no credit risk exposure. Net premium is received (not paid) since the bank is selling the more expensive, nearer to-the-money, put. Although it has a long put position that typically generates risk, it is farther out-of-the-money than the short put and therefore only has value once the short position is further in-the-money. If counterparty default occurs once the bank's long position is in-the-money the bank will not receive what it is owed; however, it will not make the larger payment to the counterparty on the short position.

BEARISH VERTICAL CALL SPREAD

Under this strategy the bank has no credit risk exposure. A bearish vertical call spread, which is the reverse of the bullish vertical call spread, is created when a bank sells a call struck closer to-the-money and buys one struck farther out-of-the-money. As such, it is a net receiver of premium and, following the logic developed for the bullish put spread above, faces no credit risk.

BEARISH VERTICAL PUT SPREAD

Under this strategy the bank has credit risk that resembles that of a bullish call spread. Since the bank purchases a put struck closer to-the-money and sells one struck farther out-of-the-money, it is a net payer of premium (which is at risk). In addition, it faces market risk exposure up to a maximum level determined by the difference between the long and short strikes. We show the equation as:

$$REE = net\ prem + (NC * (SP_{put1} - SP_{put2}))$$ (7.2)

where *net prem* is the time value component of net option premium; NC is the number of option contracts; SP_{put1} is the strike price on the closer to-the-money long put; SP_{put2} is the strike price on the farther-from-the-money short put, and $SP_{put1} > SP_{put2}$.

If the spread between the long and short puts is particularly wide (that is, in excess of that dictated by RFc), valuation can be accomplished through Equation 6.4.

MULTIPLE COUNTERPARTY TRANSACTION

It is possible for a bank to create a synthetic put or call spread by executing a long position with one counterparty and a short position (of matching size and maturity) with a second counterparty. A synthetic position generates a profit profile that is identical to the single counterparty vertical spread, assuming both counterparties continue to perform. The credit risk parameters, however, are different.

BULLISH VERTICAL CALL SPREAD

In a bullish vertical call spread, the bank is a receiver of premium (time value) equal to x and payer of premium (time value) equal to x + y. In a single counterparty transaction the net payment premium by the bank to the counterparty is simply $(x + y) - x$, or y. In a multiple counterparty transaction, the bank ignores receipt of premium x from the first counterparty and focuses on the payment it makes to the second counterparty, $x + y$. In addition, the bank does not have the benefit of a nettable transaction, so potential market risk on the synthetic spread is no longer the difference between the two strike prices times the number of contracts; rather, the full amount of the long position must be counted, since failure by the counterparty to perform once the long position is in-the-money results in loss of intrinsic value (plus remaining time value). The bank is required to perform on its short position if that leg moves in-the-money and can no longer look simply at the strike differential. The risk of this transaction is equivalent to that of a standard long call, and can be quantified by Equation 6.3.

BULLISH VERTICAL PUT SPREAD
The analysis of the bullish vertical put spread is identical to that discussed immediately above. Risk on this transaction is based on the long put established with one of the two counterparties, together with premium (time value) paid for the put; it ignores the short put and the premium received from the second counterparty. The quantification of the long put position is accomplished through Equation 6.4.

BEARISH VERTICAL CALL AND PUT SPREADS
The analysis of bearish vertical call and puts spreads follows the discussion immediately above; in both instances the credit risk is based on the long call and put legs of the synthetic spreads, which can be quantified through Equations 6.3 and 6.4.

Figures 7.19 and 7.20 illustrate bullish vertical call spreads transacted with single and multiple counterparties.

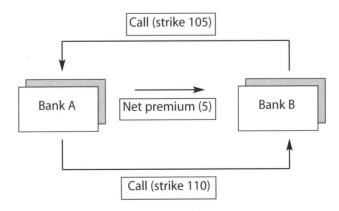

Figure 7.19 Bullish vertical call spread with a single counterparty

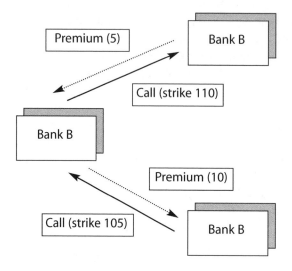

Figure 7.20 Bullish vertical call spread with multiple counterparties

Volatility strategies: compound positions

Straddles

A straddle is a combination of a put and a call struck at the same level, expiring on the same day. The credit risk of straddles focuses exclusively on long positions. A short straddle involves the sale of a put and a call with matching strikes and expiry dates and creates no credit exposure for the seller if premium is received in a normal cash-settlement time frame. Thus, our discussion focuses exclusively on long single and multiple counterparty straddles.

Single counterparty transaction

An institution that purchases a straddle exchanges premium for long positions in a put and a call struck at the same level. As with other option strategies, it faces credit exposure from premium (time value) and potential intrinsic value. In order to estimate the potential credit risk of the intrinsic value, we focus on only one of the two legs; since the put and the call in a straddle are struck at the same level it is only possible for one side to be in-the-money at any point in time. The REE equation, therefore, only values the credit risk of the put or the call, whichever is greater. Combining Equations 6.3 (for calls) and 6.4 (for puts) yields Equation 7.3:

$$REE = prem + \max(0, (NC * ((RFc * CMP) + (CMP - SP))), \qquad (7.3)$$
$$(NC * ((RFc * CMP) + (SP - CMP))))$$

Consider the following example. Bank Q purchases an at-the-money straddle on the German DAX from Dealer F, with the put and call legs struck at 1600 in a 1600 market. The premium (time value) paid for the 10,000 contracts is €1.5m, the maturity of the straddle is 12 months and the initial RFc is 22 percent. The upfront REE, per Equation 7.3, is:

$$REE = €1.5m + max(0, (10{,}000 * ((0.22 * 1600) + (1600 - 1600))),$$
$$(10{,}000 * ((0.22 * 1600) + (1600 - 1600)))))$$

$$= €1.5m + max(€3.52m, €3.52m)$$

$$= €5.02m$$

Note that in the potential intrinsic value component of REE the two figures are identical (for example, €3.52m); this is logical, since both the put and call are struck at the same level. Assume six months from now the CMP of the DAX is 1700 (that is, the call is in-the-money and the put is out-of-the-money), RFc is 15.5 percent, and premium (time value) is €750,000. The REE, via Equation 7.3, becomes:

$$REE = €750{,}000 + max(0, (10{,}000 * ((0.155 * 1700) + (1700 - 1600))),$$
$$(10{,}000 * ((0.155 * 1700) + (1600 - 1700)))))$$

$$REE = €750{,}000 + max(€3.64m, €1.63m)$$

$$= €4.39m$$

If, at maturity, the DAX finishes at 1750, only the call portion of the straddle has value; the put expires worthless. One day prior to maturity (when RFc and premium (time value) are both zero) the risk is:

$$REE = €0 + max(0, (10{,}000 * ((0.0 * 1750) + (1750 - 1600))), (10\,000$$
$$* ((0.0 * 1750) + (1600 - 1750)))))$$

$$= €0 + max(€1.5m - €1.5m)$$

$$= €1.5m$$

If Dealer F defaults at this point, Bank Q loses € 1.5 m: the intrinsic value of the call. The put is out-of-the-money and therefore carries no credit risk at the point of default. It is easy to imagine the opposite scenario, where the put finishes in-the-money and the call expires worthless; Equation 7.3 takes account of this as well.

Multiple counterparty transaction

A bank can create a synthetic straddle by entering into a long call with one counterparty and a long put (with identical strike and maturity parameters) with a second counterparty. From a credit standpoint the risk assigned to the transaction depends on whether an institution views the trades as a single strategy, knowing that only one side can be in-the-money at any point in time. If it does, it can continue to utilize Equation 7.3, substituting the sum of the premium (time value) paid (which should theoretically be close to the original premium paid for the single counter-party transaction above). Direct application of Equation 6.3 for the call leg and Equation 6.4 for the put leg might be considered unnecessarily conservative if a bank is truly viewing the positions as a straddle, albeit with different counterparties. Default by one of the two counterparties cannot yield a situation that is worse than the one estimated via Equation 7.3 for a single institution. For instance, if the call moves in-the-money but the put counterparty defaults, a bank only loses the remaining portion of its premium (time value) (which is already accounted for through Equation 7.3). If the call counterparty defaults when the option is in-the-money, the bank loses premium (time value) plus the intrinsic value of the call, which is already reflected via Equation 7.3. Returning to the original example above, we can separate the call and put and evaluate via Equations 6.3 and 6.4 (remembering to divide the premium (time value) between the two counterparties). Under this scenario we obtain the following results:

Call risk:
$$REE = €750{,}000 + \max(0, (10{,}000 * ((0.22 * 1600) + (1600 - 1600))))$$

$$= €750{,}000 + €3.52m$$

$$= €4.27m$$

Put risk:
$$REE = €750{,}000 + \max(0, (10{,}000 * (0.22 * 1600) + (1600 - 1600))))$$

$$= €750{,}000 + €3.52m$$

$$= €4.27m$$

Total risk:
$$REE = €4.27m + €4.27m$$

$$= €8.54m$$

Thus, REE of €8.54 m (versus €5.02m at inception via Equation 7.3), represents a significant overstatement of potential credit risk.

Strangles

A strangle is a combination of a put and a call with different strikes but the same expiry. A strangle, like a straddle, only generates credit risk for buyers of the spread. Since straddles and strangles are structurally similar the approaches to credit risk quantification are also quite similar.

Single counterparty transaction

In establishing a strangle with a single counterparty, a bank exchanges premium for a long position in a put and a call struck at different levels. As with a straddle, REE includes premium (time value) paid plus the potential intrinsic value of the greater of the put or the call (since only one side can be in-the-money at exercise). We can, in fact, utilize Equation 7.3 to calculate the REE of a long strangle.

Consider the following example: Bank B purchases a 12-month strangle on crude oil from Bank Z for US$100,000 in premium (time value). The CMP of crude oil is US$20/barrel, the call is struck at US$22 and the put is struck at US$17 (that is, the call is struck closer to-the-money than the put). The straddle is composed of 100,000 contracts (which pay off at US$1/contract for simplicity), and the 12-month RF for crude oil is 20 percent. The REE of this position, via Equation 7.3, is:

$$REE = US\$100,000 + max(0, (100,000 * ((0.20 * 20) + (20 - 22))),$$
$$(100,000 * ((0.20 * 20) + (17 - 20)))))$$

$$= US\$100,000 + (US\$200,000, US\$100,000)$$

$$= US\$300,000$$

Since the put is farther out-of-the-money the Equation only values the risk of the call (adjusted for current moneyness) plus premium (time value). Assume nine months into the trade crude oil falls to US$15/barrel, RFc is 10 percent and premium at risk is US$20,000; the REE becomes:

$$REE = US\$20,000 + max(0, (100,000 * ((0.10 * 15) + (15 - 22))),$$
$$(100\,000 * ((0.10 * 15) + (17 - 15)))))$$

$$= US\$20,000 + (-US\$550,000, US\$350,000)$$

$$= US\$370,000$$

Note that the call has moved out-of-the-money, leaving Bank B with no credit exposure on that portion of the strangle; this implies the put is moving further in-the-money, increasing B's credit risk exposure on the put leg. It also illustrates why risk should not be attributed to both legs of the structure.

Multiple counterparty transaction

A bank can create a synthetic strangle by establishing long put and call positions with different institutions. Since the theoretical premia paid for the two legs should approximate the premium paid for the single counterparty strangle, and since only one side of the transaction can end in-the-money (or be in-the-money during the life of the trade, when default occurs) we need only attribute risk to the put or call, whichever is closer to-the-money. Given these parameters, the risk of a multiple counterparty strangle can be calculated via Equation 7.3. The logic followed is identical to that of a multiple counterparty straddle, where separate risk calculations for both the put and the call (via Equations 6.3 and 6.4) might be considered overly conservative.

Butterfly spreads

A butterfly is a package of four puts or calls which expire at the same time; the buyer of a butterfly purchases low and high strike options and sells middle strike options, while the writer sells low and high strike options and purchases middle strike options. The long butterfly typically results in a premium debit.

Single counterparty transaction

A long call or put butterfly with a single counterparty generates REE from premium (time value) and potential intrinsic value (which is capped by the strikes of the options rather than RF). We can consider the following scenarios for a long call butterfly: if CMP is below the lowest strike, all options are worthless. If it is above the highest strike, the gains from the long low strike and high strike calls are exactly offset by losses from the two short middle strike calls. Thus, the only opportunity for profit (and, therefore, credit risk) occurs when the CMP is between the two long strikes. In fact, the greatest profit and credit risk occurs when CMP is precisely equal to the two middle strikes, as the difference between the long low strike and the short middle strike is maximized. Thus, the REE calculation for long positions is shown as:

$$REE = prem + (NC * (SP_{call\ mid} - SP_{call\ low})) \qquad (7.4)$$

for calls, and

$$REE = prem + (NC * (SP_{put\ high} - SP_{put\ mid})) \qquad\qquad (7.5)$$

for puts,

where *prem* is the time value component of option premium; *NC* is the number of option contracts; $SP_{call\ mid}$ is the strike price of the short middle strike call; $SP_{call\ low}$ is the strike price of the long low strike call; $SP_{put\ high}$ is the strike price of the long high strike put, and $SP_{put\ mid}$ is the strike price of the short middle strike put.

Consider the following example. Bank F buys a call butterfly on a bond (currently trading at 99) from Securities Dealer ABC for US$100,000 in premium (time value); the transaction size is 100,000 contracts (with a payoff of US$1/contract). Through the butterfly, F is long a call at 100, short two calls at 105, and long a call at 110. The initial, and maximum, REE on this transaction, via Equation 7.4, is

REE = US$100,000 + (100,000 * (105 – 100))

= US$100,000 + US$500,000

= US$600,000

If the CMP of the bond moves to 105 immediately after trade date and ABC defaults, F loses US$100,000 of premium (time value) plus the anticipated payout of the butterfly, US$500,000. If, during the life of the transaction, CMP rises to 110 and ABC defaults, F simply loses the remaining time value portion of its premium; although it expects to receive US$1m ((110 – 100) * 100,000) from ABC on the long calls, it will not pay the US$1m ((105 – 100) * 2 * 100,000) it owes ABC on the short calls, and therefore faces no additional loss. If CMP only reaches 109 before default, F is due US$900,000 ((109 – 100) * 100,000), but expects to pay US$800,000 ((109 – 105) * 2 * 100,000); F therefore loses the remaining portion of its premium plus US$100,000 of intrinsic value. It should be clear, then, that Equation 7.4 represents the maximum risk a bank can face on a long call butterfly. The approach is identical for long put butterflies, utilizing Equation 7.5. Note that if a bank wants to take account of the short position once it moves in-the-money (which subtracts from total REE), it can simply subtract the intrinsic value of the short positions from Equations 7.4 or 7.5, being careful to adjust for the greater number of options. As with call or put spreads, if the differential between the butterfly strikes is larger than the amount indicated by RFc, an institution can value the structure as an independent long position. Most butterflies, however, are written with narrower, as opposed to wider, strike differentials.

Assuming premium is received upfront, a short position in a butterfly generates no credit risk exposure. Although the seller is long two middle strike options, it is short the low and high strike options and, as such, faces no risk. Adapting the example above for a short put-based butterfly, we can consider the following: Bank F sells Dealer ABC a put butterfly where it is short a low strike option at 90, short a high strike option at 100 and long two middle strike options at 95. If CMP moves between 100 and 95, F owes ABC 5 points. If CMP moves below 95 (but not to 90), F's long puts move in-the-money but it is still a net payer to ABC (for example, if CMP moves to 93, F is due 4 $((95 - 93) * 2)$ from ABC, but still owes ABC 7 $(100 - 93)$). ABC therefore has risk to F, not vice versa. Finally, if CMP moves below the low strike of 90, the payoff nets to zero, implying no risk to F. Thus, short butterflies carry no risk if they are transacted with a single counterparty and premium is received upfront.

Multiple counterparty transactions

If a synthetic long butterfly is established with multiple counterparties, the individual components must be analyzed separately. Since the strategy involves the establishment of long and short positions in either puts or calls with different counterparties, and since the positions cannot legally be netted out as they can through a single counterparty transaction, each leg must be analyzed on its own. In the case of a long butterfly, a bank's risks include premium (time value) and the intrinsic value associated with the long low and high strike positions; these may be evaluated by Equations 6.3 and 6.4. The two short middle options are, of course, of no credit concern to the bank once premium is received, and can be ignored.

In the case of a short synthetic butterfly, a bank can dismiss the effect of the short low and high strike options but must account for the two long middle strike options; this implies normal REE associated with long positions, which can be quantified through Equations 6.3 and 6.4.

Condor spreads

A condor is a package of four puts or calls that expire on the same date. The buyer of a condor purchases low and high strike options and sells middle low and middle high strike options, while the writer sells low and high strike options and purchases middle low and middle high strike options. The risk analysis of condors is similar to the analysis of butterflies described above; this should not be surprising, since a condor is simply a butterfly with wider strike middle options.

Single counterparty transaction

A long call or put condor with a single counterparty generates REE from premium (time value) and potential intrinsic value (which is capped by the strikes of the options rather than RF). The maximum credit risk on the intrinsic value is based on the difference between the long low strike and the short middle strike. In the case of a call condor, the maximum profit (and credit risk) is reached at the middle strike low call, and in the case of a put condor it is reached at the middle strike high put.

Consider the following example. Bank Z buys a long call condor from Bank J on stock EFG (100,000 contracts (US$1/contract)) for US$500,000 in premium (time value). The long call strikes are set at 100 and 110, while the short middle strikes are set at 103 and 107; assuming CMP is 99, the position is out-of-the-money for Z. Once CMP moves to 103, J owes Z US$300,000 ((103 − 100) * 100,000). As CMP moves to 105, J owes Z US$500,000 ((105 − 100) * 100,000) but Z owes J US$200,000 ((105 − 103) * 100,000), resulting in a net gain of US$300, 000 for Z. As CMP moves to 108, J owes Z US$800,000 ((108 − 100) * 100,000) but Z owes J US$500,000 ((108 − 103) * US$100,000) on one option, and US$100,000 ((108 − 107) * 100,000) on a second option, for a total of US$600,000. This implies a net gain of US$200,000 for Z. Once CMP moves past 110, the positions equal zero, with no gain for either party. Thus, the maximum risk Z encounters is the difference between the long low strike call and the short middle strike low call (this presumes that the strikes are set at "even" intervals between long and short positions which is normal market convention). The REE for a long call condor is equal to:

$$REE = prem + (NC * (SP_{call\ mid\ low} - SP_{call\ low})) \qquad (7.6)$$

For puts, the equation focuses on the difference between the long high strike put and the short middle strike high put:

$$REE = prem + (NC * (SP_{put\ high} - SP_{put\ mid\ high})) \qquad (7.7)$$

where *prem* is the time value component of option premium; *NC* is the number of option contracts; $SP_{call\ mid\ low}$ is the strike price of the short middle low strike call; $SP_{call\ low}$ is the strike price of the long low strike call; $SP_{put\ high}$ is the strike price of the long high strike put; and $SP_{put\ mid\ high}$ is the strike price of the short middle high strike put.

Note that although a short condor with a single counterparty includes two long middle strike high/low puts or calls, the overall package of options generates no credit risk for the seller once premium is received.

Multiple counterparty transactions

As with the synthetic butterfly discussed above, the establishment of a synthetic condor with several institutions requires an examination of the individual long positions in a normal framework such as that presented via Equations 6.3 and 6.4; the logic for evaluating the individual option components is discussed in the section above. A short condor with multiple counterparties requires risk analysis based on the long middle strike high/low calls or puts (per Equations 6.3 or 6.4).

Time spreads

A time spread is a combination of a long option and short option with equal strikes but different expiries; a time spread can be created by buying the near month and selling the far month, or vice versa, and can be executed in multiples (rather than just one buy against one sell).

Single counterparty transaction

In creating a long time spread, a bank is long a far month option and short a near month option; since the long option has greater time value, the position results in a net payment of premium. A bank is therefore exposed to loss of premium (time value) as well as the potential intrinsic value of the long option; these risk elements can be quantified by Equations 6.3 or 6.4. This analysis assumes a bank preserves the long position once the short position expires; if it unwinds the trade when the short option expires, there is arguably no credit risk except premium (time value). For instance, if Bank X pays Bank JKL US$200,000 to enter into a ¥/US$ time spread (on 100,000 contracts) where it sells an at-the-money yen call for two month delivery and buys an at-the-money yen call for four month delivery, it faces a potential loss if JKL defaults after the short option expires but before the long option expires (again, assuming it preserves the long position once the short option expires); X is therefore exposed to the credit risk attributable to a long call position. If we assume the short and long calls are struck at ¥100/US$ (in a market trading at ¥100/US$), the risk factor for a four month ¥ trade is 14.5 percent and the net premium (time value) paid is US$200,000, the risk via Equation 6.3 is:

$$REE = US\$200,000 + \max(0, (100,000 * ((0.145 * 100) + (100 - 100))))$$

$$= US\$200,000 + US\$1.45m$$

$$= US\$1.65m$$

The two-month call X sells to JKL has no bearing on what X expects to receive (if anything) from JKL at, or near, maturity. Thus, Equations 6.3 and 6.4 are appropriate for long call and put time spreads, respectively. Note that the premium (time value) paid above is net, not gross.

Short time spreads, which consist of a long position in the near month and a short position in the far month, result in a premium inflow to the seller. Although the long near month call or put in the spread can be quantified by Equations 6.3 or 6.4, the quantification of premium (time value) exposure is dependent on the conservatism of an institution: the liberal approach subtracts from REE the premium received from the short position, while the conservative approach ignores receipt of premium and simply values the market risk portion of the long option without adjustment. These are shown as:

$$REE = (NC * ((RFc * CMP) + (CMP - SP))) - prem \text{ or } 0 \qquad (7.8)$$

for calls, and

$$REE = (NC * ((RFc * CMP) + (SP - CMP))) - prem \text{ or } 0 \qquad (7.9)$$

for puts.

Some might view this as overly conservative, and suggest that a short time spread has no risk once premium is received. Under this approach an institution might feel if the spread is documented as a single nettable trade, any default by the counterparty on the bank's near month long position once it moves in-the-money is offset by the bank's far month short position, which by definition is also in-the-money (since the spreads are constructed with the same strikes). Thus, the two positions net to zero, where a gain on the long position lost through counterparty default is offset by the payment due the defaulting counterparty on the short position. This presumes the transaction is appropriately documented as a single transaction giving right of offset against future amounts which might be due the defaulting counterparty on an in-the-money short leg (where a bankruptcy receiver is unable to "cherry pick" the short position). It is for the reader to determine which approach is most logical for a particular situation.

Multiple counterparty transactions

As with most other multiple counterparty transactions we have discussed in this chapter, the long or short time spread focuses on the long position established at either the near or far month, per risk Equations 6.3 and 6.4. Since these are discrete transactions with individual counterparties, netting cannot be used to offset (or eliminate) credit risk exposure; full valuation of long positions (whether for the near or far months) should be employed.

Backspreads

A backspread is a strategy created by combining long and short options with different strikes but identical expiries; the long position is comprised of a larger number of options with lower moneyness, while the short position consists of a smaller number of options with greater moneyness (this, again, preserves delta neutrality). The risk discussion below relates only to the long backspread; a short backspread is, in fact, a ratio vertical spread and is covered in the section immediately following.

Single counterparty transaction

When an institution establishes a backspread with a single counterparty, the premium it receives from selling the nearer-to-the-money options is generally greater than the premium paid for the purchase of a larger quantity of farther out-of-the-money options; as such, premium (time value) can be set to zero or subtracted from REE. Potential REE therefore relates strictly to possible risk on the intrinsic value of the backspread. The quantification of this component is best illustrated by first reviewing an example. Consider a Treasury bond call backspread between Bank TUV and Dealer DEF where TUV purchases 100,000 call contracts (US$1/contract) struck at 105 and sells 50,000 call contracts struck at 100. If CMP moves from 99 to 101, the short position moves in-the-money. When CMP reaches 105, TUV owes DEF US$250,000 ((105 − 100) * 50,000). However, once CMP reaches 110 the profit profile begins to shift. Though TUV owes DEF US$500,000 ((110 − 100) * 50,000), it expects an equal payment from DEF ((110 − 105) * 100,000), for a net of zero. When CMP moves to 115, the rate of gain increases: TUV's payout equals US$750,000, but its receipt is US$1m, for a net gain of US$250,000. Thus, TUV is exposed to DEF once the long positions move heavily in-the-money. Until they pass the point of outpacing the value of the short positions, however, there is no credit risk. Thus, credit risk evaluation focuses on the maximum movement of the long position (times the number of contracts, which is central to backspreading), less the amount payable on the short positions, less premium received (or zero, in the more conservative case). We document the risk via Equation 7.10 for calls:

$$REE = (NC_{long} * ((RFc * CMP) + (CMP - SP_{long}))) - \\ (NC_{short} * ((RFc * CMP) + (CMP - SP_{short}))) - prem \text{ or } 0 \quad (7.10)$$

and Equation 7.11 for puts:

$$REE = (NC_{long} * ((RFc * CMP) + (SP_{long} - CMP))) - \\ (NC_{short} * ((RFc * CMP) + (SP_{short} - CMP))) - prem \text{ or } 0 \quad (7.11)$$

where *prem* is the time value component of option premium; NC_{long} is the number of option contracts associated with the long position; SP_{long} is the strike price associated with the long position; *NC* short is the number of option contracts associated with the short position; and SP_{short} is the strike price associated with the short position.

Returning to the example above, if we assume on trade date that RFc is 20 percent, the CMP of the Treasury bond is 99, and TUV receives US$100,000 in premium (time value) for selling the nearer to-the-money calls, the resulting REE is:

$$REE = (100,000 * ((0.20 * 99) + (99 - 105))) - (50,000 *((0.20 * 99) + (99 - 100))) - US\$100,000$$

$$= (US\$1.38m) - (US\$940,000) - US\$100,000$$

$$= US\$340,000$$

If, during the life of the trade, CMP moves to 115, RFc declines to 10 percent and premium (time value) decays to US$50,000, the new REE is

$$REE = (100,000 * ((0.10 * 115) + (115 - 105))) - (50,000 *((0.10 * 115) + (115 - 100))) - US\$50,000$$

$$= (US\$2.15m) - (US\$1.325m) - US\$50,000$$

$$= US\$775,000$$

REE begins to rise because the intrinsic value of the long calls, multiplied by the greater quantity of contracts, outweighs the value of the lower strike, lower volume short calls. If DEF defaults at this point TUV loses US$250,000 (US$1m ((115 - 105) * 100,000) less US$750,000 ((115 - 100) * 50,000)), less the remaining time value of premium. If DEF does not default, the REE equation values the actual intrinsic value of the back-spread, and includes a potential factor which allows for the CMP to move even further during the remaining life of the trade (before default occurs). For instance, if CMP rises to 120 just prior to maturity (when RFc is zero and premium has decayed to zero), the REE is

$$REE = (100,000 * ((0.0 * 120) + (120 - 105))) - (50,000 * ((0.0 * 120) + (120 \ 2 \ 100))) - US\$0$$

$$= (US\$1.5m) - (US\$1m) - US\$0$$

$$= US\$500,000$$

If default occurs at this point, TUV loses, with certainty, US$500,000 on the net difference between the long and short positions.

Multiple counterparty transactions

In order to evaluate the risk of multiple counterparty transactions, we simply need to isolate the long and short positions. The bank has no risk exposure on the short positions. On the long positions, however, it can value the risk in the same fashion as any long put or call position, via Equations 6.4 or 6.3, respectively. Note that although the single counterparty backspread results in a net inflow of premium (as a result of selling more expensive options, albeit in lower quantity), the long position established with an institution as a way to create a synthetic backspread results in an outflow of premium (which cannot be legally offset by inflow from the sale of the more expensive options).

Ratio vertical spreads

A ratio vertical spread, like the backspread, involves long and short options with different strikes but identical expiries. Unlike a backspread, however, a ratio vertical spread consists of a long position in a smaller number of options with greater moneyness, and a short position in a larger number of options with lower moneyness (this, too, preserves delta neutrality).

Single counterparty transaction

When an institution establishes a ratio vertical spread it pays premium for the smaller number of more valuable options. REE is therefore based on premium (time value) and potential intrinsic value. As with backspreads, potential REE on the intrinsic value component is best illustrated by tracking the effect of the underlying on the long and short positions defining the spread.

Consider a transaction where Bank KLM purchases from Dealer ABC 100,000 call contracts (US$1/contract) on stock XYZ struck at 100, and sells ABC 200,000 call contracts struck at 105. Though KLM sells 200,000 105 calls, the 100,000 100 calls it purchases are struck closer-to-the-money and are therefore more expensive; this results in a net outflow of premium (a figure which is included in the REE computation). If CMP rises to 105, KLM expects a payout of US$500,000 ((105 − 100) * 100,000). As CMP rises above 105, however, the ratio of sold versus purchased calls begins to shift the profit profile from a gain to a loss for KLM. For example, if CMP reaches 115, KLM expects a payoff of US$1.5m ((115 − 100) * 100,000); however, because KLM has a short position as well, it owes ABC US$2m ((115 – 105) * 200,000). There is thus a net outflow of US$500,000 to ABC (and no longer any credit risk except time value of premium). This logic is, of course, the reverse of what we have discussed immediately above. The maximum risk for KLM, therefore, is the point at which market price and volume are maximized; this occurs when the short position is precisely at-the-money. Thereafter, risk declines until it is negative, implying ABC has credit risk exposure to KLM, not vice versa. Once this occurs, the only item at risk to the bank is the time value component of premium (which arguably should not be counted, as if there is counterparty default the amount the bank owes its counterparty on a net basis is likely to exceed the premium at stake). Note that the ratio of bought versus sold contracts is important in determining how much price movement is required before exposure becomes negative. We discuss this at greater length in the example below. The REE equations for ratio verticals are shown as:

$$REE = prem + (NC_{long} * (SP_{short\ call} - SP_{long\ call})) \qquad (7.12)$$

for calls, and

$$REE = prem + (NC_{long} * (SP_{long\ put} - SP_{short\ put})) \qquad (7.13)$$

for puts,

where $prem$ is the time value component of option premium; NC_{long} is the number of long option contracts; $SP_{short\ call}$ is the strike price of the short call; $SP_{long\ call}$ is the strike price of the long call; $SP_{long\ put}$ is the strike price of the long put, and $SP_{short\ put}$ is the strike price of the short put.

In the example above, if we assume premium paid is US$500,000, maximum REE is:

REE =   US$500,000 + (100,000 * (105 – 100))

    =   US$500,000 + US$500,000

    =   US$1m

If ABC defaults when CMP is equal to the strike of the short call, KLM loses up to US$1m (depending on the remaining time value of premium). While the above represents the maximum level of risk attributable to the transaction, an institution can also value the risk on an ongoing basis as the difference between the long and short positions. To do so, it is can utilize Equation 7.14 for calls:

$$REE = prem + \max(0, ((NC_{long} * (CMP - SP_{long})) - (NC_{short} * (CMP - SP_{short}))))$$

(7.14)

and can use Equation 7.15 for puts:

$$REE = prem + \max(0, ((NC_{long} * (SP_{long} - CMP)) - (NC_{short} * (SP_{short} - CMP))))$$

(7.15)

For instance, if the CMP of stock XYZ in the example above moves to 107 (and premium decays to US$250,000), REE becomes:

$$REE = US\$250,000 + \max(0, ((100,000 * (107 - 100)) - (200,000 * (107 - 105))))$$

$$= US\$250,000 + (US\$700,000 - US\$400,000)$$

$$= US\$250,000 + US\$300,000$$

$$= US\$550,000$$

This is less than the US$1m calculated above, which is a maximum REE figure. We do not employ RFc in this calculation, since the maximum risk is bounded on the upside by the short position established in the ratio vertical, rather than market movements. Note further that we take the greater of zero or the market risk portion of the equation because, as CMP moves further in-the-money, the buy-sell ratio causes the risk to become negative (that is, the bank is not expecting performance from its counterparty; it is, in fact, expecting to perform for its counterparty).

Multiple counterparty transactions

As in the case of backspreads, a synthetic ratio vertical created by dealing with more than one institution requires examination of the long and short positions. On the higher volume short positions the bank is a receiver of premium and faces no credit risk exposure, while on the lower volume, more expensive, long positions the bank is a payer of premium and faces normal credit risk exposure attributable to a long call or put position; such can be evaluated via Equations 6.3 or 6.4.

Synthetics

From a credit risk perspective, synthetics created by combining long or short options and long or short underlyings do not require any special analysis. For instance, if an institution is long the underlying and long a put, it is actually long a synthetic call. Since the credit risk evaluation does not focus on the long underlying (as there is no credit risk inherent in the position so long as the issuer of the underlying does not default), the focus is solely on evaluating the long put (via Equation 6.4, for example). Although the relationship of the underlying and the put translates into a synthetic instrument that acts like a long call, this is irrelevant to the credit officer. From a risk management standpoint it may well be a consideration, as it might affect the direction and posture of hedging. However, from a credit perspective we need only focus on the original long option, not the resulting synthetic option.

To summarize the discussion we have presented above, it should be clear that the most vital step in the credit risk analysis of compound option strategies is to determine the potential payoffs that might be generated during the course of a given transaction. This assists in determining whether maximum risk should be calculated via a risk factor, whether it should be capped as a result of the sale of another option, whether premium (time value) is ever at risk, and so on. In addition, when creating a synthetic strategy with multiple counterparties, it is important to decompose the package of options to the individual transaction level so that long and short positions can be viewed separately and risk attributed accordingly.

CHAPTER 8

The Credit Risk of Complex Options

In Chapter 6 we reviewed methods of quantifying the risk of standard put and call options and in Chapter 7 we discussed the nature and risk of various compound option strategies. We continue the theme in this chapter by exploring the nature, use, and risk of complex options. While many of these options were regarded as rather "exotic" only a few years ago, some have become quite common in the financial markets of the twenty-first century. Despite their growing popularity, however, the instruments are not always simple to understand, price, or hedge. Some are particularly challenging to deal with; hence the need for a thorough understanding of their characteristics and risks.

We define complex options as derivatives with structural enhancements which result in payoff or protection profiles that are different than those of vanilla puts and calls. The structural differences can relate to the nature and determination of the payoff path, the starting or ending point of the contract, the timing of the premium payment, the method of establishing the strike price, payout, and so on. Although there are various ways of categorizing complex options, we divide our discussion into the broad classes of path dependent and path independent options.[1]

- *Path dependent options* are derivatives whose value at exercise depends on the price of the underlying market reference at earlier time periods.

- *Path independent options* are derivatives whose value at exercise depends only on the price of the underlying market reference at exercise.

Our discussion focuses on the product description and credit risk evaluation of the following path dependent and independent derivatives:

Path dependent options

- barrier options

- Asian (average price/average strike) options

- floating strike lookback options

- options on the maximum/minimum

- high–low options

- partial lookback/reset options

- ladder options

- cliquet options

- shout options

- installment options.

Path independent options

- binary options[2]

- rainbow/multi-index options
    - options on the best-worst of n-assets and cash
    - options on the best-worst of n-assets
    - multiple strike options
    - spread options
    - basket options

- compound options

- chooser options

- contingent premium options

- deferred payment American options

- quanto options

- forward start options

- exploding options

- power options.

Unlike many of the complex swaps we consider in Chapter 10, most dependent/independent options can be written on a broad range of asset classes (for example, debt, equity, currency, commodity, credit, and even "new" asset references such as temperature, inflation, macroeconomic variables, and so on); our discussion is thus general. Certain variations or extensions exist within some of these broad classes and, where relevant, we shall consider them as well. Table 8.1 summarizes common complex options, alternate names, and variations.

Table 8.1 Complex option variations

Option	Also known as	Variations
Barrier option	Regular knock-in option (or Up and in option) (Down and in option) Regular knock-out option (Up and out option) (Down and out option)	Reverse knock-in option (or Kick-in option) (Reverse up and in option) (Reverse down and in option) Reverse knock-out option (Kick-out option) (Reverse up and out option) (Reverse down and out option) Partial barrier option (Discrete barrier option) Point barrier option Outsider barrier option
Asian/average price option	–	Geometric average price option Arithmetic average price option
Asian/average strike option	–	Geometric average strike option Arithmetic average strike option

Table 8.1 Continued

Lookback option	Floating strike lookback option	Partial lookback option (Reset option) (Extendible option)
Options on the maximum/ minimum	Call on the maximum Put on the minimum (Fixed strike lookback option)	High–low option
Ladder option	Fixed strike ladder option (Modified ladder option)	Floating strike ladder option
Cliquet option	Ratchet option	–
Shout option	Fixed strike shout option (Modified shout option)	Floating strike shout option
Installment option	–	–
Binary option	Digital option	All-or-nothing option (European binary option) (Cash-or nothing option) (Asset-or-nothing option) Binary–barrier option (One-touch option) (Cash-or-nothing at hit option) (Cash-or-nothing at expiry option) (Asset-or-nothing at hit option) (Asset-or-nothing at expiry option)
Rainbow option	Multi-index option	Option on best/worst of n-assets and cash Option on best/worst of n-assets Multiple strike option (Dual strike option) Spread option (Outperformance option, Underperformance option, Difference option) Yield curve option Credit spread option Basket option

Table 8.1 Continued

Compound option	Nested option	Call on a call Call on a put Put on a call Put on a put
Chooser option	Choice option Preference option	Regular chooser option Complex chooser option
Contingent premium option	Pay later option Cash on delivery option When-in-the-money option	–
Deferred payment American option	–	–
Quanto option	Guaranteed exchange rate option Quantity adjusted option	–
Forward start option	–	Deferred strike option
Exploding option	Binary–barrier spread option	–
Power option	Leveraged option Turbo option	Squared power option Cubed power option

PRODUCT DESCRIPTION

Path dependent options

Barrier options

A *barrier option* is a derivative that either creates, or extinguishes, an underlying European option when a market price reaches a predetermined barrier level. Barrier options are not new products; they have been in existence since the late 1960s but gained considerable popularity throughout the 1990s and into the millennium.[3] The four main barrier categories include:

- *Up and out option*: an option is cancelled (out) if the underlying price rises above a certain barrier (up).

- *Down and out option*: an option is cancelled (out) if the underlying price falls below a certain barrier (down).

- *Up and in option*: an option is created (in) if the underlying price rises above a certain barrier (up).

- *Down and in option*: an option is created (in) if the underlying price falls below a certain barrier (down).

The first two instruments are known as knock-out options and the latter two as knock-in options. Note that puts and calls are available within each of the four categories, creating eight different barrier combinations. In addition to the definitions above, certain institutions use a more precise level of description to reflect the level of intrinsic value gained or lost as barriers are triggered. When barriers are set out-of-the-money (for example, barrier < strike for a call and barrier > strike for a put), options are considered "regular" knock-ins or knock-outs. When barriers are set in-the-money (for example, barrier > strike for a call and barrier < strike for a put), options are considered *reverse knock-ins* or *reverse knock-outs* (or kick-ins or kick-outs). Table 8.2 summarizes the available combinations of regular and reverse barriers and the effect of a barrier being triggered.

Traditional barrier options utilize European options as the underlying payoff instrument.[4] Thus, if an option is created (that is, the option knocks-in once the barrier is triggered) the purchaser assumes a position in a European put or call. If an option is not extinguished (that is, the option is not knocked-out as the barrier is not triggered) the purchaser retains a position in a European put or call. We can summarize the payoffs for barriers as follows:

Table 8.2 Barrier options

Option	Class	Effect
Down and out call	Regular knock-out	Out-of-the-money option extinguished
Up and out put	Regular knock-out	Out-of-the-money option extinguished
Down and in call	Regular knock-in	Out-of-the-money option created
Up and in put	Regular knock-in	Out-of-the-money option created
Up and out call	Reverse knock-out	In-the-money option extinguished
Down and out put	Reverse knock-out	In-the-money option extinguished
Up and in call	Reverse knock-in	In-the-money option created
Down and in put	Reverse knock-in	In-the-money option created

- *Down and in call*: max (0, (CMP – SP)), when CMP ≤ barrier, or else rebate[5] (as in the last chapter, SP is the strike price and CMP is the current market price of the underlying at expiry (for example, the terminal value)).

- *Down and in put*: max (0, (SP – CMP)) when CMP ≤ barrier, or else rebate.

- *Down and out call*: max (0, (CMP – SP)) when CMP ≥ barrier, or else rebate.

- *Down and out put*: max (0, (SP – CMP)) when CMP ≥ barrier, or else rebate.

- *Up and in call*: max (0, (CMP – SP)) when CMP ≥ barrier, or else rebate.

- *Up and in put*: max (0, (SP – CMP)) when CMP ≥ barrier, or else rebate.

- *Up and out call*: max (0, (CMP – SP)) when CMP ≤ barrier, or else rebate.

- *Up and out put*: max (0, (SP – CMP)) when CMP ≤ barrier, or else rebate.

Since the purchaser of a barrier stands to lose some of its traditional economic benefits (for example, the option may be extinguished or may never be brought into existence) the premium paid is less than it is for a European option with the same strike and maturity parameters; in fact, the lower cost is one of the main motivations for entering into barrier transactions and one of the reasons they have proven so popular. The seller, in contrast, receives less premium income but faces a smaller probability of having to provide the buyer with a payoff (for example, the underlying option may never be brought into existence or it may be extinguished).[6]

Consider the following examples of barrier options:

- A bank purchases a six-month, at-the-money Nikkei call struck at 18,000 with a down and out barrier at 17,000; if the Nikkei falls below 17,000 the call ceases to exist. Assume during the next six months the Nikkei falls to 16,500 and then rebounds to 19,000; the call is knocked out and the bank receives no payout (if it had purchased a vanilla European index call it would have received a payout of 1000 times the relevant number of contracts).

- A bank purchases a 12-month up and in put on the S&P 500 with a barrier of 575 and a strike price of 565, in a market trading at 560.

Assume during the next 12 months the S&P 500 trades up to 580 and then falls to 550. The bank's knock-in put generates a gain of 15 (times the relevant number of contracts), since the upper barrier of 575 is breached and a European put (with a strike of 565) is created.

■ A bank purchases a 12-month up and in call on the FTSE 100 with a barrier of 3500 and a strike price of 3300 (for example, a reverse knock-in call option). During the next 12 months the FTSE rises to 3700 and ends at 3600. The bank receives a payment of 300 (times the relevant number of contracts) since the reverse knock-in call is created once the 3500 level is hit.

Figure 8.1 illustrates the payoff of an up and out call option and Figure 8.2 illustrates the flows of a down and in put option.

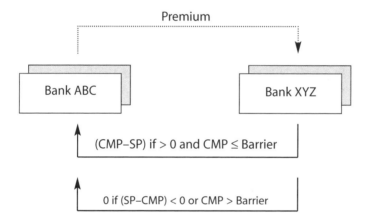

Figure 8.1 Up and out call option

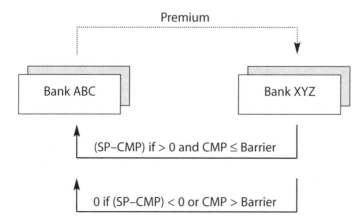

Figure 8.2 Down and in put option

Two additional barrier structures warrant brief mention: the partial barrier and the outsider barrier. A *partial barrier option* (also known as a discrete barrier option) is identical to the structure described above except that the barrier exists only during the prespecified time (rather than the entire life of the transaction); if the barrier is not triggered during the stated period, it disappears entirely and the purchaser is left with either a standard European option (if the derivative did not knock-out) or no position (if the derivative did not knock-in). Another type of partial barrier is one that only exists during certain fixing periods (for example, the last day of each month for the entire maturity of the transaction). In the extreme, a partial barrier becomes a point barrier option, or a barrier option that can only be triggered on a single day. An *outside barrier option* is a multivariate derivative with payoff and trigger references that are drawn from different markets. While a standard barrier knocks-in or out and generates a payoff based on the movement of a single reference (if created or not extinguished), an outside barrier is created or extinguished by a third reference. For instance, an outsider barrier on the Nikkei may be created (knocked-in) by movement of ¥/US$ rather than the Nikkei; if the currency rate moves to a certain level and triggers the outside barrier, a standard European Nikkei index option is created. While these are interesting adaptations of the barrier structure, we shall not consider them further.

Asian/average price options

The family of Asian, or average, derivatives includes average price and average strike options. An *average price option* is a derivative that provides the buyer with a payoff based on the differential between a predetermined strike price and the average price of an underlying market reference during a prespecified averaging period (often referred to as the "Asian tail"). The payoff of an average price call is max (0, (CMP(avg) – SP)) and the payoff of an average price put is max (0, (SP – CMP(avg))), where CMP(avg) is the average price of the underlying market reference derived over the averaging period. In contrast to European options, average price options permit an investor to obtain a payoff that is derived over an entire period rather than a single point in time (for example, maturity); this helps reduce the uncertainty of the final payoff (it may also mean, of course, a lower payoff than a European option; however, average price options are typically used to reduce the uncertainty surrounding payoff). The average price path for the option can be calculated on either a geometric or arithmetic basis. The averaging period for the derivative is flexible and can be negotiated between buyer and seller; such periods are often set equal to the final days or weeks before maturity of the option (for example, in a typical six-month or 12-month option the averaging period might consist of the last two to four weeks of the transaction), but longer periods and earlier starting points are also possible. Note that as the period becomes shorter and closer to the expiry of the option, the average price option approaches the price and payoff of a standard European option. Average price options are, in general, cheaper than vanilla European options.

Consider the following example: broker ABC purchases an average price put from Dealer KLM on 50,000 shares of stock XYZ; the six-month put has an averaging period covering the final 30 days of the transaction and is struck at US$30/share in a market trading at US$33 (i.e. 10 percent out-of-the-money). At the conclusion of the six-month period XYZ shares are trading at US$30/share (having rallied sharply in the three days prior to expiry); the geometric average during the preceding 30 days is US$26/share. The average price put therefore generates a payoff to ABC of US$200,000 ((30– 26) * 50,000). Note that if ABC purchases a European put, the contract expires worthless (it is possible, of course, to imagine a sharp decline in the price of XYZ just prior to expiry, which would cause the European put to end with greater value than the average price put). Figure 8.3 illustrates the payoff of an average price put option.

Asian/average strike options

An *average strike option*, the second derivative in the Asian option family, provides a buyer with a payoff equal to the difference between the price of the underlying at maturity and an average strike price computed over a predetermined averaging period; as above, the average can be geometric or arithmetic. The payoff of an average strike call is max (0, (CMP – SP(avg))) and the payoff of an average strike put is max (0, (SP(avg) – CMP)), where SP(avg) is the average strike price derived over a specified averaging period.

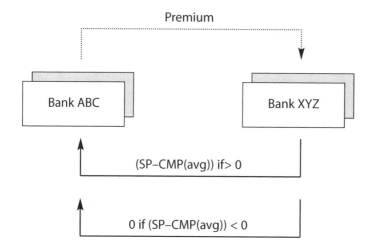

Figure 8.3 Average price put option

Let us consider the average strike option using details from the example above. Under the terms of the average strike trade, ABC purchases a six-month put option on 50,000 shares of XYZ and sets the strike equal to the average price during the last 30 days of the transaction. If the average equals US$26/share (which becomes the strike of the option) and the terminal price is US$30/share (for example, a sharp rally just prior to maturity), the option expires worthless. If, however, the terminal price falls below the average strike of US$26 to, say, US$22/share, the payoff to ABC is US$200,000 ((US$26 – US$22) * 50,000). Figure 8.4 illustrates the payoff of an average strike put option.

Floating strike lookback options

A *lookback option* is a derivative which generates a payoff by "looking back" over the price path of the underlying market reference to determine the lowest buying price (for calls) or the highest selling price (for puts); this type of derivative is often referred to as a floating strike lookback, since the strike is effectively set at the conclusion of the transaction in order to generate the maximum gain (note that floating strike lookback options are distinct from fixed strike lookback options (also known as calls on the maximum and puts on the minimum) which we discuss in the section immediately following).[7]

Through the floating strike mechanism, a lookback call permits an institution to buy the underlying market reference at the lowest price recorded during the life of the transaction, while a lookback put permits it to sell the underlying market reference at the highest price recorded. The payoff of a lookback call is max (0, (CMP – CMP(min))) and the payoff of a lookback

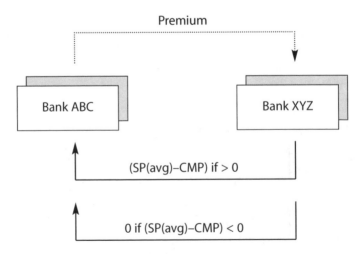

Figure 8.4 Average strike put option

put is max (0, (CMP(max) – CMP)), where CMP is the terminal price of the market variable, CMP(max) is the highest observed price of the market variable, and CMP(min) is the lowest observed price of the market variable. Given the payoff flexibility characteristic of lookbacks, these derivatives are more expensive than vanilla European options.

Consider the following example. Bank UVW purchases a six-month lookback call on the Australian All Ordinaries Share Price Index ("All Ords") that is trading at 2200 at the start of the transaction. During the next six months the All Ords falls to a low of 2000, reaches a high of 2800, and ends at 2500. The payoff to UVW on the lookback call is 500 (2500 – 2000), which is equal to the terminal value of the All Ords (2500) less the minimum level of the index (2000, which becomes the strike). If UVW purchases a lookback put instead of a call its payoff equals 300 (2800 – 2500), which is the difference between the maximum level of the All Ords (2800, which becomes the strike) and the terminal value of index (2500). Figure 8.5 illustrates the flows of a floating strike lookback call option.

Options on the maximum/minimum

Options on the maximum/minimum (categorized as a call on the maximum and a put on the minimum) are closely related to lookback options. Indeed, as indicated above, such derivatives are often referred to as fixed strike lookbacks or modified lookbacks, since they generate a payoff by "looking back" over the entire price path of the underlying market reference to generate maximum and minimum points. Unlike floating strike lookbacks, however, options on the maximum/minimum carry fixed strike prices set at the inception of the trade, and generate a maximum payout by taking the maximum or minimum level achieved by the underlying reference during the life of the

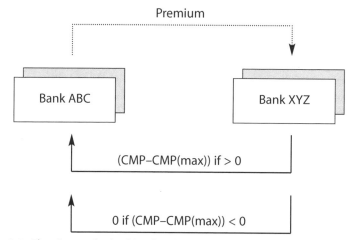

Figure 8.5 Floating strike lookback call option

transaction. *Calls on the maximum* generate a payoff based on the maximum price achieved by the underlying market reference during the life of the trade; this is denoted by max (0, (CMP(max) – SP)). *Puts on the minimum* generate a payoff based on the minimum price achieved; this is denoted by max (0, (SP – CMP(min))).

Consider the following example. Dealer JKL believes the Nikkei 225 index will decline over the coming six months and wants to ensure it receives the maximum payoff on the downside. Accordingly, it purchases from Bank ABC an at-the-money Nikkei 225 put on the minimum, with a fixed strike price of 19,000 and a maturity of six months; the payoff of the option equals the difference between the strike price and the minimum value of the Nikkei 225 over the next six months, times ¥1000 (an arbitrary multiplier set between JKL and ABC). During the next six months the Nikkei trades at a high of 21,000 and a low of 16,500, and ends at 17,500. Although the Nikkei ends at 17,500, the payoff to JKL from its put on the minimum equals ¥2.5m, based on the minimum 16,500 level attained by the Nikkei during the life of the transaction. Figure 8.6 illustrates the payoff of a put option on the minimum.

High–low options

As we might surmise from its name, a *high–low option* (a variation of the lookback structure described above) provides a payoff equal to the difference between the highest and lowest points achieved by the underlying market reference during the life of the transaction. While an option on the maximum–minimum (for example, a fixed strike lookback) generates a payoff equal to the difference between the strike price and the maximum (for calls) or the strike price and the minimum (for puts), a high–low option

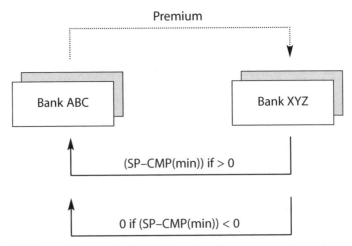

Figure 8.6 Put option on the minimum

generates a payoff equal to the sum of the highest point against a "strike" and the lowest point against the same "strike." In this respect the option provides a "two-way" payoff, and can be viewed as a package of a call on the maximum and a put on the minimum, struck at the same level (note that while we draw this parallel here, we cannot do the same in the REE framework as we necessarily assume maximum market movement for each individual option over the entire life of the transaction; we discuss this in more detail later in the chapter). The payoff of a high–low option is given simply as (CMP(max) – CMP(min)).

Consider the following example. Bank EFG purchases from Dealer QRS a 12-month high–low option on the S&P 500 (which is trading at 580 on trade date); the payoff is based on the differential between the high and low of the S&P during the next 12 months, times a multiplier factor of 5000 (an arbitrary factor set between EFG and QRS). During the next 12 months the S&P rises to a high of 600 and declines to a low of 520; the payoff to EFG is therefore US$4m ((600 – 520) * 5000). Note that if EFG purchases an at-the-money call on the maximum, the payoff equals the difference between the strike price and the highest price achieved, or US$1m ((600 – 580) * 5000); if it purchases an at-the-money put on the minimum, the payoff equals the difference between the strike price and the lowest price achieved, or US$3m ((580 – 520) * 5000). We can see, then, that the payoff of the high–low option is precisely equal to the sum of the payoffs of a call on the maximum and a put on the minimum, struck at identical levels. Figure 8.7 illustrates the payoff of a high–low option.

Partial lookback/reset options

A *partial lookback option* is another variation of the lookback option.[8] While the lookback option we have discussed above permits the purchaser to "look back" during the life of the transaction and identify the point which provides the greatest gain (by resetting the strike to the level which maximizes the

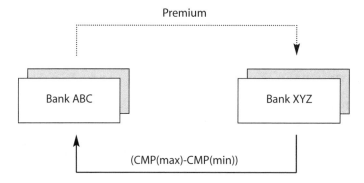

Figure 8.7 High–low option

gain), the partial lookback permits the purchaser to reset the strike at a prespecified time. Under a typical structure the purchaser resets the strike at the current market level if the option is out-of-the-money; in effect, the purchaser is permitted to convert an out-of-the-money contract into one that is precisely at-the-money (with a maturity equal to the remaining time of the original transaction). If the option is in-the-money during the reset period no change in the strike price is possible (or even desirable, since the option already has intrinsic value). At expiry, a partial lookback call pays off max (0, (CMP – SP), (CMP – SP(reset))) while a partial lookback put pays off max (0, (SP – CMP), (SP(reset) – CMP)), where SP(reset) is the reset strike price. As indicated, a typical partial lookback only allows for a single reset opportunity, though in certain instances multiple resets can be negotiated. In the extreme, as reset periods tend towards infinity, a partial lookback becomes a conventional floating strike lookback. Partial lookbacks are more expensive than vanilla options since they provide the purchaser with additional payoff flexibility; they are, however, cheaper than conventional lookbacks since they do not guarantee payoff of the maximum gain generated during the life of the option. Note that a variation on this structure is the extendible option, which lets the purchaser reset the option at the current market or exercise the option based on the last strike reset; the extendible option has multiple reset periods.

Consider the following example. Bank CDE purchases a partial lookback call on 100,000 shares of stock QRS; the option is struck at-the-money (US$100) and the maturity of the transaction is two years. At the end of year one CDE can reset the option at the current market level if the price of QRS is below US$100. Assume the following two scenarios. Scenario one: at the end of year one the price of QRS is US$80 and at the end of year two it is US$150. Under this scenario, the payoff to CDE is US$7m ((US$150 – US$80) * 100,000) since the call strike resets at US$80 (it is out-of-the-money during the reset period). Scenario two: at the end of year one the price of QRS is US$110 and at the end of year two it is US$150. Under this scenario the payoff to CDE is US$5m ((US$150 – US$100) * 100,000) since the call strike does not reset (it is in-the-money during the reset period). Figure 8.8 illustrates the payoff of a partial lookback call option.

Ladder options

A *ladder option* (like the cliquet and shout options we discuss below) is a structured derivative that automatically "locks in" intrinsic value once prespecified market levels (or "rungs," as they are often called) are reached. If the market subsequently retraces (for example, declines for a call or rises for a put), the purchaser preserves the intrinsic value that has already been locked in.

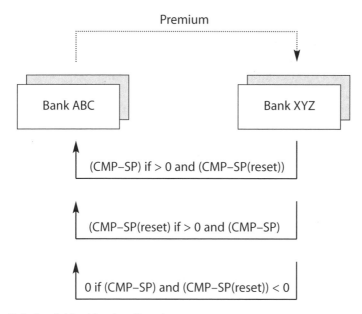

Figure 8.8 Partial lookback call option

There are two basic forms of ladder option: the *fixed strike ladder option* (also known as a modified ladder) and the *floating strike ladder option*. While both are structurally similar in locking in gains prior to maturity, a fixed strike ladder features a strike price that is set on trade date, while a floating strike ladder features no predefined strike. Payoff of a fixed strike ladder is generated at maturity by comparing the strike price against the terminal price and the ladder rungs; the greater of the two becomes the payout. The payoff of a fixed strike ladder call is thus max (0, (CMP – SP), (highest rung – SP)) and the payoff of a ladder put is max (0, (SP – CMP), (SP – lowest rung)). Comparing the terminal price against the ladder rungs at maturity generates payoff of a floating strike ladder. The payoff of a floating strike ladder call is thus max (0, (CMP – min (lowest rung, CMP))) while the payoff of a floating strike ladder put is max (0, (max (highest rung, CMP) – CMP)). While both types of ladder are utilized in the derivative markets, we shall concentrate our examples and REE discussion on fixed strike ladders, knowing that analysis can easily be adapted to accommodate the floating strike version. Regardless of the specific structure, the number of rungs in the ladder option is flexible and can be negotiated between the buyer and seller; as we might expect, the greater the number of rungs the more expensive the option, as each breach of a rung allows the purchaser to realize a greater amount of value. In the extreme, as the number of rungs tends towards infinity, the payoff profile and price of the option approach that of a floating strike lookback option (for example, the ladder locks in all the gains achieved during the life of the transaction, in the same way a lookback option pays off based on the minimum purchase price (for calls) or maximum selling price (for puts)).

Consider the following example. Bank ABC buys from Dealer UVW a ladder call (1000 contracts) referencing the Hang Seng Index. The 12-month option is struck at 10,000 (the current level of the index) and has rungs at 10,500 and 11,000. During the life of the option the Hang Seng rises to 11,100 and ends at 10,300. The payoff of the ladder call at expiry equals HK$1m ((11,000 – 10,000) * 1000) since ABC locks in gains up to 11,000, the second rung of the ladder. Figure 8.9 highlights the payoff of a ladder call option.

Cliquet options

A *cliquet option*, also known as a ratchet option, is a structured derivative that generates a payoff that is similar to the ladder and shout options. Unlike the ladder option (which locks in gains once prespecified values are reached), the cliquet option locks in gains at prespecified time intervals (to the extent the option has intrinsic value at each evaluation point); such gains are not lost if the market subsequently retraces. If the option is out-of-the-money on a particular evaluation date, the strike is reset at the lower market level and future payout is adjusted to reflect the new strike level.[9] Payoff of a cliquet call that remains at, or above, the strike during the entire trade is max (0, (CMP – SP), (highest cliquet – SP)), while the payoff of a cliquet put is max (0, (SP – CMP), (SP – lowest cliquet)). Payoff of a

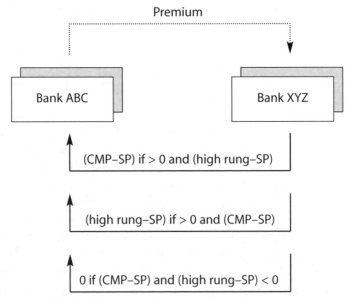

Figure 8.9 Ladder call option

cliquet call that resets out-of-the-money during the trade is max (0, (CMP – SP(reset)), (highest cliquet – SP(reset)), while the payoff of a cliquet put is max (0, (SP(reset) – CMP), (SP(reset) – lowest cliquet)). Cliquets can be structured with any number and frequency of evaluation periods (for example, weekly, monthly, quarterly, semi-annually, annually); the greater the frequency of evaluation, the more expensive the option. In the extreme, as cliquet intervals tend towards infinity, the payoff profile and price of the option approaches that of a conventional floating strike lookback.

Consider the following example. Bank EFG buys a six-month cliquet put on the US 30-year Treasury bond, with monthly evaluation intervals and an at-the-money strike price of par; the payoff is based on the price differential times US$100,000. Assume that during the next six months 30-year Treasury bond prices are as follows: Month 1: 100; Month 2: 100; Month 3: 100; Month 4: 98.5; Month 5: 98; and, Month 6: 100. Based on the price path of the Treasury bond, the cliquet generates a payoff of US$200,000 ((100 – 98) * 100,000), since the price of the underlying reaches a low of 98 during the Month 5 evaluation period (note that the bank locks in minimum gains in month four as well, though these are eventually exceeded by the gains in month five). If the Treasury price drops to 96 during the life of the transaction (but not on an evaluation date), the maximum payoff is still US$200,000 (note that if EFG purchases a more expensive lookback put it realizes the larger gain generated by a price decline to 96). Figure 8.10 highlights the flows of a standard at-the-money cliquet put option.

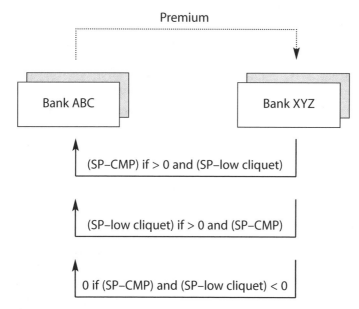

Figure 8.10 Cliquet put option

Shout options

The *shout option* is a third derivative that locks in gains prior to expiry. Like its peers, the shout option gives a purchaser the ability to crystallize gains achieved during the life of the transaction. Unlike ladder options (which lock in gains based on the breach of prespecified market levels) or cliquet options (which lock in gains based on the passage of time), shout options lock in gains at any market level or at any time; the gains are triggered when the purchaser "shouts" for gains to be locked in. Shout options are available in two distinct forms, the *fixed strike shout option* (also known as a modified shout option) and the *floating strike shout option*. A fixed strike shout features a strike price that is set on trade date, while a floating strike shout has no predefined strike. At maturity a fixed strike shout compares the strike price against the shout level and the terminal price and allocates a payout to the larger of the two. The payoff of a shout call is thus max (0, (CMP – SP), (shout – SP)) and the payoff of a shout put is max (0, (SP – CMP), (SP – shout)). Comparing the terminal price against the shout level at maturity generates payoff of a floating strike shout. The payoff of a floating strike shout call is thus max (0, (CMP – min (shout, CMP))), and the payoff of a floating strike shout put is max (0, max ((shout, CMP) – CMP)). Although both fixed and floating strike shouts are prevalent in the market we shall concentrate our discussion, examples, and REE analysis on the more popular fixed strike version. While any number of shouts can theoretically be incorporated in a given structure, in practice most options feature a single lock-in opportunity. In the extreme, as the number of shout periods approaches infinity, the option assumes the payoff profile and price of a conventional floating strike lookback.

Consider the following example. Bank JKL purchases a 12-month shout put on the yen (¥ put/US\$ call), struck at-the-money (¥100/US\$). During the 12-month period the yen strengthens to a high of ¥95/US\$, weakens to a low of ¥108/US\$, and ends at ¥107/US\$. Assume JKL shouts at ¥106/US\$ and locks in, at that time, certain gains of ¥6/US\$ per contract. Since the terminal value of the yen is ¥107/US\$, the final payoff to JKL equals ¥7/US\$. Note that if JKL times the market perfectly and shouts at ¥108/US\$, it locks in gains of ¥8/US\$, despite the subsequent strengthening in the yen. Figure 8.11 highlights the payoff of a shout put option.

Installment options

An *installment option* is a derivative that permits the purchaser to pay the seller premium on a periodic, or installment, basis, rather than upfront. Once the last installment payment is made (that is, the premium is fully paid off) the seller grants the buyer full benefits of a vanilla European put or call with trade characteristics specified at contract date (which is generally when the

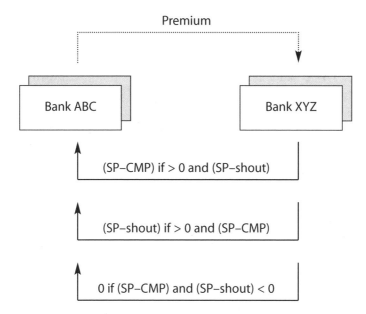

Figure 8.11 Shout put option

first installment payment is made). When an option buyer is not convinced of the need to enter into an underlying option trade (for example, it may be awaiting receipt of a contingent cash flow), an installment option surfaces as a sensible alternative; by not fully committing to the transaction via payment of upfront premium, the buyer has the ability to cancel the contract and save on remaining premium expense. If, at any time during the installment payment period, the buyer determines it no longer needs or wants the underlying option, it simply ceases to make payments and the contract is cancelled. If, however, the need for the option becomes apparent, the buyer continues paying until the premium is fully paid – at which point it obtains the speculative or hedge benefits of the underlying option. Note that installment options are cheaper than contingent premium options (discussed below), since interim payments are required. It should also be noted that installment options can be created to commence immediately (for example, at trade date) or at a forward date; in either event, the buyer cannot claim the benefits of the option until all premium payments are made.

Consider the following example. Company VWX will face a €/US$ foreign exchange exposure in six months if it is awarded a sales contract. Rather than being exposed to foreign exchange risk when, and if, it receives the contract, VWX intends to hedge through the purchase of an at-the-money European currency option. After discussing alternatives with its advisor, Bank FGH, VWX discovers that the premium of the European option will cost US$600,000. Given the uncertainty surrounding the sales contract the company enters into an installment option with FGH, where it pays FGH US$100,000 per month, over six months, to reserve the right to enter into a €/US$ currency option (note that the option is assumed to be forward, not spot, starting, though we could easily imagine the opposite scenario). VWX can cancel the contract at any time by ceasing to make installment payments. Assume that in three months, after it has made US$300,000 in installment payments, VWX learns that it has not been awarded the sales contract and will not require hedging cover. It lets its next installment payment lapse and FGH cancels the underlying contract. By entering into the installment option VWX only loses US$300,000, instead of US$600,000, of premium. Figure 8.12 highlights the payoff of an installment call option.

Path independent options

Binary options

A *binary option*, often referred to as a digital option, is a derivative that provides the purchaser with a discontinuous payoff or protection profile. Unlike a conventional option, which provides a continuum of payoffs depending on the position of the underlying price in relation to the strike price, a binary option has no such continuum; the payoff for in-the-money binary puts and calls is simply M, where M is a predetermined amount unrelated to the specific moneyness of the contract. Institutions that require a fixed payoff that is influenced only by whether the strike has been breached

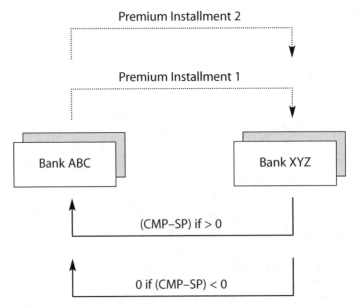

Figure 8.12 Installment call option

usually employ binary options; such options form the "building blocks" of the popular range floater structures we noted in Chapter 1 (and similar instruments such as "tower bonds," accrual notes, day-count notes, and so on).

The two classes of binary options are the *cash-or-nothing option* and the *asset-or-nothing option* (sometimes known collectively as all-or-nothing options). Instead of providing a terminal payoff of max (0, (CMP – SP)) for a call, or max (0, (SP – CMP)) for a put, the cash-or-nothing option (either a put or call) generates a cash payoff of max (0, Mc), where Mc is a prespecified cash amount. An asset-or-nothing option is identical to the cash-or-nothing option except it settles in physical rather than cash (the underlying must, of course, be an asset which can be settled physically). An in-the-money asset-or-nothing call requires delivery of cash in exchange for the asset, while an in-the-money asset-or-nothing put requires delivery of an asset in exchange for cash. The payoff of an asset-or-nothing option is simply max (0, Ma), where Ma is a prespecified asset amount. Since cash-or-nothing and asset-or-nothing options must end in-the-money to generate the fixed cash or asset payoff M, they are often known as European binary options.

In addition to standard European binary options, hybrid *binary–barrier options*, often referred to as one-touch options or American binary options, are also available (as we mentioned at the beginning of the chapter, these hybrids represent a combination of path dependent-independent options and might, arguably, be included in the path dependent section above; for continuity, however, we find it easier to include the discussion in this section). The one-touch option provides a prespecified cash or asset payoff M if the option moves in-the-money at any time during the life of the transaction (payoff is not dependent on the price of the underlying in relation to the strike at expiry, as is required for European binaries); once the option "touches" the strike (barrier) and becomes an in-the-money derivative, it locks in prespecified gains and pays off either immediately (at hit options) or at expiry (at expiry options). Binary–barriers are available in various classes based on puts/calls, cash/asset, and at hit/at expiry; in all instances options must be struck out-of-the-money at trade date; barriers are, of course, set equal to the strike prices. Table 8.3 summarizes available combinations.

Consider the following example. Bank Z buys a UK£5m cash-or-nothing put on the FTSE 100 struck at 3600 in a current market of 4000, implying an 11 percent out-of-the-money contract; payoff to Z, if the option ends in-the-money, is £5m. At expiration assume the FTSE falls to 3400, indicating the option is 5.5 percent in-the-money. With a conventional put, Bank Z receives 5.5 percent of UK£5m, or UK£275,000. Since this is a cash-or-nothing put, however, Bank Z receives the full UK£5m (it is, of course, possible to structure a cash-or-nothing option with a payoff different than the notional of the transaction). Let us also consider an example of the one-touch option.

Table 8.3 Binary–barrier option cominations

Cash-or-nothing at hit call option	Up and in cash-or-nothing at hit option
Cash-or-nothing at hit put option	Down and in cash-or-nothing at hit option
Cash-or-nothing at expiry call option	Up and in cash-or-nothing at expiry option
Cash-or-nothing at expiry put option	Down and in cash-or-nothing at expiry option
Asset-or-nothing at hit call option	Up and in asset-or-nothing at hit option
Asset-or-nothing at hit put option	Down and in asset-or-nothing at hit option
Asset-or-nothing at expiry call option	Up and in asset-or-nothing at expiry option
Asset-or-nothing at expiry put option	Down and in asset-or-nothing at expiry option

Assume Bank Z purchases a UK£5m FTSE cash-or-nothing at hit put with the strike/barrier set at 3600. Over the life of the transaction the FTSE moves to a low of 3400 and ends at 3700. Under a European binary (such as the one described immediately above), the option expires out-of-the-money, with no payoff to Bank Z. With the cash-or-nothing at hit option, however, Bank Z is entitled to the full UK£5m as soon as the FTSE breaches the 3600 barrier. Figure 8.13 highlights the payoff of a cash-or-nothing at hit put option.

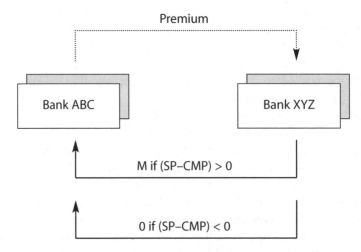

Figure 8.13 Cash-or-nothing at hit put option

Rainbow/multi-index options

The family of *rainbow options* (or multi-index options) is broad-based and includes a series of derivatives whose payoff depends on the performance of more than one underlying reference. The references may be drawn from the same or different asset classes/markets. In this section we describe several of the most common rainbow options, including options on the best/worst of n-assets and cash, options on the best/worst of n-assets, multiple strike options, spread options, and basket options.

Options on the best/worst of n-assets and cash

The general class of *options on the best/worst of n-assets and cash* includes derivatives that generate payoffs based on the largest gain from a series of assets and cash, or the smallest gain from a series of assets and cash; the assets in the portfolio can be drawn from similar, or different, markets. Since the option contains no strike price the purchaser always earns a return, unless it sets the cash parameter equal to zero (which is unlikely). The payoff of an option on the best of n-assets and cash is given as max (CMP1, CMP2, . . . CMPn, C), where the portfolio includes n assets (with CMP representing the terminal price of each) and a fixed amount of cash C. The payoff of an option on the worst of n-assets and cash is given as min (CMP1, CMP2, . . . CMPn, C).

Let us consider the following example. Securities Firm JKL wants to express a view on the performance of three different stocks and receive a

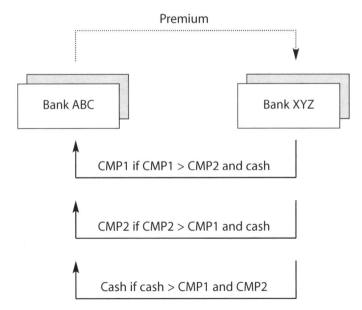

Figure 8.14 Option on the best of two assets and cash

payoff based on the best of the three; to protect itself from a downward move in the market, it also wants to make certain it receives a minimum cash payment of US$100,000. To monetize this view JKL purchases an option on the best of three stocks (10,000 shares equivalent) and cash. For ease we assume that the three reference stocks underlying the option, stocks A, B, and C, are each trading at US$10/share on trade date. Consider the following two scenarios. Scenario one: at maturity of the transaction, stock A trades at US$15/share, stock B at US$12/share, and stock C at US$9/share. JKL receives a payoff of US$150,000 (that is, stock A's price of US$15 * 10,000 shares); this represents the best performing asset in the portfolio, and is even greater than the minimum cash payment of US$100,000. Scenario two: at maturity of the transaction, stock A ends at US$9/share, stock B at US$8/share, and stock C at US$7/share; in this case JKL receives the US$100,000 fixed cash payment since it is the best performing asset in the portfolio. Figure 8.14 illustrates the payoff of an option on the best of two assets and cash.

Options on the best/worst of n-assets

Options on the best/worst of n-assets are similar to the derivatives described immediately above, with two exceptions: the options provide no "guaranteed" minimum cash payoff (denoted by C in the payoff formula above) and all market price movements are compared against a preset strike level in order to generate a payoff; it is possible, therefore, for these options to end with no value. Index references may be from the same market (for example, two equities) or from different markets (for example, an equity and a bond); when considering references from two different markets, care must be taken to equate strikes and contract multipliers.[10] As with options on the best/worst of n-assets and cash, options on the best/worst of n-assets provide the purchaser with additional opportunities to achieve gains; in exchange for this flexibility the option purchaser is required to pay a greater premium. Four different versions exist:

■ *Call on the best of n-assets*: which gives the holder the right to purchase the underlying asset worth the most at expiry; the payoff is given by max $(0, \max((CMP1, CMP2, \ldots, CMPn) - SP))$.

■ *Call on worst of n-assets*: which gives the holder the right to purchase the underlying asset worth the least at expiry; the payoff is given by max $(0, \min((CMP1, CMP2, \ldots, CMPn) - SP))$.

■ *Put on the best of n-assets*: which gives the holder the right to sell the asset worth the most at expiry; the payoff is given as max $(0, (SP - \max(CMP1, CMP2, \ldots, CMPn)))$.

- *Put on the worst of n-assets*: which gives the holder the right to sell the asset worth the least at expiry; the payoff is given as max (0, (SP – min (CMP1, CMP2, . . ., CMPn))).

In each case the "portfolio" includes n-assets with terminal price CMP.

Let us consider the following example. Bank BCD wants to take a view on the worst performing of a series of industrial stocks; to do so it purchases a put on the worst performing of four stocks (based on 100,000 shares equivalent). Assume on trade date stock U trades at US$70/share, stock V at US$65/share, stock W at US$66/share, and stock X at US$68/share; the strike of the option is set at US$60. (Note that although certain stocks are struck slightly closer to the money, BCD may feel strongly that those struck farther out-of-the-money have a greater chance of falling sharply and is thus comfortable with the structure. It should be noted that these options can also be made more "uniform" by converting relative performance into percentage terms; for simplicity, however, we use an example in dollar terms). Assume 12 months hence, at the conclusion of the transaction, stock U trades at US$55/share, stock V at US$57/share, stock W at US$72/share, and stock X at US$69/share. Based on the terminal prices BCD receives a payoff of US$500,000 (100,000 * (US$60 – US$55)) from Stock U, which is the worst performing of the four securities. (Note that only one other stock, V, ends in-the-money; all others end out-of-the-money). Figure 8.15 highlights the payoff of a put option on the worst of two assets.

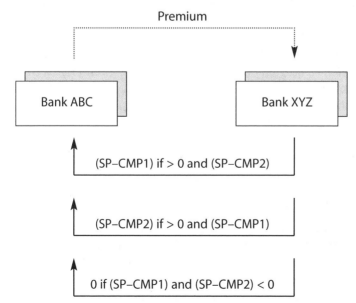

Figure 8.15 Put option on the worst of two assets

Multiple strike options

A *multiple strike option* is a derivative that generates a payoff based on the best performing of a series of assets, each with its own strike price and underlying price (options referencing only two assets/strikes are commonly known as dual strike options). In this regard a multiple strike option can be viewed as a portfolio of individual call or put options with payoff determined by the single call or put which returns the largest economic gain over the life of the deal; if all options in the portfolio end out-of-the-money, the multiple strike option expires worthless. The structure of a multiple strike option allows inclusion of references from identical or different asset classes; the correlative effects incorporated in the pricing generally yields a derivative that is cheaper than the sum of the individual components. The payoff of a multiple strike call is given by max $(0, (CMP1 - SP1), (CMP2 - SP2), \ldots (CMPn - SPn))$, while the payoff of a multiple strike put is given by max $(0, (SP1 - CMP1), (SP2 - CMP2), \ldots (SPn - CMPn))$.

Consider the following example. Dealer LMN is interested in obtaining the potential upside of the best performing of a series of Treasury bonds; though it believes Treasury prices will rise, it is uncertain which issue will perform the best, so it purchases a multiple strike call on three bonds: Bond A, currently priced and struck at 100, Bond B, currently priced and struck at 103, and Bond C, currently priced and struck at 95. It thus has a mini-portfolio of at-the-money bond options, with final payoff based on the best performing of the three (times an arbitrary multiple of US$100,000). Assume six months hence Bond A is trading at 105, Bond B at 104 and Bond C at 101. Through the multiple strike option LMN receives a payoff of US$600,000 (US$100,000 * (101 – 95)) from the best performing asset, Bond C; the first bond generates a payoff of US$500,000 while the second bond generates no gain. This example is structured in price terms; as with other rainbow options, multiple strike options can be created in percentage terms, which is helpful when comparing across asset classes. Figure 8.16 illustrates the payoff of a multiple strike call option.

Spread options

A *spread option* (also known as a difference option, outperformance option, or underperformance option) is a derivative that generates a payoff based on the spread, or differential, between two reference indexes from similar or different markets. While vanilla options generate a payoff based on the direction (and often terminal value) of a single reference, spread options pay off based on the direction of the spread between two references. Popular spread options include those based on the difference between two equity indexes, the shape of the yield curve,

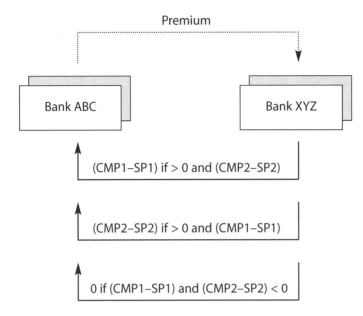

Figure 8.16 Multiple strike call option

and the movement of credit-risky instruments; we consider all three cases below. The payoff of a standard spread call option is max (0, (CMP1 – CMP2 – SP)) and the payoff of a spread put option is max (0, (SP – CMP1 – CMP2)), where CMP1 references the price of underlying index 1 and CMP2 references the price of underlying index 2.

Consider the following example. Bank TUV purchases an at-the-money spread option that pays off based on the maximum differential between the Singaporean Straits Times Index (STI) and the Thai Stock Exchange of Thailand Index (SET); the STI is trading at 2300 and the SET is trading at 1300, indicating a spread of 1000 points. The maturity of the option is 12 months and the payoff is equal to the spread times an arbitrary multiplier of US$10,000, as long as the spread exceeds the strike of 1000; if it trades below 1000 the option expires worthless (note that this structure provides a currency-protected payoff through a quanto option, which we discuss at greater length later in the chapter). Under the structure the relative level and direction of each market is less relevant than the size and volatility of the spread between the markets. For instance, if the STI drops by 100 points but the SET drops by 200 points, the spread widens and the option moves in-the-money; if the STI remains unchanged and the SET rises by 200 points the spread narrows and the option moves out-of-the-money. If, 12 months hence, the STI rises to 2400 and the SET falls to 1200, the payoff to Bank TUV is US$2m (((2400 – 1200) – 1000) * US$10 000). Figure 8.17 illustrates the payoff of a spread call option.

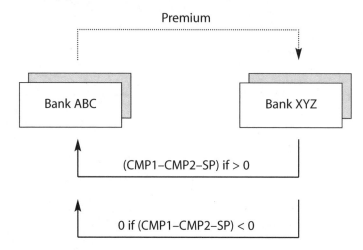

Figure 8.17 Spread call option

A *yield curve option* is another type of spread option that is commonly used in the financial markets. A yield curve option, as the name suggests, is a spread option that provides a buyer with a payoff based on the shape of the yield curve. While an investor can buy and/or sell two separate options referencing different points on a yield curve to achieve the same results, the ease of having the transaction embedded in a single instrument has a great deal of investor appeal. More importantly, the premium paid by the buyer is lower since correlation is factored into the pricing. A yield curve option can be structured in price or yield terms, though the latter tends to be a more popular dealing convention. Viewed strictly in terms of yield, we summarize, in Table 8.4 various yield curve scenarios required to take advantage of movements in an upward sloping yield curve (adjustments would obviously need to be made for less common flat yield curves, inverted yield curves or "kinked" yield curves). Thus,

Table 8.4 Yield curve scenarios

Scenario	Short-end yields	Long-end yields
Steepening	Constant	Rising
Steepening	Falling	Constant
Steepening	Falling	Rising
Flattening	Constant	Falling
Flattening	Rising	Constant
Flattening	Rising	Falling

an institution expecting short-end yields to remain constant or fall, and long-end yields to increase or remain unchanged, is anticipating a steepening; to monetize this view it can purchase a yield curve option which generates a payoff once the curve steepens above the level indicated by the strike of the option.

Consider the following example. Bank Z is expecting a flattening between the two and ten-year Treasury yields (that is, it is expecting the two-year yield to remain constant or rise and the ten-year yield to fall or remain constant). To profit from this view it purchases from Dealer NOP a six-month at-the-money yield curve option which provides a payoff of US$10,000 per basis point once the spread moves through the strike; the current spread between the two references is 55 basis points in yield terms (which is also the strike price). Six months from now the yield on the two-year Treasury rises by 20 basis points while the yield of the ten-year Treasury remains constant; the spread is therefore 35 basis points and the payoff to Bank Z is US$200,000 ((0.55 – 0.35) * 10,000).

The credit spread option, an integral component of the credit derivatives market, compares the differential between a credit-risky instrument such as a corporate bond or loan, and a risk-free benchmark such as a high quality government bond.[11] Credit spread puts are purchased by institutions that believe the credit quality of an issuer will deteriorate – as reflected in the widening of a company's bond credit spread against the risk-free benchmark. Sellers of credit puts believe an issuer's credit quality will remain stable/improve, and they generate premium income if this view proves to be correct (alternatively, they may be selling puts as part of an overall credit portfolio risk management exercise). Credit spread calls, in contrast, are purchased by institutions that believe the credit quality of an issuer will improve. In order to buy or sell a credit option, the target credit must have some traded debt security that can be used as a reference; this should ideally be sufficiently liquid to provide a fair assessment of market value. Credit spread options can be settled in cash or physical; an investor long a physical settlement credit put can deliver bonds or loans to the seller at a predetermined price/spread if the option is exercised. Options can be price or spread-based (in spread-based options the final payoff must be adjusted for the price sensitivity of the spread through a duration factor, which is simply a reflection of the average maturity of the bond's cash flows).[12]

Consider the following example. Bank MNO believes Company ABC is a deteriorating credit and wishes to take a view on the deterioration. It purchases a US$10m spread-based credit put (struck at-the-money) from Bank JKL. The tenor of the credit put is 12 months and references ABC's publicly quoted five-year bond, which currently trades at a spread of 200 basis points over Treasuries. Assume that 12 months from now, when the ABC bond has four years left to maturity (and a duration of approximately three), ABC's credit quality deteriorates and the spread widens to 350 basis points over Treasuries. Bank MNO exercises the option on a cash-settlement basis and earns US$450,000 ((0.035 − 0.02) * 3 * US$10m), adjusted for present value. If ABC's credit quality improves, its spread might tighten within 200 basis points; under this scenario MNO's credit put expires worthless.

Basket options

A *basket option* is a derivative that allows the purchaser to obtain, in a single structure, a payoff based on the performance of a combination of related or unrelated assets. Combining a series of underlying assets into a basket generates a payoff based on appreciation (call), or depreciation (put), of the group of assets against a predetermined strike level; correlations among the assets in the basket generally result in a derivative that is cheaper than the sum of options on the individual components of the basket. The payoff of a basket call is max (0, (CMP(basket) − SP(basket))) while the payoff of a basket put is max (0, (SP(basket) − CMP(basket))), where SP(basket) is the strike price of the basket and CMP(basket) is the terminal price of the basket.

Consider the following example. An investor believes the Asian equity markets will rise over the next six months but is uncertain which one will perform the best (and whether, in fact, one might decline); as such, it purchases a basket call encompassing the Nikkei 225, Hang Seng, and STI indexes (assigning one-third weighting to each one, or perhaps some other weighting if it feels strongly that one of the indexes will rise by a greater amount). If, at expiry, the weighted value of the group of indexes exceeds the basket strike price, the investor receives the difference (times 10,000 contracts, at US$1/contract). If the group of indexes does not move up (or if one moves down sharply and forces the weighted average of the entire package below the strike) the investor receives no payout. Assume on trade date the Nikkei is trading at 22,000, the Hang Seng at 10,000 and the Straits Times at 2400, to yield a strike price of 11,350. If, at the conclusion of the transaction, the Nikkei is quoted at 23,000, the Hang Seng at 9000, and the Straits Times at 2700, the payoff to the investor is US$1m ((11,450 − 11,350) * 10,000)). Although the Hang Seng declined during the evaluation period the other two reference indexes rose sufficiently to generate a payoff to the investor (note, once again, that this structure includes a currency-protected payoff via a quanto option). Figure 8.18 illustrates the payoff of a basket call option.

Credit basket options have become very popular in recent years. Such derivatives can be structured to give investors a payoff based on the best performing of a series of credits; they can also be used to give intermediaries

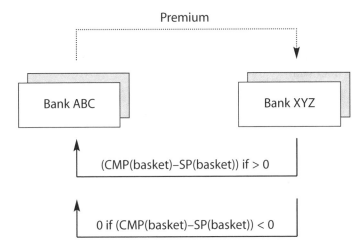

Figure 8.18 Basket call option

or portfolio managers a payoff based on the worst performing credit – often one that defaults. Knowing this, it is possible to use credit basket options to actively manage portfolios of credit risk, as we shall discuss in Chapter 13. Use of credit default correlations in pricing the basket option generally results in pricing that is lower than an equivalent strip of individual credit options, adding to the appeal of the structure.

Compound options

A *compound option* (also known as a nested option) is an option on an option. Though compound options have been in existence for several decades they have been applied to a broader variety of assets/markets in recent years and are now commonly used in the derivative markets.[13] A compound option gives the purchaser the right, but not the obligation, to buy or sell an underlying put or a call. Under a standard transaction, terms of the original option and the underlying option are agreed in advance of a trade. The purchaser of the compound pays the seller an initial premium payment on trade date; if the original option is in-the-money at expiry the purchaser can exercise into the underlying option, settling the additional premium at that time. Alternatively, if the original option is out-of-the-money it simply lets it expire. Under a standard compound structure the premium on the underlying option is determined based on the strike price and current price of the market reference of the underlying option; the strike price of the original compound option is then set as a function of the premium of the underlying option. An institution might purchase a compound option if it faces uncertainty over prices/rates or other events that could affect future asset/liability or input/output streams. Buying an option on an option locks in a certain level of protection without committing the institution to a transaction it might not actually require; it also enables the institution to save on premium payments for a contingent event that may not occur.

There are four types of compound options:

- *Call on a call*: giving the purchaser the right to buy a call on a specified date; the option payoff is max (0, (prem(UL) – SP(t))) at expiry of the original option at time t and, if exercised into the underlying option, max (0, (CMP – SP)).

- *Call on a put*: giving the purchaser the right to buy a put on a specified date; the option payoff is (max (0, (prem(UL) – SP(t))), followed by max (0, (SP – CMP)).

- *Put on a put*: giving the purchaser the right to sell a put on a specified date; the option payoff is (max (0, (SP(t) – prem(UL))), followed by max (0, (SP – CMP)).

- *Put on a call*: giving the purchaser the right to sell a call on a specified date; the option payoff is max (0, (SP(t) – prem(UL))), followed by max (0, (CMP – SP)).

In all cases prem(UL) is the premium of the underlying option, SP(t) is the strike price of the original option (expiring at time t) and is set as a function of the underlying option's premium; SP and CMP, as always, relate to the strike and current market price of the underlying transaction. While most compound options involve two European derivatives, it is possible to structure transactions with American or complex derivatives (making valuation and pricing much more difficult).

Consider the following example. Bank X purchases a call on a call on stock ABC (currently trading at US$50/share) which gives it the right to purchase a call from Bank Y struck at US$55/share in 12 months; the premium of the underlying option is US$1/contract and the strike price of the original compound call is US$1.25. If, 12 months from now, stock ABC is trading above US$55/share, the underlying option moves in-the-money (perhaps with a premium equal to US$2) and has value to X; X can exercise the compound option at the strike of US$1.25 (when the value is equal to US$2) and receive a call struck at US$55/share; upon doing so it pays Y the additional premium required. If stock ABC is trading below US$55/share the underlying option has no value to X and the original option expires worthless. Figure 8.19 illustrates the payoff of a compound call option.

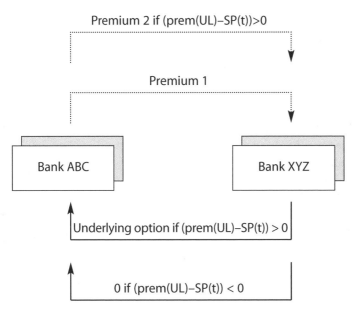

Premium 2 if (prem(UL)–SP(t))>0

Premium 1

Bank ABC

Bank XYZ

Underlying option if (prem(UL)–SP(t)) > 0

0 if (prem(UL)–SP(t)) < 0

Figure 8.19 Compound call option

Chooser options

A *chooser option* (also known as a preference option) is a derivative that provides the purchaser with flexibility in selecting the specific characteristics of an underlying option within a given time frame. With a *regular chooser option* the buyer can select between a put and a call (where both options have identical strikes and maturities). Once the selection is made, the buyer assumes a long position in a vanilla European option and forwards the seller the required premium payment. (Note that the initial position of a regular chooser is very similar to that of a long straddle, discussed in Chapter 7, which provides the buyer with both a put and a call at the same strike level; the difference between a chooser and a straddle is, of course, that once the purchaser of a chooser selects either a put or a call leg, the other disappears, whereas the purchaser of a straddle retains both legs until maturity. As a result of the decreased flexibility, the chooser is considerably less expensive than an equivalent straddle.) The payoff of a regular chooser at choice date is max (call (SP1, T1), put (SP1, T1)), followed by max (0, (CMP – SP1)) at expiry if a call is chosen and max (0, (SP1 – CMP)) if a put is chosen, where SP1 is the strike and T1 is the maturity.

With a *complex chooser option* the buyer is accorded even greater flexibility, being able to select between a call with predefined strike price SP1 and maturity T1 and a put with strike price SP2 and maturity T2. At choice date the buyer assumes a long position in the derivative selected and pays the option seller any premium due. The payoff of a complex chooser at choice date is max (call (SP1, T1), put (SP2, T2)), followed by max (0, (CMP – SP1)) at expiry if a call is chosen and max (0, (SP2 – CMP)) if a put is chosen.

Chooser options are particularly useful when the outcome of a particular event might have a significant impact on future prices/volatilities. Rather than locking in a specific upfront transaction, which may or may not result in optimal gain or protection given a current scenario, the chooser allows deferral of key details, which can be crystallized as time clarifies a given situation or event.

Consider the following example. Bank ABC purchases a regular chooser from Bank PQR; PQR grants ABC a 30-day window, during which ABC decides whether to establish a 12-month ¥ put/US$ call or a ¥ call/US$ put struck at ¥100/US$. At the conclusion of the 30-day period, yen trades at ¥95/US$. Since the yen has appreciated against the dollar, ABC elects to enter into a long ¥ call/US$ put struck at ¥100/US$; ABC thus has an in-the-money option at the point of selection. Note that ABC's decision may be unrelated to the market level of ¥/US$ during the choice period. Instead, it may related to knowledge of specific asset or liability flows (or potential market events) occurring during the 30-day choice period; thus, the purchaser will not always automatically select the option which is more valuable on choice date. Figure 8.20 illustrates the flows of a regular chooser option.

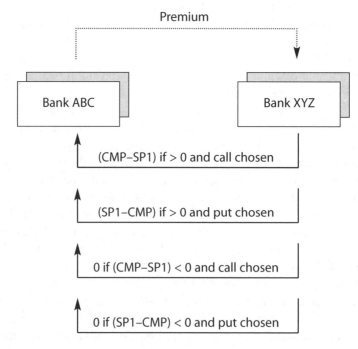

Figure 8.20 Regular chooser option

Contingent premium options

A *contingent premium option* (also known as a pay later option, a cash on delivery option, or a when-in-the-money option) is a derivative that allows the buyer of the option to defer payment of premium until, and if, the option moves in-the-money. If the option remains out-of-the-money over the life of the transaction the buyer is not required to make a premium payment to the seller. If the option moves in-the-money the buyer is obliged to exercise the contract and pay the seller premium, regardless of the intrinsic value (that is, even if exercise results in a gain which is smaller than the premium due to the seller, exercise must take place). From the buyer's perspective this derivative has the advantage of not requiring the payment of upfront premium for an option which may ultimately end with no value; from the seller's perspective the option generates a greater amount of premium than would be earned through the sale of a vanilla structure.

Consider the following example. Dealer XYZ purchases a six-month contingent premium call from Bank DEF on US$10m worth of 30-year Treasury bonds for US$100,000 in premium; the option is struck at a price of 101. Let us assume two scenarios. Scenario one: in six months the 30-year Treasury bond trades at a price of 105; XYZ exercises the call for an economic gain of approximately US$395,000 and pays DEF US$100,000 in premium. Scenario two: in six months the 30-year bond trades at 100; in this instance XYZ's contingent call expires worthless and DEF receives no premium payment. Figure 8.21 illustrates the payoff of a contingent premium call option.

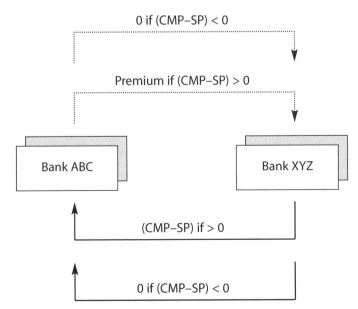

Figure 8.21 Contingent premium call option

Deferred payment American options

A *deferred payment American option* (DPA option) is a derivative that results in the deferral of intrinsic value until the maturity of the option, regardless of when exercise occurs. Through a DPA a buyer enters into an American exercise option with a final maturity at time t. If the option moves in-the-money during the life of the transaction the buyer can exercise and is entitled to the intrinsic value, as with any conventional American option. Rather than paying out the intrinsic value upon exercise, however, the option seller defers payment until the original expiration of the option. This means the seller has use of the buyer's funds until time t, while the buyer is left with a financial gain it cannot utilize until the original expiry date is reached. In exchange for the deferred payment of funds, the buyer effectively pays the seller a smaller premium (for example, through a rebate based on the time value of money).

Consider the following example. Bank JKL purchases a 12-month €/US$ DPA call option from Dealer CDE. Six months from trade date, JKL elects to exercise the option as it is heavily in-the-money; it does so, locking in an economic gain of US$3m. Rather than paying JKL the US$3m at the point of exercise, Dealer CDE retains the funds for its own use until the original contract date is reached, six months hence; at that point JKL receives the US$3m it is due. Figure 8.22 illustrates the payoff of a DPA call option.

Quanto options

A *quanto option* (also known as a guaranteed exchange rate contract or a quantity adjusted option) is a derivative that allows the purchaser to fix a foreign exchange rate and eliminate currency risk from the payoff

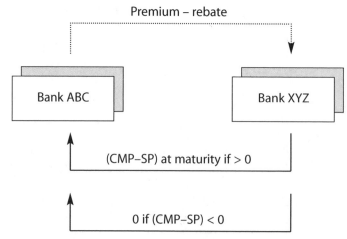

Figure 8.22 Deferred payment American call option

of an underlying market reference. This is particularly useful if the investor fears currency movements are likely to detract from gains generated by an underlying transaction, or when it believes that spot rates are likely to be different than implied forward rates suggest. The payoff of a quanto call is fixed FX * max (0, (CMP(f) – SP(f))) and the payoff of a quanto put is fixed FX * max (0, (SP(f) – CMP(f))), where fixed FX is a predetermined foreign exchange rate and CMP(f) and SP(f) relate to the current market price and strike price of a foreign currency reference.

Consider the following example. Bank TUV, resident in the United States, invests in the Swiss Market Index (SMI) via a dollar quanto put; it needs to receive any gains forthcoming from its put in dollar terms, and does not want such gains eroded by adverse movement of the dollar against the franc. Through the quanto, TUV fixes the CHF/US$ rate at the inception of the trade at CHF1.5/US$. Assume that the SMI put moves in-the-money at maturity, generating CHF1.5m of gains; in this instance the quanto converts TUV's gains from CHF1.5m into US$1m. Note that if TUV does not obtain currency protection through the quanto, and spot CHF/US$ at maturity equals CHF2/US$, conversion of SMI depreciation back into dollars results in only US$750,000 of dollar gains (the opposite scenario can, of course, be considered, where CHF/US$ strengthening generates even greater gains for TUV; the point of the quanto, however, is to eliminate the uncertainty). Note that since the gains from the put at exercise are uncertain on trade date, the amount of required foreign exchange cover is unknown at the commencement of the transaction. Figure 8.23 illustrates the effects of a quanto option on a put structure.

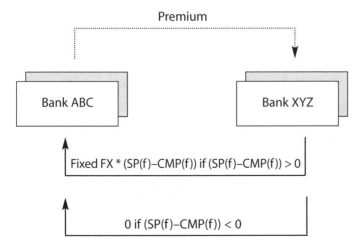

Figure 8.23 Quanto option on put structure

Forward start options

A *forward start option*, as the name suggests, is a derivative that is contracted between buyer and seller at time t and commences at time t +1. Such an option can be useful if a buyer needs to match asset or liability flows that are expected to arise in the future. The purchaser of a forward start option is required to pay the seller premium at contract date, despite the fact that the transaction does not commence until some future time; all terms surrounding the option (such as underlying, strike, notional, forward start date, maturity date, and so on) are agreed and contracted at the time premium is paid. In most cases forward start options are structured to begin as at-the-money transactions on the forward start date; this, however, is not a strict requirement.

A subclass of the forward start option is the *deferred strike option* (or variable strike option). A deferred strike option begins on trade date t when the buyer pays the seller premium. Under terms of the contract, the final maturity of the option is established at time t, but the strike remains undefined until a forward date t + 1. On the forward date the strike is set as a specific function of the current market price (for example, 105 percent of the current market, the current market less 50 basis points, the current market plus 100 index points, and so on). Once the strike is specified, the deferred strike option becomes a conventional European option with the selected strike.

Consider the following example. Bank JKL purchases a UK£10m forward start call option on a ten-year gilt from Dealer MNO for UK£250,000 in upfront premium. The forward start option is structured to commence in six months and mature six months after the forward start date (12 months after the initial trade date). The option will carry an at-the-money strike (that is, the cash price of ten-year gilts six months hence, in price terms), and is exercisable only at maturity. Six months hence JKL's gilt option commences, with an at-the-money strike of 100 and a final maturity of six months. At maturity the ten-year gilt trades at 102; JKL exercises the option, purchases the gilts for UK£10m from MNO and sells them in the market for a UK£200,000 profit.

Exploding options

An *exploding option* is a call or put spread that locks in gains once a strike level is breached. In the last chapter we discussed vertical call and put spreads, created by buying a closer-to-the-money strike option and selling a farther out-of-the-money strike option (long spread), or vice versa (short spread). Spreads are often created using European options; while this can give the purchaser a cheaper position, it also means intrinsic value which might exist cannot be realized until expiry (unless the spread is sold). Indeed, the spread may move in-the-money during the life of the transaction and move back out-of-the-money at expiry, meaning the investor loses any gains achieved. Spreads can, of course, be created using American options (permitting exercise whenever the buyer believes its value has been maximized); however, the added flexibility results in a more expensive package. The exploding option acts as a solution to this problem by giving the spread buyer gains once the short leg of the spread moves in-the-money (indicating the value of the spread has been maximized); at this point the transaction is automatically terminated (it "explodes") and gains are locked in (this occurs regardless of the original maturity of the transaction and the price of the spread at maturity). It is worth noting that this structure is equivalent to a call or put spread with an embedded binary–barrier option (in fact, it is sometimes referred to as a binary–barrier spread).

Consider the following example. Securities Firm GHI wishes to purchase an S&P 500 call spread (5000 contracts at US$1/contract), and wants possible gains accruing from the spread to be locked in once they have been realized. Rather than entering into a conventional European call spread GHI purchases a 12-month exploding option from Bank PQR. The option provides GHI with a long call struck at 600 and a short call struck at 650. Eight months from trade date the S&P 500 moves from 600 to 655; over the next four months it retraces to 635. With the exploding option, GHI's gains on the transaction are automatically realized in the eighth month when the S&P 500 crosses the short call strike of 650; GHI receives a payoff of US$250,000 ((650 – 600) * 5000) at this point (note that if GHI purchases a standard European call spread the payoff is US$175,000 ((635 – 600) * 5000)). Figure 8.24 illustrates the payoff of an exploding call option.

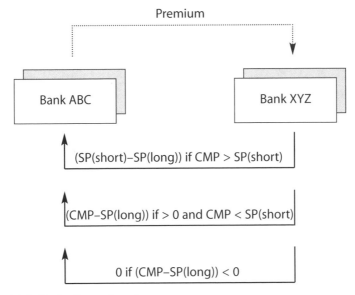

Figure 8.24 Exploding call option

Power options

A *power option* (also known as a leveraged option or a turbo option) is a derivative that provides the purchaser with an exponential payoff. While we know that the payoffs of standard call and put options are max (0, (CMP – SP)) and max (0, (SP – CMP)), respectively, the payoff of a power call option is max (0, (CMP^x – SP)) and the payoff of a power put option is max (0, (SP – CMP^x)), where x is the relevant exponent or "power." Though a buyer can theoretically obtain any exponential payout, in practice most dealing remains limited to *squared power options* (also known as two-power options, paying (CMP^2 – SP) or (SP – CMP^2)) and *cubed power options* (also known as three-power options, paying (CMP^3 – SP) or (SP – CMP^3)); exponential payoffs greater than this can be particularly risky. In exchange for this potential payoff, the purchaser pays the seller a significant premium.

Consider the following example. Dealer STU purchases a squared power put on 10,000 shares of stock CDE from Bank X. The option is struck at US$100 in a US$12 market, and pays off based on the difference between the square of the underlying price and the strike price at maturity. At maturity the price of CDE falls to US$9/share. The payoff to STU on the power put is US$190,000 ((US$100 – US$9^2) * 10,000); if the price of CDE falls to US$7/share the payoff increases to US$510,000 ((US$100 – US$7^2) * 10,000). Thus, a movement of only US$2/share has a substantial impact on the payoff of the transaction. Figure 8.25 illustrates the flows of a squared power call option.

Multi-derivative packages

We have described above several of the most commonly utilized complex options. Given both the demands of end users and the technical and

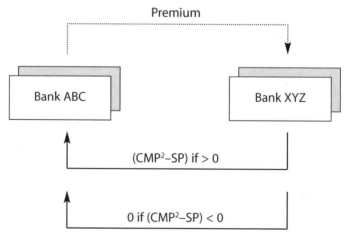

Figure 8.25 Squared power call option

marketing expertise of financial intermediaries, it comes as no surprise that complex options are often combined into multi-option packages to generate even more specific (or esoteric) payoff or protection profiles. (Indeed, some of the examples we have reviewed above already combine multiple complex options. For instance, any complex option that is "quantoed" can be regarded a multi-derivative package; similarly, the binary–barrier option is a package of a binary option and a barrier option.) It is therefore not unusual to see packages featuring "variations on the theme," including:

■ multiple barrier options

■ power barrier options

■ average price barrier options

■ basket shout options

■ compound power options

■ quanto lookback options.

Since the potential combinations of multi-derivative packages are limited only by the needs of end users and creativity of intermediaries, we only consider a few additional examples in this section, including multiple barriers and power barriers.

At the beginning of this chapter we discussed the barrier option. While single barriers are extremely common in the financial markets, multiple barriers also attract considerable attention. A *multiple barrier*, as the name suggests, is a derivative package that contains several knock-in or knock-out options. For instance, a *twin-in barrier option* is a package that creates an underlying European option when the market either rises above, or falls below, one of the two barriers. Likewise, a *twin-out barrier option* is a package with an underlying option that is extinguished when the market rises above, or falls below, one of the barriers.

Consider the following example. Bank QRS purchases a twin-in barrier which creates a European call option struck at 100 if the price of stock HIJ (currently quoted at 100) rises above 110 or falls below 95; if the stock trades between 95.1 and 109.9 during the life of the trade QRS does not gain the benefit of the underlying option. If the stock price rises above 110 QRS owns a European call struck 10 points in-the-money, and if it falls below 95, QRS owns a European call struck five points out-of-the-money. The advantage of this structure is that the creation of the underlying option is not strictly dependent on market direction but also on market volatility (we can draw parallels between this structure and a long straddle). In return for the added flexibility QRS pays a greater amount of premium than it would for a single knock-in.[14] Many other variations of multiple barriers can be arranged in accordance with an institution's view of likely market movements and/or its specific hedging or investing requirements.

The power option described immediately above can be combined with a barrier option to produce a *power barrier option* (or power knock-in/ power knock-out). This results in a derivative package with an exponential payoff profile coupled with discontinuities as an option is either created or extinguished. While all barrier options are characterized by sharp, discontinuous profiles, the presence of an exponential factor creates even more dramatic profiles. Consider the following example. Dealer XYZ purchases a two-power knock-in call (1000 contracts) on stock ABC. The stock currently trades at US$50, the strike price is US$5400 and the barrier is set at US$60 (where the option knocks-in out-of-the-money). Unlike a conventional knock-in, once the barrier is exceeded the payoff of the power knock-in is not the difference between the current price and strike price but the difference between the square of the current price and the strike price. Assume at maturity of the transaction ABC trades at US$80. At US$60 the barrier is triggered and XYZ owns an out-of-the-money two-power call; at maturity, the terminal price of US$80 generates a payoff of US$1m (($US80^2 – US$5400) * 1000). We can imagine the reverse of the transaction, where XYZ purchases a two-power knock-out put (on 1000 contracts) which extinguishes at US$60 (against a strike of US$4900 and a CMP of US$90). If CMP trades from US$90 to US$70, the power knock-out moves at-the-money; once CMP moves to US$61, XYZ's power knock-out has intrinsic value of US$1.2m ((US$4900 – US$$61^2$) * 1000). Once CMP drops to US$60 the power knock-out extinguishes and XYZ is not entitled to a payoff.

Again, we stress that many of the other options described above can be purchased in unique combinations that provide for very specific results. Such packages of can also be embedded in bonds or notes, or standard interest, currency rate, commodity, credit, or equity swaps.

CREDIT RISK QUANTIFICATION

The complex options described in the preceding section are impacted by movements in underlying reference prices or rates. As a result, they are defined as market risk products and must be adjusted through the risk equivalency method to generate an estimate of actual and potential credit risk. As in the previous chapter, the risk equivalency calculation focuses on the risk factor RF in the relevant risk equation.

The method we use to quantify the credit risk of many of the complex options discussed above begins with the general equations developed in Chapter 6. We recall from that discussion that a bank's credit exposure in dealing in OTC options occurs when it is purchaser; short options generally expose the bank to no credit risk once premium is received (for the purposes of this chapter we assume option purchases and sales are executed with premium paid and received upfront).[15] As a reminder, the equations developed in Chapter 6 for valuing credit risk of contract-based options are given as:

$$REE = prem + \max(0, (NC * ((RFc * CMP) + (CMP - SP)))) \qquad (6.3)$$

for calls, and

$$REE = prem + \max(0, (NC * ((RFc * CMP) + (SP - CMP)))) \qquad (6.4)$$

for puts,

where *prem* is the time value component of option premium; *RFc* is a constantly adjusted risk factor; *NC* is the number of option contracts; *CMP* is the current market price, and *SP* is the strike price.

The REE calculations and examples in this section are based on contracts rather than notional; readers interested in examining risk from a notional standpoint can easily adapt the examples for notional terms per our discussion in Chapter 6.

Path dependent options

Barrier options

A barrier option is a derivative that creates or extinguishes an underlying European option once a barrier level is reached. Our discussion of the credit risk of knock-ins and knock-outs focuses on the various "in" and "out" combinations.

Up and in option

In this structure an option is created if the market moves up through a barrier. The credit risk associated with this derivative includes premium (time value) plus the market risk attributable to a European option, assuming the option is created. If the barrier is reached and the option is activated (either out-of-the-money (knock-in) or in-the-money (reverse knock-in)), the bank purchasing the option faces normal credit risk associated with a European put or call with specific moneyness; the option purchaser will look to the option seller to perform on the European option once it is created. A conservative stance suggests the option should be valued regardless of whether it ever comes into existence. Since a bank valuing credit risk typically wants to quantify a plausible worst-case scenario, such an approach appears reasonable. A less conservative method suggests the potential market risk on the option should only be counted when and if it comes into existence; until this occurs, only premium (time value) should be considered at risk. The first version is, of course, precisely equal to the form given in Equations 6.3 and 6.4, when the barrier is equal to the strike level; if the strike is not equal to the barrier, the relevant comparison against CMP is the strike price (rather than the barrier).

Equations 8.1A and 8.1B reflect the REE for calls when the barrier is equal to the strike:

when CMP< Barrier
$$REE = prem \qquad\qquad (8.1\text{A})$$

when CMP > Barrier
$$REE = prem + \max(0, (NC * ((RFc * CMP) + (CMP - Barrier)))) \quad (8.1\text{B})$$

Equations 8.2A and 8.2B reflect the REE for puts when the barrier is equal to the strike:

when CMP < Barrier
$$REE = prem \qquad\qquad (8.2\text{A})$$

when CMP > Barrier
$$REE = prem + \max(0, (NC * ((RFc * CMP) + (Barrier - CMP)))) \quad (8.2\text{B})$$

where *Barrier* is the barrier level at which the option becomes activated: and all other terms are as defined earlier

Let us consider the following example. Bank C purchases a six-month reverse up and in call (50,000 contracts) on the S&P 500 with a strike of 600 and a barrier of 610 in a market trading at 575. Bank C pays the call writer, Bank F, US$250,000 of premium (time value). Note that if the underlying European option is created it will already have intrinsic value (that is, 610 – 600). If the initial RFc is 14 percent, Bank C can value the risk of the transaction as:

$$REE = \text{US\$250m} + \max(0,(50{,}000 * ((0.14 * 575) + (575 - 600))))$$

$$= \text{US\$250m} + 0 \text{ or } (50{,}000 * ((80.5) + (225)))$$

$$= \text{US\$250m} + \text{US\$2.775m}$$

$$= \text{US\$3.025m}$$

Note that Barrier, 610, is replaced by SP, 600, since the two are not equal. This type of approach is clearly most conservative as it assumes the barrier will be breached and the European call created. If Bank C does not wish to value the option until the barrier is hit, it simply allocates the US$250,000 time value component of premium against credit limits. If CMP reaches the barrier at 610, it immediately adds the additional exposure against F's credit lines.

Up and out option

In this structure an option ceases to exist once an upper barrier is reached; if the barrier is not reached, the option generates a payoff equivalent to a standard European put or call. The credit risk associated with this derivative consists of premium (time value) paid, plus potential intrinsic value until the option is extinguished (if ever). If the barrier is breached, the option extinguishes and the transaction terminates, with no further performance required by the seller. If the barrier is not breached the option continues to exist in standard European form, with intrinsic value (and, hence, credit risk) to the buyer. In this instance, however, the maximum level that can be attained before the option is extinguished dictates the maximum amount of credit exposure (that is, just fractionally below the barrier level). The exposure is highlighted in Equations 8.3 for calls and 6.4 for puts (for reasons discussed below):

$$REE = prem + (NC * (Barrier - SP)) + \min(0, (NC * (CMP - SP))) \quad (8.3)$$

With an up and out call, the strike price SP must be less than the barrier or there is no incentive for a bank to purchase the structure. If the barrier is 100 (that is, the call is knocked out) and the SP is 100 (or greater), the bank will not receive an economic benefit (that is, CMP − SP) because the call is extinguished; the call only has value to the buyer when CMP is greater than SP and SP is less than the barrier.

For puts, we need only refer to Equation 6.4 to obtain an estimate of REE. Since an up and out put extinguishes when the barrier is breached by the CMP, this indicates the option is moving further out-of-the-money (implying reduced credit risk) until it is eventually eliminated. For this reason it is only necessary to value the normal credit risk on the put, as in Equation 6.4. As the put moves further in-the-money, it is moving further away from the barrier; there is therefore no likelihood it will be extinguished and more chance that it will be exercised. This implies increased reliance on the performance of the seller.

Let us consider the following example. Bank S purchases from Bank GHI a six-month up and out call on the DAX (10,000 contracts), struck at

2500 in a 2400 market, with a barrier at 2650. Bank S pays €100,000 in premium (time value). The maximum risk attributable to the option is:

$$REE = €100{,}000 + (10{,}000 * (2650 - 2500)) + \min(0, (10{,}000 * (2400 - 2500)))$$

$$= €M100{,}000 + (10{,}000 * 150) + \min(0, (10{,}000 * (- 100)))$$

$$= €100{,}000 + €1.5m + (- €1m)$$

$$= €600{,}000$$

If the DAX option moves in-the-money during the life of the transaction (that is, any value above 2500), S experiences increasing credit exposure, to a maximum level of 2650. The maximum loss S can sustain in the event GHI defaults (just prior to the barrier being breached) is €1.5m, plus the remaining premium (time value). If the barrier of 2650 is breached the option extinguishes and all credit exposure disappears. Note that in this equation we also subtract the out-of-the-money portion of the transaction. It is possible, of course, to exclude the out-of-the-money portion of the equation and simply value the maximum exposure that can be encountered (that is, the difference between the barrier and SP).

Down and in option

In this structure a European option is created once a barrier is breached on the downside. The approach taken to valuing credit risk exposure in this instance is similar to the up and in option described above, where a bank can opt for a conservative or liberal view. In more conservative terms, a bank includes both the time value component of premium and the potential market exposure of an option which may, or may not, come into existence; this can be adjusted for moneyness. Under the liberal approach, a bank values the premium (time value), only adding in the option's market exposure if the barrier is hit. The risk equations used in this analysis are similar to those illustrated in Equations 8.1 and 8.2 above, except for an inversion of the conditions that compare the barrier and CMP levels. Equations 8.4A and 8.4B for calls are shown as:

when CMP > Barrier
$$REE = prem \tag{8.4A}$$

when CMP < Barrier
$$REE = prem + \max(0, (NC * ((RFc * CMP) + (CMP - Barrier)))) \tag{8.4B}$$

Equations 8.5A and 8.5B for puts are shown as:

when CMP > Barrier
$$REE = prem \tag{8.5A}$$

when CMP < Barrier
$$REE = prem + \max(0, (NC * ((RFc * CMP) + (Barrier - CMP)))) \tag{8.5B}$$

Again, *Barrier* is replaced by SP if the two are not equal.

Let us consider the following example. Bank LMN purchases a 12-month down and in put (5000 contracts) on the Hang Seng for HK$200,000 in premium (time value); the option is struck at 10,500 in a 10,800 market, and has a barrier at 10,400. Based on an RF of 30 percent the REE is equal to:

$$REE = \text{HK\$200,000} + \max(0, (5000 * ((0.30 * 10,800) + (10,500 - 10,800))))$$

$$= \text{HK\$200,000} + \max(0, (5000 * ((3240) + (2300))))$$

$$= \text{HK\$200,000} + \text{HK\$14.7m}$$

$$= \text{HK\$14.9m}$$

The initial REE of HK$14.9m is updated on a constant basis through an adjustment to RFc and premium time value, which continues to decay. If the Hang Seng falls to 10,401, the option moves in-the-money but has no value to the buyer; if the barrier is breached during the life of the trade the option at that moment is HK$500,000 in-the-money (that is, it is a reverse down and in put). From the less conservative point of view highlighted in Equation 8.5A, the only risk exposure attributed to the option is premium (time value) of HK$200,000 until the underlying price of the Hang Seng falls below the barrier (if ever).

Down and out option

In this structure an option is extinguished once a barrier is breached on the downside. From a risk perspective the analysis of a down and out option is similar to the up and out option discussed above. Specifically, until the option's barrier is breached the buyer faces normal option risk (that is, premium (time value) plus the potential market movements on the put or call itself). Once again, the limiting factor in determining maximum credit risk is the barrier, rather than RF; once breached, the option ceases to exist and credit risk exposure disappears. Equation 8.6 summarizes the credit risk equivalency for down and out puts:

$$REE = prem + (NC * (SP - Barrier)) + \min(0, (NC * (SP - CMP)))   (8.6)$$

Just as the up and out put REE equation focuses on the risk attributable to a normal put option, the down and out call REE is based on the standard risk formula reflected in Equation 6.3. Once again, a down and out call becomes ineffective once CMP falls below the barrier; as this occurs the call moves farther out-of-the-money and therefore carries no credit risk other than premium (because the call only has value once CMP is greater than SP, which means it is moving away from the knock-out barrier). Once the barrier is reached and the call is knocked out, all credit risk disappears.

Let us consider the following examples. Bank A purchases from Bank RST 10,000 down and out put contracts (¥1/contract) on the Nikkei 225, struck at 18,000 in a 19,000 market, with a barrier at 16,000. The premium (time value) is ¥1m and transaction maturity is nine months. Credit risk exposure of this option, per Equation 8.6, is:

$$REE = ¥1m + (10,000 * (18,000 - 16,000)) + \min(0, (10,000 * (18,000 - 19,000)))$$

$$= ¥1m + (10,000 * 2000) + \min(0, (10,000 * (-1000)))$$

$$= ¥1m + ¥20m + -¥10m$$

$$= ¥1m + ¥10m$$

$$= ¥11m$$

If the put travels to its minimum level before knockout, 16,001, and RST defaults, A loses a total of nearly ¥20m plus the remaining time value component of premium. Note that the equation above adjusts for the current moneyness of the option; since the option is out-of-the-money, the full ¥20m of potential payout is not reflected. Institutions opting for a more conservative allocation against credit limits may ignore the adjustment for moneyness (for example, the second component of the equation). Again, no risk factors are utilized since the determining factor of maximum market movement is not the potential movement in the Nikkei, but the lower bound on the knock-out.

If Bank A purchases a call, instead of a put, with the same trade details above (and assuming an initial RFc of 17.5 percent), the REE equals:

REE $= \yen1m + \max(0, (10,000 * ((0.175 * 19,000) + (19,000 - 18,000))))$

$\quad = \yen1m + \max(0, (10,000 * ((3325) + (1000))))$

$\quad = \yen1m + \yen43.25m$

$\quad = \yen44.25m$

As the CMP moves away from the barrier of 16,000, the call moves further in-the-money. Thus, upside risk is not confined to the difference between the strike and the barrier, as in the case of the put; rather, it is dependent on upside market movements dictated by RFc. As the CMP moves down to the barrier the call moves farther out-of-the-money; depending on the time left to maturity (which is reflected, as we know, by an ever-declining RFc) the only amount at risk may be the remaining time value of premium. This, in turn, equals zero once the down and out barrier is reached.

Asian/average price options

An average price option is a derivative that provides a payoff equal to the difference between the strike price and the average price of the underlying reference over a prespecified period. The determination of REE for an average price option can take one of several forms. Under the most conservative approach, an institution can simply apply Equation 6.3 for average price calls and 6.4 for average price puts. Since the RF in the equation is designed to quantify the maximum market movement in the underlying reference variable, it obviously captures the average market movement derived over the averaging period; in all cases the terminal value of the underlying reference, as predicted by RF, will exceed the average value of the underlying, yielding a more conservative REE computation. This particular approach might be especially useful for average options that tend towards a standard European option (that is, short averaging periods close to expiry). For average price options based on an extended averaging period (for example, one which begins to approach the entire life of the transaction), use of an average worst case (or expected) RF, instead of a terminal worst case (or expected) RF, might be appropriate.[16]

Consider the following example. Bank XYZ purchases from Dealer MNO a 12-month average price call (10,000 contracts) on stock DEF for US$200,000 of premium (time value); the option is struck at US$100 in a US$100 market. Using an RF of 50 percent, the standard call option Equation 6.3 generates REE of US$700,000; this might be an appropriate estimate if the averaging period is particularly short and concentrated towards the end of the transaction. Alternatively, average worst-case REE equals

US$535,000; this estimate might be appropriate if the averaging period is particularly long (perhaps approximately the entire maturity of the option).

Asian/average strike options

An average strike option is a derivative that generates a payoff equal to the difference between the terminal price and an average strike price determined by the path of the underlying over a prespecified period. Quantifying the REE of an average strike option is more challenging than it is for an average price option, primarily because the strike price is not known in advance and its value is dependent on an average over a period of time. Some comfort can be taken, however, in knowing that the REE of an average strike option will, in all cases, be lower than the REE for a corresponding European option of the same maturity (for the reasons described above). As before, standard REE can be used for average strike options that feature short averaging periods, while average REE can be employed for options with very long averaging periods. Since the strike price is unknown on trade date, we make the simplifying assumption in both cases that it is equal to the current market price on trade date, and the terminal value of CMP is predictable through the RF process. Alternatively, we can develop a more precise framework, such as the one outlined in the note for average price options.

Floating strike lookback options

A floating strike lookback option provides the buyer with a payoff based on maximum market movement experienced during the life of the transaction. This generates maximum economic gain, and thus maximum credit risk, at maturity. One means by which to estimate the credit risk of a lookback is to quantify the option through Equations 6.3 and 6.4. Since the RF framework provides information on the maximum expected market movement during the life of the option we can be quite certain (to the appropriate confidence level) that the figure obtained from RF incorporates the value of the actual payoff at the conclusion of the option. Thus, no changes are required to the underlying risk formulae.

Although the same risk equations can be utilized, we note certain timing differences between lookbacks and conventional options. In order for a bank purchasing a conventional option to lose the maximum amount estimated by REE it must suffer counterparty default when the option has moved to the maximum in-the-money point indicated by RF; naturally, the two events are not likely to coincide with frequency. Thus, while a bank might sustain a loss due to counterparty default, it is unlikely to be the maximum loss predicted by REE. With a lookback, however, timing of default is most critical at maturity since this point always reflects the maximum value of the option (that is, at maturity the parties look back and determine the maximum value of the option and effect a payment based on such a review). Therefore, any risk officer considering lookbacks must be sensitive to the final maturity of the transaction, since this is when maximum risk occurs.

Options on the maximum/minimum

Options on the maximum or minimum permit the buyer to generate a gain equal to the difference between the strike and the maximum (for calls) or minimum (for puts) of the underlying market reference during the life of the transaction. Quantifying the REE of options on the maximum/minimum is based on use of standard call and put Equations 6.3 and 6.4. Under the REE framework, we assume the underlying market variable governing a call on the maximum or put on the minimum generates maximum market movement to the upside or downside. Accordingly, the maximum payout on either option is based on the maximum market movement indicated by RF. As with floating strike lookbacks above, the timing of counterparty default in a call on the maximum or a put on the minimum is most critical at maturity, since the derivatives generate maximum payoff at the conclusion of the transaction (through a "hindsight" review of the maximum or minimum points). As such, options on the maximum/minimum are more credit-sensitive to default timing than conventional options.

Consider an example where Bank JKL purchases a six-month Nikkei put on the minimum (1000 contracts at ¥1/contract) from Bank ABC. Assume the six-month Nikkei 225 RF is 18 percent and the premium (time value) paid for the option is ¥1m. Under standard Equation 6.4 the upfront REE of the put on the minimum is:

$$REE = \text{¥1m} + \max(0, (1000 * ((0.18 * 19{,}000) + (19{,}000 - 19{,}000))))$$

$$= \text{¥1m} + (1000 * 3420)$$

$$= \text{¥1m} + \text{¥3.42m}$$

$$= \text{¥4.42m}$$

The maximum REE JKL expects to face with ABC during the life of the transaction is ¥4.42m. Assume the Nikkei falls to a low of 16,500 and ends at 17,500; if ABC defaults at the conclusion of the transaction, JKL experiences a credit loss of ¥2.5m ((19,000 – 16,500) * 1000) despite the fact that the index ends 1000 points above the minimum (note that there is no longer any premium time value at risk as the entire amount decays by maturity).

High–low options

A high–low option is a derivative which pays the difference between the high and low points achieved by the underlying reference during the life of the option. Accordingly, to estimate the REE of a high–low option we focus on the maximum and minimum points attained by the reference between trade date and maturity. For instance, beginning at a market level m, the variable can move up to point CMP(u) and down to point CMP(d). The difference between CMP(u) and CMP(d) generates the payoff of the option. Through the RF framework we can estimate a maximum move to CMP(u) by (CMP * (1 + RF)); we can also estimate a movement to CMP(d) by (CMP * (1 − RF)). The difference of the two must equal the maximum payoff under the option. We note, however, that once CMP(u) is attained, the relevant starting point for the downward calculation is not CMP, but CMP(u); the minimum point which can therefore be achieved is (CMP(u) * (1 − RF)). For example, if the starting point for evaluation in a 12-month trade is 100 and the annual RF is 33 percent (for example, 20 percent volatility, 90 percent confidence level), CMP(u) equals 133; the payoff of a call on the maximum would equal 33. If the maximum is reached at the six-month mark, CMP(u) equals 123 (for example, 100 * (1+ (0.20 * 1.65 * $\sqrt{0.5}$))); if the downward movement is maximized from that point on, CMP(d) is 94.7 (123 * (1 − (0.20 * 1.65 * $\sqrt{0.5}$))). The payoff under this scenario equals 28.3 (123 − 94.7). As the time interval for upward or downward movement is drawn to trade date or maturity date, the estimated payoff via the RF framework tends to increase slightly; instead of taking the square root of the maturity, we are "overcompensating" by taking the square root of two separate time intervals which, by definition, is greater (note that we make a simplifying assumption about the distribution of the variables, as discussed later in the chapter). The movements, however, approximate the maximum market movement estimated by a continuous up or down move in the standard REE framework; as such, it is entirely reasonable to utilize standard Equations 6.3 or 6.4 to generate an exposure estimate of the high–low option.

Partial lookback/reset options

A partial lookback option is a derivative that resets during its life if it is out-of-the-money on reset date. Although partial lookbacks can be structured in slightly different ways (for example, single reset period, multiple reset periods, reset on a prespecified date, reset at any time, and so on), we focus our REE evaluation on a single reset lookback, where the option is effectively "re-written" at-the-money if it is out-of-the-money on the reset date. In addition to premium (time value) paid to secure the option, the REE analysis focuses on two distinct items: how far the market moves by the prespecified reset date, and how much it moves from reset date to maturity date. This approach is very similar to the one discussed above for high–low options. For a partial lookback we first apply the RF to CMP to determine the maximum upward–downward movement of the underlying between trade date and reset date. From that point on, the original strike price is replaced with a new strike price (equal to the level estimated by the RF), and a new RF (reflecting the remaining time to maturity) is applied to the current market price to provide an estimate of the maximum expected terminal value of the underlying. As discussed in the section on high–low options, in most cases this value will be equal to, or less than, the REE computed for a standard option; as such, Equations 6.3 and 6.4 can be used to generate an REE estimate for partial lookback calls and puts, respectively.

Ladder options

A fixed strike ladder option is a derivative that locks in gains once the underlying reference reaches prespecified market levels. In addition to premium (time value) the REE quantification of a ladder option focuses on the location of the "rungs" of the ladder in relation to the maximum market movement of the underlying (as estimated through RF). Using standard REE call and put Equations 6.3 and 6.4, we can quantify the upfront REE of a ladder in the same manner as a vanilla put or call. The critical difference between a ladder option and a conventional option occurs once a given rung is reached: when this happens the fractional risk exposure attributable to the transaction becomes actual exposure and is never reduced, even if the market subsequently retraces. In order to reflect the value of the option that is effectively "locked in," we reclassify the difference between the strike price and ladder rungs as realized value (actual exposure) once the market level breaches each rung. The remaining REE of the transaction can then be calculated based on a "new" option struck at the last rung reached, calibrated for the remaining time to maturity. Once each rung is passed, the new REE can be calculated through Equation 8.7 for calls:

$$REE = prem + RV + \max(0, (NC * ((RF_{cn} * CMP) + (CMP - SP_n)))) \quad (8.7)$$

and 8.8 for puts:

$$REE = prem + RV + \max(0, (NC * ((RF_{cn} * CMP) + (SP_n - CMP)))) \quad (8.8)$$

where: RV is the realized value that is locked in at each rung; RF_{cn} is the constantly adjusted risk factor for the "new" option; SP_n is the strike price for the "new" option: and all other terms are as defined above.

Consider the following example. Bank X purchases, from Bank Y, a six-month ladder call on 10,000 shares of stock ABC for US$80,000 in premium (time value). The option is struck at US$50 in a US$50 market and has a single rung at US$60. Given an initial RF of 46 percent, the REE, per Equation 6.3, is:

$$REE = US\$80,000 + \max(0, (10\ 000 * ((0.46 * 50) + (50 - 50))))$$

$$= US\$80,000 + US\$230,000$$

$$= US\$310,000$$

Since the transaction has just commenced, REE is comprised solely of potential intrinsic value plus the time value component of premium. Assume three months into the deal the stock price rises to US$61, breaching the first ladder rung. The minimum payoff Bank X will receive at maturity is US$100,000 ((60 – 50) * 10,000), regardless of the terminal value of stock ABC. At this stage X's credit exposure to Y is, with certainty, US$100,000; this is the variable RV reflected in Equation 8.7. As a second step, X can view its exposure as the sum of the realized value (US$100,000), the remaining time value portion of premium paid (assume US$40,000), and the potential market exposure of a "new" three-month option struck at the rung level of US$60. The total REE is summarized by Equation 8.7 as:

$$REE = US\$40,000 + US\$100,000 + \max(0, (10,000 * ((0.33 * 61) + (61 - 60))))$$

$$= US\$140,000 + US\$211,300$$

$$= US\$351,300$$

Note that this figure is close to the *ex ante* calculation of US$310,000. In addition to a more conservative readjustment for the remaining time period, which causes a proportionally higher RF, a notable point is that the composition of REE has changed. At inception of the transaction REE comprises fractional exposure, while three months into the deal nearly half of the REE is actual, rather than fractional, exposure. More importantly, this is a minimum level of credit exposure X faces throughout the remaining life of the deal, as it is locked in by the ladder structure. Naturally, if the stock price of ABC never rises to the ladder rung or, indeed, drops below the initial strike, the REE attributable to the transaction is identical to that of any vanilla call. Ladders with multiple rungs can be evaluated in the same fashion. As each ladder rung is breached and gains are locked in, fractional exposure can be converted into actual exposure and the REE of a "new" option, based on the latest rung to be breached and the remaining time to maturity, can be computed. As discussed earlier in the chapter, ladder options can also be created in floating strike form; the equations above can be adapted to accommodate the floating strike version of this option.

Cliquet options

A cliquet option locks in gains once the underlying reference passes prespecified time periods. Given the similarities between cliquets and ladder options, the REE determination is identical to that described in the section immediately above. We begin by quantifying the REE of a cliquet through standard Equations 6.3 and 6.4. As before, we assume the underlying market variable will move to the maximum level predicted by the relevant RF; this generates an upfront REE that is the same as that of a vanilla call or put. As specific time intervals are passed, and assuming that at each point the cliquet is in-the-money, the fractional exposure is converted into actual exposure that is never reversed (regardless of subsequent market movements). As with ladder options, it is possible to then rewrite the REE of an in-the-money cliquet via modified Equations 8.7 and 8.8 (for example, the sum of realized actual exposure, remaining premium (time value), and the specific REE of a "new" option struck at the market level on evaluation date (the "new" option reflects the remaining, rather than original, maturity of the transaction). The same process can be repeated for each subsequent cliquet evaluation period. Note that if the option is out-of-the-money during a prespecified time interval, the strike resets to the lower (for calls) or higher (for puts) market level; maximum credit exposure does not change, however, as we have quantified maximum upward or downward movements via RF (that is, smaller movements, even for a "new" option struck at-the-money, are already contained within the REE estimate). The interim REE can simply be quantified by standard Equations 6.3 or 6.4, reflecting an option struck at-the-money with a lower RFc and shorter time to maturity.

Consider the following example. Bank QRS purchases a six month cliquet call (3000 contracts) on the All Ordinaries from Securities Firm UVW for A$100,000 in premium (time value); the option is struck at-the-money (2000) and contains monthly evaluation intervals. Using a six-month RF of 32 percent, the upfront REE using Equation 6.3 is:

$$REE = \text{A\$100,000} + \max(0, (3000 * ((0.32 * 2000) + (2000 - 2000))))$$

$$= \text{A\$100,000} + \text{A\$1,920,000}$$

$$= \text{A\$2,020,000}$$

Assume during the first interval the All Ords declines to 1900. In this instance, no actual exposure exists (for example, there is no mark-to-market, or intrinsic, value to QRS) and the option resets to the new lower market level of 1900. In this example the only REE to account for is the potential market risk of a new at-the-money option struck at 1900, with five months remaining until maturity, plus residual time value of premium. During the second interval assume the All Ords rises to 2100. Using Equation 8.7, REE is now comprised of the realized value (measured from 1900 to 2100), the remaining premium (time value) and the potential market risk assigned to a new at-the-money option struck at 2100 (with four months to maturity). As with the ladder option, the cliquet's risk is now appropriately split into actual and fractional components, where the actual exposure represents true credit exposure that never declines. As before, the conservative readjustment of RF for the remaining time period provides a slightly higher adjustment to remaining REE. If, during subsequent evaluation periods, there is a further rise in the index, the same process is repeated (that is, the intrinsic value is locked in as actual exposure, and a new fractional exposure is determined based on an option struck at the market level during the evaluation period, with an adjustment for the remaining maturity of the transaction).

Shout options

A shout option is a derivative that locks in gains when the purchaser "shouts" and crystallizes intrinsic value; given the structural similarities between ladders, cliquets, and shouts, we employ a methodology similar to the one detailed above in order to quantify the REE of the fixed strike version of the shout. As before, the initial step focuses on determining the maximum possible market movement for a shout call or put using standard vanilla call and put Equations 6.3 and 6.4. While the most conservative view suggests the purchaser shouts once the market reaches a maximum as indicated by RF, timing of the market is unlikely to be that perfect. As such, the REE process can be split into a second phase, which occurs once the buyer has shouted and locked in gains. In the second phase, actual exposure is locked in for the remaining life of the transaction and the remaining fractional exposure is recomputed based on a "new" option struck at the market level at which the shout occurred, with an adjustment for the remaining time to maturity. If the deal incorporates multiple shouts, the same process can be repeated each time a shout occurs. The ongoing risk can thus be quantified using modified Equations 8.7 and 8.8. The same process can also be adapted to accommodate floating strike shouts.

Installment options

An installment option is a derivative that permits the purchaser to pay premium in installments (rather than upfront), and cancel the underlying contract at any time by ceasing any payments that remain. Since an installment option is a European option with premium paid over a period of time, the risk attributable to the option can be approximated through standard Equations 6.3 and 6.4; the RF is based on the time period between the start date and the final maturity of the transaction (where the start date depends on whether the underlying option is forward or spot starting). Unlike standard options, however, the premium (time value) component of the REE equation reflects the fractional portion paid at each installment date, rather than the full amount paid under a conventional option. From the standpoint of the installment option seller, the receipt of premium in deferred fashion might be construed as credit risk. This, however, is likely to be an overly conservative treatment since, by its very construction, the installment option always stands a chance of being cancelled. If the buyer misses an installment payment, through financial difficulties or lack of need, the seller simply cancels the option under the terms of the agreement.

Consider the following example. Bank CDE purchases an installment put (10m contracts) from Bank PQR on CHF/$ (that is, CHF put/$ call) for total premium of CHF600,000, payable in two monthly installments of CHF300,000 each. The underlying option is struck at-the-money (CHF1.60/$), carries a 12-month maturity, and commences on trade date (spot start); the RF attributable to 12-month CHF/$ is 13 percent. The upfront REE, per Equation 6.4, is given as:

$$REE = CHF300,000 + max(0, (10m * ((0.13 * 1.60) + (1.60 - 1.60))))$$

$$= CHF300,000 + CHF1.3m$$

$$= CHF1.6m$$

Only the first installment of the premium (time value) payment is counted as REE. If Bank PQR defaults between trade date and the second installment date, CDE loses its fractional premium payment plus any actual exposure. Note that for ease we show REE spanning the full maturity of the transaction (rather than until the second installment period). Once the second installment period is reached, and CDE forwards a further CHF300,000 in premium to gain the full effects of the currency option, its total REE will equal premium (less the portion attributable to normal time decay) plus fractional exposure of the option.

Path independent options

Binary options

A binary option is a derivative that generates a discontinuous payoff once a strike price is exceeded. From a credit risk perspective it is vital to focus on the maximum amount a bank expects to receive if the price of the underlying reference breaches the strike price at expiry (conventional binary) or prior to expiry (one-touch binary, or binary–barrier (we again remind the reader that the binary–barrier subset of this group is actually a path dependent derivative)). Given the binary nature of the payoff, these derivatives are relatively straightforward to analyze from a credit risk perspective. In a cash-or-nothing or asset-or-nothing option the payout equals either a fixed cash or asset amount M (if the strike is breached), or zero (if the strike is not breached). The purchaser of a long cash or asset-or-nothing option expects to receive a fixed amount M from the seller once the strike is reached, and therefore faces credit risk exposure to the seller. In addition to relying on the option seller for delivery of the fixed amount M if the instrument moves or ends in-the-money, the option buyer may be paying a significant premium for the potential benefit (depending on the fixed amount M receivable under the contract). The REE for a binary call or put is given as:

$$REE = prem + M \qquad (8.9)$$

where *prem* is the time value component of option premium and *M* is the fixed cash or asset amount of the trade (as agreed between buyer and seller).

Note that the standard RF framework is not utilized in the equation. This approach simply assumes the option will be exercised, with a full amount M due to the buyer. It is conceivable, of course, that the underlying option is struck so far out-of-the-money that it is virtually certain to end without value; in this instance a bank may wish only to consider the time value component of premium paid as potential credit risk. It should be noted that these approaches can also be applied to binary–barriers. However, for the general class of binary–barrier at expiry options there is a delay between exercise and receipt of cash or physical proceeds, indicating that maximum market movement and counterparty default need not coincide to produce the worst case credit loss.

Let us consider the following example. Bank Q purchases from Dealer CDE a six-month cash-or-nothing call on the S&P 500 struck at 600 (in a 540 market), which pays off a fixed cash amount of US$3m if the option ends in-the-money. Q pays US$1m of premium (time value) for the derivative. The associated REE, per Equation 8.9, equals US$4m; if CDE defaults when the S&P index is over 600, Q loses the remaining portion of premium (time value) plus the fixed US$3m payment.

Rainbow/multi-Index options

Rainbow options are broadly defined as derivatives that generate payoffs based on the relative performance of two or more indexes. We consider, in this section, the REE estimation for options on the best/worst of n-assets and cash, options on the best/worst of n-assets, multiple strike options, spread options, and basket options

Options on the best/worst of n-assets and cash

Options on the best/worst of n-assets and cash are derivatives that deliver to the buyer the largest or smallest gains from one of several assets and a prespecified amount of cash. REE quantification is based on premium (time value) and the maximum or minimum market movement associated with any individual asset in the structure, or cash. Although the risk officer considering a best/worst of option does not know in advance which specific asset will generate the best or worst performance, one approach focuses on the asset which exhibits the highest historical volatility, under the assumption that such volatility will exist into the future and drive the underlying asset to its maximum or minimum point (it may also be necessary to compare high price/low volatility and low price/high volatility assets to make sure the most "damaging" case is captured). The gain attained by any individual asset represents, of course, the buyer's anticipated payoff; it also represents the maximum credit exposure the buyer has to the seller of the option. If the volatility evaluation yields a potential economic payoff which is less than the fixed cash amount C (for best of options), or greater than the fixed cash amount C (for worst of options), the buyer expects to receive the cash amount as its payoff; this, then, represents its credit risk exposure. Note that on an ongoing basis assets can be substituted dynamically to reflect the current best/worst performers; in addition, RFc and premium (time value) can be adjusted downward as time to maturity declines. The formula for an option on the best of n-assets and cash is summarized in Equation 8.10:

$$REE = prem + \max(C, (NC * \max(((1 + RF_{c1}) * CMP_1), \ldots, \qquad (8.10)$$
$$((1 + RF_{cn}) * CMP_n))))$$

The REE formula for an option on the worst of n-assets and cash is summarized in Equation 8.11:

$$REE = prem + \min(C, (NC * \min(((1 - RF_{c1}) * CMP_1), \ldots, \qquad (8.11)$$
$$((1 - RF_{cn}) * CMP_n))))$$

where *prem* is the time value component of option premium: C is the fixed cash payoff; NC is the number of option contracts; RF_{c1} is the risk factor associated with the first asset; CMP_1 is the current market price associated with the first asset; RF_{cn} is the risk factor associated with the n-th asset; and CMP_n is the current market price associated with the n-th asset.

Note that Equations 8.10 and 8.11 do not include specific strike prices since the options carry no predetermined strikes and always end with a minimum, non-zero, value. Interestingly, the payoff for an option on the worst of n-assets and cash is structured so that the purchaser receives the minimum of the relevant assets/cash; as such, this is a unique situation where credit risk exposure focuses on the minimum, rather than maximum, market movements of the assets in the portfolio and attributes credit risk exposure to the smallest, rather than largest, amount obtained.

Consider the following example. Bank RST purchases from Dealer LMN 100,000 contracts on the best performing of stock X, stock Y, and US$300,000 cash. Stock X trades at US$10/share and has an RF of 30 percent, while stock Y trades at US$10/share and has an RF of 60 percent. The *ex ante* REE, including US$200,000 of premium (time value), equals:

$$REE = US\$200,000 + \max(US\$300,000, (100,000 * \max(((1.30) * 10), ((1.60) * 10))))$$

$$= US\$200,000 + \max(US\$300,000, US\$1.3m, US\$1.6m)$$

$$= US\$1.8m$$

Based on the RF framework, stock Y is assumed to be the *ex ante* best performing asset, capable of generating a potential gain – and therefore credit exposure – of US$1.6m over the life of the transaction (plus premium). Assume that just prior to maturity, when premium (time value) has decayed to zero and RFc is zero, stock X trades at US$6/share and stock Y trades at US$8/share. The payoff to RST is US$800,000; if LMN defaults at this point, RST loses this amount with certainty.

Options on the best/worst of n-assets

Options on the best/worst of n-assets are derivatives that generate an economic gain by comparing underlying prices of various assets against a single, predetermined, strike price. The asset generating the largest gain (that is, either the best or worst performing) provides the option buyer with the relevant economic payoff. If all underlying reference prices end below the strike price (for calls) or above the strike price (for puts), the option expires worthless. Unlike the options discussed above, options on the best/worst of n-assets do not guarantee minimum cash payment. For purposes of this discussion we focus on the two most popular versions of the structure: the call on the best of n-assets and the put on the worst of n-assets. These two derivatives provide purchasers with the largest potential economic gains and, hence, largest potential credit exposures (REE estimates for a call on the worst of n-assets and a put on the best of n-assets can easily be derived from the equations below).

REE quantification of these derivatives is based on premium (time value) plus market risk associated with the differential between the strike and the best (or worst) performing reference asset. Since the risk officer considering this derivative does not know in advance which asset will produce the greatest gain, it can follow an approach conceptually similar to the one summarized in Equations 8.10 and 8.11 above. To begin, the buyer can identify the volatility of each individual reference asset and assume such volatility will carry the asset to its maximum or minimum point during the life of the trade. As a second step, each asset can be compared against the preset strike price to determine which generates the maximum economic gain and, hence, credit exposure. Since the review of credit exposure is a dynamic process, maximum REE is likely to change over the course of the transaction, as markets begin to favor specific assets in the portfolio. Nonetheless, in most instances interim credit exposure should be less than that predicted by the upfront REE computation. Note that the payoff of a put on the worst of n-assets is distinct from the option on the worst n-assets and cash discussed above. In the case of the option on the worst of n-assets and cash, we have developed an REE framework based on minimum market movement, but for the put on the worst of n-assets we generate an REE framework based on maximum market movement; this provides REE estimates that are consistent with the payoff of the underlying derivatives. The REE equation for a call on the best of n-assets is shown as:

$$REE = prem + \max(0, (NC * \max(((((1 + RF_{c1}) * CMP1), \ldots, \qquad (8.12)$$
$$((1 + RF_{cn}) * CMP_n)) - SP)))$$

The REE for a put on the worst of n-assets is shown as:

$$REE = prem + \max(0, (NC * (SP - \min(((1 - RF_{c1}) * CMP1), \ldots, \qquad (8.13)$$
$$((1 - RF_{cn}) * CMP_n)))))$$

Consider the following example. In order to express a specific view on individual equities in a portfolio, Investment Bank XYZ purchases a put on the worst of three stocks from Bank JKL. The put is based on 100,000 contracts and matures in six months; premium (time value) paid for the option is US$100,000. The assets underlying the option include stock Q (with an RF of 35 percent and current price of US$20/share), stock R (RF of 40 percent, CMP of US$25/share), and stock S (RF of 50 percent, CMP of US$30/share). The strike price of the put is set at US$18 (note that although S has the highest RF, it is also struck furthest from the money). Based on Equation 8.13 the upfront REE is:

REE = US$100,000 + max(0, (100,000 * (18 – min(((1 – 0.35) * 20), ((1 – 0.4) * 25), ((1 – 0.5) * 30))))))

= US$100,000 + max(0, (100,000 * (18 – min(13, 15, 15))))

= US$600,000

Assume that, just prior to maturity, Q trades at US$17/share, R at US$16/share and S at US$22/share. If ABC defaults at this point (when RFc is zero and time value has decayed to zero), the economic loss to XYZ is:

REE = US$0 + max(0, (100,000 * (18 – min(17, 16, 22))))

= US$200,000

Multiple strike options

A multiple strike option is a derivative that generates a payoff based on the best or worst performing of a group of assets in a portfolio. Since each underlying asset has its own strike price, the structure can be viewed as a mini-portfolio of options. The REE estimate focuses on premium (time value) and market risk associated with individual asset prices and strike prices contained within the structure. The market risk quantification is based on the volatility and moneyness of each individual component, and REE is assigned on the basis of maximum projected value. As only one component can carry maximum value (and hence maximum credit risk) at any point in time, it is necessary to identify the component that meets this requirement, both upfront and continuously. The REE for multiple strike calls can be estimated via Equation 8.14:

$$REE = prem + max(0, NC * (max(((RF_{c1} * CMP1) + (CMP_1 - SP_1)), \ldots, + ((RF_{cn} * CMP_n) + (CMP_n - SP_n)))))) \qquad (8.14)$$

while the REE for puts can be computed through Equation 8.15:

$$REE = prem + max(0, (NC * (max(((RF_{c1} * CMP_1) + (SP_1 - CMP_1)), \ldots, + ((RF_{cn} * CMP_n) + (SP_n - CMP_n)))))))) \qquad (8.15)$$

Consider the following example. Dealer DEF wants to receive the gains from the best performing of three bonds. To do so, it purchases from

Bank PQR a 12-month multiple strike call (20,000 contracts) for US$150,000 in premium (time value). The option returns the greatest economic gains achieved by one of three securities: Bond A (which trades at 95 and carries an RF of 25 percent), Bond B (which trades at 97 and carries an RF of 30 percent), and Bond C (which trades at 94 and carries an RF of 35 percent). Each component of the option is struck at-the-money. The initial REE of this transaction, per Equation 8.14, is:

$$REE = US\$150,000 + \max(0, (20,000 * \max(((0.25 * 95) + (95 - 95)),$$
$$((0.30 * 97) + (97 - 97)), (0.35 * 94) + (94 - 94))))$$

$$= US\$150,000 + US\$658,000$$

$$= US\$808,000$$

Assume that just prior to maturity (when RF and premium (time value) are both equal to zero), Bond A is quoted at 98, Bond B at 94, and Bond C at 98. The REE is now equal to:

$$REE = US\$0 + \max(0, (20,000 * \max((98 - 95), (94 - 97), (98 - 94))))$$

$$= US\$0 + (20,000 * \max(3, -3, 4))$$

$$= US\$80,000$$

If PQR defaults at this point DEF loses, with certainty, US$80,000, which is the payoff it is anticipating from the best performing of the assets in the multiple strike structure.

Spread options

A spread option provides a payoff based on the spread, or differential, between related, or unrelated, reference assets. The REE quantification for spread options (and basket options, discussed below) is more complex than the conventional one-factor derivatives we have discussed because, though we have assumed underlying market variables in the RF framework are lognormally distributed, it is not possible for two lognormally distributed market variables to be combined (added, subtracted, or otherwise manipulated) to obtain a lognormally distributed spread. To overcome this difficulty, we must make certain assumptions on how to treat the spread movement. Several alternatives exist, though all have some limitations:

■ Assume that the spread itself is an asset price which is lognormally distributed (the spread is an asset which follows, for instance, a geometric Brownian motion); while this permits use of the RF framework, it also suggests that spreads cannot be negative, which may be restrictive.

■ Assume the spread is distributed normally (or in some other fashion), rather than lognormally; this, as we might expect, requires adjustments to the RF framework and is a mathematically complex undertaking.

■ Utilize a two-factor approach, which involves examination of the distribution of each of the two variables and use of correlations; this process is based on assumptions about the size and direction of correlation, a measure which is notoriously unstable and difficult to observe.

Though simplified, we present our discussion based on the first alternative, which says the reference spread itself is a stochastic asset that can be estimated via a spread-based RF. As we are primarily concerned with obtaining maximum credit exposure of the spread, we will not concern ourselves with scenarios where the spread has no value to the purchaser (for example, when it falls below zero). The starting point of this analysis begins by deriving an RF for the spread itself; once known, RF is applied to the current spread level (which we denote CS) to determine the maximum possible market value of the spread during the life of the transaction.[17] Added to this component is the current intrinsic value of the spread (if any) obtained by subtracting the strike spread (SS) from CS (CS – SS) for call spreads, and the current spread from the strike spread (SS – CS) for put spreads; in order not to violate the negative boundary restriction, the value is set to zero if it is negative. The results are then applied to the number of contracts to obtain a potential REE for the intrinsic value component of the option. Premium (time value) is added to the equation to obtain a total REE. Not surprisingly, the equations immediately below are very similar to original Equations 6.3 and 6.4. The equation for call-based spread options is:

$$REE = prem + \max(0, (NC * ((RFc * CS) + \max(0, (CS - SS))))) \qquad (8.16)$$

and the equation for put-based spread options is:

$$REE = prem + \max(0, (NC * ((RFc * CS) + \max(0, (SS - CS))))) \qquad (8.17)$$

where CS is the current spread; SS is the strike spread; and all other terms are as defined above.

Consider the following example. Dealer QRS has been tracking the spread between stock A (currently trading at US$100) and stock B (currently trading at US$110). Past history of spread movements reveals it has been as narrow as US$8 and as wide as US$14; QRS feels the spread is due to widen and, as such, purchases from Bank TUV a six-month spread call option (100,000 contracts) struck at US$10, for US$100,000 in premium (time value). The six-month RF of the spread itself is estimated at 54 percent. Based on Equation 8.16, the upfront REE of this transaction is:

$$REE = \text{US}\$100{,}000 + \max(0, (100{,}000 * ((0.54 * 10) + \max(0, (10 - 10))))) $$

$$= \text{US}\$100{,}000 + \text{US}\$540{,}000$$

$$= \text{US}\$640{,}000$$

Assume that at maturity of the transaction the spread is trading at US$13.50. If TUV defaults at this point QRS sustains an economic loss of US$350,000 (100,000 * (13.50 – 10)). (Note that premium (time value) has decayed to zero and no longer adds to REE; likewise, future market movements of the spread are zero as the transaction has reached maturity.) It should be noted that the equations above could easily be adapted to take account of spread movements of fixed income yields. As indicated, this is a very basic and simplified, but workable, estimate of the risk of a spread option; readers are encouraged to review alternate methods to obtain additional results.

We indicated earlier that the increasingly popular credit spread option is a subset of the broader class of spread options and generates a payoff based on the improvement or deterioration of a reference issuer's credit quality. While credit options can be structured in price or spread terms, we concentrate our REE discussion on spread-based derivatives. The REE of spread-based credit options can be estimated through a variation of standard call and put Equations 6.3 and 6.4. An institution which has purchased a credit option is primarily concerned with maximum movement of the underlying reference credit spread during the life of the option; movement of the credit spread to an extreme point prior to default by the option seller generates maximum REE. Use of RF under the standard REE framework requires appropriate volatility information; while data on the historical volatility of credit spreads is increasingly available, it can be limited so care must be taken when computing relevant statistics.

While Equations 6.3 and 6.4 form the core of the REE computation, several refinements are required for spread-based structures. First, an adjustment must be made to take account of the price sensitivity of the underlying bond from the time of option exercise to final maturity of the reference bond; this is most often done via a standard duration measure. Second, the payoff terms in the equation are inverted to take account of the usual inverse price-yield relationship. Finally, since credit options are often based on notional, rather than contracts, we include a variable representing the notional of the transaction. These changes are reflected in Equation 8.18 for credit call options:

$$REE = prem + \max(0, (N * dur * (((1 + RFc) * CMS) + (SS - CMS)))) \tag{8.18}$$

and 8.19 for credit put options:

$$REE = prem + \max(0, (N * dur * (((1 + RFc) * CMS) + (CMS - SS)))) \tag{8.19}$$

where *dur* is the expected duration of the underlying reference bond at the maturity of the option; *CMS* is the current market spread (over a risk free benchmark); *SS* is the strike spread (over a risk free benchmark); and all other terms are as defined above

The equations can be adapted for credit options based on price, rather than spread, terms; they can also be converted into contracts, though this is a less popular dealing convention. Note also that the expected duration is based on the simplified model for European credit options; since the option is exercisable only at maturity, the duration is based on the time between option expiry and bond maturity. Consideration of an American option demands a more accurate calculation of duration, which is based on the point of exercise rather than option expiry; such information is not known in advance.

Consider the following example. Bank WXY believes Company A's credit quality is due to deteriorate and purchases a 12-month credit put from Bank CDE on US$5m notional. The volatility of A's credit spread is computed at 60 percent per year; the 90 percent confidence level, one year RF is determined to be 99 percent. The underlying reference bond has seven years until maturity (and will have six years until maturity at option expiry, with an estimated duration of approximately five (though this is dependent on the price of A's bond at expiry)). WXY purchases the credit put struck at a spread of 300 over Treasuries in a market trading at 290 over (ten basis points out-of-the-money) for US$100,000 in premium (time value). The initial REE, per Equation 8.19, is:

$$REE = US\$100,000 + \max(0, (US\$5m * 5 * ((1.99 * 0.029) + (0.029 - 0.03))))$$

$$= US\$100,000 + (US\$5m * 5 * ((0.0577) + (-0.001)))$$

$$= US\$1,517,500$$

Based on the REE framework the RF suggests that, over the next 12 months, the spread of A can widen by 287 basis points over the current spread of 290 basis points, to a maximum of 577 basis points. If this occurs, the payoff to WXY equals US$1.42m (577 basis points * 5 * US$5m). Assume that just prior to expiry (when RFc and premium (time value) are effectively zero and the sole credit exposure comes from the actual exposure component of the equation), the spread is trading at 450 basis points over Treasuries. Equation 8.19 yields REE of

$$REE = \ US\$0 + max(0, (US\$5m * 5 * ((0 * 0.045) + (0.045 - 0.03))))$$

$$= \ US\$750,000$$

If CDE defaults at this point, WXY sustains an actual economic loss of US$750,000.

It should be noted that the framework above is applicable to spread-based options that provide the buyer with a continuum of payoffs based on credit deterioration, including default. Options that provide a pure binary payoff based on whether a reference credit defaults must be evaluated through a different framework that does not factor in a continuum of credit deterioration. This follows along the lines of the binary option discussion above, and centers on replacing the fixed cash–asset payoff of M with an estimated post-default payment anticipated from the seller of the option. (The structure can also be analyzed through the default swap framework developed in Chapter 10; we shall not duplicate the discussion in this chapter, but refer the reader to the section on default swaps for a complete review and analysis of the REE for binary default structures).

Basket options

A basket option provides a payoff based on the weighted average performance of a group of assets against a predefined strike. As with spread options discussed above, the REE of basket options is more challenging to determine since lognormally distributed variables defining the basket cannot be manipulated to generate a lognormally distributed basket. Once again, we must consider the alternatives (that is, assume the basket is an asset which is lognormally distributed, assume the components of the basket follow the normal, or some alternate, distribution, utilize a two-factor framework with correlations, and so on). For illustrative purposes we continue to assume that a basket of reference assets is, in fact, a single asset that follows a geometric Brownian motion (emphasizing again the limitations that accompany this approach). Rather than isolating the RFs of individual components of the basket and adding them together, we assume we can compute the RF of the basket as a whole and insert the result into the overall REE framework. Once complete, the process is virtually identical to the one we have discussed for spread options. Under our simplifying assumption the relevant equations are:

$$REE = prem + \max(0, (NC * ((RFc * CMP_{basket}) + \max(0, (CMP_{basket} - SP_{basket})))))$$ (8.20)

for basket call options, and

$$REE = prem + \max(0, (NC * ((RFc * CMP_{basket}) + \max(0, (SP_{basket} - CMP_{basket})))))$$ (8.21)

for basket put options, where: CMP_{basket} is the current market price of the basket; SP_{basket} is the strike price of the basket, and all other terms are as defined above.

Note that in computing the CMP_{basket} and SP_{basket} as a stochastic asset, appropriate basket weightings are utilized (and held constant).

Consider the following example. Bank JKL wants to receive the payoff on the downside of a basket of four industrial stocks, W, X, Y, Z. It purchases from Dealer FGH a 12-month at-the-money basket put (100,000 contracts) on the four stocks for US$150,000 in premium (time value). The basket is comprised of equal one-quarter weightings of each stock (stock W trades at US$10/share, stock X at US$15/share, stock Y at US$20/share, and stock Z at US$18/share); the weighted value of this basket is, therefore, US$15.75. After analyzing past volatilities of the basket as an entire asset, the RF for a 12-month transaction is determined to be 55 percent. Based on this information, the REE of the basket put is computed as:

$$REE = US\$150,000 + \max(0, (100,000 * ((0.55 * 15.75) + \max(0, (15.75 - 15.75)))))$$

$$= US\$150,000 + US\$866,250$$

$$= US\$1.02m$$

Assume at the maturity of the transaction the basket is trading at a level of US$13.50. The payoff to JKL equals US$225,000 (100,000 * (15.75 − 13.50)). If FGH defaults at this point, JKL sustains a certain loss of this magnitude.

Once again, it is important to stress that converting a basket into a single asset and utilizing it in the standard REE framework is based on simplifying assumptions. While the process is efficient and yields an estimate of credit exposure, readers are encouraged to review alternate methodologies.

Compound options

A compound option is a derivative on a second derivative; as noted above, there are four basic variations, including calls on puts and calls, and puts on puts and calls. The credit risk evaluation of a compound option is a multistep process that can be viewed with varying degrees of conservatism. In order to analyze the situation we recall what occurs under each structure:

- Call on call: a long call position is generated if the original option is exercised.

- Call on put: a long put position is generated if the original option is exercised.

- Put on call: a short call position is generated if the original option is exercised.

- Put on put: a short put position is generated if the original option is exercised.

When a bank purchases a compound option, credit risk is twofold: premium (time value) paid for the original option, plus the market risk attributable to the original option. If the original option moves in-the-money, the buyer exercises its option and enters into the underlying option. Thus, if the option seller defaults once the original option is in-the-money, the bank as purchaser of the compound structure loses the remaining time value of its premium and the economic value of the original option (recall that the economic value will be the difference between the strike price of the original option and the price of the underlying option which is, itself, dependent on the price of the underlying reference against the underlying strike price). This risk can be quantified per standard Equations 6.3 or 6.4. Note that the SP and CMP used in this stage relate to the SP and CMP of the premiums, not the underlying reference. For instance, if a bank purchases a call on a put, the strike of the original call might be US$1; the CMP of the original call relates to the current premium of the underlying option (perhaps it is US$0.50, based on an underlying reference price of US$20 and underlying strike price of US$15, indicating the original option is still out-of-the-money). As the underlying reference price falls, say to US$10, the CMP of the underlying's premium may rise to US$1.25 which, against an SP of US$1, indicates the original option is in-the-money. This can, of course, be valued by our original equations. Although exercise of the original option does not result in either cash or physical settlement, it does result in the creation of an underlying option that, at the moment of exercise, has

some economic value (for example, in the example above the put reference has fallen from US$20 to US$10, suggesting US$5 of intrinsic value
along with remaining time value).

It is important to consider what occurs once the original option is exercised: if the purchaser of the compound enters into a call on a call or a call
on a put and exercises the option at expiry, it pays a new premium and
obtains a standard long position in a new call or put; credit risk can be
quantified by standard Equations 6.3 and 6.4, assuming the underlying
options are standard structures (if they are not, then alternate formulae
corresponding to the type of underlying options (such as those presented in
this chapter) may be used). From a credit risk perspective, the buyer continues to face the original compound option seller; its second premium
payment is now at risk (the first one is no longer relevant) and it faces
normal credit exposure (based on the underlying market reference rather
than the underlying option premium value) as it looks to the seller for
continued performance. An institution can, therefore, treat the REE of a
call on a call or a call on a put with at least two degrees of conservatism: it
can value the premium and market risk exposure of the underlying option
(for example, it assumes the option moves to a maximum level as estimated
by RF, at which time exercise occurs, generating normal call or put risk),
or it can value the premium and market risk exposure of the original option
plus the premium and market risk exposure of the long underlying option
generated through the exercise of the original option. In all cases the REE
of the underlying option dominates. If the purchaser of the compound
enters into a put on a put or a call, the analysis shifts; in this instance, the
purchaser becomes the seller of the underlying option upon exercise, and
faces no credit risk once the original option is exercised, assuming the original seller (who undertakes a long position in the option) pays premium in
an upfront fashion.

From the perspective of the original seller the analysis is, again, distinct.
If the seller of a compound option sells either a call on a call or a call on a
put, it has no credit risk exposure to the buyer once premium is received. If
the original option moves in-the-money for the purchaser and it exercises, but
never forwards the second premium payment for the new long option, the
seller simply cancels the underlying option contract and saves itself an
economic payout (for example, it does not create the second option, which
already has intrinsic value to the buyer). If, however, the seller of the
compound option sells either a put on a put or a put on a call, it faces credit
risk exposure to the buyer if the original option moves in-the-money and
exercise occurs. Once this happens, the purchaser of the compound becomes
the seller of a standard put or call, while the seller of the compound becomes
the purchaser of a standard put or call. In this instance REE can be determined through standard Equations 6.3 and 6.4. From a credit limit allocation

standpoint the compound seller can again approach this structure with vary-ing degrees of conservatism: if it has sold a put on a put or call, it only faces credit exposure when it becomes the purchaser of the underlying option, which occurs when the original option moves in-the-money and is exercised. From a conservative perspective, the seller of a compound put may wish to attribute upfront REE to its credit limit, on the assumption that the original compound will move in-the-money and the purchaser will exercise; it is then left with no alternative but to take the original purchaser's credit risk. Under a less conservative approach the seller may wish to attribute credit risk to the purchaser's credit limits once exercise occurs; if exercise of the original compound put never occurs, the seller will never assume a long position in the underlying option.

In our discussion throughout this text we have noted that credit risk of options arises when an institution is long, not short. In the special case of a short compound option involving puts on calls or puts on puts, the origi-nal seller of the compound may find itself with a long position in a put or a call if the original compound buyer exercises its compound put; this exception must be borne in mind.

Chooser options

A chooser option is a derivative that allows the purchaser to customize details of the option during a set time period. A regular chooser permits the buyer to choose between a call and a put with identical strike prices and maturities, while a complex chooser permits the buyer to choose between a call with strike price SP1 and maturity T1 and a put with strike price SP2 and maturity T2. Since the specific parameters of a chooser option by defi-nition remain imprecise at trade date, it is difficult for a credit officer to assign a precise credit risk value to the derivative at the outset; only when the bank makes its final choice will the risk officer have sufficient infor-mation to judge the risk of the transaction. Until a choice is made, however, it is perfectly reasonable for a credit officer to compute REE for both the put and call components and select the larger of the two as its *ex ante* REE (so that a credit decision can be made); once the final choice is made, the REE shifts to the instrument selected. In the case of a regular chooser, upfront REE for a call and put with identical features can be quantified by standard Equations 6.3 and 6.4 (or Equation 7.3 for long straddles). For a complex chooser an analyst needs to review the specific strikes and matu-rities to obtain relevant RFc's, utilize such RFc's to compute REE (through Equations 6.3 and 6.4), and assign the larger of the two values against credit limits.

Consider the following example. Bank TUV purchases a complex chooser from Bank EFG on 100,000 barrels of West Texas Intermediate

(WTI) crude oil which permits it to enter into a six-month call struck at US$19/barrel or a six-month put struck at US$18/barrel; the market for WTI crude is currently US$19/barrel. TUV pays EFG US$100,000 premium (time value) for the chooser and choice date is set for 30 days after trade date. Based on a six-month RFc of 30 percent, the REE of the call element of the chooser is computed, via Equation 6.3, as:

REE = US$100,000 + max(0, (100,000 * ((0.30 * 19) + (19 − 19))))

= US$670,000

The put element of the chooser is computed through Equation 6.4 as:

REE = US$100,000 + max(0, (100,000 * ((0.30 * 19) + (18 − 19))))

= US$470,000

The upfront REE assigned to EFG's credit lines is therefore US$670,000 (the larger of the two REEs). In 30 days the price of WTI rises to US$21/barrel; feeling oil will continue to rise, TUV converts its chooser into a European call with a strike of US$19 and five months until maturity. Based on a new RFc of 27 percent and US$70,000 of time value of premium, the new REE is:

REE = US$60,000 + max(0, (100,000 * ((0.27 * 20) + (20 − 19))))

= US$700,000

The new REE allocated to EFG's credit lines is US$700,000. From this point forward, TUV monitors the REE performance of a standard European call on WTI crude and ignores the put component, which is no longer relevant. Note that any additional premium due must be factored into the equation.

Contingent premium options

A contingent premium option is a derivative that allows the purchaser to defer payment of premium until the option moves in-the-money; if the underlying option never moves in-the-money the seller receives no premium. The REE of a standard put or call can be quantified by Equations 6.3 or 6.4; these equations, as we have discussed, include premium (time value) as a component of overall risk, since this is an amount immediately paid to the option seller. In a contingent option, premium may never be paid. If it is not paid, it means the option has no intrinsic value and, therefore, a bank will not look to the writer for performance. Thus, the buyer of a contingent option may treat the credit risk with varying degrees of conservatism. If it believes the option will eventually move in-the-money (perhaps it is struck close to-the-money), it may value credit risk per standard Equations 6.3 and 6.4. If it does not wish to value the premium until the option moves in-the-money, it can simply assign credit risk exposure to the potential intrinsic value component of the option (based on equations 6.3 or 6.4, less the premium component) and add premium to REE when it is paid. If the premium is not paid until the exercise of the option, perhaps in net payment form, it may choose never to count it as risk since the protective flow it is anticipating from its option is partially offset by the premium due the writer. In the least conservative form, a purchaser might choose not to assign any risk to the transaction. Although this is obviously a very liberal approach to risk valuation, a bank might opt for this process if the contingent option it is purchasing is very short term and very far out-of-the-money, with no real chance of ending in-the-money (such a deep out-of-the-money option might be purchased to prevent financial loss due to an extremely sharp upward or downward movement in rates or prices). Since no premium is paid upfront, as in a standard option, it might be argued that there is no real chance for credit risk exposure to develop. Naturally this scenario changes if there is a large movement in the underlying reference. In either event it is perhaps a little naive not to assign any risk to the transaction, but we present the view for the reader's consideration.

We know the seller of a standard option faces no credit risk once premium is received; since this typically happens within a five-day framework, no credit risk exposure is incurred. This, as discussed, is standard treatment for all short option positions (with a few exceptions, as already indicated). For the seller of a contingent option the risk is clearly different: since premium is not received within five business days (unless the option moves in-the-money during that time frame), this amount is at risk. Once again, an institution selling a contingent option has several choices on how it wishes to value the credit risk. In the most conservative stance it might consider delayed receipt of premium as its risk. Once premium is received (that is, when the option moves in-the-money), which may be several months or years in the future, risk may then be set equal to zero. This is clearly a conservative approach; if the option moves in-the-money and the counterparty does not deliver the required premium, the bank writing the option will not honor its commitment under the contract. Since the option will have intrinsic value to the defaulting purchaser, the writer will not deliver that value. A second, less conservative, view assigns no risk to the extended settlement of the premium since non-receipt can be offset by non-payment under the option. The main issue is whether the intrinsic value of the option more than offsets the premium. If it does not the bank, as writer, still sustains a loss equal to the net difference between $(CMP - SP)$ – premium, for a call, and $(SP - CMP)$ – premium, for a put.

Deferred payment American options

A deferred payment American (DPA) option requires the buyer of the option to forego use of an economic gain realized through the exercise of an in-the-money contract until some future date (which is the original maturity date of the option). In exchange for giving up the right to use the intrinsic value immediately, the buyer pays the seller a smaller premium (which is based on estimated time value of money). From a credit risk standpoint we can evaluate the risk of a deferred payment put or call as we would any other conventional option, via standard Equations 6.3 or 6.4. The premium (time value) element incorporated in the calculation is likely to be smaller than that of a regular option, but still presents risk to the buyer. In addition, potential market risk on the intrinsic value exists and can be estimated through the RF framework. Thus, credit risk to the buyer of a DPA will approximate the risk of a conventional option.

Although the risk calculation is the same, risk officers must be aware of one additional element. As in the case of the lookback options discussed above, the critical time for counterparty failure in a DPA does not occur when intrinsic value has reached its peak; rather, it comes from the moment of exercise until maturity of the transaction, since the purchaser expects to receive the payoff at maturity. While we are normally concerned with market risk moving to a maximum point at the time of default, with a DPA the maximum market movement and time of default need not coincide. Thus, while risk quantification does not change, it is important to be aware of the final time horizon and the fact that maximum market movements and default need not occur simultaneously.

Quanto options

A quanto option is a derivative incorporated into a broader note or swap/option structure which converts proceeds at the conclusion of a transaction into a desired home (or target) currency at a predetermined rate; it thus protects a derivative purchaser from foreign exchange risk. From a risk quantification standpoint it is relatively easy to assign a risk factor to account for the potential market movements of converting from, for example, yen into dollars or euros into sterling. Since the quanto involves setting a fixed exchange rate on trade date, for use at some future point (for example, maturity), the risk to the purchaser is an adverse movement in the currency rate that generates a loss if counterparty default occurs. For instance, if Bank X has a quanto which converts yen proceeds from the Nikkei 225 into dollars at a fixed rate of ¥125/US$ and the counterparty defaults when the ¥/US$ rate has moved to ¥135/US$, X sustains a loss in converting the yen proceeds into dollars at the new spot rate (since US$ has depreciated versus ¥). If X is due ¥100m from index appreciation, which equals US$800,000 based on the fixed ¥125/US$ rate specified by the quanto, conversion via the new spot of ¥135/US$ yields net proceeds of US$770,000, or US$30,000 less than anticipated; this presumes, of course, that proceeds from the ¥ appreciation/US$ depreciation have been credited to X's account prior to default. If default occurs before local currency credit takes place, the loss sustained by X equals the foregone index appreciation plus any remaining time value of premium plus the foreign exchange loss. Risk of a quanto, then, adds to the total potential risk sustainable by X; it is not a replacement for other types of risk.

There are two difficulties in quantifying the *ex ante* credit risk of a quanto. The first challenge is the unknown amount of economic value that may ultimately be converted into the reference currency at the predetermined rate. On trade date, a bank entering into a quanto structure is uncertain how much gain, if any, will require conversion at maturity. If a bank purchases a call on an index and the index rises, it needs to convert the differential between the current price and the strike price, times the number of contracts or notional; if the index falls, no currency conversion is required. The proceeds for conversion are clearly dependent on the intrinsic value of the call.

The second difficulty reverts to the discussion on multiple index options above (given that a quanto is, effectively, a type of multiple index option). Specifically, we know from earlier that the sum of two lognormally distributed variables (that is, the underlying variable and the foreign exchange variable) is not itself lognormally distributed. This means, once again, that alternate assumptions must be used to estimate the risk on the quanto portion of a derivative structure. As before, we can assume the risk of the entire package (for example, the quanto and underlying derivative) is a single stochastic asset which can be observed in the market and modeled via the RF framework – though in this instance the resulting spread is likely to be particularly difficult to handle. Alternatively, we can assume the combination of the two references follows an alternate distribution, or can be modeled in a two-factor framework with correlations.

All of these approaches have certain drawbacks and there is no ideal solution. In practice, certain institutions elect simply to assign an "add-on" factor to the underlying risk being converted; since the foreign exchange risk introduced in the event of default is often minor compared with the market risk of the underlying reference, this might be regarded as sufficiently accurate for credit risk estimation purposes, and it is obviously very simple to implement. In most cases potential losses from the underlying derivative being "quantized" are far greater than potential losses from the quanto itself (note, for instance, in the example above that the loss from the underlying Nikkei call amounts to US$800,000, while the loss from the foreign exchange movement is only an incremental US$30,000). To the

extent that an institution follows the simple add-on approach, it can estimate its risk via

$$REE_{fx} = (REE_{orig} - prem) * RF_{fx} \qquad (8.22)$$

where *prem* is the time value component of option premium; REE_{fx} is the risk
equivalent exposure attributable only to the quanto; REE_{orig} is the risk equivalent exposure associated with the original trade; and RF_{fx} is an add-on risk
factor for FX market movements.

This equation reflects the maximum foreign exchange market risk exposure an institution can encounter on the trade by applying the add-on factor
to the REE of the underlying derivative being quantized (note that premium
(time value) is excluded as it is not converted in the process). As indicated
above, this currency exposure component is in addition to the normal REE
of the underlying derivative, which dominates overall transaction REE. The
add-on approach is attractive because it provides a very straightforward and
workable method of estimating what is often modest incremental risk. The
drawback is that it is overly simplified and not mathematically rigorous. A
more precise approach would focus on alternate distributions or a two-factor
model with correlations; the reader may wish to explore such alternatives.

Forward start options

A forward start option is a derivative that is contracted on trade date but
commences at a future time. The credit risk exposure of a forward start
option can be estimated using standard call and put Equations 6.3 and 6.4; in
order to use these equations we assume the strike level at the forward start
date is a function of the market movement estimated by RF at the inception
of the transaction. Note that the RF employed must reflect the entire tenor of
the transaction, from trade date until maturity date, where the forward start
date is a point between the two. As the forward start date is passed and the
option commences, an adjustment to the REE figure may be required to
reflect the actual starting point. Assuming use of RF provides for maximum
market movement over the life of the transaction, however, we can be quite
comfortable that worst-case credit exposure is being captured.

Consider the following example. Assume Investment Bank XYZ wishes
to take a speculative view on the NASDAQ, but prefers to wait three months
before entering into the transaction. It purchases a forward start call from
Bank FGH for US$200,000 (time value of premium), which provides a
payout equal to the differential between the strike and the terminal value of
the NASDAQ, times an arbitrary multiplier of US$1000. The index is
currently trading at 1100 and carries an annual volatility of 30 percent (and
a 15-month, 90 percent RF of 55 percent). The forward start option is

contracted to commence in three months and mature 12 months after the forward date; the call will be struck at-the-money in three months time. Since XYZ is uncertain of the precise strike level of the NASDAQ three months hence, it can only generate an estimate of its REE on the transaction, and will make an adjustment once the transaction is under way; the most conservative approach is to assume the option is struck at-the-money on trade date. For this example, assume XYZ calculates its REE based on an at-the-money option on trade date. The REE, by Equation 6.3, is given as:

$$REE = US\$200,000 + max(0, ((US\$1000 * (0.55 * 1100) + (1100 - 1100))))$$

$$= US\$200,000 + US\$605,000$$

$$= US\$805,000$$

Assume that three months from now, at commencement of the option, the NASDAQ is trading at 1200. XYZ readjusts its REE to include the new market level and the remaining time to maturity (the latter impacting the RF). For purposes of this example, assume the RF declines to 49.5 percent and the remaining time value of premium is US\$150,000. Given a sufficient level of conservatism the new REE should not, in general, exceed the *ex ante* REE already computed. In this instance the REE equals:

$$REE = US\$150,000 + max(0, ((US\$1000 * (0.495 * 1200) + (1200 - 1200))))$$

$$= US\$150,000 + US\$594,000$$

$$= US\$744,000$$

For the remainder of the transaction the REE can be adjusted to reflect declining time to maturity and possible increase in actual exposure as the NASDAQ moves further in-the-money. Note that for the special case of the deferred strike option (that is, the forward start option with a strike set as a predefined function of the market level on selection date) an adjustment to the intrinsic value, reflecting the nature of the strike reset, is warranted, as this is likely to add/subtract from potential intrinsic value and, hence, potential credit exposure.

Exploding options

An exploding option is a call or put spread that locks in gains once both strikes (from long and short positions) are breached. The REE quantification for an exploding call or option is based on the methodology introduced in Equations 7.1 and 7.2 in Chapter 7. Under the long call/put spread equations, the conservative REE evaluation suggests the spread moves to its maximum point (for example, breaching both the long and short strikes) to provide maximum credit exposure. The same logic applies to exploding options, but is made even more realistic by the fact that gains are locked in once the upper strike (for calls) or lower strike (for puts) is breached (for example, gains are not given up if the market retraces, as they might under a European spread).

Power options

A power option, which generates an exponential payoff, can create a substantial credit risk exposure for the purchaser. As with other options, the first element of credit risk is premium (time value), which may be considerable (given the potentially large payoff of the transaction). The second element of risk is the potential intrinsic value of the transaction. Since a power option involves an exponential payout, the credit exposure associated with intrinsic value can quickly grow very large – and, the greater the exponent, the more rapid the increase in exposure. In order to adjust the REE equation to take account of the payoff profile of power options (for example, $(CMP^x – SP)$ for a power call and $(SP – CMP^x)$ for a power put, where x is the relevant exponent), we adapt Equations 6.3 and 6.4 as follows:

$$REE = prem + \max(0, (NC * (((1 + RFc) * CMP)^x) – SP)) \qquad (8.23)$$

for calls, and

$$REE = prem + \max(0, (NC * (SP – ((1 – RFc) * CMP)^x))) \qquad (8.24)$$

for puts, where x is the exponent; and all other terms are as defined above

Consider the following example. Bank X buys a squared power call (100,000 contracts) from Dealer ABC on stock JKL, with a CMP of US$10 and a strike price of US$160; premium (time value) paid equals US$300,000 and maturity of the transaction is two years. The 12-month RF computed for the stock is 25.6 percent, indicating a two-year RF of 36.2 percent. The initial REE of the transaction, per Equation 8.23, equals:

$$REE = US\$300{,}000 + \max(0, (100{,}000 * (((1 + 0.362) * 10)^2 – 160)))$$

$$= US\$300{,}000 + US\$2.5m$$

$$= US\$2.8m$$

Assume that with six months until maturity JKL is trading at US$11.50/share, the new RFc is 18.1 percent and premium has decayed to US$100,000. In this instance REE equals:

REE = US$100,000 + max(0, (100,000 * (((1 + 0.181) * 11.50)^2 − 160)))

= US$100,000 + US$2.41m

= US$2.51m

If ABC defaults at this point X loses, with certainty, US$100,000 of remaining time value of premium but no intrinsic value (that is, the option is not yet in-the-money); the remaining US$2.41m allows for the remaining possibility of market movement, adjusted for the exponential payout. Assume one day prior to maturity, when no more market movements can occur and premium (time value) has decayed to zero, the price of JKL is US$13.50/share. The REE becomes:

REE = US$0 + max(0, (100,000 * (((1 + 0.0) * 13.50)^2 − 160)))

= US$0 + US$2.2m

= US$2.2m

If ABC defaults, X sustains an actual loss of US$2.2m, which is the current value of the power option. It is rather clear to see that even small movements in the underlying can result in significant payoff and, hence, credit exposure.

Multi-derivative packages

As indicated in the product description section above, many of the complex derivatives we have discussed can be combined into multiple packages to create derivatives with even more specific payoff/protection profiles. From an REE perspective it is usually necessary to "dissect" the components of the package and review the nature and source of credit risk. Once this is accomplished the amount of exposure in the package can be determined. Note that in certain instances risk is bounded by barriers (rather than RF-driven market movements), in other instances payoffs (and risk) increase exponentially until a barrier is reached, and so on. Since we have already reviewed many of the major products and their risks in the sections above, we shall not analyze the myriad combinations of multiple options further; obviously, care must always be taken when reviewing the risk of any package.

The discussion in this chapter should help demonstrate that the credit risk of complex options can be significant. Such derivatives can carry long maturities and are often based on indexes or prices that exhibit substantial volatility, which together compound the effects of REE. It is vital, therefore, for the credit officer dealing with complex options to isolate and consider every aspect of credit risk generated by such derivatives.

CHAPTER 9

Quantifying Swap Credit Risk

The prevalence of vanilla and exotic swaps in the financial system means that the calculation of swap credit risk exposure remains a vital topic for financial institutions, corporate end users, and regulatory agencies. Given the complex characteristics of swap contracts, it comes as no surprise that there is no single accepted way of computing swap credit risk; much ultimately depends on the views and preferences of individual institutions and regulators. Though methodologies vary, we can consider two broad approaches: calculation of risk exposure for regulatory purposes and calculation of risk exposure for internal measurement and management purposes. In certain instances these approaches may be similar. This occurs primarily when an institution falls under a regulatory jurisdiction that enforces a specific methodology and it chooses to apply the same guidelines to its internal management process. In fact, a uniform approach is possible through the BIS's IRB advanced approach, as we have discussed in Chapter 3 (indeed, greater consistency is a driving force behind the new risk capital regime). If a national regulator approves an institution's models for assessing the probability of counterparty default and the estimated amount of exposure that might exist at the point of default, then the regulatory approach is precisely equal to the internal management approach. However, in other cases the approaches may be different; this occurs when there is no governing regulatory guideline (for example, an institution does not fall under the jurisdiction of the BIS and its capital framework) or a firm prefers to utilize regulatory risk calculations for regulatory capital and reporting purposes, and internal risk calculations for internal credit allocation, credit pricing, and risk-adjusted performance purposes.

Since we have already considered general regulatory approaches to swap credit risk estimation, we focus our attention in this chapter on general quantification approaches that might be used as a supplement or substitute to the regulatory approach. In addition, we present a sample methodology for computing swap risk to provide some practical perspective on the topic. We will apply various concepts developed in this chapter in our discussion of complex swap products in Chapter 10.

There are many ways of estimating swap credit risk. The topic lends itself to a certain amount of subjectivity, driven by the use of parameters that vary from institution to institution (and which are often defined and crystallized through the risk governance process). That said, most swap credit risk frameworks consist of two components: actual exposure and fractional exposure. As discussed earlier (and as highlighted in our discussion on options) each plays a vital role in initial decision-making and ongoing risk management. While this framework is similar in concept to the BIS's original CEM process (which, as already mentioned, includes a mark-to-market component and a credit risk "add on" component), the detailed approaches of the two methodologies can yield different results; this is particularly true regarding risk factors, where significant differences can arise. We discuss actual and fractional swap exposure in greater detail in the following sections. Note that we present our discussion in terms of generic interest rate swaps, knowing that the same concepts apply equally to other types of swap transactions.

ACTUAL EXPOSURE OF SWAP CONTRACTS

The *actual exposure* component of swap credit risk is used to quantify the ongoing replacement cost of a transaction. The measure typically includes the mark-to-market value of the swap and accrued interest receivable under the swap. The mark-to-market (MTM) component is generally the dominant portion of actual exposure and provides an indication of the ongoing market value of a swap; it can be computed through various formulae, including those given by Equations 9.1 and 9.2:

$$MTM = \sum_{x=1}^{p} \left[\frac{N * (r_n - r_0)}{(1 + r)^x} \right] \tag{9.1}$$

where r_n is the new swap rate in period x; r_0 is the original swap rate; p is the number of years until maturity; and N is the notional of the swap.

If the swap involves semi-annual payments, r_n and r_0 are divided by two, and if it involves quarterly payments, r_n and r_0 are divided by four; the periods to maturity are also adjusted. We may thus expand the equation into a more generic form:

$$MTM = \sum_{x=1}^{p} \left[\frac{N * \frac{(r_n - r_0)}{t}}{\left[1 + \frac{r_n}{t} \right]^x} \right] \tag{9.2}$$

where t is the frequency of payments per year under the swap (1 for annual pay, 2 for semi-annual pay, 4 for quarterly pay, and so on) and p is now the number of periods until maturity.

The equations above represent the market value, or economic replacement cost, of the swap and may be positive (implying credit exposure) or negative (no credit exposure), depending on the direction of rates between trade date and default. The equations effectively measure the difference between the original coupon and the new coupon (times the notional), from the time of default until the maturity of the originally contracted swap, discounted back to the present at the new rate. This represents the loss or gain in entering into a new swap in a new rate environment.

Very often the MTM approach is expressed in terms of a net present value (NPV). The NPV of a swap at default, for a fixed rate payer, is shown as:

$$NPV_{Fix\ Pay} = NPV_{OP} - NPV_{NP} \tag{9.3}$$

where NPV_{OP} is the NPV of the swap based on the originally contracted payments and NPV_{NP} is the NPV of the swap based on the new replacement payments.

$NPV_{Fix\ Pay}$ may be positive or negative, depending on whether rates have risen or fallen between trade date and time of default. From the standpoint of a fixed rate payer, this figure becomes negative if rates rise, implying a loss. Intuitively this makes sense because, in the event of default, the fixed payer needs to establish a new series of fixed payments in a higher (more costly) interest rate environment. For a fixed rate receiver, we reverse the terms:

$$NPV_{Fix\ Rec} = NPV_{NP} - NPV_{OP} \tag{9.4}$$

If rates fall (that is, NPV_{NP} is less than NPV_{OP}), a fixed rate receiver loses money; this is shown by a negative result. Again, this makes sense: in the event of default the fixed rate receiver needs to replace the swap in an environment where fixed rates, and therefore receipts, are lower.

The general formula for the NPV of a fixed rate annuity is:

$$NPV_{Fixed} = PMT \left[\dfrac{1 - \left[\dfrac{1 + \dfrac{r}{t}}{} \right]^{-n}}{\dfrac{r}{t}} \right] \tag{9.5}$$

where PMT is the periodic fixed payment under the swap; r is the relevant interest rate; t is the frequency of payments per year under the swap, and n is the number of payments to be made until maturity.

The NPV valuation of floating rates is considerably more involved and requires the calculation of a forward–forward rate. Although valuing the

NPV of an entire swap (that is, fixed and floating) is vital for swap pricing and hedging purposes, for our purposes we only need to focus on the NPV of the fixed stream (under the assumption that when we value the NPV of a swap, there is another fixed rate available which guides the calculation of the actual economic replacement cost, which we have termed $NPV_{Fix\ Pay}$ or $NPV_{Fix\ Rec}$ above).

In order to calculate $NPV_{Fix\ Pay}$ or $NPV_{Fix\ Rec}$ we focus on the expected payment PMT under the original and new rates, since this cash flow ultimately determines whether more or less will be paid or received. When discounting via the relevant interest rate r above, however, we utilize the new rate in existence at the time of default. The equation above indicates that the amount a fixed payer stands to gain or lose is simply the difference between the amount it originally expected to pay (NPV_{OP}) and the amount it is now required to pay (NPV_{NP}); both terms are discounted back to the present using the new rate, in order to account for the time value of money. The reverse is applied for a fixed receiver scenario.

We can easily show that the MTM and NPV equations are equivalent. Consider the following example. Bank X enters into a five-year, US$100m interest rate swap with Bank Q, where X pays 10 percent fixed annually and receives 12 month Libor. Assume that two years hence, when the swap still has three years until maturity, Q defaults. Fixed rates at the time of default are 12 percent, indicating that if Bank X wants to replace the swap it must do so at a higher rate (which generates a loss). Under this scenario the MTM to X is positive, implying exposure to the counterparty and a credit loss; the NPV result is negative, again signifying a credit loss to X.

By Equation 9.2 the rounded MTM value of the swap is:

$$MTM = ((US\$100m * (0.12 - 0.10)/(1 + 0.12)^1 + (US\$100m * (0.12 - 0.10)/(1 + 0.12)^2 + (US\$100m * (0.12 - 0.10)/(1 + 0.12)^3)$$

$$= US\$1,786,000 + US\$1,594,000 + US\$1,424,000$$

$$= US\$4,805,000$$

This amount represents today's economic cost of replacing the original 10 percent fixed pay swap in an environment where rates are 12 percent; note that time to maturity is three, instead of five, years. By Equations 9.3 and 9.5 the NPV of the swap (at original and new payment levels) is:

$$NPV_{OP} = US\$10m * ((1 - ((1 + 0.12)^{-3}))/0.12) = US\$24,025,000$$

$$NPV_{NP} = US\$12m * ((1 - ((1 + 0.12)^{-3}))/0.12) = US\$28,830,000$$

$$NPV_{\text{Fix Pay}} = NPV_{\text{OP}} - NPV_{\text{NP}} = US\$24{,}025{,}000 - US\$28{,}830{,}000$$

$$= -US\$4{,}805{,}000$$

Not surprisingly, these two values are identical and show X losing just over US\$4.8m.

In addition to the cash flow calculations above, the actual exposure component generally includes *accrued interest receivable* (AIR). AIR exists when an institution pays coupons more frequently than it receives them. For instance, if an institution pays quarterly and receives annually, and its counterparty defaults after receiving the first three quarterly payments but before making its own larger annual payment, it faces a loss equal to the AIR. The AIR can be calculated via the following:

$$AIR = N * \left[\frac{r}{PayF} * \frac{(PayF - RecF)}{RecF} \right] \qquad (9.6)$$

where r is the interest rate; $PayF$ is the pay frequency; $RecF$ is the receive frequency; and N is the notional of the swap.

In most instances if AIR is negative (that is, the bank receives more frequently than it pays, implying a risk exposure benefit), the resulting receivable is set to zero rather than subtracted from the total REE equation. (Note that AIR is reset at zero once a complete payment cycle is finished, for example, every year.)

As indicated at the beginning of this section, the sum of the MTM and AIR components is collectively referred to as actual exposure (AE). We summarize the process to this point as:

$$AE = MTM + AIR \qquad (9.7)$$

where *MTM* is the current mark-to-market value of the swap as defined above; and *AIR* is the accrued interest receivable as defined above.

The primary benefit of the actual exposure component of swap risk is that it reflects the true economic cost of replacing a swap. That is, it indicates exactly how much will be gained or lost at the point of counterparty default. It is computationally easy to derive MTM/AIR on a continuing basis and simple to track if proper systems are in place. The drawback of AE is that it provides no indication of the impact of future rate movements on a swap transaction; this affects initial decision-making and ongoing exposure management. For instance, an analyst considering a par transaction on trade date faces an actual exposure of zero, as rates will not yet have moved (note that if the swap is an off-market premium or discount structure there may be actual exposure on trade date; for standard par swaps, however, actual exposure is zero). Under these circumstances the analyst has no method of valuing the future risk exposure inherent in the swap and cannot make a rational credit decision. Likewise, it is difficult for an institution to set appropriate pricing and capital levels when potential movements are not factored into the equation. In practice, many banks utilize actual exposure in conjunction with fractional exposure, discussed immediately below, to value the total risk of a swap.

FRACTIONAL EXPOSURE OF SWAP CONTRACTS

The second component of the swap credit risk framework is represented by fractional exposure (FE). *Fractional exposure* (also known as "potential market risk," "presettlement risk," or "time-to-decay risk") estimates the potential future market movements that might affect the value, and therefore credit exposure, of a swap; this, of course, is the same RF approach we have used throughout the text, and can be defined as:

$$FE = RF * N \tag{9.8}$$

where RF is the swap risk factor and N is the notional of the swap.

Note that this equation is identical to the original REE equation highlighted in Chapter 5; this is because FE equals REE at the inception of the swap, before market movements have had an opportunity to impact the value of the transaction. The FE component, which can be computed through various methods, estimates the maximum amount a bank might lose if its counterparty defaults at some point in the future. With this information a credit officer has the *ex ante* information required to make a rational credit decision; in addition, knowledge of fractional exposure permits greater accuracy in pricing and capital allocation. While the FE component is critical to the swap risk quantification process, its derivation is subjective. Various methods of implementing FE exist (along with various ways of creating parameter inputs to generate the risk factors which yield FE), meaning differences in swap risk estimates arise between institutions. Below we describe in summary form three of the most popular approaches: the historical method, the option method, and the simulation method.

The first quantification approach we outline is the *historical method*, whereby an institution employs historical rate movements to estimate FE. Under this framework, an institution obtains a history of interest rate (or swap rate) movements (for example, one, two, three, four, five-year swap rates, and so on), determines the distribution of rates, and computes the mean and variance of each rate. Following an adjustment to a prespecified confidence level, it projects swap rates forward (perhaps at semi-annual or annual intervals). Using these statistically projected rates, it then revalues a swap at each forward point and discounts back to the present; the largest exposure obtained during the revaluation process becomes the FE assigned to the swap transaction. Statistically projected rates can be summarized as risk factors and applied to the notional of other swaps with the same fixed rate and maturity parameters.

The second approach is the *option method*, which centers on estimating swap risk through an option pricing framework.[1] Under the option method, a swap is viewed as a package of options that gives the holder the right to buy a fixed rate bond and sell a floating rate note (or vice versa); the options are exercised jointly in the event of counterparty default, but only if they are in-the-money.[2] For instance, default by the fixed rate payer is equal to the simultaneous exercise of a call to buy a fixed rate bond and a put to sell a floating rate note, but only if rates have fallen (for example, bond prices have risen). The options can be priced through a binomial framework, for example, and the resulting values can be used as an estimate of potential credit exposure. Note that as volatility and time, two key inputs in any option-pricing model, increase, the resulting value of the options, and hence swap credit exposure, increases. This is consistent with our discussion in Chapter 5, where the two key elements defining RF are volatility and time to maturity. A variation of this model is based on the hypothetical purchase of a series of swaptions that replicate the flows of the swap; the swaptions are exercisable only if the counterparty defaults on the underlying swap. The theoretical premia paid for this strip of swaptions, obtained from a swaption-pricing model, is then used as an estimate of the fractional credit exposure on the underlying swap.[3]

A third approach to valuing fractional exposure is the *simulation method*, which follows from the discussion in Chapter 6. As noted earlier, one of the most common numerical procedures for projecting the movement of random variables is Monte Carlo simulation, which can be adapted to handle the simulation of interest rates in order to generate an estimate of swap credit risk. A typical approach to the process begins with an assumption that rates move randomly over time but that possible values can be defined in terms of a particular distribution (for example, normal, lognormal) with certain mean and variance. Given a predefined statistical distribution, confidence levels, starting rate, time intervals, and the mathematical relationship of future rate movements, a random generation of an artificial future path can be created, with swap replacement costs calculated at each interval (perhaps semi-annually or annually, until maturity); such periodic calculations are generally discounted back to the present. Thousands of realizations yield a set of discounted swap replacement costs, and the average is used as a representation of the discounted replacement cost at each select time interval during the life of the swap. The sum of average discounted replacement costs yields a risk factor that can be used to calculate FE.[4] Note that in the simulation process certain methodologies focus on average replacement cost (based on average rate movements) while others opt for maximum replacement cost (based on peak rate movements, which is clearly more conservative). We provide a more detailed example of a general method by which to value future rates, and to utilize such rates to derive risk factors later in the chapter.

SWAP CREDIT RISK IN A COMPLETE FRAMEWORK

Combining the actual exposure and fractional exposure components described above into a single framework provides an estimate of initial and ongoing swap credit risk. Utilizing the equations above, we can summarize the complete risk of a swap as:

$$REE = FE + AE \tag{9.9}$$

Expanding the individual terms, this becomes:

$$REE = (RF * N) + (MTM + AIR) \tag{9.10}$$

On trade date, when no AE exists, the equation condenses to the standard REE equation introduced in Chapter 5:

$$REE = (RF * N) \tag{5.13}$$

Let us consider the following example. Bank CDE enters into a US$50m, three-year par fixed–floating interest rate swap (matched, semi-annual payments) with Bank UVW; the RF of the transaction is 5 percent (obtained, perhaps, through a simulation process). The initial REE of the transaction, per Equation 9.10, is:

REE = (0.05 * US$50m) + (0 + 0)

   = US$2.5m

Thus, the initial REE allocated by CDE against the credit limits of UVW is US$2.5m. Note that since the market has not yet moved, the MTM component equals zero. In addition, since payments are made on a matched basis, the AIR component equals zero (and remains zero throughout the life of the transaction).

   Assume at the end of the second year the MTM has moved in CDE's favor by US$800,000. Given a new RF of 1 percent (reflecting the remaining time until maturity), the REE becomes:

REE = (0.01 * $50m) + (US$800,000 + 0)

$\qquad$ = US$1.3m

If UVW defaults at this point CDE loses, with certainty, US$800,000, which is the MTM value of the swap; the additional US$500,000 represents the potential exposure for the remaining twelve months of the swap's life.

The reader will note that the initial, and ongoing, REE of the swap is a small fraction of the notional of the deal. This is true because at no time in an interest rate swap are notional amounts exchanged. This means that it is most appropriate to evaluate credit risk exposure through the risk equivalency framework; the same process can be applied to currency swaps, although the final exchange of principal heightens risk considerably. The maximum risk point for a cross currency swap occurs at the end of the transaction, while in an interest rate swap it occurs one-half to one-third of the way through the transaction (we discuss this point in greater detail at the end of the chapter). Equation 9.10 can be adjusted to accommodate different types of swaps, such as discount/premium swaps, forward swaps, zero coupon swaps, and so on. Although these are important instruments within the derivative product framework, we shall not discuss them further.[5] However, in the next chapter we shall adapt Equation 9.10 as we review and quantify the credit risk of complex swaps. Figure 9.1 summarizes much of the discussion above (based on the simulation approach to valuing swap credit risk).

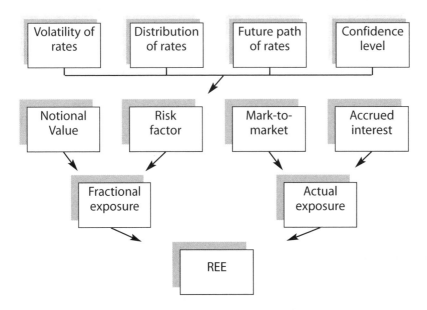

Figure 9.1 The simulation approach to credit risk valuation

A MODEL FOR CALCULATING SWAP CREDIT RISK

We have noted a number of ways by which swap risk can be calculated and have further indicated that there is no single correct way to value the FE portion of a transaction; much ultimately depends on the views of a particular institution. However, to relate our summary discussion to industry practice, we present a more detailed method of swap risk computation in the section that follows.

The model

The main components of any simulation-based potential market exposure model are:

- a method by which to simulate or project future interest rate movements

- an equation by which to compute the replacement cost based on simulated future rates.

The combination of the two allows the development of a risk factor for a swap with particular maturity and rate parameters; it is, effectively, a percentage measure of fractional exposure for a swap with those parameters. When RF is applied to the notional of a swap, we obtain an REE that is comprised solely of FE on trade date. Over time, as RFs decline, FE declines (though PE may increase if the swap's mark-to-market value increases).

Our process thus begins by establishing a method to simulate future interest rates. For instance, the binomial option-pricing model suggests "up" and "down" movements of a stochastic variable that can be described by:[6]

$$u = e^{\sigma\sqrt{\tau/n}}$$
(9.11)

and

$$d = e^{-\sigma\sqrt{\tau/n}}$$
(9.12)

with probabilities defined by

$$q = \frac{1}{2} + \frac{1}{2}[(\mu/\sigma)\sqrt{\tau/n}]$$
(9.13)

where σ is the standard deviation; μ is the expected return; n is a time increment; and τ is the time to maturity.

Rendleman and Bartter[7] have adapted these equations for modeling interest rate movements by incorporating several simple assumptions: namely, the growth rate of the stochastic variable (the interest rate) is constant, the volatility of the variable is constant, and the market price of risk is constant; for our purposes, these assumptions are acceptable.[8] The Rendleman and Bartter equations are given by:

$$u = e^{s\sqrt{\Delta t}} \tag{9.14}$$

and

$$d = e^{-s\sqrt{\Delta t}} \tag{9.15}$$

where s is the volatility and Δt is a small time increment.

With this model we focus on the upward movement of rates for fixed rate payers (which is when risk increases), and the downward movement of rates for fixed rate receivers (which is when risk increases). Adapting these equations to the terms used in Chapter 5, we can state that Δt represents the time change in small intervals. In a Markov process a long interval becomes T, which is precisely equal to the time dimension we have utilized earlier, representing a cumulative, rather than interval, time frame. In Chapter 5 we define the standard deviation of rates via historical volatility HV, after an adjustment to the appropriate confidence level. Utilizing this terminology, we adjust the two equations as follows:

Upward movements:
$$u = e^{HV\sqrt{T}} \tag{9.16}$$

Downward movements:
$$d = e^{-HV\sqrt{T}} \tag{9.17}$$

With these equations providing information on the possible direction of future rates, we set new rates equal to original rates times the upward (or downward) movement estimated by the equations above. For a fixed rate payer this equals:

$$r_n = r_0 * e^{HV\sqrt{T}} \tag{9.18}$$

And, for a fixed rate receiver, equals:

$$r_n = r_0 * e^{-HV\sqrt{T}} \tag{9.19}$$

If we assume original rates are 10 percent and historical volatility of interest rates is 16 percent (lognormally distributed and adjusted to a 90 percent confidence level), we obtain the results highlighted in Table 9.1. (Note that the process above can be incorporated into a broader Monte Carlo simulation, where a large number of realizations yields an average value for the future path of interest rates at select points in time).

This becomes the first component of the potential market exposure framework for swaps. We now turn our attention to the replacement cost calculation. As discussed above, a standard replacement cost equation sums the difference between the new coupon on the swap (r_n) and the original coupon on the swap (r_0) over the number of periods remaining until maturity, and discounts back by the new coupon rate (that is, the coupon rate in existence at the time of

Table 9.1 Calculated up/down rate movements (percentages)

Time	r_0	r_n (up)	r_n (down)
0.5	10.00	11.19	8.93
1.0	10.00	11.74	8.52
1.5	10.00	12.16	8.22
2.0	10.00	12.54	7.97
2.5	10.00	12.88	7.76
3.0	10.00	13.19	7.57
3.5	10.00	13.49	7.41
4.0	10.00	13.77	7.26
4.5	10.00	14.04	7.12
5.0	10.00	14.30	7.00
5.5	10.00	14.55	6.87
6.0	10.00	14.80	6.76
6.5	10.00	15.00	6.65
7.0	10.00	15.27	6.55
7.5	10.00	15.50	6.45
8.0	10.00	15.72	6.36
8.5	10.00	15.94	6.27
9.0	10.00	16.16	6.19
9.5	10.00	16.37	6.10
10.0	10.00	16.58	6.02

default). The equation provides an estimate of how much it will cost to replace a swap in the future (at the time of default), utilizing simulated future rates.

The use of the replacement cost equation is standard within the financial industry, and may be defined as:

$$r_d = \sum_{x=1}^{p} \left[\frac{\frac{(r_n - r_o)}{t}}{\left[1 + \frac{r_n}{t} \right]^x} \right] \tag{9.20}$$

where r_n is the new rate in period x; r_0 is the original rate; p is the number of periods until maturity; and t is the frequency of payments under the swap.

We may also wish to show the results of the equation above (which we term the calculated replacement cost) in today's terms. This is accomplished by discounting the result from Equation 9.20 using r_0:

$$r = \frac{r_d}{(1 + r_o)^q} \tag{9.21}$$

where q is the period in which the default occurs.

We term this the discounted replacement cost. The maximum result obtained through Equation 9.21 is the risk factor RF for a swap with a specific final maturity and original starting rate; this may also be thought of as the maximum replacement cost likely to be encountered during the life of the swap.

With a framework for calculating upward and downward rate movements and a replacement cost equation, we can complete an example that demonstrates the full development of a swap risk factor. Highlighted in Table 9.2 are the calculated rate movements for a five-year fixed-floating semi-annual interest rate swap, based on 16 percent historical volatility and a 10 percent original rate for the fixed rate payer.

Utilizing the calculated rates from Table 9.2 in Equation 9.20 (recalling that we compare r_n with r_o at each semi-annual period), we obtain a discounted calculation for each semi-annual period of the five-year swap. The results are shown in Table 9.3.

Adding the calculated replacement cost terms above for each time period yields r_d, the total calculated replacement cost. Discounting back using r_o gives us the discounted replacement cost, r. These results are given in Table 9.4.

From the table we note the maximum value of r is 5.2 percent, occurring in year 1.5. This indicates that the maximum replacement cost (and, hence, the maximum risk) likely to be encountered under the above scenario is 5.2 percent of the notional amount of the swap. We can therefore say the RF for a five-year, 10 percent fixed payer swap is 5.2 percent.

Table 9.2 Calculated rate movements (percentages)

Time	r_0 (%)	r_n (up) (%)
0.5	10.00	11.19
1.0	10.00	11.74
1.5	10.00	12.16
2.0	10.00	12.54
2.5	10.00	12.88
3.0	10.00	13.19
3.5	10.00	13.49
4.0	10.00	13.77
4.5	10.00	14.04
5.0	10.00	14.30

Table 9.3 Discounted replacement costs

(%)	No. of periods remaining in swap life								
n	1	2	3	4	5	6	7	8	9
0.5	0.37	0.39	0.41	0.43	0.46	0.48	0.51	0.54	0.57
1	0.55	0.58	0.62	0.65	0.69	0.73	0.77	0.82	
1.5	0.72	0.76	0.81	0.86	0.91	0.96	1.00		
2	0.88	0.94	0.99	1.06	1.12	1.20			
2.5	1.05	1.12	1.19	1.27	1.35				
3	1.24	1.32	1.41	1.50					
3.5	1.44	1.53	1.64						
4	1.65	1.76							
4.5	1.89								
5	0.00								

The reader may note that the maximum risk under in transaction occurs in year 1.5, rather than at maturity as a result of the *diffusion and amortization effect*. If we plot the maturity of the swap transaction on the x-axis and the replacement cost along the y-axis, we observe that maximum risk occurs approximately one-third to one-half way through the transaction. This inter-

Table 9.4 Calculated and discounted replacement costs

Time	$r_d(\%)$	$r(\%)$
0.5	4.1	4.0
1	5.4	4.9
1.5	6.0	5.2
2	6.2	5.1
2.5	6.0	4.7
3	5.5	4.1
3.5	4.6	3.3
4	3.4	2.3
4.5	1.9	1.2
5	0.0	0.0

action is highlighted in Figure 9.2, where we illustrate swap replacement curves for a five-year transaction (based on 16 percent volatility and a 10 percent starting rate). The diffusion and amortization effect arises because simulated future rates used in the calculation of replacement cost will not have had a chance to move sufficiently in the early periods of a swap to pose the greatest economic loss (the "diffusion" effect); and insufficient payments remain to be made toward the end of the swap to pose the greatest economic loss ("amortization" effect). Accordingly, the greatest economic loss occurs at some point in between, when rates have had a chance to move and there are still a number of swap payments remaining to be made. Depending on the historical volatility used, the maximum replacement cost occurs one-third to one-half through the life of the swap. We can see in the example above that the maximum point on the five-year swap under 16 percent volatility is reached in Year 1.5, precisely one-third through the life of the transaction.

Once the equations above have been used to produce the series of replacement costs (discounted back to today's value), it is relatively easy to create a table of risk factors that can be used to determine swap risk. Such tables might encompass a range of likely swap rates and maturities; for each rate and maturity, the maximum replacement cost calculated by the method above becomes the risk factor for that maturity. For instance, we might create a table with a range of fixed rates, for example, 5–12 percent, and a range of maturities, for example, 1–15 years (we can also replicate the procedure for fixed receiver swaps where simulated rates are based on Equation 9.19; this yields a slightly different set of RFs). The relevant RF (or replacement cost) is then multiplied by the notional to obtain REE. Knowing that the fractional

Replacement cost (%)

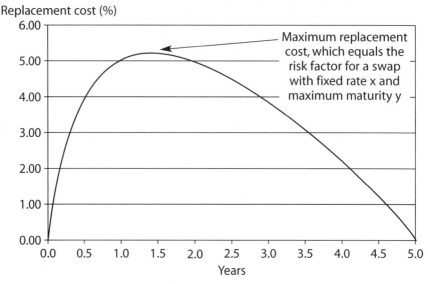

Figure 9.2 Swap replacement cost curve

exposure decays over the life of a swap, it is entirely appropriate for the RFs to be lowered to reflect the fractional exposure attributable to the remaining maturity of the transaction.

Highlighted in Table 9.5 are sample RFs generated by the model we have described above. The factors are based on Treasury rates with a 16 percent historical volatility (adjusted to a 90 percent confidence level). Factors are shown for fixed rates from 5 to 12 percent, and for maturities from one year to ten years. As detailed earlier, the RF for a given swap with fixed rate x and final maturity y is simply the maximum replacement cost for a swap with those characteristics when the adjusted historical volatility is 16 percent. For example, based on our model, a ten-year, 10 percent fixed rate swap will have a maximum replacement cost of 10.7 percent, occurring in Year Three. Therefore, the relevant factor, encompassing the maximum point of risk, is 10.7 percent. A credit officer considering a US$100m swap with such parameters would assign an REE of US$10.7m.

EMPIRICAL FINDINGS ON SWAP RISK FACTORS

We have noted above a variety of ways by which swap risk factors can be derived and have presented one model for doing so. However, knowing that there is no single correct way by which to value swap risk (since each institution operates under a different set of requirements, constraints, and opinions), we highlight below findings obtained by researchers in the development and application of their own models.

Table 9.5 Sample risk factor for interest rate swaps (%) (fixed payer)

Year	1	2	3	4	5	6	7	8	9	10
5%	0.3	0.8	1.0	1.5	2.3	3.9	4.9	5.8	7.2	7.6
6%	0.3	1.0	1.8	2.7	3.6	4.6	5.6	6.6	8.1	8.5
7%	0.4	1.1	2.1	3.0	4.1	5.1	6.2	7.3	8.8	9.3
8%	0.4	1.3	2.3	3.4	4.5	5.6	6.7	7.8	9.4	9.9
9%	0.5	1.4	2.5	3.7	4.9	6.1	7.2	8.3	9.9	10.4
10%	0.5	1.5	2.7	3.9	5.2	6.4	7.6	8.7	10.3	10.7
11%	0.6	1.7	2.9	4.2	5.5	6.8	8.0	9.1	10.6	11.1
12%	0.6	1.8	3.1	4.5	5.8	7.1	8.3	9.4	10.9	11.3

Federal Reserve/Bank of England

The Federal Reserve and the Bank of England were among the first to develop a methodology for creating swap risk factors.[9] The two regulators examined the average replacement cost of a pair of matched swaps, as well as the maximum replacement cost of a single swap, utilizing a simulation procedure. The maximum replacement cost factors are shown in Table 9.6.

Key assumptions: 90 percent confidence level, lognormal distribution, 18.2 percent volatility, 9 percent initial interest rate.

Table 9.6 Federal Reserve/Bank of England

Yrs	1	2	3	4	5	6	7	8	9	10
RF%	0.5	1.5	2.8	4.3	6.0	7.8	9.6	11.5	13.4	15.3

Arak, Goodman, and Rones

Arak, Goodman, and Rones (1986) have presented a model that simulates maximum exposure and yields the risk factors given in Table 9.7 (for a semi-annual fixed payer/floating receiver swap).

Key assumptions: upward sloping yield curve and volatilities based on active Treasuries in 1985, short term rates which follow a random path with no drift coefficient.

Table 9.7 Arak, Goodman, and Rones

Yrs	2	3	4	5	7	10
RF%	1.43	2.69	4.17	5.94	9.51	15.08

Whittaker

Whittaker (1987) has presented an option-based model that yields the risk factors given in Table 9.8a (for a semi-annual fixed receiver/floating payer swap).

Risk factors for a matched pair of swaps are shown in Table 9.8b.

Key assumptions: Cox, Ross, and Rubinstein (1979) option pricing model, lognormal distribution, 22 percent volatility to seven years, 23 percent volatility beyond seven years.

Table 9.8a Whittaker									
Yrs	1	2	3	4	5	6	7	8	9	10
RF%	0.23	0.56	0.86	1.18	1.50	1.81	2.11	2.45	2.77	3.09

Table 9.8b Whittaker									
Yrs	1	2	3	4	5	6	7	8	9	10
RF%	0.43	1.13	1.79	2.48	3.15	3.82	4.45	5.22	5.91	6.57

Ferron and Handjinicolaou

Ferron and Handjinicolaou (1987)[10] have presented a lognormal simulation-based model that yields the risk factors shown in Table 9.9.

Key assumptions: lognormal distribution, 20 percent volatility, 9 percent initial interest rate.

Table 9.9 Ferron and Handjinicolaou					
Yrs	1	3	5	7	10
RF%	0.12	0.76	1.49	2.18	3.13

Muffet

Muffet (1986) has presented a simulation-based model that calculates the average replacement cost for a matched pair of five year fixed-floating swaps as 1 percent; once adjusted to a 90 percent confidence level, the average replacement cost rises to 2 percent. For a single fixed payer swap (not adjusted to a 90 percent confidence level), the maximum (rather than average) replacement cost is 2 percent.

Key assumptions: lognormal distribution, 18 percent volatility, 90 percent confidence level, 9 percent initial interest rate.

Hull

Hull (1989) has presented a simulation-based model that generates the risk factors given in Table 9.10 (for a fixed receiver/floating payer swap).

Key assumptions: 20 percent volatility, flat term structure, and an initial interest rate of 5 percent with zero growth and constant volatility.

Table 9.10 Hull				
Yrs	2	5	10	15
RF%	0.30	1.20	3.20	5.50

Giberti, Mentini, and Scabellone

Giberti, Mentini, and Scabellone (1993) have presented a simulation model to calculate credit exposures for interest rate and currency swaps. The average replacement costs for fixed payer/floating receiver swaps are shown in Table 9.11a. The maximum replacement costs for fixed payer/floating receiver swaps are shown in Table 9.11b.

Key assumptions: reference distribution derived from historical observations of empirical data, not from a prespecified distribution (that is, normal, lognormal), 95 percent confidence level.

Table 9.11a Giberti, Mentini, and Scabellone		
Yrs	1	2	3
RF%	1.09	1.44	1.29

Table 9.11b Giberti, Mentini, and Scabellone		
Yrs	1	2	3
RF%	2.52	4.79	4.33

The quantification process we have presented in this chapter, though based on interest rate swaps, can be adapted for other swap-related products constructed on different underlying references. We shall use aspects of this framework in our discussion on complex swaps in the next chapter and again when we consider portfolio risk management issues in Part III.

CHAPTER 10

The Credit Risk of Complex Swaps

While vanilla swaps are extremely well established in the financial markets and have become an essential building block of corporate risk management, various complex swap structures have been created in recent years and are becoming increasingly popular as well. In this chapter we describe and analyze a number of these instruments, building on the credit risk quantification methods described in the last chapter.

In previous chapters we have considered derivative structures as generically as possible to demonstrate how they might be used across a range of underlying markets and references. In this chapter we are required to narrow our discussion slightly and analyze complex swaps in terms of the markets in which they are normally used; we find that not all swap structures are applicable to all underlying reference markets – hence our narrower focus. In particular, we describe and analyze structures that are found primarily in the interest rate, currency, credit, equity, and "new asset class" markets. More specifically, we consider:

Interest rate and currency markets

- Inverse floater swaps.

- Leveraged swaps.

- Differential swaps.

- Variable principal swaps:
  - amortizing swaps
  - accreting swaps

– mortgage swaps

– index principal swaps/reverse index principal swaps.

Credit markets

■ Credit forwards.

■ Default swaps.

■ Total return swaps.

Equity markets

■ Equity index swaps.

■ Volatility swaps.

Other markets

■ Inflation swaps.

■ Electricity swaps.

■ Temperature swaps.

We shall not discuss other "non-standard" structures such as putable and callable swaps, forward swaps, premium-discount swaps, or zero coupon swaps, as these have been described in a previous volume.[1] In the first section of this chapter we provide product description on each swap instrument (summarized in Table 10.1) and in the second section we discuss the credit risk quantification of each instrument.

PRODUCT DESCRIPTION

Interest rate and currency market references

The interest rate and currency swap markets, which are the most established and advanced sectors of the OTC derivative market, feature a range of complex swap structures that have become widely used by a broad range of intermediaries and end users. Though the list of transactions and variations is extensive, we focus our discussion on several key instruments,

Table 10.1 Complex swap variations

Swap	Also known as	Variations
Interest rate and currency market references		
Inverse floater swap	Reverse swap Reverse floater swap	Leveraged inverse floater swap
Leveraged swap	Power swap Ratio swap	–
Differential swap	Diff swap Quanto swap	–
Variable principal swap	–	Amortizing swap Accreting swap Mortgage swap Index principal swap Reverse index principal swap
Credit market references		
Credit forward	–	–
Default swap	–	First-to-default swap Basket swap (Credit portfolio swap)
Total return swap	Total rate of return swap	–
Equity market references		
Equity index swap	–	Call swap Put swap Call/put swap
Volatility swap	–	Realized volatility swap Variance swap
Other market references		
Inflation swap	CPI swap, RPI swap, HICP swap	Zero coupon inflation swap Annual inflation swap
Electricity swap	–	–
Temperature swap	Degree day swap	Heating degree day swap Cooling degree day swap Average temperature swap

including inverse floater swaps, leveraged swaps, differential swaps, and variable principal swaps.

Inverse floater swaps

An *inverse floater swap* (also known as a reverse swap or reverse floater swap) is a derivative used to take advantage of, or protect against, movements in a particular yield curve. An inverse floater swap exchanges a floating rate index for a fixed rate less the same floating rate index. The general form of the flows is

Pay or receive: (x% fixed – floating index)

Receive or pay: floating index

Consider the following example. Bank XYZ believes US short-term rates will rise (either the yield curve will flatten as short rates rise or the entire curve will move up in a parallel fashion); to monetize this view, it enters into an inverse floater swap where it receives six-month US$ Libor flat and pays 15 percent minus six-month US$ Libor flat. Through this structure the inverse flows (for example, x percent fixed – floating index) move opposite the floating index flows. If six-month Libor rises, XYZ receives a greater payment, just as it would under any standard swap; however, it also makes a smaller payment, since 15 percent minus an increasing Libor rate generates a smaller coupon payment. In this example XYZ's pay and receive legs benefit from an upward movement in rates, and suffer from a downward movement. Thus, the correct view allows the bank to magnify gains, while an incorrect view compounds losses. This is essentially a mechanism by which to leverage a particular position and view (in fact, in our credit risk discussion below we demonstrate that a leverage approach is useful when considering the credit risk exposure of these transactions).

In addition to utilizing inverse floater swaps to express a view on a given curve, they are also used to hedge asset or liability flows that are structured in the same fashion. Since the mid-1990s, for example, various government agencies and corporations have issued inverse floating rate notes (or warrants exercisable into notes with inverse floating coupons). A swap, such as the one described above, can hedge a position in the underlying note. Figure 10.1 illustrates the flows of an inverse floater swap.

Leveraged swaps

A *leveraged swap* (also known as a power swap or ratio swap) is a derivative that features payments and/or receipts which are adjusted by a

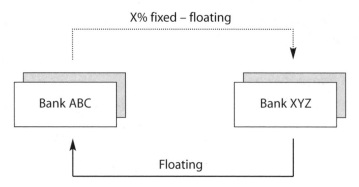

Figure 10.1 Inverse floater swap

leverage, or multiplier, factor. These swaps are structured to magnify one side of the transaction payout; as a result of this "magnification" the effects of rate movements are compounded. Leverage can be applied to virtually any type of swap (for example, traditional fixed/floating swaps, inverse floating swaps, currency swaps, and so on) and can be defined in any manner. The actual leverage payout formulae can either be simple and transparent or complex and opaque.

Let us consider several examples of the leveraged swap structure. Assume Bank LMN believes US$ Libor rates will decline; rather than book a standard vanilla swap, it elects to leverage its view by entering into a structure where it pays (2 * 6-month Libor) in exchange for a fixed rate. Since the net present value of a par swap equals zero at inception, the fixed payment LMN receives under the transaction is significantly higher than that of a vanilla swap. Assume for simplicity that six-month Libor and fixed swap rates are both 7 percent on trade date. Ignoring present value and credit pricing considerations, we assume LMN contracts to pay the leveraged Libor flow in exchange for 14 percent fixed. If the bank's view is correct and six-month rates fall by 100 basis points, to 6 percent, it pays 12 percent and receives 14 percent; the net effect of the leverage is to compound the gain by an extra 100 basis points. If Libor falls 200 basis points, to 5 percent, it pays 10 percent and receives 14 percent; the net differential is thus 400 basis points (under a vanilla swap the downward move in Libor to 5 percent only generates a gain of 200 basis points).

We can easily consider the opposite scenario: if Libor rises by 200 basis points, to 9 percent, the bank's payment equals 18 percent and its receipt 14 percent, indicating a net outflow of 400 basis points (200 basis points more than a vanilla swap). Note that LMN could incorporate greater leverage into the swap by multiplying the Libor flow by three, four, five, or more times; alternatively, it could square or cube the Libor flow (or insert Libor into an esoteric formula). As we might expect, the greater the leverage multiplier, the greater the potential gain or loss, and use of extremely large leverage factors can therefore be very risky. Figure 10.2 illustrates the pay/receive flows for a swap involving two, three, and four times leverage.

In our second example, we enhance the inverse floater swap described above by incorporating a leverage factor. Consider a transaction where Dealer STU, the inverse rate payer, pays 25 percent – (3 * six-month Libor) and receives six-month Libor + 50 basis points. Assuming six-month Libor moves to 6 percent on the first reset date, STU pays 7 percent (25 percent – (3 * 6 percent)) and receives 6.50 percent, for a net gain of 50 basis points. If Libor rises to 7 percent, STU only pays 4 percent, and receives 7.50 percent, for a net gain of 350 basis points. Thus, a 100 basis point upward move in Libor rates allows STU to save 300 basis points on its pay flow and earn 100 basis points on its receive flow (which is what it was expecting in any event, since the receive component is not leveraged). If, in contrast, Libor falls to 5 percent, then STU pays 10 percent (25 percent – (3 * 5 percent)) (300 basis points above the starting point) and receives 5.5 percent (100 basis points below the starting level); this results in a net payment of 450 basis points and demonstrates, rather clearly, the effects of leverage.

As indicated above, leveraged structures are generally utilized to compound the effects of a certain view of the market (and only rarely to hedge a structured asset or liability). Many of the dramatic derivative losses of the early to mid-1990s were based on the use of leverage in a variety of swap structures; in many instances the payoff formulae used to

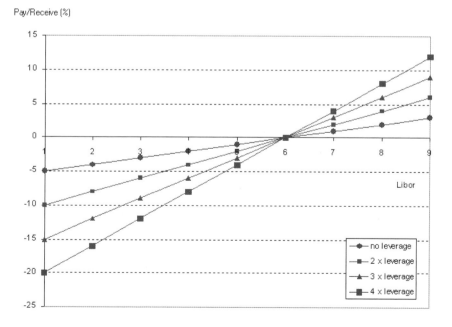

Figure 10.2 Pay/receive flows of leveraged swaps

compute pay or receive flows were complex and the true effects of leverage not always immediately apparent (particularly in absence of detailed and extensive scenario analysis).[2] Figures 10.3 and 10.4 illustrate the flows of the two leveraged swaps described above (with "n" degree of leverage).

Differential swaps

A *differential swap* (also known as a diff swap or a quanto swap) is a derivative that references interest rates in two different currencies, but calls for periodic payment on a net basis in a single currency; such a swap is often thought of as a package of an interest rate swap and a "quantized" swap (similar to the quanto options discussed in Chapter 8). Differential swaps have gained substantial popularity in recent years as intermediaries and investors attempt to capitalize on the movement in foreign money market rates (for example, foreign currency Libor) without assuming currency exposure.

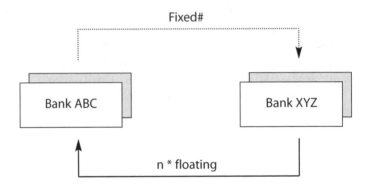

Figure 10.3 Leveraged swap
where Fixed is a function of the leverage factor n in order to generate an NPV of 0.

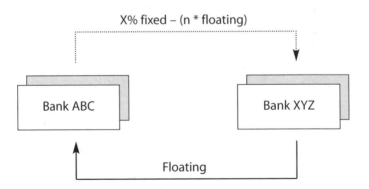

Figure 10.4 Leveraged inverse floater swap

Consider the following example. Bank ABC contracts with Dealer JKL to enter into a differential swap where it receives six-month Euribor and pays six-month US$ Libor plus a spread, all in dollars. Since the flows are payable in a single currency (dollars in this case), ABC takes no currency risk. (Note that in a differential swap there is typically a spread either added to or subtracted from one leg, reflecting the interest differential between the two currencies.) Establishing a differential position suggests ABC is attempting to take advantage of inaccuracies in implied forward rates. In this particular example, ABC may believe the Euribor curve will not fall as far, or the dollar curve will not rise as high, as implied rates suggest. As long as this holds true, ABC continues to benefit from the economics of the spread without being exposed to the direction of €/US$ foreign exchange rates.

Note that differential swaps are often combined with leveraged and/or inverse floating swaps to create additional speculative opportunities. A bank, for instance, may enter into a transaction to pay 15 percent minus (2 * ¥ Libor), in exchange for receiving US$ Libor less a spread, all in dollars. In this instance the bank hopes the short end of the ¥ Libor curve rises against (or remains above) the US$ Libor curve, since an increase in the leveraged inverse yen index subtracts from the required payment and means a greater differential. Figure 10.5 illustrates the flows of a generic differential swap, while Figure 10.6 highlights the construction of a US$ Libor/Euribor differential swap.

Variable principal swaps

A *variable principal* swap is a derivative transaction that is based on a dynamic notional principal amount that varies by time or the triggering of some event. Since the notional principal amount dictates the amount payable and/or receivable, any variation will have an impact on the amount paid or received (rate changes will also affect payables/receivables, of course). Several types of variable principal swaps are actively traded in the

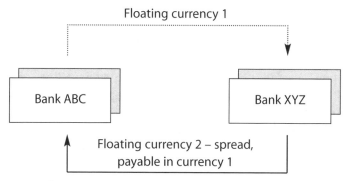

Figure 10.5 Differential swap

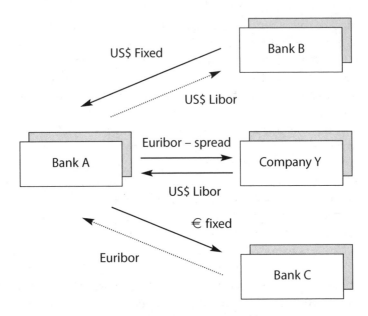

Figure 10.6 Creation of a US$ Libor/Euribor differential swap

market including the amortizing swap, accreting swap, mortgage swap, index principal swap, and reverse index principal swap. We consider each of these in greater detail below.

Amortizing swaps

An *amortizing swap* is a derivative that is based on a periodically declining notional principal balance. While standard swaps carry fixed notional principal balances until maturity, amortizing swaps feature dynamic notional principal balances that decline on a preset basis at select intervals. An amortizing swap is often used when an institution needs to swap an exact series of flows from a particular asset or liability with a declining principal balance (for instance, airlines utilize amortizing swaps to hedge flows under aircraft leases, which typically amortize on a preset schedule); the ability to customize interest receipts or payments to match dynamic flows from source assets or liabilities provides end users with greater precision in asset/liability management efforts. It should be noted that a swap amortization schedule need not necessarily be straight line; any type of principal reduction can be constructed and swapped, though an even flow of reductions tends to be most common.

Consider an example where Bank CDE enters into an amortizing swap where it pays fixed rates in exchange for floating rates, based on a declining principal balance. Under the terms of the transaction the principal begins at US$100m and amortizes on a straight line basis for each of the five years of the swap; by the final year of the swap the reference balance amounts to only US$20m, indicating interest payments exchanged (or netted) on remaining payment dates are significantly smaller than at the inception of the trade. Note that mortgage swaps and index principal swaps, treated below, are versions of the amortizing swap structure. Figure 10.7 illustrates the flows of a generic amortizing swap which amortizes from notional N at time t, to notional N – X at time t + 1, N – X – Y at time t + 2, and so on.

Accreting swaps

An *accreting swap* is the reverse of an amortizing swap. This transaction features a notional principal that increases with the passage of time, suggesting that the value exchanged and potential credit risk also grow over time. Accreting swaps can be used to match the cash flows of a given structured transaction or financing. For instance, if a company is going to draw down increasing amounts of funding under a revolving credit facility, and wants to make sure that all new amounts are hedged, it might enter into

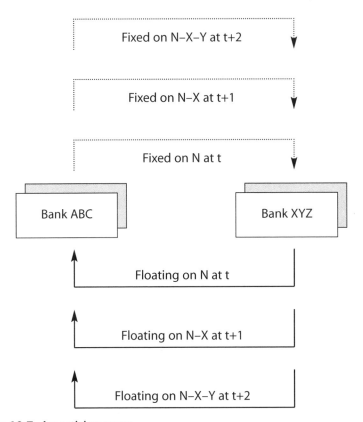

Figure 10.7 Amortizing swap

an accreting swap that grows in size with each new pre-planned drawdown. Apart from the schedule of notional principal increases, the structure of the accreting swap is identical to the amortizing swap.

Mortgage swaps

A mortgage swap, which is a subclass of the amortizing swap structure detailed above, is a derivative designed to replicate the flows found in a specific pool of mortgage-backed securities (MBS). MBS, which are formed by pooling individual residential or commercial mortgages, are very sensitive to interest rate changes that can impact notional principal balances. For instance, as rates decline, borrowers tend to pre-pay their outstanding mortgages so that they can refinance at lower rates; as pre-payments occur, the notional balance of the MBS declines in tandem. In contrast, when rates rise pre-payments slow as borrowers seek to preserve their existing borrowings, meaning that the notional balance of the MBS remains relatively unchanged. Mortgage swaps seek to match the flows of such MBS pools, and can thus serve as a hedge or synthetic investment.

A typical mortgage swap provides an investor with a fixed rate (for instance Treasuries plus a spread), "decompounded" and paid monthly, in exchange for payment of a monthly floating rate (typically US$ Libor). The notional principal of the swap amortizes (just as the principal in an MBS amortizes through principal repayments by the ultimate home-owner) at a rate equivalent to the amortization level of specific MBS issues (for example, Federal National Mortgage Association (FNMA) 9 percent securities). The amortization level may be calculated, for example, by taking the amortization rates of all FNMA 9s issued between a specified time period and projecting future amortization based on various interest rate pre-payment scenarios. Through these parameters the swap flows (including the declining balance) duplicate the flows generated by the physical securities.

There are various other ways of creating a mortgage swap. For instance, the swap might duplicate a specific security, or a pool of mortgage-backed securities (that is, a collateralized mortgage obligation, or CMO, which is comprised of pools of MBS). In a CMO swap an investor might pay US$ Libor and receive a fixed coupon; the swap notional amortizes on a schedule determined by Public Securities Association (PSA) pre-payment rates, tied to a monthly amortization factor. Another common structure involves the synthetic replication of a FNMA adjustable rate mortgage (ARM) pass-through based on the 11th District Cost of Funds Index (COFI). Under this swap, the investor pays US$ Libor and receives floating COFI on a notional amount which amortizes at a rate equal to the amortization of FNMA COFI ARM pass-throughs.

Figure 10.8 illustrates the flows of a generic mortgage swap which amortizes from notional N at time t, to notional N – X at time t + 1, and so on, based on the amortization schedule of the reference MBS.

Index principal swaps/reverse index principal swaps

An *index principal swap* (IPS) (also known as an index amortizing rate (IAR) swap), is another subcategory of the amortizing swap discussed above and is commonly used to manage asset-liability flows or express specific views on the volatility of interest rates. Under a standard IPS structure, the notional principal of the swap amortizes on a set schedule as Libor (or Constant Maturity Treasuries (CMT) or some alternate floating index) declines. For instance, if rates fall by 50 basis points by the next reset period, the notional might reduce by 20 percent; if rates fall by 100 basis points, the notional might reduce by 40 percent, and so on. Rather than a straight step-level (that is, 20 or 40 percent amortization based on 50 or 100 basis point movements in Libor), the amortization can be calculated through a formula in order to take account of small changes in rates (that is, one or five basis points). While the notional of an IPS amortizes if floating rates fall, it remains constant if rates rise or remain stable; in this case the swap retains the characteristics of a plain vanilla transaction with full notional principal. In an IPS, the bank paying the floating rate is said to be the purchaser of the swap; in exchange for paying the floating rate, it receives a fixed rate that is typically set above market levels. The above market rate is the bank's compensation for effec-

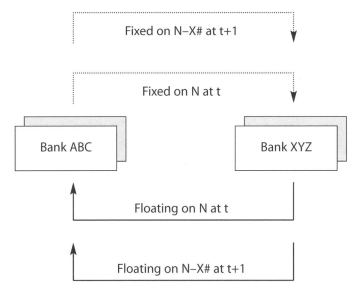

Figure 10.8 Mortgage swap
Where X is a function of the actual or anticipated amortization schedule of the reference MBS.

tively having written a strip of binary options (that is, if floating rates fall to a certain level the binary option moves in-the-money and triggers amortization); the seller of an IPS pays the above market fixed rate and receives the floating rate. IPSs typically have a *lockout period* during which no amortization takes place, regardless of the movement in rates; this period generally lasts for the first few years of a multi-year transaction. They also usually feature a "cleanup call" that terminates the swap if the floating rate index declines through all amortization barriers during the lockout period.

The purchaser of an IPS (as floating rate payer) favors stable rates. If rates fall sharply, the notional of the swap amortizes (indicating the average life falls) and reinvestment occurs at lower rates. If floating rates rise sharply, the swap retains its full notional value and the floating rate payer sacrifices the opportunity to invest at higher rates. The seller of an IPS (as floating rate receiver) favors either rising or falling rates for the opposite reasons. Figure 10.9 illustrates the flows of a generic IPS which amortizes from notional N at time t, to notional N − X at time t + 1 if the first floating rate binary level is breached on the downside, to N − X − Y at time t + 2 if the second floating rate binary level is breached, and so on.

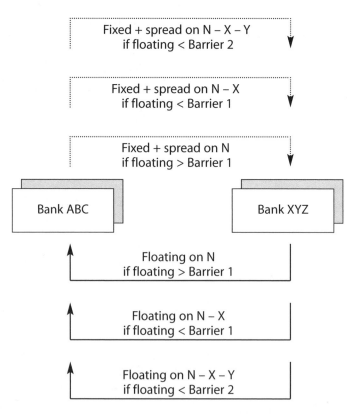

Figure 10.9 Index principal swap

In addition to standard IPSs, there is also a market for *reverse index principal swaps* (reverse IPSs); the derivatives are often used to hedge portfolios of IPSs or mortgage swaps. As the name indicates, reverse IPSs perform in a manner opposite to that of the IPS described above and can thus be considered a type of accreting swap. Specifically, if floating rates fall the notional of the reverse IPS increases, meaning interest payments increase. If floating rates remain stable, the notional principal balance remains unchanged. Figure 10.10 highlights the flows of a reverse IPS.

Credit market references

The broad category of credit derivatives includes credit options (which we discussed in Chapter 8) and a series of credit forward and credit swap-related products. In this section we discuss three of the most common credit swap instruments: credit forwards, default swaps, and total return swaps (it should be noted that total return swap structures can be applied to a broader range of markets and products, though they are very prevalent in the credit markets). These three structures, together with credit options, form the fundamental "building blocks" of the credit derivative market.

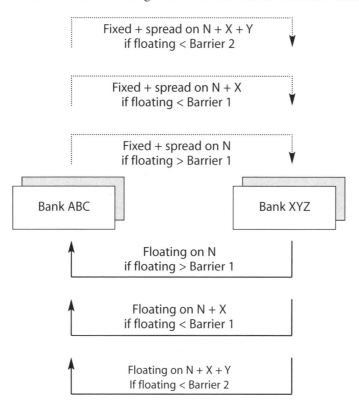

Figure 10.10 Reverse index principal swap

Credit forwards

A *credit forward* is a single period bilateral contract that references the appreciation or depreciation of an issuer's credit quality in either price or spread terms, up to, and including, the point of default. Under a typical credit forward an institution can take a view on an issuer's credit by entering into a forward with a second institution that has the opposite view. A buyer contracts with a seller to purchase a given reference bond at an agreed forward date and forward price (or spread against a risk-free benchmark); if the underlying credit improves (for example, the bond price rises or the credit spread narrows) the buyer realizes a gain and the seller a loss. If an institution believes a credit will deteriorate, it sells the reference bond at an agreed forward date and forward price (or spread); if the underlying credit deteriorates (for example, the bond price falls or the spread widens), the seller realizes a gain and the buyer sustains a loss. The extreme event in this situation relates to counterparty default; if the reference credit defaults, the price of the obligation will fall (or spread widen) dramatically; the payoff to the seller will relate to the value assigned to the reference obligation in bankruptcy.

In addition to using credit forwards to take a view on the direction of an issuer's credit quality, forwards can also be used to manage portfolios of credit exposures; we shall discuss this at greater length in Part III. Credit forwards (which can be settled in cash or physical) carry maturities ranging from several months to several years and can be structured to reference either the target bond's price or spread; forwards which are structured in spread terms include a duration adjustment to account for the basis point price sensitivity of the underlying reference bond.

Consider the following example. Bank HIJ believes Company XYZ's credit will deteriorate over the next 12 months; in order to capitalize on this view it sells Bank ABC a 12-month credit forward based on US$10m of four year XYZ bonds, with the forward set at a spread of 200 basis points over Treasuries. The forward pays off based on the differential between the spread at maturity and the contracted forward spread. Assume XYZ's credit quality deteriorates by the end of the transaction and its bonds trade at a spread of 300 basis points over Treasuries (note that the duration at this point is equal to two). As a result of the credit deterioration, HIJ receives a payment of US$200,000 from ABC (US$10m * 2 * (0.03 – 0.02)). Since a forward is a bilateral contract, we note that if XYZ's credit improves over the life of the contract – as reflected, for instance, by a tightening of the spread to 100 over Treasuries – ABC receives a payment of US$200,000 from HIJ (US$10m * 2 * (0.02 – 0.01)). Figure 10.11 illustrates the flows of a generic price-based credit forward (such structures often pay off as a percentage of appreciation or depreciation against a notional value).

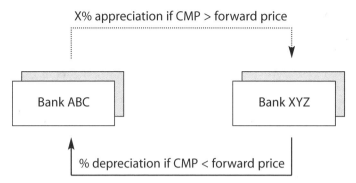

Figure 10.11 Credit forward

Default swaps

The *default swap*, one of the original instruments of the credit derivative market, is a bilateral, multi-year derivative used to transfer credit risk between two parties. Default swaps can be used to take a specific speculative view on the probability of credit default or protect/hedge an underlying credit position. Under a standard default swap a counterparty with excess credit exposure on its book pays a second counterparty a periodic fee (often a fixed number of basis points against a notional amount) in exchange for a lump sum or periodic floating payment if the underlying reference counterparty defaults on an obligation. The default payment is typically based on the difference between the pre and post-default price of the reference credit's publicly traded debt. Note that in this section, and the one which follows on total return swaps, we define "buyer" as the party purchasing credit protection, for example, making a payment in exchange for a potential payoff if the underlying reference credit defaults; in purchasing such protection the buyer becomes "short the credit" and benefits economically on the position if the credit deteriorates. The "seller" is defined as the party selling the credit protection; in selling the protection it becomes "long the credit," benefiting economically on the position if the credit improves and losing if the credit deteriorates.

Consider the following example. Bank ABC has US$30m of credit exposure with Company XYZ and wants to enter into a default swap referencing XYZ's credit (perhaps it is concerned about XYZ's financial position or wishes to free credit lines to engage in more business with the company). It contracts with Securities Firm JKL to buy a default swap; under the swap ABC pays JKL 25 basis points running on US$30m notional for two years. In exchange, JKL provides ABC with a contingent payment if XYZ defaults on any of its obligations during the two year period; the security for determining the contingent payment is XYZ's five-year fixed rate Eurobond, currently trading at par. Let us assume two scenarios. Scenario one: over the next two years XYZ remains current on its liabilities (including the five-year Eurobond and all of its credit obligations with Bank ABC). Under this scenario JKL earns a fixed fee of US$150,000 and is not required to make a payment to ABC. Scenario two: XYZ experiences financial difficulties and defaults on one or more of its liabilities; once default occurs, the reference Eurobond trades at a price of 50 among distressed debt dealers. ABC receives only a fractional portion of the US$30m due from XYZ (let us assume that, as a senior unsecured creditor, it eventually recovers 50 cents on the dollar, or $15m). Under the terms of the default swap, however, JKL makes a payment of approximately US$15m to ABC (((100 – 50)/100) * $30m) meaning ABC recoups its loss; the payment from JKL might be made as a lump sum or an annuity, depending on the specific terms of the agreement. Note that this example is simplified; the trading price of the reference bond post-default and the recoveries on current obligations are unlikely to match precisely, so there may be a net gain or loss to ABC. Figure 10.12 illustrates the flows of a typical default swap.

An extension of the default swap (which references a single credit) is the first-to-default swap, which groups together several credits and then provides a payoff based on the default of any single one. Though any number of credits can be included in the portfolio, payment is only made on the first reference credit that defaults; if others default, no further payment is made.

Consider the following example: Portfolio Manager RST, seeking to protect the overall credit quality of its portfolio (which has outstanding credit exposure to Company ABC (steel industry), Company DEF (media industry), and Company STU (auto industry)), might purchase a first-to-default swap covering ABC, DEF, and STU. If DEF defaults, it will receive a compensatory payment defined by the characteristics of the trade; if STU then defaults, the

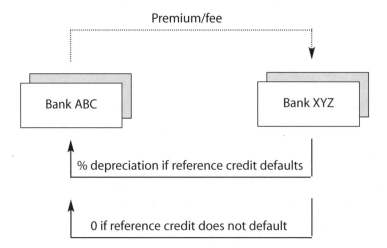

Figure 10.12 Default swap

portfolio manager receives no further payment. While this appears to be simply a mini-portfolio of individual default swaps, the correlative effects that exist between individual credits generally result in a cheaper level of pricing (unless, perhaps, all of the credits are taken from a deeply troubled industry). A more generalized version of this structure is a *basket swap* (also known as a credit portfolio swap), which bundles together a variety of credits and provides payout for every one that ultimately defaults.

Total return swaps

The *total return swap* (TRS) has emerged as a popular derivative that can be used to synthetically replicate and transfer the price appreciation/depreciation of a reference asset. Though virtually any asset can serve as a reference, the instrument has been used widely in the credit markets, hence our inclusion of the TRS under the credit category.

A standard credit-based TRS provides credit protection for one party (the buyer) and a synthetic off balance sheet position in a risky bond (or an entire portfolio of bonds) for a second party (the seller). Through the TRS a buyer transfers the economics, and hence credit exposure, of the risky bond, meaning that it effectively purchases credit deterioration/default protection; the seller, in contrast, receives the economics of the risky bond, indicating that it has synthetically purchased the instrument. Under a standard TRS the buyer of the swap pays the seller a flow which reflects the coupon on a third-party reference bond; in exchange, the seller passes the buyer a smaller flow (often Libor-based). In addition, at maturity of the transaction the current price of the bond is compared to a predetermined starting price: if the price has declined (a possible sign of credit deterioration), the seller pays the buyer a lump sum payment reflecting the depreciation; if the price has risen, the buyer pays the seller a lump sum payment reflecting the appreciation. The seller thus has a synthetic long position in the bond without actually holding the security on its balance sheet; it receives appreciation and periodic interest payments reflecting the coupons from the bond and pays depreciation. The buyer, in turn, hedges its exposure to the issuer of the bond. If, for example, the bond issuer defaults, the buyer of the TRS loses on its own balance sheet inventory position (or related credit exposure) but receives a compensatory lump sum payment from the seller. If the bond issuer performs, the buyer of the TRS is repaid on the bond (or related credit exposure) by the issuer, but makes a lump sum payment to the seller of the TRS in an amount reflecting the appreciation. Note that most TRS maturities range from six to 24 months, though longer-term transactions can be negotiated. And, although interim payments are exchanged (for example, bond coupons for a Libor payment) the main economic payoff generally relates to the capital gain/loss at the conclusion of the transaction (indeed, in our risk discussion below, though the incremental spread exchanged periodically features in the computation, the main REE focus is on bond appreciation/depreciation occurring at final maturity).

Consider the following example. Bank PQR has a US$50m position in Company ABC's three-year bond, which is trading at 95 (the same level where PQR originally purchased the bond). Since PQR wants to reduce its exposure to ABC (without selling the bond outright) it enters into a 12-month, US$50m TRS with Dealer XYZ. Under the terms of the agreement PQR pays XYZ a fixed quarterly coupon (reflecting the coupon of the ABC bond) in exchange for Libor flat. In addition, in 12 months the two parties will exchange a final lump sum payment; if the price of ABC's bond is greater than 95, PQR will pay XYZ appreciation as a percentage of the agreed level times the US$50m notional (note that it may also be structured as a percentage of par against the notional, or an absolute price increase times the number of bonds involved; various conventions can be used, but the economic effect is always the same). If the price is less than 95, XYZ will pay PQR depreciation on the same basis.

Consider the following two scenarios. Scenario one: 12 months from now ABC's credit quality improves and the reference bond trades at 100; in addition to having passed the incremental coupon to XYZ, PQR pays XYZ a lump sum of approximately US$2.5m. PQR, however, has sold its own bond for a similar gain and sustains no loss (and, in the process, may have had the opportunity of entering into incremental credit-sensitive business with ABC). Scenario two: near the end of the 12-month period ABC encounters financial difficulties and defaults on its obligations; upon default its bond trades at distressed levels of 45. In this instance PQR sustains a loss of approximately US$26m on its inventory position. It expects, however, to receive approximately US$26m from XYZ under the terms of the TRS when the transaction matures (note that we have simplified the timing considerations for simplicity; in reality the default on the underlying reference bond and the maturity of the TRS are unlikely to coincide so there are likely to be timing mismatches). Figure 10.13 highlights the flows of a credit-based total return swap.

Equity market references

The equity derivative market, comprised of both equity related options and equity swaps, has been in existence since the early 1990s (many of the compound strategies and complex options we have described in Chapters 7 and 8 are bought and sold on equity references, for example, single stocks, baskets, portfolios, and broad indexes). Investment and portfolio managers seeking to hedge or synthetically replicate equity market returns actively use equity swap structures. Within this category we consider equity index swaps and volatility swaps.

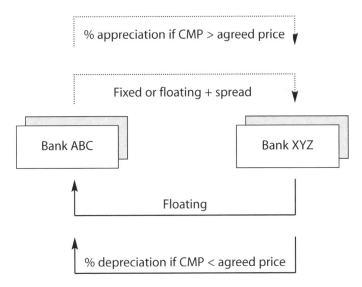

Figure 10.13 Total return swap

Equity index swaps

An *equity index swap* is a derivative that provides an investor or intermediary with specific exposure to, or protection against, a range of equity instruments. The fundamental equity swap allows one or both swap parties to achieve gains based on the appreciation or depreciation in a single equity, basket of equities, or an equity index; maturities typically range from one to five years, though transactions can be structured with shorter or longer terms.

In a typical equity index swap, the buyer of the swap pays the seller premium in exchange for appreciation or depreciation in the relevant index, which might be a specific stock, a sector basket, or a broad market index. The premium may be paid as an upfront cash payment or a series of periodic payments spread over the life of the swap (often in the form of a Libor flow); the latter tends to be a popular convention. If the buyer receives index appreciation, it is effectively long an *equity call swap* (that is, it receives value as the market price of the index rises above a certain strike price); if it receives depreciation, it is long an *equity put swap* (that is, it receives value as the market price of the index falls below a certain strike price). The seller does not pay the buyer if there is no appreciation (for the call swap) or depreciation (for the put swap). Note that certain equity swaps are also structured as bilateral contracts. For instance, one party may contract with a second party to receive appreciation and pay depreciation; this is equal to the first party purchasing a call swap and selling a put swap, which is precisely equivalent to the TRS described above. The net premium payment (whether upfront or periodic) depends on the relative "strike" levels and intrinsic value of the two market references.

Given the customized nature of the equity index swap market, an institution can readily gain exposure or protection through alternate swap structures, including straddles, strangles, and spreads. For instance, a firm may wish to receive index appreciation or depreciation (along with dividends) through the swap; this is the equivalent of owning a straddle (equal strikes) or strangle (different strikes). As before, in return for this payoff the buyer pays the seller premium in the form of an upfront sum or periodic Libor flow. Figure 10.14 illustrates a generic equity call swap while Figure 10.15 reflects a combination equity call–put swap (where the call is struck further in-the-money and neither party receives dividends).

Payment in an equity swap can be exchanged periodically or at maturity. For instance, two institutions may arrange to compare the strike with the index level prevailing at quarterly intervals, and net settle in one direction or the other; the process can then be repeated at the next evaluation period, and so on, until maturity. This can be viewed as a package of forwards, since the index differential is settled each quarter and then continues until the next period, when another measurement and settlement occurs. Alternatively, the two institutions might choose not to compare the index values at any time during the life of the transaction except maturity. At maturity an examination takes place and one party makes the required payment – effectively a single period forward contract.

As indicated above, the equity swap market is very flexible. We can consider an example of various ways in which Bank Q, currently holding a portfolio of US Treasury notes yielding 5.5 percent, can participate in the appreciation of a given index, say the Nikkei 225, by entering into an equity swap with Bank Z. Depending on Bank Q's view of the Nikkei, it may exchange the interest received from the bonds for appreciation in the Nikkei

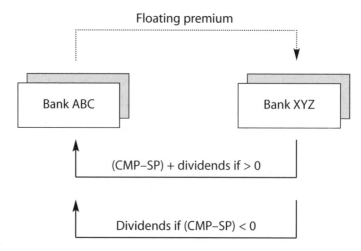

Figure 10.14 Equity call swap

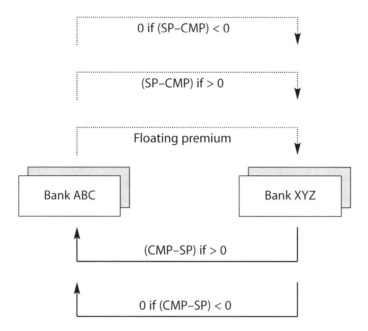

Figure 10.15 Equity call–put swap

(for example, perhaps buying an in-the-money call swap struck at 19,000 in a market trading at 20,000). Alternatively, if it believes the Nikkei's upside potential is limited it might cap its upside gain by writing a call at a higher strike (for example, 24,000), in exchange for premium income which enhances total return (for example, a call spread swap). If, however, Q feels the market will continue to rise and does not wish to cap the upside (but still desires premium income), it may write an equity put swap (that is, pay Bank Z depreciation in the index below, say, 17,000) and earn premium (for example, a collar swap). If two years from now the Nikkei is at 22,000 and Bank Q selected the first scenario, it realizes a gain of approximately 15.7 percent, which is superior to the gain from the Treasury notes (11 percent assuming no compounding). If two years from now the Nikkei is at 16,000 and Bank Q selected the third scenario, it realizes no gain on the transaction except premium received from selling the put swap at 16,000. In addition, it foregoes 11 percent in interest on the Treasury notes and makes a 5.9 percent payment to Bank Z for index depreciation.

Volatility swaps

Volatility swaps, derivative contracts that are typically structured as single period forwards, reference the movement of volatility evident in an equity index (rather than the absolute price or level of the index itself). Through the contract an institution makes, or receives, a payment that is based on the level of turbulence occurring in the market. This can be useful when trying to hedge an entire portfolio of equities or index contracts, or taking a specific view on the possible level and direction of volatility, just as a buyer/seller of straddles, strangles, butterflies, or condors might in the options markets; unlike these option strategies, however, the volatility swap features no exchange of premium. Although the equity volatility swap is a relatively new element of the derivative markets (having been introduced in late 1998), it has become very popular as it permits very direct and efficient treatment of volatility exposures (indeed, the market has become much more "two-sided" and bid-offer spreads are narrowing steadily). Contract maturities range from less than one year out to five years; longer transactions are possible, though still rare. Volatility references are typically based on large blue-chip stocks or major indexes, where the availability of quality volatility information on which to base payment/receipt calculations is readily available (and where alternate risk management hedging tools are available for dealers).[3]

Different types of volatility swaps are available in the marketplace; two of the most popular include the realized volatility swap and the variance swap. A *realized volatility swap* is a linear contract that generates a payoff based on the difference between realized volatility and implied volatility. Realized volatility is the floating volatility of the underlying reference index evident over the life of the transaction, while implied volatility is the fixed volatility rate contracted between buyer and seller at the start of the transaction. A *variance swap*, in contrast, is a non-linear contract that generates a payoff based on the difference between the square of the realized volatility and the square of the implied volatility. Since it is nonlinear, it provides the purchaser with *positive convexity*, meaning losses and gains are not symmetric (for example, when realized variance is greater than implied variance gains are greater, and when realized variance is less than implied variance losses are smaller); the seller is obviously exposed to *negative convexity*.

Consider an example of a realized volatility swap. Investment Manager OPQ owns a diversified portfolio of UK equities that very nearly replicates the FTSE-100 index. Concerned about potential market turbulence over the next 24 months, it wants to protect its portfolio. Although OPQ has investigated the use of options strategies it has also discussed a volatility swap on the FTSE-100 index with its banker, Investment Bank ABC. It decides to enter into a 24-month volatility swap, where it will receive a payment in two years (at UK£100,000 per index volatility point) if FTSE-100 realized volatility is above the current implied level of 15 percent, and will make a payment if it is below 15 percent. We can now imagine two scenarios. Scenario one: the FTSE-100 remains very tranquil, moving up and down only gradually; realized volatility at the end of the transaction amounts to 12 percent, requiring OPQ to pay ABC UK£300,000. However, OPQ's own portfolio has not been impacted by the turbulence (which was the risk it was seeking to protect against). Scenario two: the FTSE-100 goes through a period of tremendous market instability, with volatilities spiking up to 25 percent during some quarterly periods; realized volatility at the end of the period amounts to 19 percent, meaning OPQ receives UK£400,000 from ABC. Though OPQ's investment portfolio may have sustained some financial damage (depending on which stocks went up or down), the investment manager receives a compensatory payment from ABC. Figure 10.16 illustrates a standard implied volatility swap between two parties.

Other market references

Given the creativity of the financial engineering community it comes as no surprise that various other "new" swaps have been created in recent years. While most of these are not yet widely used, they appear to fill a market need and may ultimately become part of the "mainstream" of financial derivatives. In this section we consider certain swaps that are available on other market references, including inflation, electricity, and temperature.

Inflation swaps

The market for *inflation swaps* (sometimes referred to as consumer price index (CPI) swaps (US), retail price index (RPI) swaps (UK), or harmonized index of consumer prices (HICP) swaps (Eurozone)) has developed gradually since the mid-1990s as a variety of end users and intermediaries have sought to protect against, or take advantage of, actual changes in inflation. Activity in swaps has been boosted, in some cases, by issuance of inflation-linked securities by various government authorities (the Treasuries/Central Banks of the USA, UK, France/EU, and Sweden, among others, all have active inflation-linked bond issuance programs, some dating back to the 1980s). The market is also strengthened by the existence of two-sided

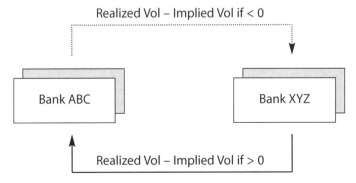

Figure 10.16 Realized volatility swap

activity: first, natural payers of inflation (or sellers of inflation swaps), for example, those whose revenues are positively correlated with changes in inflation such as municipal/state/regional government authorities with taxing power, utilities, and other firms with monopoly/oligopoly power that can pass price increases on to customers; and second, natural receivers of inflation (or buyers of swaps), for example, those whose revenues are negatively correlated with changes in inflation, such as industrial companies with core commodity inputs, insurance companies, or pension funds. Intermediaries are also able to hedge one side of an inflation swap with the inflation-linked securities, helping promote a certain amount of activity. Bid-offer spreads are very wide and transaction maturity is often quite long (for example, five to ten years or more); settlement typically occurs on a lagged basis (for example, three to nine months), as official government statistics reflecting the measure of inflation take time to compile. Various inflation swap structures have been arranged in recent years and we consider two of the most common: the zero coupon inflation swap, and the annual inflation swap.

The *zero coupon inflation swap* is a bilateral, multi-year contract agreed between two parties. Under a standard zero coupon swap, one party pays a fixed inflation rate (established on trade date) and receives a variable inflation rate at maturity (based on actual movements in the official inflation index); though the exchange of payments occurs only at maturity, the variable amount accretes during the life of the trade. This structure is, in essence a single-settlement, forward contract.

Consider the following example. Company ABC, seeking to lock-in certain production costs, enters into a zero coupon inflation swaps where it pays fixed inflation at 3 percent per annum over three years and receives, from Bank XYZ, variable inflation (based on lagged CPI) on US$100m notional. No payments will be exchanged until the end of year three. Over the intervening period actual inflation (the variable leg) registers at 4 percent, 5 percent, and 3 percent at each of the year end periods. Company ABC thus receives a payment of US$3m from XYZ at the end of year three. (Note that we ignore some of the PV-based timing differences related to lags for purposes of clarity.)

The *annual inflation swap* is a bilateral, multi-year contract that calls for an exchange of payments based on changes in the inflation index occurring over the prior year. The swap is thus similar to a package of forwards that settle every year (as discussed in the equity section above). Returning to the previous example, we note that at the end of year one ABC would be entitled to a payment of US$1m (1 percent inflation differential), at the end of year two it would receive US$2m (2 percent inflation differential) and at the end of year three it would receive no payment. (We again ignore the PV-based timing differences from lags.) Figure 10.17 illustrates the flow of a zero coupon inflation swap.

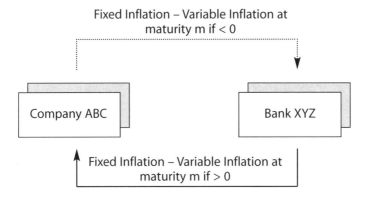

Figure 10.17 Zero coupon inflation swap

Electricity swaps

While swaps have been available on various energy-based commodity indexes for the past two decades (for example, fixed/floating physical swaps and non-physical ("paper") swaps on crude oil, natural gas, coal, fuel oil, jet fuel, and gas oil), the deregulation of global electricity markets – in North America, Europe, and parts of Asia – from the mid-1990s through the millennium, has led to greater volatility in electricity prices. As a consequence, end users and intermediaries have sought to manage electricity risks more actively and have done so through instruments such as electricity swaps (as well as OTC/listed electricity options).

The market for electricity swaps is most active in the USA, Canada, UK, Germany, and parts of Scandinavia, and is typically centered on an exchange of fixed for floating electricity prices (based on the average, rather than spot, level of a recognized pricing index). Most transactions are settled financially rather than physically, generally every month or quarter (to coincide with billing cycles). While most activity is concentrated in shorter maturities of less than one year, longer-term transactions are possible. Some electricity swaps reference "on peak" prices (for example, the daily 16-hour period of high demand) and others "off-peak" prices (the remaining eight-hour period).

Consider the following example: Company XYZ, an industrial firm whose production process requires significant amounts of electricity (which it purchases on a spot basis every month), is concerned that electricity prices are set to rise as a result of possible network transmission repairs and rising summer temperatures. In order to protect itself, it wants to lock in the monthly price it pays for peak-load electricity over the next 12 months, and arranges with Bank MNO to pay – on a notional block of 50 megawatts (MW) – fixed electricity at US$25/megawatt hour (MWh); in exchange it will receive the average monthly floating electricity index. During the first two months the floating index remains under US$25/MwH, requiring XYZ to pay MNO; the company, however, faces lower electricity input costs for its production processes, and has thus hedged its position. During the next ten months, however, electricity prices climb steadily, reaching a high of US$40/Mwh; for each monthly evaluation period, MNO receives a compensatory payment from XYZ, which it uses to offset the higher costs it faces in its production process. Figure 10.18 reflects the flows of a peak load electricity swap.

Temperature swaps

The market for non-catastrophic weather derivatives has grown rapidly since the late 1990s, primarily through end user and intermediary interest in *temperature swaps* and options. Indeed, although the weather risk management market in its entirety includes transactions on precipitation, wind, and streamflow, the vast majority of business is centered on temperature.[4] Temperature contracts are available as listed futures and options as well as OTC options, compound option strategies, and swaps.[5] While the market for OTC options is particularly active, we shall focus our discussion on temperature swaps, which are often created synthetically by packaging multiple options (further to our discussion from Chapter 7).

Interest in managing temperature risk has developed as firms have come to realize that it is an economic variable that can have an impact on revenues, expenses, assets, and liabilities (just as interest rates or currency prices might); indeed, temperatures can be quite volatile and create significant risk management issues for companies with temperature-sensitive exposures. For instance, an energy company that must contractually supply more energy to customers during a heat wave may not have sufficient capacity to do so and may be forced to purchase additional electricity in a more expensive spot market. Creating a temperature-based hedge, where the company receives a compensatory payment when temperatures are

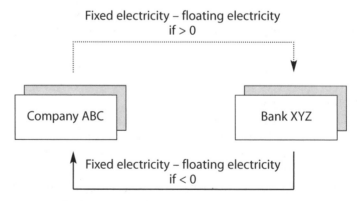

Figure 10.18 Peak electricity swap

very high, can help offset some of the loss incurred in spot power market purchases. Many other types of industries are sensitive to hot or cold temperature conditions and can thus use temperature derivatives to help mitigate risks (retailing, hospitality, airlines, transportation, municipalities, construction, agriculture, and so forth).

Most activity is centered in locations where temperature data is reliable, including North America and Western Europe. In fact, the measurement of temperature in the United States occurs through various indexes (which are the underlying measures used in temperature derivatives), including Tmax (the maximum daily temperature), Tmin (the minimum daily temperature), heating degree days (HDDs), cooling degree days (CDDs), and energy degree days (EDDs). HDDs are determined by computing the average of the daily high and low temperatures and subtracting the result from 65 degrees F (or 18 degrees C, though alternate Centigrade bases are used) the "benchmark" temperature (above which cooling comes into use and below which heating comes into use). CDDs subtract 65 from the daily average.[6] EDDs are simply a cumulative total of HDDs and CDDs.

In Western Europe and other regions indexes are based on average daily temperatures rather than the HDD or CDD index. In fact, the form of calculation varies between countries, but generally centers on the average of the high and low temperatures recorded every hour of a given day. Regardless of the specific temperature index employed, the resulting figure is typically multiplied by some nominal amount (for example, US$ per HDD/CDD or UK£ per average temperature) to generate a payment flow. Though most temperature indexes are computed on a daily basis, derivative contracts generally make use of the cumulative result of these daily observations to determine payoffs; the cumulative period relates primarily to a portion of a heating or cooling season (for example, May–September (cooling) or October–April (heating)), though multi-year contracts that reset are becoming increasingly evident.

The temperature swap (and option) market is governed by two unique characteristics that have a bearing on economic payoffs (and, as we shall note later in the chapter, credit risk exposure). The first feature is that the payoffs on most contracts are limited by explicit caps, meaning that even if the underlying temperature reference rises to a level that would generate a payoff in excess of the cap, no such payment will be made. The second feature is that, unlike various other financial variables that can theoretically rise without limits (and fall to zero), temperature variability is bounded by natural forces. Thus, temperatures cannot rise above particular levels without limit; they are capped and eventually revert, in line with seasonal changes.

Consider the following example. Company QRS, seeking to protect against warm summer temperatures in a particular city (but willing to pay if temperatures remain cool) enters into a three-month CDD swap with Bank EFG whereby it will receive a payment if cumulative CDDs over the period exceed 3000 and will make a payment if they fall below 3000. The swap pays out at US$10,000/CDD, up to a maximum cap of US$3m. After an overly hot summer the cumulative CDD index stands at 3200, meaning EFG makes a payment of US$2m to QRS ((3200 − 3000) * US$10,000). Note that if the CDD index had increased above 3300, the maximum payment to QRS would have been capped at US$3m, per terms of the swap contract. Alternatively, had the CDD index fallen below 3000, QRS would have made a payment to EFG (again, capped at US$3m). Many other variations of the temperature swap can be constructed, including those that pay off based on maximum or minimum temperatures on a specific day (rather than a cumulative tempera-ture over time), those that permit some level of "participation" (for example, gains and losses are shared between the two swap counterparties), and so on. Figure 10.19 illustrates the flows of a CDD swap.

CREDIT RISK QUANTIFICATION

The swap instruments described above are all impacted by movements in market prices or references. In order to produce an estimate of credit risks, they must be adjusted through the risk equivalency process. The quantifi-cation of credit risk in the complex swap structures described above focuses on the general equations cited in Chapter 9, including:

$$REE = (RF * N) + (MTM + AIR) \tag{9.10}$$

and the more general equation, introduced in Chapter 5, which is employed at the inception of a trade (when no MTM exposure exists):

$$REE = RF * N \tag{5.13}$$

In addition to variations on Equations 9.10 and 5.13 (which we use primarily

Cumulative CDDs − fixed CDDs if > 0

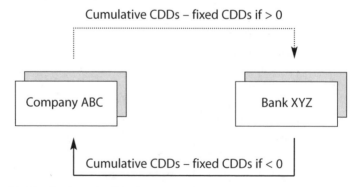

Company ABC   Bank XYZ

Cumulative CDDs − fixed CDDs if < 0

Figure 10.19 Cooling degree day swap

for interest rate and currency-based swap structures), the quantification of various other swaps outlined above (for example, equity call or put swaps, which are effectively swaps with embedded options) relies on variations of Equations 6.3 to 6.6 developed in Chapter 6. As a reminder, these are given by Equations 6.3 and 6.5 for calls and 6.4 and 6.6 for puts:

$$REE = prem + \max(0, (NC*((RFc * CMP) + (CMP - SP)))) \qquad (6.3)$$

$$REE = prem + \max(0, (NC*((RFc * CMP) + (SP - CMP)))) \qquad (6.4)$$

$$REE = prem + \max\left[0, \left[N * \left[\frac{(RFc * CMP)}{SP} + \frac{(CMP - SP)}{SP}\right]\right]\right] \qquad (6.5)$$

$$REE = prem + \max\left[0, \left[N * \left[\frac{(RFc * CMP)}{SP} + \frac{(SP - CMP)}{SP}\right]\right]\right] \qquad (6.6)$$

where: *prem* is the time value component of option premium; *NC* is the number of contracts; *N* is the notional; *RFc* is a constantly adjusted risk factor; *CMP* is the current market price; and *SP* is the strike price.

Note that regardless of the specific formulae utilized, care must be taken when using RFs for single, versus multiple, period transactions. As we noted in Chapter 9 multiple period transactions, such as interest rate and currency swaps, utilize RFs that take account of future payment periods. Single period transactions, such as forwards, are based on RFs that take account only of a single payment period. In situations where multiple settlement periods are used (for example, a package of forwards) the *ex ante* REE process remains generally unchanged, though the actual exposure changes as interim "settlement payments" are arranged.

Interest rate and currency references

Inverse floater swaps

An inverse floater swap is a derivative that has the effect of leveraging, or magnifying, a movement in rates. That is, an upward movement in the floating rate index causes the payer of the inverse to pay less and receive more, while a downward movement causes the payer of the inverse to pay more and receive less; this knowledge is useful when estimating credit risk exposure. A reasonable starting point in the analysis process sets the pay and receive flows equal to one another under the assumption that, if priced correctly, the two components are economically equivalent at inception. To do this we note that:

(x percent fixed – floating) = floating

With simple algebra we may conclude that:

x percent fixed = floating + floating, or

x percent fixed = (2 * floating)

This is equal to two swaps of (floating, (x percent fixed/2)) and demonstrates the leveraging effect of the structure. Let us now assume the fixed rate x is set equal to 15 percent and the floating rate to 12-month Libor flat. By the framework above,

(15 percent − 12-month Libor) = 12-month Libor

which is equivalent to saying that a 15 percent fixed pay swap is equal to receiving 2 * 12-month Libor flat. In order to place this in terms of the REE framework, we can think of this as being equal to a pair of 7.5 percent fixed pay/Libor receive swaps. Thus, if the risk factor for a 5-year, 7.5 percent fixed pay swap is 4.3 percent, the risk on this transaction is equal to 2 * 4.3 percent, or 8.6 percent. Intuitively, this should make sense, since an upward move in rates when an institution pays the inverse results in a gain on the receive leg (implying greater credit risk exposure) and a decline on the pay leg (also implying greater credit risk exposure). If counterparty default occurs when rates have risen, an institution needs to replace the structure in a rate environment where it originally expected to receive more and pay less; its economic loss is thus greater than that of a standard swap structure. We summarize the REE of an inverse floater swap as:

$$REE = ((LF * RFc) * N) \tag{10.1}$$

where LF is the leverage factor and all other terms are as defined above.

LF is calculated algebraically by setting the inverse leg equal to the floating leg, and solving for the number of swaps that can be "extracted" from the original structure. The RF utilized in the equation above is simply equal to the risk factor for a standard swap with the maturity and fixed rate of a "non-leveraged" structure. It should also be noted that instead of leveraging the risk factor it is possible to leverage the notional by the same LF; the REE impact is identical.

Leveraged swaps

A leveraged swap is a derivative that generates a payoff by magnifying the movement of an underlying reference index. Given this structure, quantification of credit risk exposure follows the logic outlined immediately above.

Specifically, it is necessary to identify the degree of leverage inherent in the underlying transaction; in certain instances this will be apparent, at other times it will be somewhat more complex. Even in the most complicated swaps, however, it is possible to "reverse engineer" the structure by decomposing the transaction into individual swaps (just as we have done above). Once this is accomplished a specific leverage factor can be isolated and applied in Equation 10.1 above.

Let us consider an example using a leveraged inverse floater swap. The credit exposure analysis follows the same process outlined above, where the leveraged inverse pay flow is set equal to the floating receive flow and a leverage factor is computed; once the leverage factor is known, it is applied to the standard risk factor for a swap with a "non-leveraged" fixed rate.

Consider a swap where Bank TUV enters into a US$100m, three-year leveraged inverse floater swap with Dealer XYZ. TUV pays 25 percent – (3 * 6-month Libor) in exchange for six-month Libor flat. The decomposition is equal to:

(25 percent – (3 * 6 month Libor)) = 6-month Libor

25 percent – (3 * 6 Libor) + 6-month Libor

25 percent – 4 * 6-month Libor

This is equivalent to four swaps with a fixed rate of 6.25 percent, indicating a leverage factor LF of four. Assuming the risk factor for a three-year, 6.25 percent fixed swap is 1.9 percent, the REE of the transaction is:

REE = ((4 * 0.019) * US$100m)

    = (0.076 * US$100m)

    = US$7.6m

This is, of course, equivalent to leveraging the notional of the transaction rather than the risk factor (US$400m * 1.9 percent, or US$7.6m). As indicated earlier, the same equation can be used for any leveraged structure once the transaction is separated into its component pieces. Figure 10.20 highlights the decomposition of a leveraged inverse floater swap.

Differential swaps

A differential swap is a derivative that references floating rate indexes in two currencies but generates a payoff in a single currency; this structure permits

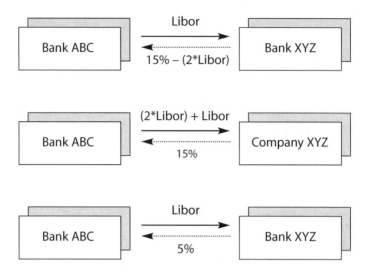

Where this step consists of three swaps

Figure 10.20 Decomposing a leveraged inverse floater swap

swap participants to take a view of foreign currency money market rates without incurring foreign exchange risk. The credit risk of a differential swap, as we might expect, is based on the spread differential that exists between two floating rate indexes at the time of counterparty default. If default occurs when the differential is positive (that is, the bank receives more than it pays) a credit loss results, and if it occurs when the differential is negative (that is, the bank pays more than it receives), no credit loss arises.

Knowing that the payoff of a differential swap is based on the movement of two distinct variables leads us to conclude that the credit risk valuation process faces the same hurdles we considered in certain multi-index options in Chapter 8. Specifically, we know from our previous discussion that the sum or difference of two lognormally distributed variables (for example, two Libor rates) is not lognormal. This means certain assumptions must be made in order to generate an REE for the swap. As before, we can assume the differential (or spread) between the two assets (for example, the Libor rates) is an asset that follows a particular path (and can therefore be implemented in the RF framework); this means, of course, that the differential cannot be negative, which remains a rather restrictive assumption. Alternatively, we can assume the process adheres to an alternate distribution and make necessary alterations to the risk evaluation framework; this may be a particularly difficult mathematical task if the distribution is esoteric. Finally, we may assume some level of correlation between the two reference assets and attempt to model the spread in a two-factor framework; this necessarily means assumptions need to be made regarding the size and stability of correlations, which is an imprecise exercise. In addition, two-factor models are typically more complex and time-consuming to implement. Although somewhat simplistic we present, for purposes of this discussion, an analysis based on the first process. That is, we assume the differential between the reference rates is itself a stochastic asset, with a calculable RF (based on the past volatility of the "asset"); this RF is then introduced into the REE framework. The process is summarized as:

$$REE = (RF_{diff} * N)$$ (10.2)

where RF_{diff} is the risk factor attributable to a differential spread computed as a single asset and N is the notional of the swap.

Consider the following example. Bank A enters into a US$100m differential swap where it receives 12-month Euribor flat (currently quoted at 6 percent) from Bank X, and pays 12-month US$ Libor (currently 4 percent) plus a spread. The swap has a maturity of three years and the payments are made annually, in dollars. Based on the past history of the differential as an asset, Bank A determines the appropriate RF is 4 percent.[7] Through the standard REE equation Bank A estimates its credit exposure on the transaction as US$4m (0.04 * US$100m). If default occurs once the spread widens from A's perspective (that is, the Euribor curve rises and the dollar curve falls), the swap is in-the-money to A and it loses an amount quantifiable by a standard replacement cost equation, adjusted for the specific Euribor and US$ Libor references. (Note that differential swaps are occasionally executed in leveraged form; in such instances Equation 10.2, with the leverage factor LF, can be used. As before, it is essential to decompose the total number of swaps embedded in the leveraged structure to obtain the relevant factor LF.)

We stress, once again, that this example is based on the simplifying assumption that the Libor differential is a stochastic asset and that negative values are not permitted. While this approach does not yield a precise reading of risk exposure, it generates an estimate of the relative amount of risk an institution faces and is likely to be an acceptable working tool. Those feeling the assumptions are too restrictive can investigate alternatives based on different distributions or two-factor models with correlation inputs (recognizing, of course, the limitations of such approaches).

Variable principal swaps

Amortizing swaps

An amortizing swap is a derivative that features a declining notional principal balance. Since interest payments are not based on the full notional principal for the entire length of the swap, the credit risk of an amortizing transaction is lower than that of a vanilla swap; a conservative risk assessment can thus set the risk of the amortizing deal equal to the risk of a vanilla deal with the same rate and final maturity parameters. If an institution prefers to be more accurate and realistic, however, it may wish to consider an alternative risk estimate methodology, such as the average life framework or the average exposure framework (in either terminal or expected form, as discussed in Chapter 5). Note that in addition to the average life approach there are other ways to estimate amortizing swap exposure; for instance, we might view an amortizing structure as a strip of zero coupon swaps or forward starting coupon swaps of varying maturities and notional values (which reflect the amortization schedule) and calculate risk accordingly. We shall not discuss these in detail.

Let us consider an example that illustrates the REE computation based on the average life method. Bank X enters into a five-year fixed-floating amortizing swap, where it pays 10 percent fixed on annual basis and receives 12-month Libor, on a US$100m starting balance; the first amortization occurs at the beginning of year two, so that the first payment exchange at the end of year one is based on the full US$100m. The notional amortizes on a straight-line basis, meaning the principal reduces by US$20m each year; the final interest payment, at the end of year five, is based on US$20m notional. The schedule of amortizing principal is given in Table 10.2.

The average life method focuses on the weighted average life of the swap, measured in years. The average life can be determined by the following formula:

$$Average\ life = \Sigma(Time * Amount\ prepaid) / \Sigma\ Amount\ prepaid \qquad (10.3)$$

Returning to the example above, we calculate the average life of the swap and illustrate the results in Table 10.3.

By Equation 10.3, the average life is equal to 3.5 years (US$280m/ US$80m). Utilizing this information, we can assign a risk factor to the transaction that is based on the average life of the swap rather than its final

Table 10.2 Amortization schedule

End of year	Notional principal outstanding (millions)
1	$100
2	$80
3	$60
4	$40
5	$20

Table 10.3 Average life results (millions)

Year	Remaining notional	Amount prepaid	Time * amount prepaid
1	$100	$0	$0
2	$80	$20	$40
3	$60	$20	$60
4	$40	$20	$80
5	$20	$20	$100
Total		$80	$280

maturity. Utilizing the risk factors highlighted in Chapter 9, the REE of a five-year, 10 percent fixed pay swap is US$5.2m (based on a 5.2 percent risk factor). In contrast, a 3.5-year, 10 percent fixed pay swap yields REE of approximately US$3.3m (based on a 3.3 percent risk factor). Thus, the straight line-amortizing swap carries less risk than a standard five-year swap (which is logical, since interest payments (and therefore potential replacement costs) are declining). It is important to highlight that although the risk is based on an average life of 3.5 years, cash flows (albeit small ones) are present until maturity in Year Five. As a final note, it should also be clear that the amortization schedule need not conform to a straight-line basis or any regular or orderly decline; an average life can be calculated for any set of cash flows. To summarize, the REE of an amortizing swap using the average life method is:

$$REE = (RF_{AL} * N) \tag{10.4}$$

where: RF_{AL} is the risk factor associated with the average life of the swap and N is the notional of the swap.

Note that similar results can be obtained by utilizing the average exposure framework developed in Chapter 5. For instance, if the unadjusted five-year swap risk of US$5.2m (as indicated above) is based on terminal worst-case exposure, then the transformation into average worst-case exposure yields REE of nearly US$3.5m, which is a close approximation of the US$3.3m derived via the average life method.

Accreting swaps

An accreting swap is a mirror image of the amortizing swap, with notional principal growing, rather than declining, as particular time or trigger points are passed. Determining the credit risk on an accreting structure requires that attention be given to two forces: the principal balance and the RF. In a standard interest rate swap the "diffusion and amortization" effect we discussed in the last chapter means peak risk generally occurs one-third to one-half into the life of the transactions; this is because insufficient rate movements occur in the early part of the swap to generate maximum risk and insufficient payments remain to be made in the latter part of the swap to generate maximum risk. However, in an accreting structure the two forces that act to maximize risk are at work jointly, meaning maximum risk occurs at the end of the swap, when market rates have theoretically moved to their maximum point, and the notional principal balance has increased to its greatest level. If an institution has to replace the transaction at maturity due to counterparty default, it will be doing so when the notional balance and theoretical market movements have both been maximized, meaning potential credit risk is at its greatest point. For instance, in a simple three-year accreting swap that starts with a balance of US$50m and grows by an additional US$50m at the end of Year One (to US$100m), Year Two (to US$150m), and Year Three (final maturity, US$200m), the last payment exchange will be the largest. And, we know from our discussion on the development of RFs that the longer the time to maturity, the greater the chance for market movements, the higher the RF. Thus, the most conservative stance we can take is to compute REE through standard Equation 5.13 by setting N equal to the fully accreted notional principal and RF equal to the market move reflecting terminal maturity; thereafter we can begin adjusting the RF down as each subsequent payment passes and the chance for market movements declines, but retain the notional principal unchanged at the maximum accreted level.

Mortgage swaps

A mortgage swap, which is a subset of the amortizing swap discussed above, is a derivative that synthetically replicates the flows of an MBS. Although a given mortgage swap may have distinct features which must be recognized (particularly if non-Libor floating rate indexes are utilized), the standard mortgage swap structure can be examined in light of several key characteristics: fixed rate paid or received (generally monthly), final swap maturity and, most importantly, the anticipated amortization schedule of the MBS and, hence, underlying swap. We have seen above that straight-line amortization of a swap lowers REE against a benchmark vanilla interest rate swap. Similarly, the amortizing characteristics of a mortgage swap generate a lower REE figure than a plain vanilla structure.

As indicated in the product description above, most mortgage swaps which duplicate specific FNMA, GNMA or FHLMC issues typically amortize on a monthly basis; this is in keeping with the monthly amortization of the actual MBS (or pool of MBSs). In order to estimate the REE on these transactions, we need to determine the amortization schedule that lowers the principal balance of the swap. Once the actual declining balance of the swap is calculated we can evaluate REE via the average life method (or alternate process). It is worth noting that in a five-year mortgage swap, with monthly amortization of principal, there are 60 known or estimated changes in the balance. Using the average life approach indicated above means the task is likely to be quite onerous and unnecessarily precise. In fact, it may be sufficiently accurate to determine the risk based on a balance that declines every quarter or semi-annual period. Amortization of mortgage swap notionals is not an exact science; pre-payment levels often vary from those originally estimated. Nonetheless, it is unlikely that risk will be understated if an average life (or comparable) methodology is utilized; in a worst-case scenario, there may be some overstatement if amortization occurs faster than originally anticipated. Any such overstatement, however, is likely to be modest and should not impact credit decisions or exposure management.

It should be noted that the procedures above are applicable for mortgage swaps involving a fixed flow (based on Treasuries) against Libor. When a mortgage swap involves two floating rate indexes against an amortizing principal, it is more accurate to replace standard fixed-floating risk factors for floating risk factors that are representative of two floating rate indexes (which represents basis risk). Basis risk factors are typically lower than standard interest rate swap factors, as movements in two floating rate indexes are more closely correlated.

Index principal swaps/reverse index principal swaps

An index principal swap (IPS) is a derivative that amortizes as interest rates fall through predefined levels. If the floating rate reference does not decline through these levels, the IPS does not amortize; in this situation the credit risk facing the floating rate payer (whom we designate the seller) is identical to that of any vanilla interest rate swap (we can ignore the effects of the above market rate it is receiving from the buyer; if the bank receives the above market rate for the binary options embedded in the IPS it will not perform on its obligation (that is, amortize the swap) if its counterparty defaults). The buyer, however, pays an above market fixed rate and must account for this extra risk, particularly if it pays the higher rate during the multi-year lockout period, only to have its counterparty default as amortization is due to begin. We may show the relevant formulae for IPS sellers and buyers as:

$$REE = (RFc * N) \qquad (5.13)$$

and

$$REE = (RFc * N) + NPV_{am} \qquad\qquad (10.5)$$

respectively, where NPV_{am} is the net present value of the above market rate paid over the life of the transaction and all other terms are as defined above.

Instead of counting the NPV as a lump sum added to REE, the buyer may adjust the RFc to show the higher above market rate it is paying.

This is clearly the most conservative stance that a firm can take regarding the credit risk of IPSs. We know from the amortizing swaps and mortgage swaps discussed above that when amortization occurs REE declines; this also occurs with IPSs. Thus, the worst-case credit scenario for an IPS arises when the full notional remains outstanding for the entire deal (that is, the binary options remain out-of-the-money). If we wish to account for the changing exposure of the transaction once the floating rate falls through a particular threshold (following the lockout period), we can adjust the risk factor RF to reflect the new average life of the transaction (or utilize an alternate amortization quantification technique). Since amortization implies a lower average life (which implies a lower RF), the adjustment can easily be made to the equation above (where the new RFc is based on average life rather than final maturity).

Reverse IPSs, like the generic accreting swap mentioned above, feature a notional principal balance that increases as the floating rate index breaches prespecified levels; since this is the reverse of the IPS, it must be analyzed in a slightly different fashion. The worst-case credit scenario for the purchaser of the reverse IPS occurs when the floating rate index falls and the notional of the swap increases. In this instance the purchaser is left with a derivative position that carries a greater amount of REE than the position on trade date. The conservative approach to the valuation of REE therefore focuses on the maximum notional that can be experienced during the life of the transaction; this approach assumes the floating rate reference levels are breached and the binary options generate an increase in the notional principal. Of course, institutions feeling this approach is too conservative can assign REE to the original notional of the swap, and increase the REE allocation as it becomes likely one or more of the reference levels will be breached.

Consider the following example. Bank ABC enters into a reverse IPS with Dealer QRS based on a US$100m starting notional principal balance. The five-year swap contains trigger levels which create a US$10m increase in the principal balance for each ten basis point decline in US$ Libor, to a maximum of US$150m (five trigger points). Assuming the risk of a five-year, 7 percent interest rate swap is 3 percent, ABC may elect to assign total REE of US$4.5m (0.03 * US$150m) against QRS's credit lines, based on an assumption that all five Libor barriers will be breached.

Credit market references

Credit forwards

A credit forward is a bilateral, single-period derivative that generates a payoff based on the differential between spot and forward credit prices or spreads. The REE evaluation of a credit forward is based on the maximum expected movement in the reference bond during the life of the transaction. We consider both spread and price-based equations in this section. In order to generate a maximum REE figure, we require information on the potential future movement of the target credit; importantly, the volatility data must only reflect the movement of the credit component of the bond (that is, it should exclude movement attributable to interest rate changes). Since the payment on a credit forward is two-sided (that is, the bond may increase or decrease in value), REE must be assigned against credit limits whether a bank is long or short the forward. As indicated earlier in the chapter, spread-based transactions include a duration multiplier that reflects the basis point sensitivity of the spread; since this determines payoff, it must also be incorporated into the credit risk estimate. The spread-based REE for an institution purchasing a single-period forward is defined through Equation 10.6:

$$REE = N * dur * (FS - ((1 - RFc) * CMS)) \qquad (10.6)$$

The REE for an institution selling a single-period forward is defined through Equation 10.7:

$$REE = N * dur * (((1 + RFc) * CMS) - FS) \qquad (10.7)$$

where *dur* is the duration of the underlying reference bond; *CMS* is the current market spread of the reference bond (against a risk-free benchmark); *FS* is the contracted forward spread of the reference bond (against a risk-free benchmark); and all other terms are as defined above.

Note that callable bonds may have an upper boundary price (lower boundary spread) after which the issuer may redeem securities. However, such a boundary is often quite far from par, and almost certain to fall outside market movements predicted by RF.

Consider the following example. Bank HIJ sells Dealer RST a US$100m, 12-month credit forward on four-year XYZ bonds, with a forward spread set at 200 basis points over Treasuries. If the volatility of XYZ's credit spread is 40 percent per annum, the 90 percent confidence level risk factor for a 12-month trade is 66 percent; assuming the duration of the bond at inception of the trade is three and the CMS on trade date is 180 basis points over Treasuries, the REE on the credit forward, per Equation 10.7, equals:

REE =   US$100m * 3 * (((1.66) * 0.018) – 0.020)

=   US$2,960,000

Once the transaction commences, the duration of the underlying bond will decrease, the RF will decline, and the CMS will increase or decrease; as a result, the REE of the forward changes. For instance, if six months into the trade the duration is 2.5, the RFc is 46 percent and the CMS is 210 basis points over Treasuries, the new REE is

REE =   US$100m * 2.5 * (((1.46 * 0.021) – 0.02)

=   US$2,665,000

If RST defaults at this point, HIJ sustains an economic loss of US$250,000 (0.001 * 2.5 * US$100m).

It is possible to perform the same calculation using a price, rather than spread, reference. In such cases the focus is on price volatility rather than spread volatility and a duration factor is no longer necessary. For an institution purchasing a single-period price-based forward (set as a percentage of appreciation against the forward price),[8] REE can be computed by Equation 10.8:

$$REE = N * (((((1 + RFc) * CMP) – FP)/FP) \tag{10.8}$$

An institution selling a single-period price-based forward (set as a percentage of depreciation against a forward price) can compute REE by Equation 10.9:

$$REE = N * ((FP – ((1 – RFc) * CMP))/FP) \tag{10.9}$$

where FP is the contracted forward price of the reference bond and all other terms are as defined above.

While this framework captures potential price appreciation or depreciation based on the historical volatility of bond prices (or credit spreads), it does not capture the outright default risk inherent in the transaction. While default by a reference credit may be reflected by gradual deterioration in credit quality and associated decline in the bond price (or a widening of the credit spread), it can also be reflected by a sudden move; the bond of a reference credit may trade at a price in the mid-90s one day before default and in the mid-50s one day after default. Such a sharp move is not necessarily predicted by the RF framework, as it may be a five or ten standard deviation event, rather than the one or two standard deviation events we have been dealing with. As a result, the event risk surrounding a default can be difficult to model and incorporate into a standard REE framework. One possible solution is for the seller of a credit forward (who is short the credit) to assume the reference bond will default. Under this scenario a full payment will be due from the buyer. This raises the issue of where the defaulted bond will trade and how much REE to apply against the buyer's credit limits. Since every default and bankruptcy situation is unique, it is impossible to predict, *ex ante*, the trading level of a defaulted bond for a given counterparty. A reasonable estimate, however, might be drawn from a combination of historical distressed debt trading levels and historical recovery levels. If, for example, senior unsecured creditors are known to recover an average of 48 cents on the dollar in default scenarios, and distressed debt dealers generally concur with the assessment, the seller may wish to apply a discount of 52 (100 less recoveries, which is the economic loss it might sustain) to its notional position and assign the resulting value against the buyer's credit limits. If the reference credit defaults, the seller, who is short the credit, expects a compensating payment from the buyer, who is long the credit, in an amount equal to the difference between the agreed value of the bond at the beginning of the transaction and the value of the bond post-default.[9] Once again, this approach is conservative and estimates credit exposure based on default rather than simple deterioration.

Equation 10.10 summarizes the REE for an institution selling a single-period price-based credit forward based on outright default (and is again computed as a percentage depreciation against the forward price):

$$REE = N * ((FP - ((1 - rec) * 100)) / FP) \qquad (10.10)$$

where N is the notional of the forward; FP is the contracted forward price; and rec is the expected recovery level on the bond (in percentage terms).

If Bank STU sells a US$10m credit forward to Dealer XYZ at a contracted forward price of 95 (and assumes a 48 percent recovery rate) the REE to STU, assuming default on the underlying reference bond, equals

$$REE = US\$10m * ((95 - ((1 - 0.48) * 100))/95)$$

$$= US\$10m * 0.452$$

$$= US\$4.52m$$

That is, if the underlying reference issuer defaults, and the bond trades at distressed levels reflecting expected recoveries, the anticipated gain to STU from selling the forward (against the forward price) is US$4.5m. If XYZ, long the forward, defaults on its forward contract, STU loses this amount. This depends on the assumption that the underlying bond will trade at levels reflecting historical recoveries. Note that unlike Equations 10.8 and 10.9 above, Equation 10.10 is one-sided (it relates only to the seller of the forward who is short the credit, since an event of default will add value, and hence credit exposure, only to the seller).

Default swaps

A default swap is a unilateral, single period, contract that provides the buyer with protection against default of a reference credit. The REE evaluation of a default swap is based on two elements: the floating payment from the buyer of the default swap (who becomes short the credit) to the seller (who becomes long the credit) and the potential payment from the seller to the buyer if the underlying reference credit defaults. The sum of the two represents the REE the swap buyer sets against the swap seller's credit lines. As with the credit forwards discussed above, the key variable in determining REE is the trading level of the reference bond in default. Once again, one approach focuses on the trading value of the bond post-default; the trading level is likely to reflect expected recovery levels for creditors of particular classifications. It is important to note that RF is not used, as the default swap does not provide a continuum of payoffs: it is strictly a binary structure. Using historical recovery statistics (for example, for senior unsecured creditors), an institution can estimate the value of the bond post-default (just as above, this serves as an *ex ante* estimate); this, in turn, provides a measure of the payment due to the buyer of the swap. This approach is summarized in Equation 10.11, which is presented in price-based form as:

$$REE = fp + (N * (1 - rec)) \qquad (10.11)$$

where fp is the summation of floating payments the buyer pays the seller and all other terms are as defined above.

Based on this equation, we can quantify worst-case REE on a default swap as the sum of the exposure from a defaulted reference credit (which generates a receivable for the buyer of the swap) and the floating payments made to the seller of the default swap. If the seller subsequently defaults, the buyer sustains a loss on both the default-related payment expected from the seller and the floating "premium" payments made to the seller in consideration of the transaction. This is, of course, extreme, since it assumes defaults by both the underlying reference credit and the swap seller. A more realistic approach might give some "allowance" to default correlations that exist between the reference credit and the counterparty; in fact, this is a central technique of the portfolio credit risk models we consider in Part III.

It should be noted that, unlike credit forwards and credit-based total return swaps, the default swap is unilateral: the buyer of the swap faces credit exposure to the seller but the reverse never occurs, since at no time is the buyer obligated to pay the seller appreciation in the underlying reference credit (as it might under a credit forward or total return swap). If the seller ceases to receive floating rate payments from the buyer, it simply cancels the transaction. Note that this type of default structure shares certain similarities with the binary version of credit puts discussed in Chapter 8, which provide a payoff based solely on default (rather than deterioration). In fact the two instruments are virtually identical, except for the nature and timing of premium payments.

Consider the following example. Dealer JKL wishes to lower its credit exposure to Company PQR (a BBB-rated entity) and enters into a default swap with Bank Z. The reference security in the transaction is PQR's three-year bond, which currently trades at par. Under terms of the transaction JKL enters into a US$10m, 12-month default swap with Z, for which it pays the equivalent of US$100,000 of floating payments. Unlike standard credit forwards or credit options, which provide a continuum of payoffs as PQR's credit deteriorates, JKL expects only to receive a payment from Z if PQR defaults. As such, it takes the most conservative approach in valuing REE; reviewing historical information it determines average recoveries for senior unsecured creditors are 40 (implying an economic loss of 60 on default). Through Equation 10.11 it calculates its REE as

$$REE = US\$100,000 + (US\$10m * (1 - 0.4))$$

$$= US\$6.1m$$

Thus, JKL assigns US$6.1m of REE against Bank Z's credit limits; importantly, the transaction also releases JKL's credit exposure to PQR (this is a vital aspect of risk mitigation, as discussed in Chapter 13). Assume that during the life of the transaction PQR defaults, at which time the reference bond trades at 55 among distressed dealers (implying estimated recovery of 55 and economic loss of 45). At this point JKL's underlying exposure to PQR is in jeopardy and it is certain to sustain a loss (the magnitude of which depends on the size of the exposure it has to PQR at the time of default). To compensate, however, JKL receives a payment of US$4.5m (US$10m * (1 − 0.55)) from Z. If Z fails to perform on its default swap contract with JKL, JKL suffers losses from its exposure to both PQR and Z. Once again, this approach is particularly conservative since it presumes default by both the reference credit and the swap counterparty; correlations can be used to offset a portion of the exposure.

The REE attributable to first-to-default swaps follows along very similar lines. Indeed, no particular adjustment needs to be made, because the derivative structure only provides for a single payment: the one coming from the first credit to default. If the payment is based on the difference between par and the estimated amount in recovery, the focus remains on the estimated recovery value, rather than the specific credit that defaults. Naturally, if recovery values vary widely among industries, a conservative view would assign REE based on the lowest possible recovery value; except for this, the approach is the same as discussed above. Though some differential might exist in the probability of default (which might indicate which credit is more apt to pay out) our concern at this stage is on the REE component; we will introduce probabilities of default in Part III of the book. The same approach can be taken for basket swaps unless there is a particular reason to believe multiple credits will default, in which case a summation across credits can be considered.

Total return swaps

A total return swap (TRS) is a derivative that produces a synthetic off-balance sheet position in an underlying risky bond for one party (the seller). In the context of credit derivatives, it also provides a second party (the buyer) with protection against the deterioration or default in a reference credit. Though TRSs have intervening settlement periods related to the basic fixed/floating or floating/floating interest flows on the coupon/Libor legs, the main REE focus is on the capital gain/loss occurring at transaction maturity. In that sense the REE evaluation of the TRS is not markedly different from that of the credit forward discussed above. In fact, the primary difference centers on the incremental spread paid by the buyer of the TRS (who is short the credit) to the seller (who is long the credit); the incremental spread is simply the difference between the fixed/floating bond coupon and the floating Libor leg. If the payment of the incremental spread occurs at periodic intervals during the life of the TRS, this represents additional credit exposure the buyer faces with the seller. If the incremental spread is paid only at maturity it can effectively be ignored (as it is likely to be netted out in any final exchange; that is, if the seller defaults on the potential bond depreciation payment, the buyer will withhold its final spread payment). Assuming the incremental spread is payable at periodic intervals, the buyer may develop an estimate of the spread and employ price-based Equation 10.12 to reflect the potential credit exposure (assuming the underlying bond depreciates but does not default); this equation is based on the percentage depreciation of the reference credit as a percentage of the agreed price:[10]

$$REE = N * ((AP - ((1 - RFc) * CMP))/AP) + incs \qquad (10.12)$$

where *AP* is the agreed price under the TRS; *incs* is the incremental spread (in dollar terms) paid by the buyer to the seller during periodic intervals (not at maturity); and all other terms are as defined above.

This equation reflects the dollar sum of the incremental coupon spread paid to the seller as well as the potential exposure accruing from a decline in value in the underlying reference bond (as a percentage of the agreed price). Recall from earlier that the decline in value is predicted via RF, which reflects historical credit volatilities. It should be emphasized that, like the credit forward above, the seller of a TRS faces credit exposure to the buyer since it stands a chance of receiving a payment if the underlying reference bond appreciates in value. The seller may thus reflect its exposure via Equation 10.13 (defraying a portion of its exposure through the incremental spread it is receiving from the buyer, if desired):

$$REE = N * ((((1 + RFc) * CMP) - AP)/AP) - incs \text{ or } 0 \qquad (10.13)$$

If the maturity of the TRS coincides with the maturity or call date of the underlying bond and the redemption-callable value is set at par (or some other figure), the upside payment due the seller will be bounded; as a result, the credit exposure the seller faces may be capped as well. This, however, is a special situation that is unlikely to occur with frequency.

Consider the following example. Bank TUV enters into a 12-month US$20m TRS with Securities Firm CDE based on Company XYZ's publicly traded bond (currently quoted at 97). TUV pays CDE an incremental spread (equal to 50 basis points per semi-annual period, payable at the end of six months and at maturity) plus potential appreciation in the reference bond, and receives depreciation from CDE; the TRS provides CDE with gains over 95 and TUV with gains below 95. Based on the historical credit price volatility of XYZ's bond (together with a confidence level adjustment), the RF is calculated at 20 percent per annum; this suggests the bond may move to a maximum of 116 (absent redemption at par or some other amount) and a minimum of 77.6 (absent default). The upfront REE from TUV's perspective is calculated via Equation 10.12 as:

$$REE = \text{US\$20m} * ((95 - ((1 - 0.20) * 97))/95) + \text{US\$100,000}$$

$$= \text{US\$3.76m}$$

Note that the incremental spread component is US$100,000 since TUV only faces a single interim payment (the final coupon payment coincides with settlement at maturity). The REE from the perspective of CDE, ignoring the receipt of the incremental spread in six months, is equal to US$4.28m. If 12 months from now XYZ's credit deteriorates and the bond trades at 90, TUV expects a payment of US$1.05m ((US$20m * (95 – 90)/95), which represents depreciation as a percentage of the agreed price). If CDE defaults TUV sustains an actual loss of US$1.15m (incremental coupon plus bond depreciation).

The equations above focus on the possible risk exposure arising from bond depreciation or appreciation. We turn now to the case of bond default. As with default swaps and credit forwards the buyer of the TRS faces maximum payout from the seller if the underlying reference credit defaults on its obligation. In order to reflect this eventuality, we can use a modified form of Equation 10.11, which makes certain assumptions regarding the trading level of the bond in default (again based on expected recoveries for senior unsecured creditors). Replacing the floating payment component in Equation 10.11 with the incremental spread reference, the relevant equation becomes:

$$REE = incs + (N * (1 - rec)) \tag{10.14}$$

Equity market references

Equity index swaps

An equity index swap is a customized derivative that provides an institution with specific exposure to, or protection against, movements in individual equities, baskets, or broad market indexes. Our discussion of REE for equity swaps begins with the simple call or put swap. Recall from above that in a call (put) swap a bank receives appreciation (depreciation) in an equity index with no corresponding payment to the counterparty if the index depreciates (appreciates); in certain structures a bank may also be entitled to receive dividends from the underlying reference. In exchange for the right to receive potential appreciation (depreciation) and/or dividends, the bank pays its counterparty premium (time value), either upfront or on a periodic basis (in the form of a Libor flow against the notional amount of the trade). A bank's risk in entering into equity call-put swaps is, therefore, threefold:

■ premium (time value) paid to the seller

■ potential dividends receivable from the seller

■ potential gains from index appreciation/depreciation.

As indicated, the premium payment may be in the form of a known lump sum or a periodic Libor flow over the life of the transaction or at maturity (note:

in the case of periodic flows, a bank needs to estimate the maximum expected Libor movement during the life of the transaction. Such an estimate might focus on current Libor plus the anticipated upward movement that might occur during subsequent payment periods (for example, as estimated via the adjusted historical volatility framework, or through a forward–forward rate process); alternatively, it might simply wish to estimate the representative premium by pricing a vanilla option with the same trade parameters, using market-quoted implied volatilities). Potential appreciation/depreciation may be estimated by the standard risk factor RF, while potential dividend receipts can be approximated through historical data. The REE equation for an institution purchasing an equity swap is therefore summarized as:

$$REE = (RF * N) + div + (prem \text{ or } \Sigma \ (Libor_{max} * N)) \qquad (10.15)$$

where $Libor_{max}$ is the maximum anticipated Libor rate during the transaction (or the relevant period); div is the anticipated dividend payment (converted into dollar value as an estimated percentage of historical dividend payments times notional); and all other terms are as defined above.

This equation is useful primarily for equity swaps struck at-the-money, as no allowance is made for the moneyness of the transaction; the equation above does not highlight any potential increase in actual (mark-to-market) exposure as a result of moneyness. We discuss an alternate approach that takes account of this in the section below.

The timing of Libor-based premium is important when estimating the credit risk of the transaction. Transactions structured with premium payable on a net basis at maturity reduce credit risk by not forcing the swap purchaser to deliver a payment before anticipated performance by the swap seller; even periodic flows occurring during the life of the transaction are preferable to upfront payments. If premium is payable on a net basis at the appropriate evaluation date (or maturity) it can be excluded from the equation above (as it does not present additional credit risk to the buyer). In such instances REE can be determined by the following equation:

$$REE = (RF * N) + div \qquad (10.16)$$

Consider the following example. Bank Z enters into a 12-month index call swap on the Hang Seng with Bank QRS whereby it receives index appreciation and dividends. The current level of the index is 10,000, the notional of the transaction is HK$10m, and premium (time value) is equal to six-month Hong Kong Interbank Offer Rate (Hibor) flat, payable in equal installments at the end of six and 12 months. The credit risk to Bank Z equals potential appreciation in the Hang Seng over the next 12 months along with dividends and the first premium payment. Using the RF framework, Bank Z determines the 12-month Hang Seng RF is 38.4 percent. Historical dividends equal 3.2 percent and Hibor currently trades at 5.5 percent (this is the amount payable in six months' time; note that the 12-month payment is not considered because, if QRS defaults on the final payment, Z simply withholds its final premium payment). The credit risk to Z on this transaction, per Equation 10.15, equals:

$$REE = (0.38* \text{ HK\$10m}) + \text{HK\$320,000} + \text{HK\$550,000}$$

$$= \text{HK\$4.67m}$$

This analysis assumes the call swap moves from its at-the-money point of 10,000 to 13,800, the maximum level estimated by RF. If QRS defaults at this point (just prior to maturity), Z loses index appreciation, dividends and the first installment of its premium payment.

As indicated above, a risk value that is lower or higher than the one reflected in 10.16 can be assigned if a particular swap is executed in or out-of-the-money. This logic parallels the discussion in Chapter 6 on in and out-of-the-money options. If, for example, Bank Z enters into the call swap outlined above but only receives appreciation above 10,500, it is effectively entering into a call swap which is out-of-the-money on trade date; the swap has farther to travel before it moves in-the-money and therefore carries lower credit exposure. The opposite is true for an in-the-money equity swap, which begins with greater risk exposure. To take account of the intrinsic value of an equity swap and value the moneyness (for example, actual, or MTM exposure) of the transaction on an ongoing basis, an institution can apply Equation 10.17 for call swaps:

$$REE = \left[N * \left[\frac{RFc * CMP + CMP - SP}{SP \qquad\qquad SP} \right] \right] + div + prem \text{ or } \Sigma(Libor_{max} * N) \tag{10.17}$$

and Equation 10.18 for put swaps:

$$REE = \left[N * \left[\frac{RFc * CMP + SP - CMP}{SP \qquad\qquad SP} \right] \right] + div + prem \text{ or } \Sigma(Libor_{max} * N) \tag{10.18}$$

These equations, which are slight adaptations of those presented in Chapter 6, allow an institution to track the ongoing exposure resulting from an increase or decrease in intrinsic value.

Returning to the example above, and utilizing Equation 10.17, we obtain the following REE:

$$REE = (HK\$10m \; * \; (((0.384 \; * \; 10{,}000)/10{,}500) + ((10{,}000 - 10{,}500)/$$
$$10{,}500))) + HK\$320{,}000 + HK\$550{,}000$$

$$= \; (HK\$10m \; * \; (0.365 + (20.047))) + HK\$870{,}000$$

$$= \; HK\$3.18m + HK\$870{,}000$$

$$= \; HK\$3.27m$$

This compares with risk of HK\$4.67m from the original example. As we might expect, the above is relevant when equity swaps are struck deep in or out-of-the-money, and helps ensure risk is not understated or overstated by a significant amount. (The reader should recall from the discussion in Chapter 6 that the RFcs in Equations 10.17 and 10.18 are calibrated by an amount that reflects the additional in or out-of-the-money portion of the transaction. If desired, CMP in the numerator may be replaced by SP to preserve the original RFc.)

Returning to our previous discussion on call swaps, the risk discussion presented in Equations 10.17 and 10.18 does not hold true if a bank is payer (instead of receiver) of index appreciation (that is, seller of the call). In such instances the bank's counterparty expects performance from the bank should the index move in-the-money. A bank must therefore focus only on receipt of premium. If it occurs in upfront fashion the trade can be viewed as normal cash settlement risk; if the counterparty fails to deliver the premium within a five-day time frame, the bank simply unwinds the transaction. If, however, payment of premium follows the more traditional equity swap convention and is paid in a Libor stream over the life of the transaction (or at maturity), the bank may wish to estimate the anticipated value of the Libor stream and count that figure as its risk. Some might ignore the risk of the Libor stream by assuming that if Libor is not received, payment for appreciation in the index will not be made. However, if no appreciation occurs and the Libor flow is not received, the bank will have effectively lost money.

Having described a risk valuation approach for an institution that is long an equity put or call swap, we now turn to the special case where an institution is long an equity put or call swap and short an equity call or put swap (that is, a bank is receiver of either depreciation or appreciation, and payer of the opposite; this is equivalent to the synthetic positions we discussed in Chapter 6). From a credit risk standpoint we can divide the issue into four parts, where the bank is:

■ receiver of appreciation and payer of depreciation (and Libor premium)

■ receiver of depreciation and payer of appreciation (and Libor premium)

- receiver of appreciation (and Libor premium) and payer of depreciation

- receiver of depreciation (and Libor premium) and payer of appreciation.

The Libor premium payments are clearly dependent on the moneyness of each element of the equity swap. Note that we ignore dividends for simplicity, though the reader may factor them into the equations per the discussion above.

When a bank is receiver of index appreciation and payer of index depreciation and Libor, the analysis focuses solely on the long call swap, which can be quantified by Equations 10.15 or 10.17. The fact that the bank is also a payer of depreciation does not enter into the credit risk consideration, as the short put swap does not add exposure. If a bank is receiver of index depreciation and payer of index appreciation and Libor, the analysis again focuses solely on the long put swap, which can be quantified by Equations 10.16 or 10.18; the short call swap is, again, irrelevant.

If, in contrast, a bank is receiver of depreciation and Libor premium and payer of appreciation, the analysis shifts. In a worst-case credit scenario the reference index falls and the bank expects to receive depreciation below the strike. The same risk factor framework discussed above captures this element. In addition, the bank must consider the nature and timing of the premium payment. If it is an upfront payment, this amount can be subtracted from the risk equivalent exposure, if desired (for example, it is money in hand which can be used to defray any future amounts due from the counterparty which are not forthcoming because of default). Note that the bank continues to ignore the short call swap, for the reasons cited above. The resulting formula is an adaptation of Equation 10.18:

$$REE = \left[N * \left[\frac{RFc * CMP + SP - CMP}{SP} \cdot \frac{SP - CMP}{SP} \right] \right] - prem \text{ or } 0 \qquad (10.19)$$

If the bank is receiver of appreciation and Libor premium and payer of depreciation, it ignores the short put swap and simply focuses on the long call swap, adjusted for the effects of premium receipt. This is given through an adaptation of Equation 10.17:

$$REE = \left[N * \left[\frac{RFc * CMP + CMP - SP}{SP} \cdot \frac{CMP - SP}{SP} \right] \right] - prem \text{ or } 0 \qquad (10.20)$$

If the swap contains a normal Libor premium flow that occurs during the life of the transaction (or at maturity), it is important that the additional exposure be reflected in the risk calculation, since failure to receive premium in a normal cash time frame implies an additional amount at risk. Once again, this is a variable that can be estimated using an adjusted historical volatility measure, forward-forward rate analysis, or approximated by the amount of lump sum premium associated with a long-dated option with similar parameters.

Let us consider the following example. Bank A enters into a US$100m 12-month equity swap with Bank X where it receives appreciation in the S&P 500 over 640 and pays depreciation below 625; with the market trading at a level of 635, the call is 0.8 percent out-of-the-money and the put is 1.6 percent out-of-the-money, so Bank A pays Bank X six-month Libor less 75 basis points, semi-annually (assume that six-month Libor at trade date is 2.75 percent and is estimated to rise to 3.10 percent in six-months); it pays the Libor flows on trade date and in six months. Note for simplicity there is no exchange of dividends. Based on these parameters (and utilizing an S&P RF of 25.6 percent) the initial REE of the transaction from Bank A's perspective is:

$$REE = (US\$100m * (((0.256 * 635)/640) + ((635 - 640)/640)))) + (0.0218 * US\$100m)$$

$$= US\$24.6m + US\$2.18m$$

$$= US\$26.78m$$

Thus, the total risk on a US$100m transaction, where Bank A expects to receive appreciation in the S&P 500 in one year against payment of premium (six-month Libor less 75 basis points every semi-annual period) plus depreciation in the S&P 500, is equal to just under US$27m. Note, once again, that Bank A faces no credit risk on the index depreciation component of the transaction. From Bank X's standpoint REE is based on gains from index depreciation which Bank A may be required to pay plus the second Libor payment (recall that the first one is received on trade date). The initial REE facing Bank X equals US$25.58m (US$1.18m (for the second premium payment) and US$24.4m (for index depreciation)); X can elect to subtract the original premium from REE if it so desires.

Twelve months from now we can assume two scenarios: Scenario one: the S&P reaches a high of 662 at maturity. Bank A, as receiver of appreciation, is entitled to the 3.4 percent appreciation over the strike and receives a gross payment from Bank X; if Bank X defaults at this point, A loses, with certainty, US$3.4m. Scenario two: the S&P falls to 600 at maturity. Bank A, as payer of depreciation, finds the index is 4 percent below the put strike price of 625 and so is required to pay Bank X US$4m for depreciation. If Bank A defaults at this point, X loses, with certainty, US$4m.

In our discussion immediately above we have focused on transactions where an index is evaluated at one point in time, namely maturity of the swap; in this case we can consider the transaction to be a single period forward (although Libor payments might occur periodically). This means the strike and market level of the index are compared at the conclusion of the transaction, at which time a payment is made. When a transaction is structured as a single period forward the potential for actual exposure to accumulate is greater (though *ex ante* REE remains unchanged). An equity swap can also be structured as a portfolio of linked forward transactions with the strike and market prices compared and settled at periodic intervals. At each evaluation period the two parties review the current level of the index against the strike price and settle a payment. Following this interim evaluation and settlement the transaction proceeds until the next evaluation period and the process is repeated. Any transaction structured as a series of multiple forwards with periodic settlement has the effect of not allowing the mark-to-market (for example, intrinsic value or current replacement cost) to build up; the periodic settlement effectively crystallizes MTM value on an ongoing basis. Of course, it is still necessary to take account of future exposure through the REE framework on the presumption that default could happen in the future, but the MTM value can be segregated and effectively ignored once each current period payment is made.

Volatility swaps

A volatility swap, which is generally structured as a single period forward, obtains its value from the movement in an underlying volatility, rather than price or rate, index. While different volatility references can be used (for example, single stock volatility, basket volatility, index volatility) and various forms of volatility indexes can be computed (for example, realized volatility, variance), the determination of REE follows along the lines we have discussed above (for instance, the credit exposure generated when a firm is owed money under the volatility contract). Accordingly, the equations we have presented earlier can be adapted for the volatility reference, with RF applied to realized volatility to provide an estimate of the maximum value, and thus exposure, that might be generated. The main task centers on determining the appropriate RF for the volatility indicator; given sufficient data, however, this can be derived (with the usual adjustments made for maturity and confidence level). Since the volatility swap market typically trades on the basis of number of contracts times the number of volatility points per contract, we make slight modifications to our previous equations. Thus, when an institution is a purchaser of a realized volatility swap (for example, generating a profit, and thus credit exposure, as realized volatility exceeds implied volatility) it can use Equation 10.21:

$$REE = NC * VP * (((1 + RF) * RV) - IV) \qquad (10.21)$$

And, when it is a seller of the swap (for example, generating a profit, and thus credit exposure, as realized volatility drops below implied volatility), it can make use of Equation 10.22:

$$REE = NC * VP * (IV - ((1 - RF) * RV)) \qquad (10.22)$$

where VP is the volatility points per contract; IV is the implied volatility agreed on trade date; RV is the realized volatility; and all other terms are as defined above.

Terms are quoted in points, rather than percentages, in accordance with market convention; the equations above can certainly be adapted to convert the framework into percentage terms. Note that the reverse positions are of no concern from a credit risk perspective. Thus, if the purchaser of the swap experiences a decline in volatility (for example, $RV < IV$) it has exposure to the seller, not vice versa; conversely, if the seller of the swap experiences a rise in volatility (for example, $RV > IV$) it has exposure to the purchaser, not vice versa. Note further that the equations can be adapted to handle the variance swap, which is simply realized volatility squared less implied volatility squared (see also our discussion on power options in Chapter 8).

Consider the following example. Portfolio manager UVW wishes to receive a payment in one year if DAX volatility rises above its current implied level of 20 percent and is willing to pay if volatility declines; the trade is 10 contracts in size, with each contract paying €100,000 per volatility point. Based on its historical examination of implied DAX volatility, UVW computes a 90 percent RF of 25 percent. Per Equation 10.21 it computes REE as:

$$REE = 10 * €100,000 * (((1 + 0.25) * 20) - 20)$$

$$= €1,000,000 * 5$$

$$= €5m$$

Thus, if DAX volatility rises during the next 12 months to reach 25 percent (as estimated through the RF) the volatility swap is worth €5m to UVW, and if XYZ defaults at this point, UVW will lose that amount.

Other market references

Inflation swaps

An inflation swap requires the exchange of fixed and variable inflation, either at the end of a multi-year period (that is, a zero coupon inflation swap) or every year (that is, annual inflation swap). Though transactions are bilateral we are interested in examining positions that generate positive credit exposure; this occurs when variable inflation is above the fixed benchmark for a fixed inflation payer, and below the fixed benchmark for a fixed inflation receiver. Unlike certain other swaps and forwards discussed above, inflation swaps typically do not typically involve the payment/receipt of a periodic "Libor flow"; this element can therefore be ignored.

A key dimension of the REE process relates to development of an appropriate RF value for the inflation index. While some aspect of this might relate to historical inflation patterns, it is also likely to take account of future macroeconomic policy, monetary and fiscal pressures, and so on. Indeed, unlike most of the other variables we have considered in this book, period-to-period inflation data often reflects modest volatility and must be supplemented by "forward looking" economic analysis. Any RF should reflect this fact.

From an REE perspective we can, once again, adapt the equations developed above to handle inflation variables. For the institution acting as a fixed inflation payer the relevant equation is shown as:

$$REE = N * (((1+RFc) * Infl_{var}) - Infl_{fix}) \qquad (10.23)$$

And, for an institution that is a fixed inflation receiver the equation is:

$$REE = N * (Infl_{fix} - ((1 - RFc) * Infl_{var})) \qquad (10.24)$$

Where: $Infl_{fix}$ is the fixed inflation rate agreed on trade date; $Infl_{var}$ is the variable inflation rate; and all other terms are as defined above.

Once again, we are not concerned with the reverse scenarios (for example, falling inflation for a fixed payer and rising inflation for a fixed receiver), as these generate no credit exposure. Note that the equations above ignore the effects of computation lags for simplicity.

Consider the following example. Company V wants to receive the variable rate inflation over a three-year period on a US$100m notional zero coupon inflation swap, and is willing to pay Bank X 5 percent fixed inflation in return (which is also the current period inflation rate). Based on a long-term study of inflation patterns and an examination of economic forecasts, Company V believes that the relevant three-year inflation RF is 20 percent. No payments will be exchanged between V and X until the maturity of the transaction. Based on Equation 10.23, V's upfront REE allocation is:

$$REE = US\$100m * ((1 + 0.20) * 0.05) - 0.05)$$

$$= US\$100m * ((1.20) * 0.05) - 0.05)$$

$$= US\$100m * 0.01$$

$$= US\$1m$$

The computation of risk on the annual inflation swap is quite similar to the analysis presented above. Though the full risk horizon must be considered (for example, three years) when developing *ex ante* REE, the annual settlement feature that characterizes the structure reduces the build-up of actual exposure. Since the annual swap is actually comprised of a series of linked forwards, our framework focuses on the REE derived through the standard multi-year RF and, on a continuous basis, takes account of the settled MTM component.

Electricity swaps

An electricity swap (typically structured as a series of periodically settled forward contracts) calls for the exchange of fixed and floating power prices based on a recognized index. Again, though the electricity swap contract is bilateral, our credit exposure analysis focuses on transactions where floating prices are above the agreed fixed price for the fixed price payer and below the fixed price for the fixed price receiver. The reverse positions are of no concern from a credit risk perspective. Thus, if the floating prices fall below the fixed price the purchaser of the swap has exposure to the seller, not vice versa. Conversely, if the floating prices rise above the fixed price the seller of the swap has exposure to the purchaser, not vice versa. Since market convention calls for periodic settlement, actual exposure does not accumulate beyond a given settlement period, though the full risk of the transaction must still be considered for decision-making and ongoing risk management purposes (for example, an event of default might occur after any particular settlement has passed, but before maturity).

A fixed price payer can use Equation 10.25 to compute REE:

$$REE = MWh * (((1 + RFc) * CPP) - FPP) \tag{10.25}$$

While a fixed price receiver can use Equation 10.26 as the appropriate measure:

$$REE = MWh * (FPP - ((1 - RFc) * CPP)) \tag{10.26}$$

Where *MWh* is megawatt hours (which can be further decomposed into the megawatt power block times the relevant number of peak or off-peak hours); *RFc* is a constantly adjusted risk factor; *CPP* is the current power price; and *FPP* is the fixed power price.

As a reminder, the development of a power-based RF must focus on the volatility of prices over an averaging period, rather than just the spot movement; this is consistent with market convention.

Consider the following example: Energy company GHI wishes to protect against rising power prices over the next quarter by entering into an electricity swap on 120,000 MWh (total peak hours), paying a fixed rate of US$30/MWh (which is also the current market price) and receiving the average floating electricity price from Bank ABC. Per Equation 10.25 the initial REE, assuming a three-month RF of 10 percent, is:

$$REE = 120{,}000 * (((1 + 0.10) * US\$30) - US\$30)$$

$$= 120{,}000 * (US\$33 - US\$30)$$

$$= US\$360{,}000$$

The *ex ante* REE is thus US$360,000. As each monthly settlement period passes, the actual exposure component can be removed and the remaining REE (based on remaining MWh as well as the new CPP and RFc) can be applied.

Temperature swaps

Temperature swaps provide for payments that depend on whether the relevant temperature index (for example, CDD, HDD, Tmax, Tmin, averaged daily, and so on) is above, or below some fixed level at the conclusion of the transaction. From a credit risk perspective we again focus on situations where the temperature index rises above a predetermined fixed index level (for a fixed payer) and falls below the fixed level (for a fixed receiver); the reverse positions generate no credit risk.

The index used in temperature swaps is generally accumulated during a seasonal period (for example, winter or summer) (the exception occurs with "single day" Tmax or Tmin contracts, which reflect a single point in time); payout is then a function of the cumulative total of the index, adjusted by some sensitivity multiplier (for example, US$ or € per degree or degree day). The most common temperature swaps can therefore be viewed as single period forward contracts (though multi-year swaps are becoming more common, they are "restarted" at pre-defined levels every year, in line with our comment earlier that seasonal temperatures are "mean reverting" due to natural forces).

The analysis of credit exposure focuses on the maximum value the index can take during a particular seasonal period. However, we cannot necessarily apply the same financially modeled RFs to the framework because a temperature index, while certainly stochastic, does not follow the same diffusion process of an equity or currency price, for instance. Indeed, the temperature index cannot continue to rise or fall beyond some natural boundary, meaning the shape of the distribution is likely to be different and the maximum movement predicted through a diffusion process will be different. In addition, since most transactions are seasonal in nature (for example, three to six months) there are limits as to how far the index might travel under the standard RF framework. We also recall from the discussion above, that the temperature swap market commonly trades with "caps" or payout limits; thus, regardless of how far a given temperature index might travel, it will still be limited by a contractual payout boundary. Nonetheless, an RF-based REE framework can still be considered, as long as it is properly synchronized to the particulars of temperature data movements. This approach is most appropriate when the payout cap on a derivative is quite large and a firm does not want to over-allocate credit exposure.

For a payer of the fixed temperature index the relevant REE is shown as:

$$REE = DV * (((1 + RFc) * TempC) - TempF) \qquad (10.27)$$

For a receiver of the fixed temperature index the equation is:

$$REE = DV * (TempF - ((1 - RFc) * TempC)) \qquad (10.28)$$

Where DV is degree value; RFc is a constantly adjusted risk factor; $TempF$ is the fixed value of the temperature index; and $TempC$ is the cumulative value of the temperature index.

Thus, to compute the REE of a temperature swap (using any particular reference temperature index), an institution can take one of several approaches. Under the most conservative approach, it can simply assign as its REE the maximum payable under the payout cap of the contract, by assuming that the temperature index will rise to the maximum point during the life of the trade and that its counterparty will default. Alternatively, it can apply Equations 10.27 or 10.28 after gaining some understanding of the RF process for temperature indexes.

Consider the following example. Energy Company BCD enters into an HDD swap with Bank WXY to receive the cumulative HDD index of a particular city when it rises above 3500 HDDs (at US$10,000/HDD, to a maximum of US$3m). The conservative method calls for BCD to allocate US$3m of REE against WXY's credit limits. The company makes no particular assumptions on whether the cumulative HDD index will rise to 3800 (the

level of the index which equates to maximum payout), it just assumes that it
will. Under a less conservative, though perhaps more realistic (and more
intensive), approach, BCD might examine the underlying temperature data
and develop an RF that indicates how far the HDD index might travel during
the life of the trade. For instance, if it concludes that the 95 percent confidence level RF is 5 percent (since the trade is only one season long) and that
its mean reverts from that point on (for example, temperatures begin to warm
up once again), then it can apply Equation 10.27.

Under the example the REE is computed as:

$$REE = US\$10,000 * (((1.05) * 3500) - 3500)$$

$$= US\$10,000 * ((3675 - 3500)$$

$$= US\$10,000 * 175$$

$$= US\$1.75m$$

The *ex ante* REE is thus US\$1.75m based on the use of an RF of 5 percent. If
BCD feels that a normal season is likely to occur it may wish to use this more
realistic approach, which allocates less REE than the maximum payout of the
contract allows. Again, care must be taken in developing RFs related to the
movement of temperature indexes, as they have unique characteristics.

In addition to the complex swap structures discussed in this chapter, it
should be clear that many other compound packages of derivatives can be
created by combining swaps and options. Indeed, the combinations are
virtually limitless: Libor lookback swaps, range forward/corridor swaps,
leveraged equity swaps with quantos or barriers, and so on. From a risk
quantification perspective it is again necessary to review the individual
components of the derivative package and isolate specific sources of credit
risk; many of the formulae presented in Part II can provide guidance.
Whether a risk officer is dealing with the instruments detailed above, or
one of the "variations on the theme," care must obviously be exercised
when considering such transactions. Swap risk is generally long term in
nature and represents a vital and sensitive extension of credit. Not all
complex swap transactions are suitable for all counterparties, and caution
must be taken to ensure that credit decisions result in prudent action for
bank and counterparty alike.

Having reviewed the potential credit risk arising from individual
complex options, swaps and strategies in Part II, we turn our attention in
Part III to broader portfolio management issues. This helps us understand
how portfolios of derivatives (and other credit-risky instruments) can be
evaluated and managed in a broader framework.

Credit Portfolio Risk Management Issues

CHAPTER 11

Credit Risk Management of Derivative Portfolios: Quantitative Issues

The ongoing management of derivative credit exposures represents an integral component of the risk control framework. Once an institution has identified and quantified its credit risks, it needs to ensure they are actively and appropriately managed. While risk identification and measurement, which we have discussed at length in Parts I and II, are critical elements of the governance and control process, they must be supplemented by active and continuous risk management. As shall note in Part III, the active credit risk management process is both quantitative and qualitative.

- In this chapter we consider various quantitative portfolio issues, including the aggregation of individual transactions into discrete counterparty portfolios, the aggregation of counterparty portfolios across businesses, and the computation of portfolio credit losses for reserve and regulatory/ economic capital allocation purposes.

- In Chapter 12 we supplement the quantitative discussion by examining the state of credit risk portfolio models, including first and second-generation model advances that have been made in recent years.

- In Chapter 13 we turn our attention to qualitative portfolio issues, including dynamic management of credit exposures (for example, risk mitigation, scenario analysis, limit adjustment) and various ancillary topics (such as lengthening transaction maturities, transaction motivation/suitability, and willingness versus ability to pay).

In considering portfolio credit exposures we must extend our discussion at certain points to consider exposures arising from all of a firm's credit-sensitive business: not only derivatives, but also funded and contingent loans, bonds, money market/deposit instruments, repurchase agreements, and so forth. This is the most relevant approach as it provides a consolidated view of a firm's credit risks: any instrument or transaction susceptible not only to default, but also deterioration. Indeed, as we shall note later, the application of capital and portfolio optimization techniques requires this type of consolidation. Though many of the examples we use in this chapter relate to derivative exposures specifically, it should be understood that the framework can easily be extended to incorporate risks arising from linear transactions, such as funded loans with REE of 100 percent, repo financing transactions (marked daily) with REE of 1–10 percent (depending on the underlying collateral security), unfunded/contingent commitments with REE of 25–50 percent (depending on nature of commitment), and so forth.

Proper analysis and management of credit exposures on a portfolio, rather than transaction-specific, basis provides a more realistic view of a bank's true credit exposure with a given counterparty. For instance, simple aggregation of the REE inherent in multiple transactions with a single counterparty can overstate a bank's exposure and lead ultimately to bad decisions and resource misallocation. Development of portfolio management techniques is thus an integral aspect of the credit risk management process; we discuss this issue in the first section below. Monitoring credit transactions solely on an REE basis can likewise lead to confusion about transaction return and required capital; this becomes problematic when attempting to allocate scarce credit resources between competing transactions and businesses. Conversion of REE into expected and unexpected credit losses provides a vital link to profitability and capitalization, and permits more accurate decision-making; we discuss this issue in the second section.

CONSOLIDATING INDIVIDUAL CREDIT EXPOSURES INTO PORTFOLIOS

Aggregation of credit exposures and the evaluation of credit risk on a portfolio basis are among the most critical areas of credit risk management. The measurement and management of portfolio credit risk has become particularly important as institutions strive to manage resources and risks more accurately and efficiently; by doing so, they can ensure exposures are not overstated (which might otherwise divert profitable incremental business) or understated (which might otherwise generate a "misbalanced," and potentially problematic, exposure to a given counterparty).[1] By understanding the effects of a portfolio of trades on counterparty exposure, it becomes clear that diversified business with a given client (that is, activity on both sides of the market, across markets, and across products) and among different clients helps reduce potential exposures. Reduction of exposures also leads to lower potential credit losses.

There are various ways of combining and managing portfolios of credit exposures. While a rigorous review of all methods is well beyond the scope of this text, we shall briefly describe and consider three fundamental approaches:[2]

- *The incremental summation approach*: which groups single counterparty transactions into a portfolio and aggregates across transaction-specific REEs to generate a total counterparty portfolio REE.

- *The simulation approach*: which simulates an entire portfolio of counterparty transactions to produce a total counterparty portfolio REE.

- *The hybrid approach*: which utilizes the summation and simulation approaches in combination to produce a total counterparty portfolio REE.

Again, for clarity, we shall limit our illustration of counterparty portfolio techniques to derivative transactions. It should be clear, however, that a portfolio of credit-sensitive transactions could easily include other instruments (with relevant REEs, ranging from 1 percent to 100 percent, as discussed above). Thus, a bank might have a portfolio of credit-sensitive transactions with Company ABC as reflected in Table 11.1.

Table 11.1 Company ABC credit portfolio

Derivative books:
  5-year interest rate swaps
  3-year cross currency swaps
  1- year Nikkei barrier options

Loan book:
  5-year fixed rate loan

Fixed income trading books:
  9-month commercial paper inventory
  5-year bond inventory

Financing book:
  1-year US Treasury repurchase agreements

Foreign exchange book:
  6-month forward $/¥ transactions

These would form an essential part of any portfolio analysis ; they cannot, and should not, be ignored in the portfolio risk analysis exercise, though we shall omit them for clarity.

Before beginning our discussion, we present a typical sequence of events confronting an analyst considering a credit decision. Charting this process provides an understanding of the trade-off between speed and accuracy in the credit decision framework; this, in turn, indicates why certain trade-offs exist in the selection of portfolio aggregation and management techniques.

Under a typical credit "workflow" at a financial institution, an analyst first receives a request from a derivative trader or marketer regarding a specific transaction with a client.

- If the counterparty is not already covered by the analyst, financial information is generally obtained and an analysis performed to determine internal credit rating and appropriate credit limits. An analyst then computes transaction REE and determines whether the maturity of the deal is within the bank's overall policy guidelines (for example, certain institutions only permit unsecured term exposure for counterparties with particular credit ratings). If the counterparty does not meet term guidelines an analyst may request use of a risk mitigating technique (for example, collateral, recouponing, termination option, and so on, as discussed at greater length later in the book). If a bank uses a risk-adjusted return framework it can also examine the potential profitability of the transaction against corporate hurdle rates. At this point the analyst can approve, reject, or restructure the transaction.

- If the counterparty is already covered by the analyst, an internal credit rating and credit limits are likely to exist. If so, the analyst calculates the REE of the transaction and compares the figure against current limits to determine credit availability. Since some business/exposures already exist, the risk evaluation process also focuses on whether the contemplated transaction adds to, subtracts from, or leaves unchanged, a counterparty's current potential credit exposure. In some cases incremental transactions can lower overall exposure (particularly when an enforceable netting agreement is in place); in other instances, however, incremental transactions generate no such benefit and represent additional risk to the bank. After reviewing these portfolio exposures, and considering maturity guidelines and profit hurdles, the analyst is in a position to approve, reject, or restructure the transaction.

Against this background a trading desk must often deal with urgent transaction execution for the counterparty; this becomes particularly critical in the face of volatile markets, where a transaction may not be economical once a market moves by even a modest amount. In such an environment, the best portfolio aggregation method might be one that can be implemented easily and used quickly; a decision-making framework based on a time-consuming aggregation processes may be inappropriate. There are, naturally, instances where an analyst has a greater amount of time for analysis and decision-making. This is particularly true when a potential transaction is highly structured, or when execution is not dependent on specific market levels. In such cases an analyst might have enough time to do a very rigorous and comprehensive review of all relevant portfolio factors, without being concerned about specific time pressures; the credit process thus permits use of more extensive and accurate, though time-consuming, portfolio aggregation methods. Figure 11.1 summarizes the typical credit workflow process.

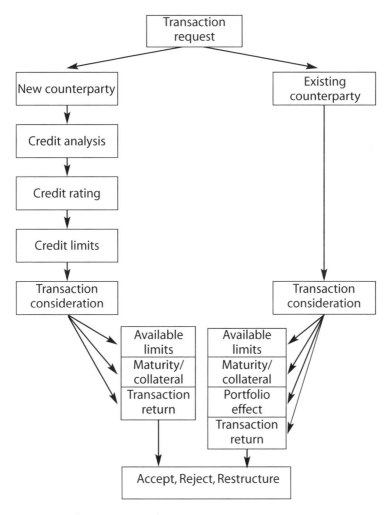

Figure 11.1 Credit transaction decision process

The point of this introductory discussion is to illustrate that institutions need to consider trade-offs when quantifying and managing portfolios of credit exposures. As we shall note below, the simulation process, while elegant and quite accurate, can be time-consuming – even with advanced computing power and efficient computational algorithms – and may not be suitable as a working tool. Simple aggregation and incremental summation, while easy and inexpensive to employ as a quick decision-making tool, can result in oversimplification and misinterpretation of true exposures, and may not provide the most accurate information necessary. Some combination of the two can be a workable "middle ground," but has shortcomings of its own.

Incremental summation approach

A common and relatively simple method of combining and evaluating a portfolio of credit exposures is the incremental summation approach. There are various ways of implementing this technique and we shall discuss several in this section.

The most basic form of incremental summation aggregates the REE of individual transactions (as obtained through the quantitative process described at length in this book, or through other methodologies) to create a total portfolio REE; incremental transactions are then added to the total portfolio REE as they arise. This framework is easy to implement but quite flawed, for at least three reasons.

■ If a bank is active with a counterparty on both sides of a market (for example, it has both fixed payer and receiver interest rate – or currency, commodity, equity, credit – swaps with the counterparty), a simple summation of transactions within the portfolio, and incremental trans-actions against the portfolio, implies increasing credit exposure whether the market rises or falls; this is clearly impossible. If the market rises, it increases exposure on certain transactions and lowers it on others, and vice versa. Under no circumstances can an upward (or downward) market movement increase exposure on all trades in the portfolio at the same time. Failure to recognize this results in significant overstatement of exposure.

■ If a bank has in place a legally enforceable netting agreement with a counterparty, it benefits from the full effects of net (not total) exposure in bankruptcy; aggregation that fails to recognize this benefit will again lead to overstatement.

■ A simple summation approach does not accurately account for the timing of peak exposures which, in a diversified portfolio, will occur at different times; pure summation simply adds the peak exposure of one deal to the peak exposure of a second deal, and so on, regardless of when they occur or mature (we discuss this point in greater detail below as it is also a flaw found in a more advanced summation approach).

An example helps illustrate the first two shortcomings of the simple summation approach. Assume a bank has an existing swap transaction where it pays six-month Libor and receives 6 percent fixed; the fractional exposure attributable to the deal is US$2m. Suppose next month rates decrease by ten basis points and the bank adds a second, offsetting transaction where it receives six-month Libor and pays 5.90 percent fixed. If the incremental trade is considered at execution date, it adds no actual exposure (for example, the market has not moved) but adds US$2.5m of fractional exposure. These positions are reflected in Table 11.2.

Strict summation of these trades indicates potential exposure of US$5m. If swap rates move upward during the life of the two transactions credit exposure increases on the bank's fixed payer transaction (for example, if the counterparty defaults when swap rates are 50 or 100 basis points higher, it costs the bank more to replace its fixed payer swap in the new, higher rate, environment) and decreases credit exposure on the bank's fixed receiver transaction (for example, if the counterparty defaults when rates are 50 or 100 basis points higher, the bank can replace its fixed receiver swap at a higher rate); the reverse occurs if rates decline. To suggest that both transactions simultaneously add potential exposure is impossible and results in an overstatement. In addition, the framework above does not account for the treatment of net exposures. As we have discussed at several points in this text, use of a master agreement, in a jurisdiction that legally accepts netting, permits institutions to use net exposure computations with confidence. Failure to employ netting in the determination of portfolio risk leads to a misallocation of credit exposures against counterparty credit limits.

Knowing that simple summation of incremental and existing transactions inflates credit exposure (and makes no intuitive sense from a market direction

Table 11.2 Incremental summation approach: sample portfolio 1

Bank pays	Bank receives	Actual exposure	Fractional exposure	Potential exposure
6-month Libor	6.00%	$0.5m	$2.0m	$2.5m
5.90%	6-month Libor	$0.0m	$2.5m	$2.5m
Total		$0.5m		$5.0m

standpoint), we must consider an alternate method of incorporating incremental transactions into the portfolio. Since market direction can negatively impact only one trade in a pair of "offsetting" trades, dividing derivative transactions into distinct categories that reflect opposing pay and receive streams can generate a more accurate aggregation. The groupings might include fixed interest payments and fixed interest receipts, currency "A" payments and currency "A" receipts, and so on, by broad product classification (for example, US interest rates, Japanese interest rates, ¥/$ currency rates, £/€ currency rates, and US equity indexes). By splitting potential exposures into two distinct categories, an institution is better able to compare total, gross, and net potential exposures; this provides a more accurate credit management tool and a more precise exposure figure that takes account of activity on both sides of a market and enforceable netting arrangements. Note that while this method is an improvement over the simple summation approach, it also has certain shortcomings that we discuss below.

Consider the scenario depicted in Table 11.3, which captures the transactions detailed above once they are under way.

We begin by defining the following exposure classes:

■ *Total potential exposure*: the sum of fixed pay and receive potential exposures (as in the previous example).

■ *Gross potential exposure*: the greater of the fixed pay and receive potential exposures.

■ *Net potential exposure*: the difference between the fixed pay and receive potential exposures.

■ *Portfolio mark-to-market (MTM)*: the sum of actual exposures.

Under the basic summation strategy mentioned above, the total potential credit exposure applied against counterparty limits is US$2.3m. We know

Table 11.3 Incremental summation approach: sample portfolio 2

Bank pays	Bank receives	Actual exposure	Fractional exposure	Potential exposure
6-month Libor	6.00%	$1.0m	$0.9m	$1.9m
5.90%	6-month Libor	($1.0m)	$1.4m	$0.4m
Total		$0.0m		$2.3m

this overstates potential risk, since market moves will alternately increase exposure on one transaction and lower it on the other. Instead of utilizing the total of the two potential exposures, we can use the greater of the two (gross) or the difference of the two (net). Use of one versus the other is dependent on the enforceability of netting within a particular jurisdiction, as discussed below. What is immediately apparent, however, is that by using either gross or net potential exposure, only one side of the potential credit exposure is allocated against limits; this is obviously a much more sensible and equitable approach, since market moves can only increase exposure on one side of the market at any point in time.

In the example above, gross potential exposure (greater of fixed pay and receive potential exposures) is US$1.9m and net potential exposure (net of fixed pay and receive potential exposures) is US$1.5m. Gross potential exposure might be an applicable measure in instances when a bank doubts its ability to net counterparty claims successfully in the event of counterparty default, believing a bankruptcy receiver will "cherry pick" by assigning value to contracts that benefit the bankrupt company while dismissing those that are detrimental. The bank's doubt may relate to the lack of governing documentation (for example, signed master agreements) or lack of legal comfort that the jurisdiction accepts netting. Certain institutions might choose to take an even more conservative stance by defining gross potential exposure as the greater of fixed pay and receive potential exposures plus the actual exposure of the lesser of the fixed pay and receive exposures. Net potential exposure is an applicable measure in situations where a bank has a signed master swap agreement and is active in a jurisdiction that accepts netting; therefore it has no fear of being "cherry picked" and is confident that treatment in bankruptcy will focus on net actual exposures. Where potential exposure is divided into two components there is no overstatement of potential exposures as a result of market movements. As only the greater (or the net) of the two exposures is used, we are not assuming a market impossibility (for example, a move in a single direction increasing exposure on both sides). This approach represents a more realistic use of the incremental summation process. Table 11.4 provides a more detailed examination of this concept.

It is easy to imagine applying the same framework to a portfolio of currency derivatives. For instance, assume a bank has a portfolio of Japanese yen currency swaps, vanilla currency options, and barrier options, as listed in Table 11.5.

Under this example, use of gross or net potential currency exposure (depending on an institution's ability to net), instead of total potential exposure, results in a meaningful reduction in credit limit usage. More importantly, it ensures an institution's risk profile is being managed more accurately, which will have an impact on portfolio management and optimization.

Table 11.4 Incremental summation approach: sample portfolio 3

Bank pays	Bank receives	Actual exposure	Fractional exposure	Potential exposure*	
				Receive fixed	Pay fixed
6-month Libor	6.00%		$1.0m	$0.9m	$1.9m
5.90%	6-month Libor	($1.0m)	$1.4m	$0.4m	
	Total actual exposure			$0.0m	
	Total potential exposure			$2.3m	
	Gross potential exposure			$1.9m	
	Net potential exposure			$1.5m	

* If actual exposure + fractional exposure < 0, then potential exposure = 0.

Table 11.5 Incremental summation approach: sample portfolio 4

Type	Bank pays	Bank receives	Actual exposure	Fractional exposure	Potential exposure*	
					Receive $	Pay $
Barrier	¥	$	$2.0m	$4.5m	$6.5m	
E-call	¥	$	$1.5m	$1.4m	$2.9m	
Swap	$	¥	($1.2m)	$6.9m		$5.7m
A-call	$	¥	$0.0m	$1.2m		$1.2m
E-call	$	¥	($1.3m)	$0.8m		$0.0m
	Total actual exposure				$1.0m	
	Total potential exposure				$16.3m	
	Gross potential exposure				$9.4m	
	Net potential exposure				$2.5m	

* If actual exposure + fractional exposure < 0, then potential exposure = 0.

It is entirely appropriate to extend this analysis to other non-derivative, credit sensitive transactions that might exist in the bank's credit portfolio. In some cases the same "dual" market movement applies. For instance, a bank might have a US Treasury repo and a reverse repo with a counterparty;

movement in Treasury rates can only impact one of the two positions at a time, so the approach is precisely the same as we have described for derivatives (particularly when governed by a repurchase netting agreement). Alternatively, it might have a funded loan position in the counterparty's credit and a short position in its bond, meaning that a movement in the counterparty's credit spreads cannot hurt or help both positions at the same time. In other cases the dual market movement will not be relevant and the exposure simply counts as its relevant REE against the portfolio total (for example, a funded loan or long bond position with no offset). The framework is thus applicable to other credit products.

Having developed a general methodology for dividing exposures into two separate components, so that gross and net potential exposures become a realistic way of measuring a portfolio of transactions, it is relatively straightforward to determine the effect of an incremental transaction on a counterparty portfolio. Under this process an analyst calculates REE for a new transaction, determines whether it qualifies as a pay rate/currency/index or receive rate/currency/index and aggregates accordingly. In certain instances the proposed transaction increases gross/net exposures, in other instances it reduces exposures. As indicated above, the ability to weigh an incremental transaction against the counterparty portfolio during the trade evaluation process becomes an important tool in the management of exposures.

Consider the following example. Bank DEF has a portfolio of US interest rate derivatives with a counterparty as highlighted in Table 11.6.

Table 11.6 Incremental summation approach: sample portfolio 5

Type	Bank pays	Bank receives	Actual exposure	Fractional exposure	Potential exposure*	
					Receive fixed	Pay fixed
Swap	5.00%	Libor	$3.0m	$4.5m		$7.5m
Swap	4.00%	Libor	($1.0m)	$2.2m		$1.2m
Swaption	Libor	6.00%	($3.2m)	$6.5m	$3.3m	
Swaption	7.00%	Libor	$2.0m	$4.2m		$6.2m
		Total actual exposure			$0.8m	
		Total potential exposure			$18.2m	
		Gross potential exposure			$14.9m	
		Net potential exposure			$11.6m	

* If actual exposure + fractional exposure < 0, then potential exposure = 0.

In evaluating a request to approve an incremental trade, the analyst at DEF must first ascertain whether the transaction adds to, subtracts from, or leaves unchanged, overall exposures. Based on the discussion above, it should be clear that if DEF enters into a derivative trade where it receives fixed rates, it will not add to its gross potential exposure – it will, in fact, lower its exposure. For instance, if DEF enters into a new interest rate swap where it receives 6.50 percent fixed and pays Libor, the REE of the trade at inception is US$3m (where potential exposure equals fractional exposure since actual exposure is still zero). The complete portfolio, including the incremental transaction, is illustrated in Table 11.7.

By incorporating the new fixed receiver transaction into the portfolio based on the incremental summation approach, DEF's gross potential exposure remains unchanged and its net potential exposure declines by US$3m. Note that in this example, and the one which follows, we define gross potential exposure as the greater of the fixed pay and receive potential exposures; we do not consider the more conservative method defined above – for example, greater of the fixed pay and receive potential exposures plus the actual exposure of the lesser of the fixed pay and receive exposures. Only total potential exposure increases but this, as we have already explained, is not a valid measure of aggregate risk exposure. If the incremental transaction involves DEF paying, rather than receiving, a fixed rate, it is clear that gross potential and net potential exposures increase. The

Table 11.7 Incremental summation approach: sample portfolio 6

Type	Bank pays	Bank receives	Actual exposure	Fractional exposure	Potential exposure*	
					Receive fixed	Pay fixed
Swap	5.00%	Libor	$3.0m	$4.5m		$7.5m
Swap	4.00%	Libor	($1.0m)	$2.2m		$1.2m
Swaption	Libor	6.00%	($3.2m)	$6.5m	$3.3m	
Swaption	7.00%	Libor	$2.0m	$4.2m		$6.2m
Swap	Libor	6.50%	$0.0m	$3.0m	$3.0m	
Total actual exposure					$0.8m	
Total potential exposure					$21.2m	
Gross potential exposure					$14.9m	
Net potential exposure					$8.6m	

* If actual exposure + fractional exposure < 0, then potential exposure = 0.

new portfolio, featuring the incremental fixed payer swap, is illustrated in Table 11.8.

Under this scenario the incremental fixed payer swap adds to both gross and net potential exposure; there is no offsetting benefit from the trans- action (in fact, there is incremental usage of credit limits). These examples help emphasize that care must be taken when considering the effects of incremental transactions on existing portfolios; in certain cases new deals represent net additions to risk, while in other instances they can mitigate risk (assuming netting is valid).

Extending this framework to the next logical step, we can create sub- portfolios by markets/products for a given counterparty (for example, a subportfolio of US interest rate derivatives, a subportfolio of ¥/$ currency derivatives, and so on, including subportfolios of non-derivatives). Simply adding across these subportfolios by gross or net potential exposure to yield a total counterparty exposure may, in certain instances, be misleading. Since many markets are highly correlated, either positively or negatively, it is wrong to simply assume that correlations will equal zero over the life of the transactions. Depending on the composition of the portfolio and the nature and magnitude of the correlation, credit exposure may increase or decrease as transactions are added; the overall portfolio is expanded or underlying markets shift.

Consider the following example. Bank A has two portfolios, one

Table 11.8 Incremental summation approach: sample portfolio 7

Type	Bank pays	Bank receives	Actual exposure	Fractional exposure	Potential exposure*	
					Receive fixed	Pay fixed
Swap	5.00%	Libor	$3.0m	$4.5m		$7.5m
Swap	4.00%	Libor	($1.0m)	$2.2m		$1.2m
Swaption	Libor	6.00%	($3.2m)	$6.5m	$3.3m	
Swaption	7.00%	Libor	$2.0m	$4.2m		$6.2m
Swap	6.50%	Libor	$0.0m	$3.0m		$3.0m
		Total actual exposure			$0.8m	
		Total potential exposure			$21.2m	
		Gross potential exposure			$17.9m	
		Net potential exposure			$14.6m	

* If actual exposure + fractional exposure < 0, then potential exposure = 0.

comprised of derivatives where it is a fixed payer of US rates and a second where it is a fixed payer of Euro rates. Based on an assumed correlation of zero between US and Euro swap rates, the gross potential exposure is calculated as US$15m. However, by assuming correlation of +0.4 between the swap rates (that is, if US rates rise by 100 basis points Euro rates will rise by 40 basis points), gross potential exposure of the two portfolios increases to US$19m; intuitively this makes sense since Bank A is a payer on the same side (that is, fixed) in both portfolios. As correlation rises to 0.9, the exposure of the two portfolios increases to US$23m.

Consider now the situation where Bank A has two portfolios: one contains a series of US fixed payer derivatives while the second contains Euro fixed receiver derivatives; this, of course, is the opposite of the first example. Assuming no correlation between US and Euro swap rates, the gross potential exposure is determined to be US$12m. If correlation rises to 0.4, gross potential exposure of the two portfolios declines to US$9m; this occurs because Bank A is a fixed payer in one portfolio and a fixed receiver in the second. As correlation rises to 0.9, gross potential exposure declines further, to US$7m, for the same reasons. This framework can be extended to accommodate portfolios that are negatively correlated. Tables 11.9 and 11.10 highlight the effects of correlation on sample portfolios.[3]

We can see through these simple examples that introducing correlations in the incremental summation approach helps provide a more accurate view of portfolio exposures. Correlations are also employed in the simulation

Table 11.9 Sample portfolio 1 with correlations

Portfolios	Correlation	Gross potential exposure
US fixed pay/Euro fixed pay	+0.0	$15m
US fixed pay/Euro fixed pay	+0.4	$19m
US fixed pay/Euro fixed pay	+0.9	$23m

Table 11.10 Sample portfolio 2 with correlations

Portfolios	Correlation	Gross potential exposure
US fixed pay/Euro fixed receive	+0.0	$12m
US fixed pay/Euro fixed receive	+0.4	$9m
US fixed pay/Euro fixed receive	+0.9	$7m

approach and alternate aggregation methodologies to achieve the same results (and can be implemented in any aggregation methodology via the equation highlighted in Note 3). Care must be taken, of course, in selecting, measuring and updating correlations. As we shall discuss in the next chapter, correlation parameter inputs are vital in every first and second-generation credit portfolio risk model. Unfortunately, they can be quite unstable, particularly in the face of financial stress (which is precisely when they are most important for the quantification and management of exposures); the LTCM crisis noted in Part I reinforces this point, and serves as a reminder that market and credit risk models, no matter how sophisticated, must be used with caution, and with full awareness of assumptions, sensitivities, and potential shortcomings.

Despite the relative appeal of the more "realistic" incremental summation approach (for example, one which distinguishes between total, gross, and net potential exposures) it has certain flaws. For instance, by condensing an entire portfolio of trades down to a single number (whether gross or net potential exposure), rather than a profile of exposures over time, the effects of netting may not be properly understood. For example, a long-term trade with positive potential exposure may be partly offset by a short-term trade with zero potential exposure (as a result of a large negative MTM); in reducing the portfolio to a single number an analyst may derive false comfort from an exposure figure that changes dramatically once the short-term trade matures. In addition, if an institution utilizes average, rather than worst-case REE (in the form of a single number), it is effectively adding together different averaging periods (for example, a one-year transaction/averaging period and a ten-year transaction/averaging period) and this is mathematically suspect. Finally, as indicated earlier, if an institution simply adds together the peak REE from all transactions in the portfolio, it overstates total portfolio exposure.

Consider the following example. Bank XYZ has two Japanese interest rate derivatives in its portfolio. Transaction one is a three-year cap referencing six-month ¥ Libor that has just passed the final reset period in-the-money; it has six months until maturity and is worth US$7m to Bank XYZ. Since the final reset period has passed, credit exposure remains unchanged until XYZ receives the US$7m from its counterparty at maturity, six months hence. Transaction two is a new six-year ¥ swaption which has no actual exposure (for example, it has just been booked) but has US$15m of fractional exposure (with the peak US$15m occurring approximately one-third through the life of the transaction, in year two). Under an incremental summation methodology the potential exposure of the portfolio is US$22m, which is equal to the peak exposures XYZ experiences on each transaction (US$7m and US$15m). In fact, this overstates exposures by simply taking peak exposures, regardless of when they occur, and adding them together. A more accurate method adds the peak exposure in evidence at any particular forward point. For instance, the six-month peak exposure is US$7m from the cap, and perhaps US$8m from the swaption, for a total of US$15m (rather than US$22m). The inability of the incremental summation approach to take account of the timing of peak exposures is clearly a drawback. Figure 11.2 illustrates a portfolio of three forward-based derivative transactions of varying maturities; the exposure differential between a pure summation of peak exposures and a summation against forward points is very apparent.

Knowing that an incremental summation approach, which condenses exposures to a single figure and adds peak exposures occurring at different points in time, is flawed, we can consider the development of a process based on the forward point exposures described above. Specifically, we can continue to aggregate exposures by distinguishing between pay–receive flows and incorporating correlations, but extend the framework by including an entire forward point exposure profile which changes on a dynamic basis as actual exposure increases or decreases and fractional exposure declines. Implementation of this type of framework permits management based on aggregate forward point exposures rather than peak worst-case exposures, and allows for review and analysis of an entire continuum of exposure over time; this is helpful in the overall risk management process (note that under this framework the exposure applied against credit limits

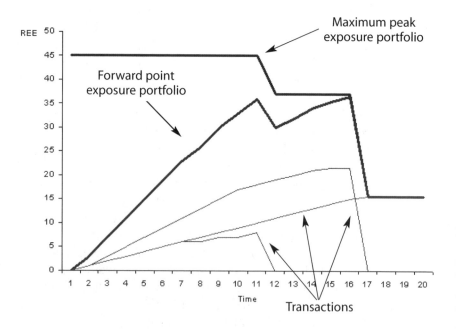

Figure 11.2 Maximum peak and forward point exposures

is the peak of the forward point exposure portfolio). The benefits of this approach are apparent when reviewing, for example, the effects of the trades noted above as time passes and markets begin to move. Illustrated below are two "snapshots" of the portfolio at select points in time. Consider Figure 11.3, which traces the three transactions after two periods have elapsed. Note that one of the transactions generates no credit exposure since the mark-to-market value of the transaction is sufficient to offset fractional exposure. Figure 11.4 depicts the three transactions after one more period has elapsed; in this instance the mark-to-market value of one of the transactions overwhelms the remaining fractional exposure, causing the entire forward point profile for the transaction to become negative. Institutions preferring a more conservative approach might choose to bound transaction profiles at zero.

While clearly not as sophisticated (or accurate) as the simulation approach outlined below, the incremental summation approach (in either condensed or forward point form) is appealing because the effect of new transactions on existing portfolios can be incorporated with speed and efficiency, without waiting for an extensive computer simulation to generate results (for example, entire credit risk profiles of every transaction in the counterparty portfolio, based on simulations of stochastic market variables). In a market of competitive bidding, "live" trades, and urgent credit decisions, the incremental summation approach can be viewed as an acceptable working tool, recognizing that in certain situations portfolio exposures will still be overstated.

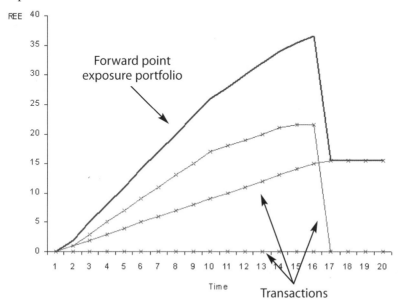

Figure 11.3 Forward point exposures 1

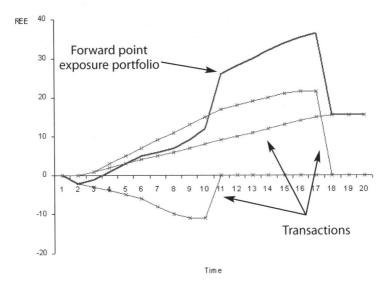

Figure 11.4 Forward point exposures 2

Simulation approach

As indicated earlier in the text, simulation methods are often used to compute REE of credit transactions with stochastic exposure levels. Use of a simulation process (to project the future path of key market variables and revalue derivatives at select future points based on the paths generated by the market variables) is a very effective means of calculating REE. In addition to using simulation to determine REEs for individual derivative transactions (which assists the credit officer in arriving at an initial credit decision), it can also be used to value the potential exposure of an entire counterparty portfolio of transactions (again, derivatives as well as linear credit instruments). Simulation can also be used to value exposures of multiple counterparties, as we shall note below and in the next chapter.

The process employed is similar to that used in analyzing individual transactions, except that the effects of stochastic market variables on the cash flows (and potential cash flows) of dozens, hundreds, or even thousands of transactions can be examined in unison. While simulation techniques vary between firms, a common process, as described earlier in the book, follows these steps:

■ The market variables impacting the underlying transactions are identified and defined.

■ The future paths of the stochastic market variables are defined.

- The length of the discrete time period and the starting values of the stochastic variables are chosen.

- A confidence level is selected.

- A path for each stochastic variable is created (based on the information specified above and by drawing a random number from a sample).

- The values of the stochastic variables generated by each path are used to value the portfolio of transactions at each time period up until the terminal point.

- A new set of random numbers is generated and new paths are determined; the value of the portfolio of transactions is recalculated.

- The process is repeated tens of thousands of times and average periodic and terminal values of the portfolio of transactions are determined.

- The difference between the average periodic and terminal values of the portfolio and the initial value of the portfolio provides an estimate, to the pre-specified confidence level, of the potential credit exposure of the portfolio.

As part of the simulation process, the effects of netting and collateral can be incorporated into the overall portfolio. Transactions that offset existing deals (that is, those on the "opposite" side of the market, actual or synthetic shorts, hedging longs, and so forth) can be subtracted from overall portfolio exposures to generate net portfolio credit exposure.

Simulation techniques for portfolio credit exposures are found throughout the academic and technical literature. For example, Lawrence has proposed an approach based on a "portfolio credit vector" (a risk profile for a given portfolio of derivatives) that is updated with a simulation of an incremental transaction as it is received from a trading desk.[4] The portfolio credit vector allows easy manipulation of incremental transactions within a portfolio and does not overstate overall portfolio risk (as a total potential exposure–summation approach might; for example, it does not aggregate exposures which peak at different maturities and does not condense risk into a single number); this process also takes account of the effects of netting. The drawback, of course, is the fairly significant computing power and time required to generate a simulation of the proposed transaction. The same is true of other credit portfolio simulation approaches (for example, Aziz and Charupat (1998), Iscoe, Kreinin, and Rosen (1999), Arvantis and Gregory in Ong (1999), and others, some of which we shall discuss in greater detail in the next chapter): while they can generate useful results, all require computing power of some consequence.

This brings us back to the topic we raised at the beginning of this chapter. Analysts often do not have time to generate the required simulated credit exposure when dealing with "live" trades. The speed of market movements and the need to respond to client requests on a real-time basis may render this an unworkable solution. It is true, of course, that highly structured transactions (for example, very large derivatives with potentially significant credit risks) are often days or weeks in the making, so that an immediate decision may not be required. In such cases there is enough time for full transaction and portfolio simulation. Assuming "live" transactions are the norm, however, an institution may need to weigh the advantages and disadvantages of utilizing transaction simulation within the portfolio framework. As always, there is no single correct answer, simply a range of options and trade-offs (for example, time, cost, accuracy), which an institution must consider prior to implementation of a risk control framework.

Hybrid approach

The hybrid approach combines elements of the incremental summation framework described earlier with the simulation approach outlined above. In this instance, we assume an existing portfolio of transactions with a given counterparty is transformed into a portfolio credit vector through the simulation process. This means that each time an incremental transaction is approved and booked it is "absorbed" into the overall portfolio simulation process generated by the bank's systems infrastructure. Before a new transaction is approved and booked, however, it is viewed as an incremental trade by the analyst and simply added to the existing counterparty portfolio credit vector. This approach has the benefit of permitting the analyst to employ a relatively straightforward, and quick, decision methodology (for example, the REE framework with subsequent aggregation against a portfolio credit vector), while deriving the benefits of the more accurate (though time-consuming) simulation approach. As indicated, once the new credit transaction is approved and booked, it is included in the bank's overnight simulation run (which might be generated automatically through a batch process). At the start of the next trading day the analyst has access to an updated portfolio credit vector, which includes the previous day's incremental swap trade.

In addition to the three approaches outlined above, there are numerous other ways of aggregating and evaluating portfolios of derivative credit risk.[5] As we might expect, each has its own advantages and disadvantages: what an analyst gains in speed may be sacrificed in accuracy, and vice versa. It is thus necessary for each institution to analyze its credit transaction flows, computing resources, its comfort with assumptions (on correlation, addition of peak exposures occurring at different times, and so on) to determine which portfolio aggregation technique is most suitable.

PORTFOLIOS OF COUNTERPARTIES

While multiple derivative and linear credit transactions with a single counter-party combine to form a portfolio of exposures with that counterparty, multiple counterparty portfolios combine to form an institution's entire credit-sensitive business. We have indicated that diversification of trades with a single counterparty (for example, activity on both sides of the market, and/or across different markets) can be beneficial in reducing potential credit exposures and, ultimately, losses; diversification of trades across a broad range of counterparties can also reduce potential exposures and losses. The idiosyncratic, or counterparty specific, nature of counterparty credit risk means there is little correlation between the performance of one counterparty and another. This low correlation means that diversification of exposures across a broad number of counterparties, industries, and geographic regions is an effective means of managing overall credit risk and can result in lower expected credit losses in a bank's credit-sensitive business. While empirical data in support of this is still limited, certain studies suggest the default corre-lation between two investment grade companies is only 0.01.[6] This implies strong opportunities for diversification across counterparties, industries, and countries. Of course some exceptions could occur within the swap dealing community, causing correlations to rise and credit risk concentrations to increase. The frequently cited "domino-effect" remains a concern: default by one dealer impacting the performance ability of other dealers exposed to the defaulting bank, and so on. In fact, default correlation in such instances would be significantly higher than empirical studies might suggest. The marketplace came close to testing this notion during the 1998 collapse of LTCM. In fact the possibility of a systemic collapse caused by the failure of dealers, hedge funds, and other financial institutions to perform on their credit and market risk-sensitive obligations was perceived to be large enough that the *de facto* "private sector bailout" of LTCM was viewed as a necessity.

The counterparty portfolio management process therefore relies on the use of correlations between individual counterparties. The credit portfolio models that we consider in the next chapter require counterparty correlation matrixes in order to make possible effective portfolio management; considerable time, effort, and research have gone into the development of these processes. We shall consider general techniques for implementing such processes in the next chapter, but for now we stress that the correlation input parameter is a key driver in the portfolio risk management framework. Most models are extremely sensitive to correlation inputs, so extreme care must be used when gathering and utilizing them. Managing credit risk exposures across counterparties is, of course, the ultimate goal of active credit portfolio management. While it is helpful and necessary to be able to manage risk exposures with any single counterparty, the ability to manage the entire credit-sensitive business of an institution (including management of regulatory and economic capital and optimization of the overall portfolio) is generally the end goal of any sophisticated institution.

QUANTIFYING CREDIT LOSSES

Expected and unexpected derivative credit losses

Throughout this text we have dealt with the concept of credit exposure as represented by actual exposure and fractional exposure (and potential exposure, or REE, as the sum of the two). As we have already discussed, potential exposure is the worst-case credit loss a bank faces if the market moves to a maximum point in favor of the bank (as determined through the REE process) and the counterparty defaults at the moment of maximum movement. Under this scenario a bank loses an economic amount equal to that suggested by REE at the inception of the transaction.

The figure cannot, however, be interpreted as the probable, or expected, credit loss facing a bank should a counterparty default on a derivative transaction (or, in continuing with our extension of the credit framework, any credit-sensitive transaction with some associated REE). In order to arrive at an estimate of expected credit loss we must employ a framework that incorporates the amount of potential exposure a bank faces (as estimated by REE) and the likelihood, or probability, its counterparty will default during the life of the transaction. In addition, the framework must indicate whether any amount will be recovered following default and bankruptcy proceedings. When these three elements (summarized in Figure 11.5) are combined possible credit losses can be quantified.

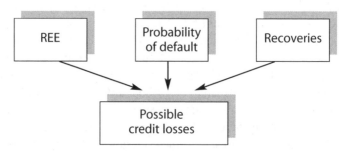

Figure 11.5 Derivation of possible credit losses

Once a bank has information on possible credit losses it can utilize the data in a broader framework to determine the amount of reserves and capital necessary to support individual transactions, portfolios of transactions, or an entire business. Ultimately, this type of framework can be used in developing more objective and uniform risk-adjusted performance metrics, which are particularly useful when comparing profitability across transactions and businesses and attempting to optimize the firm's risky portfolios.

As indicated in Chapter 1, risk-adjusted returns are an essential component of financial management. Risk-takers (for example, traders) are subject to greater scrutiny on the profitability of their businesses for at least two reasons: first, institutions are increasingly aware of the need to manage their own capital actively and blunt measures such as return on assets and return on equity no longer provide managers with the quality of information required to evaluate the true risk-adjusted profitability of a given business. Second, in an era of growing derivatives volume and lengthening transaction maturities, counterparty credit limits sometimes become scarce; this requires a framework by which to "redirect" credit limits to those transactions which provide the greatest risk-adjusted returns.

As mentioned, the calculation of expected and unexpected credit losses arising from derivative portfolios (or portfolios of financial instruments) is obtained by combining three distinct components: credit risk exposure of the transaction (or portfolio of transactions), probability of counterparty default, and recoveries in default (often defined as one less the recovery rate in order to crystallize a net loss figure). This is summarized as

Credit Loss = Credit Risk Exposure * Probability of Default * (1 – Recoveries)

For ease, we shall condense the concept into the following equation:

$$CL = REE * P(def) * (1 - rec) \qquad (11.1)$$

Utilizing this framework and basic statistics, it is possible to divide the concept of credit loss into "expected" and "unexpected" components. *Expected credit losses* are those that are most likely to occur in the normal course of business, and are represented by the mean of a particular distribution of credit losses. *Unexpected credit losses* are those that are unlikely to occur, and are represented by a point several standard deviations away from the mean. Expected and unexpected credit losses are most often utilized for determining the amount of reserves and capital an institution might apply to its businesses; we discuss this at greater length later in the chapter.

Financial institutions employing the expected and unexpected credit loss framework can turn to various methodologies (with varying degrees of complexity and sophistication) to obtain the parameters in Equation 11.1;

some methodologies rely on historical information while others depend on use of more sophisticated simulation processes.

Credit risk exposure

The first parameter in the credit loss framework is credit risk exposure, or the amount of actual and fractional exposure that might exist during the life of a transaction. This parameter is, of course, the very REE figure we have discussed throughout the text and is the essential starting point in determining how much a bank may lose if its counterparty defaults.[7] As discussed in Chapter 5, the specific REE methodology can focus on terminal worst-case credit exposure (through use of REE(twc)) and terminal expected credit exposure (through use of REE(te)), or average worst-case credit exposure (through use of REE(awc)) and average expected credit exposure (REE(ae)). Expected and worst-case exposures can be used to determine expected and unexpected credit losses.

As we also indicated in Chapter 5, a firm can use a simulation process, rather than a volatility-based framework, to obtain REE; results obtained from such an approach can be readily applied to the credit loss framework. The simulation process gives rise to a distribution of REE over the life of a given transaction, which can then be incorporated into the expected loss framework. A full simulation analysis may yield a more accurate REE figure but requires greater computing resources and time.

Regardless of the specific approach used to generate REE figures, it is possible to determine an entire probability distribution for credit risk exposure on trade date, and generate future probability distributions over time (for example, a complete distribution of REE every semi-annual period until the maturity of the transaction(s)); the REE probability distributions (initial, interim, and terminal) contain expected and worst-case REE points which can be used in the overall loss framework. Creation of an REE distribution thus forms the first step in generating the combined credit loss distribution function. Figure 11.6 illustrates a sample REE probability distribution.

Probability of counterparty default

The second parameter used in the credit loss equation is the probability of default. This variable is critical in crystallizing the magnitude of dollar credit loss on a transaction (or portfolio of transactions) if a counterparty fails to perform as expected. Use of probability of default in the expected loss framework begins with the assignment of an internal or external credit rating or credit score to a particular counterparty. As noted in Chapter 3, larger institutions generally perform their own internal credit analyses and assign ratings to individual counterparties; ratings can then

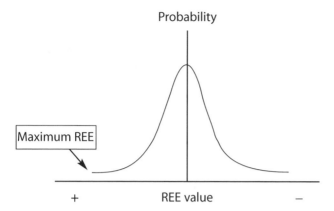

Figure 11.6 REE probability distribution

be used as a representation of the likelihood of default (by drawing on an institution's own default data or default information compiled by the external rating agencies or other data providers). Thus, if Company X is determined to carry a "C" rating (on a scale of "A" (best) to "F" (worst)), and the bank's historical records indicate that C-rated credits have historically defaulted at an average annual rate of 1 percent, the institution can assign this probability of default to a specific transaction or portfolio with Company X. Note that the A–F scale is simplified; financial institutions that perform their own credit analyses/scorings often do so with far greater precision or granularity (perhaps 10–20 rating categories). If an institution does not have the resources necessary to rate its own counterparties it may be required to use ratings data provided by agencies such as Standard and Poor's, Moody's, Fitch, and Dominion Bond Rating Service. (Recall, however, that firms that relinquish the credit analysis and rating process to a third party may be weakening an element of their governance process.) Institutions that rate their own counterparties independently may still choose to use default statistics provided by the agencies, as their own corporate default experience may be insufficient to provide adequate statistical information.

Tables 11.11 and 11.12 contain data on average cumulative default rates from Standard and Poor's and Moody's. Cumulative default is defined as the probability of default over an entire time period (for example, the life of a given transaction). The data provide an indication of the default probabilities for each rating category over a period of one to ten years, and can be utilized as a proxy for probability of counterparty default in a given derivative transaction (or portfolio of transactions). For instance, an institution considering a five-year swap with a BBB+/Baa1 rated counterparty, knows that, on an historical basis, such counterparties have a 2.33 percent

Table 11.11 Standard and Poor's cumulative average default rates

Rating	Yr. 1	Yr. 2	Yr. 3	Yr. 4	Yr. 5	Yr. 6	Yr. 7	Yr. 8	Yr. 9	Yr. 10
AAA	0.00	0.00	0.03	0.06	0.10	0.17	0.25	0.38	0.43	0.48
AA+	0.00	0.00	0.00	0.08	0.17	0.27	0.38	0.38	0.38	0.38
AA	0.00	0.00	0.00	0.05	0.14	0.22	0.35	0.49	0.60	0.71
AA−	0.02	0.08	0.19	0.32	0.46	0.62	0.80	0.96	1.07	1.20
A+	0.06	0.12	0.25	0.45	0.58	0.74	0.90	1.09	1.35	1.60
A	0.05	0.14	0.21	0.33	0.51	0.68	0.85	1.06	1.32	1.67
A−	0.04	0.20	0.43	0.60	0.85	1.13	1.50	1.77	2.08	2.31
BBB+	0.35	0.81	1.31	1.84	2.33	2.93	3.37	3.77	4.22	4.66
BBB	0.34	0.74	1.03	1.61	2.24	2.82	3.43	4.16	4.77	5.46
BBB−	0.43	1.36	2.42	3.95	5.59	7.07	8.28	9.19	9.90	10.88
BB+	0.52	1.97	4.22	6.11	7.56	9.12	10.82	11.56	12.90	14.00
BB	1.16	3.54	6.35	8.70	10.86	13.04	14.49	16.12	17.67	18.73
BB−	2.07	5.74	9.54	13.20	16.30	19.16	21.31	23.28	25.03	26.45
B+	3.29	8.93	14.10	18.44	21.45	23.83	26.38	28.41	29.91	31.48
B	9.31	18.14	24.37	28.45	31.68	34.32	35.94	37.36	38.56	39.56
B−	13.15	23.28	31.31	36.62	40.18	42.86	45.79	47.83	48.50	49.23
CCC	27.87	36.02	41.79	46.26	50.46	52.17	53.60	54.36	56.16	57.21
IG	0.13	0.34	0.57	0.87	1.20	1.52	1.83	2.13	2.41	2.72
NonIG	5.17	10.27	14.81	18.46	21.31	23.67	25.71	27.36	28.83	30.07

Source: B. Brady, *Corporate Defaults Peak in 2002*, March 2003, Standard & Poor's Ratings Services. Reproduced with permission of Standard & Poor's, a division of The McGraw-Hill Companies, Inc.

(Standard and Poor's) or 1.80 percent (Moody's) chance of defaulting, on average, over the five-year period. This information can then be used to create a distribution of default rates for use in the expected credit loss framework, as discussed below.[8] Table 11.13 provides additional information on Moody's average one-year default rates, which are particularly relevant for short-term transactions. Note that the rating agencies also produce marginal default statistics, which reflect the incremental probability of default from one time period to the next. Marginal default probabilities can also be incorporated into the expected credit loss framework, as we discuss later in the chapter.

Table 11.12 Moody's cumulative average default rates*

Rating	Yr. 1	Yr. 2	Yr. 3	Yr. 4	Yr. 5	Yr. 6	Yr. 7	Yr. 8	Yr. 9	Yr. 10
Aaa	0.00	0.00	0.00	0.05	0.17	0.24	0.31	0.40	0.40	0.40
Aa1	0.00	0.00	0.00	0.17	0.17	0.28	0.28	0.28	0.28	0.28
Aa2	0.00	0.00	0.05	0.15	0.33	0.40	0.48	0.57	0.68	0.81
Aa3	0.05	0.07	0.13	0.21	0.29	0.38	0.38	0.38	0.38	0.48
A1	0.00	0.02	0.24	0.37	0.47	0.57	0.62	0.72	0.78	0.93
A2	0.03	0.09	0.24	0.48	0.68	0.89	1.04	1.41	1.73	1.86
A3	0.04	0.21	0.34	0.47	0.62	0.84	1.15	1.34	1.57	1.75
Baa1	0.21	0.60	1.02	1.40	1.80	2.10	2.39	2.56	2.77	2.90
Baa2	0.15	0.46	0.84	1.56	2.24	2.89	3.47	3.99	4.61	5.50
Baa3	0.50	1.27	2.05	3.15	4.23	5.40	6.52	7.55	8.25	8.97
Ba1	0.70	2.11	3.76	5.82	7.61	9.64	10.93	12.23	13.01	13.96
Ba2	0.65	2.34	4.72	7.30	9.42	11.01	13.00	14.44	15.61	15.92
Ba3	2.38	6.60	11.49	16.22	20.70	24.98	28.59	32.32	36.05	39.29
B1	3.33	9.73	16.14	22.05	27.56	32.77	38.42	42.50	46.26	49.97
B2	7.14	15.99	23.43	29.57	34.49	37.94	40.40	42.57	44.96	47.37
B3	11.97	21.97	30.41	37.92	44.40	49.26	53.64	58.21	61.39	62.60
Caa–C	23.65	36.95	47.47	55.61	60.99	66.16	69.72	74.94	78.07	81.73
IG	0.09	0.26	0.48	0.77	1.05	1.31	1.55	1.79	2.00	2.21
NonIG	5.48	11.25	16.59	21.34	25.38	32.03	32.03	34.77	37.08	38.99

* Issuer weighted.

Source: Moody's Investors Service (2003), *Default and Recovery Rates of Corporate Bond Issuers*. © Moody's Investors Service, Inc. and/or its affiliates. Reprinted with permission. All rights reserved.

Alternate means of determining default probabilities are available. Certain methodologies focus on ratio analysis–ratio scores to determine whether a given counterparty matches the profile of an institution that has defaulted with known probability. Institutions may also use information from the publicly traded equity and debt markets to arrive at default probabilities. For instance, analytics firm Moody's KMV has developed an expected default frequency (EDF) approach to estimating default probabilities from equity prices; we discuss this further in Chapter 12. Another approach is to track the movement of credit spreads of risky debt against

Table 11.13 Moody's one-year default rates, 1992–2002

Rating	1992	1993	1994	1995	1996	1997	1998	1999	2000	2001	2002
Aaa	0.00	0.00	0.00	0.00	0.00	0.00	0.00	0.00	0.00	0.00	0.00
Aa	0.00	0.00	0.00	0.00	0.00	0.00	0.00	0.00	0.00	0.00	0.00
A	0.00	0.00	0.00	0.00	0.00	0.00	0.00	0.00	0.00	0.16	0.16
Baa	0.00	0.00	0.00	0.00	0.00	0.00	0.12	0.10	0.38	0.19	1.22
Ba	0.30	0.55	0.24	0.69	0.00	0.19	0.63	1.01	0.89	1.56	1.53
B	9.03	5.71	3.81	4.80	1.44	2.11	4.22	5.92	5.44	9.48	5.11
Caa	26.67	28.57	5.13	11.57	13.99	14.67	15.09	20.44	19.65	34.45	29.45
IG	0.00	0.00	0.00	0.00	0.00	0.00	0.04	0.03	0.13	0.13	0.49
NonIG	4.84	3.51	1.94	3.32	1.67	2.05	3.43	5.68	6.06	10.60	8.33

a risk-free benchmark For instance, Gluck has proposed a technique which compares spreads on zero-coupon corporate and US Government debt to derive the probability of default (given a known recovery rate for the corporate issuer).[9] The formula for such an approach is given by Equation 11.2:

$$P(def) = (Z_r - Z_t)/((1 + Z_r) * (1 - rec)) \tag{11.2}$$

where Z_r is the yield on a risky corporate zero coupon bond; Z_t is the yield on a risk-free US Treasury zero coupon bond; and *rec* is the expected recovery rate.

While this, and other, spread–ratio-based models are useful in computing default probabilities we shall not consider them further in the text.

In addition to using historical statistics, equity implied models, or spread–ratio models to generate a distribution of default probabilities, another popular technique involves credit migration/ratings transitions. Credit migration estimates the future path of credit quality and, by extension, defaults. The process begins with a counterparty's current credit rating; then, knowing the distribution of credit ratings over time (derived, for example, through ratings transition matrices or bond cohorts, described below), a firm can construct a distribution of possible future credit ratings. It can then map a profile of possible future ratings against future defaults and exposures to determine possible credit losses.

Standard and Poor's and Moody's publish transition matrices which provide data on the probability that a counterparty of a given rating will transition to an alternate rating group; this information indicates the likelihood that a counterparty's rating will improve or deteriorate. Tables 11.14 and 11.15 illustrate the one-year transition matrices from Standard and Poor's and Moody's; as an example, the probability of migrating from a BBB/Baa to BB/Ba over a one-year period equals 4.39 percent (Standard and Poor's) and 4.70 percent (Moody's). An associated process, known as the cohort technique, groups counterparties by rating and tracks the default performance of each rating group over time.[10]

Table 11.14 Standard and Poor's one-year transition matrices

To:	AAA	AA	A	BBB	BB	B	CCC	D	NR
AAA	89.37	6.04	0.44	0.14	0.05	0.00	0.00	0.00	3.97
AA	0.57	87.76	7.30	0.59	0.06	0.11	0.02	0.01	3.58
A	0.05	2.01	87.62	5.37	0.45	0.18	0.04	0.05	4.22
BBB	0.03	0.21	4.15	84.44	4.39	0.89	0.26	0.37	5.26
BB	0.03	0.08	0.40	5.50	76.44	7.14	1.11	1.38	7.92
B	0.00	0.07	0.26	0.36	4.74	74.12	4.37	6.20	9.87
CCC	0.09	0.00	0.28	0.56	1.39	8.80	49.72	27.87	11.30

Table 11.15 Moody's one-year transition matrices

To:	Aaa	Aa	A	Baa	Ba	B	Caa–C	Default	WR
Aaa	88.37	6.31	0.96	0.20	0.01	0.00	0.00	0.00	4.15
Aa	1.17	86.99	5.75	0.63	0.15	0.02	0.00	0.07	5.21
A	0.07	2.36	86.09	4.78	0.62	0.10	0.02	0.12	5.82
Baa	0.04	0.25	3.92	82.66	4.72	0.65	0.09	0.29	7.38
Ba	0.01	0.08	0.42	4.76	78.41	5.38	0.50	1.11	9.33
B	0.00	0.04	0.14	0.56	5.86	75.99	3.22	3.67	10.52
Caa-C	0.00	0.02	0.03	0.32	1.21	4.59	71.72	13.27	8.84

Knowing how credit rating cohorts evolve provides useful information on migration of credit quality; this in, turn, can be factored into the future distribution of counterparty defaults. Alternative processes focus on the derivation of forward default rates as a means of computing possible default distributions; we shall consider some of these in the next chapter.[11]

Regardless of the specific method employed, it is possible to derive an entire probability distribution of default rates on trade date and generate future probability distributions (reflecting the path of future default rates) over time (for example, a complete default distribution every semi-annual period until the maturity of the transaction(s)); it is generally appropriate to create a complete series of distributions for each individual credit rating category. The default probability distributions (initial, interim, and terminal) contain expected and unexpected default rates that can be applied in the expected credit loss framework; such distributions form the second component needed to develop the overall credit loss distribution function discussed below. Figure 11.7 illustrates a sample default rate probability distribution for a given credit grade; default rate distributions are typically skewed and do not assume the appearance of a standard normal distribution.

Recoveries in default

The third parameter required in the calculation of credit losses is the amount an institution might recover following counterparty default. This measure is critical because it provides a measure of the *ex post*, rather than *ex ante*,

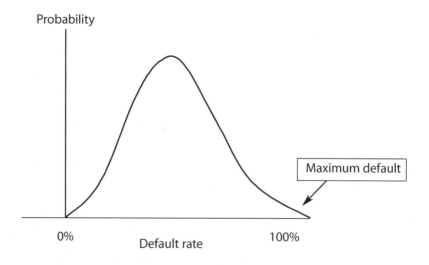

Figure 11.7 Default rate probability distribution

amount that will be lost in the event of default; thus, it is likely to be a better reflection of the true economic loss that will ultimately be sustained by an institution holding a defaulted obligation. Since there is often a residual value assigned to the assets of a company in bankruptcy that provides creditors with partial repayment of amounts due, it is logical to include a parameter that captures this effect. Since recoveries defray the amount of a potential credit loss it is appropriate to adjust REE through (1 minus recoveries), as indicated in Equation 11.1 above.

The level of recovery in default is often derived from historical statistics, but can also be determined via simulation. Historical recovery information may be obtained from data supplied by the public rating agencies or from proprietary data accumulated by a bank from its own default and recovery experience. Regardless of the source of the statistics or the type of simulation method used, it is clear that senior secured creditors can expect to recover a greater amount than senior unsecured, subordinated, or junior subordinated creditors.[12] Although much depends on specific derivative structures and the nature of client relationships, most non-collateralized derivatives are classified as a senior unsecured claims; collateralized derivatives are obviously classified as senior secured claims.[13] Table 11.16 illustrates historical recovery information from Moody's.

As with REE and default rates, we are primarily interested in generating a complete probability distribution function of recovery rates over time. Through specific examination of recovery statistics it is possible to derive a recovery rate distribution on trade date, and generate future probability distributions (reflecting the path of future recovery rates) over time (for example, a complete recovery rate distribution every semi-annual period

Table 11.16 Default recovery statistics, 1982–2002

Category	Average recovery (% of face value)
Senior secured bank loan	61.6
Senior secured	53.1
Senior unsecured	37.4
Senior subordinated	32.0
Subordinated	30.4
Junior subordinated	23.6

Source: Moody's Investors Service (2003), *Default and Recovery Rates of Corporate Bond Issuers*. © Moody's Investors Service, Inc. and/or its affiliates. Reprinted with permission. All rights reserved.

until the maturity of the transaction(s)). The recovery rate probability distributions (initial, interim, and terminal) contain recovery levels that can be applied in the expected credit loss framework; such distributions represent the third, and final, component used to create the overall credit loss distribution function. Figure 11.8 illustrates a sample recovery rate probability distribution. As with the default distribution above, the recovery rate distribution is generally skewed and does not assume the appearance of a standard normal distribution.

Confidence levels

As discussed in Chapter 5, statistical confidence levels are often employed to reflect the likelihood that a given event will or will not occur with a specified degree of confidence. In calculating credit losses, it is important to utilize a confidence level in order to be certain, to specific percentages, that a given credit loss will remain within some boundary a given percent of the time. Use of confidence levels, particularly as related to the credit policies employed by a bank, is an important means of determining the differential between expected and unexpected credit losses, as discussed in the paragraphs below.

For institutions requiring use of a 97.5 percent confidence level, a two standard deviation interval is appropriate; those requiring an even more conservative level need a higher standard deviation interval. By multiplying the standard deviation of the credit loss by the statistical z factor (see Chapter 5), an institution ascertains a "worst-case" credit loss and can therefore determine its unexpected credit losses. Rather than adjusting the expected loss directly, a bank might choose to utilize the same confidence

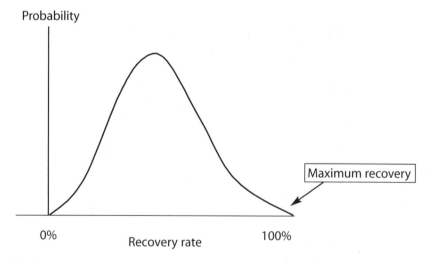

Figure 11.8 Recovery rate probability distribution

interval and apply the confidence level either to the underlying risk factor or the probability of default. Each has the effect of generating expected and worst-case loss points on the distribution of credit losses, though the results are generally somewhat different.

Computing expected and unexpected credit losses: alternative approaches

Using the distributions generated for REE, default rates, and recovery rates (at trade date, select points in time, and maturity), credit loss distributions can be generated over the same time intervals. Once these discrete distributions are determined, a summary distribution can be calculated. We assume for simplicity that the distributions discussed henceforth are the terminal summary distributions. In effect, the credit loss distribution is a joint probability distribution function comprised of the three functions described above, with certain assumptions regarding the independence of the three variables (discussed at greater length below). Figure 11.9 illustrates the creation of a credit loss distribution.

Once the credit loss distribution function has been developed, a bank has a foundation for describing and calculating expected and unexpected credit losses for both single transactions and broader portfolios. *Expected credit*

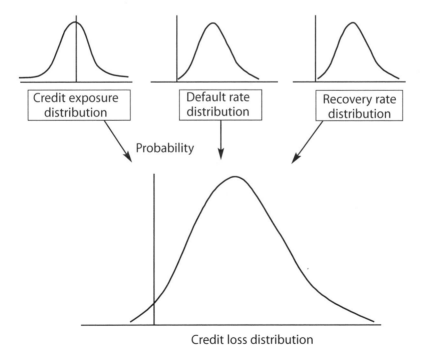

Figure 11.9 Creation of a credit loss distribution function

loss (ECL) represents the mathematical expectation of losses a bank might sustain in the course of its dealings with counterparties of a given rating. Since ECL represents the average, or mean, of losses in the credit loss distribution function, it can be noted in the distribution in Figure 11.10 as the point with the highest probability of occurrence.

In its simplest form ECLs can be defined through a variation of Equation 11.1. as:

$$ECL = REE_{exp} * P(def_{exp}) * (1 - rec) \qquad (11.3)$$

where REE_{exp} is the average or terminal expected risk of the transaction (for example, REE_{ae} or REE_{te}); $P(def_{exp})$ is the expected probability of counterparty default; and *rec* is the expected recovery rate.

In deriving ECLs we focus on the expected (rather than worst-case) risk exposure in order to ensure appropriate reference to an average, rather than extreme, point on the credit loss distribution. The same holds true for the probability of counterparty default, where we reflect the expected (rather than worst-case) probability that a counterparty of a given rating will default. As noted below, use of extreme points for either REE or probability of default can be employed in determining worst-case credit losses. It is also worth stressing that this method of computation assumes independence between the size of the potential credit exposure (REE) and the probability of default (P(def)).[14] In other words, REE and default probabilities are uncorrelated, meaning that an increasing REE does not result in an increasing probability of counterparty default. This, in general, is a reasonable assumption. Swap dealers, for instance, have substantial potential

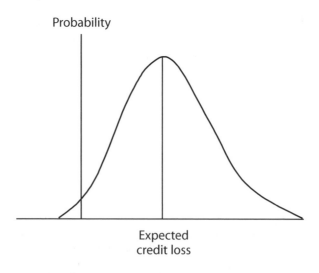

Figure 11.10 Expected credit losses

credit exposures but do not default more frequently as a result of such exposures, and do not default more frequently as the exposures increase (default evidence from the market would appear to support this assumption). This assumption might be violated when an institution has a great deal of exposure with a very small, or perhaps very weak, counterparty (for example, a highly leveraged hedge fund). The burden of the exposure (coupled, perhaps, with a rather sudden, detrimental, move in rates or index prices) might be sufficient to force the counterparty to default. Although diligence on the part of the credit officer may preclude a bank from extending substantial unsecured derivative credit exposure to a weak counterparty, it is possible for the counterparty to have similar derivative credit exposures with multiple financial institutions. The total of these exposures could be enough to trigger default, invalidating the independence assumption. (Recall from Chapter 2 that a form of this occurred during the 1998 Russia/hedge fund crisis.) A second assumption we employ for ease is that recoveries are equal to zero when evaluating ECL; once ECL has been computed, we multiply by (1 – recovery rate) to determine net ECL. Since these two assumptions are sufficiently realistic for our purposes, we use them in our discussion below. Those desiring a more comprehensive and detailed approach (without independence assumptions) need to integrate across the combined probability function, which is a considerably more complex, but still tractable, mathematical process.[15]

Based on the discussion above, let us consider the following example. Bank A has a 12-month FX barrier transaction with Counterparty X that carries an expected REE of US$10m. Counterparty X is a BBB-rated institution, and historical default statistics suggest a 0.5 percent probability of default in the coming 12-months. The recovery rate for senior unsecured creditors is 65 percent. Based on this information, Bank A determines the ECL of the transaction is:

$$ECL = US\$10m * 0.5 \text{ percent} * (1 - 0.65)$$

$$= US\$17,500$$

That is, based on the REE of the barrier and the expected default and recovery statistics, Bank A can expect to lose US$17,500. With this information the bank can evaluate the reserves required to support the transaction.

Focusing on marginal default probabilities and dynamic credit risk exposure, rather than cumulative default probabilities and static credit risk exposure, refines the computation of ECL. By utilizing marginal default data, we can create an equation that computes the ECL at each specified point in time and discounts back to yield a present value of the ECL. Consider Equation 11.4:

$$ECL = PV\sum_{T=1}^{n}(Ree_{exp(t)} * P(def_{exp(t)}) * (1 - rec)) \qquad (11.4)$$

where $Ree_{exp(t)}$ is the expected risk exposure for a given time period t (for example, as indicated through a constantly adjusted average risk factor $RFc(exp(t))$) in either average or terminal form), and $P(def_{exp(t)})$ is the expected marginal probability of default for a given time period t.

Note that we do not apply a marginal recovery rate to each discrete time t, but assume recoveries are static and achievable as estimated in any time period t.

While ECLs (calculated in either marginal or cumulative form) represent the anticipated credit losses a firm faces in entering into a derivatives transaction or running an entire derivatives book, such as the cost of running the business, it is critical to understand the level of unanticipated credit losses a firm may face. Unexpected credit losses, or UCLs, are the risk of running the business, and these may by calculated by determining the worst-case credit losses (*WCCLs*) and subtracting from ECLs.[16] Equation 11.5 highlights the basic equation for computing UCLs.

$$UCL = WCCL - ECL \qquad (11.5)$$

where *WCCL* is defined and discussed at greater length below.

WCCL, which is used to compute UCL, is a point represented at the extreme right-hand tail of the credit loss function based on a given confidence level parameter. Figure 11.11 illustrates a sample WCCL in relation to the ECL (the point of maximum probability, as discussed above).

WCCLs are most often estimated as a set number of standard deviations from the ECL. The number of standard deviations used in the computation (that is, the percentage confidence level) is typically driven by bank policy and related to the unexpected credit loss coverage required by the institution, consistent with the risk appetite defined by the firm's board. WCCLs can be computed in several ways. The first approach involves an adjustment to REE (via the risk factor) so that it reflects the worst-case scenario. As discussed in Chapter 5, the standard risk factor RF can be adjusted by the appropriate z factor to incorporate the required confidence level. Worst-case REE can be calculated in either terminal or average form, depending on an institution's view of each approach. The critical point to note is that if terminal exposures are used to calculate ECLs (for example, REE_{te}), then they must also be used to calculate WCCLs (for example, REE_{twc}). Likewise, if average exposures are used to determine ECLs (for example, REE_{ae}) they must also be used to determine WCCLs (for example, REE_{awc}). The generic form of the equation is similar to the one in Equation 11.3 above for ECLs:

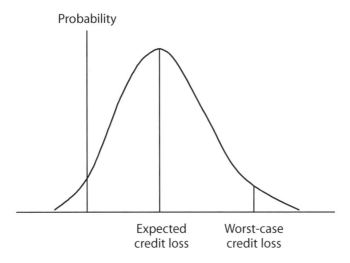

Figure 11.11 Worst-case credit losses

$$WCCL = REE_{wc} * P(def_{exp}) * (1 - rec) \tag{11.6}$$

where REE_{wc} is the worst-case REE (in either terminal or average form (for example, REE_{twc} or REE_{awc})) and all other terms are as defined above.

Note that while the exposure is adjusted to an extreme point, the default probability remains unchanged (and reflects the expected default probability for a counterparty of a given rating category).

A second method of computing WCCL uses expected REE instead of worst-case REE, but adjusts the default probability to a given confidence level which reflects an extreme, rather than expected, default probability; the worst-case default probability may be the worst-case default probability for a counterparty of a given rating based on historical observation or one drawn from the default distributions discussed above. This approach is contained in Equation 11.7:

$$WCCL = REE_{exp} * P(def_{wc}) * (1 - rec) \tag{11.7}$$

where REE_{exp} is the expected REE (in either terminal or average form (for example, REE_{te} or REE_{ae}) and $P(def_{wc})$ is the worst-case probability of default.

A third method focuses directly on the dispersion of the ECL (which, as we know, is influenced by the dispersion of REE and/or probability of default). Knowing the probability distribution and standard deviation of expected credit losses, we need only apply a confidence level factor consistent with policy to obtain the WCCL. The fundamental equation is given as:

$$WCCL = z * \sigma_{ECL} \tag{11.8}$$

where σ_{ECL} is the standard deviation of the ECL and z is a confidence level factor.

Equations 11.6, 11.7, and 11.8 each yield slightly different results. What is most important, however, is that each provides a methodological means of defining a confidence level-based boundary. Knowing this upper bound (that is, WCCL), we can determine the magnitude of unexpected credit losses to a given level, and make certain decisions about the allocation of capital. Before describing unexpected credit losses, let us present a uniform example that uses each of the equations we have just discussed.

Assume Bank ABC has booked an inverse floater swap with Company XYZ. XYZ is an A-rated credit and (based on historical default statistics) might be expected to default only 0.20 percent of the time; worst-case defaults for A-rated credits, however, have been as high as 0.40 percent. Recoveries for senior unsecured creditors are estimated to be 60 percent. The expected REE on the inverse floater swap is US$6.5m, while the worst-case REE (adjusted to two standard deviations) is US$10m. By Equation 11.3, the ECL on this transaction is:

$$ECL = US\$6.5m * 0.002 * (1 - 0.60)$$

$$= US\$5200$$

The WCCL, per Equation 11.6, is estimated as:

$$WCCL = US\$10m * 0.002 * (1 - 0.60)$$

$$= US\$8000$$

And, per Equation 11.7, is:

$$WCCL = US\$6.5m * 0.004 * (1 - 0.60)$$

$$= US\$10,400$$

If the standard deviation of the ECL is known to be US$3500, the WCCL, per Equation 11.8 (to the 97.5 percent confidence level), is

$$WCCL = 2 * US\$3500$$

$$= US\$7000$$

Although these approaches yield slightly different figures the discrepancies are likely to be traced to the use of variables that may not correspond to precisely the same confidence level driven by policy.

While expected credit losses are the mathematical expectation of credit losses likely to be sustained by an institution, unexpected credit losses represent the dispersion, or variance, of credit losses. When counterparty default occurs the actual loss a bank sustains will be far greater than the amount suggested by the expected loss. True default risk, as captured by the UCL, can therefore be defined as the deviation of the actual loss from the ECL.

Suppose a bank enters into two derivative trades with a given counterparty. Based on the trade parameters and the credit rating of the counterparty, an analyst determines that the ECL for the first trade is US$50,000 and the UCL is US$50,000. The ECL for the second trade is also US$50,000, but the UCL is US$500,000. The standard deviation of losses in the second trade is obviously much higher. Given this information, an institution has to make sure the second transaction receives more capital and earns more profit, since the actual losses sustained in the event of default will be considerably higher than in the first trade. Knowing the UCL, it is possible to determine the appropriate level of capital to set aside for a given transaction or portfolio of transactions; we discuss this concept below.

It should be noted that UCLs could be computed directly by knowing the probability of counterparty default, REE, variance of REE, and recoveries. For instance, Kealhofer has proposed the following simplified formula for the direct computation of UCLs:[17]

$$UCL = \sqrt{Pdef(1 - Pdef)E^2\ REE + Pdef\ \sigma^2 REE} * (1 - rec) \qquad (11.9)$$

Ong has defined a similar process:[18]

$$UCL = REE * \sqrt{Pdef * \sigma^2_{(1 - rec)} + (1 - rec)^2 * \sigma^2_{P(def)}} \qquad (11.9)$$

These formulae demonstrate that, for a given change in credit risk exposure, unexpected credit losses are an increasing function of the probability of counterparty default.

Words of caution are necessary at this point. First, the use of a confidence level to obtain UCL and WCCL only tells us that a credit loss is expected to be less than, or equal to, some threshold amount x percent of the time, where x is 95 percent, 99 percent, 99.9 percent (or any other confidence level selected). It does not, however, tell us anything about how large the losses will be the remaining 5 percent, 1 percent, or 0.1 percent of the time (the area in the right of the tail, as in Figure 11.11). Second, we have indicated at various points in the text, the framework is based on assumptions regarding statistics and probability distributions, and the behavior of markets and counterparties. It is incumbent upon any firm using these tools to stress-test them and understand what happens when assumptions breakdown, for example, when the credit loss distribution has fatter tails than expected, volatilities are greater than expected, and correlations are lower than expected. Any of these can ultimately impact ECLs, UCLs, and WCCLs – and, thus, reserves, capital, and profitability. Due care is therefore an absolute requirement.

Figure 11.12 illustrates expected, unexpected, and worst-case credit losses in the combined credit loss distribution; the zero credit loss point of the distribution is also highlighted.

The discussion above focuses on the computation of single transaction ECLs and UCLs. A similar approach can be taken to obtain ECLs and UCLs for an entire portfolio of trades with a given counterparty. Note that the portfolio approach requires assumptions regarding the acceptability of netting and/or the application of collateral to reduce potential exposures; it also requires correlation inputs. As we might expect, there are various other ways of computing and implementing the expected-unexpected credit loss framework.[19] Regardless of the approach, however, the variables cited above (for example, credit exposure, probability of default, and recoveries in default) always play an essential role.

Unexpected credit losses and portfolios

While we have considered risk and loss in the context of a single counterparty with one ore more transactions, financial institutions managing firmwide credit risks also have an interest in determining potential losses arising from all counterparties. This ultimately indicates how much total capital will be needed to protect against counterparty defaults and helps optimize portfolios so that risk-adjusted return is maximized.

We have noted above the UCL of a single counterparty transaction (or

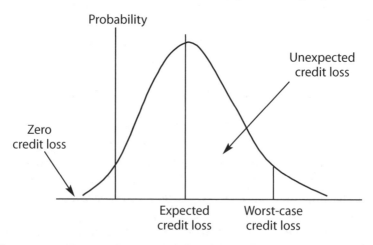

Figure 11.12 Expected, unexpected, and worst case credit losses

portfolio with the same counterparty) represents the volatility of counterparty default around the ECL. To determine the UCL for all counterparties in the portfolio, we must extend the framework to include the UCLs of each counterparty, together with the default correlations between those counter-parties. Default correlations indicate whether default by one counterparty will lead to, or in some way influence, default by another counterparty.[20] If an institution fails to take account of default correlations, it is almost certainly overstating potential UCLs, and therefore allocating too much capi-tal in support of losses that cannot occur. By extension, the portfolio will not be optimized. Accordingly, to determine portfolio UCLs we can make use of the equation given by 11.11:

$$UCL_{port} = \left[\sum_x \sum_y \rho_{x,y} \, UCL_x \, UCL_y\right]^{1/2} \qquad (11.11)$$

where UCL can be computed through one of the methods above (for example, Equations 11.5, 11.9, and 11.10); x, y represent two distinct counterparties, x and y; and $\rho_{x,y}$ is the default correlation between counterparties x and y.

Through this equation we can infer that, unless the correlation between counterparties x and y is equal to 1, portfolio UCL is not equal to a linear sum of individual counterparty UCLs. Diversification across counterparties that are not perfectly correlated means that portfolio UCL must be smaller.[21] In fact, only a portion of a counterparty's UCL contributes to the total risk of loss of the entire portfolio; the level of contribution is precisely equal to the marginal, or incremental, risk of a single counterparty to the whole portfolio. We can define a marginal risk component for any counterparty x (MR x) as:

$$MR_x = \frac{UCLx \sum_x UCL_y \, \rho_{x,y}}{UCL_{port}} \qquad (11.12)$$

The marginal risk contribution thus measures the undiversified risk element of counterparty portfolios. By knowing the risk contribution of any single counterparty – that is, by knowing MR – a firm can modify the risk profile of its portfolio by changing its risk characteristics. Extending the logic above, it is fairly easy to demonstrate that the UCL of the entire portfolio of counter-parties is simply the sum of all the marginal risk contributions of all the counterparties in the portfolio, rather than the sum of all the UCLs. The marginal risk contribution is thus intimately related to the default correlations between counterparties.

Unfortunately, it is not easy to determine the default correlations between two counterparties, and it is therefore challenging to calculate individual MRs based on correlation among all counterparties in the portfolio. As we shall note in Chapter 12, determining default correlations is at once time consuming and vitally important.[22] A firm may attempt to estimate them through historical default data (by computing pairwise correlations – an arduous task for a portfolio of any size), through a Monte Carlo simulation process, or by observing counterparty asset volatilities and variance/covariance structure. In fact, market-driven approaches focused on asset correlations appear to be most popular, and have been adopted by several of the commercially available models we discuss in the next chapter.

Ultimately, effective portfolio credit risk management demands knowledge of MRs and how they impact the overall portfolio. These help in allocating capital and identifying optimal return opportunities and the presence of any potential credit risk concentrations; that is to say, UCLs are influenced by the MRs of individual counterparties, which are related through default correlations; these correlations, in turn, determine whether any concentrations (for example, across industries, countries, and rating classes) might arise. Any credible portfolio process must therefore be capable of evaluating risk of loss across all counterparties.

Credit losses, reserves, capital, and risk adjusted profitability

As we discussed at the beginning of this text, institutions active in derivatives assume market, liquidity, credit, sovereign, operational, and legal risks. To ensure there is an appropriate balance between risks assumed and revenues earned, an institution has to generate enough profitability on, and allocate enough capital to, discrete transactions, portfolios of transactions, and/or entire businesses. While all risks must be appropriately factored into the risk–return equation, we shall focus specifically on credit risk, utilizing the concepts of ECL, WCCL, and UCL.

We know that institutions generally, and financial institutions in particular, are exposed to credit losses and expect, over the course of months and years, to experience a certain amount of them. A bank enters into a credit-sensitive transaction because that is the specific function it performs. In return for performing the function (for example, assuming a credit risk), it must be properly compensated (just as other businesses charge customers or consumers for goods or services provided). The extension of credit must be appropriately priced. Institutions that do not price their credit risks properly will find themselves burdened with credit losses (for example, by attracting too much high-risk business and not obtaining sufficient returns to cover write-offs) or driving business away (for example, attracting no business as a result of overly conservative and uncompetitive pricing). The ECL provides an indication of just how much a bank should be prepared to charge for providing its credit services (for example, as noted, the cost of running the business). ECLs can be used as a measure of the profitability reserve needed to cover likely credit losses. Reserves taken to cover ECLs can be increased as the probability of counterparty default rises (a client is downgraded) or potential risk exposures increase, and can be decreased as the probability of default declines (a client is upgraded) or potential risk exposures decline. Regardless of the specific amount or method, reserves should always be greater than ECLs.

As indicated earlier, ECLs represent only the average, or expectation, of credit losses, and reserves established to cover ECLs do not protect the bank from losses in excess of the average. In fact, a bank must ensure that sufficient capital is allocated to cover the "greater than average," or unexpected, credit losses. The UCL – again, the risk of running the business — is typically driven by a bank's risk tolerance (though regulators might also have some say), based on the maximum level of losses it wishes to cover (97.5 percent, 99 percent, and so on). Use of a confidence level dictates how much capital needs to be set aside to cover such eventualities (note that the capital allocated will also necessarily be a function of the institution's target leverage). Through this process the bank is trying to protect itself from a multiple standard deviation event. For instance, if an institution wants to be certain that it has covered 97.5 percent of unexpected credit losses (for example, a two standard deviation event on a one-tailed distribution), it needs to assign capital equal to two standard deviations of the credit loss. Certain institutions also use UCLs as a means of converting the default risk of their derivative portfolios into a common metric, such as the default risk of an AAA or AA-rated security. By setting appropriate confidence intervals, an institution can be reasonably certain that the true default risk in its derivative portfolio is equivalent to the true default risk inherent in an investment grade security (say 0.05 percent per annum, as an example; that is, aggregate derivative losses can only exceed aggregate capital 0.05 percent of the time). This common metric is then easily understood, and measured, throughout the institution's credit businesses.

To summarize, credit reserves (or credit charges, or credit provisions) are taken to cover expected credit losses, while risk capital is taken to cover unexpected credit losses. Let us consider the following example: an institution enters into an exotic option transaction with an A-rated counterparty. The ECL, as calculated through Equation 11.3, equals US$150,000, and one standard deviation of losses is determined to be US$300,000. The bank wants to ensure that it has enough capital to cover 99 percent of unexpected credit losses, which represents a 2.33 standard deviation event. Total reserves to cover the expected credit losses amount to US$150,000, and total capital to cover the 99 percent unexpected credit losses amounts to US$550,000. The bank can therefore feel comfortable that losses in excess of US$550,000 have only a 1 percent chance of occurring (though how large such losses will be that 1 percent of the time remains an unknown that is ultimately determined by the nature of the distribution).

Once reserves and capital have been allocated to a transaction, risk-adjusted performance measures can be implemented in order to compare risk-adjusted profitability across transactions and businesses. Prior to industry focus on risk-adjusted profits, simple return on asset (ROA) and return on equity (ROE) measures were the norm. With regulatory and industry attention now focused more closely on business risks, profitability targets have evolved into risk-related performance measures.[23]

One increasingly common performance measure is the risk-adjusted return on risk-adjusted capital ratio. Through this measure, an institution adjusts the gross pricing of its derivative transactions (or other credit-risky transactions) to reflect the various risks and costs associated with its business. It then divides the resulting net profit amount by the appropriate level of allocated risk capital to arrive at a risk-adjusted performance measure. This type of measurement makes it possible to compare the true risk-adjusted profitability of individual transactions and entire products or businesses, and helps financial institutions make more balanced and rational business decisions.

Assume, for instance, that Bank JKL enters into a currency swap with Company XYZ. The gross return on the swap is US$300,000. The credit reserve for the transaction (based on the computed ECL) is US$50,000, and JKL sets aside an additional US$50,000 for funding and liquidity charges. Taxes and business overhead expenses consume an additional US$80,000. The risk-adjusted capital attributable to the transaction (based on the computed UCL, to a 97.5 percent confidence level) is US$500,000 (note that we ignore specific leverage considerations and non-credit capital adjustments for clarity). Based on this information, the risk-adjusted return on risk-adjusted capital is computed as:

$$(\text{US\$300,000} - \text{US\$50,000} - \text{US\$50,000} - \text{US\$80,000})/\text{US\$500,000}$$
$$= 24\%$$

If JKL has a competing transaction with Company ABC designed to earn a gross return of US$500,000, but the transaction carries credit reserves of US$100,000, funding/liquidity costs of US$60,000, taxes/overhead expenses of US$100,000, and risk-adjusted capital of US$800,000, the risk-adjusted return on risk-adjusted capital (again, ignoring leverage considerations and non-credit adjustment to risk capital) is:

$$(\text{US\$500,000} - \text{US\$100,000} - \text{US\$100,000} - \text{US\$160,000})/\text{US\$800,000}$$
$$= 17.5\%$$

If JKL must choose between only one of these two transactions, it is apt to select the first swap on the basis of pure risk-adjusted return considerations (it must still fit within other risk governance parameters, of course, including maturity limitations, client suitability issues, and so on).

To summarize, the credit risk-adjusted performance measure can be computed via the following equation:[24]

$$RAROE = (GR - CC - FC - OHC)/RC \qquad (11.13)$$

where GR is the gross transaction return; CC is a credit charge (likely to be directly related to ECLs); FC is a funding/liquidity charge; OHC is an overhead charge; and RC is the risk capital attributable to credit considerations (likely to be directly related to UCLs).

There are other ways of calculating risk-related performance measures. The main point we wish to highlight is that the most relevant means of evaluating specific transaction return is by incorporating variables that reflect the risk being assumed by the banking institution. Unadjusted ROE or ROA measures, which make no allowance for the risk dimensions of a given business, are not sufficient measures by which to guide a business. Determining how much capital a firm is willing to risk in support of UCLs is, of course, institution-specific. Firms have different risk tolerance levels that should be defined and implemented through the governance process discussed in Chapter 3. Board directors, together with executive management, must understand the extent of losses the institution is able and willing to sustain (for example, by benchmarking to some target insolvency rate) and then enforce that maximum level through capital allocation and risk limits. For instance, the board of directors at a large bank might indicate that their target insolvency rate is 0.03 percent – meaning their probability of remaining solvent is 99.97 percent – which is approximately equal to the one-year historical default rate for AA-rated credits. The insolvency rate can then be translated into economic capital. The bank's risk limit structure must allocate that economic capital to different credit-risky businesses, including derivatives trading. Through an ongoing monitoring process it must ensure that target risk-adjusted returns are being met, in order to justify the use of allocated economic capital. As above, due caution must be exercised to take account of any simplifying statistical assumptions used to determine exposures, portfolio risks, or counterparty credit quality. Figure 11.13 summarizes the flow of a generalized credit framework, which incorporates counterparty risk assessment, transaction-portfolio REE quantification, and risk-adjusted return analysis as elements of the credit decision-making process.

While an institution can produce an objective measure of risk-adjusted performance, qualitative measures can influence the growth, profitability, and riskiness of a given derivatives business. Although it may be relatively simple for a risk officer or business manager to compare the risk-adjusted performance of competing trades and arrive at a decision based on such results, management often has additional "subjective" priorities which can lead to decisions that might be different than those suggested by pure risk-adjusted performance measures. For instance, a trading desk might trade with a counterparty for relationship reasons, even if the risk-adjusted return is lower than that of a competing trade with a second counterparty (or, indeed, lower than the internal hurdle rate of the institution). Alternatively, a desk might underprice a client trade in hopes of earning future business (for example, a type of "loss leader" strategy). Or, a desk might pursue seemingly unprofitable business if it is attempting to enter a particular segment of the derivatives market by "purchasing" market share. In these instances the subjective decision framework may overwhelm the objective decision framework; this can, over the long term, result in the misallocation of credit resources, misbalancing of derivatives portfolios and mispricing of credit risks.

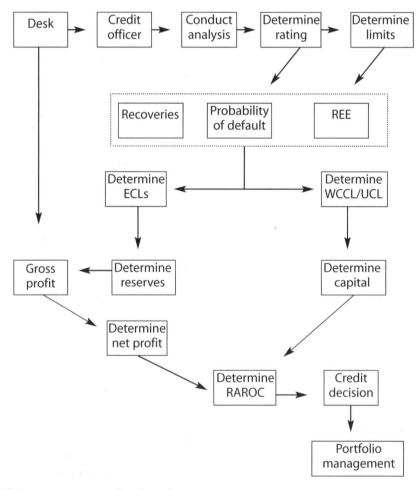

Figure 11.13 Generalized credit process

CHAPTER 12

Credit Risk
Portfolio Models

One of the most significant innovations in the field of credit risk management over the past decade has been the development of increasingly sophisticated models to quantify the credit risk, and potential losses, embedded in portfolios of credit-sensitive transactions. This, as we have noted in previous chapters, provides the basis for allocating and managing regulatory and economic capital on a portfolio-wide basis and properly managing a diversified portfolio of credit exposure.

In this chapter we build on the discussion introduced in Chapter 11, reviewing progress that has occurred in credit portfolio modeling in recent years. We commence with a brief introduction on market-risk based value-at-risk models (which were a catalyst in the development of, and migration to, similar credit models) and then consider general features of the generic credit portfolio model. We then turn our attention to two broad classes of models in use:

■ First-generation credit portfolio models developed in the mid to late-1990s, which estimate possible portfolio credit losses based on a dynamic credit ratings process and fixed (or deterministic) exposure computation.

■ Second-generation credit portfolio models, which began appearing at the turn of the millennium (and continue to be developed up to the present time), which estimate portfolio credit losses through the use of dynamic ratings and stochastic credit exposures.

VALUE-AT-RISK AND REGULATORY MODELS

Credit portfolio models trace their origins back to the value-at-risk (VAR) framework developed in the early to mid-1990s by several leading financial institutions (including JP Morgan – which produced the first commercially viable VAR platform, RiskMetrics™ – CSFB, and Deutsche Bank) and was presented as an attempt to estimate the potential losses contained in a portfolio of diverse market risks. Through a VAR framework, financial institutions quantify the change in value of a portfolio of risks (for example, directional, curve, volatility, spread) on the basis of assumptions regarding the distribution of market risk variables, the collection and application of correlations between market risk variables, and the selection of a time-horizon (liquidation period) and statistical confidence level.[1] Based on these parameters an institution that marks-to-market every day can generate an estimate of gains or losses.

For instance, if a bank determines that its 99 percent, ten-day VAR is US$100 million, then it expects, with 99 percent certainty, that the value of the portfolio of market risks will not gain or lose more than US$100 million over that ten-day period. Unfortunately, VAR provides no information on how large the gain or loss might be the remaining 1 percent of the time; if the curve has particularly "fat tails," the resulting 1 percent loss may be very large. In addition, it requires that all of the assumptions related to correlations and distributions remain intact – something which may not always be realistic, as numerous institutions discovered during the 1998 LTCM meltdown: as LTCM neared the point of collapse, market correlations broke down, liquidity dried up, and statistical distributions indicated the existence of much "fatter" tails than most had expected – meaning actual market risk losses well in excess of what might have been estimated through a typical VAR framework.

Despite these shortcomings, VAR was widely adopted during the mid to late-1990s and now serves as an accepted way of aggregating a diverse pool of market risks and estimating its impact on operations (though most firms have learned to use it as just one of several analytical tools in the risk management toolkit). Importantly, VAR provides a link into the capital required to support these risks. As we have already noted in Chapter 4, in a rather radical (but very welcome) move, the BIS, through the 1996 Basel Capital Amendment, accepted use of the internally-developed models to estimate the amount of capital required for a given market risk portfolio.[2] Though the VAR framework (including models and process) must still be scrutinized and approved by relevant regulatory authorities, it brings the capital allocation process closer to the reality of financial institution management. Firms need not apply rigid or unrealistic formulas (which may not be linked to the reality of business and markets); they can use the models they actually employ to help manage risks. This means that regulatory capital and economic capital are brought closer together, and a firm does not need to artificially manage its capital on two fronts.

With the 1996 Accord as a precedent, market practitioners began lobbying for similar treatment of credit risk portfolios; many institutions were eager to employ internal credit models, rather than mandated regulatory formulas, in managing credit risk capital allocations. This, as we have already noted, is an important component of the new Basel Capital Accord IRB approach, and the use of internally developed credit risk portfolio models – under the foundation or advanced approaches – is now permitted for capital allocation purposes. Below we consider the basic elements that are required for the construction of a generic credit portfolio model, including one that would be consistent with the general parameters of the IRB approach. We then turn our attention to several first and second-generation credit portfolio models to consider, in summary form, how they function.

THE IDEAL GENERIC CREDIT PORTFOLIO MODEL

Though market risk models are generally simpler to create and implement than credit risk models – and are certainly in a much more advanced state of development – generic credit portfolio models are becoming more sophisticated with each passing year, and are gradually moving toward an "ideal" standard. The challenge in credit modeling relates to multiple risk drivers/factors that are required to make a framework meaningful and the extensive calibration and validation that is required to verify results. For instance, credit models must take account of:

■ Counterparty credit quality, which depends on macroeconomic factors (for example, state of the economy, inflation, interest rates) and idiosyncratic factors (for example, state of the counterparty's financial condition, quality of management).

■ Individual dynamic credit risk parameters (for example, default probabilities, recoveries, ratings migration, credit correlations), which impact concentration and diversification.

■ Dynamic exposure parameters (for example, stochastic REE and collateral profiles driven by the same market variables influencing other elements of the model).

Any model built around these elements must be sound (built via accurate analytics) and useful (capable of providing necessary information on the construction of the credit risk portfolio, minimum capital required for protection, and so on). When designing any type of credit portfolio model (for use within an institution as a risk/business management and capital allocation tool) it is essential that the platform remain sufficiently flexible to allow for enhancement and refinement. We have noted throughout the text the considerable advances that have taken place in the derivative market over the past few years. Any model that is not scalable and adaptable (in the context of the full spectrum of credit-sensitive products, including financings, loans, bonds, and structured products, as well as the derivatives we have discussed in this text) will soon be of limited use. The internal and regulatory review must therefore ensure flexibility in design and implementation.

A credible credit portfolio risk model must adequately capture credit exposures and associated losses by focusing on concentration risk, spread risk (where spread risk forms a key nexus of market and credit risk), default risk, downgrade risk (where default risk is a subset of downgrade risk), recovery (loss given default) rates, and credit event correlations (both systemic/macro and idiosyncratic). The impact of netting, collateral, termination options, and other risk mitigants must also be incorporated. With these elements the model can be used for:

- Expressing overall credit risk exposures (including solvency and concentrations) and setting limits to constrain them (for example, a risk management and governance tool).

- Defining the amount of capital needed to cover unexpected credit losses (for example, a capital management tool).

- Managing/optimizing the composition of the portfolio in order to maximize risk adjusted returns (for example, a business management tool).

To be a true portfolio tool all sources of credit risk must be captured and weighed on an equal basis. Increasingly, this means bringing every exposure towards a forward mark-to-market process (for example, loans with embedded options, typically held in a "lower of cost or market" rather than MTM book, must be absorbed into the overall portfolio and valued the same way as any other credit instrument). Obviously, collecting, collating, and aggregating all of this data is a non-trivial task – but an essential one, and therefore worth the time, cost, and effort. The goal of the portfolio model must be quantification of portfolio credit exposures and the probability distribution of future credit losses, just as we have discussed in the last chapter. Once these have been developed a firm has the means of managing credit risks and concentrations, quantifying expected and unexpected credit losses, allocating capital, and optimizing its overall portfolio.

In an ideal world the generic portfolio model should comprise two components – dynamic credit exposure computation and application of portfolio default and migration probabilities – in order to yield a complete framework. The first critical step in the modeling process centers on computing the REE of a counterparty portfolio in a stochastic, rather than deterministic, fashion (as noted below, most first-generation portfolio models are limited by their reliance on deterministic REEs, a problem that second-generation models have sought to overcome). The credit portfolio REE must include the credit exposure arising from all transactions with a counterparty, taking account of the netting and collateral benefits we have discussed earlier in the book. While a credit portfolio REE can be derived from the regulatory "add-on" approach, we have indicated its shortcomings. An analytic process or simulation-based approach, with risk factor drivers related to a firm's own market risk VAR process (to ensure internal consistency and draw the two disciplines together) is preferable. The raw output from this dimension of the model, REEs, can then be used for many of the credit risk management, credit limit, and reporting functions that accompany any credit function.

The specific portfolio default component of the modeling effort can take one of two forms: structural models or intensity models. *Structural models*, originally put forth by Black and Scholes in 1973 and Merton in 1974 (and since extended and adapted), determine counterparty default by an underlying process that describes the value of the counterparty in terms of assets, liabilities, and capital structure. Default is said to occur when a particular boundary value (for example, liability threshold) is reached. *Intensity models*, in contrast, model time of default with a particular intensity and uncertain time horizon; such models have no direct reference to a firm's value, but derive the probability of the event as an instantaneous likelihood of default (sometimes known as the "hazard rate").

The definition of a credit loss centers on whether the model is quantifying only defaults (a *credit default model* or *loss-based model*) or migrations and defaults (a *credit mark-to-market model* or *NPV model*, where default is one unique state within the model). The former only considers credit losses arising from actual default – meaning it does not take into account market information such as the term structure of credit spreads – while the latter allows for losses that occur through continuous credit deterioration up to, and including, the point of default. Not surprisingly, a credit default model is generally easier to develop and implement, though is less useful as it only considers the "extreme" credit scenario (which may be acceptable in the context of "hold-until-maturity" derivative contracts and loans, but too constraining for "realizable" derivative contracts, traded bonds, loans, and so forth). As in the VAR context, the definition of a credit time horizon is a reflection of the change in the portfolio value over some period. The choices vary and can extend from a discrete (and somewhat artificial) time frame, such as six months or one year, to the final maturity of the transactions in the portfolio. In practice, many models are based on a one-year horizon, which is consistent with the one-year default probabilities that are often computed internally or externally. Specification of these two elements means that the model can estimate changes in credit portfolio value – from defaults and/or credit deterioration – over a given time period.

After these have been defined, the model must generate a probability density function (PDF) of future credit losses, so that losses associated with a given percentile of the distribution can be determined. This takes us back to our discussion of ECL, WCCL, and UCL from Chapter 11. Again, ECL represents the mean of the loss distribution and UCL the variability in losses (computed to some relevant confidence percentile, minus the ECL). To generate the PDF of future credit losses the model must travel through a multi-step process:

- Individual counterparty credits in the portfolio must be classified by rating (either internal or external/agency ratings).

- The probability that counterparties will migrate to different rating states over the time horizon must be computed (recalling that in the credit default model only the default probability is required, while in the credit mark-to-market model the *transition probabilities* are required (for example, the probabilities of moving from rating class to rating class)).

- The estimated amount of credit exposure for each counterparty must be determined from the portfolio REE component mentioned above; this would include, for example, notional value for drawn loans or funded bonds, some fractional REE value for contingencies or undrawn commitments, and stochastic, consistently determined, REE for derivatives, all with accurate representation of collateral and netting.

- For each rating category and credit exposure in that category, the value of the position must be determined. In the credit default model this is the loss given default (LGD) percentage (or 1 less the recovery rate, as we have discussed), while in the credit mark-to-market model this is more likely to be a spread-based revaluation reflecting the current level of default risk.

To generate the PDF of future credit losses it is necessary to consider the entire credit portfolio, meaning that it is important to consider correlations between individual counterparty losses as noted in the last chapter. By understanding default correlations, a firm can determine the risk contribution of each counterparty exposure to the portfolio UCL, which is necessary in order to manage capital and risk-adjusted returns properly.[3] This means that the model must capture the variability in, and the correlation between, rating transition probabilities, REE, and credit valuations. In a practical sense these correlations and variances are driven by risk factors related to multiple variables: country, industry, economic state, interest rates, macroeconomic indicators, equity prices, and so forth. Unfortunately, credit correlations cannot be observed in the market directly, meaning other solutions must be found. It is possible to use aggregate time series to infer correlations, but this is only suitable for basic portfolio analysis since aggregate data is generally only available at high levels (that is, not at the counterparty level, meaning insufficient granularity). Alternatively, correlations can be determined through a model that uses observable financial inputs and translates them into correlations; this is a common technique in Merton-based models.[4] Under a Mertonian model default occurs when the market value of a counterparty's assets falls below the market value of its liabilities (as summarized in Figure 12.1). Through this framework, asset value correlations, which are observable in the marketplace (for example, equity prices, balance sheet construction) can be converted into credit risk correlations. Correlations involving macro variables such as interest rates and inflation can be determined through factor models. Though different models use different sets of risk factors, generally driven through some type of mathematical process, this step has a considerable impact on the final shape of the PDF. If the form of the PDF is assumed, results can be computed analytically; alternatively, the PDF can be developed through Monte Carlo simulation (for example, simulating the underlying risk factors to determine default and transition probabilities).

Knowing the PDF, a firm can establish a capital charge based on a set percentile of the loss distribution over the specified time horizon as we indicated in the last chapter (that is, the capital required to support a portfolio

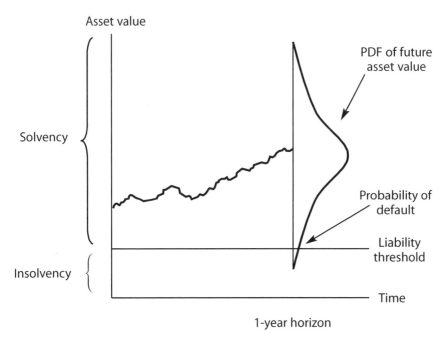

Figure 12.1 PDF of future asset value and probability of default

based on an estimate of the distribution of future credit losses); the output from this dimension of the model – for example, how much capital is needed to support UCLs – becomes the capital management tool. It can also be combined with credit pricing parameters and modern portfolio management techniques (such as in a Markowitz/Sharpe framework) to optimize the overall credit portfolio – for example, where and how to allocate scarce credit resources – and becomes the business management dimension of the model.

Any model must be governed by appropriate standards related to prudency and analytics. Prudency standards center on the general capital parameters set by individual regulators and are designed to ensure a sufficient level of capital exists to cover UCLs. Appropriate standards are generally based on credit losses, time horizon, and confidence level percentile (for example, if the desire is to remain in the realm of the mid to strong-investment grade, then a 99 percent confidence level, approximately equal to the 1 percent default probability normally associated with investment grade credits, is appropriate). As noted, analytic standards must be sufficiently flexible to allow for customization and enhancement. However, certain fundamental traits must exist in every credit risk model, including:

- Accurate default and transition probabilities that cover economic cycles (and are sensitive to the fact that transitions between ratings are correlated to some degree across counterparties).

- Empirical verification of correlations.

- Robust computation of exposure (with relevant stress scenarios, for example, fully drawn commitments or actual derivative exposure approaching the worst-case future exposure estimates).

- Cohesive use of a market model (for example, the model used to generate REE risk factors for interest rates, currencies, equities, commodities, and so forth is the same model used to generate market risk sensitivities and VAR estimates).

- Consistent use of exposure correlations (for example, when the market variable impacts a given counterparty exposure, it impacts all exposures with the same variable).

- Accurate revaluation of assets (for example, exposures change in value and variability as credit quality changes).

Naturally, the model must be fed by a "clean" trade/counterparty database and include accurate corporate hierarchies and aggregations.

Credit portfolio models generally cannot be backtested or validated in the same way as market VAR processes, primarily because the market horizons (credit cycles) are much longer (though, again, some second-generation models have sought to overcome this hurdle). This means alternative validation procedures have to be employed, including verification of mathematical integrity by independent parties and benchmarking of individual parameters (for example, default probabilities, recoveries, correlations, and exposures) against market sources. The validation process must also examine the control process surrounding the credit portfolio model, ensuring that sufficient checks and balances exist in the form of independent risk management, internal audit, financial control, reporting, technology audit, version control, and so forth. The end result should be a credit risk portfolio model that can be used both for credit and business management and capital allocation purposes. Figure 12.2 summarizes the inputs and outputs of the generic credit risk portfolio model.

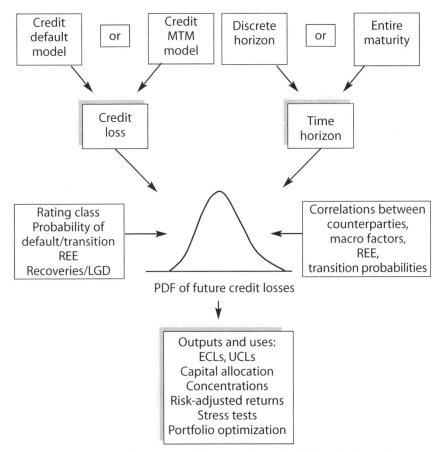

Figure 12.2 Inputs and outputs of the generic credit risk portfolio model

AN OVERVIEW OF SPECIFIC CREDIT RISK PORTFOLIO MODELS

First-generation portfolio models

With the generic model process as background we now consider, in summary form, some of the first-generation commercial risk models that have been created by various institutions over the past few years. Since we are primarily interested in understanding general approaches and differences, our overview is necessarily condensed; readers are urged to consult the underlying technical documents for each of the models (these are listed in the Reference section).

Four models – CreditMetrics, CreditRisk+, PortfolioManager, and Credit-PortfolioView (many of which appeared within a very short-time frame in the late 1990s) – are limited versions of the process described above.[5] These first-generation models represent an attempt to set banking book capital against the tail risk of systemic factors. Some of the models – such as CreditMetrics and Moody's KMV Portfolio Manager – take a Merton-based option approach, using a firm's capital structure (directly or indirectly) to estimate the likelihood of default. This type of model can be relevant for firms with counterparties that are publicly traded, since the underlying asset correlations can be derived from publicly quoted equity prices. Others – such as CreditRisk+ – are actuarial and use default rate volatilities from historical experience rather than market prices. These might be relevant for firms with counterparties that are not publicly traded or with credit sensitive portfolios that are illiquid. Use of historical default rates results in a process that is more computationally tractable, as loss distributions can be computed analytically, rather than by simulation.

It is important to note that the first-generation models discussed below are relevant primarily for non-linear instruments (for example, credit instruments excluding derivatives); this is because the models lack the capability to simultaneously treat stochastic credit parameters and market variable parameters (for example, interest rates underlying derivative contracts) cohesively. Since derivatives require simultaneous derivation of credit exposure and loss distribution, stochastic rates are needed to assess derivative credit risks. Accordingly, users must make certain decisions on implementation, such as, use of deterministic REE inputs. The second generation of portfolio models attempts to eliminate this limiting factor by creating a cohesive linear/derivative exposure and capital evaluation framework.

JP Morgan/CreditMetrics

JP Morgan introduced its CreditMetrics model in April 1997. The Credit-Metrics framework, which follows the Merton process, is a credit mark-to-market model that focuses on movement within credit rating bands over a specific time horizon, using simulation or analytic approximations. The process models the full forward distribution of values of a credit portfolio, with changes in values related only to credit migration (for example, interest rates and other market variables are evolved deterministically). The resulting "credit VAR" (as the output is known) is then simply a percentile distribution related to the desired confidence level. The model assumes no market risk, since forward values are derived from deterministic forward curves – meaning credit risk is analyzed apart from market risk (a feature which does not allow consistent market/credit risk drivers and cannot thus treat derivative exposures appropriately).

The CreditMetrics model first specifies rating categories and the transition probabilities between each category; the rating system can be internal or external and all counterparties within a rating category are considered to be homogenous (for example, an AA bank has the same transition and default probabilities as an AA industrial company). A time horizon is then defined and a forward curve for each credit category, along with a recovery rate in the event of default, developed (thus, if a bank uses ten credit qualities to define its portfolio, it creates ten credit spread curves to value the credit portfolio in all states). Thereafter the model creates a forward distribution of changes in the portfolio due to credit migration. The resulting credit VAR is extremely sensitive to assumed changes in correlations, so these need to be as accurate as possible. CreditMetrics uses equity prices as a proxy for asset value of the firm (the latter not being observable); this, again, is a critical assumption. The model estimates the correlation of equity returns and then infers the correlation between changes in credit quality from the distribution of equity returns. Once the model has correlations between asset returns, the probability of both counterparties being in any combination of ratings can be computed.[6] Caution needs to be exercised with the CreditMetrics model (as well as others) as it relies heavily on transition probabilities that are based on average historical default frequencies and patterns of migration.

CSFB CreditRisk+

CSFB's model, introduced in October 1997, follows an actuarial approach and focuses on credit default risk rather than credit migration; default risk is assumed to be an exogenous process. Unlike the approach taken by JP Morgan and Moody's KMV, the CreditRisk+ model does not relate default probabilities to a counterparty's capital structure and makes no assumptions about the cause of default; either default occurs (with probability P) or it does not occur (probability (1–P)). In fact, default rates are modeled as continuous random variables and volatility estimates are driven by macro factors and sector analysis (to capture defaults for each rating group). Given a portfolio with many counterparties, the probability of default for any single one is small and the number of defaults in any period is independent of the number occurring in any other period; this behavior can be represented conveniently by a Poisson distribution. Such behavior means that credit portfolio diversification is important.

The overall framework is fairly easy to implement (as it is a closed-form system) and is based on the two essential steps that define any actuarial/insurance model: frequency and severity of default losses. Default probabilities and the volatility of those probabilities yields the frequency of defaults, while credit exposures and recovery rates generate the severity of losses; the combination allows the generation of a distribution of default losses for a given period (the model also allows for extension to multiple periods). Since only defaults are considered, the model has fewer input estimates. The shortcoming, of course, is an inability to model credit migration; credit deterioration is ignored so exposure for each counterparty is fixed, and not dependent on changes in credit quality. Note that CSFB introduced its follow-on model framework, PortfolioRisk+, in early 2002. The new model contains a number of enhancements (including its "saddle point" methodology allowing non-normal distributions to be added up without the need for simulation).

Moody's KMV PortfolioManager

Moody's KMV is one of the pioneers of credit portfolio modeling. The company introduced the CreditMonitor module in 1991 and the Portfolio-Manager module in 1993, several years before competitors joined the race (the platform was originally developed by analytics firm KMV, which was acquired by Moody's in 2002). Like CreditMetrics, PortfolioManager is an option-based adaptation of Merton, focusing on the capital structure of the firm – though the underlying assumptions and drivers used by Moody's KMV are different, and include the use of much more granular default information. As in any Merton model, the PortfolioManager process is centered on the assumption that the credit default process originates internally and, once assets fall below the critical liability threshold, default occurs. Moody's KMV has compiled an extensive database that it uses to assess default probabilities and create migration/default loss distributions. The process is based on an expected default frequency (EDF) for each counterparty, instead of average historical transition frequencies for each rating class (as is common in the other credit portfolio models); this implies a greater level of name-specific granularity, and perhaps a more accurate and useful representation of the "real world" (and is also of benefit when considering the Basel IRB's granularity factor). In addition, the model centers on credit deterioration leading up to default as a continuous process, rather than a discrete one as might be implied by periodic ratings changes, leading, arguably, to a more realistic interpretation of the operating environment. As a result of these differences, the Moody's KMV model results in a skew in the mean default rates versus the median (when compared to Moody's KMV's process, the average historical default rate used in other models overstates the default rate for a typical counterparty).

The central component of PortfolioManager is the EDF, which is a function of a company's capital structure, volatility of asset returns, and current asset value (EDFs include transition probabilities so that each is actually associated with a credit spread curve already). To obtain an EDF (for example, an implied risk of default), the model uses a counterparty's publicly quoted stock price and the structure of its balance sheet.[7] The asset value and asset return are estimated (the former being lognormally distributed) and, since only the stock price can be observed daily, it becomes the primary driver; the value of a counterparty's assets is thus a function of the observed stock value and the volatility of asset returns. The model assumes that a counterparty's capital structure is based on equity, short-term debt and perpetual debt and requires the leverage ratio of the capital structure, average debt coupon, and the risk free rate as inputs. Applying analytic schemes, the model finds the value of the equity and its volatility.

In order to avoid certain perceived inaccuracies in computing the actual probability of default, Moody's KMV computes a so-called "distance to default," which is defined as the number of standard deviations between the mean of the distribution of the asset value and a "default point" taken to be the par value of current liabilities plus 50 percent of total long-term debt. The distance to default is then mapped to actual probabilities of default for each time horizon to generate the EDF. The model then finds the distance to default of a particular magnitude for all counterparties; the number of defaulting parties in that group at particular time horizons becomes the implied default probability (that is, the EDF) for that time horizon. The EDF can, of course, be compared to rating agency default probabilities.[8] Like CreditMetrics, KMV derives its asset return correlations by linking into idiosyncratic and systemic factors related to country, industry, and region.

McKinsey CreditPortfolioView

McKinsey's CreditPortfolioView (CPV) was introduced in November 1997 as a discrete, multi-period, multi-factor default model based on macroeconomic factors. Like CSFP's model, the McKinsey approach ignores credit migration risk and focuses only on default risk. Default probabilities are conditional on the state of pre-defined macroeconomic variables; the underlying premise is that when the economy weakens, credit downgrades/defaults increase, and when it strengthens, downgrades/ defaults decrease. There is thus an explicit linkage between the state of the economy and default probabilities.

Under the CPV platform, default probabilities are modeled in a framework where independent variables are based on a country-specific index (for example, current or lagged macro variables). The variables are specified in advance for each country and calibrated at the country/industry level. The model simulates the distribution of specific default probabilities and makes an adjustment to migration probabilities to take account of the economic state; it requires default data for each country/industry and then uses its own procedure to adjust the default matrix.

Empirical research indicates that economic capital for sample credit risk portfolios evaluated through the models above varies, sometimes considerably (though results are bounded on the upside). However, when the same default probabilities are used the results start to converge, demonstrating just how sensitive the models are to key input parameters. Despite these differences the benefit of these models almost certainly lies in how results change over time, rather than in the absolute magnitude of the numbers; that is, whether the credit risk portfolio is getting more or less risky over time, and what implications that might have for credit risk management, risk appetite, and capital allocation. The models can be very valuable as benchmarking tools. Calibrating data, and understanding the sensitivity of parameter inputs in the portfolio model, must be a key area of focus when using any of these models. Proper inputs, including default probabilities, transition probabilities, recovery rates, credit spreads/forward curves, and correlations, are essential in obtaining good results. An institution must therefore be convinced that the model can handle these data parameters robustly and, where a high degree of sensitivity between input and output exists, must ensure the input variables are appropriate and results are stressed. Deriving false comfort from outputs when uncertain about the quality of inputs is obviously dangerous.

The models we have focused on are concerned primarily with determining the amount of capital a firm should allocate against a portfolio of credit risks and how to optimize the risk/return of the portfolio. There are, of course, other types of credit parameters that need to be modeled in order to create an effective credit risk process, even for firms focused primarily on linear credit businesses. These include credit pricing of individual transactions that feed into the portfolio, credit rating/scoring benchmarks, loan loss reserve computations, valuation of illiquid securities and positions, and so on. These should be treated consistently and cohesively with other parts of the credit risk portfolio modeling process to ensure no discrepancies appear that might lead to bad credit management decisions.

The four models summarized above (and in Table 12.1 below) are just a sampling of some of the work that has been done by financial institutions, consulting firms, and others; there are various other first-generation credit portfolio models in the marketplace (for example, those created by CIBC and Deutsche Bank), each with its own features, strengths, and weaknesses.

Second-generation credit portfolio models

In order to build on the structure and success of first-generation credit models, a second generation of analytics started appearing in the mid to late-1990s and continues to the present time.[9] These models address some of the earlier limitations arising from simplifying assumptions or technical constraints, and thus attempt to represent more accurate, and sophisticated,

Table 12.1 Summary of credit portfolio risk models

Model/approach	Inputs	Outputs
CreditMetrics/ Credit mark-to-market	Default probabilities (constant) Transition probabilities Credit spreads Correlations Recovery rates (random) Credit exposures	Economic capital Distribution of returns Loss percentiles
CreditRisk+/ Credit default	Default probabilities Default rate volatility Recovery rates (LGD) Credit exposures	Economic capital Distribution of losses Loss percentiles
PortfolioManager/ Credit mark-to-market	Transition probabilities (EDF, asset prices) Credit spreads Correlations Recovery rates (random) Credit exposures	Economic capital Distribution of returns Return on risk capital
CreditPortfolioView/ Credit default	Macroeconomic variables Default probabilities Transition probabilities (macro) Credit spreads Recovery rates (random) Credit exposures	Economic capital Distribution of returns Loss percentiles Return on risk capital

views of credit losses. Most focus on developing a cohesive framework that unites stochastic market variables, credit migration, and credit default and are similar to the generic framework we outlined at the beginning of the chapter. It is worth noting that not all firms require such sophisticated capabilities. In particular, firms that deal primarily with linear credit portfolios or are comfortable with deterministic derivative REE inputs into the credit exposure component may already have the capabilities they need with first-generation models. However, those that actively deal in derivatives and want to manage their portfolio credit exposures and capital allocations dynamically are likely to require a greater level of sophistication.

One of the most important elements of second-generation models centers on the development of a framework for considering market and credit risks jointly. This is necessary in order to ensure consistency in the treatment of firm-wide risks, and in the uniform derivation of stochastic credit risk exposures and default behaviors. Various second-generation models based on simulation techniques bring together the market and credit risk disciplines; indeed, market risk models are effectively a subset of credit-based portfolio simulation models. The outputs focus, in the first instance, on market-driven stochastic credit portfolio exposures (the element missing from first-generation models), and are then adapted to take account of credit losses and/or capital by applying default and transition probabilities, recovery rates, correlations, and so forth. Risk measures need not be tied to scenario or valuation analytics, so they are more flexible (for example, the output can include a 99 percent worst-case portfolio exposure that can be used to manage credit risk limits internally and can also include a one-year average exposure that can be used to manage economic capital, both from the same underlying engine, ensuring consistency). A proper simulation approach must make use of a stable joint process that describes long-term behavior of market risk factors and should be calibrated to historical data (including weak economic/credit cycles). And, as the lessons of LTCM have demonstrated, appropriate treatment of collateral lags, and collateral/exposure correlations have to be incorporated into the framework. In this section we consider several pioneering second-generation models (for example, Algorithmics Mark-to-Future, Jobst and Zenios), and urge the reader to consider others listed in the Reference section.[10]

Algorithmics Mark-to-Future

One of the earliest of the second-generation credit portfolio models was initially proposed by Iscoe, et al., and commercially adopted by risk technology and analytics firm Algorithmics as the Mark-to-Future (MtF) model.[11] The MtF model is a multi-step Mertonian, simulation-based process that considers market and credit risks jointly, across time and scenarios. The model captures stochastic credit exposures, collateral, and recovery rates – some of the fundamental items missing in the first-generation models –and is thus intended to provide a more consistent, and realistic, picture of credit exposures and losses (and integrate with a firm's market VAR process); though the portfolio component is based on defaults, it is extendible to migration.

The MtF approach centers on the definition of market risk scenarios (for example, asset prices) and credit risk scenarios (for example, systemic factors), which together represent micro and macro-events. A scenario can be applied to an instrument or a counterparty, so becoming part of a table; each part of the table thus has a vector of risk factor-dependent instrument/ counterparty measures based on a given scenario and time horizon. Each set of tables comprises a cube; the cube can be thought of as multiple portfolios. To create the exposure (and, ultimately, loss) outputs, the MtF model follows several steps, beginning with the generation of scenarios for individual market and credit risk factors. This is followed by computation of counter-party exposures, recoveries, and losses (computed under each scenario) and determination of default and transition probabilities conditioned on the scenario path, up to a specific point in time. Correlations between counter-parties are computed by the joint variance of conditional probabilities across scenarios. Thereafter, the scenario-conditional portfolio loss distributions can be derived (through a convolution process that takes the credit loss and probability of loss, for each counterparty, conditioned on each scenario, to yield the conditional portfolio losses; in practice this is done through Monte Carlo simulation). This leads to the final step, an aggregation of losses across all scenarios (effectively the unconditional distribution of portfolio credit losses through the average of the condition loss distribution). The MtF approach is thus intended to handle estimates of credit exposure and portfo-lio credit risk loss consistently, so that the market risk factors that drive a firm's market VAR also determine the stochastic REEs. With this output it is then possible to determine the appropriate economic or regulatory capital required to support the portfolio, or to use portfolio theory tools to optimize the overall portfolio.[12]

Jobst and Zenios

Jobst and Zenios have proposed a combined portfolio model (ratings-based, stochastic intensity), that integrates different sources of risk (consistent with empirical observations), establishes correlations among different credit and market risk factors, considers the probability of extreme events, and values the portfolio at the end of specified time horizons through simulation.[13] Under the model, the simulation framework first generates interest rate or spread scenarios (also known as "economic scenarios") which are applied to all instruments in a given class. Transactions are then priced conditional on economic scenarios according to an intensity-based pricing model (rating and default scenarios are simulated over time); additional simulations generate rating scenarios (idiosyncratic, by transaction/rating class) and recoveries in default.

The general process thus begins by defining the dynamic economic (market and credit) variables, including market prices of bonds, default-free and credit-risky term structures and spreads, transition matrixes, seniority classifications, and recovery rates. Market data flows into the pricing framework, an intensity-based model with parameter estimates of stochastic processes (including historical spread and default data). Credit variables are input into the credit event model (based on correlated Markov chains), which includes a recovery rate process. The pricing and credit event models are run through a simulation process to determine the default free short-rate, credit spreads, credit migrations and defaults, and recovery payments; a security pricing component, based on risk-neutral probabilities, values the portfolio at different horizons. The outputs thus include future portfolio valuations for use in optimization, holding period return calculations, and capital allocations. Though the model is based on linear credit instruments, it can accommodate a range of derivative instruments in a consistent manner as well.

More credit portfolio models will be developed over the coming years and should continue to become more sophisticated and accurate. Advances in computing power, improvements in analytic techniques, better access to data, and increased transparency in the credit markets will contribute to better portfolio management tools. That said, many of the tools already available are sufficiently useful and robust to allow for more precise management of credit exposures than ever before. Indeed, versions of these may ultimately form part of the BIS IRB advanced approach methodologies. When coupled with proper judgment, as well as some of the "qualitative" portfolio risk issues we consider in the next chapter, they provide an institution with a central component of a prudent governance process.

CHAPTER 13

Credit Risk Management of Derivative Portfolios: Qualitative Issues

In the last two chapters we have discussed various techniques for quantifying credit exposure on a portfolio basis. In this chapter we continue the theme by addressing a number of qualitative issues related to the management of derivative portfolios. In the first section we explore the dynamic management of derivative exposures. This can be accomplished through credit risk mitigation techniques, credit risk simulations/scenario analyses, and dynamic limit adjustment; such active risk management is generally supported by comprehensive credit technologies. In the second section we consider a range of ancillary credit risk management issues that risk officers are increasingly required to address. These topics include counterparty motivation for entering into derivative transactions (and the suitability of entering into such transactions, which takes us back to our legal risk discussion in Chapter 2), relevance of credit analysis in an era of lengthening transaction maturities, and problems posed by a counterparty's unwillingness to perform on its derivative obligations (rather than its financial inability to perform, which is the domain of traditional credit analysis). The quantitative aspects of credit portfolio risk management presented in Chapters 11 and 12 and the qualitative aspects presented in this chapter combine to form an overall framework for the ongoing management of derivative credit risk exposures.

MANAGING DERIVATIVE CREDIT EXPOSURES DYNAMICALLY

Credit risk management departments of institutions at the forefront of derivatives are increasingly involved as key partners in managing credit exposures.

While "conventional" credit departments have traditionally focused on analysis of counterparty credit quality, evaluation, and approval/rejection of transaction credit risk, and monitoring of exposures, it is increasingly important in a world of scarce credit resources, finite capital, and demanding shareholders that a bank's credit capacity be utilized in the most effective manner possible; this means credit resources must be actively managed and that credit divisions must be proactive participants in the process.

Dynamic credit exposure management can be accomplished through various mechanisms, including:

- credit risk mitigation techniques to manage increasing or changing exposures

- credit stress/scenario analyses to determine credit capacity and areas of potential credit concern

- multiple limits to control different components of credit exposure.

The process of active risk management depends heavily on robust infrastructure, including advanced credit systems/technology and accurate data. This permits credit exposures and simulations to be considered on a frequent (though probably not real-time) basis and the results to be used with confidence.

Credit risk mitigation techniques

The first major element of dynamic credit risk management we discuss centers on the implementation and use of credit risk mitigating techniques, a topic we introduced briefly in Chapter 1. Expansion of the derivatives market over the past two decades has led to an industry-wide increase in credit-sensitive business transacted with both high and low-quality credit counterparties, while introduction of complex, leveraged, and longer-dated derivatives has led to transactions with larger amounts of REE. Though netting arrangements have been a considerable help in reducing exposures, institutions in the marketplace have tended to use greater amounts of available counterparty credit limits. As a result, the need for additional risk mitigation tools has become increasingly apparent. In practice, institutions employ several of the risk mitigation techniques, including:

- portfolio diversification

- third-party enhancements/guarantees

- collateral

- recouponing

- assignment

- intermediation

- termination/downgrade options

- netting

- credit derivatives.

Portfolio diversification

Diversification of exposure – across trades on a counterparty basis and across counterparties on an industry/country basis – is one of the most fundamental ways of mitigating risk in a credit portfolio. The end result of a proper diversification exercise is a more balanced risk profile: one that is not concentrated, and is thus not prone to excessively large losses when a single counterparty (or a group of highly correlated counterparties) defaults. More formally, and drawing from our discussion in Chapter 11, we know that the volatility of credit losses in the credit portfolio (for example, UCLs) is driven by idiosyncratic (or specific) risk and systematic risk; idiosyncratic risks are those relevant to individual counterparties, while systematic risks are those that impact the economy or macro-environment at large. Under portfolio theory, idiosyncratic risks can be reduced through diversification, leaving only systematic risks to be managed/retained. Ultimately, portfolios of credit risks are influenced by both concentrations and correlations; concentrations reveal any "lumpiness" that might exist in the portfolio, while correlations indicate the sensitivity of the portfolio to macro-factors. Idiosyncratic risks are a function of concentration while systematic risks are a function of correlation. Referring to the function illustrated in Figure 13.1, we note that as the portfolio of uncorrelated credits increases, the idiosyncratic risks decline.

Part of credit portfolio management is, then, to consider mechanisms that allow for active diversification of exposures. Examples of mechanisms that might be used include credit limits to "force" diversification by limiting the maximum amount of obligor exposure that can be held, and portfolio optimization routines that compare risks and returns to ensure the best possible balance (and limit the likelihood concentrations will build). In fact, by attempting to optimize the portfolio on a regular basis, the credit unit plays a leading role in shaping the credit risk profile of the firm. We have noted, and stress once again, the importance of correlations in the diversification exercise. Regardless of the specific model or mechanism used, correlations

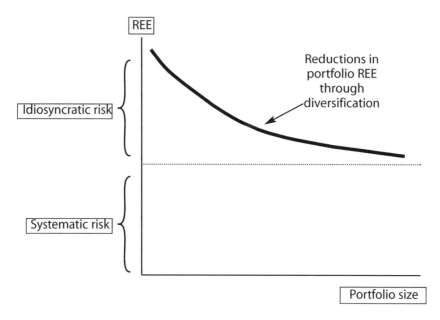

Figure 13.1 Systematic and idiosyncratic credit risks

emerge as an extremely sensitive input and must therefore be sourced and interpreted with care; failure to do so can lead to false comfort (for example, belief that the portfolio is diversified, when it is actually concentrated). Stressing the correlations, and the exposures underlying individual counter-parties (across all business units), can help provide an understanding of potential "hidden" concentrations.

Third-party enhancements/guarantees

Third-party enhancements, such as stand-by or direct-pay letters of credit, bond insurance/surety bonds, and parent (or third-party) guarantees, have been used in the financial markets for many years as a means of securing or supporting counterparty exposures. Under a typical third-party mechanism a weaker-rated counterparty pays a higher-rated support provider (typically a bank, financial institution, or insurer) a fee in exchange for an explicit guar-antee of support on its derivative obligations, to become effective in the event it is unable to perform on such obligations itself. While support is often obtained from an unrelated third party, it can also be secured from a parent company. In arranging third-party (or parent) support, a counterparty loses a portion of the economic benefit derived from entering into the transaction (for example, it pays a fee equal to a certain number of basis points to secure the support); however, if the economics (or need) for entering into the transaction are truly apparent, a counterparty may be willing to pay for the support. Once the relevant enhancement has been structured, the derivative bank effectively shifts its credit exposure from the underlying counterparty to the support provider and assumes the credit risk of the higher-rated institution (though it is likely to continue to exchange flows directly with the original counterparty until, and if, default occurs; an exception to this occurs through "direct-pay" structures, where the support provider pays the intermediary bank directly and then seeks its own payment from the underlying client).

Collateral

Collateralization – the process of taking a security interest in some asset as "protection" against a credit exposure – is one of the most commonly utilized risk reduction techniques in the derivatives industry. In fact, according to a survey conducted by ISDA at the end of 2002[1], the industry held an estimated US$437 billion in collateral.[2] Cash and government securities are the primary form of collateral received and delivered (accounting for 76 percent of collateral received and 88 percent of all collateral delivered), though corporate bonds and equities are also used (and thus factor into the pricing/haircut issues noted below). Table 13.1 summarizes the findings of the collateral survey.

Intermediaries and end users in North America and Western Europe are the most active users of collateral arrangements, while those in Japan, Southeast Asia, and various emerging nations rank behind them. Collateral arrangements can be documented through one of several standard forms, depending on the location of the counterparties and the dealing jurisdiction. These include:

Table 13.1 Derivatives collateral

Collateral type	% of total received	% of total delivered
US$ cash	37.34	44.47
€ cash	17.41	12.64
UK£ cash	4.71	5.57
¥ cash	0.82	1.32
US government securities	6.04	12.28
EU government securities	3.33	8.68
Japan government securities	1.77	2.31
Corporate bonds	5.25	3.45
Equities	11.39	0.27
All other	11.94	9.01

Source: *ISDA Margin Survey, 2002*

- 1994/2002 ISDA Credit Support Annex (documented as a pledge under New York Law)

- 1995 ISDA Credit Support Annex (documented as a title transfer under English law)

- 1995 ISDA Credit Support Deed (documented as a charge under English law)

- 1995 ISDA Credit Support Annex (documented under Japanese law)

- 2001 ISDA Margin Provisions

- German Rahmenverstrag Agreement

- French Association Française de Banque (AFB) Agreement.

As noted briefly in Chapter 4, the ISDA Credit Support Annex (CSA) is a key element of many master agreements documented under ISDA standards. The CSA contains important details on the credit parameters and relationships between two parties, for example, cross-default thresholds, credit event/downgrade provisions, collateral use and treatment, and so forth. The ISDA Credit Support Annex can form part of the 1992 Master Agreement or the 2002 revised Master Agreement.

Several fundamental issues must be considered when using collateral; these include posting collateral on an upfront or periodic basis, structuring collateral agreements on a unilateral or bilateral basis, allocating collateral for a single transaction or an entire portfolio of transactions, and determining the nature and pricing of the underlying collateral. We consider each aspect in greater detail.

Upfront versus periodic collateral

Upfront collateral is defined as collateral taken at the inception of a transaction, in an amount sufficient to cover all future market movements as indicated by the REE figure. *Periodic collateral* is defined as collateral taken at select points during the life of the transaction, in an amount approximated by the current mark-to-market level of the transaction plus some "buffer." An institution generally requires a counterparty to post upfront collateral when it does not have the operational capability to make periodic calls for collateral or prefers to secure the full amount of its calculated fractional exposure in order to avoid the possibility that its counterparty will not be able to post additional collateral at some future date (precisely when it might be most needed). Upfront collateral can be determined by an REE reflecting the final maturity date of the transaction (that is, incorporating the full potential market volatility that might affect the value of the derivative(s)). When dealing with several of the higher risk structures discussed earlier in the text, the upfront collateral requirement may be particularly large.

Some banks have the operational ability to transmit calls for additional collateral as the market value of a derivative reaches certain trigger points and/or gain enough comfort with the credit standing of a counterparty that they can reduce the upfront collateral amount by a significant amount. For instance, a bank might offer a client a 12-month derivative transaction secured by two months of upfront collateral (for example, the "buffer" or initial margin), combined with monthly marks-to-market (on the derivative and collateral) and the right to call for additional security (as a collateral call or variation margin) should changes in the market value of the derivative erode a certain percentage of the upfront security. Thus, instead of taking an upfront amount based on a full 12 months of REE, the initial amount can be adjusted downward to a smaller fraction that reflects the frequency of the mark-to-market interval plus some buffer (one month and two months, respectively); the buffer exists to provide an extra cushion against volatility in the value of the derivative/collateral as well as delays in either receiving or liquidating collateral as needed. This may prove more acceptable to the client and, assuming the bank has confidence in its ability to mark the derivative and perform collateral calls on a timely basis, can present little or no incremental risk. Care must obviously be taken in managing the entire process. As the disruptive financial events of mid-1997 and late 1998 demonstrated, market conditions characterized by illiquidity and volatility, along with counterparties that are in financial distress, can result in delays in obtaining incremental collateral (and/or liquidating collateral on hand to cover trades being closed-out); this can generate unsecured credit exposure and possible credit losses.

Unilateral versus bilateral collateral

A *unilateral collateral* arrangement requires only one of the two parties to a derivative transaction to post collateral, while a *bilateral collateral* agreement requires mutual posting. Both forms are widely used, particularly as more counterparties of roughly equal standing that want to continue doing business use collateral as a risk mitigant.[3]

A bank generally requires a unilateral collateral agreement when its counterparty's credit quality is lower or deteriorating; thus, an AA or AAA institution might require a BBB institution to post security on a one-way basis. In certain instances, however, highly rated sovereign or corporate customers require one-way collateral from banks. An extension of this is found in the construction and use of AAA-rated DPCs (discussed in Chapter 1): a key element of a DPC's enhanced rating comes from posting of collateral. Note that structuring bilateral collateral is often an alternative to entering into two-way mark-to-market/net settlement agreements, as described below.

Transaction-specific versus pooled portfolio collateral

Transaction-specific collateral is defined as collateral taken against a specific derivative deal, while *pooled portfolio collateral* is a pool of collateral securing an entire portfolio of derivatives. Collateral is generally taken on a transaction-specific basis when a counterparty is an infrequent customer of a bank. In such instances a specific collateral requirement is attached to each transaction, and termination or unwind of a particular deal results in the release of collateral associated with that deal. If a counterparty is an active client, it is common to combine collateral into a single pool for use in securing the entire portfolio. This approach has the advantage of not penalizing a counterparty for the full amount of maximum REE associated with incremental transactions (which, as noted in Chapter 11, can lead to overstatement of potential risk and, therefore, collateral). Pool agreements often include "right of substitution" language, which permits a counterparty to replace securities in the collateral pool so that it can manage its own portfolio more actively. Substitution is generally limited to securities that are defined or permitted within the agreement, such as securities with a certain rating, maturity, and structure, that do not prejudice the security standing of the institution. Thus, a counterparty is unlikely to be able to replace its US Treasury collateral with high yield bonds or mortgage residuals (unless an appropriate haircut is applied, as noted below), but it might be able to use AA corporate bonds. A pooled collateral agreement must, of course, be appropriately documented from a legal standpoint; an institution must be confident that an event of default on one transaction allows acceleration of all remaining transactions and application of the entire pool of collateral to possible losses.

Nature and pricing of collateral

Many institutions have expanded the type of collateral they are willing to accept as a result of improvements in market conditions (that is, improved liquidity, lower volatility, increased creditworthiness, and so on) and technical infrastructure (that is, improved technical ability to accept, price, and monitor collateral levels on a real-time basis). While certain institutions continue to follow a policy of only accepting cash or cash equivalents (including highly rated government securities which exhibit price stability), others have broadened the list of acceptable collateral to include corporate bonds, mortgage-backed securities, and even high yield bonds and equities. In agreeing to accept such diverse securities most institutions apply standard haircuts, or discounts, to the upfront market value in order to protect against price volatility in the collateral (the greater the riskiness and price volatility of the collateral, the greater the haircut); this provides an extra buffer or margin. Once again, the ability to price and track diverse instruments is an essential requirement before moving away from accepting only the most secure and stable instruments as security. In taking securities that exhibit greater price volatility than cash equivalents an institution incurs two dimensions of price risk: on its underlying derivative and its collateral; both must be monitored with care. This, once again, became quite evident in the aftermath of the 1998 crisis, when haircuts on riskier securities (virtually every asset apart from on-the-run government bonds from the USA, UK, EU, or Japan) were found to be insufficient to cover the growing credit exposures caused by volatile markets).

Recouponing

Periodically marking-to-market and settling the actual exposure component of derivative trades, and then rewriting transactions at current levels, is a process known as *recouponing*.[4] The procedure requires payment of a cash amount representing the accumulated mark-to-market value of a portfolio of derivatives and has the effect of reducing potential credit exposure by eliminating actual exposure within the portfolio. Marking-to-market and settling the actual exposure can be structured in several ways: the actual exposure can be evaluated on a regular basis (for example, every quarter or year) and, if positive to the bank, settled at that time; this can lead to the accumulation of an undefined amount of unsecured exposure. Alternatively, the marking and settling may only take place once a mark-to-market trigger point has been reached (for example, once the mark-to-market reaches a US$5m threshold a US$5m settlement payment is made to the party holding the in-the-money contracts); this places a defined limit on unsecured exposure. The recouponing mechanism protects the intermediary from acquiring too much exposure to what may be a lower-rated counterparty; unlike third-party support or collateral, however, a recouponing procedure does not eliminate counterparty exposure (in other words, potential future exposure remains) – it simply lowers or eliminates actual exposure periodically.

In addition to conventional unilateral agreements, bilateral agreements are increasingly prevalent, particularly between financial institutions with significant mutual exposures (where the moneyness of the exposures changes over time as additional transactions are incorporated or markets begin to move); two-way agreements are also structured between financial institutions and highly rated end users. As one might expect, a two-way agreement simply means a net settlement payment can be made by either party, depending on the direction of the positive mark-to-market. The most common bilateral agreements are structured using minimum threshold amounts rather than predetermined evaluation dates. Since the market value of a portfolio of derivatives changes over time (particularly if many of the transactions are long term in nature), both parties to the agreement may be required to make payments at different points during the life of the agreement.

Assignment

The *assignment* process involves transferring an existing derivative transaction (or portfolio) from one of the original contract parties to a third party; by assigning existing transactions, the institution initiating the action seeks to lower overall credit exposure to a particular counterparty. In certain instances the assignment process is undertaken if an institution has severe doubts regarding the continuing viability of its counterparty, while in other cases it is simply undertaken to free up credit lines or diversify the portfolio so that incremental business can be done with the same counterparty.

Regardless of the underlying motivation, third party assignments require the approval of the party from which the derivatives are being assigned, since that party will face a new institution as its own counterparty.

Consider the following example. Bank A has US$50m of net potential credit exposure with Company XYZ. As a result of policy directives, Bank A wishes to lower its potential credit exposure by US$10m, to US$40m. After receiving Company XYZ's permission, it agrees to transfer a series of derivatives to Bank C that will lower net potential exposure by US$10m. As part of the transfer process, Bank C makes a payment to Bank A in an amount equal to the mark-to-market value of the swaps being transferred (since such contracts immediately have a positive mark-to-market value to Bank C). At the conclusion of the assignment process, Bank A and Bank C have US$40m and US$10m, respectively, of net potential credit exposure with XYZ. Care must be taken in the assignment process to select transactions in the portfolio that most effectively reduce counterparty exposure. As discussed in Chapter 11, removing one or more transactions from a portfolio can have the effect of increasing, rather than decreasing, potential exposure.

Intermediation

Intermediation occurs when an institution structures a specific derivative for an end user but executes the transaction through a third-party intermediary rather than directly with the end user; the institution thus faces the intermediary as its counterparty, while the intermediary faces the end user on an identical transaction. In executing a transaction on an inter-mediated basis, the arranging institution sacrifices a certain amount of its profit, which is effectively passed to the intermediary. Intermediation may occur if the arranging institution is unwilling to face the end user directly (for credit reasons) or if it no longer has sufficient credit capac-ity to deal with the end user (its credit limits are full). Alternatively, it may occur for regulatory or tax reasons. Intermediation can be arranged on an upfront basis (prior to commencement of a deal) or during the life of a transaction.

Large financial institutions often act as intermediaries. In addition, the centralized credit clearing houses we noted in Chapter 1 (and which are structurally characteristic of the exchange-traded derivatives market) perform a basic intermediation function by accepting collateral from two derivative counterparties and then forwarding flows/payments as required during the course of a given transaction; if default occurs, the clearing house uses the collateral that has been lodged to "make whole" the other counterparty. Several clearing houses that perform the function in the listed futures and options markets now provide the same services for OTC transactions.

Termination options

Institutions periodically structure derivatives with *termination options* (sometimes known more narrowly as downgrade options), which provide an opportunity to exit transactions if counterparty credit quality begins to deteriorate. Under a typical termination option a bank negotiates the right to end a transaction at prespecified points in time (perhaps annually during the life of a multi-year derivative or in the event a particular trigger is breached). An institution can often exercise the termination option for any reason (although the implicit understanding may be that it is exercisable if the counterparty's credit deteriorates); however, in order to relate the termi-nation specifically to a counterparty's financial deterioration, the option can be written so that it is only exercisable if a counterparty's public credit rating is downgraded to a certain level (for example, below investment grade). If the credit rating remains unchanged (or improves) the derivative intermediary is not permitted to end the deal. Certain derivatives may also be structured to end if financial ratios (for example, tangible net worth, leverage, interest coverage) deteriorate below defined thresholds, not unlike financial covenants in a loan agreement. While most termination-downgrade options are unilateral (the intermediary holds the option against the counterparty), they can be written on a bilateral basis; this occurs primarily between counterparties of equal credit quality facing each other on very long-term transactions.

Netting

As we have discussed at several points in this text, netting of derivative credit risk has become one of the most popular techniques for managing counterparty exposures. The use and effectiveness of netting have increased as changes in national bankruptcy codes have been effected in recent years. As we have noted, netting is a process whereby derivative trades with a given counterparty are documented under, and governed by, a master agreement (for example, the 2002 ISDA Master, the Rahmenverstrag, the AFB). Once a master agreement is in place, all future derivative trades need only be documented through simple confirmations (rather than complete and detailed documentation); this has the advantage of reducing administrative costs and speeding the documentary process. More importantly, in the event of counterparty default in a jurisdiction that accepts netting, all trades governed by the master agreement are accelerated and all mark-to-market exposures are reduced to a single payment or receipt. If the net figure is positive to the bank, the counterparty is required to provide a net payment under bankruptcy proceedings. If other creditors exist, the bank assumes its position as a senior unsecured creditor, and attempts to recover a portion of the net payment at the conclusion of bankruptcy proceedings. This assumes, of course, the exposures are uncollateralized; if collateralized, the bank ranks as a secured creditor and is permitted to use counterparty collateral to defray/cover its losses. In fact, unlike other secured (non-derivative) creditors, it is not subject to an automatic stay in bankruptcy, meaning it can liquidate collateral immediately. If the net figure is negative to the bank, the bank is required to provide a net payment to the counterparty. Under a legally binding netting agreement in a jurisdiction that accepts netting, a bankruptcy receiver cannot "cherry pick" the portfolio. Use of net potential exposure is now generally accepted in the industry as a sensible means of managing credit limits and exposures; this has the great benefit of reducing potential exposures to the net amount that might be faced in a worst-case scenario. Recognizing the exposure benefits afforded by netting, many institutions have implemented comprehensive programs to execute master agreements with their counterparties. Once agreements are in place, credit exposures are then reduced to net measures. Regulatory capital charges also give benefit to netting.

Credit derivatives

Over the past few years, credit derivatives have emerged as an important mechanism for managing (that is, reducing or eliminating) credit exposures. We have already discussed the use of credit derivatives from the perspective of the investor. In this section we consider them as a means of protecting against default risk and releasing credit limits for the purpose of executing incremental business. While most credit derivatives used for exposure management purposes are structured to reduce, or eliminate, credit exposure to a single counterparty, certain structures – such as credit basket options, basket swaps, and first-to-default swaps – protect/hedge credit exposure to a portfolio of counterparties. When using credit derivatives it is critical for an institution to pay close attention to the legal language surrounding the transaction/agreement. Although much progress has been made since the late 1990s (when the Russian hedge fund crisis brought to the forefront many issues of legal interpretation regarding "credit events," determination of values, instrument deliverability, and so forth) due care must still be given to the legal dimension as "gray areas" remain.[5] This is particularly true when credit derivatives are being used to protect or hedge otherwise significant counterparty credit exposures.

Credit forwards

Credit forwards, which require the exchange of a payment based on the performance of a reference credit's price or spread against an agreed forward price or spread, can be used to offset or lower credit exposure to a given counterparty by providing a bank with a compensatory forward payment as its counterparty deteriorates or defaults.

Consider the following example. Bank A wishes to offset a portion of its exposure to Company C by selling Bank B a forward based on Company C's benchmark bond. Assume Bank A has US$10m of exposure with Company C and wants to protect itself from an event of severe deterioration (or outright default) in C's credit during the next 12 months. It sells Bank B a forward based on US$30m notional, using C's current five-year bond (currently trading at 90) as a reference. If the bond trades below 90 in 12 months (a sign of credit deterioration or default), A receives a payment from B equal to the percentage differential between the two prices (for example, depreciation against the forward price), times the notional. If the bond trades above 90, A makes a payment to B on the same basis.

Consider the following scenarios. Scenario one: in 12 months A's original exposure to C has grown to US$12m. C defaults and its bond trades at a distressed level of 35. Although A sustains a complete or partial loss on the original US$12m of exposure, it receives a payment from B on the short forward of US$8.3m ((90 – 65)/90 * US$30m). Thus, the forward hedges a portion of A's exposure to C and acts, in effect, as a risk-mitigating device. Note that if C defaults in six months rather than 12, the payments on the original US$12m are accelerated and A becomes an unsecured creditor of C; the forward with B is not yet due and, as such, A does not receive its gain for a further six months (at which time C's bond will trade at/above/below the price at the time of default, depending on how distressed debt dealers perceive progress on bankruptcy proceedings). Timing issues must therefore be considered. It should also be clear that an outright default is not required in order for A to receive a payment from B; simple credit deterioration is sufficient to generate a payment. Scenario two: if, at the end of 12 months, C's credit improves and the bond trades at 100, A makes a payment of US$3.3m ((90 – 100)/90 * US$30m) to B. A, in turn, receives its full payment from C. Note that since forwards are credit-sensitive transactions, the bank selling the forward to hedge the credit exposure of a given institution assumes the credit exposure of a second institution; in this example A assumes B's credit risk (B also assumes A's credit risk since the forward is a two-sided agreement).

While the discussion above focuses on protecting credit exposures, it should be equally clear that by hedging a bank is effectively creating greater credit availability with a counterparty. Thus, credit forwards (and other credit derivatives) permit incremental credit-sensitive business to be accommodated.

Let us consider a simple example reflecting the release of credit limits and the creation of credit capacity. Suppose Bank LMN has an active credit relationship with Dealer PQR. Based on the current credit portfolio, LMN has US$100m of net potential exposure and US$50m of actual exposure with PQR. Although the credit officer at LMN is comfortable with PQR as a counterparty, it does not want to increase credit limits given PQR's internal rating and financial prospects. Rather than turn away incremental business, the dealer at LMN enters into a credit forward on PQR with Bank ABC; by doing so, it frees a portion of the credit line for use in new transactions.[6] Specifically, LMN sells ABC a credit forward on US$50m of PQR's bonds; under the terms of the credit forward ABC pays LMN any percentage depreciation in PQR's bonds below the forward price of 90 in two years' time, while LMN pays any percentage appreciation. Based on this structure, LMN's credit officer feels comfortable that incremental exposures are appropriately protected by the credit forward and, as such, increases credit limits to accommodate incremental transactions. While the incremental amount of credit the officer may extend is to some degree subjective, one approach might center on the worst-case result of default by PQR within the two-year time frame. If the credit officer feels the PQR bond will trade at 45 post-default (against a forward price of 90), the net payment it would expect to receive from ABC is 50 percent of US$50m, or US$25m. In this instance the credit officer might permit a further US$25m REE of transactions to be booked with PQR, being mindful of the final maturity of the incremental derivatives against the maturity of the credit forward. Note that the credit forward is only designed to cover incremental trades; the existing portfolio of trades would still be subject to full loss (for example, the full extent of allocated, unsecured credit). There are, of course, other means by which to determine the amount of permissible incremental trading, but this is one workable solution. Figure 13.2 summarizes this structure.

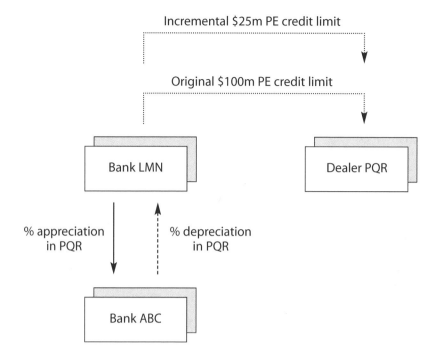

Figure 13.2 Credit forward to create credit capacity

Credit options

The protective payment flows of a short forward can be duplicated with credit spread options and default options, as we discussed in Chapter 8, without the need to make a payment should the financial position of a given counterparty strengthen. Credit puts, where a bank seeking to manage credit exposure pays the option seller premium in exchange for a payoff associated with credit deterioration/default, are routinely used to hedge credit risk and release credit limits. Under a typical credit put structure, an institution defines a credit-risky reference instrument (which will, of course, be issued by the counterparty whose risk a bank is seeking to fully or partially hedge); the payoff can be calibrated to the bond's price or spread.

Consider the following example: Bank A, once again carrying US$10m of Company C's credit risk, buys a credit put from Bank B, paying US$250,000 for a 12-month option. The strike price is spread-based (quoted as Treasuries plus 300 basis points) and the notional amount is US$30m. Six months from now, A's exposure to C increases to US$12m; C defaults and its credit spread widens to a default level of Treasuries plus 700 basis points (note that the duration at default equals five). A exercises its option with B and receives a payment of US$6m $((0.07 - 0.03) * 5 * US\$30m)$, which is used to offset a portion of the loss sustained directly with C. If C does not default on its debt

A allows the put to expire and loses US$250,000 of premium, but sustains no loss on its US$12m of exposure to C. Note that, as with forwards, standard credit puts still provide the purchaser with payment if there is credit deterioration but not outright credit default; those with a binary payoff based strictly on default rather than deterioration can also be used.

Credit swaps

Credit swaps, such as TRSs and default swaps, can also be used to mitigate credit risk. As noted earlier, a TRS provides the seller with the economics of a risky bond in off-balance sheet form and the buyer with protection against deterioration or default.[7] Under a typical TRS, the buyer pays the seller a periodic coupon (equal to the interest flow of a bond), generally in exchange for a Libor flat flow; at maturity the seller receives a payment if the ending price of the reference instrument is greater than the agreed price, while the buyer receives a payment if the ending price is below the agreed price.

Given this structure, it is relatively easy to imagine using a TRS to reduce or hedge credit exposure to a counterparty. Returning to our previous example, let us assume Bank A wants to reduce or hedge its US$10m of credit exposure to Company C. A enters into a US$30m, 12-month TRS with Bank B, where A is short the bond on Company C through the TRS (for example, paying bond coupon and appreciation over 90, and receiving depreciation under 90).

Consider two scenarios. Scenario one: at the maturity of the transaction, A's exposure to C is US$12m and C continues to perform on all of its obligations. The bond trades at 98, so A makes a payment to B in the amount of US$2.6m (((90 − 98)/90) * US$30m)) plus interim coupons; note that the payment is defrayed by the full US$12m payment A expects to receive from C. Scenario two: C defaults on its debt obligations and the reference bond trades at 50. Under this scenario A does not receive its full US$12m payment from C, but receives a payment of US$13.3m (((90 − 50)/90) * US$30m), less interim coupons, from B. In addition to hedging credit exposure, as in this example, TRSs can also be used to free credit limits. Default swaps can also be employed to hedge credit exposure and free credit limits; we shall not present an example using default swaps given the similarities such derivatives share with both long credit puts.

Basket options and swaps, first-to-default swaps, and structured notes

Rather than simply hedge credit exposure to a single counterparty, a bank might be interested in hedging an entire portfolio of credits. This typically results in cheaper and more efficient management of portfolio credit exposures. A number of different mechanisms are available to manage such credit portfolio hedging, including credit basket options, basket swaps, and first-to-default swaps; these might be arranged directly or embedded in structured notes.

As we mentioned earlier, multi-credit derivatives can be used to simultaneously provide credit portfolio protection on a number of reference counterparties. Though they are structurally similar, it is important to remember that basket options and swaps provide a payout for every counterparty that defaults, while first-to-default swaps pay out only on the first credit that fails; portfolio coverage levels are thus quite different. Rather than arranging options and swaps directly, institutions can achieve the same goals through structured notes. As discussed earlier, structured notes are simply notes or bonds with embedded short or long derivatives and can easily be adapted to reduce credit exposures to a series of counterparties. Under a typical credit-based structured note, a number of counterparties are assembled in a basket that pays an enhanced coupon as long as the reference counterparties continue to perform on their debt obligations. If one or more defaults occur, the seller of the note ceases to pay coupons and/or principal, and has thus hedged its underlying credit exposure.

Consider the following example. Bank A has large potential exposures to Banks X, Y, and Z and wants to reduce its exposure to all three. Rather than selling separate credit forwards/swaps or buying credit puts on each bank, A sells a structured note to an investor on a private placement basis. Under the terms of the note the maturity is set at seven years (which covers the longest maturity of A's swaps with the three banks) and an enhanced coupon is calculated to provide the investor with additional economic incentive for holding the credit-linked note (for example, for selling it the basket option). If there is an event of default by any one of the three institutions prior to maturity of the note, no further coupons are paid and the investor's principal is effectively forfeited.

Assume the following scenarios. Scenario one: neither X, Y, or Z defaults during the life of the note, so the investor receives principal and enhanced coupons from A; A, in turn, receives full payments from each of X, Y, and Z on individual derivatives. Scenario two: X defaults, leaving A with a loss on its derivatives with X. In exchange, however, A makes no further coupon or principal payments to the investor and, as such, has minimized its credit loss (that is, it has hedged its credit exposure).[8] It is easy to imagine developing parallel structures on a stand-alone basis, for example, through simple use of basket options or first-to-default swaps; the logic remains the same.

Though credit derivatives are a useful hedging mechanism, and become more valuable as the underlying market deepens, they cannot always be used as a risk mitigant. While liquidity in credit derivatives has grown tremendously since the late 1990s and into the millennium, structures are not available at reasonable prices on every possible reference credit, meaning that economic hedges cannot always be created. Credit derivative hedgers must also be sensitive to information disclosure that might circulate in the marketplace. For instance, if a bank is known to be actively looking for pricing on a very large corporate default option, it is "showing its hand" regarding existing or potential credit-sensitive business – information it would rather keep confidential.

Credit scenario/stress analysis

The next element of active credit risk management we discuss centers on the implementation and use of credit scenario/stress analysis. The ability to stress the nature and shape of a bank's counterparty credit portfolios provides valuable information about "doomsday" scenarios and their potential impact on financial stability. Being able to project, through computerized simulations or "what if?" scenario analyses, the path of stochastic market variables (for example, underlying market prices and rates, default probabilities, recovery rates) and, hence, the future size and concentration of credit exposure/credit losses for credit portfolios, is an important component in the active management of risk. This is especially true when considering the "unthinkable." Although high severity/low probability events are, by definition, not meant to happen with great frequency, they have occurred with alarming regularity in recent years. We need only consider the disruptive events of the 1990s and early 2000s to realize that they were often much larger than statistical distributions would have predicted (for example, they had much "fatter tails" than assumed *ex ante*). The deep and protracted bad loan problem in Japan from the 1990s into the new millennium, the emerging market crises of the mid to late-1990s, the hedge fund collapse of 1998, the largest-ever US bankruptcies of 2001–2 (for example, Enron, WorldCom), the significant UK bankruptcies/restructurings of 2001 (for example, Railtrack, Marconi), the implosion of the US energy industry in 2002, the record corporate default rates of 2001–2, and so forth, were damaging from a risk perspective.

Use of scenario analysis – particularly in situations where an analyst is concerned about the size of current and potential exposures, the credit quality of a given counterparty, the clustering or concentration of seemingly uncorrelated credit exposures, or the impact of "extreme" events – can lead to proactive decision-making on restructuring of exposures and portfolios (through implementation of credit risk mitigating techniques, increase in credit reserves/capital, reallocation of limits, purchase of deep out-of-the-money protection, and so on). Scenarios can be run through simulation processes like those mentioned in Chapters 11 and 12. For instance, a bank might use a Monte Carlo simulation to generate paths for stochastic market variables (based on criteria specified by the user and samples drawn at random from a distribution) and revalue derivative (and other credit-sensitive) portfolios at select points in time; the repetition of tens of thousands of runs generates an average valuation for a given portfolio. Such simulation, as we have already discussed, is particularly computer intensive, but yields reasonably realistic results. A bank might also make use of fabricated "what if?" scenarios. Through this process credit-risky instruments are revalued at select points in time based on user-specified (rather than simulated) stochastic market variable inputs. For instance, rather than using a mathematical model to chart the future path of US interest rates, the credit officer might simply assume that rates will move by 50 or 100 or 250 basis points across the curve during the next quarter; this allows for easy input of very extreme moves without making any assumptions about the likelihood of occurrence. Scenario analysis can also be computer intensive but does not require the creation of thousands of sample runs; since the market inputs are user-defined rather than simulated, the process permits ready use of "shock," or extreme, market scenarios.

The potential exposure framework we have discussed at length and the portfolio aggregation techniques discussed in Chapter 11 provide an indication of the current status of exposures within a given portfolio and where such exposures may go in the future (in a worst-case scenario, average case scenario, and so on). However, implementation of credit simulations/scenarios can provide analysts with even more flexibility by allowing exposures to be modeled dynamically through combinations of extreme market and default scenarios. For instance, simulations/scenarios can be employed to project the:

■ Direction of counterparty credit exposure at select points in time (for example, prior to maturity of certain trades and after the maturity of others) for an entire portfolio of same-product trades and, assuming correlations, multiple product trades (including linear credit-risky instruments, such as undrawn funding commitments).

■ Direction of credit exposure at select points in time for single or multiple counterparties within an industry or region.

■ Effect of portfolio credit exposure as barriers and digitals are triggered into existence or extinguished and removed from the portfolio.

■ Direction of credit exposure for instantaneous multiple standard deviation moves in single or multiple markets (again, utilizing correlation assumptions).

■ Expected and unexpected credit losses, given both projected or assumed market moves and instantaneous default at select points in time.

■ Migration of credit quality and its impact on expected and unexpected credit losses, credit reserves and capital.

For instance, a credit officer evaluating the current exposure a bank has with a particular counterparty might be especially concerned with a steepening (or a complete upward shift) in the US yield curve, as the bank might be a significant fixed rate payer to the counterparty. Perhaps the portfolio of trades with the counterparty also includes numerous out-of-the-money ¥/US$ reverse knock-in options that will create substantial exposure once select ¥/US$ levels are breached. In addition, the credit officer might be concerned about the financial condition of the counterparty, having followed the counterparty's financial deterioration over the prior months. A comprehensive scenario analysis can provide information on several different issues. For example, by moving the US curve upwards by 50 basis points and ¥/US$ rates by ¥10/US$, and then recomputing the market value of the entire portfolio of swaps and barriers, the credit officer may discover actual exposure rises from US$10m to US$35m. Assuming an instantaneous default by the counterparty following these market moves, the credit officer may feel that exposure is excessively large. Note that the scenarios being run may be extreme and in excess of that predicted by the REE framework (that is, stress-testing based on five or ten, rather than two or three, standard deviation market moves); that, however, is precisely the point of running such "unthinkable" market scenarios. By using them, the credit officer becomes more sensitive to the true effect of a sudden, very low-probability, upward movement in interest and currency rates. The results of the scenario analysis, coupled with the credit officer's own view about the potential deterioration of the counterparty, might then lead to certain proactive steps being taken to manage the exposure or protect the firm (for example, requiring the desk to take additional credit reserves, assigning or collateralizing exposures, purchasing default protection from a third party, and so on). This is just one simple example of how an institution can use the simulation-scenario process; there are other ways of using this framework. For instance, a bank might:

■ Apply similar scenarios to all of its counterparties in a given industry or country, in order to understand the potential impact of industry-wide or country-wide collapse (such as we have seen in the energy sector or various emerging market nations).

■ Stress the entire credit exposure portfolio regularly by examining various risk drivers and applying a range of stress scenarios – from the highly likely to the highly unlikely.

■ Investigate the sensitivity of the portfolio to stressed correlation patterns in order to discover pockets of "hidden concentration" that might become apparent in the face of a crisis situation.

In order to make the exercise particularly useful, it can be helpful to run the same stress scenarios on a regular basis (for example, every month or quarter). By tracking the changes in the results from period to period (rather than just the absolute magnitude) a firm can determine whether it is becoming more or less credit risky in particular sectors or countries, which is very useful management information. In addition, it is often helpful to "ground" such scenarios in extreme moves that have actually occurred in the past, particularly when results are being reviewed by senior management. While it is simple enough to create any number of hypothetical scenarios, it can be especially helpful when others can relate to them; consider, for example, stress scenarios that duplicate the 1987 stock market crash, or the LTCM/Russian crisis, and so forth. Doing this lets senior management understand that such "extreme" low probability events have actually happened, and that the exercise is by no means a purely theoretical one.

Dynamic allocation of credit resources

A third area of active risk management centers on the dynamic allocation of credit resources. Once a firm has defined its credit risk appetite it must set appropriate limits for all credit-based products in order to allocate and control its appetite; though all credit limits are vital, we confine our discussion to those related to derivatives. While many institutions grant overall derivative credit limits based on internal ratings and/or financial resource data (total asset size, total capital size, and so on), specific limit measurement and management techniques can vary widely. For instance, limits might be based on total potential exposure, gross potential exposure, or net potential exposure; in certain cases, they may actually be centered on net actual exposures. Despite the misleading nature of "notional" amounts of derivatives, some firms (particularly end users) still set limits based on notional amounts. This, unfortunately, may not be particularly useful or meaningful, because — as we have discussed earlier – there is often little correlation between the notional size and credit risk exposure of a derivative. There is no single correct approach to setting and managing limits, and much depends on an individual institution's approach towards the credit management process. Regardless of the approach, there appears to be a general trend towards more dynamic management of credit resources; the availability of improved technologies and more comprehensive risk mitigation techniques have helped make this a reality.

Single limit structure

The single limit structure is fundamental to many institutions active in derivatives. Under this arrangement, the credit division sets and controls all credit limits and manages to a single figure, such as gross or net potential exposure. Credit officers may approve transactions in advance of trading, and exposures can be allocated against limits as they are utilized (in a manner consistent with the specific incremental transaction and portfolio aggregation techniques employed by the institution). This type of approach to limit management tends to be rather one-dimensional.

Multiple limit structure

Institutions that manage derivative portfolios more actively often use a multiple limit structure. Under this approach, a credit division may set an overall derivative credit limit per counterparty (for example, gross or net potential exposure). It may sub-allocate a portion of the limit as a "trading desk limit" which individual derivative traders utilize without prior approval from the credit division. This means derivative traders must have credit risk quantification tools in order to calculate *ex ante* credit exposure; once credit risk exposure has been computed it can be applied by traders to the trading desk limit and used to determine the allocation of appropriate credit reserves and capital. This process also requires a system capable of indicating, on a relatively dynamic basis, remaining limit availability (which is necessarily a function of current potential exposure). The trading desk sub-allocation limit can be designed as a fixed percentage of the overall credit limit established by the credit officer (for example, perhaps 70 percent or 80 percent of the total). Once the trading desk approaches its allocated limit the credit officer reviews the acceptability of additional exposures. While in the 20 to 30 percent "buffer zone," a trader can still execute derivative transactions, but must do so by obtaining approval from a credit officer. It is while in the buffer zone that the credit officer and the derivative trader can review exposures and determine how best to manage incremental deals (by requesting collateral, assigning or recouponing certain existing deals, purchasing credit puts from a third party, and so on). Rather than focusing strictly on potential exposure limits, the multiple limit structure might be based on both actual (MTM) exposure limits and potential exposure limits. An analyst may grant larger potential exposure limits if it has the flexibility to manage actual exposures more proactively; for instance, if the credit officer has the ability to enforce risk mitigating techniques as actual exposures begin to rise, he or she may feel more comfortable granting larger potential exposures to the trading desk.

Credit charge structure

Certain institutions operate under a credit charge structure, with the credit division charging trading desks internally for use of credit limits. The credit division acts, in essence, as a "shadow" profit center (though one that theoretically operates near "break even" if it is functioning correctly). For example, a credit officer may establish overall credit limits (perhaps based on expected credit losses or actual exposure) and set internal profit hurdle rates that a desk must earn and pay to the credit division. The hurdle rates required by the credit division are, in large part, a function of a counterparty's internal credit rating and probability of default. Thus, a transaction with an A-rated credit carries a higher charge than the same transaction with an AA, but a lower charge than a BBB. In addition, incremental transactions within the same ratings class that cross a certain threshold level might attract higher credit charges to compensate for an increase in the overall level of credit exposure (for example, increased concentrations). This type of credit allocation structure requires implementation of an expected–unexpected credit loss framework and a risk-adjusted performance process, as well as rigorous internal credit analysis and complete confidence in the ability of a trading desk to price, in either actual or shadow form, the appropriate credit charges on trades. Mispricing of credit resources is a critical issue: if a credit division charges too little, it will have insufficient "revenues" to cover the actual credit losses that will ultimately arise; if it charges too much, the trading desk will find itself in an uncompetitive situation against other dealers in the market.

Regardless of the specific limit structure used to manage exposures, there must be a strong linkage into the risk governance issues discussed in Chapter 3. That is, the limits granted (and periodically adjusted) must be directly related to the risk tolerance specified by the board of directors. If limits permit too much risk-taking, creating exposures (and potential losses) that are well in excess of what the firm has defined as its maximum tolerance, then the governance process is clearly flawed. Exposures accommodated under limit allocations must always be reported back through the management hierarchy, so that those in executive management and the board of directors are ultimately aware of actual exposures. Exceptions and violations must likewise be handled through proper procedures that reflect sound internal controls and provide for appropriate senior management visibility, particularly as related to large concentrations and troublesome exposures.

Technology and the effective management of exposures

In order for dynamic credit risk management to be effective a firm must have an appropriate technology base. Many of the ideas regarding quantitative and qualitative management of derivative credit exposures work well in theory, but fail in practice if credit technology is unable to support the computation of risk and distribution of information. If proper systems are not available, the dynamic management of credit exposures is difficult (and, arguably, impossible); but, if they exist, then the risk management topics we have discussed above are achievable.

While there are many ways of designing systems platforms to accomplish the tasks indicated above (detailed discussion is well outside the scope of this book), fundamental requirements of a technology base most often center on:

- Credit analytic engines, with the functionality to draw in transaction details from individual business units, compute credit exposures, and run simulations/scenarios.

- Credit databases, with a clean population of indicative data (for example, ratings, defaults, recoveries, trade and counterparty identifiers).

- Credit monitoring interfaces, with functionality to see both trade level detail as well as portfolio aggregations.

Information must be accessible by authorized parties at a moment's notice (meaning flexible communications based on networking and use of corporate intranets, for example), and sufficiently flexible that it can be converted from an analyst's decision-making tool into a senior manager's information tool.[9] Instantaneous access, however, does not mean true real-time capabilities.

Credit analytic engine

A credit analytic engine forms the centerpiece of any credit technology platform. It is the essential element that permits computation of credit exposures through different analytic/simulation schemes, including those we have discussed in earlier chapters. Though architecture can vary widely, an engine must be able to draw in transaction level data (such as might be found on a trade ticket, including notional amount, transaction type, derivative type, maturity, strike price, currency, and so on) and access internally developed (or externally purchased) analytic/simulation routines to compute current and potential exposures, determine capital attributions, and so forth.

- *Exposure engine*: the starting point for many credit analytic platforms is a module that permits transaction and portfolio-based computation of current and potential exposures. Such an exposure engine is most likely to be the primary mechanism by which trade level detail from individual business units is accessed; such data, coupled with indicatives from the credit database mentioned below, permits initial computation of trade exposures. These can then be incorporated into portfolios so that counterparty portfolio exposures can be determined (often by accessing the simulation engine noted immediately following).

■ *Simulation/scenario engine*: we have discussed at several points in the text how simulation capabilities can be utilized in the credit risk management process; they can be used to generate risk factors or REEs for initial credit decision-making; credit migration paths for the expected and unexpected credit loss framework; portfolio credit exposures (portfolio credit vectors) for measurement of overall counterparty exposures; and, simulation-scenario analyses for projecting various future credit exposure and credit loss scenarios.

■ *Calculators*: a key element in the dynamic management of credit exposures includes understanding how risk exposure changes through an incremental transaction in order to respond to trading desk requests with speed and confidence. A credit analytic engine that provides on-line capabilities for analyzing the risk of incremental derivative transactions "on-the-fly" is essential in being able to achieve this goal. For instance, calculators that generate relevant REE figures for many of the complex derivatives discussed in this text (as well as plain vanilla derivatives such as interest rate and currency swaps, bond options, caps/floors, swaptions, and so on) are useful for analysts faced with immediate credit decisions. The REE for a given product can be derived in many ways; we have presented certain possibilities in this text, but it is clear that many other alternatives are available. To the extent an institution can accommodate an evaluation framework into a risk calculator, the speed and consistency of decision-making can improve.

While determination of REE is critical, it is important that calculators also be able to compute transaction return. We discussed in Chapter 11 the importance of determining expected and unexpected credit losses and mapping the results into the risk-adjusted performance framework. A credit calculator which is able to develop information on REEs, ECLs, and UCLs should also absorb information on gross return, liquidity/funding charges, and overhead charges. Together with additional policy-related directives regarding the bank's appetite for default risk as well as its target leverage, the calculator can generate information such as risk-adjusted return on risk-adjusted capital (and similar measures). The availability of this on-line information provides the risk officer (and/or trader) with the ability to compare competing transactions, and ultimately helps the bank ensure it is undertaking credit-risky business that maximizes risk-adjusted return.

Credit database

A credit database is essential for accurate computation, aggregation, and reporting of exposures. Indeed, any bank pursuing IRB approval under either the basic or advanced methodologies must demonstrate the existence of a robust and properly controlled credit database. This dimension of credit technology provides information that can be used in exposure computation, simulation, risk analysis, decision-making, and management information reporting. A credit database is likely to include comprehensive indicative data, including counterparty/security identifiers, corporate hierarchies, internal and external credit ratings, netting documentation flags, collateral flags, historical default probabilities (derived from rating agency information and/or proprietary bank information), historical recoveries (perhaps by level of subordination if rating agency information is employed), credit spread information, and so on; it may also compile important trend information, such as the historical path of internal credit ratings and historical credit limit usage. The database can also provide the simulation engine with supplemental market and volatility information required to generate runs.

Credit monitoring interface

Though a credit analytic engine and a credit database are the essential "nuts and bolts" needed to compute credit exposures, users still require a practical mechanism by which to view and interpret results. This can be accomplished through a credit-monitoring interface, a tool that can be used to view/analyze and report exposures. From an internal credit monitoring perspective, the interface permits a credit officer to call-up, by counterparty, all relevant trade-level credit exposure information. For derivatives this can include parameters such as:

- gross actual exposure

- net actual exposure

- net actual exposure, net of collateral (where applicable)

- gross fractional exposure

- gross potential exposure

- net potential exposure

- expected and unexpected credit losses.

Note that "on/off" switches that reflect netting/no netting and collateral/no collateral conditions can be helpful in understanding the effect of removing netting and collateral.

Depending on the specific techniques employed in the management of limits, it may also include information such as:

■ gross/net potential (REE) exposure limit

■ actual exposure limit

■ maximum maturity limit

■ maximum expected credit loss limit

■ collateral (incremental or pooled), including current market value

■ mark-to-market agreement, including dollar or time trigger points

■ termination/downgrade option dates or trigger points

■ credit derivative hedges.

Ancillary on-screen information for the counterparty might include:

■ internal rating or credit score

■ external ratings

■ status of master agreement/documentation.

As indicated, the system should provide trade level and portfolio views. The aggregation of portfolio exposures should permit review of data by industry, region, country, credit rating, and so on, to ensure appropriate management of portfolio concentration risks. Institutions obviously do not look at derivative counterparty exposures in isolation from other exposures (such as corporate inventories, spot currency exposures). Though they may have different means of aggregating and highlighting counterparty credit risks, institutions must include all counterparty credit exposures as a part of effective credit risk monitoring and management. (This, of course, is consistent with the treatment of portfolio exposures in the credit portfolio models we described in Chapter 12.)

To be effective and link into proper governance practices, a firm's technology must be very robust. The platform must have proper security and controls to ensure that it remains independent of front-office activities, and appropriate offsite redundancies to protect against business interruption and broader disasters. It should be subject to regular internal and external audits (on underlying code, analytics processes (to minimize model risk), data integrity, and so on). It is worth noting that "off-the-shelf" technology packages providing much of the functionality cited above have improved dramatically in recent years. Any third party system a firm might employ needs to be properly vetted from an internal perspective and must have proper links into the credit database and internal audit/finance controls.

To summarize aspects of the discussion above, Figure 13.3 illustrates distinct elements of the dynamic credit risk management process.

ADDRESSING ANCILLARY CREDIT RISK MANAGEMENT ISSUES

In the remainder of this chapter we conclude with thoughts on ancillary issues that credit officers must often consider during the course of their analysis and evaluation of derivative transactions.

Transaction motivation and suitability

In previous chapters we have introduced a framework that provides the risk officer with possible means of quantifying derivative credit risks. Such information, as we have seen, is vital in order for an officer to make reasoned credit decisions. The amount of potential credit exposure that must be allocated against credit limits, and which is ultimately included in the credit portfolio, however, forms only one element of the credit decision. Assuming a credit officer has completed a rigorous credit analysis of the counterparty and reviewed the quantitative risk aspects of the transaction under consideration, he or she must still consider a number of critical issues before arriving at a final decision; one of these issues relates to transaction motivation/suitability. Although counterparties enter into derivative transactions for a variety of reasons, we may summarize the primary motivating factors as

■ hedging

■ arbitraging/yield enhancing

■ speculating.

In the course of transaction analysis and decision-making, it is advisable for credit officers to focus on the reason a client is contemplating the execution of a particular derivative.

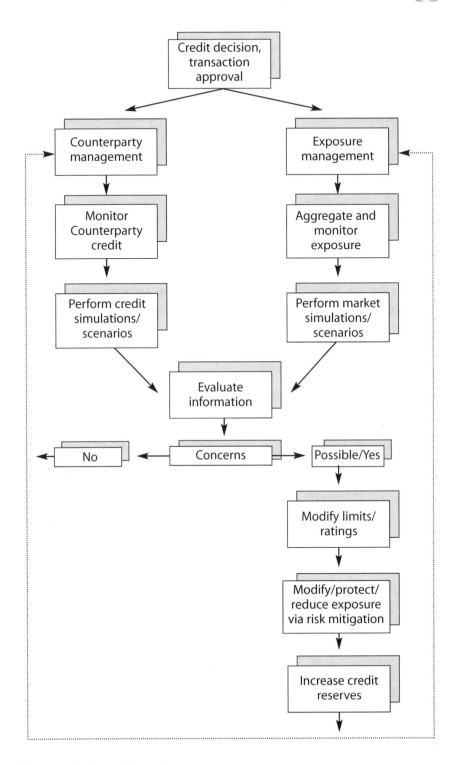

Figure 13.3 Dynamic credit exposure management

Hedge

Counterparties enter into a *hedge* transaction in order to protect assets, liabilities, revenues, or expenses from movements in a particular market or reference. Derivative transactions executed for legitimate hedging purposes are generally thought to be the soundest, and most "benign," from a credit perspective. A credit officer analyzing a proposed transaction often takes greater comfort when a derivative is executed as a hedge, because a hedge is established in order to protect a company from movement in an underlying market.[10] If a hedge is properly constructed, gain on the underlying flow will be offset by loss on the derivative, and vice versa, so that no meaningful financial deterioration is likely to result; indeed, derivatives employed for hedging purposes can often improve a client's financial position. Note that improperly constructed derivative hedges can be financially damaging; care must therefore be taken to ensure the hedge operates as it is intended to (this can often be accomplished through scenario analysis/stress-testing). Hedge transactions are typically seen as suitable and appropriate for a broad range of counterparties.

Arbitrage/yield enhancement

A counterparty might enter into an *arbitrage/yield enhancement* transaction in order to obtain incremental earnings (or lower funding costs) on a low-risk basis; low-risk derivative transactions executed to take advantage of discrepancies/anomalies in markets and provide incremental yield can easily be created. A credit officer considering a low-risk derivative arbitrage/yield enhancing transaction (for example, one that is not highly leveraged) is likely to take reasonable comfort from such a strategy, particularly if it is clear that the downside risk of loss to the counterparty is limited. It should be emphasized, of course, that certain transactions thought of as "yield enhancing" (for example, writing options in order to generate additional premium income) may not be low risk, so care must be taken in the evaluation process. True unleveraged (or only modestly leveraged) arbitrage transactions are generally seen as suitable for a broad range of counterparties.

Speculation

Counterparties enter into *speculation* in order to generate income by taking a particular view of a market. Derivative transactions executed to take an outright position in market direction or volatility are generally thought to be the riskiest of the strategies discussed in this section, as they can generate large gains or losses and are often constructed with minimal, or no, downside protection (indeed, many carry maximum leverage). Speculation via derivatives can be particularly dangerous for counterparties that lack the financial resources to support significant financial losses. Highly leveraged derivative transactions, which represent the "pinnacle" of speculation, can be particularly damaging if not properly understood and managed, and must always be viewed with a skeptical eye by credit officers (and end users). Purely speculative transactions are generally seen as suitable only for those institutions with sufficient financial resources to sustain potential losses and enough financial knowledge to understand their nature and the risks being undertaken. Counterparties that insist on these types of transactions should be thoroughly vetted from a "suitability" perspective, as noted below.

Analyzing the fundamental motivation for entering into a derivative transaction helps credit officers (as well as account officers/derivatives marketers and legal officers) determine whether a transaction is suitable for a given counterparty. Derivatives that are based on speculation (leveraged or otherwise) are of particular concern. These are the very transactions that have, over the past two decades, been a significant source of losses for end users and intermediaries (for example, the legal/suitability losses related to Orange County, Procter and Gamble, Kingdom of Belgium, and so forth, noted in Chapter 2). This does not mean counterparties (particularly end users) should not engage in speculative derivative transactions. Many counterparties have the acumen and resources to support such speculative transactions and should be free to express a market view in any form they choose; as long as risks and returns are appropriately disclosed and considered, there is little for a credit officer to be concerned about. Other institutions, however, may not possess the same expertise or resources; it is in these instances that the credit officer must apply extra diligence. While weaker counterparties are equally free to express their own market views (and can certainly do so through derivatives), it is incumbent upon those involved (at both intermediaries and client institutions) to ensure the nature and risks of the transactions are thoroughly discussed and analyzed. In the extreme, as speculative positions move sharply against counterparties (and sharply in favor of intermediaries), credit exposures increase and credit concerns become heightened (these transactions, not coincidentally, are often the ones at the center of legal friction). Transactions that can materially impact the financial standing of a bank's counterparty are clearly of concern to the credit officer, as they can jeopardize the counterparty's ability to repay; secured transactions may therefore be a necessity. Understanding motivations for entering into derivative transaction is thus a critical element of the credit process.

Credit analysis and lengthening transaction maturities

We know that the world of derivatives has changed dramatically since the early 1980s. In addition to the introduction and use of increasingly complex products, many of which we have discussed in this book, transaction maturity has been lengthening on a steady basis. During the late 1980s and into the 1990s, the liquid swap markets of the financial system (for example, the United States, Japan, Germany, and the UK) quoted transactions out to a maximum of ten years. From the mid-1990s it became increasingly common to see vanilla transactions in the major markets quoted to 12, 15, 20, and even 30 years; the trend has continued into the millennium.

This market characteristic gives rise to several challenges. From a pure market risk perspective, we must question the validity and stability of pricing methods on long-term transactions. Since yield curves and other market references are generally not well developed beyond 10 to 15 years (with rare exception, such as the US interest rate market), there is a need to implement "subjective" mechanisms in pricing long-term transactions or place greater reliance on "assumption-driven" mark-to-model techniques. This may involve extrapolating existing curves to the longer maturities (which may result in significant valuation volatility) or using other proxies (such as long-term government or corporate bonds). Hedging can also become problematic; the absence of two-way flow or suitable long-term hedge liquidity might lead to use of "*stack and roll*" *hedges* (such as hedges constructed in the short-term liquid maturities that are rolled with each contract expiry, which can give rise to curve risk) or the use of substitutes (which can leave the bank exposed to significant basis risk).

From a credit risk perspective there are also considerable challenges in long-term derivative transactions. While credit analysis is a critical discipline for financial institutions its scope, by definition, is limited. Even the most talented financial analysts have difficulty projecting the financial performance of a given counterparty far into the future; projecting the possible creditworthiness of a counterparty 7, 10, or 15 years hence is a practical impossibility. Yet the financial industry demands such analysis (and the resulting decision-making), since end users and other intermediaries increasingly look to dealers and banks for unsecured, unaltered risk on 10, 15, and 20-year derivatives (note that this same analysis impacts all credit-sensitive business, though unsecured loans often contain financial covenants which provide some semblance of protection).

There is no simple solution to this issue. The credit officer must obviously continue to perform the best credit analysis possible and should continually keep abreast of actual or perceived changes in credit quality. He or she must also attempt to structure risk mitigation whenever possible in order to obtain some form of exit or protection should a counterparty begin to deteriorate during an extended maturity transaction. Altering the profit recognition on such transactions, as well as the economic incentives applied to traders and marketers, may also be an effective means of policing extended maturity business. In addition, specific incremental credit reserves can be created for extended maturity transactions. From a governance perspective, executive management and board directors should explicitly sanction long-term business (after they have understood the potential downside that can be created through credit-intensive, illiquid, unhedgeable risks) and be kept apprised of exposures as they build towards the firm's stated tolerance levels. Although this is a complex problem (which is likely to become even more challenging as maturities extend even further over the coming years) the most appropriate solution may be to enforce a combination of the ideas mentioned above.

Counterparty willingness versus ability to perform

One of the most dramatic topics to surface in the derivatives industry of the 1990s and early millennium has been the distinction between a counterparty's "willingness to perform" and its "ability to perform." We highlight this topic since non-payment (that is, default) by a counterparty on a derivative obligation, for any reason, is generally assumed to be the responsibility (or fault) of the credit division. Common assumptions suggest that if a counterparty does not perform on its obligation, it must be as a result of financial difficulties. The financial community has discovered in recent years that counterparties may choose not to honor their derivative obligations for reasons other than financial distress. Managing this issue from an internal standpoint is critical.

Ability to perform centers on a counterparty's financial capacity to perform on its obligations and is the essence of credit analysis. It forms the fundamental question that every credit officer must address in considering the extension of credit to a client. A rigorous financial analysis (supplemented, in certain instances, by on-site due diligence) provides answers regarding a counterparty's ability to perform on its financial obligations (including derivatives). Where ability to perform is questionable as a result of weak financial standing, the analyst may turn to one of the risk-mitigating techniques discussed above, or may choose not to extend any credit at all (even on a secured basis). This is the primary function of any credit division.

Willingness to perform relates to a counterparty's intent to perform on its obligations and is unrelated to its financial capability; indeed, "willingness" is not generally thought to be the direct responsibility of the credit division. However, failure to address this topic at some level within a bank can lead to economic losses that are identical to those arising from pure counterparty default; it may also involve protracted legal encounters and reputational damage. Although it is difficult to assign a precise definition to willingness to perform, it is generally taken to mean a counterparty's desire to deal in good faith on the derivative obligation into which it has entered. Unwillingness to perform results in non-payment on a derivative (or portfolio of derivatives) for reasons other than financial complications or difficulties. Unwillingness to perform may arise if a counterparty feels:

- It has lost too much money on a given transaction.

- It was misled into entering into a transaction that provided no economic benefit (or a benefit different from that originally sought).

- It did not understand the risk it was undertaking when entering into the transaction and/or was misinformed about the initial/ongoing risks of the transaction.

As indicated in Chapter 2, there have been cases of counterparties unwilling to perform on derivative obligations as a result of all three items.[11]

There is no perfect solution to the willingness to perform question. While an analyst can do his or her best to determine the financial strength of the counterparty and its projected ability to perform on derivatives at various points in the future, there is little to suggest that formal analysis provides information on whether an institution will ultimately be unwilling to perform on its obligations for non-credit reasons. Past history of unwillingness to pay can be determined and may be of some use; understanding the counterparty's motivation for entering into the transaction, as discussed above, can also prove helpful (for example, it is often the extreme speculative positions or the "erroneously constructed" hedges that generate losses and complications leading to an unwillingness to perform). Much, however, is ultimately left to the way a given market moves and the way a particular derivative structure is assembled and marketed. What is clear is that those within a bank involved in derivatives should make every effort to be as forthright and detailed as possible about the potential risks and rewards associated with a given derivative structure. In order to provide further scrutiny and stronger governance controls, some institutions may choose to create specialized procedures/committees to consider and then approve/reject derivative transactions that meet certain "high risk" parameters (for example, nature of client, potential downside of transaction from the client's perspective, client's legal authority to deal in such transactions, and so forth). This discipline, which adds an extra layer of "checks and balances," can be useful (though not perfect) in vetting out transactions that might ultimately subject a bank to client "unwillingness to pay." It is equally important for client institutions to be in a position to identify risks being assumed by entering into given transactions and measure the economic effects of the transactions once under way. Diligence, patience, and caution from end users and intermediaries will invariably go a long way in avoiding situations where counterparties might be unwilling to perform on contracted obligations. This will ensure continued growth, innovation, and participation in the derivatives market.

In concluding this work it remains only to re-emphasize that the derivatives market place offers important risk management and profit opportunities for all participants; opportunities are made more interesting and beneficial when derivatives are thoroughly understood and properly employed.

APPENDIX 1

Option Valuation

We have mentioned at several points in this text the importance of option pricing and valuation in the work of derivative product and credit professionals. The seminal work in the area of option valuation is the 1973 article by Black and Scholes entitled "The Pricing of Options and Corporate Liabilities," where the authors develop an analytic solution to the valuation of European options on non-dividend paying stocks. The simplifying assumptions used to develop the equation include unlimited borrow and lending at a constant risk-free rate, full access to short-selling, an underlying asset which follows a continuous time stochastic process, and frictionless markets with no taxes or transaction costs.[1]

It is not our intent in this appendix to develop a detailed explanation of the mathematics of the Black–Scholes model; in addition to the original article, there are many works that do an excellent job of explaining its quantitative aspects. Instead, we provide a very brief overview of the main points of the model and illustrate, with a few simple examples, the computation of option prices and comparative statics based on the model.

To commence, we define in advance several of the terms used in the equations below (note that we make a few changes to the notation from earlier in the text; most notably, CMP becomes S, and SP becomes X):

c is the value of a European call.

p is the value of a European put.

S is the stock price.

$S_{(T)}$ is the terminal stock price.

X is the strike price.

τ is the time to maturity.

r is the risk-free rate.

m is the expected return of the stock.

s is the standard deviation of the return.

We begin our outline by defining the value of a European call at expiry as

$$c(S_T, X, \tau) = \max(0, S_T - X) \tag{A1.1}$$

The value of the call today is simply the discounted value of the expected payoff at expiry:

$$c(S_T, X, \tau) = e^{-r\tau} E(\max(0, S_T - X)) \tag{A1.2}$$

As indicated above, stock prices under the Black–Scholes model follow a stochastic process; in this case prices follow a geometric Brownian motion, where the returns of the stock prices are lognormally distributed. Under the lognormal distribution the expected value of the stock at maturity of the option is:

$$E(S_T) = Se^{\left[\mu - \frac{\sigma^2}{2}\right]\tau} \tag{A1.3}$$

where the price of the stock, S, increases by the instantaneously compounded expected return μ less half the variance of the stock price. In the equation above, σ is the standard deviation of the expected return. Under risk neutrality, one of the key elements of the Black–Scholes framework, the value of the expected return, can be ignored. This occurs because an investor can create a risk-free portfolio by combining a short position in a call option (-c) with a delta equivalent amount of stock (ΔS); the perfect correlation between the call and the stock over a very small time period means gains on the call are offset by losses on the stock and vice versa. Therefore, the value of the option is not influenced by the expected return, and investors' risk preferences need not be considered; this greatly simplifies the pricing framework. Knowing that stock prices are distributed lognormally, we return to the equation presented in Chapter 5:

$$\ln(S_T) \rightarrow \phi\left[\ln(S) + \left[\mu - \frac{\sigma^2}{2}\tau\right], \sigma\sqrt{\tau}\right] \tag{A1.4}$$

Under risk neutrality, μ is replaced with the risk-free rate, r, yielding:

$$\ln(S_T) \to \phi\left[\ln(S) + \left[r - \frac{\sigma^2}{2}\tau\right], \sigma\sqrt{\tau}\right] \tag{A1.5}$$

Returning to equation A1.2, it is necessary to solve for the value of c:

$$c(S_T, X, \tau) = e^{-r\tau}\int_X^\infty (S_T - X)g(S_T)dS_T \tag{A1.6}$$

After a rather extensive mathematical exercise, equation (A1.6) yields the familiar Black-Scholes call valuation equation:

$$c(S_T, X, \tau) = S\,N(d_1) - Xe^{-r\tau}N(d_2) \tag{A1.7}$$

where $N(d_1)$ and $N(d_2)$, defined below, represent the cumulative probability distribution function for a standardized normal variable. The N(d) values can be obtained from standard tables of probability functions.
The values of d_1 and d_2 are shown as:

$$d_1 = \frac{\ln\left[\frac{S}{X}\right] + \left[r + \frac{\sigma^2}{2}\right]\tau}{\sigma\sqrt{\tau}} \tag{A1.8}$$

and:

$$d_2 = \frac{\ln\left[\frac{S}{X}\right] + \left[r - \frac{\sigma^2}{2}\right]\tau}{\sigma\sqrt{\tau}} \tag{A1.9}$$

where d_2 may also be expressed as:

$$d_2 = d_1 - \sigma\sqrt{\tau} \tag{A1.10}$$

Through this formula, we can value a European call option on a non-dividend paying stock, under the constraints detailed above.
Knowing the above, and employing put–call parity, which effectively says that due to boundary conditions and arbitrage:

$$c + Xe^{-rt} = p + S \tag{A1.11}$$

it is relatively easy to solve for the Black-Scholes equation for puts:

$$p(S_T, X, \tau) = Xe^{-r\tau}N(-d_2) - SN(-d_1) \tag{A1.12}$$

Let us consider a numerical example in order to demonstrate the model. Assume we want to purchase a 90-day European call on a stock with a current price of 20 and a strike price of 22 (that is, it is 9 percent out-of-the-money). Recall that τ is adjusted to a fraction of a year if the volatility measure is annualized; in this case τ equals 0.25 years. The risk free rate is 4 percent and the volatility of the stock is 20 percent.

The fair value of the call, based on the equations above, is:

$$d_1 = (\ln(20/22) + (0.04 + (0.20^2/2) * 0.25))/(0.20 * \sqrt{0.25})$$

$$= ((-0.0953) + (0.015))/0.10$$

$$= -0.803$$

$$d_2 = -0.803 - 0.10 = -0.903$$

$$c = 20 * N(-0.803) - 22 * (0.99) * N(-0.903)$$

Using statistical tables we determine the probabilities associated with $N(d_1)$ and $N(d_2)$:

$$c = 20 * (1 - 0.7967) - 22 * 0.99 * (1 - 0.8238)$$

$$= 4.066 - 3.837$$

$$= 0.229$$

Thus, one call on the stock is worth nearly US$0.23.

If we apply the same procedure to an in-the-money call (that is, the price S is now US$24, instead of US$20, with the strike remaining at US$22), the value of the call rises:

$$d_1 = (\ln(24/22) + (0.04 + (0.20^2/2) * 0.25))/(0.20 * \sqrt{0.25})$$

$$= ((0.087) + (0.015))/0.10$$

$$= 1.020$$

$$d_2 = 1.020 - 0.10 = 0.920$$

$$c = 24 * N(1.020) - 22 * (0.99) * N(0.920)$$

$$= 24 * 0.8461 - 22 * (0.99) * 0.8212$$

$$= 20.306 - 17.885$$

$$= 2.421$$

As we would expect, the value of the in-the-money call is much higher than the out-of-the-money call (at US\$2.42 vs. US\$0.23) as it already has intrinsic value.

Earlier we have described the comparative statics delta, gamma, vega, and theta; these statics measure an option's sensitivity to changes in the stock price, volatility, and time. Utilizing the Black–Scholes model, we highlight equations that measure these statics (note that we shall not consider rho, sensitivity of the option's value to a change in the risk-free rate, as the effects of rho on a stock option are generally negligible when compared with the other statics; nor will we consider "higher order" statics, such as "charm," "speed,"' and "color").

It can be shown that delta, which is the change in the option's price for a unit change in the stock price, is equal to the first derivative of the option price with respect to the stock price:

$$\Delta_c = \frac{\delta C}{\delta S} = N(d_1) \tag{A1.13}$$

The quantity we obtain from $N(d_1)$ above is precisely equal to delta. We shall not explore the mathematics behind this, but we may interpret the above as saying that a short call is delta-hedged by an amount of long stock equal to $N(d_1)$; conversely, a long call is delta-hedged by an amount of short stock equal to $N(d_1)$. The equation for puts is:

$$\Delta_p = \frac{\delta P}{\delta S} = -N(-d_1) \tag{A1.14}$$

Returning to the second example above, we note that the result obtained from $N(d_1)$ is equal to 0.846. This means that to delta hedge a short call the portfolio requires long position of 0.846 shares of stock; alternatively, to delta-hedge a long call the portfolio requires a short position of 0.846 shares of stock. This also means that if the stock rises by US\$1, the value of the call increases by US\$0.846.

Gamma, which is the change in the delta of the option for a unit change in the stock price, is the first derivative of delta with respect to the stock price, or the second derivative of the option price with respect to the stock price. This may be shown, for calls, as:

$$\Gamma_c = \frac{\delta \Delta_c}{\delta S} = \frac{\delta^2 C}{\delta S^2} = \frac{1}{S\sigma\sqrt{r}} N'(d_1) \tag{A1.15}$$

where

$$N'(d_1) = \frac{1}{\sqrt{2\pi}} e^{\frac{-d_1^2}{2}}$$ (A1.16)

The first derivative of $N(d_1)$ is the standard normal density function.
    The gamma of a put is:

$$\Gamma_p = \frac{\delta\Delta_p}{\delta S} = \frac{\delta^2 P}{\delta S^2} = \frac{1}{S\sigma\sqrt{\tau}} N'(d_1)$$ (A1.17)

which is precisely equal to the gamma of a call.
Returning to the example above, we calculate the gamma of the call as

$$\Gamma = 1/(24 * (0.20 * \sqrt{0.25})) * N'(d1)$$

$$= 0.4167 * N'(d1)$$

$$N'(d1) = 1/(2.507) * e^{-(0.520)}$$

$$= 0.2371$$

$$= 0.4167 * 0.2371$$

$$= 0.0988$$

Thus, for a US$1 increase in the stock price, the delta of the option rises by US$0.099.
    Theta, which is the change in the option's price for a change in time, is simply the derivative of the option price with respect to time until maturity. This, for a call option, is shown as:

$$\theta_c = \frac{\delta C}{\delta \tau} = -\frac{S\sigma}{2\sqrt{\tau}} N'(d_1) - rXe^{-r\tau} N(d_2)$$ (A1.18)

Where $N'(d_1)$ and $N(d_2)$ are defined above. Note the derivative of the call option price with respect to the price, if positive, yields a value greater than 0. The positive value of the derivative says that an option with a longer time to maturity, τ, has more value than an option with a shorter τ. However, we are interested, via theta, in determining how the price of the option deteriorates as time to maturity decreases (through some small interval τ), hence use of a negative in the equation above.

The theta for puts is given as:

$$\theta_p = \frac{\delta P}{\delta \tau} = \frac{S\sigma}{2\sqrt{\tau}} \, N'(d_1) + rXe^{-r\tau} N(-d_2) \qquad (A1.19)$$

Note that in the special case of an at-the-money European put, theta may not be negative; much depends on the interaction between τ and the present value of the strike price.

In our example, the theta of the call is equal to:

$$\theta = - ((24 * 0.20)/(2 * \sqrt{0.25})) * 0.2371 - (0.04 * 22 * 0.99 * 0.8212)$$

$$= - (4.8) * 0.2371 - 0.7154$$

$$= - 1.138 - 0.7154$$

$$= - 1.853$$

This means that if the time to maturity for the call increases by one year, the value of the call increases by US$1.853. We may also say that the actual daily decay in the value of the call is simply equal to US$1.853/365, or US$0.005. For one day's passage of time, the value of a long call option declines by US$0.005 (holding volatility, the underlying stock price, and the risk free rate constant); this is precisely equal to the time decay discussed throughout the text.

Vega (also known as "kappa" or "lambda") measures the change in the option's price for a change in the volatility of the underlying stock. The vega calculation for calls and puts is shown as:

$$V_{c \, or \, p} = \frac{\delta C}{\delta \sigma} = \frac{\delta P}{\delta \sigma} = S\sqrt{\tau} \, N'(d_1) \qquad (A1.20)$$

If vega is high, the option's value is very sensitive to small changes in volatility; if vega is low, the option's value is less sensitive to such changes. In our example, we can show the value of vega as

$$V = 24 * \sqrt{0.25} * 0.2371$$

$$= 2.845$$

Thus, for a unit increase in the volatility of the underlying stock (for example, from 20 to 21), the price of the call increases by US$0.028; for an increase from 20 to 30 percent, the price of the call increases by US$0.2845, and for an increase from 20 to 120 percent, the price rises by US$2.845.

This appendix is intended only as a brief primer on Black–Scholes. Readers are strongly urged to consult other references – Haley and Schall (1979), Hull (1989), Cox and Rubinstein (1985), Merton (1990), Gibson (1991), Dubofsky (1992), Eades (1992), Stoll and Whalley (1993), and Wilmott, Dewynne, and Howison (1995) among many others – for a comprehensive review of the Black–Scholes framework.

Twenty Questions for the Derivatives Desk

Listed below is a series of 20 questions that a risk officer can review with a derivatives specialist seeking credit approval for a transaction. By resolving these questions, the risk officer helps identify unique risk characteristics that may exist.

Swap-related derivatives

1. What is the size of the transaction, in notional terms? Does principal decrease or increase at any time and, if so, on what basis? Is the notional ever exchanged (for example, as in a currency swap)?

2. What is the maturity of the transaction? Are there periodic options to terminate?

3. What determines the payment of interim coupons/flows (for example, type of reference index)? Are there payment mismatches in either direction?

4. Are any of the swap payments or receipts structured in an off-market fashion? If so, how and why?

5. Is there a leverage component to the payments and/or receipts? How is the leverage defined? What is the impact of the leverage under different market conditions?

6. Does the swap contain any embedded options? How do such options affect or influence payments and/or receipts?

7. Is the payoff of the swap currency-protected?

Option-related derivatives

8. What is the size of the transaction, in notional or contract terms?

9. What is the maturity of the transaction?

10. How is the option exercised (for example, European, American, Bermudan)?

11. If the option is being purchased, how is premium being paid (for example, upfront, amortized, contingent)?

12. What is the relative starting price and strike price of the structure? Is the strike price set in a non-standard fashion (for example, deferred, forward, floating)?

13. What determines the payoff of the option? Does the option feature a payoff profile that adds or extinguishes exposure rapidly (for example, reverse knock-in/knock-out) or otherwise locks-in exposure (for example, cliquet, ladder, shout)?

14. Is there a leverage component to the payoff and, if so, how is it defined? What is the impact of the leverage under different market scenarios?

15. Is the payoff of the option currency-protected?

General

16. What is the client's motivation for entering into this transaction? Does the transaction require preparation and review of scenario analyses?

17. Are term sheets available and designed to convey details of the transaction in a clear fashion?

18. Has the client signed, or will it sign, standard documentation (including a master agreement)?

19. Does this transaction carry any special legal, operational, risk management, or credit considerations or does it require any special attention?

20. Does this transaction warrant the allocation of supplemental credit reserves and/or credit capital for any reason?

ISDA 2002
Master Agreement

As we have noted in the text, netting is an essential element of prudent and accurate credit risk management, and demands the use of a master agreement in a jurisdiction that recognizes the legal basis of netting. To provide additional detail on the matter we have included in this appendix the ISDA 2002 Master Agreement (Multicurrency Cross Border) referenced in Chapter 4.

The 2002 ISDA Master Agreement included in this section is reproduced with kind permission of ISDA; the Agreement is copyrighted and cannot be reprinted without permission of ISDA.

International Swaps and Derivatives Association, Inc.

2002 MASTER AGREEMENT

dated as of..

.... and ....

have entered and/or anticipate entering into one or more transactions (each a "Transaction") that are or will be governed by this 2002 Master Agreement, which includes the schedule (the "Schedule"), and the documents and other confirming evidence (each a "Confirmation") exchanged between the parties or otherwise effective for the purpose of confirming or evidencing those Transactions. This 2002 Master Agreement and the Schedule are together referred to as this "Master Agreement".

Accordingly, the parties agree as follows:–

1   Interpretation

(a)   *Definitions.* The terms defined in Section 14 and elsewhere in this Master Agreement will have the meanings therein specified for the purpose of this Master Agreement.

(b)   *Inconsistency.* In the event of any inconsistency between the provisions of the Schedule and the other provisions of this Master Agreement, the Schedule will prevail. In the event of any inconsistency between the provisions of any Confirmation and this Master Agreement, such Confirmation will prevail for the purpose of the relevant Transaction.

(c)   *Single Agreement.* All Transactions are entered into in reliance on the fact that this Master Agreement and all Confirmations form a single agreement between the parties (collectively referred to as this "Agreement"), and the parties would not otherwise enter into any Transactions.

2.   Obligations

(a)   *General Conditions.*

(i)   Each party will make each payment or delivery specified in each Confirmation to be made by it, subject to the other provisions of this Agreement.

(ii)   Payments under this Agreement will be made on the due date for value on that date in the place of the account specified in the relevant Confirmation or otherwise pursuant to this Agreement, in freely transferable funds and in the manner customary for payments in the required currency. Where settlement is by delivery (that is, other than by payment), such delivery will be made for receipt on the due date in the manner customary for the relevant obligation unless otherwise specified in the relevant Confirmation or elsewhere in this Agreement.

(iii)   Each obligation of each party under Section 2(a)(i) is subject to (1) the condition precedent that no Event of Default or Potential Event of Default with respect to the other party has occurred and is continuing, (2) the condition precedent that no Early Termination Date in respect of the relevant Transaction has occurred or been effectively designated and (3) each other condition specified in this Agreement to be a condition precedent for the purpose of this Section 2(a)(iii).

(b) *Change of Account.* Either party may change its account for receiving a payment or delivery by giving notice to the other party at least five Local Business Days prior to the Scheduled Settlement Date for the payment or delivery to which such change applies unless such other party gives timely notice of a reasonable objection to such change.

(c) *Netting of Payments.* If on any date amounts would otherwise be payable:–

(i) in the same currency; and

(ii) in respect of the same Transaction,

by each party to the other, then, on such date, each party's obligation to make payment of any such amount will be automatically satisfied and discharged and, if the aggregate amount that would otherwise have been payable by one party exceeds the aggregate amount that would otherwise have been payable by the other party, replaced by an obligation upon the party by which the larger aggregate amount would have been payable to pay to the other party the excess of the larger aggregate amount over the smaller aggregate amount.

The parties may elect in respect of two or more Transactions that a net amount and payment obligation will be determined in respect of all amounts payable on the same date in the same currency in respect of those Transactions, regardless of whether such amounts are payable in respect of the same Transaction. The election may be made in the Schedule or any Confirmation by specifying that "Multiple Transaction Payment Netting" applies to the Transactions identified as being subject to the election (in which case clause (ii) above will not apply to such Transactions). If Multiple Transaction Payment Netting is applicable to Transactions, it will apply to those Transactions with effect from the starting date specified in the Schedule or such Confirmation, or, if a starting date is not specified in the Schedule or such Confirmation, the starting date otherwise agreed by the parties in writing. This election may be made separately for different groups of Transactions and will apply separately to each pairing of Offices through which the parties make and receive payments or deliveries.

(d)   *Deduction or Withholding for Tax.*
(i)   *Gross-Up.* All payments under this Agreement will be made without any deduction or withholding for or on account of any Tax unless such deduction or withholding is required by any applicable law, as modified by the practice of any relevant governmental revenue authority, then in effect. If a party is so required to deduct or withhold, then that party ("X") will:–

(1)   promptly notify the other party ("Y") of such requirement;

(2)   pay to the relevant authorities the full amount required to be deducted or withheld (including the full amount required to be deducted or withheld from any additional amount paid by X to Y under this Section 2(d)) promptly upon the earlier of determining that such deduction or withholding is required or receiving notice that such amount has been assessed against Y;

(3)   promptly forward to Y an official receipt (or a certified copy), or other documentation reasonably acceptable to Y, evidencing such payment to such authorities; and

ISDA® 2002

(4)   if such Tax is an Indemnifiable Tax, pay to Y, in addition to the payment to which Y is otherwise entitled under this Agreement, such additional amount as is necessary to ensure that the net amount actually received by Y (free and clear of Indemnifiable Taxes, whether assessed against X or Y) will equal the full amount Y would have received had no such deduction or withholding been required. However, X will not be required to pay any additional amount to Y to the extent that it would not be required to be paid but for:–

(A)   the failure by Y to comply with or perform any agreement contained in Section 4(a)(i), 4(a)(iii) or 4(d); or

(B)   the failure of a representation made by Y pursuant to Section 3(f) to be accurate and true unless such failure would not have occurred but for (I) any action taken by a taxing authority, or brought in a court of competent jurisdiction, after a Transaction is entered into (regardless of whether such action is taken or brought with respect to a party to this Agreement) or (II) a Change in Tax Law.

(ii)   *Liability.* If:–

(1)   X is required by any applicable law, as modified by the practice of any relevant governmental revenue authority, to make any deduction or withholding in respect of which X would not be required to pay an additional amount to Y under Section 2(d)(i)(4);

(2)   X does not so deduct or withhold; and

(3)   a liability resulting from such Tax is assessed directly against X,

then, except to the extent Y has satisfied or then satisfies the liability resulting from such Tax, Y will promptly pay to X the amount of such liability (including any related liability for interest, but including any related liability for penalties only if Y has failed to comply with or perform any agreement contained in Section 4(a)(i), 4(a)(iii) or 4(d)).

3.   Representations

Each party makes the representations contained in Sections 3(a), 3(b), 3(c), 3(d), 3(e) and 3(f) and, if specified in the Schedule as applying, 3(g) to the other party (which representations will be deemed to be repeated by each party on each date on which a Transaction is entered into and, in the case of the representations in Section 3(f), at all times until the termination of this Agreement). If any "Additional Representation" is specified in the Schedule or any Confirmation as applying, the party or parties specified for such Additional Representation will make and, if applicable, be deemed to repeat such Additional Representation at the time or times specified for such Additional Representation.

(a)   *Basic Representations.*

(i) *Status.* It is duly organised and validly existing under the laws of the jurisdiction of its organisation or incorporation and, if relevant under such laws, in good standing;

(ii) *Powers.* It has the power to execute this Agreement and any other documentation relating to this Agreement to which it is a party, to deliver this Agreement and any other documentation relating to this Agreement that it is required by this Agreement to deliver and to perform its obligations under this Agreement and any obligations it has under any Credit Support Document to which it is a party and has taken all necessary action to authorise such execution, delivery and performance;

(iii)   **No Violation or Conflict.** Such execution, delivery and performance do not violate or conflict with any law applicable to it, any provision of its constitutional documents, any order or judgment of any court or other agency of government applicable to it or any of its assets or any contractual restriction binding on or affecting it or any of its assets;

(iv)   **Consents.** All governmental and other consents that are required to have been obtained by it with respect to this Agreement or any Credit Support Document to which it is a party have been obtained and are in full force and effect and all conditions of any such consents have been complied with; and

(v)   **Obligations Binding.** Its obligations under this Agreement and any Credit Support Document to which it is a party constitute its legal, valid and binding obligations, enforceable in accordance with their respective terms (subject to applicable bankruptcy, reorganisation, insolvency, moratorium or similar laws affecting creditors' rights generally and subject, as to enforceability, to equitable principles of general application (regardless of whether enforcement is sought in a proceeding in equity or at law)).

(b)   **Absence of Certain Events.** No Event of Default or Potential Event of Default or, to its knowledge, Termination Event with respect to it has occurred and is continuing and no such event or circumstance would occur as a result of its entering into or performing its obligations under this Agreement or any Credit Support Document to which it is a party.

(c)   **Absence of Litigation.** There is not pending or, to its knowledge, threatened against it, any of its Credit Support Providers or any of its applicable Specified Entities any action, suit or proceeding at law or in equity or before any court, tribunal, governmental body, agency or official or any arbitrator that is likely to affect the legality, validity or enforceability against it of this Agreement or any Credit Support Document to which it is a party or its ability to perform its obligations under this Agreement or such Credit Support Document.

(d)   **Accuracy of Specified Information.** All applicable information that is furnished in writing by or on behalf of it to the other party and is identified for the purpose of this Section 3(d) in the Schedule is, as of the date of the information, true, accurate and complete in every material respect.

(e)   **Payer Tax Representation.** Each representation specified in the Schedule as being made by it for the purpose of this Section 3(e) is accurate and true.

(f)   **Payee Tax Representations.** Each representation specified in the Schedule as being made by it for the purpose of this Section 3(f) is accurate and true.

(g)   **No Agency.** It is entering into this Agreement, including each Transaction, as principal and not as agent of any person or entity.

4.   **Agreements**

Each party agrees with the other that, so long as either party has or may have any obligation under this Agreement or under any Credit Support Document to which it is a party:–

(a)   **Furnish Specified Information.** It will deliver to the other party or, in certain cases under clause (iii) below, to such government or taxing authority as the other party reasonably directs:–

(i)   any forms, documents or certificates relating to taxation specified in the Schedule or any Confirmation;

(ii)   any other documents specified in the Schedule or any Confirmation; and

(iii)   upon reasonable demand by such other party, any form or document that may be required or reasonably requested in writing in order to allow such other party or its Credit Support Provider to make a payment under this Agreement or any applicable Credit Support Document without any deduction or withholding for or on account of any Tax with such deduction or withholding at a reduced rate (so long as the completion, execution or submission of such form or document would not materially prejudice the legal or commercial position of the party in receipt of such demand), with any such form or document to be accurate and completed in a manner reasonably satisfactory to such other party and to be executed and to be delivered with any reasonably required certification,

in each case by the date specified in the Schedule or such Confirmation or, if none is specified, as soon as reasonably practicable.

(b)   **Maintain Authorisations.** It will use all reasonable efforts to maintain in full force and effect all consents of any governmental or other authority that are required to be obtained by it with respect to this Agreement or any Credit Support Document to which it is a party and will use all reasonable efforts to obtain any that may become necessary in the future.

(c)   **Comply With Laws.** It will comply in all material respects with all applicable laws and orders to which it may be subject if failure so to comply would materially impair its ability to perform its obligations under this Agreement or any Credit Support Document to which it is a party.

(d)   **Tax Agreement.** It will give notice of any failure of a representation made by it under Section 3(f) to be accurate and true promptly upon learning of such failure.

(e)   **Payment of Stamp Tax.** Subject to Section 11, it will pay any Stamp Tax levied or imposed upon it or in respect of its execution or performance of this Agreement by a jurisdiction in which it is incorporated, organised, managed and controlled or considered to have its seat, or where an Office through which it is acting for the purpose of this Agreement is located ("Stamp Tax Jurisdiction"), and will indemnify the other party against any Stamp Tax levied or imposed upon the other party or in respect of the other party's execution or performance of this Agreement by any such Stamp Tax Jurisdiction which is not also a Stamp Tax Jurisdiction with respect to the other party.

5.   Events of Default and Termination Events

(a)   **Events of Default.** The occurrence at any time with respect to a party or, if applicable, any Credit Support Provider of such party or any Specified Entity of such party of any of the following events constitutes (subject to Sections 5(c) and 6(e)(iv)) an event of default (an "Event of Default") with respect to such party:–

(i)   **Failure to Pay or Deliver.** Failure by the party to make, when due, any payment under this Agreement or delivery under Section 2(a)(i) or 9(h)(i)(2) or (4) required to be made by it if such failure is not remedied on or before the first Local Business Day in the case of any such payment or the first Local Delivery Day in the case of any such delivery after, in each case, notice of such failure is given to the party;

(ii)   **Breach of Agreement; Repudiation of Agreement.**

(1)   Failure by the party to comply with or perform any agreement or obligation (other than an obligation to make any payment under this Agreement or delivery under Section 2(a)(i) or 9(h)(i)(2) or (4) or to give notice of a Termination Event or any agreement or obligation under Section 4(a)(i), 4(a)(iii) or 4(d)) to be complied with or performed by the party in accordance with this Agreement if such failure is not remedied within 30 days after notice of such failure is given to the party; or

(2)   the party disaffirms, disclaims, repudiates or rejects, in whole or in part, or challenges the validity of, this Master Agreement, any Confirmation executed and delivered by that party or any Transaction evidenced by such a Confirmation (or such

action is taken by any person or entity appointed or empowered to operate it or act on its behalf);

(iii) *Credit Support Default.*

(1)   Failure by the party or any Credit Support Provider of such party to comply with or perform any agreement or obligation to be complied with or performed by it in accordance with any Credit Support Document if such failure is continuing after any applicable grace period has elapsed;

(2)   the expiration or termination of such Credit Support Document or the failing or ceasing of such Credit Support Document, or any security interest granted by such party or such Credit Support Provider to the other party pursuant to any such Credit Support Document, to be in full force and effect for the purpose of this Agreement (in each case other than in accordance with its terms) prior to the satisfaction of all obligations of such party under each Transaction to which such Credit Support Document relates without the written consent of the other party; or

(3)   the party or such Credit Support Provider disaffirms, disclaims, repudiates or rejects, in whole or in part, or challenges the validity of, such Credit Support Document (or such action is taken by any person or entity appointed or empowered to operate it or act on its behalf);

(iv)   *Misrepresentation.* A representation (other than a representation under Section 3(e) or 3(f)) made or repeated or deemed to have been made or repeated by the party or any Credit Support Provider of such party in this Agreement or any Credit Support Document proves to have been incorrect or misleading in any material respect when made or repeated or deemed to have been made or repeated;

(v)   *Default Under Specified Transaction.* The party, any Credit Support Provider of such party or any applicable Specified Entity of such party:–

(1)   defaults (other than by failing to make a delivery) under a Specified Transaction or any credit support arrangement relating to a Specified Transaction and, after giving effect to any applicable notice requirement or grace period, such default results in a liquidation of, an acceleration of obligations under, or an early termination of, that Specified Transaction;

(2)   defaults, after giving effect to any applicable notice requirement or grace period, in making any payment due on the last payment or exchange date of, or any payment on early termination of, a Specified Transaction (or, if there is no applicable notice requirement or grace period, such default continues for at least one Local Business Day);

(3)   defaults in making any delivery due under (including any delivery due on the last delivery or exchange date of) a Specified Transaction or any credit support arrangement relating to a Specified Transaction and, after giving effect to any applicable notice requirement or grace period, such default results in a liquidation of, an acceleration of obligations under, or an early termination of, all transactions outstanding under the documentation applicable to that Specified Transaction; or

(4)   disaffirms, disclaims, repudiates or rejects, in whole or in part, or challenges the validity of, a Specified Transaction or any credit support arrangement relating to a Specified Transaction that is, in either case, confirmed or evidenced by a document or other confirming evidence executed and delivered by that party, Credit Support Provider or Specified Entity (or such action is taken by any person or entity appointed or empowered to operate it or act on its behalf);

(vi)   ***Cross-Default*** . If "Cross-Default" is specified in the Schedule as applying to the party, the occurrence or existence of:

(1)   a default, event of default or other similar condition or event (however described) in respect of such party, any Credit Support Provider of such party or any applicable Specified Entity of such party under one or more agreements or instruments relating to Specified Indebtedness of any of them (individually or collectively) where the aggregate principal amount of such agreements or instruments, either alone or together with the amount, if any, referred to in clause (2) below, is not less than the applicable Threshold Amount (as specified in the Schedule) which has resulted in such Specified Indebtedness becoming, or becoming capable at such time of being declared, due and payable under such agreements or instruments before it would otherwise have been due and payable; or

(2)   a default by such party, such Credit Support Provider or such Specified Entity (individually or collectively) in making one or more payments under such agreements or instruments on the due date for payment (after giving effect to any applicable notice requirement or grace period) in an aggregate amount, either alone or together with the amount, if any, referred to in clause (1) above, of not less than the applicable Threshold Amount;

(vii)   ***Bankruptcy.*** The party, any Credit Support Provider of such party or any applicable Specified Entity of such party:–

(1) is dissolved (other than pursuant to a consolidation, amalgamation or merger); (2) becomes insolvent or is unable to pay its debts or fails or admits in writing its inability generally to pay its debts as they become due; (3) makes a general assignment, arrangement or composition with or for the benefit of its creditors; (4)(A) institutes or has instituted against it, by a regulator, supervisor or any similar official with primary insolvency, rehabilitative or regulatory jurisdiction over it in the jurisdiction of its incorporation or organisation or the jurisdiction of its head or home office, a proceeding seeking a judgment of insolvency or bankruptcy or any other relief under any bankruptcy or insolvency law or other similar law affecting creditors' rights, or a petition is presented for its winding-up or liquidation by it or such regulator, supervisor or similar official, or (B) has instituted against it a proceeding seeking a judgment of insolvency or bankruptcy or any other relief under any bankruptcy or insolvency law or other similar law affecting creditors' rights, or a petition is presented for its winding-up or liquidation, and such proceeding or petition is instituted or presented by a person or entity not described in clause (A) above and either (I) results in a judgment of insolvency or bankruptcy or the entry of an order for relief or the making of an order for its winding-up or liquidation or (II) is not dismissed, discharged, stayed or restrained in each case within 15 days of the institution or presentation thereof; (5) has a resolution passed for its winding-up, official management or liquidation (other than pursuant to a consolidation, amalgamation or merger); (6) seeks or becomes subject to the appointment of an administrator, provisional liquidator, conservator, receiver, trustee, custodian or other similar official for it or for all or substantially all its assets; (7) has a secured party take possession of all or substantially all its assets or has a distress, execution, attachment, sequestration or other legal process levied, enforced or sued on or against all or substantially all its assets and such secured party maintains possession, or any such process is not dismissed, discharged, stayed or restrained, in each case within 15 days thereafter; (8) causes or is subject to any event with respect to it which, under the applicable laws of any jurisdiction, has an analogous effect to any of the events specified in clauses (1) to (7) above (inclusive); or (9) takes any action in furtherance of, or indicating its consent to, approval of, or acquiescence in, any of the foregoing acts; or

(viii)   ***Merger Without Assumption.*** The party or any Credit Support Provider of such party consolidates or amalgamates with, or merges with or into, or transfers all or substantially all its assets to, or reorganises, reincorporates or reconstitutes into or as, another entity and, at the time of such consolidation, amalgamation, merger, transfer, reorganisation, reincorporation or reconstitution:–

(1)   the resulting, surviving or transferee entity fails to assume all the obligations of such party or such Credit Support Provider under this Agreement or any Credit Support Document to which it or its predecessor was a party; or

(2)   the benefits of any Credit Support Document fail to extend (without the consent of the other party) to the performance by such resulting, surviving or transferee entity of its obligations under this Agreement.

(b)   ***Termination Events.*** The occurrence at any time with respect to a party or, if applicable, any Credit Support Provider of such party or any Specified Entity of such party of any event specified below constitutes (subject to Section 5(c)) an Illegality if the event is specified in clause (i) below, a Force Majeure Event if the event is specified in clause (ii) below, a Tax Event if the event is specified in clause (iii) below, a Tax Event Upon Merger if the event is specified in clause (iv) below, and, if specified to be applicable, a Credit Event Upon Merger if the event is specified pursuant to clause (v) below or an Additional Termination Event if the event is specified pursuant to clause (vi) below:-

(i)   ***Illegality.*** After giving effect to any applicable provision, disruption fallback or remedy specified in, or pursuant to, the relevant Confirmation or elsewhere in this Agreement, due to an event or circumstance (other than any action taken by a party or, if applicable, any Credit Support Provider of such party) occurring after a Transaction is entered into, it becomes unlawful under any applicable law (including without limitation the laws of any country in which payment, delivery or compliance is required by either party or any Credit Support Provider, as the case may be), on any day, or it would be unlawful if the relevant payment, delivery or compliance were required on that day (in each case, other than as a result of a breach by the party of Section 4(b)):–

(1)   for the Office through which such party (which will be the Affected Party) makes and receives payments or deliveries with respect to such Transaction to perform any absolute or contingent obligation to make a payment or delivery in respect of such Transaction, to receive a payment or delivery in respect of such Transaction or to comply with any other material provision of this Agreement relating to such Transaction; or

(2)   for such party or any Credit Support Provider of such party (which will be the Affected Party) to perform any absolute or contingent obligation to make a payment or delivery which such party or Credit Support Provider has under any Credit Support Document relating to such Transaction, to receive a payment or delivery under such Credit Support Document or to comply with any other material provision of such Credit Support Document;

(ii)   ***Force Majeure Event.*** After giving effect to any applicable provision, disruption fallback or remedy specified in, or pursuant to, the relevant Confirmation or elsewhere in this Agreement, by reason of force majeure or act of state occurring after a Transaction is entered into, on any day:–

(1)   the Office through which such party (which will be the Affected Party) makes and receives payments or deliveries with respect to such Transaction is prevented from performing any absolute or contingent obligation to make a payment or delivery in respect of such Transaction, from receiving a payment or delivery in respect of such Transaction or from complying with any other material provision of this Agreement relating to such Transaction (or would be so prevented if such payment, delivery or compliance were required on that day), or it becomes impossible or

impracticable for such Office so to perform, receive or comply (or it would be impossible or impracticable for such Office so to perform, receive or comply if such payment, delivery or compliance were required on that day); or

(2)   such party or any Credit Support Provider of such party (which will be the Affected Party) is prevented from performing any absolute or contingent obligation to make a payment or delivery which such party or Credit Support Provider has under any Credit Support Document relating to such Transaction, from receiving a payment or delivery under such Credit Support Document or from complying with any other material provision of such Credit Support Document (or would be so prevented if such payment, delivery or compliance were required on that day), or it becomes impossible or impracticable for such party or Credit Support Provider so to perform, receive or comply (or it would be impossible or impracticable for such party or Credit Support Provider so to perform, receive or comply if such payment, delivery or compliance were required on that day),

so long as the force majeure or act of state is beyond the control of such Office, such party or such Credit Support Provider, as appropriate, and such Office, party or Credit Support Provider could not, after using all reasonable efforts (which will not require such party or Credit Support Provider to incur a loss, other than immaterial, incidental expenses), overcome such prevention, impossibility or impracticability;

(iii)   *Tax Event.* Due to (1) any action taken by a taxing authority, or brought in a court of competent jurisdiction, after a Transaction is entered into (regardless of whether such action is taken or brought with respect to a party to this Agreement) or (2) a Change in Tax Law, the party (which will be the Affected Party) will, or there is a substantial likelihood that it will, on the next succeeding Scheduled Settlement Date (A) be required to pay to the other party an additional amount in respect of an Indemnifiable Tax under Section 2(d)(i)(4) (except in respect of interest under Section 9(h)) or (B) receive a payment from which an amount is required to be deducted or withheld for or on account of a Tax (except in respect of interest under Section 9(h)) and no additional amount is required to be paid in respect of such Tax under Section 2(d)(i)(4) (other than by reason of Section 2(d)(i)(4)(A) or (B));

(iv)   *Tax Event Upon Merger.* The party (the "Burdened Party") on the next succeeding Scheduled Settlement Date will either (1) be required to pay an additional amount in respect of an Indemnifiable Tax under Section 2(d)(i)(4) (except in respect of interest under Section 9(h)) or (2) receive a payment from which an amount has been deducted or withheld for or on account of any Tax in respect of which the other party is not required to pay an additional amount (other than by reason of Section 2(d)(i)(4)(A) or (B)), in either case as a result of a party consolidating or amalgamating with, or merging with or into, or transferring all or substantially all its assets (or any substantial part of the assets comprising the business conducted by it as of the date of this Master Agreement) to, or reorganising, reincorporating or reconstituting into or as, another entity (which will be the Affected Party) where such action does not constitute a Merger Without Assumption;

(v)   *Credit Event Upon Merger.* If "Credit Event Upon Merger" is specified in the Schedule as applying to the party, a Designated Event (as defined below) occurs with respect to such party, any Credit Support Provider of such party or any applicable Specified Entity of such party (in each case, "X") and such Designated Event does not constitute a Merger Without Assumption, and the creditworthiness of X or, if applicable, the successor, surviving or transferee entity of X, after taking into account any applicable Credit Support Document, is materially weaker immediately after the occurrence of such Designated Event than that of X immediately prior to the occurrence of such Designated Event (and, in any such event, such party or its successor, surviving or transferee entity, as appropriate, will be the Affected Party). A "Designated Event" with respect to X means that:–

(1)   X consolidates or amalgamates with, or merges with or into, or transfers all or substantially all its assets (or any substantial part of the assets comprising the business conducted by X as of the date of this Master Agreement) to, or reorganises,

reincorporates or reconstitutes into or as, another entity;

(2)   any person, related group of persons or entity acquires directly or indirectly the beneficial ownership of (A) equity securities having the power to elect a majority of the board of directors (or its equivalent) of X or (B) any other ownership interest enabling it to exercise control of X; or

(3)   X effects any substantial change in its capital structure by means of the issuance, incurrence or guarantee of debt or the issuance of (A) preferred stock or other securities convertible into or exchangeable for debt or preferred stock or (B) in the case of entities other than corporations, any other form of ownership interest; or

(vi)   *Additional Termination Event.* If any "Additional Termination Event" is specified in the Schedule or any Confirmation as applying, the occurrence of such event (and, in such event, the Affected Party or Affected Parties will be as specified for such Additional Termination Event in the Schedule or such Confirmation).

(c)   *Hierarchy of Events.*

(i)   An event or circumstance that constitutes or gives rise to an Illegality or a Force Majeure Event will not, for so long as that is the case, also constitute or give rise to an Event of Default under Section 5(a)(i), 5(a)(ii)(l) or 5(a)(iii)(l) insofar as such event or circumstance relates to the failure to make any payment or delivery or a failure to comply with any other material provision of this Agreement or a Credit Support Document, as the case may be.

(ii)   Except in circumstances contemplated by clause (i) above, if an event or circumstance which would otherwise constitute or give rise to an Illegality or a Force Majeure Event also constitutes an Event of Default or any other Termination Event, it will be treated as an Event of Default or such other Termination Event, as the case may be, and will not constitute or give rise to an Illegality or a Force Majeure Event.

(iii)   If an event or circumstance which would otherwise constitute or give rise to a Force Majeure Event also constitutes an Illegality, it will be treated as an Illegality, except as described in clause (ii) above, and not a Force Majeure Event.

(d)   *Deferral of Payments and Deliveries During Waiting Period.* If an Illegality or a Force Majeure Event has occurred and is continuing with respect to a Transaction, each payment or delivery which would otherwise be required to be made under that Transaction will be deferred to, and will not be due until:–

(i)   the first Local Business Day or, in the case of a delivery, the first Local Delivery Day (or the first day that would have been a Local Business Day or Local Delivery Day, as appropriate, but for the occurrence of the event or circumstance constituting or giving rise to that Illegality or Force Majeure Event) following the end of any applicable Waiting Period in respect of that Illegality or Force Majeure Event, as the case may be; or

(ii)   if earlier, the date on which the event or circumstance constituting or giving rise to that Illegality or Force Majeure Event ceases to exist or, if such date is not a Local Business Day or, in the case of a delivery, a Local Delivery Day, the first following day that is a Local Business Day or Local Delivery Day, as appropriate.

(e)   *Inability of Head or Home Office to Perform Obligations of Branch.* If (i) an Illegality or a Force Majeure Event occurs under Section 5(b)(i)(l) or 5(b)(ii)(l) and the relevant Office is not the Affected Party's head or home office, (ii) Section 10(a) applies, (iii) the other party seeks performance of the relevant obligation or compliance with the relevant provision by the Affected Party's head or home office and (iv) the Affected Party's head or home office fails so to perform or comply due to the occurrence of an event or circumstance which would, if that head or home office were the Office through which the Affected Party makes and receives payments and deliveries with respect to the relevant Transaction, constitute or give rise to an Illegality or a Force Majeure Event, and such failure would otherwise constitute an Event of Default under Section 5(a)(i) or 5(a)(iii)(1) with respect to such party, then, for so long as the relevant event or circumstance continues to exist with respect to both the Office referred to in Section 5(b)(i)(1) or 5(b)(ii)(1), as the case may be, and the Affected Party's head or home office, such failure will not constitute an Event of Default under Section 5(a)(i) or 5(a)(iii)(1).

6.   **Early Termination; Close-Out Netting**

(a)   ***Right to Terminate Following Event of Default.*** If at any time an Event of Default with respect to a party (the "Defaulting Party") has occurred and is then continuing, the other party (the "Non-defaulting Party") may, by not more than 20 days notice to the Defaulting Party specifying the relevant Event of Default, designate a day not earlier than the day such notice is effective as an Early Termination Date in respect of all outstanding Transactions. If, however, "Automatic Early Termination" is specified in the Schedule as applying to a party, then an Early Termination Date in respect of all outstanding Transactions will occur immediately upon the occurrence with respect to such party of an Event of Default specified in Section 5(a)(vii)(1), (3), (5), (6) or, to the extent analogous thereto, (8), and as of the time immediately preceding the institution of the relevant proceeding or the presentation of the relevant petition upon the occurrence with respect to such party of an Event of Default specified in Section 5(a)(vii)(4) or, to the extent analogous thereto, (8).

(b)   ***Right to Terminate Following Termination Event.***

(i)   ***Notice.*** If a Termination Event other than a Force Majeure Event occurs, an Affected Party will, promptly upon becoming aware of it, notify the other party, specifying the nature of that Termination Event and each Affected Transaction, and will also give the other party such other information about that Termination Event as the other party may reasonably require. If a Force Majeure Event occurs, each party will, promptly upon becoming aware of it, use all reasonable efforts to notify the other party, specifying the nature of that Force Majeure Event, and will also give the other party such other information about that Force Majeure Event as the other party may reasonably require.

(ii)   ***Transfer to Avoid Termination Event.*** If a Tax Event occurs and there is only one Affected Party, or if a Tax Event Upon Merger occurs and the Burdened Party is the Affected Party, the Affected Party will, as a condition to its right to designate an Early Termination Date under Section 6(b)(iv), use all reasonable efforts (which will not require such party to incur a loss, other than immaterial, incidental expenses) to transfer within 20 days after it gives notice under Section 6(b)(i) all its rights and obligations under this Agreement in respect of the Affected Transactions to another of its Offices or Affiliates so that such Termination Event ceases to exist.

If the Affected Party is not able to make such a transfer it will give notice to the other party to that effect within such 20 day period, whereupon the other party may effect such a transfer within 30 days after the notice is given under Section 6(b)(i).

Any such transfer by a party under this Section 6(b)(ii) will be subject to and conditional upon the prior written consent of the other party, which consent will not be withheld if such other party's policies in effect at such time would permit it to enter into transactions with the transferee on the terms proposed.

(iii)   ***Two Affected Parties.*** If a Tax Event occurs and there are two Affected Parties, each party will use all reasonable efforts to reach agreement within 30 days after notice of such occurrence is given under Section 6(b)(i) to avoid that Termination Event.

(iv)   **Right to Terminate.**

(1) If:

(A)   a transfer under Section 6(b)(ii) or an agreement under Section 6(b)(iii), as the case may be, has not been effected with respect to all Affected Transactions within 30 days after an Affected Party gives notice under Section 6(b)(i); or

(B)   a Credit Event Upon Merger or an Additional Termination Event occurs, or a Tax Event Upon Merger occurs and the Burdened Party is not the Affected Party,

the Burdened Party in the case of a Tax Event Upon Merger, any Affected Party in the case of a Tax Event or an Additional Termination Event if there are two Affected Parties, or the Non-affected Party in the case of a Credit Event Upon Merger or an Additional Termination Event if there is only one Affected Party may, if the relevant Termination Event is then continuing, by not more than 20 days notice to the other party, designate a day not earlier than the day such notice is effective as an Early Termination Date in respect of all Affected Transactions.

(2) If at any time an Illegality or a Force Majeure Event has occurred and is then continuing and any applicable Waiting Period has expired:–

(A)   Subject to clause (B) below, either party may, by not more than 20 days notice to the other party, designate (I) a day not earlier than the day on which such notice becomes effective as an Early Termination Date in respect of all Affected Transactions or (II) by specifying in that notice the Affected Transactions in respect of which it is designating the relevant day as an Early Termination Date, a day not earlier than two Local Business Days following the day on which such notice becomes effective as an Early Termination Date in respect of less than all Affected Transactions. Upon receipt of a notice designating an Early Termination Date in respect of less than all Affected Transactions, the other party may, by notice to the designating party, if such notice is effective on or before the day so designated, designate that same day as an Early Termination Date in respect of any or all other Affected Transactions.

(B)   An Affected Party (if the Illegality or Force Majeure Event relates to performance by such party or any Credit Support Provider of such party of an obligation to make any payment or delivery under, or to compliance with any other material provision of, the relevant Credit Support Document) will only have the right to designate an Early Termination Date under Section 6(b)(iv)(2)(A) as a result of an Illegality under Section 5(b)(i)(2) or a Force Majeure Event under Section 5(b)(ii)(2) following the prior designation by the other party of an Early Termination Date, pursuant to Section 6(b)(iv)(2)(A), in respect of less than all Affected Transactions.

(c)   **Effect of Designation.**

(i)   If notice designating an Early Termination Date is given under Section 6(a) or 6(b), the Early Termination Date will occur on the date so designated, whether or not the relevant Event of Default or Termination Event is then continuing.

(ii)   Upon the occurrence or effective designation of an Early Termination Date, no further payments or deliveries under Section 2(a)(i) or 9(h)(i) in respect of the Terminated Transactions will be required to be made, but without prejudice to the other provisions of this Agreement. The amount, if any, payable in respect of an Early Termination Date will be determined pursuant to Sections 6(e) and 9(h)(ii).

(d) *Calculations; Payment Date.*

(i) *Statement.* On or as soon as reasonably practicable following the occurrence of an Early Termination Date, each party will make the calculations on its part, if any, contemplated by Section 6(e) and will provide to the other party a statement (1) showing, in reasonable detail, such calculations (including any quotations, market data or information from internal sources used in making such calculations) (2) specifying (except where there are two Affected Parties) any Early Termination Amount payable and (3) giving details of the relevant account to which any amount payable to it is to be paid. In the absence of written confirmation from the source of a quotation or market data obtained in determining a Close-out Amount, the records of the party obtaining such quotation or market data will be conclusive evidence of the existence and accuracy of such quotation or market data.

(ii) *Payment Date.* An Early Termination Amount due in respect of any Early Termination Date will, together with any amount of interest payable pursuant to Section 9(h)(ii)(2), be payable (1) on the day on which notice of the amount payable is effective in the case of an Early Termination Date which is designated or occurs as a result of an Event of Default and (2) on the day which is two Local Business Days after the day on which notice of the amount payable is effective (or, if there are two Affected Parties, after the day on which the statement provided pursuant to clause (i) above by the second party to provide such a statement is effective) in the case of an Early Termination Date which is designated as a result of a Termination Event.

(e) *Payments on Early Termination.* If an Early Termination Date occurs, the amount, if any, payable in respect of that Early Termination Date (the "Early Termination Amount") will be determined pursuant to this Section 6(e) and will be subject to Section 6(f).

(i) *Events of Default.* If the Early Termination Date results from an Event of Default, the Early Termination Amount will be an amount equal to (1) the sum of (A) the Termination Currency Equivalent of the Close-out Amount or Close-out Amounts (whether positive or negative) determined by the Non-defaulting Party for each Terminated Transaction or group of Terminated Transactions, as the case may be, and (B) the Termination Currency Equivalent of the Unpaid Amounts owing to the Non-defaulting Party less (2) the Termination Currency Equivalent of the Unpaid Amounts owing to the Defaulting Party. If the Early Termination Amount is a positive number, the Defaulting Party will pay it to the Non-defaulting Party; if it is a negative number, the Non-defaulting Party will pay the absolute value of the Early Termination Amount to the Defaulting Party.

(ii) *Termination Events.* If the Early Termination Date results from a Termination Event:–

(1) *One Affected Party.* Subject to clause (3) below, if there is one Affected Party, the Early Termination Amount will be determined in accordance with Section 6(e)(i), except that references to the Defaulting Party and to the Non-defaulting Party will be deemed to be references to the Affected Party and to the Non-affected Party, respectively.

(2) *Two Affected Parties.* Subject to clause (3) below, if there are two Affected Parties, each party will determine an amount equal to the Termination Currency Equivalent of the sum of the Close-out Amount or Close-out Amounts (whether positive or negative) for each Terminated Transaction or group of Terminated Transactions, as the case may be, and the Early Termination Amount will be an amount equal to (A) the sum of (I) one-half of the difference between the higher amount so determined (by party "X") and the lower amount so determined (by party "Y") and (II) the Termination Currency Equivalent of the Unpaid Amounts owing to X less (B) the Termination Currency Equivalent of the Unpaid Amounts owing to Y. If the Early Termination Amount is a positive number, Y will pay it to X; if it is a negative number, X will pay the absolute value of the Early Termination Amount to Y.

(3)   *Mid-Market Events.* If that Termination Event is an Illegality or a Force Majeure Event, then the Early Termination Amount will be determined in accordance with clause (1) or (2) above, as appropriate, except that, for the purpose of determining a Close-out Amount or Close-out Amounts, the Determining Party will:–

(A)   if obtaining quotations from one or more third parties (or from any of the Determining Party's Affiliates), ask each third party or Affiliate (I) not to take account of the current creditworthiness of the Determining Party or any existing Credit Support Document and (II) to provide mid-market quotations; and

(B)   in any other case, use mid-market values without regard to the creditworthiness of the Determining Party.

(iii)   *Adjustment for Bankruptcy.* In circumstances where an Early Termination Date occurs because Automatic Early Termination applies in respect of a party, the Early Termination Amount will be subject to such adjustments as are appropriate and permitted by applicable law to reflect any payments or deliveries made by one party to the other under this Agreement (and retained by such other party) during the period from the relevant Early Termination Date to the date for payment determined under Section 6(d)(ii).

(iv)   *Adjustment for Illegality or Force Majeure Event.* The failure by a party or any Credit Support Provider of such party to pay, when due, any Early Termination Amount will not constitute an Event of Default under Section 5(a)(i) or 5(a)(iii)(1) if such failure is due to the occurrence of an event or circumstance which would, if it occurred with respect to payment, delivery or compliance related to a Transaction, constitute or give rise to an Illegality or a Force Majeure Event. Such amount will (1) accrue interest and otherwise be treated as an Unpaid Amount owing to the other party if subsequently an Early Termination Date results from an Event of Default, a Credit Event Upon Merger or an Additional Termination Event in respect of which all outstanding Transactions are Affected Transactions and (2) otherwise accrue interest in accordance with Section 9(h)(ii)(2).

(v)   *Pre-Estimate.* The parties agree that an amount recoverable under this Section 6(e) is a reasonable pre-estimate of loss and not a penalty. Such amount is payable for the loss of bargain and the loss of protection against future risks, and, except as otherwise provided in this Agreement, neither party will be entitled to recover any additional damages as a consequence of the termination of the Terminated Transactions.

(f)   *Set-Off.* Any Early Termination Amount payable to one party (the "Payee") by the other party (the "Payer"), in circumstances where there is a Defaulting Party or where there is one Affected Party in the case where either a Credit Event Upon Merger has occurred or any other Termination Event in respect of which all outstanding Transactions are Affected Transactions has occurred, will, at the option of the Non-defaulting Party or the Non-affected Party, as the case may be ("X") (and without prior notice to the Defaulting Party or the Affected Party, as the case may be), be reduced by its set-off against any other amounts ("Other Amounts") payable by the Payee to the Payer (whether or not arising under this Agreement, matured or contingent and irrespective of the currency, place of payment or place of booking of the obligation). To the extent that any Other Amounts are so set off, those Other Amounts will be discharged promptly and in all respects. X will give notice to the other party of any set-off effected under this Section 6(f).

For this purpose, either the Early Termination Amount or the Other Amounts (or the relevant portion of such amounts) may be converted by X into the currency in which the other is denominated at the rate of exchange at which such party would be able, in good faith and using commercially reasonable procedures, to purchase the relevant amount of such currency.

ISDA® 2002

If an obligation is unascertained, X may in good faith estimate that obligation and set off in respect of the estimate, subject to the relevant party accounting to the other when the obligation is ascertained.

Nothing in this Section 6(f) will be effective to create a charge or other security interest. This Section 6(f) will be without prejudice and in addition to any right of set-off, offset, combination of accounts, lien, right of retention or withholding or similar right or requirement to which any party is at any time otherwise entitled or subject (whether by operation of law, contract or otherwise).

7.   Transfer

Subject to Section 6(b)(ii) and to the extent permitted by applicable law, neither this Agreement nor any interest or obligation in or under this Agreement may be transferred (whether by way of security or otherwise) by either party without the prior written consent of the other party, except that:–

(a)   a party may make such a transfer of this Agreement pursuant to a consolidation or amalgamation with, or merger with or into, or transfer of all or substantially all its assets to, another entity (but without prejudice to any other right or remedy under this Agreement); and

(b)   a party may make such a transfer of all or any part of its interest in any Early Termination Amount payable to it by a Defaulting Party, together with any amounts payable on or with respect to that interest and any other rights associated with that interest pursuant to Sections 8, 9(h) and 11.

Any purported transfer that is not in compliance with this Section 7 will be void.

8.   Contractual Currency

(a)   *Payment in the Contractual Currency.* Each payment under this Agreement will be made in the relevant currency specified in this Agreement for that payment (the "Contractual Currency"). To the extent permitted by applicable law, any obligation to make payments under this Agreement in the Contractual Currency will not be discharged or satisfied by any tender in any currency other than the Contractual Currency, except to the extent such tender results in the actual receipt by the party to which payment is owed, acting in good faith and using commercially reasonable procedures in converting the currency so tendered into the Contractual Currency, of the full amount in the Contractual Currency of all amounts payable in respect of this Agreement. If for any reason the amount in the Contractual Currency so received falls short of the amount in the Contractual Currency payable in respect of this Agreement, the party required to make the payment will, to the extent permitted by applicable law, immediately pay such additional amount in the Contractual Currency as may be necessary to compensate for the shortfall. If for any reason the amount in the Contractual Currency so received exceeds the amount in the Contractual Currency payable in respect of this Agreement, the party receiving the payment will refund promptly the amount of such excess.

(b)   *Judgments.* To the extent permitted by applicable law, if any judgment or order expressed in a currency other than the Contractual Currency is rendered (i) for the payment of any amount owing in respect of this Agreement, (ii) for the payment of any amount relating to any early termination in respect of this Agreement or (iii) in respect of a judgment or order of another court for the payment of any amount described in clause (i) or (ii) above, the party seeking recovery, after recovery in full of the aggregate amount to which such party is entitled pursuant to the judgment or order, will be entitled to receive immediately from the other party the amount of any shortfall of the Contractual Currency received by such party as a consequence of sums paid in such other currency and will refund promptly to the other party any excess of the Contractual Currency received by such party as a consequence of sums paid in such other currency if such shortfall or such excess arises or results from any variation between the rate of exchange at which the Contractual Currency is converted into the currency of the judgment or order for the purpose of such judgment or order and the rate of exchange at which such party is able, acting in good faith and using commercially reasonable procedures in converting the currency received into the Contractual Currency, to purchase the Contractual Currency with the amount of the currency of the judgment or order actually received by such party.

(c) **Separate Indemnities.** To the extent permitted by applicable law, the indemnities in this Section 8 constitute separate and independent obligations from the other obligations in this Agreement, will be enforceable as separate and independent causes of action, will apply notwithstanding any indulgence granted by the party to which any payment is owed and will not be affected by judgment being obtained or claim or proof being made for any other sums payable in respect of this Agreement.

(d) **Evidence of Loss.** For the purpose of this Section 8, it will be sufficient for a party to demonstrate that it would have suffered a loss had an actual exchange or purchase been made.

9. **Miscellaneous**

(a) **Entire Agreement.** This Agreement constitutes the entire agreement and understanding of the parties with respect to its subject matter. Each of the parties acknowledges that in entering into this Agreement it has not relied on any oral or written representation, warranty or other assurance (except as provided for or referred to in this Agreement) and waives all rights and remedies which might otherwise be available to it in respect thereof, except that nothing in this Agreement will limit or exclude any liability of a party for fraud.

(b) **Amendments.** An amendment, modification or waiver in respect of this Agreement will only be effective if in writing (including a writing evidenced by a facsimile transmission) and executed by each of the parties or confirmed by an exchange of telexes or by an exchange of electronic messages on an electronic messaging system.

(c) **Survival of Obligations.** Without prejudice to Sections 2(a)(iii) and 6(c)(ii), the obligations of the parties under this Agreement will survive the termination of any Transaction.

(d) **Remedies Cumulative.** Except as provided in this Agreement, the rights, powers, remedies and privileges provided in this Agreement are cumulative and not exclusive of any rights, powers, remedies and privileges provided by law.

(e) **Counterparts and Confirmations.**

(i) This Agreement (and each amendment, modification and waiver in respect of it) may be executed and delivered in counterparts (including by facsimile transmission and by electronic messaging system), each of which will be deemed an original.

(ii) The parties intend that they are legally bound by the terms of each Transaction from the moment they agree to those terms (whether orally or otherwise). A Confirmation will be entered into as soon as practicable and may be executed and delivered in counterparts (including by facsimile transmission) or be created by an exchange of telexes, by an exchange of electronic messages on an electronic messaging system or by an exchange of e-mails, which in each case will be sufficient for all purposes to evidence a binding supplement to this Agreement. The parties will specify therein or through another effective means that any such counterpart, telex, electronic message or e-mail constitutes a Confirmation.

(f) **No Waiver of Rights.** A failure or delay in exercising any right, power or privilege in respect of this Agreement will not be presumed to operate as a waiver, and a single or partial exercise of any right, power or privilege will not be presumed to preclude any subsequent or further exercise, of that right, power or privilege or the exercise of any other right, power or privilege.

(g) **Headings.** The headings used in this Agreement are for convenience of reference only and are not to affect the construction of or to be taken into consideration in interpreting this Agreement.

(h)   *Interest and Compensation.*

(i)   *Prior to Early Termination.* Prior to the occurrence or effective designation of an Early Termination Date in respect of the relevant Transaction:–

(1)   *Interest on Defaulted Payments.* If a party defaults in the performance of any payment obligation, it will, to the extent permitted by applicable law and subject to Section 6(c), pay interest (before as well as after judgment) on the overdue amount to the other party on demand in the same currency as the overdue amount, for the period from (and including) the original due date for payment to (but excluding) the date of actual payment (and excluding any period in respect of which interest or compensation in respect of the overdue amount is due pursuant to clause (3)(B) or (C) below), at the Default Rate.

(2)   *Compensation for Defaulted Deliveries.* If a party defaults in the performance of any obligation required to be settled by delivery, it will on demand (A) compensate the other party to the extent provided for in the relevant Confirmation or elsewhere in this Agreement and (B) unless otherwise provided in the relevant Confirmation or elsewhere in this Agreement, to the extent permitted by applicable law and subject to Section 6(c), pay to the other party interest (before as well as after judgment) on an amount equal to the fair market value of that which was required to be delivered in the same currency as that amount, for the period from (and including) the originally scheduled date for delivery to (but excluding) the date of actual delivery (and excluding any period in respect of which interest or compensation in respect of that amount is due pursuant to clause (4) below), at the Default Rate. The fair market value of any obligation referred to above will be determined as of the originally scheduled date for delivery, in good faith and using commercially reasonable procedures, by the party that was entitled to take delivery.

(3)   *Interest on Deferred Payments.* If:–

(A)   a party does not pay any amount that, but for Section 2(a)(iii), would have been payable, it will, to the extent permitted by applicable law and subject to Section 6(c) and clauses (B) and (C) below, pay interest (before as well as after judgment) on that amount to the other party on demand (after such amount becomes payable) in the same currency as that amount, for the period from (and including) the date the amount would, but for Section 2(a)(iii), have been payable to (but excluding) the date the amount actually becomes payable, at the Applicable Deferral Rate;

(B)   a payment is deferred pursuant to Section 5(d), the party which would otherwise have been required to make that payment will, to the extent permitted by applicable law, subject to Section 6(c) and for so long as no Event of Default or Potential Event of Default with respect to that party has occurred and is continuing, pay interest (before as well as after judgment) on the amount of the deferred payment to the other party on demand (after such amount becomes payable) in the same currency as the deferred payment, for the period from (and including) the date the amount would, but for Section 5(d), have been payable to (but excluding) the earlier of the date the payment is no longer deferred pursuant to Section 5(d) and the date during the deferral period upon which an Event of Default or Potential Event of Default with respect to that party occurs, at the Applicable Deferral Rate; or

(C)   a party fails to make any payment due to the occurrence of an Illegality or a Force Majeure Event (after giving effect to any deferral period contemplated by clause (B) above), it will, to the extent permitted by applicable law, subject to Section 6(c) and for so long as the event or circumstance giving rise to that Illegality or Force Majeure Event continues and no Event of Default or Potential

Event of Default with respect to that party has occurred and is continuing, pay interest (before as well as after judgment) on the overdue amount to the other party on demand in the same currency as the overdue amount, for the period from (and including) the date the party fails to make the payment due to the occurrence of the relevant Illegality or Force Majeure Event (or, if later, the date the payment is no longer deferred pursuant to Section 5(d)) to (but excluding) the earlier of the date the event or circumstance giving rise to that Illegality or Force Majeure Event ceases to exist and the date during the period upon which an Event of Default or Potential Event of Default with respect to that party occurs (and excluding any period in respect of which interest or compensation in respect of the overdue amount is due pursuant to clause (B) above), at the Applicable Deferral Rate.

(4) *Compensation for Deferred Deliveries.* If:–

(A) a party does not perform any obligation that, but for Section 2(a)(iii), would have been required to be settled by delivery;

(B) a delivery is deferred pursuant to Section 5(d); or

(C) a party fails to make a delivery due to the occurrence of an Illegality or a Force Majeure Event at a time when any applicable Waiting Period has expired,

the party required (or that would otherwise have been required) to make the delivery will, to the extent permitted by applicable law and subject to Section 6(c), compensate and pay interest to the other party on demand (after, in the case of clauses (A) and (B) above, such delivery is required) if and to the extent provided for in the relevant Confirmation or elsewhere in this Agreement.

(ii) **Early Termination.** Upon the occurrence or effective designation of an Early Termination Date in respect of a Transaction:–

(1) *Unpaid Amounts.* For the purpose of determining an Unpaid Amount in respect of the relevant Transaction, and to the extent permitted by applicable law, interest will accrue on the amount of any payment obligation or the amount equal to the fair market value of any obligation required to be settled by delivery included in such determination in the same currency as that amount, for the period from (and including) the date the relevant obligation was (or would have been but for Section 2(a)(iii) or 5(d)) required to have been performed to (but excluding) the relevant Early Termination Date, at the Applicable Close-out Rate.

(2) *Interest on Early Termination Amounts.* If an Early Termination Amount is due in respect of such Early Termination Date, that amount will, to the extent permitted by applicable law, be paid together with interest (before as well as after judgment) on that amount in the Termination Currency, for the period from (and including) such Early Termination Date to (but excluding) the date the amount is paid, at the Applicable Close-out Rate.

(iii) **Interest Calculation.** Any interest pursuant to this Section 9(h) will be calculated on the basis of daily compounding and the actual number of days elapsed.

10. Offices; Multibranch Parties

(a)   If Section 10(a) is specified in the Schedule as applying, each party that enters into a Transaction through an Office other than its head or home office represents to and agrees with the other party that, notwithstanding the place of booking or its jurisdiction of incorporation or organisation, its obligations are the same in terms of recourse against it as if it had entered into the Transaction through its head or home office, except that a party will not have recourse to the head or home office of the other party in respect of any payment or delivery deferred pursuant to Section 5(d) for so long as the payment or delivery is so deferred. This representation and agreement will be deemed to be repeated by each party on each date on which the parties enter into a Transaction.

(b)   If a party is specified as a Multibranch Party in the Schedule, such party may, subject to clause (c) below, enter into a Transaction through, book a Transaction in and make and receive payments and deliveries with respect to a Transaction through any Office listed in respect of that party in the Schedule (but not any other Office unless otherwise agreed by the parties in writing).

(c)   The Office through which a party enters into a Transaction will be the Office specified for that party in the relevant Confirmation or as otherwise agreed by the parties in writing, and, if an Office for that party is not specified in the Confirmation or otherwise agreed by the parties in writing, its head or home office. Unless the parties otherwise agree in writing, the Office through which a party enters into a Transaction will also be the Office in which it books the Transaction and the Office through which it makes and receives payments and deliveries with respect to the Transaction. Subject to Section 6(b)(ii), neither party may change the Office in which it books the Transaction or the Office through which it makes and receives payments or deliveries with respect to a Transaction without the prior written consent of the other party.

11. Expenses

A Defaulting Party will on demand indemnify and hold harmless the other party for and against all reasonable out-of-pocket expenses, including legal fees, execution fees and Stamp Tax, incurred by such other party by reason of the enforcement and protection of its rights under this Agreement or any Credit Support Document to which the Defaulting Party is a party or by reason of the early termination of any Transaction, including, but not limited to, costs of collection.

12. Notices

(a)   *Effectiveness.* Any notice or other communication in respect of this Agreement may be given in any manner described below (except that a notice or other communication under Section 5 or 6 may not be given by electronic messaging system or e-mail) to the address or number or in accordance with the electronic messaging system or e-mail details provided (see the Schedule) and will be deemed effective as indicated:–

(i)   if in writing and delivered in person or by courier, on the date it is delivered;

(ii)   if sent by telex, on the date the recipient's answerback is received;

(iii)   if sent by facsimile transmission, on the date it is received by a responsible employee of the recipient in legible form (it being agreed that the burden of proving receipt will be on the sender and will not be met by a transmission report generated by the sender's facsimile machine);

(iv)   if sent by certified or registered mail (airmail, if overseas) or the equivalent (return receipt requested), on the date it is delivered or its delivery is attempted;

(v)   if sent by electronic messaging system, on the date it is received; or

(vi) if sent by e-mail, on the date it is delivered,

unless the date of that delivery (or attempted delivery) or that receipt, as applicable, is not a Local Business Day or that communication is delivered (or attempted) or received, as applicable, after the close of business on a Local Business Day, in which case that communication will be deemed given and effective on the first following day that is a Local Business Day.

(b)   *Change of Details.* Either party may by notice to the other change the address, telex or facsimile number or electronic messaging system or e-mail details at which notices or other communications are to be given to it.

13.   Governing Law and Jurisdiction

(a)   *Governing Law.* This Agreement will be governed by and construed in accordance with the law specified in the Schedule.

(b)   *Jurisdiction.* With respect to any suit, action or proceedings relating to any dispute arising out of or in connection with this Agreement ("Proceedings"), each party irrevocably:–

(i) submits:–

(1)   if this Agreement is expressed to be governed by English law, to (A) the non-exclusive Jurisdiction of the English courts if the Proceedings do not involve a Convention Court and (B) the exclusive jurisdiction of the English courts if the Proceedings do involve a Convention Court; or

(2)   if this Agreement is expressed to be governed by the laws of the State of New York, to the non-exclusive jurisdiction of the courts of the State of New York and the United States District Court located in the Borough of Manhattan in New York City;

(ii) waives any objection which it may have at any time to the laying of venue of any Proceedings brought in any such court, waives any claim that such Proceedings have been brought in an inconvenient forum and further waives the right to object, with respect to such Proceedings, that such court does not have any jurisdiction over such party; and

(iii) agrees, to the extent permitted by applicable law, that the bringing of Proceedings in any one or more jurisdictions will not preclude the bringing of Proceedings in any other jurisdiction.

(c)   *Service of Process.* Each party irrevocably appoints the Process Agent, if any, specified opposite its name in the Schedule to receive, for it and on its behalf, service of process in any Proceedings. If for any reason any party's Process Agent is unable to act as such, such party will promptly notify the other party and within 30 days appoint a substitute process agent acceptable to the other party. The parties irrevocably consent to service of process given in the manner provided for notices in Section 12(a)(i), 12(a)(iii) or 12(a)(iv). Nothing in this Agreement will affect the right of either party to serve process in any other manner permitted by applicable law.

(d)   *Waiver of Immunities.* Each party irrevocably waives, to the extent permitted by applicable law, with respect to itself and its revenues and assets (irrespective of their use or intended use), all immunity on the grounds of sovereignty or other similar grounds from (i) suit, (ii) jurisdiction of any court, (iii) relief by way of injunction or order for specific performance or recovery of property, (iv) attachment of its assets (whether before or after judgment) and (v) execution or enforcement of any judgment to which it or its revenues or assets might otherwise be entitled in any Proceedings in the courts of any jurisdiction and irrevocably agrees, to the extent permitted by applicable law, that it will not claim any such immunity in any Proceedings.

14. **Definitions**

As used in this Agreement:–

"Additional Representation" has the meaning specified in Section 3.

"Additional Termination Event" has the meaning specified in Section 5(b).

"Affected Party" has the meaning specified in Section 5(b).

"Affected Transactions" means (a) with respect to any Termination Event consisting of an Illegality, Force Majeure Event, Tax Event or Tax Event Upon Merger, all Transactions affected by the occurrence of such Termination Event (which, in the case of an Illegality under Section 5(b)(i)(2) or a Force Majeure Event under Section 5(b)(ii)(2), means all Transactions unless the relevant Credit Support Document references only certain Transactions, in which case those Transactions and, if the relevant Credit Support Document constitutes a Confirmation for a Transaction, that Transaction) and (b) with respect to any other Termination Event, all Transactions.

"Affiliate" means, subject to the Schedule, in relation to any person, any entity controlled, directly or indirectly, by the person, any entity that controls, directly or indirectly, the person or any entity directly or indirectly under common control with the person. For this purpose, "control" of any entity or person means ownership of a majority of the voting power of the entity or person.

"Agreement" has the meaning specified in Section 1(c).

"Applicable Close-out Rate" means:–

(a) in respect of the determination of an Unpaid Amount:–

    (i) in respect of obligations payable or deliverable (or which would have been but for Section 2(a)(iii)) by a Defaulting Party, the Default Rate;

    (ii) in respect of obligations payable or deliverable (or which would have been but for Section 2(a)(iii)) by a Non-defaulting Party, the Non-default Rate;

    (iii) in respect of obligations deferred pursuant to Section 5(d), if there is no Defaulting Party and for so long as the deferral period continues, the Applicable Deferral Rate; and

    (iv) in all other cases following the occurrence of a Termination Event (except where interest accrues pursuant to clause (iii) above), the Applicable Deferral Rate; and

(b) in respect of an Early Termination Amount:–

    (i) for the period from (and including) the relevant Early Termination Date to (but excluding) the date (determined in accordance with Section 6(d)(ii)) on which that amount is payable:–

        (1) if the Early Termination Amount is payable by a Defaulting Party, the Default Rate;

        (2) if the Early Termination Amount is payable by a Non-defaulting Party, the Non-default Rate; and

        (3) in all other cases, the Applicable Deferral Rate; and

(ii) for the period from (and including) the date (determined in accordance with Section 6(d)(ii)) on which that amount is payable to (but excluding) the date of actual payment:–

(1)   if a party fails to pay the Early Termination Amount due to the occurrence of an event or circumstance which would, if it occurred with respect to a payment or delivery under a Transaction, constitute or give rise to an Illegality or a Force Majeure Event, and for so long as the Early Termination Amount remains unpaid due to the continuing existence of such event or circumstance, the Applicable Deferral Rate;

(2)   if the Early Termination Amount is payable by a Defaulting Party (but excluding any period in respect of which clause (1) above applies), the Default Rate;

(3)   if the Early Termination Amount is payable by a Non-defaulting Party (but excluding any period in respect of which clause (1) above applies), the Non-default Rate; and

(4)   in all other cases, the Termination Rate.

"Applicable Deferral Rate" means:–

(a)   for the purpose of Section 9(h)(i)(3)(A), the rate certified by the relevant payer to be a rate offered to the payer by a major bank in a relevant interbank market for overnight deposits in the applicable currency, such bank to be selected in good faith by the payer for the purpose of obtaining a representative rate that will reasonably reflect conditions prevailing at the time in that relevant market;

(b)   for purposes of Section 9(h)(i)(3)(B) and clause (a)(iii) of the definition of Applicable Close-out Rate, the rate certified by the relevant payer to be a rate offered to prime banks by a major bank in a relevant interbank market for overnight deposits in the applicable currency, such bank to be selected in good faith by the payer after consultation with the other party, if practicable, for the purpose of obtaining a representative rate that will reasonably reflect conditions prevailing at the time in that relevant market; and

(c)   for purposes of Section 9(h)(i)(3)(C) and clauses (a)(iv), (b)(i)(3) and (b)(ii)(l) of the definition of Applicable Close-out Rate, a rate equal to the arithmetic mean of the rate determined pursuant to clause (a) above and a rate per annum equal to the cost (without proof or evidence of any actual cost) to the relevant payee (as certified by it) if it were to fund or of funding the relevant amount.

"Automatic Early Termination" has the meaning specified in Section 6(a).

"Burdened Party" has the meaning specified in Section 5(b)(iv).

"Change in Tax Law" means the enactment, promulgation, execution or ratification of, or any change in or amendment to, any law (or in the application or official interpretation of any law) that occurs after the parties enter into the relevant Transaction.

"Close-out Amount" means, with respect to each Terminated Transaction or each group of Terminated Transactions and a Determining Party, the amount of the losses or costs of the Determining Party that are or would be incurred under then prevailing circumstances (expressed as a positive number) or gains of the Determining Party that are or would be realised under then prevailing circumstances (expressed as a negative number) in replacing, or in providing for the Determining Party the economic equivalent of, (a) the material terms of that Terminated Transaction or group of Terminated Transactions, including the payments and deliveries by the parties under Section 2(a)(i) in respect of that Terminated Transaction or group of Terminated Transactions that would, but for the occurrence of the relevant Early Termination Date, have been required after that date (assuming satisfaction of the conditions precedent in Section 2(a)(iii)) and (b) the option rights of the parties in

respect of that Terminated Transaction or group of Terminated Transactions.

Any Close-out Amount will be determined by the Determining Party (or its agent), which will act in good faith and use commercially reasonable procedures in order to produce a commercially reasonable result. The Determining Party may determine a Close-out Amount for any group of Terminated Transactions or any individual Terminated Transaction but, in the aggregate, for not less than all Terminated Transactions. Each Close-out Amount will be determined as of the Early Termination Date or, if that would not be commercially reasonable, as of the date or dates following the Early Termination Date as would be commercially reasonable.

Unpaid Amounts in respect of a Terminated Transaction or group of Terminated Transactions and legal fees and out-of-pocket expenses referred to in Section 11 are to be excluded in all determinations of Close-out Amounts.

In determining a Close-out Amount, the Determining Party may consider any relevant information, including, without limitation, one or more of the following types of information:–

(i)　quotations (either firm or indicative) for replacement transactions supplied by one or more third parties that may take into account the creditworthiness of the Determining Party at the time the quotation is provided and the terms of any relevant documentation, including credit support documentation, between the Determining Party and the third party providing the quotation;

(ii)　information consisting of relevant market data in the relevant market supplied by one or more third parties including, without limitation, relevant rates, prices, yields, yield curves, volatilities, spreads, correlations or other relevant market data in the relevant market; or

(iii)　information of the types described in clause (i) or (ii) above from internal sources (including any of the Determining Party's Affiliates) if that information is of the same type used by the Determining Party in the regular course of its business for the valuation of similar transactions.

The Determining Party will consider, taking into account the standards and procedures described in this definition, quotations pursuant to clause (i) above or relevant market data pursuant to clause (ii) above unless the Determining Party reasonably believes in good faith that such quotations or relevant market data are not readily available or would produce a result that would not satisfy those standards. When considering information described in clause (i), (ii) or (iii) above, the Determining Party may include costs of funding, to the extent costs of funding are not and would not be a component of the other information being utilised. Third parties supplying quotations pursuant to clause (i) above or market data pursuant to clause (ii) above may include, without limitation, dealers in the relevant markets, end-users of the relevant product, information vendors, brokers and other sources of market information.

Without duplication of amounts calculated based on information described in clause (i), (ii) or (iii) above, or other relevant information, and when it is commercially reasonable to do so, the Determining Party may in addition consider in calculating a Close-out Amount any loss or cost incurred in connection with its terminating, liquidating or re-establishing any hedge related to a Terminated Transaction or group of Terminated Transactions (or any gain resulting from any of them).

Commercially reasonable procedures used in determining a Close-out Amount may include the following:–

(1)　application to relevant market data from third parties pursuant to clause (ii) above or information from internal sources pursuant to clause (iii) above of pricing or other valuation models that are, at the time of the determination of the Close-out Amount, used by the Determining Party in the regular course of its business in pricing or valuing transactions between the Determining Party and unrelated third parties that are similar to the Terminated Transaction or group of Terminated Transactions; and

(2)   application of different valuation methods to Terminated Transactions or groups of Terminated Transactions depending on the type, complexity, size or number of the Terminated Transactions or group of Terminated Transactions.

"Confirmation" has the meaning specified in the preamble.

"consent" includes a consent, approval, action, authorisation, exemption, notice, filing, registration or exchange control consent.

"Contractual Currency" has the meaning specified in Section 8(a).

"Convention Court" means any court which is bound to apply to the Proceedings either Article 17 of the 1968 Brussels Convention on Jurisdiction and the Enforcement of Judgments in Civil and Commercial Matters or Article 17 of the 1988 Lugano Convention on Jurisdiction and the Enforcement of Judgments in Civil and Commercial Matters.

"Credit Event Upon Merger" has the meaning specified in Section 5(b).

"Credit Support Document" means any agreement or instrument that is specified as such in this Agreement.

"Credit Support Provider" has the meaning specified in the Schedule.

"Cross-Default" means the event specified in Section 5(a)(vi).

"Default Rate" means a rate per annum equal to the cost (without proof or evidence of any actual cost) to the relevant payee (as certified by it) if it were to fund or of funding the relevant amount plus 1% per annum.

"Defaulting Party" has the meaning specified in Section 6(a).

"Designated Event" has the meaning specified in Section 5(b)(v).

"Determining Party" means the party determining a Close-out Amount.

"Early Termination Amount" has the meaning specified in Section 6(e).

"Early Termination Date" means the date determined in accordance with Section 6(a) or 6(b)(iv).

"electronic messages" does not include e-mails but does include documents expressed in markup languages, and *"electronic messaging system"* will be construed accordingly.

"English law" means the law of England and Wales, and "English" will be construed accordingly.

"Event of Default" has the meaning specified in Section 5(a) and, if applicable, in the Schedule.

"Force Majeure Event" has the meaning specified in Section 5(b).

"General Business Day" means a day on which commercial banks are open for general business (including dealings in foreign exchange and foreign currency deposits).

"Illegality" has the meaning specified in Section 5(b).

"Indemnifiable Tax" means any Tax other than a Tax that would not be imposed in respect of a payment under this Agreement but for a present or former connection between the jurisdiction of the government or taxation authority imposing such Tax and the recipient of such payment or a person related to such recipient (including, without limitation, a connection arising from such recipient or related person being or having been a citizen or resident of such jurisdiction, or being or having been organised, present or engaged in a trade or business in such jurisdiction, or having or having had a permanent establishment or fixed place of business in such jurisdiction, but excluding a connection arising solely from such recipient or related person having executed, delivered, performed its obligations or received a payment under, or enforced, this Agreement or a Credit Support Document).

"law" includes any treaty, law, rule or regulation (as modified, in the case of tax matters, by the practice of any relevant governmental revenue authority), and *"unlawful"* will be construed accordingly.

"Local Business Day" means (a) in relation to any obligation under Section 2(a)(i), a General Business Day in the place or places specified in the relevant Confirmation and a day on which a relevant settlement system is open or operating as specified in the relevant Confirmation or, if a place or a settlement system is not so specified, as otherwise agreed by the parties in writing or determined pursuant to provisions contained, or incorporated by reference, in this Agreement, (b) for the purpose of determining when a Waiting Period expires, a General Business Day in the place where the event or circumstance that constitutes or gives rise to the Illegality or Force Majeure Event, as the case may be, occurs, (c) in relation to any other payment, a General Business Day in the place where the relevant account is located and, if different, in the principal financial centre, if any, of the currency of such payment and, if that currency does not have a single recognised principal financial centre, a day on which the settlement system necessary to accomplish such payment is open, (d) in relation to any notice or other communication, including notice contemplated under Section 5(a)(i), a General Business Day (or a day that would have been a General Business Day but for the occurrence of an event or circumstance which would, if it occurred with respect to payment, delivery or compliance related to a Transaction, constitute or give rise to an Illegality or a Force Majeure Event) in the place specified in the address for notice provided by the recipient and, in the case of a notice contemplated by Section 2(b), in the place where the relevant new account is to be located and (e) in relation to Section 5(a)(v)(2), a General Business Day in the relevant locations for performance with respect to such Specified Transaction.

"Local Delivery Day" means, for purposes of Sections 5(a)(i) and 5(d), a day on which settlement systems necessary to accomplish the relevant delivery are generally open for business so that the delivery is capable of being accomplished in accordance with customary market practice, in the place specified in the relevant Confirmation or, if not so specified, in a location as determined in accordance with customary market practice for the relevant delivery.

"Master Agreement" has the meaning specified in the preamble.

"Merger Without Assumption" means the event specified in Section 5(a)(viii).

"Multiple Transaction Payment Netting" has the meaning specified in Section 2(c).

"Non-affected Party" means, so long as there is only one Affected Party, the other party.

"Non-default Rate" means the rate certified by the Non-defaulting Party to be a rate offered to the Non-defaulting Party by a major bank in a relevant interbank market for overnight deposits in the applicable currency, such bank to be selected in good faith by the Non-defaulting Party for the purpose of obtaining a representative rate that will reasonably reflect conditions prevailing at the time in that relevant market.

"Non-defaulting Party" has the meaning specified in Section 6(a).

"Office" means a branch or office of a party, which may be such party's head or home office.

"Other Amounts" has the meaning specified in Section 6(f).

"Payee" has the meaning specified in Section 6(f).

"Payer" has the meaning specified in Section 6(f).

"Potential Event of Default" means any event which, with the giving of notice or the lapse of time or both, would constitute an Event of Default.

"Proceedings" has the meaning specified in Section 13(b).

"Process Agent" has the meaning specified in the Schedule.

"rate of exchange" includes, without limitation, any premiums and costs of exchange payable in connection with the purchase of or conversion into the Contractual Currency.

"Relevant Jurisdiction" means, with respect to a party, the jurisdictions (a) in which the party is incorporated, organised, managed and controlled or considered to have its seat, (b) where an Office through which the party is acting for purposes of this Agreement is located, (c) in which the party executes this Agreement and (d) in relation to any payment, from or through which such payment is made.

"Schedule" has the meaning specified in the preamble.

"Scheduled Settlement Date" means a date on which a payment or delivery is to be made under Section 2(a)(i) with respect to a Transaction.

"Specified Entity" has the meaning specified in the Schedule.

"Specified Indebtedness" means, subject to the Schedule, any obligation (whether present or future, contingent or otherwise, as principal or surety or otherwise) in respect of borrowed money.

"Specified Transaction" means, subject to the Schedule, (a) any transaction (including an agreement with respect to any such transaction) now existing or hereafter entered into between one party to this Agreement (or any Credit Support Provider of such party or any applicable Specified Entity of such party) and the other party to this Agreement (or any Credit Support Provider of such other party or any applicable Specified Entity of such other party) which is not a Transaction under this Agreement but (i) which is a rate swap transaction, swap option, basis swap, forward rate transaction, commodity swap, commodity option, equity or equity index swap, equity or equity index option, bond option, interest rate option, foreign exchange transaction, cap transaction, floor transaction, collar transaction, currency swap transaction, cross-currency rate swap transaction, currency option, credit protection transaction, credit swap, credit default swap, credit default option, total return swap, credit spread transaction, repurchase transaction, reverse repurchase transaction, buy/sell-back transaction, securities lending transaction, weather index transaction or forward purchase or sale of a security, commodity or other financial instrument or interest (including any option with respect to any of these transactions) or (ii) which is a type of transaction that is similar to any transaction referred to in clause (i) above that is currently, or in the future becomes, recurrently entered into in the financial markets (including terms and conditions incorporated by reference in such agreement) and which is a forward, swap, future, option or other derivative on one or more rates, currencies, commodities, equity securities or other equity instruments, debt securities or other debt instruments, economic indices or measures of economic risk or value, or other benchmarks against which payments or deliveries are to be made, (b) any combination of these transactions and (c) any other transaction identified as a Specified Transaction in this Agreement or the relevant confirmation.

"Stamp Tax" means any stamp, registration, documentation or similar tax.

"Stamp Tax Jurisdiction" has the meaning specified in Section 4(e).

"Tax" means any present or future tax, levy, impost, duty, charge, assessment or fee of any nature (including interest, penalties and additions thereto) that is imposed by any government or other taxing authority in respect of any payment under this Agreement other than a stamp, registration, documentation or similar tax.

"Tax Event" has the meaning specified in Section 5(b).

"Tax Event Upon Merger" has the meaning specified in Section 5(b).

"Terminated Transactions" means, with respect to any Early Termination Date, (a) if resulting from an Illegality or a Force Majeure Event, all Affected Transactions specified in the notice given pursuant to Section 6(b)(iv), (b) if resulting from any other Termination Event, all Affected Transactions and (c) if resulting from an Event of Default, all Transactions in effect either immediately before the effectiveness of the notice designating that Early Termination Date or, if Automatic Early Termination applies, immediately before that Early Termination Date.

"Termination Currency" means (a) if a Termination Currency is specified in the Schedule and that currency is freely available, that currency, and (b) otherwise, euro if this Agreement is expressed to be governed by English law or United States Dollars if this Agreement is expressed to be governed by the laws of the State of New York.

"Termination Currency Equivalent" means, in respect of any amount denominated in the Termination Currency, such Termination Currency amount and, in respect of any amount denominated in a currency other than the Termination Currency (the "Other Currency"), the amount in the Termination Currency determined by the party making the relevant determination as being required to purchase such amount of such Other Currency as at the relevant Early Termination Date, or, if the relevant Close-out Amount is determined as of a later date, that later date, with the Termination Currency at the rate equal to the spot exchange rate of the foreign exchange agent (selected as provided below) for the purchase of such Other Currency with the Termination Currency at or about 11:00 a.m. (in the city in which such foreign exchange agent is located) on such date as would be customary for the determination of such a rate for the purchase of such Other Currency for value on the relevant Early Termination Date or that later date. The foreign exchange agent will, if only one party is obliged to make a determination under Section 6(e), be selected in good faith by that party and otherwise will be agreed by the parties.

"Termination Event" means an Illegality, a Force Majeure Event, a Tax Event, a Tax Event Upon Merger or, if specified to be applicable, a Credit Event Upon Merger or an Additional Termination Event.

"Termination Rate" means a rate per annum equal to the arithmetic mean of the cost (without proof or evidence of any actual cost) to each party (as certified by such party) if it were to fund or of funding such amounts.

"Threshold Amount" means the amount, if any, specified as such in the Schedule.

"Transaction" has the meaning specified in the preamble.

"Unpaid Amounts" owing to any party means, with respect to an Early Termination Date, the aggregate of (a) in respect of all Terminated Transactions, the amounts that became payable (or that would have become payable but for Section 2(a)(iii) or due but for Section 5(d)) to such party under Section 2(a)(i) or 2(d)(i)(4) on or prior to such Early Termination Date and which remain unpaid as at such Early Termination Date, (b) in respect of each Terminated Transaction, for each obligation under Section 2(a)(i) which was (or would have been but for Section 2(a)(iii) or 5(d)) required to be settled by delivery to such party on or prior to such Early Termination Date and which has not been so settled as at such Early Termination Date, an amount equal to the fair market value of that which was (or would have been) required to be delivered and (c) if the Early Termination Date results from an Event of Default, a Credit Event Upon Merger or an Additional Termination Event in respect of which all outstanding Transactions are Affected Transactions, any Early Termination Amount due prior to such Early Termination Date and which remains unpaid as of such Early Termination Date, in each case together with any amount of interest accrued or other compensation in respect of that obligation

or deferred obligation, as the case may be, pursuant to Section 9(h)(ii)(l) or (2), as appropriate. The fair market value of any obligation referred to in clause (b) above will be determined as of the originally scheduled date for delivery, in good faith and using commercially reasonable procedures, by the party obliged to make the determination under Section 6(e) or, if each party is so obliged, it will be the average of the Termination Currency Equivalents of the fair market values so determined by both parties.

"Waiting Period" means:–

(a   in respect of an event or circumstance under Section 5(b)(i), other than in the case of Section 5(b)(i)(2) where the relevant payment, delivery or compliance is actually required on the relevant day (in which case no Waiting Period will apply), a period of three Local Business Days (or days that would have been Local Business Days but for the occurrence of that event or circumstance) following the occurrence of that event or circumstance;

and

(b)   in respect of an event or circumstance under Section 5(b)(ii), other than in the case of Section 5(b)(ii)(2) where the relevant payment, delivery or compliance is actually required on the relevant day (in which case no Waiting Period will apply), a period of eight Local Business Days (or days that would have been Local Business Days but for the occurrence of that event or circumstance) following the occurrence of that event or circumstance.

IN WITNESS WHEREOF the parties have executed this document on the respective dates specified below with effect from the date specified on the first page of this document.

....

           (Name of Party)   (Name of Party)

By: ....

Name: Name:

Title: Title:

Date: Date:

..

International Swaps and Derivatives Association, Inc.

SCHEDULE
to the
2002 Master Agreement

dated as of..

between .... and ....

("Party A")	("Party B")
[established as a [COUNTERPARTY TYPE]]	*[established as a [COUNTERPARTY TYPE]]*
[with company number [NUMBER]]	*[with company number [NUMBER]]*
[under the laws of [JURISDICTION]]	*[under the laws of [JURISDICTION]]*
*[acting through its [BRANCH]]**	*[acting through its [BRANCH]]**

Part 1. **Termination Provisions.**

(a)　***"Specified Entity"*** means in relation to Party A for the purpose of:–

Section 5(a)(v), ...

Section 5(a)(vi), ...

Section 5(a)(vii), ...

Section 5(b)(v), ...

and in relation to Party B for the purpose of:–

Section 5(a)(v), ...

Section 5(a)(vi), ...

Section 5(a)(vii), ...

Section 5(b)(v), ...

---

*　Include if applicable.

(b) *"Specified Transaction"* [will have the meaning specified in Section 14 of this Agreement.][means ....
....]*

(c) The *"Cross-Default"* provisions of Section 5(a)(vi) [will][will not]* apply to Party A
[will][will not]* apply to Party B
[*"Specified Indebtedness"* [will have the meaning specified in Section 14 of this Agreement.][means ....
....]*

"Threshold Amount" means ....
....]**

(d) The *"Credit Event Upon Merger"* provisions of Section 5(b)(v)
[will][will not]* apply to Party A
[will][will not]* apply to Party B

(e) The *"Automatic Early Termination"* provision of Section 6(a)
[will][will not]* apply to Party A
[will][will not]* apply to Party B

(f) *"Termination Currency"* [will have the meaning specified in Section 14 of this Agreement.][means ....
....]*

(g) *Additional Termination Event* [will][will not]* apply. [The following will constitute an Additional Termination Event:–...
....
....
....

For the purpose of the foregoing Termination Event, the Affected Party or Affected Parties will be:– ....
....]***

Part 2. **Tax Representations.******

(a) *Payer Representations.* For the purpose of Section 3(e) of this Agreement, [Party A and Party B do not make any representations.][:–
[[(i)] [Party A] [and] [Party B] [each] make[s] the following representation:–

It is not required by any applicable law, as modified by the practice of any relevant governmental revenue authority, of any Relevant Jurisdiction to make any deduction or withholding for or on account of any Tax from any payment (other than interest under Section 9(h) of this Agreement) to

---

*   Delete as applicable.
**   Include if Cross-Default will apply to either Party A or Party B.
***   Include if Additional Termination Event will apply.
****   N.B.: the following representations may need modification if either party is a Multibranch Party.

be made by it to the other party under this Agreement. In making this representation, it may rely on (i) the accuracy of any representations made by the other party pursuant to Section 3(f) of this Agreement, (ii) the satisfaction of the agreement contained in Section 4(a)(i) or 4(a)(iii) of this Agreement and the accuracy and effectiveness of any document provided by the other party pursuant to Section 4(a)(i) or 4(a)(iii) of this Agreement and (iii) the satisfaction of the agreement of the other party contained in Section 4(d) of this Agreement, except that it will not be a breach of this representation where reliance is placed on clause (ii) above and the other party does not deliver a form or document under Section 4(a)(iii) by reason of material prejudice to its legal or commercial position.]*

[[(ii)] [Party A] [and] [Party B] [each] make[s] the following representation[s]:–................

....

....

....]]*

(b)   **Payee Representations.** For the purpose of Section 3(f) of this Agreement, [Party A and Party B do not make any representations.][:–

[[(i)] [Party A] [and] [Party B] [each] make[s] the following representation:–

It is fully eligible for the benefits of the "Business Profits" or "Industrial and Commercial Profits" provision, as the case may be, the "interest" provision or the "Other Income" provision, if any, of the Specified Treaty with respect to any payment described in such provisions and received or to be received by it in connection with this Agreement and no such payment is attributable to a trade or business carried on by it through a permanent establishment in the Specified Jurisdiction.

"Specified Treaty" means with respect to Party A ....

"Specified Jurisdiction" means with respect to Party A ....

"Specified Treaty" means with respect to Party B ....

"Specified Jurisdiction" means with respect to Party B ....]*

[[(ii)] [Party A] [and] [Party B] [each] make[s] the following representation:–

Each payment received or to be received by it in connection with this Agreement will be effectively connected with its conduct of a trade or business in the Specified Jurisdiction.

"Specified Jurisdiction" means with respect to Party A ....

"Specified Jurisdiction" means with respect to Party B ....]*

[[(iii)] [Party A] [and] [Party B] [each] make[s] the following representation:–

It is a "U.S. person" (as that term is used in section 1.1441–4(a)(3)(ii) of United States Treasury Regulations) for United States federal income tax purposes.]*

---

*   Delete as applicable.

[[(iv)] [Party A] [and] [Party B] [each] make[s] the following representation:–

It is a "non-U.S. branch of a foreign person" (as that term is used in section 1.1441–4(a)(3)(ii) of United States Treasury Regulations) for United States federal income tax purposes.]*

[[(v)] [Party A] [and] [Party B] [each] make[s] the following representation:–

With respect to payments made to an address outside the United States or made by a transfer of funds to an account outside the United States, it is a "non-U.S. branch of a foreign person" (as that term is used in section 1.1441–4(a)(3)(ii) of United States Treasury Regulations) for United States federal income tax purposes.]*

[[(vi)] [Party A] [and] [Party B] [each] make[s] the following representation:–

It is a "foreign person" (as that term is used in section 1.6041—4(a)(4) of United States Treasury Regulations) for United States federal income tax purposes.]*

[[(vii)] [Party A] [and] [Party B] [each] make[s] the following representation[s]:–

....

....

....]]

Part 3.   Agreement to Deliver Documents.

For the purpose of Sections 4(a)(i) and 4(a)(ii) of this Agreement, each party agrees to deliver the following documents, as applicable:–

(a)   Tax forms, documents or certificates to be delivered are[: none][:–

Party required to deliver document	Form/Document/ Certificate	Date by which to be delivered
....	....	....
....	....	....
....	....	....
....	....	....
....	....	............................]*

---

* Delete as applicable.

(b)   Other documents to be delivered are[: none][:–

Party required to deliver document	Form/Document/ Certificate	Date by which to be delivered	Covered by Section 3(d) Representation
....	....	....	[Yes][No]
....	....	....	[Yes][No]
....	....	....	[Yes][No]
....	....	....	[Yes][No]
....	....	....	[Yes][No]*

Part 4. **Miscellaneous.**

(a)   *Addresses for Notices.* For the purpose of Section 12(a) of this Agreement:–
       Address for notices or communications to Party A:–
       Address: ....
       Attention: ....
       Telex No.: .... Answerback: ....
       Facsimile No.: .... Telephone No.: ....
       E-mail:...
       Electronic Messaging System Details: ....
       Specific Instructions: ....

       Address for notices or communications to Party B:–
       Address: ....
       Attention: ....
       Telex No.: .... Answerback: ....
       Facsimile No.: .... Telephone No.: ....
       E-mail:...
       Electronic Messaging System Details: ....
       Specific Instructions: ....

---

*   Delete as applicable.

(b)   ***Process Agent.*** For the purpose of Section 13(c) of this Agreement:–

Party A appoints as its Process Agent: [not applicable][....]*
Party B appoints as its Process Agent: [not applicable][....]*

(c)   ***Offices.*** The provisions of Section 10(a) [will][will not]* apply to this Agreement.

(d)   ***Multibranch Party.*** For the purpose of Section 10(b) of this Agreement:–

Party A [is not a Multibranch Party.][is a Multibranch Party and may enter into a Transaction through any of the following Offices:–

....

....]*

Party B [is not a Multibranch Party.][is a Multibranch Party and may enter into a Transaction through any of the following Offices:–

....

....]*

[(e)   ***Calculation Agent.*** The Calculation Agent is ...., unless otherwise specified in a Confirmation in relation to the relevant Transaction.]**

[(f)]   ***Credit Support Document.*** Details of any Credit Support Document:– [none][..........

....

....]*

[(g)]   ***Credit Support Provider.*** Credit Support Provider means in relation to Party A, [none]

[...

....]*

Credit Support Provider means in relation to Party B, [none][...................................

....]*

[(h)] ***Governing Law.*** This Agreement will be governed by and construed in accordance with [English law] [the laws of the State of New York (without reference to choice of law doctrine)]*.

---

*   Delete as applicable.
**   Include if applicable.

[(i)] ***Netting of Payments.*** "Multiple Transaction Payment Netting" [will not apply for the purpose of Section 2(c) of this Agreement.][will apply for the purpose of Section 2(c) of this Agreement to [all Transactions] [the following Transactions or groups of Transactions:– ....

....]

(in each case starting from [the date of this Agreement][.....................................])]*

[(j)] ***"Affiliate"*** [will have the meaning specified in Section 14 of this Agreement.] [means

....]*

[(k)] ***Absence of Litigation.*** For the purpose of Section 3(c):–

"Specified Entity" means in relation to Party A, ...

"Specified Entity" means in relation to Party B, ...

[(l)] ***No Agency.*** The provisions of Section 3(g) [will][will not]* apply to this Agreement.

[(m)] ***Additional Representation*** [will][will not]* apply. [For the purpose of Section 3 of this Agreement, the following will constitute an Additional Representation:–

[[(i)] ***Relationship Between Parties.*** Each party will be deemed to represent to the other party on the date on which it enters into a Transaction that (absent a written agreement between the parties that expressly imposes affirmative obligations to the contrary for that Transaction):–

[(1)] *Non-Reliance.* It is acting for its own account, and it has made its own independent decisions to enter into that Transaction and as to whether that Transaction is appropriate or proper for it based upon its own judgment and upon advice from such advisers as it has deemed necessary. It is not relying on any communication (written or oral) of the other party as investment advice or as a recommendation to enter into that Transaction, it being understood that information and explanations related to the terms and conditions of a Transaction will not be considered investment advice or a recommendation to enter into that Transaction. No communication (written or oral) received from the other party will be deemed to be an assurance or guarantee as to the expected results of that Transaction.

[(2)] *Assessment and Understanding.* It is capable of assessing the merits of and understanding (on its own behalf or through independent professional advice), and understands and accepts, the terms, conditions and risks of that Transaction. It is also capable of assuming, and assumes, the risks of that Transaction.

[(3)] *Status of Parties.* The other party is not acting as a fiduciary for or an adviser to it in respect of that Transaction.]]*

[[(n)] ***Recording of Conversations.*** Each party (i) consents to the recording of telephone conversations between the trading, marketing and other relevant personnel of the parties in connection with this Agreement or any potential Transaction, (ii) agrees to obtain any necessary consent of, and give any necessary notice of such recording to, its relevant personnel and (iii) agrees, to the extent permitted by applicable law, that recordings may be submitted in evidence in any Proceedings.]**

---

*   Delete as applicable.

**   Include if applicable.

Part 5.   **Other Provisions.**

....
            (Name of Party)   (Name of Party)

By: ....   By: ....
    Name: Name:
    Title: Title:
    Date: Date:

Notes

Chapter 1. An Overview of the Derivatives Marketplace

1. The increased market volatility was due, in large measure, to the 1973 collapse of the fixed exchange rate regime previously guided by the Bretton Woods Agreement. It was followed soon thereafter by several oil price shocks.

2. Exchanges have certainly been active in creating "customized" derivative products of their own, in order to compete more effectively against the OTC sector; for instance, numerous exchanges now offer flexible options (flex options) which give users the ability to specify strike, exercise style, maturity and so forth, long-term options, overnight options, and so on. The changes have not been solely confined to product structure. The exchange sector has also expanded into new reference asset classes, such as weather (temperature), inflation, bankruptcy, microchip prices, and so forth. See Banks (2003) for additional examples.

3. *Hybrid bonds* include callable bonds, which are bonds with an embedded option giving the issuer the right to redeem the security, and putable bonds, giving the investor the right to put the security back to the issuer. Other variations exist, such as "step-up" callable bonds (which pay increasingly higher coupons until they are called).

   Convertible bonds are hybrid debt/equity securities paying a periodic coupon that contain an embedded equity option permitting the investor to convert the security into a pre-specified amount of shares (many types of convertibles exist, including zero-coupon convertibles, mandatory convertibles, and so forth).

   Exchangeable bonds are similar to convertibles, except they permit conversion into the shares of another company (often a subsidiary or affiliate of the issuer).

   Reverse convertible bonds are identical to convertible bonds, except that the right to convert the bond into equity is held by the issuer rather than the investor.

   Bonds with warrants are hybrid securities consisting of an underlying bond which pays a coupon and an attached warrant (most often an equity warrant) permitting the investor to exercise into a pre-specified amount of shares; the warrant is often detached and traded separately.

Structured notes are fixed or floating rate securities that contain embedded swaps or options; swaps and/or options can be assembled in virtually any combination in order to provide customized payoff profiles. While the combination of such notes is very broad, we summarize the main categories as follows:

a) *Range floaters*: notes paying an enhanced coupon while the floating rate reference trades within a pre-specified band; if the reference trades outside the band the investor sacrifices one day's interest for each day the reference is outside the band. More extreme versions, known as "range knock-out floaters," pay higher coupons than range floaters but cease paying interest for an entire interest period, for example one quarter, if the reference trades outside the range for a single day (we discuss digital options and knock-out options, which form the derivative core of these structures, in Chapter 8).

b) *Inverse floaters*: notes paying an enhanced coupon as a reference rate falls and a decreased coupon as a reference rate rises; these notes pay off based on a formula such as (x percent fixed minus floating), and are often leveraged to provide greater potential returns or losses (we discuss inverse floating swaps, the core derivative component of these notes, at length in Chapter 10).

c) *Leveraged floaters*: notes paying an enhanced coupon based on a leverage, or multiplier factor; the floating reference coupon is magnified by a straightforward, or complex, multiplier formula which determines payoff or loss (we discuss power options and leveraged swaps, the core derivative components of these notes, in Chapters 8 and 10, respectively).

d) *Multiple index floaters*: notes paying an enhanced coupon based on the spread between two similar or different indexes; movement of the spread in an unfavorable direction can result in loss of coupons and/or principal (we discuss multifactor options, the core derivative component of these notes, in Chapter 8).

The broad category of *collateralized debt obligations* (CDOs) has emerged as an important element of the credit derivative market of the late 1990s and new millennium. CDOs, which are available in the form of collateralized bond obligations and collateralized loan obligations, are portfolios of corporate credits that are pooled and then issued in tranches, with yields and repayment priorities arranged by class. CDOs can be created using physical bonds or loans (so-called "balance sheet" or "cash" CDOs) or credit derivatives (synthetic CDOs). Many of the credit portfolio diversification techniques we consider in Part III are applicable in the creation and evaluation of CDOs (in addition, the general category of basket default options and swaps we consider in Part II can be viewed as an off balance sheet equivalent of a balance sheet CDO). Again, we note that the act of embedding derivatives in structured products and selling the notes outright eliminates the intermediary's credit risk on the derivatives. Readers interested in considering detailed discussions on structured notes should consult Tavakoli (1998), Das (2000), or Smithson (1999).

4. Readers interested in further discussion may with to consult Banks (1993) or Smithson (1999), for example.

5. Our classification of options is based on path dependent and path independent categories, similar to one proposed by Jarrow (1995), with select additions and expansions. As we discuss in greater detail in Chapter 5, path dependent options are derivatives whose price is dependent on the level of the underlying reference at previous points in time, while path independent options are derivatives whose price is only dependent on the level of the underlying reference at exercise or expiry. There are, as one might imagine, many others means of classifying or grouping options; this is but one alternative.

6. For instance, in October 2002 Goldman Sachs and Deutsche Bank introduced options on US macroeconomic data releases, including the monthly employment report, ISM manufacturing index, producer price index, and retail sales. A buyer of an option on one of these indexes receives the difference between a strike price and the actual index number that is announced. Whereas previously a speculator or hedger seeking to act on the information could only do so indirectly, for example, by using derivatives tied to Treasury rates or Federal Funds, or other indicators likely to be influenced by the particular figures, they can now do so much more directly.

7. Fabozzi and Modigliani (1992, p. xxi).

8. Some financial intermediaries make use of *derivative product companies* (DPCs) to structurally enhance their own credit quality. DPCs, which carry external credit ratings higher than those of their financial institution sponsors, were created by some banks and securities firms in the early 1990s to transact derivatives with a broader range of counterparties and help concentrate derivative transactions in a more creditworthy segment of the market. Many AA–AAA-rated entities active in the derivative markets (often end users such as sovereigns, supranationals, and highly-rated corporates) have very strict charters or policies that only permit derivatives dealing with other AA–AAA-rated institutions. In order to serve these clients, US and foreign banks have established DPCs that can, through their structural features, gain coveted AAA–Aaa-ratings and permit dealing with higher-rated clients. Once in possession of higher credit ratings through DPCs, sponsors find themselves in a position to enter into short or long-dated, vanilla, or complex derivative transactions with a broader base of counterparties. This business comes at a price, of course; in most cases DPCs are capital-intensive entities, and this means that returns must be sufficient to cover capital allocated.

In order to achieve AAA–Aaa ratings (in instances where sponsor institutions carry ratings ranging from A to BBB) a DPC must be organized in a manner that addresses legal, risk capital, and procedural issues. From a legal perspective, a DPC must be structured as a bankruptcy-remote entity, so that if the sponsor encounters financial difficulties and files for bankruptcy, the assets of the DPC will not be included as part of the sponsor's bankruptcy; this bankruptcy-remote characteristic is vital in achieving ratings which are higher than those of the sponsor. In addition to being bankruptcy-remote, a DPC must have enough legal comfort that it can net counterparty credit exposures or, where it cannot, that it has sufficient capital to support gross credit exposures; it must also believe that it can enforce all collateral claims.

From a market risk perspective, it must minimize exposure and generally does so by engaging in "back-to-back" or mirror transactions with the sponsor, which then manages the residual market risk in the course of its regular derivatives business (note that certain DPCs manage residual market risk more actively within the structure itself).

From a credit risk perspective, a DPC is generally only permitted to deal with counterparties of a certain rating. The rating cut-off for most DPCs typically extends to the lower end of the investment grade classification (that is, BBB+/Baa1); if counterparties are downgraded below this level, swaps must be terminated or collateral must be posted. In addition, sponsors must post collateral used in "back-to-back" mirror transactions used for managing market risk.

From a capital perspective, a DPC must undergo a thorough simulation analysis to ensure sufficiency of capital under normal and extreme market conditions based on the markets and instruments in which the DPC is likely to deal. The simulation analysis focuses on (a) the risk exposures that will be generated by portfolios of transactions and (b) the default incidence of counterparties in its portfolio (net of collateral, though not recoveries). The simulation process generates, through tens of thousands of statistical runs based on select statistical inputs, a credit loss distribution function. The credit loss function provides the DPC, sponsor, and rating agencies with valuable information on expected and unexpected credit losses, and the reserves and capital required to support each (we discuss this topic at greater length in Part III).

Two primary types of DPCs exist: continuation vehicles and termination vehicles; Merrill Lynch created the first continuation DPC in 1991 (Merrill Lynch Derivative Products) and Salomon Brothers created the first termination DPC in 1993 (Salomon Swapco; Salomon is now part of Citibank). Continuation structures are those which continue to function even after a "trigger event" has occurred. Rather than terminate existing portfolios of derivatives immediately after a "trigger event," the DPC appoints a contingent manager who assumes responsibility for managing portfolios until transactions mature as originally contracted; in some cases that may extend for five, ten, or more years into the future. Continuation DPCs are generally not permitted to book incremental transactions once in a "wind-down" mode, though the contingent manager is permitted to enter into new transactions that mitigate risk. Termination structures, in contrast, are those which cease all activity once a "trigger event" occurs and accelerate/unwind all existing derivative portfolios immediately at current mid-market rates; no contingent manager is appointed and no transactions are permitted to run until maturity.

Note that there is a third type of DPC known as the "guarantee DPC;" this is a subset of the termination structure. Guarantee DPCs are not actually derivative intermediaries but are guarantors of derivative intermediaries (often the sponsor). Guarantee DPCs use in-the-money contracts from the guaranteed intermediary to pledge against payouts to contracts that are out-of-the-money (that is, where the intermediary owes its swap counterparty). Such DPCs must still adhere to structural procedures and termination events. Note that termination vehicles are generally less capital intensive than continuation vehicles. "Trigger events" for continuation and termination DPCs vary, but generally include severe downgrading or bankruptcy of the sponsor (parent), severe downgrading of the DPC itself, or breach of select operating guidelines within the DPC (for example, failure of the sponsor to post collateral, a breach of minimum capital as predicted by stress tests, and so on).

As the financial industry entered a period of recovery during the mid to late-1990s, numerous international financial institutions were upgraded back into the AA category. At the same time, various corporate and sovereign end users that had been rated as AA were downgraded as a result of industry-specific or macroeconomic events. This slowed transaction volumes flowing through DPCs for several years. However, with a weakening credit environment and a spate of financial intermediary downgrades occurring in the millennium, the trend is reversing and DPCs may once again be used more actively.

9. Certain established clearing houses, many associated with global futures and options exchanges, have extended their clearing services and technologies from the listed contract sphere to the OTC marketplace; for instance, clearers such as the London Clearinghouse, Euronext, and others now offer OTC derivative credit clearing services.

10. Full legal comfort is generally obtained only once amendments have been made to specific local bankruptcy/insolvency codes or laws (in the United States, for example, this has occurred via the US Bankruptcy Code and the Financial Institutions Reform, Recovery, and Enforcement Act).

11. It should be noted that most, though not all, of the derivative transactions considered in this book tend to be high risk in nature, by virtue of the dollar exposure they add to an institution's books, or by the long maturity horizon which they frequently cover. Credit officers and analysts considering these types of deals must always bear in mind that unaltered exposures (that is, those that have not been modified to include risk mitigating techniques) carry either a substantial quantity of risk equivalent exposure and/or a long time to final maturity. Such transactions are often not acceptable, in unsecured form, for counterparties that are of weak or deteriorating credit quality. One of the reasons the derivative market has been successful to date in avoiding significant credit losses is because of an understanding by dealers and bankers that these types of structures, in unsecured form, are generally only appropriate for institutions of high-medium credit quality. This is an element of market self-regulation we discuss in further detail in Chapter 4.

Although a great deal of business is transacted with lower credit quality counterparties, such deals are typically enhanced by one of the risk-mitigating techniques mentioned earlier. Institutions which are typically regarded as suitable for short to long-term unsecured derivative transactions (that is, those with a final maturity of one to ten years) are those which are rated by a credit department or an external rating agency in the middle to high investment grade category. Institutions which have weaker investment grade ratings are generally only regarded as acceptable for short to medium-term unsecured transactions (that is, those with a final maturity between one and three to five years). Counterparties with sub-investment grade ratings, in contrast, are often only acceptable for very short-term unsecured derivative transactions (that is, those with a final maturity of six to twelve months) or, in many instances, no unsecured transactions at all.

Chapter 2. Derivative Losses

1. Readers interested in comprehensive accounts of the role of derivatives in losses at LTCM and Enron are urged to consult Jorion (2000) and ISDA (2002a), respectively.
2. The losses put tremendous financial pressure on UBS and just five months later it was forced to "merge" with smaller rival Swiss Bank Corp to form the new UBS. The fact that Swiss Bank professionals gained most of the top derivative and management posts suggests the transaction was actually a takeover.
3. Although a detailed discussion of the nature of the internal control failures (and resulting losses) of each of these institutions is well beyond the scope of this text, we provide additional detail on several of these cases, as they provide important information on what can go wrong with internal controls:
    a) *Barings*: in 1995 unauthorized trading in yen index and interest rate futures/options contracts brought down this UK merchant bank. The unauthorized speculative trading of futures and options was based on Nikkei 225 futures/options, Japanese Government Bond futures, and Euroyen futures traded on the Singapore International Monetary Exchange (SIMEX), Nikkei 225 futures/options traded on the Osaka Stock Exchange (OSE), Euroyen futures traded on the Tokyo International Financial Futures Exchange (TIFFE), and Japanese Government Bond futures traded on the Tokyo Stock Exchange (TSE). Investigations into the incident reveal that at the time of collapse positions held by the Barings Singapore office amounted to: (1) 61,039 contracts long of Nikkei 225 index futures (in SIMEX contract equivalents), equal to US$7b notional and 49 percent of the nearby contract open interest; (2) 28,034 contracts short of Japanese Government Bond futures (in SIMEX contract equivalents), equal to US$19.65b notional and 85 percent of the nearby contract open interest; (3) 6845 contracts short of Euroyen futures, equal to US$350m notional and 5 percent of the nearly contract open interest; and (4) 71,000 contracts short of Nikkei 225 puts and calls, equal to US$7b notional (Source: *Report of the Board Bank-*

ing Supervision Inquiry into the Circumstances of the Collapse of Barings, 1995). Although notional amounts do not represent value at risk, the magnitude of the positions and the percentage of open interest are well in excess of any prudent risk guidelines. According to independent reports commissioned by the Government of Singapore and the House of Commons in the United Kingdom, the trader was able to hide trades in an "error account" (the 88888 account), which went undetected and unreconciled by the firm's control functions for a period of several years. Inadequate internal controls (including lack of separation between the trading desk and the settlements unit) coupled with flagrant unauthorized trading, were sufficient to create the devastating losses.

b)   *Daiwa Bank*: in 1995 Daiwa Bank announced losses of US$1.1b from unauthorized trading of US Treasury securities and Treasury derivatives at its New York branch. According to investigations, the trading took place over a 12-year period, during which time an internal control framework was either not in existence or unable to detect the pattern of unauthorized trading. In addition, it appears that, as with Barings, the segregation between front and back office functions was not properly delineated, with the trader responsible for the losses exercising control over settlements processes.

c)   *Sumitomo Corporation*: in mid-1996 Sumitomo Corporation announced losses of US$2.6b from unauthorized trading of London Metal Exchange copper futures from its Tokyo office. According to reports the trading occurred over an 11-year period, during which time no internal controls were in place to detect the unauthorized activity. Sumitomo ultimately sued a number of international banks (including JP Morgan, Merrill Lynch, and Credit Lyonnais) that had granted the trader credit limits to fund LME margin positions; most settled out of court.

d)   *Allfirst*: In early 2002 Allied Irish Bank (AIB) was forced to announce losses of US$691 million as a result of unauthorized trading by one of its Baltimore-based foreign exchange traders, Rusnak. AIB management indicated that the trader had manipulated controls to hide losses in Allfirst's foreign exchange trading operation over a period of five years. Specifically, Rusnak, who expected the yen to strengthen against the dollar, took dollar/yen forward foreign exchange positions that were well in excess of his authorized US$2.5 million daily loss limit; when he began posting losses (as the dollar strengthened against the yen), he attempted to cover up his errors by creating fictitious option trades. For instance, in order to generate cash to cover his losing forward positions, he sold deep-in-the-money currency options expiring within a short time frame (for example, one day) and bought the same options expiring one month out. These left the position looking flat and the overall book within risk limits, but merely delayed inevitable recognition of the bad positions.

In the aftermath of the discovery and announcement, AIB engaged former US currency comptroller Ludwig to conduct a "post-mortem." The findings revealed an almost complete collapse of internal control processes and management supervision. For instance, the company had ignored the most basic operational precautions, such as obtaining daily foreign exchange prices from independent third parties (had this occurred, controllers would have noted discrepancies and caught the fraud at a much earlier stage). In fact, the accounting department used Rusnak's own foreign exchange prices when computing his daily profit/loss statement, which meant he could manipulate them to his advantage (for example, to show profits and remain within risk limits). Furthermore, the deep in-the-money options Rusnak bought and sold carried the same prices, despite the fact they had different maturities, but controllers did not detect this discrepancy. Rusnak also exploited Allfirst's outdated risk management and trading systems, which were incapable of reporting one day expiring options, allowing for further manipulation of "hedges." Rusnak also convinced operations clerks that since no cash position resulted from the simultaneous buy/sell, they did not need to be externally confirmed with the clients (an otherwise standard practice).

4. Gay and Medero (1996).

5. For instance BT absorbed/paid an equivalent of approximately US$150m of the US$195m loss on the Procter & Gamble trades, US$67m on Air Products, US$8m on Gibson Greetings (the bank released Gibson from US$14m of payments due on the swaps in exchange for a single US$6.2m payment from Gibson), US$12 m on Federal Paper Board, and so on.

6. Mahonia was used to channel several billion dollars to Enron as financing for gas trades in the form of "prepaid swaps" that were actually loans. In many cases the gas delivered was transferred from Mahonia to JP Morgan, which then sold the gas back to Enron. Insurers providing surety bond coverage baulked at paying as they felt the transactions were "circular," flowing from Enron to Mahonia to JP Morgan and back to Enron.

7. According to US rating agency Standard and Poors, 234 global publicly rated companies defaulted on US$178 billion of debt in 2002.

Chapter 3. Risk Governance and Risk Management

1. Readers interested in the broader topic of governance may wish to consult Banks (2004).

2. Board directors obviously have many other issues with which to contend, including financial controls, audit standards, compensation, strategy, director and executive nomination, and so on; risk is but one piece of the "corporate puzzle."

3. This requirement is particularly important in a competitive environment where institutions often push to complete transactions without thoroughly understanding how credit will be repaid. For instance, it is not adequate, from either a governance or prudency perspective, to assume that a collateralized transaction requires no assessment of counterparty strength or source of repayment. Credit extensions should never be granted without full and proper counterparty assessment and a detailed understanding of primary, secondary, and tertiary sources of repayment.

Chapter 4. Regulatory and Industry Initiatives

1. Though some amount of OTC derivatives activity occurs offshore (for example, through unregulated subsidiaries of dealers, hedge funds, and so on) the very largest dealers also operate onshore and are subject to all applicable regulations. Indeed, large players almost seem to prefer operating in an environment where they are subject to scrutiny, recognizing that it is an important element of corporate governance.

2. Details were communicated in: Bank for International Settlements (1988), *International Convergence of Capital Measurement and Capital Standards*, Basle: BIS.

3. Certain inconsistencies carried on throughout the 1990s and into the new millennium. Some became very striking after credit derivatives became a mainstay of the marketplace, because the same economic credit position could be replicated in the derivatives book for a fraction of the capital charge. For instance, a bank, holding a US$100 million corporate bond, would have to allocate US$8 million in regulatory capital, but only US$2.4 million if the same position were held through a credit derivative. In order to overcome such apparent discrepancies prior to broader overhaul of the new Capital Accord, the BIS allowed certain compromise solutions.

4. It is unlikely, of course, that an institution would allocate a negative risk figure to the swap portfolio as this is not a particularly conservative means of viewing portfolio credit risk; it is more likely in such instances to set the net amount at risk equal to zero.

5. When securitization vehicles began appearing in earnest during the 1990s, they basically functioned as off-balance sheet guarantees and did not attract regulatory capital. In fact, material credit risks were not always transferred (for example, residual exposure to default, exposure to the remaining balance sheet portfolio, moral recourse, and so on), meaning good risks may have been securitized, bad ones retained, and the portfolio risk profile skewed. Regulatory scrutiny has since improved.

6. Though operational risks are vitally important in the financial world, they are well outside of the scope of this book and will not be discussed. Note that under the Three Pillars, the market risk charges put forth via the 1996 Amendment remain largely unchanged.

7. In addition, in order for a global framework to be truly effective, there must be basic standards across institutions and countries – indicating that some general level of harmonization must exist in tax and accounting rules; this is beyond the scope of a regulator such as the BIS, meaning other regulatory and industry bodies will have to take up the task – which is likely to be a time-consuming process.

8. For instance, it is now very widely known that the basic BIS "add-on" approach results in overstatement or understatement of exposures at particular points in time. There is evidence that under the BIS method, credit exposures are higher when counterparty current actual exposure is near zero and lower when current actual exposure is high, because the BIS add-on is the same regardless of the moneyness of the derivative transaction. In addition, although

the static BIS approach takes account of netting, it only does so at a point in time, rather than over the life of portfolio transactions of varying maturities.

9. Group of 30 is an industry group comprised of intermediaries, end users, and academics. Corporate default rates reached a peak in 1990–2 and remained unchallenged in size and frequency until 2002.

10. DPG includes Goldman Sachs, Merrill Lynch, CSFB, Lehman Brothers, Salomon Brothers (now a unit of Citicorp), and Morgan Stanley.

11. CRMG includes Merrill Lynch, Citibank, Morgan Stanley, Goldman Sachs, Bear Stearns, JP Morgan Chase, Lehman Brothers, CSFB, UBS, Barclays Bank, and Deutsche Bank.

12. Federal Reserve Chairman Greenspan, SEC Chairman Levitt, and Treasury Secretary Rubin publicly endorsed the efforts of the CRMG.

13. Apart from the instances of Enron as a direct credit counterparty on derivative transactions, it is worth noting that Enron was itself a reference credit on many credit derivative transactions between third parties. Indeed, Enron was the largest reference credit for a period of time, but the company's failure resulted in (a) no dispute between counterparties holding Enron-reference credit default swaps and options, and (b) no meaningful drop in the liquidity of the credit derivative marketplace; these are two important signals that suggest the credit derivative market has become quite mature.

14. For instance, the company used the Chewco SPEs to evade excess leverage, the LJM partnerships to inflate earnings and the Raptor SPEs to "hedge" financial volatility of various investments.

15. Though few used the First and Second Methods, many end users have come to rely on the Market Quotation method because they feel it provides protection from arbitrarily determined early termination values by forcing dealers to get third party quotes. In fact, end users may have been deriving some false comfort from this provision; for liquid products misvaluation can be detected quite easily, and for illiquid/complex products (including many of those discussed in this book) it is difficult to get Market Quotations, meaning that the dealer would have to make its own determination under the Market Quotation Many dealers, for their part, have noted the shortcomings of the method during periods of market stress, when all parties are searching for the same quote.

16. Many had resisted the inclusion of repos/reverses, as a delivery failure (which occurs with some frequency) could technically trigger a default under the Master Agreement. However, the 2002 version requires specified transactions to be in liquidation or acceleration (rather than the subject of delivery failure) before the Master Agreement default is triggered.

Chapter 5. Classification and Quantification of Credit Risk

1. Readers interested in focusing on aspects of counterparty credit risk analysis may wish to consult Fridson (1995) or Donaldson (1989).

2. Readers interested in analyzing such products and their associated risks are urged to consult works with a broader scope, for example, Donaldson (1989) and Banks (1993).

3. The Group of 30 (1994) follow-up survey, for instance, revealed that 96 percent of dealers and 99 percent of end users surveyed believe they should measure current (AMR) and potential (PMR) exposure of derivatives (Source: Group of 30. *Derivatives: Practices and Principles, Follow-up Surveys of Industry Practice*, 1994.)

4. Some parallel between the uncertain future value of derivatives and potential risk can also be found in the loan market through committed, but undrawn, facilities granted by a bank to its customer. When the facility is first arranged its final usage level, and therefore exposure, is uncertain. Assuming the facility is based on floating rates, the movement of rates will certainly influence the timing and magnitude of drawdown (for example, as rates decline the borrowing cost to the company declines and the probability of a drawdown rises). However, usage will also be influenced by other factors, such as corporate investment and spending programs, expansion or acquisition opportunities, business climate, and so on. In the extreme, a bank may simply choose to assume that the facility will be fully drawn at some point during its life, and therefore assign a full risk allocation against the facility. This, however, is an extremely conservative stance.

5. We provide a basic review of the Black–Scholes model in Appendix 1; in addition, the reader may wish to consult the original work by Black and Scholes (1973) for additional detail.

6. Note that not all financial prices/rates follow a lognormal distribution; for simplicity, however, we assume that the lognormal process holds true for the majority of cases.

7. Note for example Cox and Ross's *The Pricing of Options for Jump Process*, (Working paper, University of Pennsylvania, 1975) and Merton's 'Option Pricing When Underlying Stock Returns are Discontinuous' (*Journal of Financial Economics*, March 1976).

8. In generic form we may say that

$$dy = adt + bdz \tag{1}$$

where a is also known as an instantaneous rate of change in the random variable (and is sometimes referred to as μ or a drift coefficient), while b is the instantaneous standard deviation (or diffusion coefficient). Both a and b are constants. If a and b are instead functions of certain other variables, they follow what is known as an Ito process, which is defined as a(y,t) and b(y,t), where the values of a and b are functions of y and t. This is shown as

$$dy = a(y,t)dt + b(y,t)dz \tag{2}$$

We may add, further, that the random variable has an expected return of a and variance of b^2. Those familiar with stochastic calculus will recognize the standard form of Ito's Lemma as

$$dF = \left[\frac{dF}{dy}a + \frac{dF}{dt} + \frac{1}{2}\frac{d^2F}{dy^2}b^2 \right] dt + \frac{dF}{dy}bdz \tag{3}$$

For those not familiar with Ito's Lemma (or not desiring to get involved with calculus), we note simply that it is a form for solving differentials of stochastic variables (such as stock prices, time, and so on). Utilizing the equation above, where μ and σ are functions of the stock price S and time t, we substitute as follows:

$$dF = \left[\frac{dF}{dS} \mu S + \frac{dF}{dt} + \frac{1}{2}\frac{d^2F}{dy^2} \sigma^2 S^2\right] dt + \frac{dF}{dS} \sigma S dz \qquad (4)$$

(recall that the constant a from the general equation is replaced not by μ, but by $\mu*S$; likewise, constant b is replaced by $\sigma*S$).

We have said that the random variable in a Markov process is lognormally distributed. With this information, we can set the function F equal to the natural log of the underlying security price S, and incorporate the differentials. We solve the partial differentials when $F = \ln(S)$. These may be shown as

$$\frac{\delta F}{\delta S} = \frac{1}{S}, \ \frac{\delta^2 F}{\delta S^2} = -\frac{1}{S^2}, \ and \ -\frac{\delta F}{\delta t} = 0 \qquad (5)$$

Substituting back we note

$$dF = \left[\frac{1}{S}\mu S + 0 + \frac{1}{2}\left[-\frac{1}{S^2}\sigma^2 S^2\right]\right] dt + \frac{1}{S} \sigma S dz \qquad (6)$$

which equals

$$dF = \left[\mu - \frac{\sigma^2}{2}\right] dt + \sigma dz \qquad (7)$$

Earlier we said that the random variable has an expected return of a and variance of b^2. This means the change in F, from one period to the next (i.e. (T – t), or τ) is:

$$\phi\left[\left[\mu - \frac{\sigma^2}{2}\tau\right], \ \sigma^2\tau\right] \qquad (8)$$

or

$$\phi\left[\left[\mu - \frac{\sigma^2}{2}\tau\right], \ \sigma\sqrt{\tau}\right] \qquad (9)$$

We have set $F = \ln(S)$, so $\ln(S(T)) - \ln(S)$ is precisely equal to the result above (i.e. it represents the change from one period to the next). We may therefore conclude that

$$\ln(S_T) - \ln(S) \rightarrow \phi \left[\left[\mu - \frac{\sigma^2}{2} \tau \right], \sigma\sqrt{\tau} \right] \tag{10}$$

which says that the difference in the natural logs of the stock prices between time T and t is normally distributed with mean of

$$\mu - \frac{\sigma^2}{2} \tau \tag{11}$$

and standard deviation

$$\sigma\sqrt{\tau} \tag{12}$$

Finally, we may calculate from above that

$$\ln\left\{ \frac{S_T}{S} \right\} = \left[\left[\mu - \frac{\sigma^2}{2} \tau \right] + \sigma\sqrt{\tau} \right] \tag{13}$$

which equals

$$S_T = Se^{\left[\left[\mu - \frac{\sigma^2}{2} \tau \right] + \sigma\sqrt{\tau} \right]} \tag{14}$$

Readers interested in a more detailed review of the above should refer to the original work by Black and Scholes (1973), as well as discussions in Haley and Schall (1979), Hull and White (1987), Merton (1990), Gibson (1991), Field and Jaycobs (1992), Hull (1989), Hunter and Stowe (1992a), Wilmott (1993), and Dewynne and Howison (1995),– among many others.

9. Standard option pricing models require input of the strike price, underlying price, time, risk-free rate, and volatility to generate a price (for equity-related options dividends must also be input); all are observable in the market except volatility. Traders thus use quoted option prices to derive the volatility level a given option; this is implied volatility.

10. See Hull (1989), for example.

11. The reader familiar with statistics will recall that z factors are calculated via the following:

$$F(x) = P\{X \le x\} \tag{1}$$

$$= P\left[\frac{X - \mu}{\sigma} \le \frac{x - \mu}{\sigma} \right] \tag{2}$$

$$= P\left[Z \le \frac{x - \sigma}{\sigma} \right] \tag{3}$$

$$\Rightarrow \phi\left[Z= \frac{x-\sigma}{\sigma}\right] \tag{4}$$

where μ is the mean, σ is the standard deviation, and x is an observation; $\phi z(\alpha)$ is obtained from a table of z factors, for example, see Mills (1977) or Hines and Montgomery (1990). Knowing that

$$P\{Z > z_\alpha\} = 1 - \phi(Z_\alpha) = \alpha \tag{5}$$

gives us the probability the unit normal variable Z will exceed $z(\alpha)$ with probability α.

12. Recall from earlier that at inception of a trade REE = PMR; thus, on trade date, PMR = RF * N. Over time, REE = PMR + AMR, or REE = (RF * N) + AMR.

13. The mathematical derivation of this is given as:

$$RF_{awc} = \int_0^T (Z\sigma \, t^{1/2} dt)/T \tag{1}$$

$$= (z\sigma \, t^{3/2}) / (3/2) * (1/T) \tag{2}$$

$$= (z\sigma \, t^{1/2}) * (2/3) \tag{3}$$

$$= RF_{twc} * (2/3) \tag{4}$$

Knowing that RF * N = REE, we multiply both sides by the notional N to obtain

$$REE_{awc} = REE_{twc} * (2/3) \tag{5}$$

14. In deriving REE(te) we illustrate the process introduced by Mark (in Klein and Lederman, *Derivatives Risk and Responsibility*, Irwin, © 1996, p. 274), adapted for our terminology; Mark utilizes an option-pricing framework to derive terminal expected exposure, and begins by integrating:

$$RF_{te} = \int_{-\infty}^{\infty} \max (0, x) f(x) dx \tag{1}$$

where

$$f(x) = \frac{1}{\sqrt{2\pi\sigma^{*2}}} \, e^{\left[\frac{-x^2}{2\sigma^{*2}}\right]}$$

and

$$\sigma^* = \sigma\sqrt{T}$$

These equations simplify to:

$$RF_{te} = \frac{1}{2\sqrt{2\pi}}\,(2\sigma\sqrt{T}) \tag{2}$$

If we assume RF(twc) is based on a 97.5 percent confidence level this can be expressed as:

$$RF_{te} = \frac{1}{2\sqrt{2\pi}}\,RF_{twc} \tag{3}$$

Multiplying both sides by the notional N, we obtain:

$$REE_{te} = REE_{twc}/5 \tag{4}$$

15. For instance, the equation for a non-mean reverting interest rate process (for example, Ho and Lee) can be shown as $dr = \theta(t) + \sigma dz$, while a mean-reverting interest rate process (for example, Hull and White, 1987) can be shown as $dr = (\theta(t) - \alpha r)\,dt + \sigma dz$, and so on.

16. Note that confidence levels are often introduced to compare the expected value against a predetermined confidence interval. In computing the expected value of the derivative, one can also compute the standard deviation of the estimates. Adjusting this standard deviation to two or three intervals provides a range of values that the derivative can assume. To tighten the confidence interval and obtain a more accurate result of the value of the derivative, it is typically necessary to increase the number of trials or introduce an alternative technique (such as the control variate process or the antithetic variate process; see for instance Boyle (1977) or Jarrow (1995)).

17. A 2000 survey by Credit Risk Advisors of the top 25 US and European banks active in derivatives noted that the top quartile use a simulation process to compute exposures. Large European institutions often use confidence banding analytics processes, while smaller US and European institutions simply use add-on factors. As of the survey date, most had not yet incorporated collateral valuation simulation into portfolio process (only standard "haircuts") though that has begun to change.

Chapter 6. Quantifying Option Credit Risk

1. There are three exceptions to this rule: currency options, where exercise by the buyer can result in the option seller being exposed to delivery or settlement risk; compound put options, where exercise by the buyer results in the option seller assuming a long option position with the original buyer; and contingent premium options, where intrinsic value smaller than premium due can result in the option seller being exposed to the buyer's risk (we discuss the latter two cases in Chapter 8).

2. If an option is packaged within a swap structure, premium may be deferred or amortized over a longer period of time, implying different credit risk parameters (we shall explore such special cases in subsequent chapters).

3. Note that this approach is consistent with the recommendations provided by the Group of 30 in its *Derivatives: Principles and Practices* document released in 1993. For instance, in *Derivatives: Principles and Practices, Appendix I: Working Papers* (1993b, p. 20), the Credit Risk Measurement and Management Sub-committee indicates:

> [I]n contrast with swaps, purchased options with the premium paid up front initially create an immediate mark-to-market exposure equal to the option premium. If the option seller defaults immediately, the option buyer must pay another option premium to replace the option even if there has been no movement in the underlying variables.

This, by definition, means the purchased option has time value and possibly intrinsic value. Assuming the option is struck out-of-the-money or at-the-money (that is, it has no intrinsic value), the only element of option premium at risk is time value; per the recommendation by the Group of 30 this figure constitutes an initial mark-to-market exposure and, hence, a credit exposure. Although the Group of 30 does not explicitly recommend a distinction between time value and intrinsic value within the premium of a long option, the REE equations presented in this chapter (which specifically segregate the two) are consistent with the overall approach recommended in the study.

4. Perhaps the buyer has purchased the option as cheap protection against an extreme market event.

5. This logic is borne out by examining extreme cases: the equations above, for a call and put struck equally deep in-the-money on the same strike, will assign the incrementally higher risk to the call, on the assumption that the put faces a lower bound of zero but the call has an upper bound of infinity.

6. See, for instance, Arak, Goodman, and Rones (1986) or Banks (1993).

7. In: Arak, Goodman, and Rones (1986), p. 450.

8. See Mark in *Risk* (1995) and Ong in Klein and Lederman (1996), for example.

9. The specific equation used by Ong may be represented in our terminology as

$$REE = N * (|(RF * (\Delta_O + \Delta_H)| + 1/2\Gamma^2 RF^2)$$

where $\Delta(O)$ and $\Delta(H)$ relate to the deltas of the option and hedge. Ong introduces an additional level of conservatism by taking the absolute value of the delta calculation.

Chapter 8. The Credit Risk of Complex Options

1. This is consistent, for example, with the classification proposed by Jarrow (1995), with a few additions and expansions.

2. Within the section on binary options we discuss a subclass of derivatives known as binary–barrier options which are hybrid path independent/ path dependent instruments; for continuity we include them under the binary section/path independent classification, with a reminder that the path dependent characteristics of the instruments must be borne in mind.

3. See Cox and Rubenstein (1985), for example.
4. Certain parity relationships exist between knock-in and knock-out options that permit the creation of synthetic options. For instance, if a bank owns a down-and-in call and a down-and-out call (with the same barriers and parameters), it owns a synthetic vanilla call option. In general terms, a package of a knock-in and a knock-out (with identical terms) is equal to the underlying vanilla option.
5. Certain options pay a cash rebate if the barrier is triggered; if no rebate is payable, then rebate equals zero.
6. It should be noted that the market risk management characteristics of barriers generally, and reverse barriers in particular, are quite complex; hedging the deltas and gammas of such instruments can be a demanding task.
7. In fact a floating strike lookback call can be created by combining a long put on the minimum, a long at-the-money call, and a short at-the-money put; a floating strike lookback put can be created by combining a long call on the maximum, a short at-the-money call, and a long at-the-money put.
8. It should be noted that the term "partial lookback" is occasionally applied to an option that generates a payoff based on a fixed percentage of the returns generated by a conventional floating strike lookback. For instance, if a conventional floating strike lookback generates a payoff of US$100, a 60 percent partial lookback yields a payoff of US$60. Since this is a close variation of the conventional lookback discussed above, we shall not consider the structure further. In addition, we shall assume for purposes of this discussion that the term partial lookback option is applicable to the option described in this section.
9. A cliquet is often thought of as a strip of forward starting options, which pay off max (0, (CMP1 – SP1)) + max (0, (CMP2 – CMP1)) + max (0, (CMP3 – CMP2)), and so on.
10. The most common method for adjusting different assets to the same strike-price level is as follows: (a) identify the asset whose strike will be used as a reference (denominate this asset 1); (b) divide contract denomination of asset 2 by that of asset 1 to obtain a multiplier; (c) multiply asset 2's underlying price and strike price by the multiplier in the pricing equation; and (d) multiply the option's price by the contract denomination of asset 1 to obtain the final adjusted option price.

   Consider the following example. A bank can purchase the better performing of US$100,000 of S&P 500 struck at 500, which is equal to 200 units, or US$100,000 of bonds struck at 100, which is equal to 1000 units. If the S&P 500 is used as the primary reference, the multiplier is equal to 1000/200, or 5. To equate the two assets, multiply the price and strike of the bonds by 5; to arrive at the final price of the option, multiply the option price by 200.
11. Credit derivatives, which permit institutions to express a view on the specific credit performance of a particular issuer, have expanded rapidly since the turn of the millennium, and are available in numerous forms; among the most common are credit options, credit forwards, default swaps, and total return swaps. Note that credit derivatives can be used to profit

from credit spread movements or outright credit defaults, and also manage or hedge credit risk. Actively managing credit risk provides institutions with the ability to protect against counterparty default, rebalance portfolios of exposures in order to reduce concentration or correlation effects (or to achieve more appropriate risk-adjusted returns), and free credit lines in order to engage in incremental business with specific counterparties. We discuss the use of credit derivatives as risk management instruments at greater length in Chapter 13. In this section we focus on the structural and REE aspects of credit options from the perspective of an institution taking a view on credit spread movement.

12. Note that credit default options generate strictly binary payoffs, based on whether the underlying reference credit defaults rather than if spreads have widened (for example, a binary option as we have discussed earlier in the chapter, adjusted for a specific credit reference).

13. See Geske (1979), for instance.

14. Note that in the case of a twin-out barrier package the premium payable by the buyer is typically lower than that of a single knock-out option, since the presence of barriers on the upside and downside increases the probability the option will be extinguished.

15. As we indicated previously there are several exceptions to this, including short compound puts and short contingent premium options (when intrinsic value of the option is less than the expected premium payment); these are discussed at greater length in the chapter. In addition, currency options that result in exercise may expose the seller to the buyer's delivery or settlement risk; we do not consider this situation further.

16. Alternatively, we can develop an equation that reflects an average terminal price based on the starting point and length of the averaging period. This may provide unnecessary precision, but is presented as an alternate choice. For instance, we might begin by identifying the starting point of the averaging period; the initial risk factor for the transaction, RF1, which reflects market movement from the beginning of the option until the start of the averaging period, can then be computed. A second risk factor, RF2, which reflects market movement from the start of the averaging period until the conclusion of the transaction can then be determined; the difference between the variable at maturity and the variable at the start of the averaging period can be converted into an average, with the resulting figure applied to the current market price at the beginning of the averaging period. This result can then be compared against the strike price to generate an REE. In creating this type of framework care must be taken to avoid manipulation of lognormal variables in a mathematically incorrect fashion (the sum of two lognormal variables is not, for instance, lognormally distributed); this may require use of alternative statistical assumptions.

17. Note that the current spread is precisely equal to the difference between the two assets used to determine the spread; this can be denoted as (CMP1 – CMP2). Earlier in the chapter we have described the payoff of a call spread as max (0, (CMP1 – CMP2 – SP)) and a put spread as max (0, (SP – CMP1

– CMP2)); this, by extension, is equal to max(0, (CS – SS)) and max(0, (SS – CS)). In order to reflect the concept of the spread as a "self-contained asset" (following a geometric Brownian motion which is applied to the RF framework), we focus on the latter approach in our REE equations; both, however, are mathematically identical.

Chapter 9. Quantifying Swap Credit Risk

1. This process has been researched by Whittaker (1987), Das (1994), and Sorensen and Bollier (1994), among others.
2. Note that the ISDA, in its 1987 Comment Letter response to the Federal Reserve/Bank of England swap risk proposal, also made the case for viewing a pair of matched swaps as a series of at-the-money puts and calls.
3. See Das (1994).
4. It is worth noting the derivation of the BIS's CEM credit conversion factors was created utilizing simulation techniques. In a technical working paper, the Federal Reserve (FR) and Bank of England (BOE) utilized a simulation approach to derive potential credit conversion factors for capital purposes. The FR/BOE simulation utilized a lognormal distribution and generated random samples from the distribution over the life of the swap. Based on these random samples, FR/BOE calculated the value of a swap at future rates and, knowing the probability distribution function, determined appropriate confidence intervals; the end result of the process was the creation of a series of credit conversion factors. Many other researchers have incorporated simulation techniques in their studies; readers may wish to refer to obtain differing views and results on simulation (see, for example, Ferron and Handjinicolaou (1987), Muffet (1986), Hull (1989), Smith, Smithson, and Wilford (1990), Hunter and Stowe (1992a), and Giberti, Mentini, and Scabellone (1993), among others).
5. Readers interested in reviewing the credit risk aspects of vanilla swaps and basic variations may wish to consult Banks (1993).
6. Note that it can be shown that the mean and variance of the binomial process converge to the mean and variance of the lognormal diffusion process described in Chapter 5 as n moves to infinity (see Gibson, 1991).
7. See Rendleman and Bartter (1980).
8. In addition to the original paper by Rendleman and Bartter, readers may wish to reference Hull (1989), for a detailed review of the model. In addition, readers may wish to review other interest rate pricing models which model the stochastic movement of interest rates through different processes (with varying degrees of sophistication and assumptions), such as those by Black; Derman and Toy; Vasicek; Ho and Lee; Cox, Ingersoll, and Ross; Jamshidian; and Hull and White, among others.
9. The findings were presented in the 1987 technical paper "Potential Credit Exposure on Interest Rate and Foreign Exchange Rate Related Instruments."
10. Also referenced in Schwartz and Smith (1990).

Chapter 10. The Credit Risk of Complex Swaps

1. See Banks (1993).
2. Consider the following examples of "less than obvious" leverage. Gibson Greetings, which sustained rather severe losses based on its leveraged swap activity with Bankers Trust, entered into a variety of leveraged swaps, including a ratio swap where it received 5.5 percent fixed and paid $((\text{six-month Libor})^2)/6$. Assuming the transaction commenced with Libor at 5 percent, the net gain to Gibson (again, ignoring present value and credit considerations) for the first period would equal 83 basis points. A 100 basis point increase in Libor, to 6 percent, would result in a 50 basis point loss to the company, while a 200 basis point increase would result in a 266 basis point loss. Procter and Gamble, which also sustained losses based on leveraged transactions with Bankers Trust, entered into a variety of transactions (ratio swaps, "wedding bands," and so on), some of which were particularly opaque. In one swap Procter and Gamble received a fixed rate from Bankers Trust and paid commercial paper rates (CP) less 75 basis points for the first six months of the transaction. For the remaining 4.5 years of the swap, the pay flow shifted to the following formula:

   $CP - 75bps + (98.5*(5yr\ CMT/5.8) - 30yr\ Treasuries/100)$

   where *CMT* is the constant maturity Treasury rate and *30-year Treasuries* is the 30-year Treasury price (not rate).
       Beder, in Klein and Lederman (1996), provides other examples of leverage encountered in the market-place during the mid-1990s, including Swedish krona less Pibor (Paris interbank offer rate) cubed and 19,000 percent fixed less 1900 times US$ Libor (these structures have been embedded in notes, but are constructed via the same process discussed above).
3. Pure volatility-based derivatives are not, of course, new. Trading of direct foreign exchange volatility through options has been possible for many years. In addition, the listed market features a series of equity volatility contracts (for example, the DAX Volax, the S&P100 VIX, the NASDAQ 100 VXN, and so forth).
4. Readers interested in further detail on other weather-related structures may wish to consult Banks, (ed.), (2001).
5. For instance, the Chicago Mercantile Exchange and the Euronext/ LIFFE exchange feature temperature contracts.
6. The standard formulas are given as:

   Daily HDD = max (0, 65 – (Tmax + Tmin)/2))

   Daily CDD = max (0, ((Tmax+Tmin)/2 – 65))

   where Tmax is the maximum daily temperature and Tmin is the minimum daily temperature.
7. It is interesting to note that risk factors attributed to differential swaps are generally somewhat higher than those assigned to single currency basis swaps or dual currency coupon swaps (without principal exchange).

8. It should be noted that in certain cases forwards are set as a percentage appreciation against par, rather than the forward price.
9. Defaulted credits may trade below levels predicted by historical recovery statistics if the outlook for recovery is particularly poor (for example, unrealizable asset value and/or excessive leverage). However, since such information is not typically known until after the default and after distressed debt dealers have had an opportunity to analyze the specifics of bankruptcy and potential recoveries, it is of little value to analysts considering an immediate credit-related decision. It is necessary, therefore, to make a simplifying assumption that defaulted debt will trade at, or near, historical recovery levels. More conservative views can be applied as necessary.
10. As with credit forwards, certain total return swaps are structured as a percentage increase or decrease against par, rather than the agreed price. An adjustment to the formula is required in such instances.

Chapter 11. Credit Risk Management: Quantitative Issues

1. According to the 1994 Group of 30 follow-up survey, 95 percent of dealers and 98 percent of end users surveyed believe credit risk exposures to single counterparties should be aggregated and managed in aggregate form against credit limits (Group of 30, 1994).
2. Readers interested in further in-depth discussion on the topic should consult original works by authors such as Lawrence (in *Risk*, 1995), Mark (in Klein and Lederman, 1996) and Rowe (in *Risk*, 1995), among others, who have done research in the area of portfolio management.
3. Note that a more formal determination of portfolio correlations is given by the following formula:

$$\sqrt{REE_1^2 + REE_2^2 - 2 * REE_1 * REE_2 * \rho_{1,2}}$$

where: ρ is the correlation between the two references.
   Consider a portfolio of two transactions of equal risk magnitude (for example, 1) on opposite sides of the market. Under the equation above, ρ of +1 (for example, complete positive correlation) yields a net portfolio REE of zero, ρ of 0 (for example, no correlation) yields a net portfolio REE of 1.41 and ρ of -1 (complete negative correlation), yields a net portfolio REE of 2.
4. In *Risk* (1995).
5. For instance, another technique, known as the "primary risk source approach," has been put forth by Rowe (in *Risk*, 1995). This process seeks to provide a rigorous aggregation method without use of Monte Carlo simulation. Under this framework, Rowe proposes a technique that focuses on determining the value of the stochastic market variable that provides the greatest source of risk/variability in a given transaction or portfolio. The value of the variable is computed to a pre-specified confidence level at select future points during the life of the deal and is assumed to relate monotonically to the market value of the transaction. Secondary variables, which are

determined to impact the value of the transaction in only minor form, are simulated at their implied forward values. Risks from different primary sources are then aggregated using vectors, and correlations are introduced to determine additive or offsetting effects within the portfolio.

6. Kealhofer (in *Risk*, 1995) notes that, although default correlation between counterparties may be very small, it is not equal to zero; since it is not equal to zero, one cannot assume complete independence between default by one counterparty and default by a second counterparty. If complete independence were a reality, the normal distribution would be an accurate representation of the distribution of losses. Instead, the small default correlations that exist result in a distribution skewed to the right. As a result of this difference, Kealhofer points out that actual losses will be less than portfolio expected losses most of the time; large losses will occur very infrequently, but when they do occur will be greater than the median, and the probability of large losses will not be approximated by the normal distribution (suggesting that insufficient capital may be allocated to cover unexpected losses, as discussed below).

7. Extending our discussion of other credit-sensitive transactions that might exist in a portfolio of exposures, we can obviously include the relevant REE for loans, bonds, repos, and so forth.

8. Note that care must be taken in assigning a default statistic derived from a population of issuers to a single counterparty; the population default statistics carry the benefit of portfolio diversification while a single counterparty does not. A more conservative adjustment for a single counterparty may be required.

9. In Klein and Lederman, *Derivatives Risk and Responsibility*, Chicago, Irwin, 1996, p. 126.

10. The more complete definition of a cohort is based on marginal probabilities of default. For instance, a cohort may be defined as the number of issuers of a given rating originally part of a group of issuers with the same rating at the start of year Y that default in year T after cohort Y was formed, divided by the number of issuers of a given rating at the start of year Y that have not defaulted by year T.

11. For instance, Iben and Brotherton-Ratcliffe define a forward probability of default P(t) as $(1 - (1 - C(t))/(1 - C(t-1))$, where C(t) is the cumulative probability of default over t years. They then utilize P(t) to derive a loss distribution. (Source: Iben and Brotherton-Ratcliffe, "Credit Loss Distributions and Required Capital for Derivative Portfolios," reprinted with permission from *Journal of Fixed Income*, New York: Institutional Investor Inc. Publications, 1994.)

12. While default and recovery studies point to secured and senior unsecured creditors as the two groups that receive the greatest average recoveries over time, it is worth noting that the same two groups also face the largest variance in recoveries.

13. The priority of claims in US bankruptcy is structured as follows (in order of priority):
    1. Administrative expenses of the bankruptcy case.
    2. Unsecured claims incurred in the ordinary course of business once bankruptcy proceedings have begun.

3. Unsecured claims for wages and commissions earned within 90 days of bankruptcy filing.
4. Unsecured claims for employee benefits incurred within 90 days of bankruptcy filing.
5. Unsecured claims of individuals arising from deposits/prepayments for future use of goods or services.
6. Unsecured claims of the government (including taxes and penalties).
7. Secured claims with specified assets as collateral (including derivatives secured by specific collateral). Assets are liquidated in bankruptcy and used to cover the secured claims; if insufficient, the unpaid balances are treated as unsecured claims.
8. Senior unsecured claims (including unsecured derivatives); this category takes priority over subordinated claims but ranks *pari passu* with other senior unsecured obligations.
9. Other unsecured claims (including subordinated claims).
10. Other claims (including preferred stock, common stock, and so on).

14. That is, $E[P(\text{def}) * REE] = E[P(\text{def}(t))] * E[PV(REE(t))]$. If we assume that these events are not independent and that some level of correlation exists between the amount of risk exposure and the probability of default, then $E[P(\text{def}) * REE] = E[P(\text{def}(t))] * E[PV(REE(t))] + \text{Cov}[P(\text{def}), REE]$.

15. That is, we can integrate across the combined function which is denoted mathematically as:

$$\iiint REE * P(def) * (1 - rec) * \int(REE, P(def), rec) \, dREE \, dP(def) drec,$$

where the second term of the equation is a multivariate probability density function.

16. Certain regulators have also provided specific definitions of the their own. For instance, the US Office of the Comptroller of the Currency indicates: "Risk against which economic capital is allocated is defined as the volatility of earnings and value – the degree of fluctuation away from the expected level."

17. In *Risk* (1995).

18. In Ong (1999).

19. For example, the Derivatives Policy Group, cited in Chapter 1, has recommended the following approach for determining "credit capital at risk":
   a) *Current exposure*: net replacement cost for a derivative (or derivatives) with a given counterparty is computed and historic default probabilities (from the rating agencies, based on the specific internal credit score assigned to the counterparty) are applied to obtain an estimate of current credit capital at risk. The approach allows for collateral offsets and bilateral netting (where netting is legally permissible) and suggests a minimum default probability of 0.001.
   b) *Potential exposure*: potential exposure is determined through a market risk process by computing the maximum loss likely to be exceeded with a 1 percent probability over a two-week period, based on specific scenarios for given markets (using historical or implied volatilities and

correlations). The default probabilities are applied to this figure based on an internal credit score, and no allowance is made for collateral; this process generates a potential capital at risk figure.

Note that the approach followed in (b) is, effectively, a value-at-risk framework, as we discuss in the next chapter.

20. In the next chapter we shall also consider credit migration frameworks (for example, credit transitions, where the default state is but one unique state in the spectrum); correlations are also applicable.

21. It is realistic to assume that the correlation between two independent counterparties is, in most cases, less than one. Of course, we can conceive of some extreme scenarios where correlations might move towards one (for example, two hedge funds invested in similar assets and exposed to a severe market shock at the same time, which negatively impacts their financial structure), but these would be exceptions rather than the norm.

22. In general studies have shown that default correlations are low and decrease as credit ratings improve; in addition, correlations tend to decrease over long time-horizon. Studies on default correlations between industries appear to be inconclusive.

23. In 2002 Rutter Associates (henceforth Rutter) conducted a survey on behalf of ISDA, RMA, and the International Association of Credit Portfolio Managers regarding credit portfolio practices. Of the 41 major international financial institutions that responded to the survey, 90 percent used explicit risk/return measures when considering credit-related transactions; of that group, 78 percent used a risk-adjusted return on capital measure, while only 16 percent used raw ROE or ROA measures (Rutter, (2002)).

24. Note that a general version of this equation is given in Matten (1996); the reader may wish to consult the text for an in-depth review of alternate models.

Chapter 12. Credit Risk Portfolio Models

1. Readers may wish to consult Jorion (1996) for a thorough treatment of the market VAR process, including its strengths and weaknesses.

2. The computation of regulatory capital is relatively straightforward. A firm selects an x-day trading horizon to capture market moves and an x percent confidence level on a one-tailed normal distribution. Correlations between asset classes serve as inputs. The observation period for historical data is updated every quarter for prices, volatilities, and correlations. Daily VAR is computed by grossing up by the square root of the x-day trading horizon; market risk capital is then applied to the maximum of previous day's daily VAR or a regulatory multiplier M (three or four) times the average VAR over the past 60 days.

3. Using default correlations, a firm can properly aggregate risk from various assets, which will dictate the level of concentration; the level of concentration, in turn, dictates the degree of portfolio diversification.

4. Under the Merton model, default occurs when the assets of a firm fall below some pre-defined threshold, such as total liabilities. Capital is assumed to be a combination of equity and a zero coupon bond, and default only occurs at

maturity of the zero coupon bond. This assumption is then extended to include changes in credit quality.

5. Of the 80 percent of responding institutions that possessed an active credit portfolio management function in 2002 (refer to the ISDA/Rutter survey), 85 percent used a credit portfolio model to help them manage the process. Within that group, 69 percent used Moody's KMV PortfolioManager, 20 percent CreditMetrics, and 17 percent internally developed models.

6. With a large portfolio it is usually necessary to generate a full distribution of portfolio values at each credit horizon, meaning asset return thresholds must be derived for each ratings category, the correlation of asset returns must be estimated, and asset return scenarios must be developed per a joint normal distribution. For every scenario and counterparty, standard asset returns are mapped to relevant ratings per the threshold levels derived, and the portfolio is revalued using spread curves for each rating. This process is then repeated tens of thousands of times to obtain a distribution plot of portfolio values. It is then simple to obtain the relevant percentage distribution of future values.

7. Moody's KMV explicitly distinguishes between default and bankruptcy. Default occurs when an interest payment is missed or when the asset value gets to a level between the value of the liabilities and value of short-term debt. Bankruptcy occurs when a counterparty's asset value falls below the value of the liabilities and leads to liquidation or reorganization.

8. Through this mechanism the EDFs are taken as a leading indicator of credit deterioration (and possible default). Moody's KMV backtesting of the database suggests that EDFs often rise sharply and rapidly in the face of financial distress that leads ultimately to default. In this light, the framework might be more "anticipatory" than standard rating actions; since rating agencies can be slow to make ratings adjustments, the historical frequency of remaining in a rating class overstates the true probability of retaining the same credit quality. If both the probability of staying in a rating class and the probability of default are too large, the migration probabilities are likely to be too small. Moody's KMV's own view is that the probability of staying in the same rating class is one-half to one-third of the historical probability given by the agencies, except for AAA credits. Moody's KMV's probability of default is also lower, especially for lower credit quality companies. Since both CreditMetrics and Moody's KMV use Mertonian option/capital approaches but different default probability methodologies, it is not surprising that they produce different results.

9. For instance, Jarrow and Turnbull (1995) and Duffie and Singleton (1999) developed arbitrage-free pricing models for credit risk-sensitive securities, but these were not based on the valuation of portfolios at future time horizons. Work by Jarrow and Turnbull was extended to include correlation migration processes that allow the assessment of the impact of credit event correlation explicitly. However, these models assume that credit spreads only change when credit ratings change (that is, are discrete, rather than continuous), which can be a limiting factor.

10. For instance, Duffie and Pan (1999) provide an analytical approximation for VAR and other risk measures in an OTC derivative portfolio. The framework

is based on multifactor jump diffusion for default intensities and asset returns. The portfolio Delta-Gamma VAR approach (used in many VAR models) also includes the risk of changes in credit quality, up to the point of default. The model, based on a correlated default intensity process, generates approximations of probability distributions of total loss of a portfolio that is exposed to correlated default risks.

11. Iscoe, I., Kreinin, A., and Rosen, D. (1999). "An Integrated Market and Credit Risk Portfolio," *Algo Research Quarterly*, Toronto.

12. From an implementation perspective, the MtF model begins with a definition of the market and credit risk drivers. A joint default model is developed, with probabilities conditioned on scenarios. Correlations among counterparties are determined by joint variation of conditional probabilities across scenarios (the joint default model features unconditional default probabilities; the defaults reflect a "creditworthiness index" for each counterparty and result in the estimate of a multifactor model linking the index to credit drivers). Actual obligor default links the index to probabilities of default to obtain conditional default probabilities. Net counterparty exposures, recoveries and losses are then computed for each scenario. Under the stochastic exposure component of the model, exposure for each counterparty is obtained through an MtF simulation algorithm. Recoveries are also modeled stochastically, but are made independent of risk factor drivers. Then, the conditional portfolio loss distribution, conditioned on scenarios, is derived (counterparty default is assumed to be independent). Finally, losses under all scenarios are aggregated (by averaging the conditional loss distribution over all scenarios).

13. These are based on forward-looking simulations originally proposed by Mulvey and Zenios (1994) and subsequently adopted by in the Algorithmics/ MtF model.

Chapter 13. Credit Risk Management: Qualitative Issues

1. ISDA (2002b).

2. Respondents report holding US$289b of collateral; non-respondents are estimated to hold the balance.

3. According to the *ISDA Margin Survey 2002*, 60 percent of ISDA CSA New York Law and 50 percent of ISDA CSA English Law collateral agreements (the two most popular forms) were bilateral in nature.

4. Indeed, the process is very similar to the "crystallization" effect of cliquet, ladder, and shout options we discussed in Chapter 8.

5. The case of UK company Marconi is instructive in considering credit derivative "restructuring" issues. In 2002 the firm underwent a US$4b workout and restructuring (agreeing with its creditors to replace outstanding debt with a combination of cash, equity, and bonds), which led to the question as to whether a non-binding agreement to restructure can be considered a credit event under ISDA definitions. If a bank cannot settle credit derivative contracts when a company agrees to a non-binding workout, the credit protection may expire too soon; if banks have to wait for the restructuring, the underlying bonds and loans (used as references in credit derivative contracts) might have to be exchanged

for securities that may not be deliverable under a credit derivative contract (for example, equity, as in the Marconi case). Not surprisingly, ISDA takes the view that a credit event is triggered if action is "in furtherance of an arrangement for the benefit of creditors, meaning action to avoid bankruptcy." This, per ISDA, would include a non-binding agreement to restructure. Similar "default versus restructuring" arguments have occurred in other cases (for example, Argentina in 2002, which first declared a restructuring and then switched to a moratorium, confusing the market). As noted in Chapter 4, a "menu" of restructuring options is available as the issue remains the subject of debate.

6. Note that the credit derivative used to free the limit could easily be a default swap, total return swap, or credit option; all have the same effect, though certain transactions are one-sided while others are two-sided.

7. Recall from our discussion in Chapter 10 that the seller of a TRS is defined as the party that assumes a long position in the economics of a risky bond; the buyer is defined as the party buying credit protection by assuming a short position in the bond.

8. Alternative structures can also be arranged, such as those that reduce principal and/or interest for each counterparty that defaults.

9. Many advances have been made in the area of financial communications protocol and languages; a number of industry groups have joined together to develop uniform ways of communicating derivative trade information through network mechanisms, which help reduce settlement times and errors and reduce paper flow. Initiatives based on communication protocols such as FpML, FIX, and others represent an important advance in the efficient transmission of valuable financial data. Detailed review is well beyond the scope of this book, but readers should be aware that considerable advances in financial transaction communications have accompanied the era of networking and flexible computing.

10. The passage in mid-2000 of the US Financial Accounting Standards rule 133 (FAS 133), which deals specifically with derivative accounting issues, requires companies using swaps and options as a hedge to demonstrate the risk-reducing nature of the transaction in order to receive accounting offsets. As a result of this rule, many of the complex derivatives that companies once created as "hedges" may not qualify for FAS 133 hedge accounting treatment.

11. Note, for example, suspension of payments and subsequent suits filed by Air Products, Procter and Gamble, Gibson Greetings, Unipec, and Sinopec, among others. In most instances the actions have led to out-of-court settlements.

Appendix 1

1. Many subsequent articles have sought to introduce new equations or models which allow certain assumptions of the original model to be relaxed (for instance, the "no dividend" restriction was dealt with by Merton in 1973, the "no taxes/transaction costs" by Ingersoll in 1976, the "continuous stock prices" by Cox and Ross in 1976, the "European exercise only" by Roll in 1977, Geske in 1979, and Whaley in 1981, and so on).

Glossary

Ability to perform

A counterparty's financial capacity to perform on its contractual obligations. It is the essence of credit analysis and is distinguished from "willingness to perform."

Accreting swap

A swap featuring a notional principal balance that increases on a preset schedule or the triggering of an event. *See also* variable principal swap, reverse index principal swap.

Accrual note

See range floater note.

Actual exposure

The amount of credit exposure inherent in a derivative transaction; actual exposure is generally included as one of two components (along with fractional exposure) in the determination of total credit exposure. If actual exposure is positive at the time of counterparty default, a credit loss is sustained; if negative, no credit loss occurs. Actual exposure is also known as "replacement cost," "actual market risk," or "mark-to-market value."

Actual market risk

See actual exposure.

Advanced methodology

One of two credit capital allocation approaches under the BIS's Internal Ratings Based (IRB) quantification framework. Banks use internal models to determine credit losses by estimating counterparty default risk,

risk equivalent exposure, and loss given default (as well as the impact of risk mitigants and the relationship of counterparty exposures to other exposures in the portfolio). *See also* foundation methodology, internal ratings based approach.

All-or-nothing option   *See* binary option.

American binary option   *See* binary–barrier option.

American option   An option that is exercisable by the buyer at any time until, and including, maturity.

Amortizing swap   A swap featuring a notional principal balance that amortizes on a preset schedule or the triggering of an event. *See also* variable principal swap, mortgage swap, index principal swap.

Annual inflation swap   A swap involving the exchange of floating (actual) and fixed inflation at the end of each annual evaluation period. *See also* inflation swap, zero coupon inflation swap.

Arbitrage   An investment strategy, involving the simultaneous purchase and sale of two assets, that seeks to take advantage of small discrepancies between the prices or rates of the assets; the intent of the strategy is to generate a profit with a minimum amount of risk.

Asian option   An option that generates a payoff based on the average price of the underlying market reference over a predetermined averaging period (for example, Asian tail); the average path can be applied to either the price of the underlying market reference (average price option) or the strike price (average strike option) to determine the payoff. *See also* average price option, average strike option.

Asian tail   The length of the averaging period in an Asian option.

Asset-at-expiry option   A binary-barrier option that generates a payoff at expiry equal to a fixed asset M if the price of the underlying market reference breaches the strike/barrier at any time during the transaction. *See also* binary option, binary–barrier option.

Asset-at-hit option A binary-barrier option that generates an immediate payoff equal to a fixed asset M if the price of the underlying market reference exceeds the strike/barrier. *See also* binary option, binary–barrier option.

Asset-or-nothing option A binary–barrier option that generates a payoff equal to a fixed asset M if the price of the underlying market reference breaches the strike price at expiry. *See also* binary option.

Asset swap A swap involving the exchange of fixed coupons from an underlying asset for floating coupons, giving the investor a synthetic floating rate asset in a single package. An asset swap can also be structured to convert floating rate coupons into fixed rate coupons.

Assignment The process of transferring a derivative exposure from the original counterparty to a third party in order to reduce exposure.

At-expiry option A binary option that generates a payoff at expiry equal to a fixed asset or cash amount M if the price of the underlying market reference breaches the strike/barrier at any time during the transaction. *See also* asset-at-expiry option, binary–barrier option, cash-at-expiry option.

At-hit option A binary option that generates an immediate payoff equal to a fixed asset or cash amount M if the price of the underlying market reference breaches the strike/barrier at any time during the transaction. *See also* asset-at-hit option, binary–barrier option, cash-at-hit option.

At-the-money An option whose strike price (SP) is equal to the current market price (CMP). An at-the-money option has no intrinsic value but maximum time value.

Automatic stay

A legal provision barring creditors from liquidating collateral of a counterparty that has defaulted on its debt obligations; derivative contracts secured by collateral are exempt from the automatic stay provision.

Average expected risk exposure

Potential credit exposure based on the average maturity of the transaction and the expected market movement of the underlying market reference. Average expected exposure is the smallest of four classes of credit exposure. *See also* average worst-case risk exposure, terminal worst-case risk exposure, terminal expected risk exposure.

Average exposure

Credit exposure based on the average maturity of the transaction.

Average price option

An option that generates a payoff equal to the difference between an average price on an underlying market reference and a predefined strike price. *See also* Asian option, average strike option.

Average strike option

An option that generates a payoff equal to the difference between an average strike price and the terminal value of the underlying market reference. *See also* Asian option, average strike option.

Average worst-case

risk exposure

Potential credit exposure based on the average maturity of the transaction and the worst-case market movement of the underlying market reference; average worst-case exposure is the third largest of four classes of credit exposure. *See also* average expected risk exposure, terminal expected risk exposure, terminal worst-case risk exposure.

Backspread

An option strategy designed to take advantage of volatility. A long backspread is created through the sale of a smaller quantity of closer-to-the-money puts or calls and the purchase of a larger quantity of farther-from-the-money puts or calls. A short backspread is known as a "ratio vertical spread"

Barrier option

An option that extinguishes or creates an underlying European option as the price of the underlying market reference moves through a prespecified barrier. There are four versions of the barrier option, including the down and in option (an option created when the underlying market references falls through a barrier on the downside), the down and out option (an option that is extinguished when the underlying market reference falls through a barrier on the downside), the up and in option (an option created when the underlying market reference moves through a barrier on the upside), and the up and out option (an option that is extinguished when the underlying market reference moves through a barrier on the upside). *See also* down and in option, down and out option, knock-in option, knock-out option, reverse barrier option, up and in option, up and out option.

Basis risk

Risk generated from two floating indexes which track, but do not precisely replicate, one another. Basis risk is often assumed as a means of minimizing directional or volatility risk and can arise from hedging an asset with a futures contract on the same (or similar) asset, or hedging an asset with a second, similar asset.

Basis swap

An interest rate swap involving the exchange of two floating rate indexes, such as Libor and commercial paper rates or Libor and Federal Funds. The credit risk associated with two floating indexes (primarily those that are highly correlated) is generally lower than that of a standard fixed/floating interest rate swap.

Basket option

An option that generates a payoff based on the difference between the price of a basket of assets and a predefined strike price; the basket of assets may be from identical or different asset classes/markets. *See also* multi-index option.

Basket swap

A credit derivative that involves the exchange of a fixed or floating premium for a compensatory payment if one or more reference credits in a pre-defined portfolio defaults.

Bear spread

An option strategy that attempts to take advantage of bearish markets; spreads can be structured as bearish vertical call spreads (purchase of a call and sale of a second call, where the short call is struck closer-to-the-money) or bearish vertical put spreads (purchase of a put and sale of a second put, where the long put is struck closer-to-the-money). Also known as "vertical spreads," "price spreads," "money spreads."

Bermudan option

An option that can only be exercised on specific dates prior to maturity. A Bermudan option is thus more flexible than a European option, but less flexible than an American option. Also known as a "mid-Atlantic option."

Bilateral collateral

A collateral agreement between two derivative counterparties that requires either party to post security, depending on the value of the portfolio of derivative contracts and the level of unsecured credit thresholds that are established.

Binary option

An option that generates a payoff equal to a prespecified amount M if the price of the underlying market reference breaches the strike price; this derivative is also known as a "digital option" or "all-or-nothing option." A binary option can be structured to pay off in cash (a cash-or-nothing option) or the underlying asset (asset-or-nothing option) and may have a European exercise (it must end in-the-money) or American exercise (it must move in-the-money). An American exercise binary option can pay off as soon as the underlying crosses the strike price (an at-hit option) or at the expiration of the option (an at-expiry option). *See also* asset-or-nothing option, at-expiry option, at-hit option, binary–barrier option, cash-or-nothing option.

Binary–barrier option

An option that generates a payoff equal to a prespecified cash or asset amount M if the price of the underlying market reference breaches the strike price. This derivative, also known as an "American binary option," a "one-touch option," or an "at-hit/at-expiry option," is a hybrid of the barrier and binary options and generates a payoff if the underlying market reference triggers the barrier (which is also the strike) at any time during the life of the transaction. *See also* at-hit option, at-expiry option, cash-at-hit option, cash-at-expiry option, asset-at-hit option, and asset-at-expiry option.

Black–Scholes model

The fundamental closed-form option pricing model of the derivative markets, developed in 1973 by Black and Scholes to value European options on non-dividend paying stocks. The Black–Scholes framework relies on a series of assumptions (for example, continuous movement of the underlying reference, unlimited borrowing at a risk free rate, no transactions costs/taxes) to generate a price for the option.

Bonds with warrants

A structured bond comprised of a bond and associated warrants (long dated options); by selling the note with warrants the issuer lowers its effective funding costs. While the warrants, which can generally be detached and traded separately, can be issued on a range of references, they are generally linked to the issuer's stock price or a broad equity index.

Bull spread

An option strategy that attempts to take advantage of bullish markets; spreads can be structured as bullish vertical call spreads (purchase of a call and sale of a second call, where the long call is struck closer-to-the-money) or bullish vertical put spreads (purchase of a put and sale of a second put, where the short put is struck closer-to-the-money). Also known as "vertical spreads," "price spreads," "money spreads."

Butterfly spread	An option strategy designed to take advantage of volatility. Butterflies are always created with the same ratio of options (one low strike, two middle strikes, one high strike) that expire at the same time; spreads can be based on puts or calls. Short butterflies consist of short low and high strike options and long middle strike options, and long butterflies consist of long low and high strike options and short middle strike options.
Calendar spread	*See* time spread.
Call	A derivative granting the buyer the right, but not the obligation, to purchase an underlying reference security at a predefined strike price.
Call on a call	An option that grants the buyer the right to purchase an underlying call. *See also* compound option.
Call on a put	An option that grants the buyer the right to purchase an underlying put. *See also* compound option.
Call on the best of n-assets	An option that generates a payoff based on the difference between a predefined strike price and the best performing asset in a portfolio; the option permits the holder to purchase the best performing of a group of assets. *See also* multi-index option, option on the best/worst of n-assets.
Call on the maximum	An option that generates a payoff based on the difference between a predefined strike price and the highest price achieved by the underlying reference asset over the life of

the transaction. *See also* lookback option, options on the maximum/minimum.

Call on the worst of n-assets

An option that generates a payoff based on the difference between a predefined strike price and the worst performing asset in a portfolio; the option effectively permits the holder to purchase the worst performing of a group of assets. *See also* multi-index option, option on the best/worst of n-assets.

Call spread

An option strategy that is created to express a bullish or bearish directional market view; the spread requires the sale and purchase of two separate calls with different strikes. *See also* bull spreads, bear spreads.

Callable bond

A bond with embedded calls that permits the issuer to redeem the bond at a particular price level on select call dates.

Callable swap

A swap structure that gives the fixed rate payer the option to enter into an underlying swap at a future date. *See also* cancelable swap, putable swap.

Cancelable swap

A swap structure that gives the fixed rate receiver the option to terminate the underlying swap at a future date. *See also* callable swap, putable swap.

Cap

An option that generates a payoff when an underlying interest rate reference exceeds a predefined strike level.

Caption

An option on a cap, granting the purchaser the right to buy a cap. *See also* cap.

Cash-at-expiry option

A binary option that generates a payoff at expiry equal to a fixed cash amount M if the price of the underlying market reference exceeds the strike/barrier at any time during the transaction. Cash-at-expiry options are members of the binary-barrier option family. *See also* binary–barrier option.

Cash-at-hit option

A binary option that generates an immediate

payoff equal to a fixed cash amount M once the price of the underlying market reference breaches the strike/barrier. *See also* binary–barrier option.

Cash on delivery option   *See* contingent premium option.

Cash-or-nothing option   A binary option that generates a payoff equal to a fixed cash amount M if the price of the underlying market reference breaches the strike price at expiry. *See also* binary option.

Cherry pick   A process where a bankruptcy receiver or administrator attempts to have the court honor derivative contracts that benefit the defaulting counterparty, while disallowing those that harm it.

Chooser option   An option that permits the purchaser to choose between an underlying call and put (with equal strikes and maturities) between trade date and choice date. A chooser option is also known as a "regular chooser option" or "preference option." *See also* complex chooser option.

Cliquet option   An option that locks in gains at prespecified evaluation intervals if the option is in-the-money at such intervals. If the option is out-of-the-money on an evaluation date the strike resets at-the-money based on the new market level. Cliquet options are also known as "ratchet options."

Close-out netting   A netting arrangement where an institution and the defaulting counterparty agree to terminate transactions and net payments.

Collar   A spread consisting of a purchased cap/call and a sold floor/put, or vice versa. The sale of one option reduces the premium payable on the second option. *See also* zero-cost collar.

Collateralized debt obligation (CDO)   A security, comprised of pooled portfolios of corporate credits, that is issued in distinct tranches with varying ratings, yields, and repayment priorities. A CDO can be structured as a collateralized loan obligation (for example, pools of loans) or collateralized bond obligation (for example, pools of bonds), and can be created using physical instruments (balance sheet or cash CDOs) or credit derivatives (synthetic CDOs).

Collateralization

A process where an institution provides cash or some other asset with value to support the exposure created by a derivative (or other credit-risky) transaction.

Commodity swap

A swap involving the exchange of fixed and floating commodity price references. Commodity swaps can be written on virtually any physical commodity (energy products, base metals, precious metals, grains, and so on) and can be structured to settle in cash or physical.

Complex chooser option

An option that permits the buyer to choose between an underlying call (with a certain strike and maturity) and an underlying put (with a different strike and maturity) between trade date and choice date. *See also* chooser option.

Complex option

An option that is modified with respect to time, price, and/or payoff to produce very unique and specific results. *See also* path dependent option, path independent option.

Complex structured product

A financing/capital market instrument that contains embedded complex derivatives that alter risk and return characteristics in unique ways.

Complex swap

A swap that is modified with respect to time, price, notional size, and/or payoff to produce unique risk management, investment, or speculative results.

Compound option

An option that can be exercised into an underlying option. There are four different types of compound options, including a call on a call (the right to buy an underlying call), a call on a put (the right to buy an underlying put), a put on a call (the right to sell an underlying call), and a put on a put (the right to sell an underlying put). *See also* call on a call, call on a put, put on a call, and put on a put.

Compound option strategy

A package of options that provides unique and specific results. *See also* directional strategy, volatility strategy.

Condor spread

An option spread designed to take advantage of volatility. Condors are always created with the same ratio of options (one low strike, one middle low strike, one middle high strike, one high strike) that expire at the same time; spreads can be based on puts or calls. Short condors consist of short low and high strike options and long middle low and high strike options, while long condors consist of long low and high strike options and short middle low and high strike options.

Contingent premium option

An option where the purchaser is only obliged to pay the seller premium if the option ends in-the-money; if the option ends out-of-the-money the seller receives no premium payment. If the option ends in-the-money but the intrinsic value is less than the premium due to the seller, the purchaser is still obligated to exercise the option and pay the seller premium.

Convertible bond

A hybrid debt/equity security that consists of a coupon-paying bond and an embedded equity option that allows the holder to convert into a specified number of shares once a conversion level is attained. *See also* reverse convertible bond.

Convexity

A mathematical measure that quantifies the sensitivity of an instrument to large changes in price or yield (for example, the non-linear effects of market changes).

Correlation

A statistical measure that indicates the extent

to which two or more assets move in the same, or opposite, directions. Correlation is used to price and risk-manage various complex derivatives (for example, multi-index derivatives) and quantify portfolio risk exposures.

Credit default model An analytic model that is used to determine credit losses based on the probability of counterparty credit default at various points in time; a credit default model does not model losses attributable to credit deterioration, simply default. *See also* structural model, intensity model, credit mark-to-market model.

Credit default risk The risk of loss arising from a counterparty's failure to perform on its contractual obligations, including derivative contracts, loans, bonds, and other credit-sensitive instruments. *See also* credit risk.

Credit derivative A derivative that generates payoff or protection based on an underlying risky debt reference. *See also* basket swap, credit forward, credit option, default swap, first-to-default swap, total return swap.

Credit forward A single period contract that generates a payoff based on the difference between an agreed credit spread/price and the terminal credit spread/price of a risky debt reference. *See also* credit derivative.

Credit inventory risk The risk of loss arising from an issuer's financial deterioration and/or its failure to perform on an underlying loan or bond obligation. *See also* credit default risk, credit spread risk.

Credit mark-to-market model An analytic model that is used to determine credit losses based on the probability of counter-party credit deterioration at various points in time. Credit default is a specific and unique state under a mark-to-market model. *See also* credit default model, intensity model, structural model.

Credit option	An option that generates a payoff based on the difference between a risky debt credit spread/ price and a predefined strike price. In standard form, credit options generate a continuum of payoffs based on credit appreciation or depreciation; a credit option structured in binary form (as a default option) generates a payoff based solely on default by the reference credit.
Credit portfolio model	A general model that estimates credit losses arising from credit-risky portfolios; since the focus is on portfolio losses, the analytics rely on correlation estimates between counterparties comprising the portfolio. A credit portfolio model can be used as a risk management, business management, portfolio optimization, and capital allocation tool.
Credit reserve	Reserves allocated in support of expected credit losses.
Credit risk	The risk of loss arising from a counterparty's failure to perform on a transaction (also known as "credit default risk") or from credit deterioration (also known as "credit spread risk"). *See also* credit default risk, credit spread risk.
Credit support annex	An attachment to the ISDA Master Agreement framework that defines credit terms between counterparties, including credit thresholds, collateralization process, credit termination events, and so forth.
Credit spread risk	The risk of loss arising from a counterparty's credit quality deterioration (but not default), generally reflected as a widening of the spread/yield against a risk-free benchmark. *See also* credit risk.
Currency swap	A swap involving the exchange of two different currencies. A typical currency swap involves the exchange of a fixed payment in one currency for a floating payment in a second currency (although the exchange of

	two fixed or two floating payments can also be arranged). Currency swaps involve the initial and final exchange of principal, which results in a high degree of credit exposure.
Current exposure method	A regulatory method of computing derivative credit risk based on the sum of fractional credit exposure and actual exposure. *See also* fractional exposure, actual exposure.
Day count note	*See* range floater note.
Deemed risk	*See* fractional exposure.
Default option	*See* credit option.
Default swap	A swap involving the exchange of deferred premium (often in floating rate form) for a lump-sum payment if an underlying reference credit defaults. The payoff associated with this structure is similar to a binary credit option. *See also* credit derivative.
Deferred payment American option	An American exercise option that permits the seller to utilize option proceeds from the time of exercise until the original maturity of the option. In exchange for relinquishing use of proceeds until maturity, the buyer pays the seller a lower premium.
Deferred strike option	An option with a strike price set at a future time period, often as a specific function of the spot value of the underlying market reference at that time.
Delta	A change in the value of an option for a small change in the value of the underlying market reference; the value of delta is often used to create an appropriate directional hedge.
Delta hedging	The process of reducing or neutralizing the exposure of an option to market direction. Delta hedging is accomplished by establishing a delta-equivalent long or short position in the underlying reference against a long or short position in the option. Long calls are hedged with short underlying, long puts

with long underlying, short calls with long underlying, and short puts with short underlying.

Derivative product company

A highly-rated special purpose vehicle used by some financial institutions to undertake derivative transactions with counterparties demanding strong credit ratings. Through design mechanics based on capital, collateral, market risk hedging, and diversification, the derivative product company can typically attain AAA credit ratings.

Difference option

See spread option.

Differential swap

A swap involving the single currency exchange of floating rate references in two distinct currencies. The swap permits an institution to express a view on foreign interest rate movements without assuming currency risk.

Diffusion and amortization effect

A concept that indicates the maximum credit risk of an interest rate swap occurs one-third to one-half through the life of a transaction. This effect arises because simulated future rates used in the calculation of replacement cost will not have had a chance to move sufficiently in the early periods of a swap to pose the greatest economic loss (that is, the "diffusion" effect), and insufficient payments remain to be made toward the end of the swap to pose the greatest economic loss (that is, the "amortization" effect).

Diffusion process

A continuous, stochastic process, where the market variable exists in continuous time and its probability density function is continuous; the variable changes on a random and continuous basis and, as the time interval becomes larger, uncertainty in the returns increases in a predictable fashion.

Digital option

See binary option.

Directional risk

Exposure to the direction of a particular

market or reference. Also known as delta or delta risk. *See also* delta.

Directional strategy

A compound option strategy that seeks to take advantage of market direction rather than implied or realized volatility.

Discount swap

An off-market swap where one party pays a second party an upfront payment in exchange for paying below-market coupons during the life of the transaction.

Discrete barrier option

See partial barrier option.

Diversification

A risk management process that employs portfolio techniques (for example, correlations and optimization) to minimize concentrations of credit exposure and create a more balanced set of risks.

Down and in option

An option that is created if the price of the underlying market reference declines through a predefined barrier. Down and in options are members of the barrier option family. *See also* barrier option.

Down and out option

An option that is extinguished if the price of the underlying market reference declines through a predefined barrier. Down and out options are members of the barrier option family. *See also* barrier option.

Duration

A mathematical measure that quantifies the sensitivity of an instrument to small changes in price or yield (for example, the linear effects of market changes).

Economic capital

Capital that institutions allocate internally to support the financial and operational risks of their businesses (sometimes also known as "management capital"). *See also* regulatory capital.

Electricity swap

A swap involving the exchange of fixed and floating electricity prices based on the average, rather than spot, level of a recognized pricing index; most transactions are settled every month or quarter (to coincide with billing cycles), on a physical or financial basis.

Embedded option

An option that is incorporated into a note or swap to provide the investor or issuer with a unique payoff profile or lower funding cost.

Equity call swap

A swap involving the exchange of a floating rate flow for potential gains from the appreciation an equity index (stock, basket, or broad market index). *See also* equity index swap.

Equity derivative

A broad category of derivatives based on single stocks, equity baskets, and equity indexes. Equity derivatives are available as forwards, options, swaps, and derivatives/ notes with embedded options.

Equity index swap

A swap involving the exchange of a floating rate flow for appreciation or depreciation in a single equity, basket of equities, or equity index. *See also* equity call swap, equity put swap.

Equity put swap

A swap that exchanges a floating rate flow for potential gains from the depreciation of an equity index (stock, basket, or broad market index). *See also* equity index swap.

European barrier option

See point barrier option.

European option

An option that is only exercisable at maturity.

Event risk

The risk of an unexpected credit or economic event/action that can have a material impact on financial asset prices/markets.

Exchange-traded derivative

A derivative contract that is traded through a formal physical or electronic exchange. Exchange-traded derivatives, available as futures, options, and futures options with standardized terms, carry minimal credit risk (as a result of initial/variation collateral posted by all clients through a centralized clearing house).

Exotic option

See complex option.

Expected credit loss	An average, or mathematically expected, credit loss, generally determined through a combination of expected credit exposure, probability of default, and recoveries. *See also* unexpected credit loss, worst-case credit loss.
Expected exposure	Credit exposure based on a mathematically expected market movement.
Exploding option	A bullish or bearish vertical spread that generates a payoff once the two strikes defining the spread are breached. *See also* bear spread, bull spread.
Extendible option	An option that enables the purchaser to exercise an option on a particular reset date or reset the strike price to the current market level and extend the option for another reset period. This derivative is a variation of the reset, or partial lookback, option. *See also* partial lookback option.
First-to-default swap	A default swap comprised of a basket of reference credits that only entitles the purchaser a payout on the first credit that defaults; once a default occurs, the transaction effectively terminates. Since swap pricing generally takes account of reference credit correlations, the derivative is cheaper than the purchase of individual default options on the same reference credits. *See also* credit derivative.
Fixed strike ladder option	An option that locks in gains prior to expiry as the price of the underlying market reference exceeds prespecified market levels (or "rungs"); gains are not lost if the market subsequently retraces. This version of the option generates gains by comparing the terminal price and ladder rungs against a predefined strike price and allocating a gain to the larger of the two. Fixed strike ladder options are members of the ladder option family. *See also* ladder options.
Fixed strike lookback option	*See* options on the maximum/minimum.

Fixed strike shout option

An option that locks in gains at a particular market level when the purchaser "shouts"; gains are not lost if the market subsequently retraces. This version of the option generates gains by comparing the terminal price and shout level against a predefined strike price and allocating a gain to the larger of the two. *See also* shout options.

Floating strike ladder option

An option that locks in gains prior to expiry as the price of the underlying market reference exceeds prespecified market levels (or "rungs"); gains are not lost if the market subsequently retraces. This version of the option carries no preset strike price and generates gains by comparing the terminal price and ladder rungs at maturity. *See also* ladder options.

Floating strike lookback option

An option that generates a maximum gain by "looking back" over the price path of the asset and determining the point at which the greatest economic profit is created. This version of the option carries no preset strike price and generates a gain by comparing the terminal price against the lowest buying price (for calls) or highest selling price (for puts) achieved by the asset. *See also* lookback options.

Floating strike shout option

An option that locks in gains at a particular market level once the purchaser "shouts" for gains to be locked in; gains are not lost if the market subsequently retraces. This version of the option carries no predefined strike price and generates gains by comparing the terminal price and shout level at maturity. *See also* shout options.

Floor

An option that generates a payoff when an underlying interest rate reference falls below a lower strike level.

Floortion

An option on a floor, granting the purchaser the right to buy a floor.

Forward	A bilateral over-the-counter derivative that permits the purchaser to buy an asset at a predetermined forward price and forward date and the seller to sell an asset at a predetermined forward price and forward date. Forwards are available on any underlying security/asset from the fixed income, equity, currency, commodity, or credit markets and can be settled in cash or physical.
Forward rate agreement	A single period forward interest rate contract.
Forward start option	An option that is contracted on trade date t and commences on forward date t+1, with the forward start date, strike price, and final maturity parameters established on trade date. Once the forward date is reached and the transaction begins the contract assumes the characteristics of a conventional European option.
Forward swap	A swap that is contracted on trade date t and commences on forward date t+1, with the rate and final maturity parameters established on trade date. Once the forward date is reached and the transaction begins the contract assumes the characteristics of a conventional swap.
Foundation methodology	One of two credit capital allocation approaches under the BIS's Internal Ratings Based (IRB) quantification framework. Under the foundation approach, banks use internal models to determine counterparty risk of default but use BIS-supplied risk factors to compute credit risk exposures and loss given default. *See also* advanced methodology, internal ratings based approach.
Fractional exposure	The amount of future credit exposure inherent in a derivative transaction, typically included as one of two components (along with actual, or mark-to-market, exposure) in determining total credit exposure. Fractional exposure is generally estimated through statistical or

simulation methods and utilized as a measure of the potential credit exposure that might arise during the life of a transaction; it is positive at the inception of a trade and declines as maturity approaches. Fractional exposure is also known as "presettlement risk," "time-to-decay risk," or "deemed risk".

Future

An exchange-listed contract that permits the purchaser to buy an asset at a predetermined forward price and delivery date and the seller to sell an asset at a predetermined forward price and delivery date. Futures are available in standardized form on assets/securities from the fixed income, equity, currency, and commodity markets and can be settled in cash or physical (depending on contract specifications). Contracts are secured by initial margin and are marked-to-market on a daily basis by the exchange clearing-house; variation margins are posted to cover daily market movement.

Futures option

An exchange-listed option on a futures contract.

Gamma

A change in the value of delta for a change in the price of the underlying market reference. Gamma, which measures the convexity or non-linearity of option prices, is often used to measure sensitivity to large market movements.

Guaranteed exchange rate option

See Quanto.

Geometric Brownian motion

A lognormal, continuous-time stochastic process where the movement of the market variable is random in continuous time; the instantaneous return (defined as the change in the price of the variable divided by the price of the variable) has a constant mean and a constant variance.

Haircut

The upfront discount applied to the value of security taken as collateral in order to protect against price deterioration and the possibility

	of credit exposure becoming unsecured. The greater the volatility of the underlying reference security and the longer the time between valuation and collateral calls, the larger the haircut.
Hedge	A transaction that is intended to protect an underlying asset, liability, revenue, or expense from adverse movement in a particular reference index; a correctly structured hedge transaction results in gains and losses that offset one another.
High–low option	An option that generates a payoff based on the difference between the high and low prices of the underlying reference asset during the life of the transaction.
Historical method	A credit exposure computation methodology where historical rate movements are used to estimate the fractional exposure of a swap. An institution obtains a history of interest rate (or swap rate) movements, determines the distribution of rates, and computes the mean and variance of each rate. Following an adjustment to a prespecified confidence level, it projects forward swap rates, revalues the swap at each forward point, and discounts back to the present; the largest exposure obtained during the revaluation process becomes the swap's fractional exposure.
Historical volatility	A "backward looking" statistical measure of the price movement of an asset based on historical data, generally denominated in terms of variance or standard deviation. Historical volatility is often used to estimate future market moves (for example, as in a risk equivalency or value-at-risk framework). *See also* implied volatility.
Hybrid approach	A portfolio aggregation approach that combines elements of the incremental summation approach and the simulation approach. Through the process a counterparty portfolio is

periodically transformed into a portfolio credit vector through simulation; between simulation conversions each incremental trade is added to the existing counterparty portfolio credit vector as it arises. *See also* incremental summation approach, simulation approach.

Hybrid bond

The original class of structured securities (securities with embedded derivatives) that includes callable bonds (bonds with an embedded option giving the issuer the right to redeem the security) and putable bonds (bonds giving the investor the right to put the security back to the issuer).

Implied volatility

A forward-looking measure of the price movement of an asset based on data implied by traded option prices. Volatility is one of the central inputs of option pricing models but is not directly observable in the market; accordingly, traders can use observed option prices to derive the volatility implied by the prices. *See also* historical volatility.

Incremental summation approach

A simple portfolio aggregation approach that adds incremental transactions together as they arise; the process can result in overstatement of exposures and misstatement of transaction profiles. *See also* hybrid approach, simulation approach.

In-the-money

An option whose strike price (SP) is above the current market price (CMP) for puts and below the CMP for calls. An in-the-money option has maximum intrinsic value.

Index amortizing rate swap

See index principal swap.

Index principal swap

A swap with a notional principal that amortizes as a floating rate reference declines through pre-specified barrier levels. As the notional declines, fixed and floating rate payments associated with the swap become smaller. *See also* reverse index principal swap, amortizing swap.

Inflation swap	A swap involving the exchange of fixed and actual inflation rates, sometimes referred to as a consumer price index (CPI) swap (US), retail price index (RPI) swap (UK), or harmonized index of consumer prices (HICP) swap (Eurozone). *See also* annual inflation swap, zero coupon inflation swap.
Installment option	An option where the purchaser is permitted to pay the seller premium in installments, rather than upfront, and can cancel the contract at any time by suspending installment payments. If the purchaser completes all required payments, the seller grants a conventional European option with contract details as specified on trade date.
Intensity model	A form of credit default model that estimates time of counterparty default with a particular intensity and uncertain time horizon; such models have no direct reference to a firm's value but derive the probability of the event as an instantaneous likelihood of default. *See also* structural model.
Interest rate swap	A swap involving the exchange of two interest rate references. A typical interest rate swap involves the exchange of a fixed interest rate for a floating interest rate, although two floating rates can also be exchanged. Interest rate swaps do not involve the initial and final exchange of principal and thus feature less credit exposure than currency swaps. *See also* basis swap, currency swap.
Intermediation	The process of executing a derivative transaction through another party rather than directly with the end user; the intermediary, rather than the arranger, is thus exposed to the credit risk of the end user.
Internal ratings based (IRB) approach	A credit capital quantification methodology introduced under the new BIS Basle Capital Accord that replaces computation methodologies promulgated under the original 1988

Accord. The IRB approach can be implemented via the foundation or advanced methodologies, both of which permit the use of an institution's own internally developed models. *See also* advanced methodology, foundation methodology.

Intrinsic value

One of two components (along with time value) that determine the value of an option. Intrinsic value measures the current value, or moneyness, of an option; options which are in-the-money can be exercised for an immediate gain and thus have intrinsic value equal to the difference between the current market price and the strike price. Out-of-the-money and at-the-money have no intrinsic value. *See also* time value.

Inverse floater note

A structured note that provides the investor with a coupon based on an inverse rate generally defined as (x percent fixed rate minus floating rate); thus, rising rates generate a lower coupon and falling rates generate a higher coupon.

Inverse floater swap

A swap involving the exchange of a fixed rate and an inverse rate generally defined as (x percent fixed rate minus floating rate); this structure has the effect of magnifying upward or downward movements in rates since both legs of the swap move in the same direction.

Jump process

A mathematical process used to describe the movement of asset prices that are impacted by sudden, discontinuous moves. Certain option pricing models utilize a jump process, rather than a continuous stochastic process, to generate values.

Kappa

See vega.

Kick-in option

See reverse knock-in option.

Kick-out option

See reverse knock-out option.

Knock-in option

An option that is created when the price of the underlying market reference moves above or below a barrier. *See also* barrier option, down and in option, up and in option.

Knock-out option

An option that is extinguished when the price of the underlying market reference moves above or below a barrier. *See also* barrier option, down and out option, up and out option.

Ladder option

An option that locks in gains prior to expiry as the price of the underlying market reference exceeds prespecified market levels (or "rungs"); gains are not lost if the market subsequently retraces. *See also* fixed strike ladder option, floating strike ladder option.

Leveraged note

A structured note that provides the investor with an enhanced coupon based on a predefined leverage formula that multiplies the effects of market movements.

Leveraged option

See power option.

Leveraged swap

A swap that generates a payoff by multiplying one side of the transaction by a leverage factor; the use of leverage compounds the upward or downward movement of the underlying market reference. Leverage can be applied to any swap and can be defined in any fashion. Also known as "power swap," "ratio swap."

Lockout period

A time period during which an amortizing swap structure is not permitted to amortize, regardless of the movement of reference rates.

Lognormal distribution

A statistical distribution often used to characterize the distribution of asset prices. A lognormal distribution, which is skewed to the right, faces a lower bound of zero and an upper bound of infinity.

Lookback option

An option that generates a maximum gain by "looking back" over the price path of the asset and determining the point that creates the greatest economic gain. *See also* fixed strike lookback option, floating strike lookback option.

Loss-based model	*See* credit default model.
Loss given default	A dollar or percentage estimate of the amount, net of recoveries, that is expected to be lost when a counterparty defaults (for example, 1 – recovery rate).
Mark-to-market	The process of revaluing a financial transaction based on current market prices or rates. Marking-to-market is widely used in the quantification of actual derivative credit exposure as it provides an accurate indication of the current value, and hence replacement cost, of a contract.
Market risk	The risk of loss due to adverse movement in the market variable(s) of an underlying reference security or asset. Variables that can create market-based losses include direction, volatility, basis, spread, curve, time, correlation, skew, and smile.
Markov process	A stochastic process where only the current price of a variable is relevant in determining what may happen in the future; that is, previous prices, and the number of periods preceding the current observation, are irrelevant.
Master agreement	A formal agreement between two counterparties that documents the legal and credit aspects of derivative transactions (subsequent trades can then be evidenced by short-form confirmations rather than more extensive, long-form confirmations). A master agreement must be in place (and recognized legally) if credit exposures are to be quantified and managed on a net, rather than gross, basis. Common master agreements include the ISDA Master Agreement, the French AFB agreement, and the German Rahmenverstrag agreement.
Mean reversion	The tendency for interest rates, and the volatility of interest rates, to return to a mean level over the long term. Mean reversion is

incorporated into certain bond option pricing models.

Mid-Atlantic option	*See* Bermudan option.
Modified ladder option	*See* fixed strike ladder option.
Modified shout option	*See* fixed strike shout option.
Money spread	*See* bear spread, bull spread.

Monte Carlo simulation A computer-intensive statistical process that generates asset paths based on user-defined inputs and drawings from a random number generator. Monte Carlo simulation is widely used for pricing derivatives, computing credit exposures and scenarios, and measuring portfolio risks.

Mortgage swap An amortizing swap that replicates the cash flow characteristics of a physical mortgage-backed security and can thus be used as a synthetic investment or hedge for a mortgage portfolio. *See also* amortizing swap.

Multi-factor option *See* multi-index option.

Multi-index note A structured note that pays an enhanced coupon based on the performance of multiple indexes drawn from the same, or different, asset classes/markets. *See also* structured note.

Multi-index option An option that generates a payoff based on the difference between two or more reference assets and a predefined strike price; assets may be drawn from the same, or different, asset classes/markets. *See also* basket option, multiple strike option, option on the best/worst of n-assets, option on the best/worst of n-assets and cash, spread option.

Multiple barriers An option package that contains at least two barrier options. *See also* twin-in option, twin-out option.

Multiple strike option An option that generates a payoff based on the best or worst performing of a series of assets, each with a specific strike price. Option references may be drawn from the same, or different, asset classes/markets. *See also* multi-index option.

Negative convexity Any strategy or instrument that exhibits losses that are greater, and gains that are smaller, than those estimated through sensitivity measures and market movements.

Negative gamma Risk exposure to large market moves generated through the sale of puts or calls. *See also* gamma.

Netting The process of offsetting exposures and reducing payments to a single flow. In order for netting to be valid a legally acceptable master agreement must be agreed and executed by both parties. *See also* Master agreement.

Normal distribution A statistical distribution characterized by the familiar "bell-shaped" curve. A normal faces no lower or upper bounds.

Notional A common method of denominating the size of a derivative transaction, particularly for swaps and forwards. In most instances, notional is used only as a reference to compute amounts payable and/or receivable, though for currency swaps the full notional is typically exchanged on trade date and at maturity.

NPV (net present value) model *See* credit mark-to-market model

One-factor interest rate models Option pricing models that value bond options by generating an entire yield curve through a single interest rate reference (generally a short-term rate). Though such models are thought to be less accurate than two-factor models, they are simpler to implement. *See also* two-factor interest rate models.

One-touch option *See* binary–barrier option.

Option	A derivative granting the holder the right, but not the obligation, to buy or sell a reference security at a predefined strike price. In exchange for the right, the buyer pays the seller a premium. Options are available on any underlying security/asset from the fixed income, equity, currency, commodity, or credit markets, and can be bought or sold in over-the-counter or listed form. *See also* call, put.
Option method	A method where the fractional exposure of a swap is estimated through an option pricing framework. The swap is viewed as a package of options that gives the holder the right to buy a fixed rate bond and sell a floating rate note (or vice versa); the options are exercised jointly in the event of counterparty default, but only if they are in-the-money.
Option on the best/worst of n-assets	An option that generates a payoff based on the best or worst performing of a group of assets against a predefined strike price; assets may be from identical or different asset classes/markets. Options are available as calls and puts on the best of n-assets and calls and puts on the worst of n-assets. *See also* multi-index option, call on the best of n-assets, call on the worst of n-assets, put on the best of n-assets, put on the worst of n-assets.
Option on the best/worst of n-assets and cash	An option that generates a payoff based on the best or worst performing of a group of assets and cash; assets may be from identical or different asset classes/markets. Best–worst options generate a minimum payoff equal to a predefined cash amount C and do not carry strike prices; as such, they never end out-of-the-money. *See also* multi-index option.
Option on the maximum/minimum	An option that generates a maximum gain by "looking back" over the price path of the asset and determining the point that creates the greatest economic value. This version of the lookback option, also known as a "fixed strike

lookback," carries a preset strike price and generates a payoff based on the difference between the strike price and the maximum price (for calls on the maximum) or minimum price (for puts on the minimum) achieved by the asset. *See also* call on the maximum, lookback option, put on the minimum.

Original exposure method A regulatory method of computing swap credit risk that focuses solely on future credit exposure (rather than the sum of future credit exposure and actual exposure).

Out-of-the-money An option whose strike price (SP) is below the current market price (CMP) for puts and above the CMP for calls. An out-of-the-money option has no intrinsic value.

Outperformance option An option that generates a payoff based on the outperformance of a spread against a predefined strike price. *See also* spread option.

Outside barrier option A multivariate option with a barrier that is triggered by a reference that is distinct from the one defining the underlying option. *See also* barrier option.

Partial barrier option A barrier option where the barrier is only in effect during a portion of the option's life. *See also* barrier option, point barrier option.

Partial lookback option An option with a strike price that can be reset on a particular evaluation date if the option is out-of-the-money. Partial lookback options are also known as "reset options."

Path dependent option A broad category of options whose payoff at expiry is dependent on the price path of the underlying reference asset at previous points in time.

Path independent option A broad category of options whose payoff at expiry is dependent solely on the price of the underlying reference asset at expiry.

Pay later option *See* contingent premium option.

Payment netting A netting arrangement where an institution and

	its non-defaulting counterparty agree to net payments in the normal course of business.
Periodic collateral	A process where an institution takes a smaller amount of initial collateral from its counterparty but revalues and adjusts it periodically (for example, calls for additional collateral if in deficit, returns excess collateral if in surplus). *See also* upfront collateral.
Point barrier option	A barrier option where the barrier is only in effect during a single point in time. Point barrier options are also known as "European barrier options." *See also* barrier option, partial barrier option.
Pooled portfolio collateral	A collateralization technique where collateral securing a portfolio of derivatives is held in a pool that can be applied to incremental transactions and managed actively through right of substitution. *See also* transaction-specific collateral.
Positive convexity	Any non-linear strategy or instrument that exhibits losses that are smaller, and gains that are larger, than those estimated through sensitivity measures or market movements.
Potential exposure	The sum of actual exposure and fractional exposure; potential exposure is a key measure of the current and future credit exposure impacting a derivative transaction. *See also* actual exposure, fractional exposure.
Potential market risk	*See* fractional exposure.
Power barrier option	An option with an exponential payoff that is either created (knock-in) or extinguished (knock-out) when a particular barrier is breached. *See also* barrier option and power option.
Power option	An option that generates an exponential payoff. A power option raises the price of the underlying market reference to a prespecified exponent (or power) and compares the result against a predefined strike price to generate

an economic gain. Power options are also known as "leveraged options" or "turbo options."

Power swap *See* leveraged swap.

Preference option *See* chooser option.

Premium The payment made by the purchaser of an option to the seller of an option in exchange for potential gains under the option contract. Premium is comprised of time value and intrinsic value.

Premium swap An off-market swap where one party pays a second party an upfront payment in exchange for receiving above-market coupons during the life of the transaction.

Presettlement risk *See* fractional exposure.

Price spread *See* bear spread, bull spread.

Put A derivative granting the holder the right, but not the obligation, to sell an underlying reference security at a prespecified strike price.

Put on a call An option that grants the buyer the right to sell an underlying call. *See also* compound option.

Put on a put An option that grants the buyer the right to sell an underlying put. *See also* compound option.

Put on the best of n-assets An option that generates a payoff based on the difference between a predefined strike price and the best performing asset in a portfolio; the option effectively permits the holder to sell the best performing of a group of assets. Puts on the best of n-assets are members of the multi-index/rainbow option family. *See also* options on the best/worst of n-assets.

Put on the minimum An option that generates a payoff based on the difference between a predefined strike price and the lowest price achieved by the underlying reference asset over the life of the transaction. *See also* options on the maximum/minimum.

Put on the worst of n-assets

An option that generates a payoff based on the difference between a predefined strike price and the worst performing asset in a portfolio; the option effectively permits the holder to sell the worst performing of a group of assets. *See also* options on the best/worst of n-assets.

Put spread

An option strategy that is created to express a bullish or bearish directional market view; the spread requires the sale and purchase of two separate puts with different strikes; *See also* bull spreads, bear spreads.

Putable bond

A bond with embedded puts giving the investor the right to sell the bond back to the issuer at a predetermined price.

Putable swap

A swap structure giving the fixed rate payer the option to terminate the underlying swap at a future date. *See also* callable swap, cancelable swap.

Quanto option

An option that converts gains from an underlying foreign currency derivative into a target currency, at a predetermined foreign exchange rate; use of a quanto option protects an institution from exchange rate risk. Quanto options are also known as "quantity adjusted options" or "guaranteed exchange rate options."

Rainbow option

See multi-index option.

Range floater note

A structured note that provides the investor with an enhanced coupon if the floating rate reference trades within a predefined range, or band; for every day the reference falls outside the band the investor loses one day's interest. The security is effectively a standard floating rate note with a strip of embedded binary options. Also known as "accrual notes," "day count notes."

Range knock-out floater note

A structured note that pays higher coupons than a range floater but ceases paying interest for an entire interest period, for example, one quarter, if the reference trades outside the range for a single day.

Ratchet option *See* cliquet option.

Ratio horizontal spread *See* time spread.

Ratio swap *See* leveraged swap.

Ratio vertical spread An option spread that is designed to take advantage of volatility. Ratio vertical spreads are created through the purchase of a smaller quantity of closer-to-the-money puts or calls and the sale of a larger quantity of farther-from-the-money puts or calls. A long ratio vertical spread is known as a "backspread." *See also* backspread.

Realized volatility swap A swap involving the exchange of realized volatility and implied volatility. Realized volatility is the floating volatility of the underlying reference index evident over the life of the transaction, while implied volatility is the fixed volatility rate contracted between buyer and seller at the start of the transaction. *See also* variance swap.

Recouponing The process of marking-to-market and settling a portfolio of derivatives as a means of reducing actual exposure. During the process a net cash settlement is paid by the party holding the out-of-the-money contracts to the party holding the in-the-money contracts and the derivatives are then rewritten, or recouponed, at current market levels.

Regular chooser option *See* chooser option.

Regulatory capital Capital that institutions must allocate to their financial and operating risks in order to comply with regulatory requirements. *See also* economic capital, tier 1 capital, tier 2 capital.

Replacement cost *See* actual exposure.

Reset option *See* partial barrier option.

Reverse barrier option *See* reverse knock-in option, reverse knock-out option.

Reverse convertible bond A convertible security that can be exchanged from debt into equity at the option of the issuer, rather than then investor. *See also* convertible bond.

Reverse index principal swap A swap with a notional principal that increases as a floating rate reference declines through prespecified barrier levels. As the notional increases, fixed and floating rate payments associated with the swap become larger. *See also* accreting swap, index principal swap.

Reverse knock-in option A barrier option that knocks-in in-the-money. Reverse knock-in options are also known as "kick-in options." *See also* barrier option.

Reverse knock-out option A barrier option that knocks-out in-the-money. Reverse knock-out options are also known as "kick-out options." *See also* barrier option.

Rho A change in the value of an option for a change in the risk-free rate.

Risk-adjusted capital Capital allocated in support of unexpected credit losses.

Risk equivalent exposure The potential credit risk generated by a credit-risky transaction with uncertain value, such as a derivative or undrawn loan facility. For derivatives, risk equivalent exposure generally includes actual exposure (also known as "mark-to-market exposure," "replacement cost," or "actual market risk") and fractional exposure (also known as "potential market risk," "deemed risk," "time-to-decay risk," or "presettlement risk"). Risk equivalent exposure is often estimated through a statistical/ volatility framework or a simulation process. *See also* actual exposure, fractional exposure, potential exposure.

Set-off A netting arrangement where an institution and a defaulting counterparty agree to terminate derivative transactions and apply net payments against amounts due, or owed, under other financial transactions.

Shout option

An option that locks in gains at a particular market level when the purchaser "shouts"; gains are not relinquished if the market subsequently retraces. *See also* fixed strike shout option, floating strike shout option.

Simulation approach

A sophisticated, though time and resource intensive, portfolio aggregation approach that requires the generation of new credit portfolio vectors each time an incremental transaction is added to the portfolio. *See also* incremental summation approach, hybrid approach.

Simulation method

A method of estimating the fractional exposure of a swap through simulation of future interest rates. The process assumes that rates move randomly over time but that possible values can be defined in terms of a particular distribution with certain mean and variance. Given a predefined statistical distribution, confidence levels, starting rate, time intervals, and mathematical relationship of future rate movements, a random generation of an artificial future path can be created, with swap replacement costs calculated at each interval. Thousands of realizations yield a set of discounted swap replacement costs, and the average is used as a representation of the discounted replacement cost at each select time interval during the life of the swap. The sum of average discounted replacement costs generates a risk factor that can be used to calculate fractional exposure.

Speculation

A financial strategy that involves taking an outright view on a financial reference through cash or derivative instruments; resulting gains and losses can be particularly large, as they are not offset by underlying exposures/positions (as in a hedge transaction).

Spread option

An option that generates a payoff based on the difference between two reference assets and a predefined strike price; the assets may be drawn from similar or different asset classes/markets. Spread options are also known as "difference options," "outperformance options," or "underperformance options." *See also* multi-index option, outperformance option, yield curve option, underperformance option.

Square root rule

A statistical property that indicates that the standard deviation of the changes in an underlying market variable is proportional to the square root of time.

Stack and roll

A form of hedging that takes advantage of the liquidity of short-term contracts to hedge long-term exposures. Short-term contracts are "stacked" and then "rolled" into new contracts as they begin trading; though this hedge can reduce directional risk, it creates exposure to curve risk.

Stochastic process

A mathematical process used to describe continuous and dynamic movement of asset prices. Many option pricing models utilize a stochastic process to generate option prices.

Straddle

An option spread designed to take advantage of volatility. Straddles are created through the purchase or sale of options with identical strikes and expiry dates. Long straddles consist of long puts and calls struck at the same level, and short straddles consist of short puts and calls struck at the same level.

Strangle

An option spread designed to take advantage of volatility. Strangles are created through the purchase or sale of options with different strikes but identical expiry dates. Long strangles consists of long puts and calls struck at different levels and short strangles consists of short puts and calls struck at different levels.

Strap

An option strategy involving long (short) one

put and long (short) two calls with the same strike; the long strap is characterized by unlimited profit potential and limited downside risk, the short strap by limited profit potential and unlimited downside risk.

Strip

An option strategy involving long (short) one call and long (short) two puts with the same strike; the long strip is characterized by unlimited profit potential and limited downside risk, the short strip by limited profit potential and unlimited downside risk.

Structural model

A form of credit default model, originally put forth by Black and Scholes and Merton in 1973 and 1974 (and since extended and adapted), which determines counterparty default by an underlying process that describes the value of the counterparty in terms of assets, liabilities, and capital structure. Default is said to occur when a particular boundary value (for example, liability threshold) is reached. *See also* intensity model.

Structured note

A note or bond with an embedded derivative that generates a unique payoff. *See also* inverse floater note, leveraged note, multiple index note, range floater note, range knockout floater note.

Structured product

A financing/capital markets instrument that contains embedded derivatives that alter risk and return characteristics.

Swap

An over-the-counter derivative involving the periodic exchange of payments between two parties. Swaps are available on any underlying security/asset from the fixed income, equity, currency, commodity, or credit markets.

Swaption

An option on a swap. A receiver swaption grants the buyer the right to receive fixed/pay floating in swap, while a payer swaption grants the buyer the right to pay fixed/receive floating.

Synthetic option

An option position created through the combination of a long or short option on an underlying security and a long or short position in the same underlying security.

Synthetic underlying

An underlying position created through the combination of two long or short options on the same underlying security.

Temperature swap

A swap involving the exchange of fixed and floating (actual) temperatures, generally based on a cumulative index. The temperature index is often based on average degree days, heating degree days, or cooling degree days, which compare the daily average temperature recorded above/below a benchmark temperature (for example, 65 degrees Fahrenheit); the difference is accumulated during a summer or winter season and a net payment is made at the conclusion of the transaction.

Terminal exposure

Credit exposure based on the final maturity of the transaction.

Terminal expected risk exposure

Potential credit exposure based on the final maturity of the transaction and the expected movement of the underlying market reference; terminal expected exposure is the second largest of four classes of credit exposure. *See also* average expected risk exposure, average worst-case risk exposure, terminal worst-case risk exposure.

Terminal worst case risk exposure

Potential credit exposure based on the final maturity of the transaction and the worst-case movement of the underlying market reference; terminal worst-case exposure is the largest of four classes of credit exposure. *See also* average expected risk exposure, average worst-case risk exposure, terminal expected risk exposure.

Termination option

An option to terminate a derivative transaction based on the passage of time or the occurrence of a credit event (for example, ratings downgrade).

Theta	A change in the value of an option for a change in the passage of time. *See also* time decay, time value.
Third-party enhancements	Any form of support obtained from a third-party credit support provider, such as a guarantee, surety bond, or letter of credit; such enhancements are often used to increase the creditworthiness of a counter-party transaction.
Tier 1 capital	Regulatory core capital, as defined by the Bank for International Settlements, which includes common stock, retained earnings, and disclosed reserves (including loan loss reserves). *See also* economic capital, regulatory capital.
Tier 2 capital	Regulatory supplemental capital, as defined by the Bank for International Settlements, which includes hybrid securities (for example, mandatory convertibles), long-term subordinated debt with maturities greater than five years, perpetual securities, unrealized gains on investment assets and hidden reserves. *See also* economic capital, regulatory capital.
Time decay	Daily gain or loss experienced in the time value component of option premium due to the passage of time; often used as a reference to theta. *See also* theta, time value.
Time spread	An option spread designed to take advantage of volatility as related to time. Time spreads are created through the purchase or sale of options with identical strikes but different expiry dates. Long time spreads consist of short near month puts or calls and long far month puts or calls, and short time spreads consist of long near month puts or calls and short far month puts or calls. Also known as a "calendar spread" or "ratio horizontal spread."
Time-to-decay risk	*See* fractional exposure.

Time value	One of two components (along with intrinsic value) that determine the value of an option. In purchasing an option, a buyer is purchasing time for the underlying reference to move in-the-money (or further in-the-money); time value measures the remaining economic value of the option that is attributable to time. Longer term options have greater time value than shorter time options, while in-the-money and out-of-the-money options have less time value than at-the-money options. *See also* intrinsic value.
Total return swap	A swap that synthetically replicates the economic flows of a reference asset, such as a credit-risky bond or equity index. A credit-based total return swap involves the exchange of periodic fixed or floating coupons from a reference bond plus appreciation in the price of the bond for a periodic nominal floating coupon plus depreciation in the price of the bond.
Transaction-specific collateral	Collateral taken on an incremental basis in support of a discrete derivative transaction. *See also* pooled portfolio collateral.
Transition probability	The probability of a counterparty's credit rating migrating from one rating class to another; such probabilities are essential components of credit mark-to-market models.
Turbo option	*See* power option.
Twin-in barrier option	An option that is created when either an upper or lower barrier is breached. *See also* barrier option.
Twin-out barrier option	An option that is extinguished when either an upper or lower barrier is breached. *See also* barrier option.
Two-factor interest rate models	Option pricing models which value bond options by generating an entire yield curve through two interest rate references (that is, a short-term rate and a long-term rate). Though

such models are more complex to implement than one-factor models, they are generally thought to be more accurate. *See also* one-factor interest rate models.

Underperformance option

An option that generates a payoff based on the underperformance of a spread against a predefined strike price. *See also* spread option.

Unexpected credit loss

The difference between expected and worst case credit losses; alternatively, the difference between the mean of the credit loss distribution function and a point represented by multiple standard deviations from the mean. *See also* expected credit loss, worst-case credit loss.

Unilateral collateral

The process of taking a greater amount of collateral at the start of a derivative transaction in order to place less (or no) reliance on subsequent revaluations. *See also* periodic collateral.

Up and in option

An option that is created once the price of the underlying market reference rises above a predefined barrier. *See also* barrier option, knock-in option.

Up and out option

An option that is extinguished once the price of the underlying market reference rises above a predefined barrier. *See also* barrier option, knock-out option.

Upfront collateral

Collateral that is taken at the inception of a derivative transaction in an amount intended to cover potential credit exposure over some pre-determined evaluation period.

Value-at-risk

A measure of the worst-case market loss expected over a prespecified holding period, adjusted to a particular confidence level. Value-at-risk is implemented by using correlation and volatility matrices and can be quantified using historical or simulation methods.

Variable principal swap   The general class of swaps with notional principal amounts that vary according to time or the movement of a reference index. *See also* accreting swap, amortizing swap, index/ reverse index principal swap, mortgage swaps.

Variable strike option   *See* deferred strike option.

Variance swap   A swap involving the exchange of the difference between the square of realized volatility and the square of implied volatility. Since the contract is nonlinear, it provides the purchaser with positive convexity (for example, when realized variance is greater than implied variance gains are greater, and when realized variance is less than implied variance losses are smaller). *See also* realized volatility swap.

Vega   A change in the value of an option for a change in volatility.

Vertical spread   *See* bear spread, bull spread.

Volatility skew   The relationship that exists between the implied volatility of out-of-the-money calls and puts. Out-of-the-money calls generally have lower implied volatilities than out-of-the-money puts, as there are typically more call sellers than put sellers in the market.

Volatility smile   The relationship that exists between implied volatility of options and strike price. A conventional smile attributes greater implied volatility to in or out-of-the-money options.

Volatility strategy   A compound option strategy that seeks to take advantage of changes in implied or realized volatility, rather than market direction.

Volatility swap   The general class of swaps that exchanges fixed and realized volatility indexes. *See also* realized volatility swap and variance swap.

Warrant   An "option-like" derivative that is often attached to a bond issue and then detached and traded separately. The most common attached warrants provide the investor with a call on the issuer's stock, but individual warrants are also available on fixed income, equity, currency, and commodity references.

Weiner process

A stochastic process that is normally distributed with expected value of 0 and variance of 1 at each time interval t. Under a Weiner process, values at time t and t+1 have a correlation of 0 (that is, they are independent of one another; thus, a Weiner process is also a Markov process).

When-in-the-money option

See contingent premium option.

Willingness to perform

A counterparty's intent to perform on its obligations, unrelated to its financial capability.

Worst-case credit loss

A potential credit loss represented by a point multiple standard deviations from the mean (or expected) value of the credit loss distribution function. *See also* expected credit loss, unexpected credit loss.

Worst-case exposure

Credit exposure based on an extreme market movement.

Yield curve option

A spread option that generates a payoff based on the difference between two points on a yield curve against a predefined strike price. *See also* spread option.

Yield enhancement

Any financial strategy designed to increase an investor's returns; most yield enhancing techniques are intended to be low risk, for example, limited/no downside, moderate upside.

Zero-coupon inflation swap

A swap involving the exchange of floating and fixed inflation at maturity (that is, no periodic payments). *See also* annual inflation swap, inflation swap.

Zero-coupon swap

A swap involving a single payment by one party at maturity, in bullet form. In most cases the second party makes a series of interim payments up until, and including, maturity.

Zero cost collar

A spread consisting of a purchased cap/call and a sold floor/put, or vice versa. The sale of one option offsets the premium payable on the second option resulting in "zero cost." *See also* collar.

Bibliography

Aldred, P. *Convertibles and Warrants* (London: Euromoney, 1987).

Alexander, C. (ed.) *The Handbook of Risk Management and Analysis* (New York: Wiley, 1996).

Altman, E. *Corporate Financial Distress and Bankruptcy, 2nd edn* (New York: Wiley, 1993).

Antl, B. (ed.) *Swap Finance: Volume 2* (London: Euromoney, 1986).

Arak, M., Goodman, L., and Rones, A. Credit Lines for New Instruments: Swaps, Over-the-Counter Options, Forwards, and Floor–Ceiling Agreements, *Proceedings from a Conference on Bank Structure and Competition*, Federal Reserve Bank of Chicago, May 1986, pp. 437–56.

Asiamoney. *Derivatives Guide* (London: Euromoney, 1995).

Australian Financial Review. Derivatives Survey, *Australian Financial Review*, 28 January 1993.

Azarchs, T. Banks Face Manageable Risks in Derivative Business, *Standard & Poor's Creditweek*, 9 November 1992, pp. 46–51.

Bacon, K. Risk to Banks from Derivatives Still too High, *Asian Wall Street Journal*, November 1992, p. 23.

Bank for International Settlements. *International Convergence of Capital Measurement and Capital Standards* (Basle: BIS, 1988).

Bank for International Settlements. *Central Bank Survey of Foreign Exchange and Derivatives Market Activity 1995* (Basle: BIS, 1996).

Bank for International Settlements. *The Internal Ratings-Based Approach: Consultative Document* (Basel: BIS, 2001).

Bank for International Settlements. *Quarterly Review* (Basel: BIS, 2003).

Banks, E. *The Credit Risk of Financial Instruments* (London: Macmillan, 1993).

Banks, E. (ed.) *Weather Risk Management* (London: Palgrave, 2001).

Banks, E. *The Simple Rules of Risk* (London: Wiley, 2002).

Banks, E. *Exchange-Traded Derivatives* (London: Wiley, 2003).

Banks, E. *Corporate Governance* (London: Palgrave Macmillan, 2004).

Banks, E. and Dunn, R. *Practical Risk Management* (London: Wiley, 2003).

Behof, J. Reducing Credit Risk in OTC Derivatives, *Federal Reserve Bank of Chicago Economic Perspective*, January–February 1993, pp. 21–31.

Beidelman, C. (ed.) *Interest Rate Swaps*, (Homewood, Ill.: Business One Irwin, 1991).

Bennett, R. Rocket Scientists Produce a Fresh Wave of Solutions, *Euromoney*, March 1993, pp. 46–54.

Bensman, M. Derivatives: Too Damn Smart . . . *Global Custodian*, September 1992, pp. 132–7.

Bhala, R. *Perspectives on Risk Based Capital* (Tokyo: Toppan, 1992).

Black, F. and Scholes, M. The Pricing of Options and Corporate Liabilities, *Journal of Political Economy*, May–June 1973, pp 637–59.

Board of Governors of the Federal Reserve System and The Bank of England. *Potential Credit Exposure on Interest Rate and Foreign Exchange Related Instruments*, Joint Working Paper, March 1987.

Boyle, P. Options: A Monte Carlo Approach, *Journal of Financial Economics*, **4** 1977, pp 323–38

Brady, B. *Corporate Defaults Peak in 2002* (New York; Standard and Poor's Ratings Services, 2003).

Brady, S. Derivatives: Riding the US Yield Curve, *Euromoney*, April 1992a, pp. 12–13.

Brady, S. Derivatives Sprout Bells and Whistles, *Euromoney*, September 1992b, pp. 29–39.

Brookes, M. The Search for a Better Model of Volatility, *Euromoney*, March 1993, pp. 55–6.

Carty, L. and Fons, J. Measuring Changes in Corporate Credit Quality, *Journal of Fixed Income*, June 1994, pp. 27–41.

Carty, L. and Lieberman, D. (1996), *Corporate Bond Defaults and Default Rates, 1938–1995*, Moody's Special Report, January 1996, pp. 1–23.

Chase Securities. Mundane Problems, Exotic Solutions, *Euromoney*, August 1992, pp. 42–8.

Cheung, M. and Yeung, D. *Pricing Foreign Exchange Options* (Hong Kong: Hong Kong University Press, 1992).

Chew, L. A Bit of a Jam, *Risk*, September 1992a, pp. 82–93.

Chew, L. Exotic Tastes, *Risk*, October 1992b, pp. 32–6.

Chew, L. Quanto Leap, *Risk*, April 1993, pp. 21–8.

Chew, L. Protect and Survive, *Risk*, March 1994, pp. 36–41.

Chew, L. *Managing Derivative Risks* (New York: Wiley, 1996).

Chorafas, D. *Managing Derivatives Risk* (Chicago: Irwin, 1995).

Choudhury, P.S. Exchanges Take the Credit, *Risk*, November 1995, pp. 21–7.

Connolly, K. and Philips, G. *Japanese Warrant Markets* (London: Macmillan, 1992).

Cookson, R. Dangerous Liaisons, *Risk*, March 1993, pp. 30–6.

Corrigan, T. SEC and Regulators Deadlocked over Capital Requirements, *Financial Times*, 30 October 1992a, p. 34.

Corrigan, T. Growing Concern over the Dangers of Counterparty Credit, *Financial Times*, 30 November 1992b, p. 17.

Corrigan, T. SEC Issues Warning over Derivatives Operations, *Financial Times*, 2 December 1992c, p. 22.

Counterparty Risk Management Group. *Improving Counterparty Risk Management Practices* (New York: CRMG, 1999).

Cox, J., Ross, S., and Rubinstein, M. Option Pricing: a Simplified Approach, *Journal of Financial Economics*, **7** 1999, pp. 229–63.

Cox, J. and Ross, S. *The Pricing of Options for Jump Process* (Working Paper, University of Pennsylvania, 1975).

Cox, J. and Rubinstein, M. *Options Markets* (Englewood, N.J.: Prentice Hall, 1985).

Credit Suisse First Boston. *CreditRisk+ Technical Document* (London: CSFB, 1997).

Crouhy, M., Galai, D., and Mark, R. A Comparative Analysis of Current Credit Risk Models, *Journal of Banking and Finance*, **24** 2000.

Cunningham, S. (1996), The Neatness of Netting, Risk/Emerging Markets Investor, *Latin American Derivatives Supplement*, April 1996, pp. 76–80.

Das, S. *Swaps and Financial Derivatives, 2nd edn* (Sydney: Law Book Company, 1994).

Das, S. Credit Risk Derivatives, *Journal of Derivatives*, Spring 1995, pp. 7–23.

Das, S. *Credit Derivatives and Credit Linked Notes, 2nd edn* (New York: Wiley, 2000).

Dembo, R., Aziz, A., Rosen, D., and Zerbs, M. *Mark-to-Future: A Framework for Measuring Risk and Reward* (Toronto: Algorithmics, 2000).

Derivative Product Group. *A Framework for Voluntary Oversight* (New York: DPG, 1995).

Donaldson, T. *Credit Risk and Exposure in Securitization and Transactions* (London: St. Martin's, 1989).

Dubofsky, D. *Options and Financial Futures: Valuation and Uses* (New York: McGraw-Hill, 1992).

Duffie, D. *Futures Markets* (Englewood, N.J.: Prentice Hall, 1989).

Duffie, D. and Pan, J. *Analytical Value-at-Risk with Jumps and Credit Risk* (Working Paper, Stanford University, 1999).

Duffie, D. and Singleton, K. Modeling Term Structures of Defaultable Bonds, *The Review of Financial Studies*, **12**(4), 1999.

Eades, S. *Options Hedging and Arbitrage* (Chicago: Probus, 1992).

Economist. Japan's Warrant Hangover, *Economist*, 8 September 1990, pp. 95–6.

Economist. Securities Regulation: Capital Spat, *Economist*, 31 October 1992, pp. 80–1.

Euromoney. Inside the Global Derivatives Market, *Euromoney Supplement*, November 1990.

Euromoney. Derivatives: The Markets Mature, *Euromoney Supplement*, July 1991.

Fabozzi, F. and Modigliani, F. *Capital Markets: Institutions and Instruments* (Englewood, N.J.: Prentice Hall, 1992).

Falloon, W. Much Ado About Nothing, *Risk*, February 1993, p. 72.

Felgran, S. Interest Rate Swaps: Use, Risk, and Prices, *New England Economic Review*, November–December 1987, pp. 22–32.

Ferron, M. and Handjinicolaou, G. Understanding Swap Credit Risk, *Journal of International Securities Markets*, Winter 1987, pp. 135–48.

Field, P. and Jaycobs, R. (eds) *From Black–Scholes to Black Holes: New Frontiers in Options* (London: Risk Magazine, 1992).

Figlewski, S. How to Lose Money in Derivatives, *Journal of Derivatives*, Winter 1994, pp. 75–82.

Financial Times Survey. Derivatives, *Financial Times*, 8 December 1992.

Fitzgerald, M.D. *Financial Options* (London: Euromoney, 1987).

Flesaker, B., Hughston, L., Schreiber, L., and Sprung, L. Taking all the Credit, *Risk*, September 1994, pp. 104–10.

Fridson, M. *Financial Statement Analysis, 2nd edn* (New York: Wiley, 1995).

Gastineau, G. *The Stock Options Manual, 2nd edn* (New York: McGraw-Hill, 1979).

Gay, G. and Medero, J. The Economics of Derivatives Documentation, *Journal of Derivatives*, Summer 1996, pp. 78–89.

Geske, R. The Valuation of Compound Options, *Journal of Financial Economics*, 7, March 1979, pp. 63–81.

Giberti, D., Mentini, M., and Scabellone, P. The Valuation of Credit Risk in Swaps: Methodological Issues and Empirical Results, *Journal of Fixed Income*, March 1993, pp. 24–37.

Gibson, R. *Option Valuation* (New York: McGraw-Hill, 1991).

Gramm, W. Plus ça change, *Risk*, October 1992, p. 88.

Groenfeldt, T. Let the Borrower Beware, *Risk*, January 1996, p. 12.

Group of 30. *Derivatives: Principles and Practices* (Washington DC: Group of 30, 1993a).

Group of 30. *Derivatives: Principles and Practices, Appendix I: Working Papers* (Washington DC: Group of 30, 1993b).

Group of 30. *Derivatives: Principles and Practices, Follow-up Surveys* (Washington DC: Group of 30, 1994).

Haley, C and Schall, L. *The Theory of Financial Decisions, 2nd edn* (New York: McGraw-Hill, 1979).

Hansell, S. Risk Collectors, *Institutional Investor*, September 1991, pp. 69–76.

Hansell, S. and Muehring, K. Why Derivatives Rattle the Regulators, *Institutional Investor*, September 1992, pp. 103–16.

Heldring, O. Alpha Plus, *Risk*, January 1995, pp. 17–18.

Heron, D. OTC Derivatives Top $40 tln Says BIS, *Risk*, February 1996, p. 11.

Hines, W. and Montgomery, D. *Probability and Statistics in Engineering and Management Science, 3rd edn* (New York: Wiley, 1990).

Hirtle, B. Levonian, M., Saidenberg, M., Walter, S., and Wright, D. (2001), Using Credit Risk Models for Regulatory Capital: Issues and Options, *Federal Reserve Bank of New York Economic Policy Review*, March 2001.

House of Commons. *Report of the Board of Banking Supervision Inquiry into the Circumstances of the Collapse of Barings* (London: HMSO, 1995).

Hull, J. *Options, Futures and Other Derivative Securities* (Englewood, N.J.: Prentice Hall, 1989).

Hull, J. and White, A. The Pricing of Options on Assets with Stochastic Volatilities, *Journal of Finance*, **42** 1987, pp. 281–300.

Hull, J. and White, A. The Price of Default, *Risk*, September 1992, pp. 101–3.

Hull, J. and White, A. Finding the Keys, *Risk*, September 1993, pp. 109–13.

Hunter, W. and Stowe, D. Path Dependent Options, *Federal Reserve Board of Atlanta Economic Review*, March–April 1992a, pp. 29–34.

Hunter, W. and Stowe, D. Path Dependent Options: Valuation and Applications, *Federal Reserve Board of Atlanta Economic Review*, July–August 1992b, pp. 30–43.

Iben, B. and Brotherton-Ratcliffe, R. Credit Loss Distributions and Required Capital for Derivatives Portfolios, *Journal of Fixed Income*, June 1994, pp. 6–14.

Institutional Investor. Derivatives Dynamos, *Institutional Investor*, May 1991, pp. 111–16.

Institutional Investor Forum. Derivatives of the Future, *Supplement to Institutional Investor*, December 1992.

International Financing Review. IOSCO Meeting, *International Financing Review*, 31 October 1992a, p. 48.

International Financing Review. Derivative Instruments, *International Financing Review,* 31 October 1992b, p. 90.

International Financing Review. Management Fears Loss of Derivatives Control, *International Financing Review*, 5 December 1992c, p. 88.

International Financing Review. Derivative Instruments: Correlation Cornered by Risk, *International Financing Review*, 20 February 1993, p. 94.

International Swaps and Derivatives Association. *Enron: Corporate Failure, Market Success, Report of ISDA Annual General Meeting*, April 17 2002a, Berlin.

International Swaps and Derivatives Association. *ISDA Margin Survey 2002* (New York, ISDA, 2002b).

Irving, R. and Nicholls, M. Credit Ratings War Intensifies, *Risk*, March 1996, p. 8.

Iscoe, I, Kreinin, A., and Rosen, D. An Integrated Market and Credit Risk Portfolio Model, *Algo Research Quarterly*, September 1999, pp. 21–38.

Jarrow, R. (ed.) *Over the Rainbow* (London: Risk Publications, 1999).

Jarrow, R. and Turnbull, S. Credit Risk: Drawing the Analogy, *Risk*, October 1992, pp. 63–70.

Jarrow R. and Turnbull, S. Pricing Derivatives and Financial Securities Subject to Credit Risk, *Journal of Finance*, **50** 1995.

Jobst, N. and Zenios, S. *Extending Credit Risk (Pricing) Models for the Simulation of Portfolios of Interest Rate and Credit Risk Sensitive Securities* (Wharton Working Paper, 01-25, 2000).

Jorion, P. *Value At Risk* (Chicago: Irwin, 1996).

Kaufman, H. Capital Markets Regulation: Ten Reasons to Reform, *Euromoney*, November 1992, pp. 54–7.

King, W. Remodeling the Mortgage, *Institutional Investor Forum Supplement*, December 1992, pp. 30–1.

Klein, R. and Lederman, J. (eds) *Derivatives Risk and Responsibility* (Chicago: Irwin, 1996).

KMV. *Modeling Default Risk, Revised Edn* (San Francisco: KMV LLC, 2002).

Lee, P. How to Exorcise Your Derivatives Demons, *Euromoney*, September 1992, pp. 36–48.

Lee, P. A Question of Collateral, *Euromoney*, November 1995, pp. 46–50.

Leong, K. Options: Model Choice, *Risk*, December 1992, pp. 60–6.

Locke, J. Creditable Claims, *Risk*, August 1995, pp. 14–16.

Luskin, D. *Index Futures and Options* (New York: Wiley, 1987).

Makin, C. Hedging Your Derivatives Doubts, *Institutional Investor*, December 1991, pp. 93–102.

Matten, C. *Managing Bank Capital* (New York: Wiley, 1996).

Mayo, H. *Investments* (Chicago: Dryden, 1983).

McDonald, R. *Derivatives Markets* (New Jersey: Addison Wesley, 2003).

Merton, R. On the Pricing of Corporate Debt: The Risk Structure of Interest Rates, *Journal of Finance*, **2** 1974.

Merton, R. Option Pricing When Underlying Stock Returns are Discontinuous, *Journal of Financial Economics*, 1976.

Merton, R. *Continuous-Time Finance, revised edn* (Cambridge, Mass: Blackwell, 1990).

Mills, R. *Statistics for Applied Economics and Business* (Tokyo: McGraw-Hill Kogakusha, 1977).

Moody's Investors Service. *Default and Recovery Rates of Corporate Bond Issuers* (New York: Moody's Investor Services, 2003).

Muehring, K. Derivatives: Who Do You Trust? *Institutional Investor*, May 1992, pp. 51–5.

Muffet, M. Modeling Credit Exposure on Swaps, *Proceedings of a Conference on Bank Structure and Competition*, Federal Reserve Bank of Chicago, 1986, pp. 473–96.

Mulvey J. and Zenios, S. Capturing the Correlations of Fixed Income Instruments, *Management Science*, **40** 1994.

Napoli, J. Derivatives Markets and Competitiveness, *Federal Reserve Board of Chicago Economic Perspective*, July–August 1992, pp. 12–23.

Natenberg, S. *Option Volatility and Pricing Strategies* (Chicago: Probus, 1988).

Nelken, I. (ed.) *The Handbook of Exotic Options* (Chicago: Irwin, 1996).

Ong, M. *Internal Credit Risk Models* (London: Risk Books, 1999).

Options Institute (eds). *Options* (Homewood, Ill.: Business One Irwin, 1990).

Organization for Economic Cooperation and Development. *Risk Management in Financial Services* (Paris: OECD, 1992).

Parsley, M. The Raroc Revolution, *Euromoney*, October 1995, pp. 36–42.

Parsley, M. Credit Derivatives Get Cracking, *Euromoney*, March 1996, pp. 28–34.

Phillips, S. Don't Panic! Don't Panic! *Risk*, January 1993, p. 68.

Picker, I. Son of Swaps, *Institutional Investor*, February 1991, pp. 119–22.

Picker, I. The Daffier Side of Derivatives, *Institutional Investor*, February 1993, pp. 102–7.

Rendlemann, R. and Bartter, B. The Pricing of Options on Debt Securities, *Journal of Financial and Quantitive Analysis*, 15 March 1980.

Risk Publications. 5 Years of Risk, *Risk*, December 1992, pp. 35–58.

Risk Publications. *Derivative Credit Risk* (London: Risk Magazine, 1995).

Risk and Devon. *Proceedings from The Risk and Devon Conference on Equity Derivatives: Pricing, Hedging and Risk Management*, February 1993, London.

Robinson, D. LDC Derivatives: Stuck at the Crossroads, *Euromoney* 1992, October, pp. 33–44.

Robinson, D. Equity Derivatives: Tailored for All Tastes, *Euromoney*, February 1993, pp. 63–4.

Ross, S. *A Course in Simulation* (New York: Macmillan, 1991).

Rowe, D. Curves of Confidence, *Risk*, November 1993, pp. 52–6.

Rowley, A. Japanese Firms Return to No-frill Bonds, *Far Eastern Economic Review*, 21 November 1991, p. 70.

Schwartz, R. and Smith, C. (eds) *Handbook of Currency and Interest Rate Risk Management* (New York: New York Institute of Finance, 1990).

Shale, T. How ISDA Got the Message, *Euromoney*, April 1993, pp. 75–6.

Sheridan, E. The Growing Derivatives Market, *Futures Industry*, December 1992, pp. 10–14.

Shinmura, T. Derivative Trading Outpaces Watchdogs, *Nikkei Financial Weekly*, 8 March 1993, p. 15.

Shirreff, D. The Fearsome Growth of Swaps, *Euromoney*, October 1985, pp. 247–61.

Shirreff, D. Making Ends Meet, *Risk*, February 1993, pp. 16–21.

Smith, C. Option Pricing, *Journal of Financial Economics*, **3** 1976, pp. 3–51.

Smith, C., Smithson, C., and Wakeman, L. Credit Risk and the Scope and Regulation of Swaps, *Proceedings from a Conference on Bank Structure and Competition*, Federal Reserve Bank of Chicago, May 1986, pp. 166–85.

Smith, C, Smithson, C., and Wilford, S. *Managing Financial Risk* (New York: Harper and Row, 1990).

Smithson, C. Credit Derivatives, *Risk*, December 1995, pp. 38–9.

Smithson, C. *Managing Financial Risk, 3rd edn* (New York: McGraw-Hill, 1998).

Sorensen, E. and Bollier, T. Pricing Default Risk, *Financial Analysts Journal*, 1994.

Standard and Poor's. Rated Corporate Defaults Double in 1995, *Creditweek*, April 1996, pp. 44–52.

Stark, B. *Special Situation Investing* (Homewood, Ill.: Dow-Jones Irwin, 1983).

Stoll, H. and Whaley, R. *Futures and Opinions* (Cincinnati: Southwest, 1993).

Tavakoli, J. *Credit Derivatives* (New York: Wiley, 1998).

Tompkins, R. *Options Analysis, revised edn* (Chicago: Irwin, 1994).

Treanor, J. *et al.* Equity-linked Debt: From Boom to Bust, *International Financing Review, Review of the Year* 1992, pp. 156–9.

Van Duyn, A. Credit Risk for Sale, *Euromoney*, April 1995, pp. 41–4.

Waters, R. BIS Warns Banks over Growth in Derivatives Trading, *Financial Times*, 25 November 1992a, p. 19.

Waters, R. Search for Security, *Financial Times*, 23 October 1992b, p. 28.

Watts, D. Disclosure in the Dock, *Credit Magazine*, March 2002.

Wei, J. Streams of Consequence, *Risk*, January 1994, pp. 42–5.

Whittaker, J.G. *Pricing Interest Rate Swaps in an Options Pricing Framework*, Working Paper RWP, 87–02, Federal Reserve Bank of Kansas City, 1987.

Wilmott, P., Dewynne, J., and Howison, S. *Option Pricing* (Oxford: Oxford Financial Press, 1993).

Wilson, D. In Good Company, *Risk*, August 1994, pp. 35–9.

Index